Perspectives on Argument

Eighth Edition

Nancy V. Wood
University of Texas at Arlington

James S. Miller
University of Wisconsin at Whitewater

PEARSON

Boston   Columbus   Indianapolis   New York   San Francisco   Upper Saddle River
Amsterdam   Cape Town   Dubai   London   Madrid   Milan   Munich   Paris   Montreal   Toronto
Delhi   Mexico City   Sao Paulo   Sydney   Hong Kong   Seoul   Singapore   Taipei   Tokyo

Senior Acquisitions Editor: Brad Potthoff
Senior Development Editor: Marion Castellucci
Executive Marketing Manager: Roxanne McCarley
Senior Supplements Editor: Donna Campion
Senior Media Producer: Stefanie Snajder
Digital Editor: Sara Gordus
Content Specialist: Erin Reilly Jenkins
Project Manager: Shannon Kobran
Project Coordination, Text Design, and Electronic
    Page Makeup: Laserwords Private Ltd.

Design Lead: Beth Paquin
Cover Art: © Anna Henly/Getty Images; © Jean-Pierre Pieuchot/Getty Images; © Lizette Potgieter/Shutterstock; © Paula Cobleigh/Shutterstock
Senior Manufacturing Buyer: Roy L. Pickering, Jr.
Printer/Binder: R.R. Donnelley / Crawfordsville
Cover Printer: Lehigh-Phoenix Color / Hagerstown

Credits and acknowledgments borrowed from other sources and reproduced, with permission, in this textbook appear on the appropriate page within text or on pages 595–598.

Library of Congress Cataloging-in-Publication Data
Wood, Nancy V.
   Perspectives on Argument / Nancy V. Wood, University of Texas at Arlington; James S. Miller, University of Wisconsin at Whitewater. — Eighth Edition.
        pages cm.
    Includes index.
    ISBN 0-321-96426-8
1. English language—Rhetoric.   2. Persuasion (Rhetoric)   3. College readers.
4. Report writing.   I. Miller, James S.   II. Title.
    PE1431.W66 2014
    808'.042—dc23

2014004732

1 2 3 4 5 6 7 8 9 10—DOC—17 16 15 14

Student ISBN-10: 0-321-96426-8
Student ISBN-13: 978-0-321-96426-7
A la Carte ISBN-10: 0-321-97500-6
A la Carte ISBN-13: 978-0-321-97500-3

www.pearsonhighered.com

Brief Contents

Part 5   The Reader 435

Contents

Part 2   Understanding the Nature of Argument   111

Part 3   Writing a Researched Argument   327

Part 4   Further Applications: Argument and Literature 403

Part 5   The Reader   435

Major Writing Assignments

Other assignments, in addition to those listed here, appear in the Exercises and Activities sections at the ends of the chapters.

Create an Oral Argument, 360
Adapts the researched position paper for oral presentation.

Analyze an Argument in a Literary Work, 411
Analyzes the central argument made by a poem, short story, or literary essay.

Analyze an Argument About a Literary Work, 414
Takes a position on an issue associated with a literary work and argues for an interpretation.

Class Projects

Understanding Common Ground, 32

Students discover what members of their class have in common and how that could influence their choice of topics and the way they write their papers.

Argument Is Everywhere, 33

Students report on arguments they locate in a variety of contexts to demonstrate that argument can be found everywhere.

Creating Composite Lists of the Class's Reading, Thinking, and Writing Processes, 98

Students contribute strategies for reading and thinking about argument and organize them on the chalkboard under the headings *prereading*, *reading*, *reading when it is difficult*, and *postreading*; they do the same for writing argument, organizing their contributions under the headings *prewriting*, *drafting*, *writing when you get stuck*, and *rewriting*; finally, they consider how integrating reading and writing promotes critical thinking and results in better papers.

Toulmin Analyses of Examples Selected by Students, 142

Students describe the claim, support, and warrants in advertisements, cartoons, or letters to the editors.

Visual Argument Presentations, 277

Students present and explain their visual arguments to the class.

Class Debate, 303

Students select an issue and divide into three groups of affirmative, negative, and critics/respondents to conduct a debate.

Critical Reading: Reading the Letters and Reporting to the Class, 325

Students divide into groups to analyze and evaluate argumentative strategies in a written argument.

Class Symposium, 360

Students organize into small symposium groups.

Online Argument Assignments

Analyzing Argument Online, 38
Students work in groups to answer questions about arguments they locate online.

Using the Toulmin Model to Analyze an Online Argument, 137
Students locate an argument online and discuss how they might analyze it using the Toulmin model.

Analyzing Types of Claims in Online Argument, 178
Students identify the type of claim in an online argument and write a paper identifying features that are particular to the Web.

Logical and Emotional Proofs in Online Argument, 219
Students analyze and write about the use of proofs in an online Web site.

Analyzing Fallacies in Online Argument, 238
Students locate fallacies in an online argument and rewrite the argument to eliminate the fallacies and make the argument stronger.

Creating Your Own Rogerian Web Site, 296
Students identify an issue with conflicting views and create a hypothetical Web site that resolves the differences.

Preface

The most important purpose of *Perspectives on Argument* is to teach students strategies for critical reading, critical thinking, research, and writing that will help them participate in all types of argument, both inside and outside the classroom. In this eighth edition, online or digital argument is fully presented as another type of argument that students can analyze by using the same tools they use for analyzing written and visual argument. A basic assumption is that argument exists everywhere and that students need to learn to participate productively in all forms of argument (written, visual, and digital), including those they encounter in school, at home, on the job, and in the national and international spheres. Such participation is critical not only in a democratic society but also in a global society in which issues become more and more complex each year. Students who use this book will learn to identify controversial topics that are "at issue," to read texts and images and form reactions and opinions of their own, and to write argument papers that express their individual views and perspectives.

A central idea of this text is that modern argument is not always polarized as right or wrong; instead, it often invites or even imposes multiple perspectives on an issue. Another idea, equally important, is that not all argument results in the declaration of winners. The development of common ground and either consensus or compromise are sometimes as acceptable as declaring winners in argument. Students will learn to take a variety of approaches to argument, including taking a position and defending it, seeking common ground at times, withholding opinion at other times, negotiating when necessary, and even changing their original beliefs when they can no longer make a case for them. The perspectives and abilities taught here are those that an educated populace in a world community needs to coexist cooperatively and without constant destructive conflict.

What's New in the Eighth Edition?

▶ **New Analyzing Online Argument Feature.** A fully developed framework presented in Chapter 1 teaches students how to identify and analyze arguments online. In each of the chapters that follow, this same pedagogy is carried forward in the form of a recurring feature that (1) guides students through a series of logical steps for analyzing an aspect of argument in an online context, and (2) includes an activity that asks students to apply these steps to a concrete example of digital argument.

- **New Summary Charts on Argument Fallacies and Rogerian Argument.** Two new summary charts have been added to this edition. The first provides a clear and cogent summary of the principal argument fallacies, and the second gives a quick and clear overview of the key aspects of Rogerian argument.

- **New Activities for Arguing Like a Citizen.** Another recurring feature helps students understand how argument is connected to the practice of citizenship. Dividing its analysis into three discrete steps ("Thinking Like a Citizen," "Arguing Like a Citizen," and "Acting Like a Citizen"), it presents a new writing activity that asks students to connect citizenship to a specific issue and/or context.

- **New Readings and Visual Images.** More than 20 new readings and 25 new images have been selected to update the arguments throughout the book. These arguments touch upon some of the most current and controversial issues in public life today. Students will develop fresh critical and analytical understanding of issues as well as argument strategies when they read verbal and visual arguments.

- **New Thematic Sections in the Reader.** A new subsection within "Education and Learning" examines issues related to the cost of higher education. And a new subsection within "Environment and Sustainability" examines sustainability issues related to eating and food.

- **New Questions and Assignments.** New prompts that connect argument to the most current and controversial issues have been added. Also new are activities that ask students to write in greater depth about both digital argument and the relationship between argument and citizenship.

- **Streamlined and Updated Research Section.** The revamped research section includes an up-to-date presentation of both MLA and APA documentation guidelines, as well as strategies and examples for conducting research using electronic sources.

Special Features

Both instructors and students who pick up *Perspectives on Argument* have the right to ask how it differs from some of the other argument texts. They deserve to know why they might want to use this book instead of another. This text, which is targeted for first-year and second-year students enrolled in argument or argument and literature classes in two-year and four-year colleges, is both a reader and a rhetoric. Within this reader and rhetoric format are a number of special features that, when taken together, make the book unique.

- **Reading, critical thinking, and writing** are taught as integrated and interdependent processes. A chapter that combines instruction in reading and writing shows how they can be integrated to create better argument. Extensive instruction in critical reading, critical viewing, and critical thinking appear throughout. Assignments and questions that invite critical reading, critical viewing, critical thinking, and original argumentation writing appear at the end of every chapter in "The Rhetoric" and at the end of every section of "The Reader."

- **Visual argument analysis** is introduced in Chapter 1 and taught throughout the book. Students learn to apply the same ideas they have learned about written argument to visual argument as well. Images in the book are accompanied by questions for analysis and for writing, further reinforcing the concepts taught in the chapters. In Chapter 8, students learn to create their own visual arguments.

- **Digital argument analysis** is also presented in Chapter 1 and taught throughout the book. Students learn to apply the same ideas they have learned about written and visual argument to a range of online and multimedia texts.

- **Audience analysis** includes the concepts of the discourse community, the familiar and the unfamiliar audience, and Chaim Perelman's concept of the universal audience. Students are also taught to anticipate the initial degree of resistance or agreement from a potential audience along with ways to modify or change audience opinion.

- **Explanations of the elements and structure of argument** include the **Toulmin model of argument**, the **classical modes of appeal**, the **traditional categories of claims** derived from classical stasis theory, and the **rhetorical situation**. Theory is integrated and translated into language that students can easily understand and apply. For example, students learn to apply theory to recognize and analyze the parts of an argument while reading text or viewing images and to develop and structure their own ideas in writing argument or in creating visual argument.

- **Productive invention strategies** help students develop ideas for papers.

- **Library and online research is presented as a creative activity** that students are invited to enjoy. Workable strategies for research and note taking are provided along with criteria for evaluating all types of sources, including those found online. Students are taught to document researched argument papers according to the most up-to-date **MLA** and **APA styles**.

- **Exercises, class projects, and writing assignments at the ends of the chapters invite individual, small group, and whole class participation.** Collaborative exercises encourage small groups of students to engage in critical thinking, and whole class projects invite students to participate in activities that require an understanding of argument. Classroom-tested **writing assignments** include the **exploratory paper**, which teaches students to explore an issue from several different perspectives; the **position paper**, which teaches students to incorporate source material in their first position paper; the **Rogerian argument paper**, which teaches students an alternative argumentation strategy that relies on establishing common ground with the audience; the **argument analysis paper**, new to this edition, which teaches students to demonstrate their understanding of argument theory by writing an analysis of the argument strategies in a classic argument; and the **researched position paper**, which teaches students to locate outside research, evaluate it, and use it to develop an issue of their own choosing. **Examples of student papers** are provided for each major type of paper. The writing assignments in this book are models for assignments that students are likely to encounter in their other classes.

▶ **Summary Charts at the end of "The Rhetoric" present the main points of argument** in a handy format. They also integrate the reading and writing processes for argument by placing strategies for both side by side and showing the interconnections.

▶ **WHERE IS IT? A Quick Reference to Major Writing Assignments and Sample Papers by Students** appears on the inside back cover of the book to help students quickly locate frequently visited pages.

▶ **The 88 readings** in "The Rhetoric" and "The Reader" provide students with multiple perspectives on the many issues presented throughout the book. Ten of these readings are argument papers written by students.

▶ **The readings provided in "The Reader" are clustered under 14 sub-issues** that are related to the seven major general issue areas that organize "The Reader." This helps students focus and narrow broad issues. Furthermore, the readings in each sub-issue group "talk" to each other by offering different perspectives on the issue, and accompanying questions invite students to join the conversation.

Organization

The book is organized into five parts and, as much as possible, chapters have been written so that they stand alone. Thus, instructors can assign them in sequence or in any order they prefer as a supplement to their own course organization.

Part 1: Engaging with Argument. This part introduces students to issues and the characteristics of argument, written, visual, and digital, in Chapter 1; teaches them to analyze the rhetorical situation when reading, writing, and viewing arguments in Chapter 2; and provides specific strategies for integrating reading, viewing, critical thinking, and writing in Chapter 3. Writing assignments include the issue proposal, the analysis of the rhetorical situation paper, the summary-response paper, the summary-analysis-response paper, and the exploratory paper.

Part 2: Understanding the Nature of Argument. This part identifies and explains the parts of an argument according to Stephen Toulmin's model of argument in Chapter 4; explains the types of claims and purposes for argument in Chapter 5; presents the types of proofs along with clear examples and tests for validity in Chapter 6; identifies the fallacies, provides criteria for recognizing ethical argument, and teaches students to write ethical argument themselves in Chapter 7; teaches students to extend and apply in new ways what they have learned about argument to the analysis and creation of visual argument as they encounter it in all parts of their lives in Chapter 8; and explains Rogerian argument as an alternative to traditional argument and as an effective method for building common ground and resolving differences in Chapter 9. Writing assignments include the Toulmin analysis, the position paper, Rogerian argument papers, and the argument analysis paper.

Part 3: Writing a Researched Argument. This part teaches students to write a claim, clarify purpose, analyze the audience, to use various creative strategies for inventing ideas and gathering research materials in Chapter 11; and to organize, write, revise, and prepare the final manuscript for a researched position paper in Chapter 12. Oral argument is taught at the end of Chapter 12 to help students who are preparing their research papers for oral presentation to the class. Methods for locating and using resource materials in the library and online are presented in Chapter 12. An Appendix to Chapter 12 provides full instruction for documenting sources using both MLA and APA styles.

Part 4: Further Applications: Argument and Literature. Chapter 13 suggests ways to apply argument theory to reading and writing about literature. Assignments include writing papers about argument and literature.

Part 5: The Reader. This part is organized around the broad issues concerning families and personal relationships; modern technology; education and learning; race, culture, and identity; the environment and sustainability; immigration; and war and peace. Strategies and questions to help students explore issues and move from reading, viewing, and discussion to writing are also included.

Resources for Instructors and Students

MyWritingLab™ Now Available for Composition

Integrated Solutions for Writing.   *MyWritingLab* is an online homework, tutorial, and assessment program that provides engaging experiences for today's instructors and students. New features designed specifically for composition instructors and their course needs include a new writing space for students, customizable rubrics for assessing and grading student writing, multimedia instruction on all aspects of composition, and advanced reporting to improve the ability to analyze class performance.

Adaptive Learning.   For students who enter the course underprepared, *MyWritingLab* offers pre-assessments and personalized remediation so they see improved results and instructors spend less time in class reviewing the basics.

Visit www.mywritinglab.com for more information.

eTextbooks

Pearson eText.   An online version of *Perspectives on Argument* brings together the many resources of *MyWritingLab* with the instructional content of this successful book to create an enhanced learning experience for students.

CourseSmart eTextbook.   Students can subscribe to *Perspectives on Argument* at CourseSmart.com. The format of the eText allows students to search the text, bookmark passages, save their own notes, and print reading assignments that incorporate lecture notes.

Android and iPad eTextbooks.   Android and iPad versions of the eText provide the complete text and the electronic resources described above.

Instructor's Manual

The *Instructor's Manual* provides syllabi, day-by-day teaching journals, and handouts to facilitate classroom management in different types of argument classes that use *Perspectives on Argument* as the primary textbook. Because these classes and syllabi have been tested repeatedly in the classroom, they may be followed or changed and adapted with confidence. One class follows the textbook closely, another employs a considerable amount of student discussion of issues, a third includes a number of effective ways for teaching visual argument, a fourth describes a class that can be taught online as a distance education class, and the fifth describes a class that can be taught in a five-week summer session.

Other chapters in the manual provide descriptions of each chapter's contents and the exercises that accompany them, along with answers to the review questions at the end of each chapter in "The Rhetoric." Instructors can save themselves considerable time by reading these descriptions before they read the chapters themselves. A set of class handouts ready for printing is also provided.

Acknowledgments

Colleagues around the country who have provided additional ideas and recommended changes that have helped improve the first seven editions of this book include Kamala Balasubramanian, Grossmont College; Margaret W. Batschelet, University of Texas at San Antonio; Linda D. Bensel-Meyers, University of Tennessee; Benita Budd, Wake Technical Community College; Mary Cantrell, Tulsa Community College; Gregory Clark, Brigham Young University; Perry Cumbie, Durham Technical Community College; Dan Damesville, Tallahassee Community College; Carol David, Iowa State University; Kim Donehower, University of Maryland; Thomas Dukes, University of Akron; Larnell Dunkley Jr., Benedictine University; Joyce Anne Dvorak, MCC–Longview; Bob Esch, University of Texas at El Paso; Africa Fine, Palm Beach State College; Robert G. Ford, Houston Community College; Alexander Friedlander, Drexel University; Kyle S. Glover, Lindenwood University; Lynce Lewis Gaillet, Georgia State University; Richard Grande, Pennsylvania State University; William S. Hockman, University of Southern Colorado; Carrie Hoffman, University of Texas–Pan America; Tony Jack Howard, Collin College; Joanna Johnson, University of Texas at Arlington; Robert Johnson, Midwestern State University; James Kinneavy, University of Texas at Austin; Lucinda Ligget, Ivy Tech Community College of Indiana; Julie Wakeman Linn, Montgomery College; Rene Martin, Miami Dade College; Shannon Martin, Elizabethtown Community College; Elizabeth Metzger, University of South Florida; Margaret Dietz Meyer, Ithaca College; Claudia Milstead, University of Tennessee; Troy Nordman,

Butler Community College; Barry R. Nowlin, University of South Alabama; Susan Padgett, North Lake College; Martha Payne, Ball State University; Randall L. Pop-ken, Tarleton State University; Andrea Powell, Ball State University; Sue Preslar, University of North Carolina, Charlotte; Keith Rhodes, Northwest Missouri State University; Wayne Robbins, Western Carolina University; Gail Rosen, Drexel University; Raquel Scherr Salgado, University of California, Davis; John Schaffer, Blinn College; Carol Schuck, Ivy Tech Community College; William E. Sheidley, United States Air Force Academy; Heather Shippen, Duquesne University; Effie Siegel, Montgomery College; Rusty Spell, University of Texas–Pan America; Kim Stallings, University of North Carolina, Charlotte; Diane M. Thiel, Florida International University; Pat Tyrer, West Texas A&M University; Evert Villarreal, University of Texas–Pan America; Scott Warnock, Drexel University; Jim Warren, University of Texas at Arlington; Jennifer Welsh, University of Southern California; and Anna Wiley, Ivy Tech Community College. I am grateful to them for the time and care they took reviewing the manuscript.

Finally, we would also like to thank the reviewers for this edition: J. T. Bushnell, Oregon State University; Peggy Kulesz, University of Texas at Arlington; Lucinda Ligget, Ivy Tech Community College of Indiana; Byoung K. Park, Lorain County Community College; Michelle Paulsen, Victoria College; Ana Schnellmann, Lindenwood University; and Sam Zahran, Fayetteville Technical Community College.

Nancy V. Wood
James S. Miller

1

Engaging with Argument

The strategy in Part One is to introduce you to the nature of issues and the special characteristics of argument, both written and visual, in Chapter 1; to teach you to analyze the context and motivation for an argument, with special emphasis on analyzing your audience, in Chapter 2; and to teach you to develop an integrated process for reading and writing argument, in Chapter 3. The focus in these chapters is on you, and how you will engage with argument as both a reader and a writer. When you finish reading Part One:

- You will understand what argument is and why it is important in a democratic society.

- You will have found some issues (topics) to read and write about or to interpret visually.

- You will know how to analyze the rhetorical situation, including the audience, for arguments you read and write.

- You will have new strategies and ideas to help you read and view argument critically, think critically, and write argument papers.

- You will have experience with writing an issue proposal, a summary-response paper, a summary-analysis-response paper, and an exploratory argument paper.

A Perspective on Argument

After studying this chapter, you will be able to:

LO1 Explain your own perspective on argument.

LO2 Define the basic features of argument.

LO3 Describe the characteristics of traditional and consensual argument.

LO4 Identify visual arguments.

LO5 Describe the conditions of a successful argument and an unsuccessful argument.

LO6 Distinguish between ethical and unethical argument.

LO7 Define what constitutes an arguable issue in the twenty-first century.

Y ou are engaged in argument, whether you realize it or not, nearly every day. Argument deals with *issues*, ideas or topics that have not yet been settled, that invite two or more differing opinions, and that are consequently subject to question, debate, or negotiation. Pick up today's newspaper, peruse a current news magazine or Web site and read the headlines to find current examples of societal issues such as: What should be done to reduce global warming? Should the Internet be censored? To what extent should one government participate in solving the problems of other governments? How should youthful offenders be punished? Should public officials be held to higher ethical standards than everyone else? Alternatively, think of examples of issues closer to your daily experience at school: Why are you going to college? What close relationships should you form, and how will they affect your life? Which is the more important consideration in selecting a major: finding a job, or interest in the subject? Is it good or bad policy to go to school and work at the same time? How much educational debt should you undertake?

It is undeniable that we are constantly confronted with issues. But why do we care about them? Or, more to the point, how do we figure out *whether* and *why* we care? To a great extent, figuring out why we care about an argument involves figuring out how an argument works. How do we go from identifying a particular issue to figuring out our own stake in it, to creating a coherent argument of our own about the issue? Whatever the issue, every argument begins with a sense of what is important to us, what *matters*. Maybe it resonates with a particular experience we have had in our personal life. Or perhaps it raises questions or ideas we find intellectually engaging. For any issue, we need to begin with a very simple question: Why do I care?

To answer this question, we need to dig a bit into our own personal assumptions and experiences. Take, for example, the question "Should the Internet be censored?" If you wanted to better understand the stakes involved in this issue, you might begin by reflecting on your own experience with online technology. What are the particular ways, you could ask, I use online technologies? Do they help me communicate with people in ways that were not possible before? What new kinds of information do they make available, and why is such information important? Are there, conversely, any dangers or downsides to the ways I use these technologies? Do these new forms of communication pose any threat to my personal privacy? Doing this kind of personal inventory is an essential first step in figuring out our views on the more formal questions issues present. To figure out your perspective on a given issue, you need to first understand the unspoken ideas and values that shape this perspective.

Whether they seem remote or close to you, all of these issues are related to larger issues that have engaged human thought for centuries. In fact, all of the really important issues—those that address life and death, the quality of life, war and peace, the individual and society, the environment, and others like them—are discussed, debated, and negotiated everywhere in the world again and again. There are usually no simple or obvious positions to take on such important issues. Still, the positions we do take *on* them and, ultimately, the decisions and actions we take in regard *to* them can affect our lives in significant ways. In democratic societies, individuals are expected to engage in effective argument on issues of broad concern. They are also expected to make moral judgments and to evaluate the decisions and ideas that emerge from argument. Equally, they are expected to take actions based on these judgments and evaluations—to vote, to serve on a jury, to assent to or protest a policy, and so on.

The purpose of this book is to help you participate in two types of activities: the evaluation of arguments you encounter and the formulation of arguments of your own. The book is organized in parts, and each part will help you become a more effective participant in the arguments that affect your life. Part One will help you engage with argument personally as you begin to identify the issues, approaches to argument, and processes for reading and writing that will work best for you; Part Two will help you understand the nature of argument, both written and visual, as you learn more about its essential parts and how certain strategies operate in argument to convince an audience; Part Three will provide you with a process for thinking critically and writing an argument paper that requires research, critical thought, and clear presentation; Part Four will teach you to analyze uses of argument in literature; and Part Five will provide you with many good examples of effective argument to analyze and draw on as you create original argument in different styles and formats.

LO1 Explain your own perspective on argument.

What Is Your Current Perspective on Argument?

What do you think about when you see the word *argument*? It is best to begin the study of any new subject by thinking about what you already know. You can then use what you know to learn more, which is the way all of us acquire new knowledge. See the short list of five actual student responses describing some of their initial views about argument provided here. Check the responses that match your own, and add others if you like.

_____ 1. Argument attempts to resolve issues between two or more parties.
_____ 2. Argument is rational disagreement, but it can get emotional.
_____ 3. Argument can result in agreement or compromise.
_____ 4. Argument is angry people yelling at each other.
_____ 5. Argument is standing up for your ideas, defending them, and minimizing the opposition by being persuasive.

The responses in the list, with the exception of response 4, "angry people yelling at each other," are consistent with the approach to argument that appears in this book. We omit response 4 because no argument is effective if people stop listening, stop thinking, and engage in vocal fighting. "Yes, it is!"—"No, it isn't!" accompanied by a fist pounding on the table gets people nowhere.

What would happen if a society were to outlaw all forms of argument? Here are some student responses to the question. With which descriptions do you agree?

_____ 1. Everyone would think the same thing.
_____ 2. There would not be any progress.
_____ 3. There would be no new knowledge.
_____ 4. Life would be boring.

A key idea in this book is that argument is literally to be found everywhere[1] and that without it, we would have the stagnant society suggested in these student responses. You will become more aware of the ways argument impacts your life once you realize that argument can be found in virtually any context in which human beings interact and hold divergent views about topics that are at issue—from personal blogs to presidential debates, advertisements to newspaper op-eds, text messages to Facebook posts. Further, argument can appear in a variety of forms: it can be written, spoken, sung, or chanted, and it can be read, heard, or observed in pictures that are either still or moving. Argument can be explicit, with a clear purpose and position, as in an advertisement for a soft drink or a brand of blue jeans; or it can be implicit, communicating a more subtle position on an issue that the audience has to think about and figure out, as in some of the photographs taken in war zones. Most issues invite a spectrum of perspectives and views for individuals to hold. Few issues are black and white, nor can most of them be viewed in pro and con terms. Keep these complexities in mind as we now attempt to define argument, describe why it is important to study, and learn to argue well.

A Definition of Argument

LO2 Define the basic features of argument.

Since the classical era, argument theorists have defined and described argument in different ways. Whatever their differences, though, these definitions all share one crucial assumption: argument always involves an attempt to reach and influence an audience. Some definitions focus on providing convincing evidence for a point of view on a controversial issue and persuading an audience to agree with it. In this argument situation, a judge or a vote sometimes declares a winner. Examples of this type of argument can be found in courts of law where lawyers argue about whether the defendant is guilty or not guilty or in legislative assemblies where legislators argue in favor of or against new legislation. Other definitions of argument emphasize the importance of multiple views and perspectives, learning about them and making comparisons, and reasoning and gaining insights toward reaching an agreement or consensus on a position or point of view that is acceptable to everyone, at least for the present time. Examples of this type of argument can be found in policy meetings in which participants must agree on courses of action and in classrooms where students and professors reason together to establish viable solutions to puzzling questions and problems.

The definition of argument we shall use in this book is a broad one that includes both of these types of argument: *The goal of argument is to bring about a change in an audience's initial position on a controversial issue. Depending on the situation and audience, at times this goal is achieved by an arguer who presents a claim along with reasons and evidence to convince an audience to agree with the position taken [what is often*

---

[1] I am indebted to Wayne Brockriede for this observation and for some of the other ideas in this chapter. See his article "Where Is Argument?" *Journal of the American Forensic Association* 11 (1975): 179–82.

called traditional argument*]; at other times, arguers create the possibility of agreement by acknowledging different points of view and working to identify one view or a combination of views that are acceptable to most or all audience members [what is often called* consensual argument*]*. Both types of argument are taught in this book.

The basic method both types of argument share involves making a claim (expressing a point of view on an issue that is communicated by the arguer) and supporting it with reasons and evidence to convince an audience to change the way they think about the issue. All forms of productive argument include these components.

$$\boxed{\textbf{Argument}} = \boxed{\textbf{Claim}} + \boxed{\textbf{Support}}$$

LO3
Describe the characteristics of traditional and consensual argument.

Recognizing Traditional and Consensual Argument

The definition of argument presented in this chapter allows for two basic approaches to argument: the traditional and the consensual. The traditional approach to argument has been dominant in Western culture. That approach is founded in Greek classical philosophy and rhetoric. Aristotle made it clear in his book *Rhetoric,* written sometime between 360 and 334 B.C.E., that a person making an argument should find all available means of persuasion to convince an audience to change positions and agree with the arguer. You are familiar with this model of argument. You observe it every day when you watch news programs and political discussion shows on television, or when you read editorials and letters to the editor in magazines, newspapers, and the Web. When you engage in argument, orally or in writing, you probably quite naturally either consider or turn to the traditional approach.

▶ **Examples of traditional argument.** One example of traditional argument is the **public debate** among candidates for public office or among other individuals who want to convince their audiences to side with them and accept their points of view. Public debates are often televised, allowing candidates to state and explain their views on many subjects; people also write about their views, explaining how their analyses or views are better than opposing positions. The judge or decider is the viewing public or a reader, who may or may not pick a winner. *Courtroom argument,* with lawyers pleading a case (opposed sets of alleged facts) before a judge and jury, is another example of traditional argument. As in debate, lawyers take opposing sides and argue to convince a judge and jury of the guilt or innocence of a defendant. The desired outcome is that one of them wins.

Another example of traditional argument, known as *single-perspective argument,* occurs when one person develops a perspective on an issue and argues to convince a mass audience to agree with this single view. You encounter this type of argument frequently on television and in newspapers, journals, books, and public speeches. The issue and the arguer's position are usually clear. Opposing views, if referred to at all, are refuted or otherwise dismissed. An example might be a politician who wants to convince the public that marriage should exist only between a man and a woman. This arguer provides reasons and evidence and refutes the views of another politician who favors gay marriage. It may not be clear whether anyone "wins" such an argument. Polls, letters to the editor, or a change in policy may present indications about how some members of the audience have reacted.

One-on-one, everyday argument, also a type of traditional argument, can be very different from convincing a judge or a large, unspecified audience. In the one-on-one situation, the person arguing needs to focus on and identify with the other person, think about what that person wants and values, and be conciliatory, if necessary. Each participant either wins, loses, or succeeds in part. Examples might be a salesperson who wants to sell a customer a car or a student who writes a letter to convince a professor to accept a late paper.

▶ **Examples of consensual argument.** In contrast to traditional argument with its emphasis on winning, consensual argument emphasizes agreement. You will probably encounter both of these types of argument in your college classes. In *dialectic,* one type of consensual argument, two or more people participate as equals in a dialogue to try to discover what seems to be the best position on an issue. A questioning strategy is often used to test the validity of differing views. The ancient Greek philosopher Plato used this form of argument in his *Dialogues* to examine such questions as *What is truth?* and *What is the ideal type of government?* You may have seen this type of exchange referred to as "the Socratic method" because Plato's teacher, the philosopher Socrates, asks many of the questions in the *Dialogues.*

Professors sometimes use dialectic to help students think about and finally arrive at positions that can be generally accepted by most of the class. In a philosophy class, for example, the professor may ask the question *How can one establish a personal hierarchy of values?* and then describe a situation in which an individual is faced with a conflict of values. For example, Can one remain loyal to a friend if one must break a law in the process? The professor first asks class members to describe the values that are in conflict in this situation, then to compare the relative strength and importance of these values, and finally to prioritize them in a way that is agreed upon by the class. The objective is to discover, through questions and answers, a bedrock of ideas that most or all of the class can accept in common. There are no winners. There is instead a consensual discovery of a new way to look at a difficult issue. Students then may be asked to write papers in which they describe their understanding of this new consensus view.

Another type of consensual argument is *academic inquiry*. Its purpose is to discover, through reading, discussion, and writing, new views, new knowledge, and new truths about complex issues. For example, English majors engage in academic inquiry when they read, discuss, and write about their insights into the motivation of a character in a novel. Political science majors take part in academic inquiry when they find themselves contributing to a new understanding of the benefits of strong state governments. The participants in such inquiry find that there are few clear-cut, pro-and-con positions; there is no judge; the emphasis is not on winning;

anyone can participate; there are potentially as many views as there are partici-pants. The result of academic inquiry, ideally, is to reach well-founded consensus on academic and social issues. Consensus may take some time to emerge, and it may also be challenged later when someone proposes a completely new way of looking at a particular issue.

Negotiation and mediation are conducted in arenas where people must employ argument to reach consensus on plans of action that solve problems. The Pales-tinians and the Israelis, for example, cannot both claim ownership of the same land, so other solutions continue to be negotiated. Negotiation can take place between two people, one on one, or in a group meeting. A special characteristic of negotiation is that the negotiators usually represent an entire business, organiza-tion, or government, and, as a result, many people not present at the negotiating table must ultimately be as satisfied with the final agreements as the negotiators themselves. Often, negotiation involves both competition (e.g., both parties claim rights to fish in the same waters) and cooperation (they have to figure out how to make that possible). For negotiation to be successful, all those involved must state their positions, including the views or claims of the groups or governments they represent, and support them with reasons and evidence both in writing and orally. Everyone must be willing to consider alternative views and reasons and to modify their original views in order to reach consensus and resolve the problem.

Mediation is becoming a frequent alternative to a court trial. A judge assigns trained mediators to help parties who are in conflict resolve a problem that would otherwise have to be solved by a judge and possibly a jury. The mediators act as go-betweens and help the individuals involved see their problems in new ways so they can figure out how to solve them outside of the courtroom. You may be taught methods for negotiation or mediation in your business or other classes, in which case you will be able to draw on what you know about argument to help you understand and use these practices.

A final type of consensual argument you may use frequently is known as *internal argument.* Most of us argue with ourselves when we experience internal conflict because we need to increase personal motivation, make a decision, or solve a problem. New Year's resolutions, to-do lists, and time management charts are examples of internal argument and decision making. As in other forms of consensual argument, different possibilities are identified, reasons for and against are considered, and a satisfactory resolution is finally reached. Whether traditional or consensual, notice how much of argument revolves around the relationship with audience. All argument, whatever its form, is fundamentally concerned with engaging and influencing the views of others. Whether traditional or consensual, all arguments center upon a particular relationship between arguer and audience.

LO4
Identify visual
arguments.

Recognizing Visual Argument

At the beginning of this chapter, you were advised to look at the headlines of a current newspaper, news magazine, or Web site to identify some current issues. Did you also notice that many of the headlines and stories are accompanied by different kinds of visual images? Their purpose is often to reinforce or examine an idea in the written stories, making them more immediate, compelling, and convincing to audiences. Such images function as parallel visual arguments or as the visual extension of the ideas in the written argument. Other images may stand alone, making an argument themselves, without an accompanying story or essay. Stand-alone visual arguments of this type are usually accompanied by a few words to explain their significance as arguments.

Let us look at two images on page 10 that have been used to either further develop and enhance the ideas in a written argument, or to make an independent argument with only a few words of explanation to highlight the argumentative significance. As you look at these images, view them from the perspective of argument; that is, determine whether or not each image is about an issue that has not been resolved or settled and that potentially inspires two or more different perspectives or views. Describe the issue and the position the image appears to take. You will often have to infer this information because it will not always be directly stated in words either on or near the visual itself.

Figure 1.1 is one of the countless photos that appeared in newspapers, magazines, and Web sites in the days after Hurricane Sandy struck the East Coast in 2012. This storm devastated the region, killing scores of people, injuring hundreds of others, and causing extensive damage to communities up and down the Eastern Seaboard. The photograph in Figure 1.1 offers a snapshot of this damage, capturing the storm surge flooding that inundated the streets of Hoboken, New Jersey. Take a closer look at this image. What sort of message—about this storm and the devastation it wrought—does it convey? What kind of reaction does it seem designed to evoke in its viewers?

Figure 1.2 is a stand-alone visual argument that makes an argument about global warming. Notice that it is accompanied by a few words of text that explain

Steps for Reading Visual Argument

Step 1: Understanding Context: What background information do you need to know in order to read this image intelligibly?

Step 2: Describing What You See: What are the key details or features here that stand out? What images? What text? What supporting details?

Step 3: Identifying the Issue(s): Based on the picture it presents, what issue does this visual seem to be referencing? What conversation is it part of?

Step 4: Defining the Perspective: What perspective on this issue does this visual seem to take?

Step 5: Defining the Argument: How do we know what point of view the visual is taking? What specific claims about this issue does the visual seem to be making?

Step 6: Thinking in Terms of Audience: What sort of response does this visual seem to want from its viewers? What messages or lessons does it want to convey? Is it successful?

Figure 1.1 *The storm surge that followed in the wake of Hurricane Sandy flooded the streets of Hoboken, New Jersey.*

This image serves to reinforce the messages in the broader media coverage about the effect this storm had on residents of the East Coast. What issue does it address? What position does it take? What effect does it have on you as a viewer of this visual argument? What makes it effective?

Figure 1.2 *Like a polar bear adrift on a shrinking ice floe in the Arctic Ocean, many of us have held on to the dwindling hope that global warming is a vague concern for the future. As extreme weather patterns disrupt lives everywhere, it is clear that climate change is an immediate threat to our planet that must be addressed now.*

This is a photograph of a polar bear trying to get its bearings in a place where most of the ice pack in its native environment has melted. This is a stand-alone visual argument that is accompanied by a few words of explanation. View it as an argument, and read the caption. What issue does it address? What position does it take? What effect does it have on you as a viewer of this visual argument? How effective is it as a visual argument?

some of its significance as argumentation. Look at these two images, read the captions, and answer the questions that accompany them to help you think about them as arguments.

Throughout the book, you will discover that much of the same instruction that will help you read and write arguments will also help you analyze the visual argument that is present everywhere in our society. Look for visual argument on television, in newspapers and magazines, on billboards, signs, packaging, and marketing materials, in movies, Web sites, video games, and books. Your choices will likely include examples of both traditional argument and consensual argument, demonstrating that effective visual argument takes many forms. Whether written or visual, effective argument does not happen automatically. Special conditions are necessary if argument is to be effective. Let us look at some of these conditions to expand our perspective on argument even further.

Under What Conditions Does Argument Work Best?

LO5 Describe the conditions of a successful argument and an unsuccessful argument.

To work best, a productive and potentially successful argument, whether presented in writing, in speech, or in images, requires the following elements:

▶ **An issue.** An argument needs as its central focus an issue that has not yet been settled, or has become unsettled. In addition, there must be the potential for the issue to generate at least two or more views. For example, the issue of bottled water has more than two views: either in favor or against their widespread use. Between these two poles, people take a variety of positions, including the view that bottled water use may be beneficial to the environment in certain cases and detrimental in others.

▶ **An arguer.** Ideally, every argument requires a person who is motivated to initiate the argument, to take a position on the issue, to obtain and consider information, and to communicate a position to others. This person needs to develop expertise on an issue and be willing to take a risk to express his or her own ideas about it. Furthermore, the arguer should seek to go beyond the "current wisdom" about an issue and find fresh perspectives and approaches that will suggest original insights to the audience. For example, an individual arguing for tighter restrictions on bottled water needs to present fresh reasons and evidence to get people's attention and agreement. Al Gore provided such a rationale in his film about global warming, *An Inconvenient Truth*.

▶ **Audience.** An audience for an argument, whether friendly or hostile, should ideally be willing to listen to or read and consider new views or perspectives. The audience should also be capable of understanding, thinking, questioning, discussing, and answering. The arguer may be familiar with the audience's background and values or, in the case of a totally unknown audience, the arguer may have to imagine their background, motives, and values. The arguer should respect the audience and want to communicate with them. It is a compliment to draw someone into discussion on an issue, so the arguer should try to show that he or she cares about the audience, their interests, and their context or state of mind. This approach will ensure an audience who reads and listens and does not shut the arguer out or otherwise try to escape. Receptive audiences are potentially willing to change their minds, a desirable outcome of argument.[2] Consider, for example, an audience member who favors the restriction of bottled water, is an environmental activist, and is willing to think about an opposing view because a respectful fellow parent has written a letter to the editor describing the problem of plastic bottles inundating landfills.

▶ **Common ground.** Effective argument requires the establishment of some common ground between the audience and the arguer. If two parties are too far apart and share no common ground, they usually do not understand one another well enough to engage in dialogue. For example, people who disagree on the abortion issue often find themselves at a standoff, they fight rather than argue, and their disagreement sometimes results in violence. At the other extreme, if two parties are already in complete agreement, there is usually no need to argue. For example, two parents who agree that their child should go to college do not argue about that part of the child's future. Common ground may be established between an arguer and an audience through the discovery of common interests—common ideas, experiences, motives, or values—or even through recognizing common friends or enemies. As soon as two parties realize they have something in common, they can more easily achieve identification, even if it is minimal, and engage in constructive argument. Imagine, once again, two parties who disagree on bottled water use. One party believes bottled water manufacture should be forbidden in order to alleviate the environmental damage such bottles cause. The other party believes decisions about how best to protect the environment should be left to individual consumers themselves. Both agree that harming the environment is bad, and this basic agreement provides the common ground they need to begin to engage in constructive argument about bottled water use. Figure 1.3 diagrams these possible situations.

▶ **A forum.** People need forums for argument so they can feel creative and know they will be heard. Available forums include public places for argument, such as the courtroom or legislative assembly; much more widely available forums include various media, such as magazines, journals, newspapers, and other print sources, television and radio programs, movies, Web sites, the arts, photographs, and other graphic materials. College is a forum for argument. Professors and students argue in class, at meals, and in dorms and apartments. Outside speakers present argument. The argument class, with its discussions, papers, and other assignments, can be an excellent forum for practicing argument, particularly if both the students and the instructor work to create an environment in which all students participate and respect one another.

---

[2]Some of the observations in this chapter about the special conditions for argument, especially for the audience, are derived from Chaim Perelman and Lucie Olbrechts-Tyteca, *The New Rhetoric: A Treatise on Argumentation* (Notre Dame, IN: University of Notre Dame Press, 1969), pt. 1.

THE ISSUE: SHOULD RESTRICTIONS BE PLACED ON BOTTLED WATER USAGE?

Figure 1.3
*Establishing
Common Ground*

Possibility 1: *Complete agreement and no argument.*

Two individuals believe that all individual consumers should be allowed to make their own decisions regarding bottled water use. They agree that, while bottled water use may pose certain threats to the environment, this concern is outweighed by the right of consumers to exercise their own freedom of choice when making their purchases. They have nothing to argue about.

Possibility 2: *Total disagreement, no common ground, and no argument.*

One individual believes that all consumers should have the right to make their own choice about bottled water, and another believes that, because the environmental hazards such usage poses is so great, no consumer should be allowed to purchase bottled water. They disagree totally, and there is no common ground. Productive argument is nearly impossible.

Possibility 3: *Two parties discover something in common, and there is a possibility of argument.*

The two parties discover that, despite their differing views, they actually agree on the fact that bottled water use poses certain threats to the environment. One believes this threat should justify an outright ban on bottled water use, while the other believes these threats are less important than preserving individual consumer choice. They have an important point in common: they both acknowledge the connection between bottled water use and threats to the environment. Even though they may disagree on other points, this common ground creates the possibility for productive argument about what can be done to minimize the environmental dangers of bottled water use.

▶ **Audience outcomes.** Successful arguments should produce changes in the audience. At times, the arguer convinces the audience, and the members of the audience change their minds. Sometimes a successful negotiation is achieved: people find themselves in consensus, a decision is reached, and a plan of action is started. Other arguments may not have such clear-cut results. A hostile audience may be brought to a neutral point of view. A neutral audience may decide it is important to take a stand. There are times when it is a significant accomplishment just to get the audience's attention and raise the level of consciousness of those engaged. This success can lay the groundwork for a possible change of minds in the future.

How much can you expect to change people's thinking as you discuss and write about issues that matter to you and that you think are important to examine? For students in argument class, this can be an urgent question. They wonder whether they must convince their teachers and their classmates of their point of view in every paper or presentation if they are to achieve good grades. Such a demand is too great, however, since audiences and the outcomes of argument vary too much. Convincing the teacher and your fellow students that the argument paper is effective with a particular audience is a good—and probably the best possible—outcome in argument class. As one professor put it, "My ambition is to return a paper and say that I disagreed with it completely—but the writing was excellent—A!"[3]

Under What Conditions Does Argument Fail?

We have just examined the optimal conditions for argument. Now, let us look at the conditions that can cause it to flounder or fail.

▶ **No disagreement or reason to argue.** We have already seen that no argument can take place when there is no real disagreement, no uncertainty, or no possibility for two or more views. In addition, neutral people who do not have enough interest in an issue to form an opinion do not argue. Argument also cannot take place unless people perceive an issue to be a subject for argument. Orientation leaders who try to persuade students to consider one major over another will not succeed with students who have already decided on their majors.

▶ **Risky or trivial issues.** Big or risky problems are difficult for some people to argue about because they can call for radical or sizable change. Finding a new career or dissolving a longtime relationship may fit into this category, and many people, wisely or not, tend to leave such difficult issues alone rather than argue about them. Religious issues or issues that threaten global disaster are also sometimes too big, too emotional, or too scary for many people to argue about them. At the other extreme, some issues may be perceived as low risk, trivial, boring, or even ridiculous. Some family arguments fall into this category, such as what to eat for dinner or who should take out the trash. One person may care, but the rest do not.

---

[3]Hilton Obenzinger, "The Israeli–Palestinian Conflict: Teaching a Theme-Based Course," *Notes in the Margins* (Winter 1994), 12.

▶ **Difficulty in establishing common ground.** We have pointed out that arguments that lack common ground among participants are not effective. You may encounter difficulties when trying to establish common ground with those who have made up their minds on certain issues and who no longer want to listen or consider a change. Those individuals who hold fast to prejudiced beliefs about various groups of people, for example, may dismiss information that defies their favorite stereotypes. It is also difficult to argue with some religious people who take certain issues on faith and do not perceive them as subjects for argument. Finally, argument cannot take place when one party is not motivated to argue. "Don't bring that up again" or "I don't want to discuss that" puts an end to most arguments.

▶ **Standoffs or fights that result in negative outcomes.** When argument is not working, as in some of the situations just described, the outcomes are also negative. For example, a standoff occurs, the parties assert or retreat to their original views, and then refuse to be moved. In another instance, emotions may be strong, verbal fighting breaks out, and extreme views are expressed. No one agrees with anyone else. People shake their heads and walk away, or they become hurt and upset. Some individuals may become strident, wanting to debate everyone to demonstrate that they are right.

One important aim of this book is to provide you with the insight and skill to manage these negative situations so that more constructive argument can take place. As students, you are in an excellent position to overcome much of the fear, resistance, and aversion associated with difficult issues and, by using evidence and good sense, get down to work and face some of them. Understanding audience members, especially their attitudes, needs, and values, is an important first step. Another useful idea to keep in mind is that most arguers have more success with certain audiences than with others, depending on the amount of common ground. Even in the most difficult situations, some common ground can be found among people who seem to disagree on almost everything. Recent research suggests that one vehicle for establishing common ground is through narratives, with each side relating personal experiences and stories. Even the most hostile adversaries can usually relate to one another's personal experiences and find unity in the common villains, heroes, or themes in their stories. In establishing common ground through stories, participants often find that the issues themselves change or are transformed in ways that make them easier for both parties to argue.[4]

Arguing effectively in difficult situations requires a conscious effort to avoid both stereotypical reactions and entrenched behavioral patterns. Past habits must be replaced with new strategies that work better. It is sometimes difficult to make such changes because habits can be strong, but it is possible to do so, and the stakes are often high, especially when the choice is constructive argument or verbal fighting and standoffs.

---

[4]Linda Putnam, in the keynote speech to the Texas Speech Communication Association Conference, Corpus Christi, TX, October 1993, reported these results from her study of negotiations between teachers and labor union leaders.

LO6 Distinguish between ethical and unethical argument.

Distinguish Between Ethical and Unethical Argument

Throughout this book, you will be given information to help you distinguish between *ethical argument*, which approaches issues in insightful, useful, and beneficial ways, and *unethical argument*, which manipulates an audience and may even harm it. An example of an ethical argument might be a plan for an effective and economical way to rebuild an area that has been destroyed by hurricanes, floods, or fire. An example of unethical argument might be an invitation to acquire a new credit card that tempts the user to incur a huge debt with high interest that will be either difficult or impossible to pay back. A photograph of people who have acquired new clothes, new cars, and exciting new lifestyles by using their new credit cards may also accompany this second example of an unethical argument. You may recognize this image as dishonest, manipulative, and unethical, but it can still be persuasive if the viewer longs for the particular benefits promised by the new card. To assess the ethics of a given argument, we need to think about both *motive* (i.e., the goal or intention a person has in making an argument) and *outcome* (i.e., the consequences or effects on an audience who accepts or follows through on this argument). Try to keep these considerations in mind as you evaluate the ethical content of any given argument.

To help you distinguish ethical from unethical argument, consider the arguer's general approach (whether it is traditional or consensual and whether it is accompanied by visuals or not), the specific purpose of the argument (to restore a community or to make money at others' expense), the general competency and reliability of the arguers (a government bureau with access to funds or a company that makes its money by charging high interest rates), and the quantity, quality, and reliability of the information presented. Learn to detect misleading and biased information as well as information that is untrue.

Part of evaluating argument requires that you read, listen, look, and analyze objectively, without making negative prejudgments. This can be difficult when you encounter opinions and values different from your own. To help you maintain your objectivity, think of yourself as a fair, unbiased person who needs to gain information and an understanding of it before you respond. When you do respond, think of yourself as a capable and ethical arguer who is willing to evaluate and participate in argument because it is important to you and to the society in which you live.

LO7 Define what constitutes an arguable issue in the twenty-first century.

Recognizing Argument in the Twenty-First Century

What does it mean to be an arguer in the twenty-first century? And, more specifically, how has the rise of digital technology reshaped the way argument looks and works? To begin answering these questions, we need to start with an observation: the emergence of the Web has led to an explosion in the number and variety of arguments to which we are now exposed. As we have become users of this technology, we have found ourselves exposed to a seemingly limitless array of issues, ranging from the mundane to the momentous, the most intimately personal to the most sweepingly global. With little more than the click of a button, we can now take part in thousands of different discussions and arguments. From Facebook posts to political blogs, online policy debates to Web-based movie reviews, we enjoy a veritable smorgasbord of argument.

Along with an unprecedented increase in the volume and variety of argument have also come profound changes in the ways we use argument to engage with each other. Social networking tools such as Instagram and Twitter provide us with virtually instantaneous access to each other, allowing us (if we so desire) to remain in near constant conversation with counterparts throughout the world. This type of perpetual availability on a personal level is matched by the unfettered access we now enjoy to more formal sources of information and opinion. Whether it is a broadcast from the BBC, an editorial in the online version of your local paper, or an advertisement for Nike, we are constantly invited to play the role of cultural consumer. We can read a blog post as we are walking down the street, can respond to a text message while standing in the checkout line at the grocery store, can arbitrate a conflict between two friends on Facebook while simultaneously updating our plans for Friday night. There is literally no place in our lives where, if we choose, we cannot be part of the larger public conversation.

Yet, for all this newfound access and interactivity, the rise of the Web also presents its own set of unique challenges. While it has given us unprecedented access to a new universe of issues, the Web has also altered the ways we go about engaging with these issues. Along with our 24/7 exposure has come a new way of participating in argument, one that emphasizes browsing or skimming over deeper reflection. Nowadays we are more likely to engage with a given issue by darting from one link to another, traversing the surface of a discussion without necessarily delving into its underlying substance. In a world marked by perpetual distraction and interruption, where the next topic, discussion, or activity is never more than an email or Web link away, how do we ever develop the skills necessary to focus on and address an issue in a sustained, thoughtful way? While the advantages of the Web are legion, the challenges are equally numerous.

In the face of such a complex situation, we need to develop a set of tools that can help us to deal with the forms argument takes in the digital age. In the pages that follow, we will take a closer look at a framework designed to accomplish precisely this goal, one that allows us to take a more sustained and deliberate look at the way argument functions online.

GETTING STARTED: QUESTIONS AND CONSIDERATIONS TO BEAR IN MIND AS YOU THINK ABOUT ONLINE ARGUMENT

Assembled below is a quick inventory of the key issues that define the rise of Web-based argument. As you look over this list, think about how these issues influence the kinds of discussions and arguments that get waged online, and whom these discussions and arguments involve.

▶ **Volume/Variety.** The rise of the Web has led to an explosion in both the number and types of issues to which we are exposed. As we make our way through this thicket of material, it is important that we pay attention to exactly how a given issue is being defined; what does or does not make it a valid or significant issue for public debate. In a world where issues range so widely, how do we distinguish between those that matter from those that do not?

▶ **Access.** Another feature of online argument involves the ease with which we can now join an ongoing discussion of a given issue. As any number of commentators have observed, a hallmark of the Web is the degree of freedom and mobility we now enjoy. With little more than the click of a button, it is now possible for us to communicate with people from, quite literally, throughout the world, on issues that can range from the local to the global. Given this, what is the context for a given argument online? Who are the various audiences with a stake in its outcome? How do we deal with audiences who hold radically different stakes or points of view?

▶ **Relevance.** In a world where we can connect to issues and to each other so readily, argument now occupies a more immediate and personal place in our every-day lives. Indeed, the Web seems to have inaugurated a new era of what we might call *participatory argument*: a way of engaging with issues that gives us a greater stake in and ownership over the issues we discuss. In this new environment, we need to think even more about what makes a given issue important to us, and what our personal stake in it is.

▶ **Interactivity.** An additional consequence of this increased access is our ability, in this new digital age, to connect and communicate more directly with our respective audience. Perhaps the single most defining feature of the Web is the degree to which it allows us the freedom to *network*: to bond with others over a shared interest in a given issue, to exchange our views, to offer support or criticism, and to, quite often, do so instantaneously. In light of this, we might ask, how does audience feedback influence the way a given argument unfolds?

▶ **Linked Issues.** In an environment in which everything and everyone has become so interconnected, it should come as no surprise that an issue raised online often links up with a range of other related issues. Within any given argument, we need to figure out what the key issue is, and how it differs from other issues to which it is linked.

▶ **Multimodal/Multimedia.** Another feature of our online world concerns the way arguments now combine written, visual, graphic, and video elements. How do we refine our analysis to incorporate these visual and graphic elements?

▶ **Authority/Credibility.** With the rise of so many different issues online, coupled with an equivalent rise in the number of people arguing over these issues, it has become increasingly important to think about the credibility of the arguments we encounter. In an environment in which everyone is free to express her or his opinion, how do we determine the validity of a given claim? On what basis—factual, logical, or emotional—do we decide a claim is legitimate?

▶ **Polarization.** Even as it has fostered greater engagement with and participation in various issues, the rise of the Web has also increased the intensity of feelings around them. Extreme views occupy a more prominent place in our public discussions these days. Given this, how do we find common ground?

Analyzing Online Argument: An Introduction

When it comes to argument, the rise of digital culture presents both significant opportunities and pressing challenges. Because they combine so many different elements and assume so many different forms, learning to analyze these arguments effectively requires that you focus on a set of factors that are particular to the world of digital argument. The outline below provides a framework for doing just this. Examine this outline carefully, as well as the sample analysis that follows. They provide step-by-step instructions for analyzing arguments in the digital age.

▶▶▶ Think About the Context

- What type of site is it?
- Who is the author of this text?
- What background information about this author can you find?
- Does this text include any links to other texts? What related issues and/or arguments do these texts address?

▶▶▶ Identify the Genre

- What form does this argument take (i.e., Web site, video, social media post, etc.)?
- How does this form affect the argument being made?

▶▶▶ Describe the Format

- What multimedia elements (i.e., written, visual, graphic, video) does this text include?
- How do these elements interact with or relate to each other?
- How do these elements work together to present a particular argument?

▶▶▶ Speculate About Audience

- Who is the target or intended audience?
- What opportunities for audience response or feedback does it provide?
- How does such feedback affect the argument being made?

▶▶▶ Analyze and Evaluate the Claim

- What key claim is being advanced?
- What specific multimedia elements help to advance it?
- What makes these elements effective or persuasive?

continued

Analyzing Online Argument: An Introduction (*continued*)

Sample Analysis: Healthy Choices Public Service Announcement (NIH)

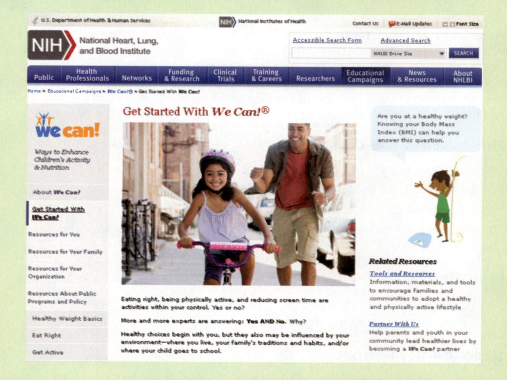

▶▶▶ Think About the Context

- This Web site was created as a joint project by the federal Department of Health and Human Services and the Ad Council, a private nonprofit organization.

▶▶▶ Identify the Genre

- This text takes the form of a public service announcement (PSA). PSAs are free messages disseminated by the media in order to raise public awareness about important social issues.

▶▶▶ Describe the Format

- This PSA combines a number of multimedia elements, including written text, visual imagery, graphics, and video.

Analyzing Online Argument: An Introduction (*continued*)

- The written text above the video screen shot offers an overview of the initiative being showcased: the "We Can" campaign, dedicated to helping children maintain a healthy weight and active lifestyle.
- The graphic to the right of the video reinforces the message about healthy eating by presenting a cartoon image of child speaking about the importance of knowing your "Body Mass Index" (BMI). And the video image of the smiling child on a bicycle reinforces the message about the benefits of an active lifestyle.

▶▶▶ Speculate About Audience

- This Web site seems to be directed toward the parents of school-age children who may be at risk of being overweight.
- By asserting the benefits of healthy eating and an active lifestyle so clearly, the Web site aims to raise awareness among parents and spur them to action.

▶▶▶ Analyze and Evaluate the Claim

- On the most general level, this Web site makes an argument about the importance of healthy eating and an active lifestyle.
- To bolster this argument, the Web site makes several additional claims. Among them: health-related choices are influenced by "environment" and "family"; children can control their own eating and exercise choices.

Activity

Choose an example of online argument. Then use the steps outlined above to analyze it in terms of context, genre, format, audience, and claim.

Engaging with Issues

To summarize, the most easily arguable issues are those that invite two or more views that are perceived by all parties as issues, that are interesting and motivating to all participants, and that inspire research and original thought. They also promise common ground among participants, and they do not appear too big, too risky, too trivial, too confusing, too scary, or too specialized to discuss profitably. You may, however, find yourself drawn to some of the more difficult issues that do not meet all of these criteria, and you should not necessarily shun them because they are difficult. You will need to work with your audience in creative ways and consider the entire context for argument, regardless of the nature of the issues you select. Most important at this point is that you identify several issues that are arguable and important to you and to your classroom audience. Identifying issues will help you keep a high level of motivation and receive the maximum instructional benefits from argument class. Finding arguable issues yourself is much better than accepting assigned issues as writing topics.

So, now the search begins. What will help you search out and select arguable issues? Issues exist in contexts, and the issues most engaging to you will probably emerge from the parts of your life that demand your greatest attention and energy. For example, people who are compellingly engaged with their professions think about work issues; new parents think about childrearing issues; dedicated students think about issues raised in class; and many teenagers think about peer-group issues. To begin the search for your issues, examine those parts of your life that demand your most concentrated time and attention right now. Also, think about the special characteristics of issues in general. Here are a few of them.

▶ **Issues are compelling.** People get excited about issues, and they usually identify with a few in particular. Most people can quickly name one or more issues that are so important and so interesting to them that they think about them often, sometimes daily. If you live in the Northwest, for example, the preservation of old-growth forests may be an issue for you. If you are preparing for a career in education, an issue you may care about might be creating equal access to quality education. Can you think of particular issues that are compelling to you?

▶ **Issues often originate in dramatic life situations.** Things happen all around us—global terrorism seems out of control, people download music and videos from the Internet but debate over what they should pay, the number of illegal immigrants entering the United States increases. As the issues around us change, we inevitably respond with questions: What should be done to stop global terrorism? How much is a song you can download from iTunes actually worth? Should U.S. borders be patrolled, or should immigrants be offered work permits? Pay attention to the stories that are newsworthy this week, and identify the issues associated with them. Select the ones that interest you the most.

▶ **Current issues can be linked to enduring issues that have engaged people for ages.** For example, the controversy about genetically engineering new plant and animal life is related to age-old issues associated with the preservation of life as it has evolved on this planet: Will genetic engineering help cure human disease? Or will genetic engineering be profoundly destructive to existing life forms? Affirmative action issues are linked to the enduring issue of whether or not all people are created equal: Will affirmative action contribute to racial profiling, or will it actually decrease discrimination? Look at Box 1.1 for additional examples of contemporary public issues we have linked with enduring issues to demonstrate the timeless quality of many of them. See if you can add examples as you read through those in the "Current" column.

Box 1.1   Examples of Current and Enduring Public Issues

▶▶▶ What Are Some Public Issues?

CURRENT ISSUES	ENDURING ISSUES
Ways and Means Issues	
Should everyone pay taxes? In what proportion to their income?	From what sources should a government obtain money, and how should it spend it?
Should free trade be limited?	
How much business profit can be sacrificed to keep the environment clean and safe?	
Should scholarships and fellowships be taxed?	
How can we reduce our dependence on foreign oil?	
How should we finance health care?	
Is the national debt too high, and, if so, what should be done about it?	
Quality of Life Issues	
Should more resources be directed to protecting the environment?	What is a minimum quality of life, and how do we achieve it?
Are inner cities or rural areas better places to live?	
How can we improve the quality of life for children and senior citizens?	
What effect will global climate change have on our lives?	

continued

Box 1.1   *(continued)*

CURRENT ISSUES	ENDURING ISSUES
Personal Rights versus Social Rights Issues	
Should individuals, the government, or private business be responsible for the unemployed? Health care? Day care? The homeless? Senior citizens? People with drug addictions? People with AIDS? Race problems? Minority problems? Dealing with criminals? Worker safety? Deciding who should buy guns?	Can individuals be responsible for their own destinies, or should social institutions be responsible? Can individuals be trusted to do what is best for society?
War and Peace Issues	
How much should the government spend on the military? Should the United States remain prepared for a major world war? Should you, your friends, or your family be required to register for the draft? To what extent should a government pursue negotiation as an alternative to war?	Is war ever justified, and should countries stay prepared for war?
Self-Development Issues	
What opportunities for education and training should be available to everyone? How well are job-training programs helping people find employment? Should undocumented workers be allowed the same opportunities to participate in society as citizens?	What opportunities for self-development should societies make available to individuals?
Human Life Issues	
Should abortions be permitted? Should capital punishment be permitted? Is mercy killing ever justifiable? Should stem cell research be allowed?	Should human life be protected under any conditions? What or who will define the limits of a person's control of his or her own life, and what or who limits a government's interest or control?

Box 1.1   (continued)

CURRENT ISSUES	ENDURING ISSUES
Foreign Affairs Issues	
Which is wiser, to support an American economy or a global economy?	In world politics, how do we balance the rights of smaller countries and different ethnic groups against the needs of larger countries and international organizations?
How much foreign aid should we provide, and to which countries?	
Should college graduates be encouraged to participate in some type of foreign service like the Peace Corps?	
Should the United States defend foreign countries from aggressors?	
Law and Order Issues	
Is the judicial system effective?	What is an appropriate balance between the welfare and protection of society as a whole and the rights of the individual?
Does the punishment always fit the crime?	
How serious a problem is racial profiling?	
How can global terrorism be eradicated?	
To what degree have we sacrificed our privacy for national security?	
Intimacy/Friendship	
Do online technologies enhance or detract from the quality of our friendships? Should there be stricter policies regulating social networking?	To what extent should our public speech or behavior be regulated?
Privacy	
What are the risks of putting so much information about ourselves online? Should people have the right to censor public information about themselves?	Is privacy a universal right?
Surveillance	
Should the government be allowed access to information about us online?	What limits should be put around government authority?
Political Activism	
Has the rise of the Web improved the quality of political campaigning?	What should be the rules governing how politicians are allowed to campaign for office?

▶ **Issues go underground and then resurface.** Public concern with particular issues is not constant. Experts may think about their issues continuously, but the public usually thinks about an issue only when something happens that brings it to public attention. How to deal with the increasing population is an example of such an issue. Experts think about that issue almost daily, but the general public may note it or think about it only when new information is released. For example, the world's population is expected to reach more than nine and a half billion by the year 2050. It has more than doubled in only fifty years, a fact that prompted a considerable amount of argument in the media, particularly about future population growth and the ability of the planet to sustain it. As one commentator stated, the media often make arguments out of the news. Persistent issues are, of course, always alive in the background and always important, but we do not think about all of them all of the time. Think back. Are there some issues that used to concern you that you have neither thought about nor read about for a long time? What are they?

▶ **Issues sometimes are solved, but then new ones emerge.** Some issues command so much public attention that the people who can do something about them finally perceive them as problems and pass laws or take other measures to solve them. As soon as an issue is solved, however, other, related issues spring up in its place. For example, for many years, people argued about what to do about health care. Much of the current health care debate revolves around the fact that millions of Americans have been uninsured, and the role the government should play has become an issue. Are there other issues of this type that might interest you? Think of problems that now seem solved, but are probably not completely solved for all people, or for all times.

▶ **Issues seem to be getting more complex.** Issues seem to become more and more complex as the world becomes more complex. In an interview, actress Susan Sarandon, who has always been engaged with social issues, stated that in the mid-to-late 1960s, when she was in college, the issues seemed simpler, more black and white. The issues at that time, for example, centered on civil rights and the Vietnam war. "We were blessed with clear-cut issues," she says. "We were blessed with clear-cut grievances. Things were not as gray as they are now."[5]

Because issues are now more complex, people need to learn to engage with them in more complex ways. The word *perspectives,* as used in this book, refers not only to a broader perspective on issues and argument itself, including viewing images and reading essays as though they were arguments when that is appropriate, but also to the variety of perspectives that individuals can take or must accommodate others taking. Few issues are black and white, and not many can be viewed in pro or con terms anymore. Most invite several different ways of looking at them and require language that reflects their complexity.

As you develop your own perspectives on the complex issues that engage you, keep in mind that it takes many years to become an expert. You will want to look at what experts say and write, though you will not have the background

---

[5]Ovid Demaris, "Most of All, the Children Matter." *Parade,* March 1, 1992, 4–5.

and information to write as comprehensively as they do. When you write your argument, you will want to research and write on a limited aspect of the issue you engage, one that you can learn enough about to argue effectively. Limiting your topic will permit you to get the information and gain the perspective to be convincing. Suggestions that can help you limit your approach to a complex issue will be made in future chapters.

Arguing Like a Citizen

Arguments are more than simply academic discussions. Issues have real-world consequences that impact how we live, the opportunities we enjoy, the ways we interact with each other. More than an abstract or formal exercise, argument is one of the most direct and vital tools we have for engaging the forces and factors that shape public life. Given this, we might well ask, What is the broader social or public significance of a given issue? How do our arguments over issues provide us with an opportunity to effect change in the world around us? How can arguing contribute to the common good?

In order to answer these questions, we need to approach argument as more than an abstract set of skills. We need instead to understand and appreciate the ways argument is woven into the fabric of our lives, informing our assumptions and actions, our values and choices. We need, in short, to see argument as an act of citizenship.

The questions outlined below offer a framework for beginning to think about argument in terms of citizenship. Considering these questions will help us better understand the real-world consequences that arguments have.

▶▶▶ Thinking Like a Citizen: Questions to Get Us Started

- Why do I care about this issue? What makes it matter to me personally? What are the factors or circumstances that determine my stake?

- Who else cares about this issue? Who are the other stakeholders? Which other individuals or groups are most likely to consider this issue important?

- What are the different perspectives on this issue others might have? How are their stakes in this issue similar to or different from my own?

- What are the factors and/or circumstances that account for these differences? How and why do people who are part of different groups or constituencies understand the significance of this issue differently?

▶▶▶ Arguing Like a Citizen: Connecting Issues to the Larger World

- How does this issue impact or affect my daily life? What difference (social, political, economic, cultural) does it make to me?

- What are the key problems or questions this issue raises for me? Are these the same problems and questions this issue raises for others?

continued

Arguing Like a Citizen (*continued*)

- What are the differences among us that a discussion over this issue might expose?
- How can these differences be bridged?

▶▶▶ Acting Like a Citizen: Putting Our Arguments Into Practice

- Where could I go in my community to see an example of this argument being waged?
- What concrete action could I take to change or improve the way this issue is debated?
- What sort of concrete action might help resolve this argument?

Example: "Should a state allow its citizens to cast their votes in elections online?"

▶▶▶ Thinking Like a Citizen

- Why do I care about this issue? What is my stake?
  I'm concerned about voter participation in elections and feel this plan would allow more voters to participate in the democratic process. My perspective is that voters should be allowed to cast votes online because it would allow more people to participate in political elections and thereby enhance the democratic process.

- Who else cares about this issue? Who are the other stakeholders? Which other individuals or groups are most likely to consider this issue important?
  Individuals running for public office have a clear stake in this question, as do groups or organizations whose interests might be affected by the outcome of a given vote: grassroots activists, corporations, or "good government" advocates whose mission is to increase participation in the political process. Incumbent politicians who may have a vested interest in preserving the status quo might also consider this issue important.

- What are the different perspectives others might have on this issue? How are their stakes in this issue similar to or different from my own?
  Corporations may have a vested interest in restricting eligible or interested voters to those more likely to side with their own views. Grassroots activists, who often struggle to gain recognition or support for their initiatives, may be in favor of such a plan because of its potential to attract more supporters to their cause.

- What are the factors and/or circumstances that account for these differences?
  Economic factors (i.e., Do I stand to gain financially with this policy?), one's place in the political process (i.e., Does this change give me greater influence?)

Arguing Like a Citizen (*continued*)

▶▶▶ Arguing Like a Citizen

- How does this issue impact or affect my daily life? What difference does it make to me?
  As a college-age student who is only now beginning to participate in politics, this issue matters a great deal to me. As someone who uses online technology in every facet of my daily life, this policy would make it much easier to care about and participate in the political process.

- What are the key problems or questions this issue raises for me? Are these problems and questions the same as those this issue raises for others?
  The key issues raised for me concern questions of convenience. In my view, one of the main reasons we do not have greater political participation has to do with the fact that voting requires so much effort. Democracy should make it easier for citizens to participate. Others, however, might consider the key concern to involve privacy. How do you preserve the confidentiality of the ballot box when peoples' votes are tallied online? Still others might harbor concerns over the issue of election fraud. Does online voting provide the same degree of security when it comes to tallying up the votes themselves?

- What are the differences among us that a discussion over this issue might expose? How might these differences be bridged?
  Clearly, an issue such as this has the potential to draw distinctions between those who benefit from the current political status quo and those who do not. Citizens who feel disenfranchised by the current process, who feel their voices are not heard in public matters, are more likely to respond positively to a proposal to make voting easier and more accessible. Conversely, those who feel the current system already provides adequate access are more likely to take an opposing view. Common ground might be found, however, if the new policy were implemented in a way that did not replace, but rather simply supplemented, the existing voting system.

▶▶▶ Acting Like a Citizen

- Where could I go in my community to see an example of this argument being waged?
  League of Women Voters; college Democrats or Republicans; advocacy organizations.

- What concrete action could I take to change or improve the way this issue is debated? What sort of concrete action might help resolve this argument?
  Take part in a "get-out-the-vote" registration drive; start a political blog designed to raise public awareness around political issues.

How Should You Engage with Issues?

Remember that *issues are everywhere*. Listen for issues in lectures and look for them in your textbooks. Ask your professors to identify the major issues in their fields. Box 1.2 illustrates some of the issues you are likely to encounter in your other

---

| **Box 1.2** | **Examples of Academic Issues Across the Disciplines** |

▶▶▶ What Are Some Academic Issues?

In Physics—Is there a unifying force in the universe? Is there enough matter in the universe to cause it eventually to stop expanding and then to collapse? What is the nature of this matter?

In Astronomy—What elements can be found in interstellar gas? What is the nature of the asteroids? What criteria should be used to identify a new planet?

In Biology—What limits, if any, should be placed on genetic engineering?

In Chemistry—How can toxic waste best be managed?

In Sociology—Is the cause of crime social or individual? Does television have a significant negative effect on society? What effects do computers have on their users?

In Psychology—Which is the better approach for understanding human behavior, nature or nurture? Can artificial intelligence ever duplicate human thought?

In Anthropology—Which is more reliable in dating evolutionary stages, DNA or fossils?

In Business—Can small, privately owned businesses still compete with giant conglomerate companies? Are chief executive officers paid too much?

In Mathematics—Are boys naturally better than girls are at learning math? Should the use of calculators be encouraged? Should calculators be allowed in testing situations?

In Engineering—How important should environmental concerns be in determining engineering processes? To what extent, if any, are engineers responsible for the social use of what they produce? How aggressive should we be in seeking and implementing alternative sources of energy? Should the government fund the development of consumer-oriented technology to the same extent that it funds military-oriented technology?

In History—Have historians been too restrictive in their perspective? Does history need to be retold, and, if so, how? Is the course of history influenced more by unusual individuals or by socioeconomic forces?

In Political Science—Where should ultimate authority to govern reside: with the individual, the church, the state, or social institutions? Is power properly divided among the three branches of government in the United States?

In Communication—How can the best balance be struck between the needs of society and freedom of expression in the mass media? How much impact, if any, do the mass media have on the behavior of individuals in society?

In English Literature—Is the concept of literature too narrowly focused in English departments? If yes, what else should be considered literature?

college classes. These are examples of issues that your professors argue about, the subjects for academic inquiry. You may be expected to take positions and develop arguments yourself on these or similar issues if you take classes in some of these fields.

As you read, try to add examples from your other courses. Read newspapers and newsmagazines, look at images to get ideas (see Figure 1.4), listen to public radio, watch television programs that hold discussions of issues, and scroll through blogs and Web sites online. Browse through some of the newly acquired books in the library and look for issues. Listen for issues in conversations and discussions with friends and family. Identify campus issues. If you attend a house of worship or belong to an organization, listen to the issues that surface there.

As you watch for and think about the issues that might engage you, start making a list of those you particularly want to learn more about. Make a corresponding list of some of the other groups or individuals who may also be interested in these topics and jot down the views they may hold. Such lists will come in handy when it is time to select topics for your argument papers and begin analyses of your potential audiences.

MAKING AN ISSUE YOUR OWN

Step 1: What do I care about? What questions or problems—whether national, political, or personal—do I find myself drawn to? Why?

Step 2: Who else cares about this, and what different kinds of views do they hold? How do these views relate to my own?

Figure 1.4 *Girls Receiving Education in Bamiyan, Afghanistan*

Step 3: Where do people talk about this? In what contexts or setting?

Step 4: What point of view on this issue do I want to communicate? How?

Step 5: What is my larger goal? Why do I want to convey this viewpoint? Who is my audience, and what effect do I want to have on their views?

Review Questions

1. What did you think of when you encountered the word *argument* as you began to read this chapter? What do you think now? **(LO1)**

2. Describe traditional and consensual argument. Give two examples of each. **(LO2)**

3. Provide three examples of your own to illustrate the statement "Argument is everywhere." One of your examples should be a visual argument. **(LO3)**

4. What are some of the conditions necessary for argument to work best? **(LO4)**

5. What are some of the conditions that may cause argument to fail? **(LO4)**

6. Give two examples of an ethical argument and two examples of an unethical argument. **(LO5)**

7. How has the role of audience changed in the world of digital argument? **(LO6)**

8. Identify four sources of arguable issues. **(LO7)**

Exercises and Activities

A. Class Project: Understanding Common Ground

1. *Build common ground with your classmates.* Create pairs of students, appoint one in each pair as the scribe, and have each pair take five minutes to discuss and record ideas, experiences, and so on that they have in common. Now create groups of four students by teaming two pairs, appoint a scribe for this group, and have the groups take five minutes to discuss and record what all four members have in common. The scribes then give one-minute reports about what each group has in common. As you listen to these reports, a sense of what the whole class has in common will emerge.

2. *Discover common ground about argument.* Return to your groups of four for five minutes and have the scribes record answers to these questions: (1) What do you think of when you hear the word *argument*? (2) What effect might finding common ground have on your ideas about argument? Finally, have the scribes take two minutes to report to the class on these findings.

3. *Write about common ground.* Write for five minutes about the common ground you think already exists in your classroom. What do you and your classmates have in common? How do you differ? How are your ideas about argument and common ground similar to or different from those of your classmates? What effect will common ground in your class have on the argument that takes place there? Discuss what you have written with the class.

B. Class Project: "Argument Is Everywhere"

1. Test the idea that argument can be found everywhere. Each member of the class should bring in an example of an argument and explain why it can be defined as argument. Each example should focus on an issue that people are still arguing about and on which there is no general agreement. Each student should also define a position on the issue, and the position should be supported with reasons and evidence. Look for examples in a variety of contexts: newspapers, magazines, the Internet, television, motion pictures, music, sermons, other college classes, conversations, and printed material you find at work, at school, and at home.

   Bring in actual examples of articles, images, letters to the editor, bumper stickers, advertisements, or other easily transportable argument formats, or provide clear and complete descriptions and explanations of argument sources you cannot bring to class, such as lectures, television shows, or billboards. Students should give two- to three-minute oral reports on the example of argument they have selected, including a description of the issue and some of the reasons and evidence offered. This is most easily achieved by completing the statement "This arguer wants us to believe . . . , because. . . ." The class should decide whether all examples described in this activity are indeed examples of argument.

2. State whether you think the argument you have provided is ethical or unethical, and say why.[6]

C. Reading, Group Work, and Class Discussion: What Makes a Good Written Argument?

Read the following two argument essays. Then, in small groups, answer the questions listed below for each of them.

1. What is the issue?

2. What is the author's position on the issue?

3. What reasons and evidence are given to support the author's position?

4. What makes each of these arguments successful?

5. What are the weaknesses in the arguments, if any?

---

[6]I am indebted to Cedrick May for the basic idea for this project.

Finally, in class discussion, compile a list of the best as well as the weakest features of argumentation in each essay. Keep a copy of this list. It is a starting point. You will add to it as you learn more about what it takes to make a good argument.

> **BEFORE YOU READ:** What is the proper role parents should play with their college-age students? How closely involved should parents be?

ESSAY #1   NO ESCAPE FROM "HELICOPTER PARENTS"*
Felix Carroll

Felix Carroll is a former staff writer for the *Albany Times Union*. He currently writes a regular column for the newspaper.

Excuse me, but you're hovering. You realize that, right?

The media, pediatricians, psychologists and even the college dean, they've all got you figured out—or so they say. They're calling you a helicopter parent. Get it? Because you hover?

You're a baby boomer, right? OK, then. Listen up, because this is what they're saying about you.

You're too obsessed with your children. You treat them like little princes and princesses—like they're No. 1, like they're MVPs. You've painstakingly planned their lives from their first play date to their first day of college.

5   They're your little Renaissance kids. You shuttle them from soccer practice, to clarinet lessons, to karate, and—because they will be going to a great college—to SAT prep class. Whoops! Speaking of which: You're late.

You inflate their egos. You give them graduation ceremonies even when it's just from preschool. You give them a trophy at the end of the season even when they lose. And by the time they get to college and are asked who their hero is, your child will say those words you long to hear: My dad. My mom.

Yes, helicopter parent, your intentions are good, but that rotor of yours is causing a din. Bring her down to terra firma. Let's talk.

A report on "60 Minutes" last fall discussed how the so-called echo boomers—the children of baby boomers, who were born between 1982 and 1995—are "over managed" and "very pressured" and treated by their parents as pieces of "Baccarat crystal or something that could somehow shatter at any point."

Indeed, Mel Levine, a professor of pediatrics at the University of North Carolina Medical School in Chapel Hill, says today's children "may well shatter."

10   He thinks children are being coddled and protected to a degree that threatens their ability later in life to strike off on their own and form healthy relationships and proper job skills.

"These parents are trying to create a really terrific statue of a child rather than a child," says Levine, author of "Ready or Not, Here Comes Life" (Simon and Schuster, 2005).

Beverly Low, dean of the first-year class at Colgate University, says that where before parents would drop their kids off to college and get out of the way, parents now constantly call her office intervening in a roommate dispute or questioning a professor's grading system.

"A lot of our students tell us, 'Hey, my mom is my best friend. My father is my best friend.' Is that a good thing? It's a different thing," she says.

But why is it happening? Mary Elizabeth Hughes, a sociologist at Duke University, says helicopter parenting may be an outward sign of economic anxiety, particularly when parents consider the uncertain job market that may await their children.

15   "They're very concerned that their kids do very well and excel at a lot of things as a result," she says.

Hughes says such parenting may reflect generational changes as well.

Many baby boomer parents came of age during the turbulent '60s where they could not help but experience social change and respond by creating new lifestyles including new forms of parenting.

Mark and Cathy Gamsjager of Greenville, N.Y., are annoyed by parents who turn their loving into hovering. But baby boomers, as a whole, may not be getting the credit they deserve, they say, particularly for some of the improvements they have brought to parenthood.

Mark Gamsjager, 42, fronts the rockabilly band The Lustre Kings. He skateboards and snowboards with his two boys, Austin, 13, and Thomas, 9.

20   They have a great relationship and have lots to talk about, he says.

But he is still their dad.

"I think there's got to be a line, you know?" he says. "You still have got to be the tough guy."

Indeed, the Gamsjagers say they try to take the best aspects of their parents— emphasizing education, independence and discipline—while improving upon their parents' shortcomings.

"I think parents make much more of an effort to be with their kids," says Cathy Gamsjager. "It seems to me that we've gotten away from everybody being an authoritarian. Not that we don't have authority over our kids, but there's more honesty. You spend more time actually talking to your kids about real things."

25   But being open and honest does not mean being a pushover, she says. "I'm not my kids' best friend," she says. "I'm their mom. I love being their mom, and I love being fun, but in the end, I totally get that I'm responsible for helping them make good choices. I'm responsible for where their lives head. I can enjoy them, but no, I can't be their friend."

For Discussion:

What are your opinions about the issue of parental involvement in the lives of their children? Is there an age limit at which this kind of involvement becomes counterproductive? If so, when? If your parents fit the model of "helicopter parenting" outlined here, would you be pleased?

> **BEFORE YOU READ:** Are there any annoying distractions in any of your classes? What are they? What could be done to eliminate them?

ESSAY #2   **THE LAPTOP ATE MY ATTENTION SPAN***
Abby Ellin

The author lives in New York and writes a regular column, "Preludes," for the *New York Times* about starting out in business.

[What is] the latest issue on business school campuses? It is not whether to start your own dot-com before graduation, but whether you should be allowed to use your laptop in the classroom as you please.

While more and more schools—especially business schools—provide Internet access in class and require students to lug their laptops with them, some are imposing rules on what their students can and cannot do with them in class.

But why, in the sedate hallways of graduate schools, is there need for debate on rules of discipline? It seems that some students, although smart enough to earn M.B.A.'s, have not figured out how the old, generally unwritten rules of conduct apply to the wired classroom. More and more students are sending instant messages to one another (chatting and note passing, 21st century–style), day trading (as opposed to daydreaming) and even starting their own companies, all in class.

The resulting commotion has annoyed many students. Jen McEnry, 28, a second-year M.B.A. student at the University of Virginia's Darden Graduate School of Business Administration, recalled that a classmate once downloaded an e-mail attachment during a finance lecture. The attachment automatically turned on the sound on the student's computer, which then delivered a booming message: "Oh my God, I'm watching porn!" Everyone roared at the practical joke, but the problem was clear.

5   "It's distracting when people are day trading, checking their e-mails or surfing the Web," Ms. McEnry said. It is even more distracting because Darden relies heavily on classroom participation.

At Columbia University, the business school's newspaper reported that a student-run "chat room" ended up on the overhead projector in the middle of class. University officials denied the report. By January, cyberspace had so intruded on classroom space at Columbia that a committee of professors and students came up with a code of professional conduct. "We're trying to find ways professors and students can use technology effectively and appropriately to create leaders," said Jeff Derman, a second-year M.B.A. student who heads the panel.

Yet how can M.B.A. students, whose average age is about 28 nationally, not know that it is rude to click away in class? After all, they presumably know not to walk out in the middle of a lecture, however boring. The rules of etiquette should not change just because of technology.

*"The Laptop Ate My Attention Span," by Abby Ellin, from *The New York Times*, April 16, 2000. Reproduced by permission of the author.

Still, some business schools have gone beyond issuing rules. Two years ago, Darden officials installed a switch in each classroom; a professor can program it to shut down the students' Net-surfing at fixed times. The students, however, found that they could override the teacher's decision by sneaking over before class and flicking the switch back on. It became a kind of game, the Battle of the Button.

The students spent hours arguing the broader issues. Should computers be banned from class? (No, we're adults! We pay to be here!) Should networks be shut off? (Of course not! Web access is an inalienable right!) Should professors be able to turn off the systems? (That's, like, so 1984!)

10   Blood started to boil: Students got mad at professors, professors got mad at students, students got mad at each other and everyone cursed technology. Why should they have to deal with all this when all they really wanted to do was learn how to be a millionaire?

Ms. McEnry proposes a standard of reasonable necessity. "If I'm expecting something important, like news about a job or something, then it's O.K. to go online," she said. "There are really pressing issues in people's lives, and they need to have access."

She is not kidding. Ms. McEnry found out that she had been elected president of the Student Association after her friends found the news on the school's Web site and told her. In class. [. . .]

At the Columbia business school, Safwan Masri, Vice Dean of Students and the M.B.A. program, takes a temperate tone. "These kids have grown up with computers; they can multitask," he said, explaining why Columbia decided against a Web shutdown switch. "We don't want to act as police. They're adults. We'd like to think they can control themselves."

I agree. Let them control themselves. If they cannot, here is my suggestion to them: Take a computer to the Metropolitan Opera. Log on. Write e-mail. Check your portfolio. At the end of the night, you will be lucky to still have a computer.

For Discussion:

Does this article describe a problem that you have experienced in your classes or labs? What do you think instructors should do? Do you think that students ever talk on cell phones or answer their beepers at inappropriate times? Elaborate. How do you think instructors should respond to that?

D. **Group Work and Class Discussion: Analyzing Visual Argument**

Look at the image reprinted in this section. You could analyze this work as a news photo or as a work of art, but you are not being asked to do that here. Instead, you will analyze it as a visual argument. Many images are subtly and deliberately persuasive, and you can learn to recognize, analyze, and evaluate them as arguments, just as you would print materials.

Organize into small groups, read the written commentary that accompanies this image, and answer these questions.

1. What is the issue?
2. How would you state the claim (the point of view on the issue that is communicated by the arguer)?
3. What reasons and evidence are given to support the position?
4. What makes the image interesting and effective as a visual argument?

Image 1: Waterfront Living

This photograph, taken in 2008, depicts a condemned home along the Atlantic coast of North Carolina's Outer Banks. Several years earlier, beach erosion in the same area forced the relocation of the nearby Cape Hatteras lighthouse approximately 2,900 feet inland from its previous oceanside location.

For Discussion: What did you first think when you looked at this photograph? How did the description of it change your perception? Do you find this photo convincing as a visual argument? What do you conclude about the alleged situation depicted here?

E. Reading, Group Work, and Class Discussion: Analyzing Argument Online

Choose an issue that is currently being debated online. Then, in small groups, answer the following questions listed below.

1. How is this issue defined and debated?

2. Who seems to be the target audience? What individuals and/or groups participate in this discussion?

3. What specific perspectives or points of view on this issue are represented?

4. How do you evaluate point of view? What are its strengths and weaknesses? Which do you find most convincing? Why?

5. Finally, as a group, discuss how this argument is different from one we might see in a more traditional format (i.e., newspaper, magazine, on TV, etc.). What specifically is different about the way issues are explored online? Are these differences for the better? How or how not?

F. Before You Write: Finding Compelling Issues for Future Argument Papers

The objective is to make a list of the issues that interest you so that you can draw possible topics from this list for future argument papers.

1. *Become acquainted with the issues that are topical in your world.* Make a list of current, debatable issues you find interesting.

2. *Report on these issues.* Individuals or pairs of students should select from this list of issues until they have all been assigned. Then follow these instructions to prepare a report for the class.

   a. Identify the content of the issue. What is it about? What key questions does it raise?

   b. Describe the rhetorical situation for each.

   c. Give a two-minute oral report in which you identify and describe the key aspects of this issue.

3. *Find "your" issues.* Most students have issues that they really care about. What are yours? Think about what has affected you in the past. Think about your pet peeves. Think about recent news items on television, in the newspaper, or online that have raised issues for you. Make a class list of the issues that concern you and the other students in your class.

4. *Identify campus issues.* What issues on campus concern you? What could be changed at your college to improve student life and learning? Make a class list.

G. **Before You Write: Applying the Twelve Tests**

Before you write about an issue, apply the twelve tests of an arguable issue that appear in Box 1.3 to make certain that it is arguable. If all of your answers are yes, you will be able to work with your issue productively. If any of your answers are no, you may want to modify your issue or switch to another one.

Box 1.3   **Twelve Tests of an Arguable Issue**

▶▶▶ **Do You Have an Arguable Issue?**

If you cannot answer yes to all of these questions, change or modify your issue.
Your issue (phrased as a question): _____

Yes _____	No _____	1. Is this an issue that has not been resolved or settled?
Yes _____	No _____	2. Does this issue potentially inspire two or more views?
Yes _____	No _____	3. Are you willing to consider a position different from your own and, perhaps, even modify your views on this issue?
Yes _____	No _____	4. Are you sufficiently interested and engaged with this issue to inspire your audience also to become interested?
Yes _____	No _____	5. Do other people perceive this as an issue?
Yes _____	No _____	6. Is this issue significant enough to be worth your time?
Yes _____	No _____	7. Is this a safe issue for you? Not too risky? Scary? Will you be willing to express your ideas?
Yes _____	No _____	8. Can you establish common ground with your audience on this issue— common terms, common background, and related values?
Yes _____	No _____	9. Will you be able to get information and come up with convincing insights on this issue?
Yes _____	No _____	10. Can you eventually get a clear and limited focus on this issue, even if it is a complicated one?
Yes _____	No _____	11. Is it an enduring issue, or can you build perspective by linking it to an enduring issue?
Yes _____	No _____	12. Can you predict one or more audience outcomes? (Think of your classmates as the audience. Will they be convinced? Hostile? Neutral? Attentive? Remember that any outcomes at all can be regarded as significant in argument.)

H. Writing Assignment: Writing a Short Argument on a Campus Issue

Select the campus issue that interests you the most, apply the twelve tests in Box 1.3, and write a 250- to 300-word argument about it. Use the two short arguments on pages 34–35 and 36–37 as models. Write a title that identifies your issue. Then make a statement (a claim) that explains your position on the issue, followed by reasons and supportive evidence to convince a college official to accept your views and perhaps take action to improve the situation.

I. Writing Assignment: Writing a One-Page Issue Proposal

Issue proposals help you organize and develop your thoughts for longer argument papers. Once you have selected an issue, test it with the twelve tests, do some background reading as necessary, and write a proposal that responds to the following four items:

1. Introduce the issue, and then present it in question form.
2. Explain why it is compelling to you.
3. Describe what you already know about it.
4. Explain what more you need to learn.

The following is an example of an issue proposal that was written by a student.*

STUDENT PAPER

#1

Prisna Virasin
Professor Wood
English 1302
2 Feb. 2014

The Barbie Controversy

Introduce the issue.

It is interesting that a small, blond, blue-eyed, plastic doll could cause an uproar. Barbie has succeeded (intentionally or not) in inciting heated opinion on whether she is fit to be the image of the perfect woman for millions of impressionable young girls. Some people have stated that Barbie's proportions are humanly impossible, with her exaggerated bustline and minuscule waist. They claim that these impossible proportions could lead girls to develop a poor body image. Barbie doll defenders state that Barbie is a part of most girls' lives

*The format shown in this paper (and similar student papers throughout this book) reflects an MLA documentation style that is modified to accommodate space limitations. For example, all MLA-style student papers are double-spaced throughout. For actual MLA guidelines and a sample student paper showing the correct, more complete MLA format, see the Appendix to Chapter 12, pages 363–383.

Present it in question form.

while they are growing up. Is Barbie bad? Does she have the power to affect girls psychologically all over the country or perhaps the world?

Explain why it is compelling to you.

I am interested in the Barbie controversy because, like many girls growing up in America, I was obsessed with Barbie when I was a child. Now, as a college student, I am very interested in female icons and their role in self-image development. I also have to fight the voices in my head telling me that I am too short and too fat, and I am not sure exactly where these voices have come from.

Describe what you already know about it.

I know that the Barbie doll product is pervasive in American society. I have never met a woman or girl who has not played with at least one Barbie. Barbie's image has appeared in McDonald's Happy Meals, in computer programs, on her own clothing line, on school supplies, and in every major American store with a toy section.

Explain what more you need to learn.

I need to do more research on the validity of the claim that Barbie affects girls' self-images either detrimentally or positively. I would like to explore the pervasiveness of Barbie internationally and compare the domestic sales figures to the international sales figures. If Barbie proves to be a detriment to girls' self-images, I would like to seek out some proposed solutions and discuss their feasibility.

The Rhetorical Situation: Understanding Audience and Context

After studying this chapter, you will be able to:

LO1 Identify the five elements of the rhetorical situation, and use these elements to analyze a written argument.

LO2 Use these five elements to analyze a visual argument.

LO3 Use these five elements to analyze an online argument.

LO4 Use these five elements to create your own written argument.

LO5 Analyze the audience of an argument.

You are probably beginning to realize by now that argument does not take place in a vacuum. Instead, a situation occurs that raises questions in people's minds and motivates them to discuss and argue in an attempt to resolve the issues and problems that emerge. For example, the price per barrel of crude oil goes up and issues emerge: How can the United States become less dependent on foreign oil? What are viable alternate energy sources? How effective are hybrid cars? Professor Lloyd Bitzer calls a situation that motivates issues and argument a *rhetorical situation*, because it stimulates discussion and encourages change. Rhetorical situations existed for the Declaration of Independence in 1776 when the issue was independence and its authors declared that the North American colonies should be independent from Great Britain, and for Abraham Lincoln's Gettysburg Address that he delivered in 1863 at the site of a famous Civil War battle. The issue was national unity. The time, place, and existing circumstances of these rhetorical situations provided the motivation for the authors of these documents to write them.[1]

---

[1]Lloyd Bitzer, "The Rhetorical Situation," *Philosophy and Rhetoric* 1 (January 1968): 1–14.

Five elements, according to Bitzer, are present in every rhetorical situation, and they can be analyzed.

In this chapter, we focus on the rhetorical situation as readers, creators of visual and multimedia argument, and writers employ it. Analyzing the rhetorical situation is an important critical reading strategy: it can be used as a tool for analysis throughout the reading process; it can be employed in a similar way to gain a fuller understanding of visual argument; and it is a potent critical thinking strategy that can help the writer plan and write a better argument.

Analyze the Rhetorical Situation When You Read an Argument

LO1 Identify the five elements of the rhetorical situation, and use these elements to analyze a written argument.

According to Bitzer, a rhetorical situation has five elements. We rearrange the elements in order to form the acronym TRACE, from the initial letters of these five elements, to help you remember them: the *text*, the *reader* or audience, the *author*, the *constraints*, and the *exigence* or cause. Now look at each of them to see how they can help you read, understand, and evaluate writing that presents an argument.

   Text. The text is the argument. Whether it is written, visual, or spoken, the text will have characteristics you can analyze. These include the type of text (essay, letter, book, image, contest, debate, etc.), the content of the text, and the format, organization, argumentation strategies, language, and style that are employed by the author.

   Reader. The potential reader or audience for the text ideally must care enough to read or otherwise take in the text and pay attention. An audience might change its perceptions as a result and, perhaps, will mediate change or act in a new way. A rhetorical situation invites such audience responses and outcomes. Most authors have a targeted or intended reading audience in mind. You may identify with the targeted audience, or you may not, particularly if you belong to a different culture or live in a different time. As you read, compare your reactions to the text with the reactions you imagine the targeted or intended reading audience might have had.

   Author. The author writes or develops an argument to convince a particular audience. You can analyze the author's position, motives, values, and degree of expertise. If you do not have direct information about the author, you will need to infer or guess at much of this information as you consider the argument text.

   Constraints. Constraints include the people, events, circumstances, and traditions that are part of the situation that constrain or limit a targeted audience and cause them to analyze and react to the situation in a particular way. Constraints also include the beliefs, attitudes, prejudices, interests, and habits that influence the audience's perceptions of the situation. The author brings another set of constraints to the situation. These include the author's character, background, available resources, and style. The limits inherent in the type of text being produced, whether written, spoken, or visual, can also provide constraints. Constraints may draw the author and audience together, or they may drive them apart. They influence the amount of common ground that will be established between an author and an audience. Look at the cartoon in Figure 2.1 for an example of constraints that are driving people apart. The constraints in this example are the basic assumptions about who governs in this family. What would you say are the father's constraints in this situation, and how do they differ from those of the rest of the family?

Here are some additional examples of constraints: (1) An audience feels constrained to mistrust the media because it thinks reporters exaggerate or lie. This constraint may cause this audience to be cynical and suspicious of an essay written by an editor that praises reporters for always writing the truth. (2) Another essay, by a famous biologist, presents the global environmental and overpopulation crisis in such catastrophic and frightening terms that a particular audience is constrained, through fear, to shut out the argument and refuse to consider it. (3) Some voters have lost their faith in political leaders. When they are mailed brochures that argue in favor of particular candidates and that ask them to support these candidates with donations, their constraints cause them to throw these materials away without looking at them.

As these examples demonstrate, a constraint can include a specific attitude or assumption on the part of an author or an audience. In addition, constraints also include those external factors—from formal rules or laws to informal social norms or traditions—that play a role in shaping these attitudes and assumptions. Here are

Figure 2.1 *Constraints in the Form of Basic Assumptions Driving People Apart*

"Because this family isn't ready to hold democratic elections—that's why!"

two more examples of constraints that may be closer to you: (1) You parked your car in a no-parking zone because you were late to class, and the police feel constrained by law to give you a ticket. You have different constraints, and you write to the hearings board that more and closer parking should be available to students to help them get to class on time. The hearings board has its own constraints, and will probably turn down your plea. (2) You believe everyone should share the household chores equally, and the person you live with disagrees. Both of you are constrained by your past experiences in living with other people, possibly by traditions that influence your ideas about gender roles in this type of division of labor, and also by perceptions about who has the most time to spend on the chores. Both parties may have to work hard to create the common ground necessary to resolve this issue. Notice how the constraints present on both sides in these examples influence the way the audience and the arguer react to the rhetorical situation and to the issues it generates.

Exigence. Exigence is the part of the situation that signals that something controversial has occurred or is present and that a problem needs to be resolved by some response from an audience. Here are some examples of exigence for argument: people become suspicious of genetically engineered foods because of negative newspaper reports; a third-world country threatens to resume nuclear testing; a football player is badly injured in a game and the fans of the opposing team cheer in delight. In all cases, something is wrong, imperfect, defective, or in conflict. Exigence invites analysis and discussion, and sometimes a written response to encourage both individual public awareness and discourse about problematic situations.

Study the following set of questions. They will help you analyze the rhetorical situation and gain insight into its component parts when you are the reader.

Text. What kind of text is it? What are its special qualities and features? What is it about?

Reader or audience. Who is the *targeted audience?* What is the nature of this group? Can they be convinced? What are the anticipated outcomes? If you are reading a historical document—for example, the Declaration of Independence—you might ask further: How did the readers at the time the text was written differ from other readers of the time or from modern readers? Were they convinced? Did they act on their convictions?

Now consider how you, *as a reader,* compare with the targeted audience and ask: *Am I typical of one of the readers the writer anticipated? What is my initial position? What are my constraints? Do I share common ground with the author and other audience members? Am I open to change? Does this argument convince me? Am I motivated to change my mind or modify the situation? How?*

Author. Who is the author? Consider background, experience, education, affiliations, and values. What is motivating the author to write?

Constraints. What special constraining circumstances will influence the reader's and the author's responses to the subject? Think about the people, events, circumstances, and traditions that are already in place along with the beliefs, attitudes, prejudices, interests, habits, and motives held by both the author and the reader that may limit or constrain their perceptions. Do the constraints create common ground, or do they drive the reader and author apart?

Exigence. What happened to cause this argument? Why is it perceived as a defect or problem? Is it new or recurring?

The student essay reprinted below addresses policies regarding cell phone use. Read the essay first and then read the analysis of the rhetorical situation that follows it. This analysis provides an example of how readers can use the rhetorical situation to help them understand argument.

BEFORE YOU READ: What are your opinions about the cell phone policies in your classes?

ESSAY #1 LET'S BAN THE CELL PHONE BAN*

Ava Guiterrez

Ava Guiterrez is a sophomore majoring in communications at the University of Wisconsin–Whitewater.

Over the last few semesters, I have repeatedly found myself face-to-face with professors who have issued the same classroom commandment: check your cell phones at the door.

The first time I encountered this rule, I was confused. Hand in my cell phone? Why? Was the professor worried that students' phones would ring nonstop, thereby interrupting her lecture? Or was she concerned that students would simply tune her out, losing ourselves in our screens instead of focusing on the material at hand?

I don't mean to suggest that concerns like these aren't valid. Professors have a right to expect that students will be attentive. But a blanket cell phone ban—imposed without any input from students—is a mistaken way to address these concerns. There are, after all, a number of ways to enlist students in a voluntary solution to the problems posed by cell phones. For example, students can simply be asked to turn phones off once they come into a classroom. Or failing this, they can be required to firmly put away their phones in pockets or backpacks.

Indeed, the fact that this cell phone ban leaves no room for commonsense compromise is what makes it so troubling. As students, we are told over and over that college is the place where we must take responsibility for our own education. Given this, it is surprising that so many instructors would institute a policy that seems designed to take responsibility away from students.

*"Let's Ban the Cell Phone Ban" by Ava Guiterrez. Reprinted with permission of the author.

5   When I asked one of my professors to explain his own no-cell-phone-in-the-classroom rule, he replied that such a policy helps students "take greater responsibility for their education." But in my opinion, this policy actually does the opposite. By making a decision that affects students without soliciting input from them, rules like the cell phone ban convey the message that instructors—not students—are really in charge. Rather than encouraging students to take ownership over their own educations, this policy tells them that their real job is simply to follow rules laid down by others.

A far more reasonable approach would be to involve students in a conversation with their instructors about what the proper limits on cell phone access should be. Rather than forcing students to surrender their cell phones on command, this type of compromise would give students the opportunity, as well as the responsibility, to set reasonable limits for themselves.

For Discussion:

What is the issue? What is the author's position on the issue? What reasons and evidence are given to support the author's position? What is your position on this issue? How much common ground do you share with your instructors on this issue?

Here is an analysis of the rhetorical situation for "Let's Ban the Cell Phone Ban."

▶ Example of an Analysis of a Rhetorical Situation from the Reader's Point of View

Text. This is an argumentative essay that provides reasons and personal experience to prove that professors should not implement a cell phone ban.

Reader or audience. The targeted readers are professors and students in classes where this policy has been implemented. The author expects the students and professors to identify with her and agree that this ban should be abolished.

Author. The author is a sophomore majoring in communications who was a student in several classes in which the cell phone ban had been put into effect.

Constraints. The author is constrained by the belief that students should be considered co-equals with professors when it comes to formulating class policy. She is also constrained by the idea that students can learn despite the potential disruption cell phones might cause. She expects her readers to hold the same beliefs.

Exigence. The student took several classes in which this cell phone ban was imposed.

Now consider how an understanding of the rhetorical situation can help you analyze images.

Arguing Like a Citizen

Take another look at the essay, "Let's Ban the Cell Phone Ban." In order to see how the argument made in this piece connects to the issue of citizenship, look at the sample analysis below. In what ways does the discussion here provide you with a starting point for "arguing like a citizen"? And how might you answer the questions that accompany this discussion?

▶▶▶ Thinking Like a Citizen

- Why do I care about this issue?
  As a college student, I have a considerable stake in the argument being made. In very immediate ways, my course grade—and by extension my overall academic record—could well depend on whether I comply with policies like a cell phone ban.

- Who else cares about this issue?
  The other major stakeholder group is the instructors who teach these courses. As the people tasked not only with creating classroom cell phone policies, but also with ensuring that such policies help further legitimate academic goals, instructors need to think about where the lines around cell phone use in the classroom should be drawn.

- What different perspectives on this issue might others have?
  While students would likely base their views on the relative inconvenience of a cell phone ban, instructors need to think about the impact this issue would have on the quality of their classroom teaching.

▶▶▶ Arguing Like a Citizen

- How does this issue affect my daily life?
  Because this issue bears so directly on my work in the classroom, it could be said to have an enormous impact on my day-to-day life as a student. Most immediately, it could affect whether I choose to bring a cell phone to class. Additionally, if I were to bring a cell phone to class, it could also impact the way I participate in classroom activities and discussions.

- What are the key problems or questions this issue raises for me?
  The key challenge posed by a mandatory cell phone ban relates to the impact such a policy would have on my participation in classroom discussions. Would I focus on the material at hand just as closely if my cell phone were more accessible to me?

▶▶▶ Acting Like a Citizen

- Where could I go in my community to see an example of this debate being waged?
  This issue could be argued in any number of campus venues, from college newspaper editorials to classroom conversations between instructors and students to casual conversations among classmates outside of class.

Arguing Like a Citizen (*continued*)

- What concrete action could I take to change or improve the way this issue is debated? *Given how relevant this issue is to students and instructors alike, the discussion over it would benefit most from a forum that brings all of the stakeholders together. Toward this end, this issue could be explored as a story in a campus newspaper, or posted as a question to be debated on a college Web site.*

Activity

Now use this same framework to analyze the argument presented in the essay "A Defense of Grade Deflation." What key issue does it address? What larger argument about this issue does it make? And how can you use the questions outlined above to connect this argument to the question of citizenship?

Analyze the Rhetorical Situation When You View a Visual Argument

LO2 Use these five elements to analyze a visual argument.

In our visual culture, natural disasters are the subject of extensive news coverage. The images photographers have sent back from disaster zones highlight not only the damage inflicted but the efforts to lend assistance. In Figure 2.2, U.S. Vice President Joe Biden offers assistance to residents of Natori, Japan, following the tsunami that devastated that country's northeastern coastline in 2011. Look at the image, read the caption that accompanies it, and consider the questions in the margin. Then read the following analysis of the rhetorical situation of the image and notice how much more you learn about this photo and its possible effect on an audience.

▶ Example of an Analysis of the Rhetorical Situation from the Viewer's Point of View

Text. This is a photograph from the tsunami zone in Japan. It is printed in an American newspaper. It depicts U.S. Vice President Joe Biden speaking to residents of Natori, Japan.

Viewer or audience. The targeted viewers are people in the United States, but also in other parts of the world, who read this newspaper either online or in print. The photographer expects the audience to be interested in what is going on in Japan in general, but also to show an interest in natural disasters of this sort. The photographer would expect a sympathetic audience who shares his humanitarian values.

Photographer or artist. This photographer works for Getty Images, a major source of digital images used by the news media.

Figure 2.2

Photograph of Vice President Joe Biden delivering a speech to Japanese citizens following the tsunami in August 2011

This image appeared as a stand-alone image in a national United States newspaper. View this photograph as an argument. How is it different from many of the images of natural disasters you have seen on television or in newspapers? How does it affect you as a viewer?

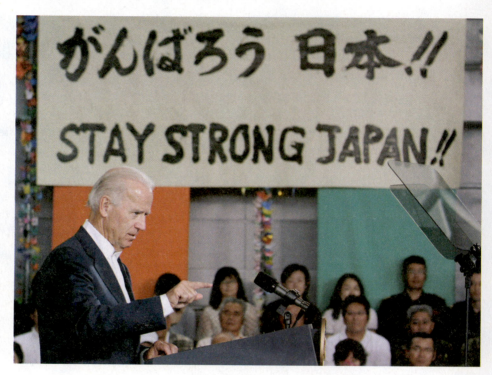

Constraints. The artist is constrained by the idea that natural disasters often bring out the best impulses in people to lend assistance. At times, good and generous acts as well as unexpected cooperation can occur in the midst of such events. He expects viewers to accept these constraints when they view his photograph, which will result in common ground with his audience.

Exigence. The aftermath of a devastating tsunami has caused great suffering among Japanese citizens.

Now, let's consider how an understanding of the rhetorical situation also helps you analyze the kinds of arguments you encounter online.

LO3 Use these five elements to analyze an online argument.

Analyze the Rhetorical Situation When You Encounter an Argument Online

In Chapter 1, you learned a series of steps for analyzing online argument. The same steps can also help you understand how the concept of the rhetorical situation applies to these arguments.

Analyzing Online Argument: TRACE

▶▶▶ Text

- What issue does this text explore? What claims does it make?
- What genre or form does the text take (i.e., Web site, video, email, social media post, etc.)?
- What multimedia elements (written, visual, graphic, video) does it include?

▶▶▶ Reader

- Who is the target viewer or audience?
- What opportunities for viewer feedback does this text provide?

▶▶▶ Author

- Who is the author or producer of this text?
- What information about the author does the text include?

▶▶▶ Constraints

- What does this information tell you about the author's perspective or bias?
- How does the text's genre or form affect the argument being made?
- How do the multimedia elements included affect the argument being made?

▶▶▶ Exigence

- What issue or event motivated the author to create this text?

Now let's look at how this revised TRACE model can be used to analyze a specific example of online argument. The BP/Horizon oil spill that occurred in the Gulf of Mexico in 2010 is considered by many to be one of the worst environmental catastrophes in American history. This spill, which released an unprecedented amount of oil into the Gulf, raised serious questions regarding our country's energy needs, our current energy consumption practices, and the effect of both on the overall health of the environment. Look at the Web site on page 52. What stands out to you about the images presented? What message about oil drilling, energy consumption, and the environment do they seem designed to convey? How does the written text, which accompanies these images, influence or reinforce this message? How is this message further affected by the links to other sources that this site includes? Once you have answered these questions, read the following analysis of the rhetorical situation presented by this Web site, and see whether you would add any further observations or interpretation.

continued

Analyzing Online Argument: TRACE (*continued*)

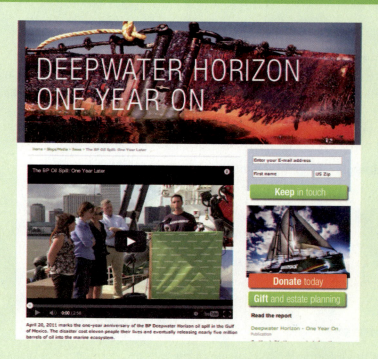

▶▶▶ Text

This is a Web site that highlights the environmental damage from the 2010 BP/Horizon oil spill in the Gulf. It was created by the environmentalist organization Greenpeace and is part of its larger campaign to raise awareness about threats to the global environment. It includes visual imagery that details the environmental damage inflicted by the spill, and documents Greenpeace's efforts to commemorate this event, as well as written text that describes the spill as a "disaster that cost eleven people their lives" and released "nearly five million barrels of oil into the marine ecosystem."

▶▶▶ Viewer or Audience

The targeted viewers for this text are people in the United States and, perhaps more particularly, Americans who live in those areas affected by the oil spill. The creators of this Web site expect the audience to be aware of the spill and the extent of the damage it has caused, and also to have concerns about the potentially long-lasting effects the spill might have. The creators would expect a receptive audience, given the widespread news coverage this oil spill received.

▶▶▶ Author

The author(s) of this Web site are the people who work for Greenpeace, an environmental advocacy organization.

Analyzing Online Argument: TRACE (*continued*)

▶▶ Constraints

The authors are constrained by their belief that oil companies pose a threat to environmental safety. Unless they are checked by environmental organizations, the authors believe oil companies are liable to deny responsibility for their actions. Evidence of this belief can be seen in the ways this Web site uses written and visual elements to convey its concerns about the effects of the oil spill. The audience is constrained by their own skepticism concerning the motives of such companies, a suspicion fueled in part by the media coverage of the BP/Horizon oil spill.

▶▶ Exigence

An oil rig collapses in the Gulf of Mexico, resulting in the release of millions of gallons of oil. The U.S. government attempts to work with BP to contain the spill, but for several months these efforts fail to stem the flow of oil into the Gulf, resulting in severe environmental damage.

Activity

Choose an example of an online argument. Then use the TRACE model outlined above to analyze the rhetorical situation.

Use the Rhetorical Situation When You Write an Argument

LO4 Use these five elements to create your own written argument.

As a writer, you can use the rhetorical situation to help you think critically and make decisions about your own writing. All five elements of the rhetorical situation are important considerations for writers. Three elements are in place before you begin to write. They are the *exigence*, the *reader or audience*, and the *constraints*. When you begin to write, the other two elements are added: you, the *author*, and the *text* that you create. Figure 2.3 provides a diagram of these five elements.

Now consider each of the five elements from the writer's point of view. Use TRACE to help you remember the elements. As a writer, however, you will think about them not in the order presented in the mnemonic but in the order suggested in the previous paragraph.

What Is the Exigence?

The exigence of a situation will provide an author with the motivation to write about an issue. Issues often emerge from real-life events that signal something is wrong. One student found a topic when a relative who had spent time in jail could not get employment after he was released. Another student from a country outside of the United States became interested in intercultural differences and decided to

Figure 2.3 The Five Elements of the Rhetorical Situation That the Writer Considers While Planning and Writing Argument

write about the relative value of retaining her own culture or assimilating with a new one. Yet another student discovered an exigence when she read a negative article about Barbie dolls and remembered her positive experiences with them when she was younger.

Such occurrences can cause the writer to ask the questions associated with exigence: *What issues, including problems or defects, are revealed? Are these new issues or recurring issues? How severe is the problem or defect?*

Who Is the Reader or Audience?

In order to be productive, arguments must create common ground and achieve some definable audience outcomes. To do this, a writer needs to analyze the audience's present opinions, values, and motives, and show as often as possible that the author shares them. Both audience and author must cooperate to a certain degree for argument to achieve any outcomes at all.

To help you understand your audience, ask: *Who are my readers? Where do they stand on my issue? How can I establish common ground with them? If they disagree with me, will they be willing to change or modify their views, or not?*

What Are Some of the Constraints?

Remember that constraints influence the ways in which both you and your audience think about the issues. What background, events, experiences, traditions, values, or associations are influencing both you and them? If you decide to write to convince an audience that has no experience with criminals to hire people with criminal records, what are their constraints likely to be? How hard will it be for them to adopt your views? On the other hand, if you are an international student who is comparing your culture with the American culture to decide how much to change and adapt to American ways, and your audience is only familiar with its own culture, what will you do to help them see this problem as you see it? If you are writing for an audience that is mostly male and has no experience with or memories of Barbie dolls, what constraints would you run into if you tried to convince them that Barbie dolls are an important part of children's experience?

To help you understand the constraints held by both you and your audience, ask: *How are our training, background, affiliations, and values either in harmony or in conflict? Will constraints drive us apart or help us build common ground? If they drive us apart, what additional information can I provide to build common ground and bring us closer together? Where will my argument appear? Will it be a paper for an instructor, a letter to a supervisor, a letter to an editor, or a post in an online chatroom? Each medium has its own requirements.*

You are in a position now to think about the remaining two elements of the rhetorical situation: you, the *author,* and the *text* you will write.

Who Is the Author?

You will now need to think of yourself as an author of argument. You may have selected one or more issues to write about at this point. Before beginning your research, reflect on what you already know about your issue and what you still need to learn. Draw on your own experience, if you have some that applies. For instance, one student might think about her relative's experiences in prison and imagine a better life for him, another might feel out of place in America and wonder how much he should change, and yet another student recalls her Barbie dolls and looks back with pleasure on the many hours she spent playing with them. Make brief notes on this experience to use later in your paper. If you have no direct experience to draw on, research, reading, and critical thinking will provide the material for your paper.

To better consider your role as the author, ask these questions: *Why am I interested in this issue? Why do I perceive it as a problem? Is it a new or old issue for me? What is my personal background or experience with this issue? What makes me qualified to write about it? Which of my personal values are involved? How can I get more information? What is my purpose and perspective? How can I make my paper convincing?*

How Should the Text Be Developed to Fit the Situation?

Your text (paper) may be written in response to an assignment in your argument class, in which case it should meticulously follow the assignment requirements. You might also write a paper for another class, a proposal at work, or a letter to the editor of a newspaper, to name a few possibilities.

Questions such as the following will help you decide what your completed argument text might look like: *What is the assignment? What final form should this paper take? Should I use an adversarial or a consensual style? How can I build common ground? Should I state the issue and my position on it right away, or should I lead up to it? How can I make my position original and interesting? What types of support should I use? How will I conclude my argument?*

▶ Example of an Analysis of a Rhetorical Situation When You Are the Writer

Exigence: What is motivating you to write on this issue? You neglected to turn in two early assignments in a course, and you suddenly realize that the zeroes you received then will lower your final grade from a B to a C. If you get a C, you will lose your scholarship. You decide to write to your instructor to find a way to raise your grade.

Reader or Audience: Who is going to read this? Your instructor (the audience) has already announced a policy of no late work. Nothing has been said about extra-credit work, however. You will try to establish common ground with the instructor by proposing an extra-credit project that will benefit not just you, but the entire class. You will describe in detail a successful experience you had with online research on your paper topic. The class is struggling with online research, the teacher wants the students to learn it, she does not have much time to teach it, and you can help fill the gap.

Constraints: Will your values and attitudes drive you and your instructor apart, or will they help you develop common ground? The instructor will have time constraints in class and may be unwilling to give you class time for your project. To address that constraint, you decide to ask for only five minutes, and you offer to prepare handouts that describe your online research in a way that will benefit your classmates.

The instructor may also have constraints about replacing missed assignments with extra-credit work. If one student is allowed to do this, she reasons, will all the others want to also? You point out that the project you are proposing is more difficult than the early assignments you missed and probably few, if any, students will want to follow your example.

You create common ground with your instructor by showing you are serious about the course and its standards. You decide to admit to your bad judgment when you failed to complete assignments, to point out that you have done well since then, and to commit to completing the remaining assignments carefully and on time. You also explain the importance of the extra-credit work to your future as a student. Without your scholarship, you will have to drop out of school. You know that you and your teacher share a desire to keep students in school. You and your instructor have common ground on that matter as well.

Author: What do you know? What do you need to learn? You are the author. You have read the class policies in the syllabus and know you have to work with them. You know you have computer expertise that many others in the class lack. You need to learn how to present what you know both orally and in written handouts to help the rest of the class.

Text: What should your argument look like? You will write a one-page proposal to your instructor in which you describe in detail what you would like to present to the class about online research. You ask that this assignment be used to raise the zero grades you received earlier in the course. You attach a second page that shows a sample of the handouts you will prepare for the class.

The class activities and writing assignments at the end of this chapter will help you use the information about the rhetorical situation that you have learned in this chapter. Before you turn to the activities and writing assignments, however, you will need additional information to help you think about and analyze an audience for an argument paper.

Conducting an Audience Analysis

LO5 Analyze the audience of an argument.

The purpose of argument is to bring about some change in an audience. Here are several additional considerations to help you understand your audience and plan your argument strategies to bring about change.

Determine the Audience's Initial Position and Consider How It Might Change

As part of your planning, speculate about what you would regard as acceptable audience outcomes for your argument. Think particularly about the degree of common ground you initially share with your audience because it is then easier to plan for audience change. There are several possibilities for initial audience positions and possible changes or outcomes.

▶ *A friendly audience.* You may be writing for a friendly audience, one that is in *near or total agreement with you* from the outset. The planned outcome is to *confirm this audience's beliefs and strengthen their commitment.* You can be straightforward with such an audience, addressing them directly and openly with your claim at the beginning, supported with evidence that they can accept. Political rallies, religious sermons, and public demonstrations by special-interest groups, such as civil rights or environmental groups, all serve to make members more strongly committed to their original beliefs. When you write for a friendly audience, you will achieve the same effect.

▶ *An undecided audience.* This audience either mildly agrees with you or mildly opposes you. They *may possess no clear reasons* for their tendencies or beliefs. Possible outcomes in this case usually include (1) *final agreement* with you, (2) *a new interest* in the issue and a commitment to work out a position on it, or (3) *a tentative decision* to accept what seems to be true for now. To establish common ground with this kind of audience, get to the point quickly and use support that will establish connections.

▶ *A neutral audience.* Other audiences may be *neutral on your issue, uncommitted and uninterested in how it is resolved.* Your aim will be to *change the level of their indifference* and encourage them to take a position. You may only be able to get their attention or raise their level of consciousness. As with other audiences, you will establish common ground with a neutral audience by analyzing their needs and by appealing to those needs.

▶ *A hostile, resistant audience.* A hostile audience, which may fully disagree with you, may also be closed to the idea of change at all, at least at first. Anticipated outcomes for such audiences might include *avoiding more hostility* and *getting people to listen and consider possible alternative views.* It is always possible that a hostile audience will have their minds *changed* or at least *compromise.* If all else fails, sometimes you can get a hostile audience to *agree to disagree,* which is much better than increasing their hostility.

▶ *An unfamiliar audience.* When you do not know your audience's position, it is best to *imagine them as neutral to mildly opposed* to your views and direct your argument with that in mind. Imagining an unfamiliar audience as either hostile or friendly can lead to extreme positions that may cause the argument to fail. Imagining the audience as neutral or mildly opposed ensures *an even tone* to the argument that *promotes audience interest and receptivity.*

▶ *A linked audience.* Linked audience refers to a reader not directly connected to or immediately participating in the discussion of a given issue, but who does have an interest in some issue that is related. This is often the case for arguments online, where the discussion of a given issue will frequently include references or links to discussions of similar issues. Imagine a neutral and unfamiliar audience that is sufficiently interested to seek additional information and perspectives regarding the issue. Supply links that will satisfy their needs and encourage them to respond positively to the argument you are making.

Think of your relationship with your audience as if it were plotted on a sliding scale. At one end are the people who agree with you, and at the other end are those who disagree. In the middle are the neutral audience and the unknown audience. Other mildly hostile or mildly favorable audiences are positioned at various points in between. Your knowledge of human nature and argument theory will help you plan strategies of argument that will address all these audience types and perhaps cause them to change their initial position on the sliding scale.

Analyze the Audience's Discourse Community

Besides analyzing your audience's initial position and how it might change, it is also useful to identify the audience's *discourse community.* An audience's affiliations can help define the nature of the audience itself. Specialized groups who share subject matter, background, experience, values, and a common language (including specialized and technical vocabulary, jargon, or slang) are known as discourse communities.

Consider discourse communities composed of all scientists, all engineers, or all mathematicians. Their common background, training, language, and knowledge make it easier for them to connect, achieve common ground, and work toward conclusions. The discourse community itself creates some of the common ground necessary for successful academic inquiry or for other types of argument.

You are a member of the university or college discourse community where you attend classes. This community is composed of reasonable and educated people who share common backgrounds and interests that enable them to inquire into matters that are still at issue. You are also a member of the discourse community in your argument class, which has a common vocabulary and common tasks and assignments. Outsiders visiting your class would not be members of this community in the same way that you and your classmates are. To what other discourse communities do you belong?

Compare argument in your class with argument at home, at work, or with your friends. The strategies for connecting with others, building common ground, and arguing within the context of each of your discourse communities can vary considerably. With some reflection, you will be able to think of examples of the ways you have analyzed and adapted to each of them already. You can improve your natural ability to work with audiences by learning several strategies for analyzing and adapting to both familiar and unfamiliar audiences.

Analyze and Adapt to a Familiar Audience

In working with a familiar audience, ask questions such as the following to learn more about them:

▶ Who are the members of your audience and what do you have in common with them?

▶ What are some of the demographic characteristics of this audience? Consider number, age, organizational affiliations, interests, and college majors.

▶ What is the present position of audience members on your issue, and what audience outcomes can you anticipate?

▶ What experience do audience members have with your issue? Ask about their knowledge and background, including both positive and negative experiences and obstacles.

▶ What beliefs, values, motives, goals, or aims about your issue do you share?

Construct an Unfamiliar Audience

Sometimes you will not be able to gather direct information about your audience because these readers will be unfamiliar to you and unavailable for study. In this case, you will need to draw on your experience for audience analysis. To do so, imagine a particular kind of audience, a *universal audience,* and write for them when you cannot collect direct audience information.

Chaim Perelman, who has written extensively about the difficulty of identifying the qualities of audiences with certainty, developed the concept of the universal audience.[2] He suggests planning an argument for a *composite audience,* one with distinct individual differences but also important common qualities. This universal audience is educated, reasonable, normal, adult, and willing to listen. Every arguer constructs the universal audience from his or her own experiences, and consequently the concept of the universal audience varies somewhat from individual to individual and culture to culture.

The construct of the universal audience can be useful when you write papers for your other college classes. It is especially useful when the audience is largely

---

[2]See Perelman and Olbrechts-Tyteca, *The New Rhetoric,* for additional details on the universal audience.

unknown and you cannot obtain much information about them. Imagine writing for a universal audience on those occasions. Your professors and classmates as a group possess the general qualities of this audience.

CONSTRUCT YOUR OWN UNIVERSAL AUDIENCE

Choose an issue and create a composite portrait of the hypothetical or universal audience you aim to address. What preexisting views on this issue does this audience hold? What constraints operate on this audience? What attitudes or assumptions influence their views? What factors influence these attitudes and assumptions? Then, based on this profile, speculate about how this audience would influence your specific strategies for making your argument.

When you complete the analysis of your audience, go back through the information you have gathered and consciously decide which audience characteristics to appeal to in your paper. You will then be in a position to gather materials for your paper that will be convincing to this particular audience. You will develop reasoning and support that audience members can link to their personal values, motives, beliefs, knowledge, and experience. Similarly, you need to show the same care in adapting to the needs of a universal audience. Since this audience is reasonable, educated, and adult, reasoning and support must be on their level and should also have broad applicability and acceptance. The universal audience inspires a high level of argumentation. *Careful research, intelligent reasoning, and clear writing style are requirements for this audience.*

Use your understanding of the rhetorical situation to help you read and to help you get ideas and plan your own argument writing. It can be useful at every stage when you are reading, thinking, and writing about issues. The Summary Chart of the Rhetorical Situation (page 421) provides a brief version of the elements of the rhetorical situation as it applies to both reading and writing. Use it as a quick reference worksheet as you read or plan and write argument.

Review Questions

1. What are the five elements in the rhetorical situation? Use TRACE to help you remember. **(LO1)**

2. How can you use the rhetorical situation to analyze an argument essay? How can you use the rhetorical situation to analyze an image? How can you use the rhetorical situation to analyze an argument online? How can you use the rhetorical situation during the planning phase of writing a paper? **(LO2, LO3, LO4)**

3. Why is the audience important in argument? What types of positions might an audience initially hold? What possible outcomes are associated with arguments directed to each of these audiences? **(LO5)**

4. What is a discourse community? To what discourse communities do you belong? How does a discourse community help establish common ground for its members? **(LO5)**

5. What is the universal audience? What are the special qualities of this audience? Why is it a useful idea? **(LO5)**

Exercises and Activities

A. **Class Discussion: Analyzing the Discourse Community for an Essay**

Read the following essay by Will Harrel. Then answer the questions for discussion that follow the essay.

> **BEFORE YOU READ:** How do you understand the term "grade deflation"? In your experience, does this term describe a widespread problem within higher education?

ESSAY #2   **A DEFENSE OF GRADE DEFLATION***

Will Harrel

Will Harrel is a student at Princeton University and a contributing writer to the *Daily Princetonian*, the campus newspaper.

While Princeton's diverse student body rarely unifies around a single issue, nearly every student seems to have rallied against grade deflation. This forces advocates of the policy—well, the few that exist—to always be on the defensive, addressing only the apparent negatives of grade deflation without discussing the benefits. I'll begin this defense of grade deflation by once again discussing the negatives, but I will conclude by finally going on the offensive.

One common complaint is that grade deflation compounds students' stress. While added pressure about grades does entail added stress, this pressure encourages students to work harder and learn more. Low standards breed low results, and grade deflation is an excellent way to increase standards. If a student knows he has a guaranteed A, he has no incentive to work harder for a better grade. It's certainly nice to relax or party, but the purpose of a university is to teach, not to entertain, so

Princeton's policies should focus on maximizing academics, not leisure. Rather than studying hard, if we want to breeze through college without much depth, receiving a high GPA and a diploma with honors, we could always go to Harvard. In the long run, however, knowledge and study skills are more useful than a high GPA. After a few years, achievement beyond graduation matters more than anything else.

Another major complaint is that grade deflation hurts our job and graduate-school prospects. While some employers and graduate schools are certainly unfamiliar with Princeton's grading system, admission rates and job placements have actually risen slightly since grade deflation was instituted, as demonstrated by statistics in the "Grading at Princeton" pamphlet. From 2004 (the last class without grade deflation) to 2009, even accounting for the economic downturn, the percentage of seniors with full-time jobs in hand actually grew slightly, from

---

*"A Defense of Grade Deflation," by Will Harrell, from *The Daily Princetonian*, March 2, 2010, © 2010. Reproduced by permission of the author.

29.4 percent to 29.6 percent. Both medical-school and law-school acceptance rates also grew, from 92.0 percent to 93.0 percent, and 25.9 percent to 34.5 percent, respectively. Moreover, Princeton sends out a letter with every transcript explaining the grading system, and employers and graduate schools know that GPAs from different schools have different meanings. For instance, MIT has a GPA scale from 5.0 to 0.0, and nobody would compare that GPA to a 4.0 scale side-by-side. Something like MIT's scale might actually be a useful next step for Princeton to clearly differentiate its grading scheme and increase awareness about grade defla-tion beyond Princeton.

On a slightly more trivial note, I've heard complaints that grade deflation renders the A-plus obsolete. While no statistics are released, Paolo Esquivel's 2009 article, "A-pluses in a time of grade deflation," mentions many examples of people with multiple A-pluses, and I know that at least two of my friends have also received A-pluses in stereotypically difficult courses. While receiving this ultimate mark is certainly difficult, it is definitely attainable.

5   Now that I have addressed the negatives of grade deflation, I must also discuss the two major benefits. First, it differentiates students more clearly in the top of the class. When everybody receives A's, employers and graduate schools have difficulty distin-guishing between the good and the excellent students. In 2001, 91 percent of Harvard seniors graduated with honors, prompting former dean and acting president of Harvard Henry Rosovksy to say, "Honors at Harvard has just lost all meaning. The bad honors is spoiling the good." This absurd "honors inflation" was certainly beneficial to the students in the 50th through 91st percentiles range, but those in the top of the class were not rewarded for their hard work. Instead,

they were clumped together with mediocre students. The bottom 9 percent of the class were essentially outcasts.

Princeton's goal should not be handing out diplomas with honors but rather should be educating students and rewarding excep-tional students for exceptional work. We have a 4.0 scale, so why would we only use 1 or 2 points of it? Grade inflation is excellent at highlighting the worst students, because so few students get low grades. By providing rigorous grading standards, Princeton highlights the best, not just the worst. For instance, because of the transcript letter, employers know that a Princeton student with a 3.7 GPA is an excellent student, and students are still being hired at similar or better rates. While grade deflation makes a 3.7 difficult, it is certainly achiev-able, and those who are able to achieve it are rewarded.

The other major benefit of grade deflation is its consistency across classes and departments. There are still certainly many kinks to be fixed in the soft quota system, but it is an excellent step in the right direction. The beauty of the system is that departments can assign a higher proportion of A grades to more competitive courses in order to maintain consistent standards across classes and departments. This allows me to place very little weight on the difficulty of grading when choosing my courses, because I know that our grades will be based on our abilities, not the professor's arbitrary grading standards. Grade deflation discour-ages people from gaming the system and taking "easy" courses in which everybody gets an A. Coupled with the new pass/D/fail policy changes, these effects now encourage students to take courses that excite them, not just ones that promise A's. While the current system is not completely flawless, the harms are negligible, and the benefits are great.

For Discussion:

Who are the members of the discourse community for this essay? In your view, how would different people in this community respond to the claims made by the author?

B. Writing Assignment: Analyzing the Rhetorical Situation in Written Argumentation

Write a 300- to 400-word paper in which you explain the rhetorical situation for "A Defense of Grade Deflation" by Will Harrel. Answer the following questions using TRACE.

1. How would you describe the text itself?
2. How would you characterize the reader or audience that the author may have had in mind while writing the essay? To what degree do you identify with this audience?
3. What do you learn about the author?
4. What are some of the possible constraints that might have influenced the author? What constraints influence you as you read this essay?
5. What is the exigence for this essay?

C. Group Work: Analyzing the Rhetorical Situation in Visual Argument

The two images on pages 64 and 66 are visual arguments that memorialize historic events. They may not appear at first to be visual arguments until you learn something about the history and original rhetorical situations in which they were situated. Both are photographs, and they are accompanied by enough explanation to help you understand the rhetorical situations in which they occurred. This will allow you to evaluate their effectiveness as visual arguments, both now and when they first appeared.

Form small groups, view each image, read the written commentary and essays that provide information about the photos, and answer the "For Discussion" questions that follow them. Then answer the following questions about their rhetorical situations. Refer back to the example of the analysis of the rhetorical situation from the viewer's point of view on pages 49–50, if you need to recall its details.

1. *Image.* What type of image is it? What are its qualities and features? What is it about?
2. *Viewer or audience.* Who do you think was targeted as the most appropriate audience at the time each photo was taken? Who might still regard each of these photos as a compelling visual argument?
3. *Photographer.* What do you know about the photographer, and what may have motivated that individual to take the photo? What might have been the intended result?

4. *Constraints.* What constraints influenced the photographer? Consider the influential events, circumstances, and traditions already in place at the time each photo was taken. Consider, also, the possible beliefs, attitudes, motives, and prejudices of the photographer. How about your constraints? Do any of your beliefs, attitudes, or prejudices seem to match those of the photographer, or are they different? Do the possible constraints you have identified create common ground between yourself and the photographer, or do they drive you apart?

5. *Exigence.* What motivated the photographer to take each of these photos? What happened? Was it perceived as a defect or problem? If yes, why? Was it new or recurring?

Image 1:
Rosa Parks Rides in the Front of the Bus

Rosa Parks riding a Montgomery, Alabama, bus in December 1956, after the Supreme Court outlawed segregation on buses.

Look at the image and read the essay that follows. It explains the history of this photograph and will provide you with the information you need to analyze the rhetorical situation.

This photograph was taken in 1956 early in the civil rights movement in Alabama when the issue was segregation in public facilities. Until this time, African American people were required to sit only at the back of public buses. A new national ruling gave them the right to sit wherever they wanted to sit. In the photograph, Rosa Parks, an African American civil rights activist, tests this new ruling by taking a seat in the front of the bus with a white man seated behind her. This is a famous photograph. It appears on the walls of buses in New York City and has come to symbolize change brought about by the movement for civil rights that continued into the next decades.

BEFORE YOU READ: What more would you like to know about the history of civil rights and racial segregation in the United States? How might this historical context affect how you view the Rosa Parks photograph?

ESSAY #3   THE CIVIL RIGHTS ERA
The Library of Congress

The following excerpt is part of the project entitled "The African American Odyssey," a historical overview of African American history created by the Library of Congress.

The post-war era marked a period of unprecedented energy against the second class citizenship accorded to African Americans in many parts of the nation. Resistance to racial segregation and discrimination with strategies such as civil disobedience, nonviolent resistance, marches, protests, boycotts, "freedom rides," and rallies received national attention as newspaper, radio, and television reporters and cameramen documented the struggle to end racial inequality. There were also continuing efforts to legally challenge segregation through the courts.

Success crowned these efforts: the Brown decision in 1954, the Civil Rights Act of 1964, and the Voting Rights Act in 1965 helped bring about the demise of the entangling web of legislation that bound blacks to second class citizenship. One hundred years after the Civil War, blacks and their white allies still pursued the battle for equal rights in every area of American life. While there is more to achieve in ending discrimination, major milestones in civil rights laws are on the books for the purpose of regulating equal access to public accommodations, equal justice before the law, and equal employment, education, and housing opportunities. African Americans have had unprecedented openings in many fields of learning and in the arts. The black struggle for civil rights also inspired other liberation and rights movements, including those of Native Americans, Latinos, and women, and African Americans have lent their support to liberation struggles in Africa.

For Discussion:

If you had no knowledge about the larger historical struggle for civil rights, how would this affect your understanding of the rhetorical situation in which the Rosa Parks photograph is situated? And how does this historical context help you better understand the rhetorical situation here? Does this context help you analyze this photo as a visual argument?

Image 2:
Auschwitz Victims of Medical Experiments

Auschwitz Exhibit at Jerusalem's Yad Vashem Holocaust Memorial

This is a photograph of an Israeli soldier in Jerusalem, Israel, who is viewing historical photographs at the Yad Vashem Holocaust Memorial Museum of Jewish victims from Auschwitz. Photojournalist David Silverman, who works for Getty Images and has been based in Israel and the West Bank since 1991, took this photo the week before the sixtieth anniversary of the liberation of Auschwitz.

The photographs in this exhibit were taken in the early 1940s during World War II at the Auschwitz concentration camp. The issues related to this image are anti-Semitism, the Holocaust, genocide, and the desire on the part of the Nazis, who ran this camp, to create a so-called master race. More than a million Jews died in the gas chambers at Auschwitz, were the victims of deadly medical experiments, or died of other causes such as starvation. Analyze the rhetorical situation for this image. How does this analysis help you perceive this image as a visual argument? What conclusions can you draw about the Holocaust, the Nazi death camps, and the individuals imprisoned there?

D. Before You Write on Your Issue: Applying the Rhetorical Situation

The worksheet on page 67 will help you understand the rhetorical situation for any issue you have selected to write about and have already tested to see whether it is arguable. Complete the worksheet by yourself. You are working with limited information, so you may need to guess at some of the answers.

E. Writing Assignment: Writing a Letter to a Specific Audience

Read the following rhetorical situation and write a letter in response to one of the four individuals in the prompts that appear immediately after it. Do not confer with other members of the class. Make sure at least some students write in response to each of the four prompts.

The Rhetorical Situation

You are enrolled in a freshman English class and your teacher allows you to be absent five times before she gives you an F for the course. If you are tardy to class three times, it counts as an absence. You have been absent five times and tardy to class twice. Your parents are angry with you for missing class so

Worksheet 1	Rhetorical Situation

1. **Exigence**
   What is motivating you to write on this issue? What happened? Why is it compelling to you?

2. **Reader or Audience**
   Who is going to read this? Where do you think they might stand on your issue right now? What are the chances of establishing common ground? What is the best approach to change their minds?

3. **Constraints**
   How do you think your training, background, affiliations, values, and attitudes about your issue are either in harmony or in conflict with those of your audience? What constraints can you use to build common ground?

4. **Author**
   What is your position or perspective on your issue? What do you already know? What do you need to learn? How can you be convincing?

5. **Text**
   What are you writing? What should it look like? What specifications do you need to follow? Review the assignment for your paper.

much, and they say that if you fail English you will have to get a job and start paying rent to live at home. Your teacher has explained that if you are tardy or absent from class one more time, she is going to fail you. You really want to do better; you are determined to change your ways.

On the way to class you have a blowout on the freeway. You pull over to change the tire and when you get the spare from the trunk, it is flat. This is not your fault, as you have just had your car serviced and the tires checked. A fellow motorist pulls over and helps you, but by the time you get a good tire on your car and drive to class, you are forty-five minutes late. You enter the classroom as quietly as you can. Your best friend raises her eyebrows. Your teacher gives you a stern look. You feel terrible.

The Writing Prompts

1. You are too embarrassed to talk to your teacher. Write her a letter to explain what happened and ask her for another chance.

2. Your parents are too angry to talk to you. Write them a letter to explain what happened and to ask their forgiveness.

3. You are very upset with the tire company. Write them a letter to explain what happened and ask for a reimbursement.

4. You do not have time to talk to your best friend after class. Write her a note to explain what happened and tell her what you intend to do about it.[3]

---

[3] I am indebted to Samantha Masterton for this assignment.

You and your classmates should now read some of these letters aloud. When you read them, do not divulge who the intended audience is. Ask the other students to guess who the intended reader of the letter is. Continue doing this until you have a sampling of all four letters and the class has guessed to whom each has been written.

Discuss the Results

What clues helped you surmise the audience for each letter? How are the letters different from each other? In your discussion, consider how each audience influenced the purpose for writing each letter, the tone of each letter, and the type and level of vocabulary used in each letter.

F. Class Discussion and Writing Assignment: Analyzing Your Class as an Audience

Learn more about your class as an audience by answering the questions listed here.

1. How many students are in your class? What are some of the qualities and features you have in common?

2. Consider some of the demographics of your class (ask for a show of hands to answer some of these): How many are traditional college-age students (18–22 years old), and how many are older, new, or returning students? Count the number of men and the number of women. How many are international students, and what countries do they represent? How would you describe the cultural diversity in the class? How many in the class agree that their heritage or native culture influences their personal life? How many are first-years and sophomores? How many are juniors and seniors? How many work part time? How many work full time? What are some of the types of work represented in class?

3. What college majors are represented in your class?

4. What are some of the groups class members belong to that are important to them? Consider political, religious, social, and living groups. Ask for students to volunteer this information.

5. What are some of the special interests and hobbies of class members? Make a list.

Using this class survey data, write as full a description of your classroom audience as you can. Which of the issues that you have considered writing about would immediately interest them? Why? Which would they find less interesting? Why? What could you provide in your paper to increase their interest?

Reading, Thinking, and Writing about Issues

After studying this chapter, you will be able to:

LO1 Describe and put into practice the steps for beginning a writing assignment.

LO2 Define the six types of argument purpose and apply them to written, visual, and online argument.

LO3 Create comprehensive notes for a given reading.

LO4 Create a plan for revising your own written argument.

LO5 Write examples of summary, summary-analysis, and exploratory essays.

LO6 Develop skills for peer review.

LO7 Apply the skills of summary, summary-analysis, and exploration to visual argument.

This chapter teaches strategies to help you complete assignments that require reading, thinking, and writing about issues. You can combine these three activities as you use the strategies taught here in writing three types of argument papers, explained later in this chapter: (1) the summary-response paper; (2) the summary-analysis-response paper; and (3) the exploratory paper.

Most people like their current reading and writing processes and are able to describe them. Try it. First, imagine that your professor has given you a difficult scholarly article to read. You must understand it, think about it, and remember the main ideas. How do you proceed with such an assignment? What do you typically do *before you read, while you are reading, when you encounter difficult passages,* and *after you finish reading?*

Now imagine writing a college paper on a subject that requires some research but also a considerable amount of critical thinking on your part. How would you *get started, write the first draft, break through writer's block* (if that occurs), and *rewrite and revise your paper?*

As you read through the strategies in this chapter, bear in mind that *readers are often actively thinking and writing as they read,* and that *writers, in turn, are often reading and thinking as they write.*

LO1 Describe and put into practice the steps for beginning a writing assignment.

Getting Started on a Writing Assignment

Here is an example of a typical writing assignment.

> Write a five- to six-page, typed, double-spaced argument paper in which you iden-tify an issue, take a position on the issue, make a claim, and support it so that it is convincing to an audience of your peers. Do as much reading as you need to do, but plan to draw material from three to five sources in writing your paper. Use MLA style to document your sources and prepare your bibliography.

ANALYZE THE ASSIGNMENT AND ALLOCATE TIME

Before you begin work on a writing assignment for an argument paper, take some time to organize a workspace equipped with the materials you will need. Then take a few minutes to understand the assignment and schedule sufficient time to com-plete it. Begin by dividing the assignment into small, manageable parts: assign a sufficient amount of time for each part and set deadlines for completing each part.

IDENTIFY AN ISSUE, NARROW IT, AND TEST IT

The assignment just described directs you to identify an issue on which to write. You may start with a broad issue area such as education, technology, immigration, or the environment, but you will need to find a more narrow and specific issue to write about within this broad area. The map in Figure 3.1 shows one technique for generating more specific issues related to a broad issue area. A group of students created this map to help them find specific issues about race. Reading about your issue can also uncover a particular aspect or interpretation that you want to explore. You may also take a position on the issue and write a tentative claim. Add reasons for your position on the claim, if you can at this point. Keep your audience in mind as you do so.

DO SOME INITIAL WRITING, READING, AND THINKING

Get off to a strong start by using some of these suggestions.

Write Down Everything You Now Know about Your Issue

As soon as you have an issue in mind, begin to make notes. This practice guarantees that some of the material in your paper will be your original ideas. Do you have an idea right now about the position you think you may take on your issue? Can you list some reasons for it? Can you think of some examples?

ISSUES RELATED TO RACE

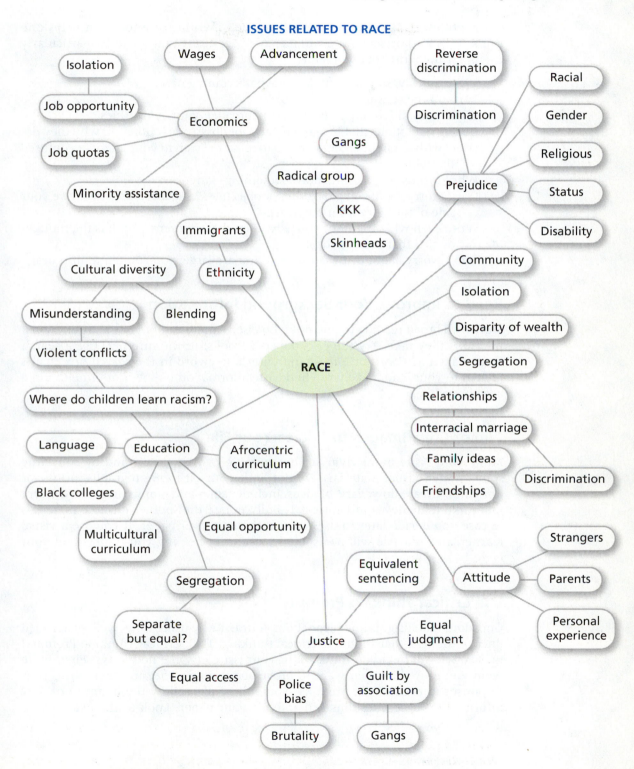

Figure 3.1 *A Map Can Help You Discover Specific Related Issues for Paper Topics*

A professional writer describes this type of writing as a tool that helps one think. This author sets out a number of suggestions that could be particularly useful for the writer of argument.

Write quickly, so you don't know what's coming next.

Turn off the censor in your head.

Write from different points of view to broaden your sympathies.

Collect quotations that inspire you and jot down a few notes on why they do.

Write with a nonjudgmental friend in mind to listen to your angry or confused thoughts.

When words won't come, draw something—anything.

Don't worry about being nice, fair, or objective. Be selfish and biased; give your side of the story from the heart.

Write even what frightens you, *especially* what frightens you. It is the thought denied that is dangerous.

Don't worry about being consistent. You are large; you contain multitudes.[1]

Read to Improve Your Background Information

Start with broad reading to find out who else is interested in your issue and what positions they take. Try the encyclopedia, books, or the Internet. Use a search engine such as *Google* or *Yahoo!* and enter a keyword in the search box that is related to your issue to begin to find basic information online. Continue to write as you read.

Clip or Copy Images to Add to Your File

Make your issue more vivid and memorable in your own mind by collecting some related visual materials. Do not limit yourself to photographs, prints, or drawings. Create flowcharts of ideas, include tables and graphs, or make concept maps like that shown in Figure 3.1. Fully notate the sources of these materials in case you decide later to use some of them in your paper. If you are a visual learner, this practice will be especially useful in helping you understand your issue.

Use Critical Thinking Prompts

Get additional insights and ideas about your issue by using some well-established lines of thought that stimulate critical thinking. The "Critical Thinking Prompts" in Box 3.1 will help you think about your issue in some new ways. First, write what you now think you want to prove about your issue, and then write your responses to each of the prompts. You will be pleased by the quantity of new information these questions generate for your paper. Look at the example on page 74 to get started.

---

[1]Marjorie Pellegrino, "Keeping a Writer's Journal," *Writer*, June 1992, 27.

Box 3.1   Use These Prompts to Help You Think Critically about Your Issue

▶▶▶ Critical Thinking Prompts

What is your issue? _____

Use some, but not all, of these prompts to help you think about it.

1. *Associate it.* Consider other related issues, broader issues, or enduring issues. Also associate your issue with familiar subjects and ideas.

2. *Describe it.* Use detail. Make the description visual if you can by forming pictures in your mind or by looking at the visual materials you have collected in your file and then describing them.

3. *Compare it.* Think about items in the same or different categories. Compare your issue with topics you know or understand well. Compare what you used to think about the issue with what you think now. Give reasons for your change of mind.

4. *Apply it.* Show practical uses or applications. Show how it can be used in a specific setting.

5. *Divide it.* Illuminate your issue by dividing it into related issues or into parts of the issue.

6. *Agree and disagree with it.* Identify the extreme pro and con positions and reasons for holding them. List other approaches and perspectives. Say why each position, including your own, might be plausible and in what circumstances.

7. *Consider it as it is, right now.* Think about your issue as it exists, right now, in present time. What is its nature? What are its special, contemporary characteristics?

8. *Consider it over a period of time.* Think about your issue in the past as well as how it might present itself in the future. Does the issue change? How? Why?

9. *Decide whether it is a part of something bigger.* Put it in a larger category, and consider the insights you gain as a result.

10. *Analyze it.* Consider its parts and assess how the parts are related.

11. *Synthesize it.* Put it back together in new ways so that the new whole is different. Ask if it is clearer and better than the old whole.

12. *Evaluate it.* Decide whether it is good or bad, valuable or not valuable, moral or immoral, ethical or unethical. Give evidence to support your evaluation.

13. *Elaborate on it.* Add and continue to add explanation until you can understand the issue more easily. Give some examples to provide further elaboration.

14. *Project and predict.* Answer the question, "What would happen if . . . ?" Extend its frame outward and its meanings and possibilities forward.

15. *Ask why, and keep on asking why.* Examine every aspect of your issue by asking why.

▶ Example of How to Use Critical Thinking Prompts

What is your issue? My issue is old-growth forests. I want to preserve those on the western coast of the United States.

Associate it. This is an enduring environmental issue. It is associated with other environmental issues, including reducing greenhouse gases that cause global warming and saving wildlife like the spotted owl, deer, and the other animals that live in these forests. It is also associated with preserving natural beauty and the history of these areas.

Describe it. These trees are as much as 3,200 years old. The giant sequoias in California, for example, are huge, majestic trees that can reach heights of 325 feet. People standing among them appear to be very small, and when they look up, they can barely see the tops. Even the sky seems farther away than usual. It is awe-inspiring to walk among these trees because of their size, their age, and their beauty.

Compare it. Saving these forests from logging is similar to preserving natural lakes, national forests, and other wilderness areas from commercial interests.

These responses will give you the idea. As you work through all the prompts, you will find that some are more productive than others for a particular issue. Use as many as you can. If you do not yet know enough to respond to some prompts, add information later when you have done more reading.

LO2 Define the six types of argument purpose and apply them to written, visual, and online argument.

Read to Develop Arguments for Your Paper

As you start reading in more detail, you will need to learn to recognize written argument.

RECOGNIZING ARGUMENTATION PURPOSE IN WRITTEN ARGUMENT

Some texts are obviously intended as argument, and others conceal their argumentation purpose, making it more difficult to recognize. Think of a continuum that includes six types of purpose, ranging from obvious argument at one extreme to objective writing at the other. Each of the six types reflects not only a different authorial intention but also a different relationship between the author and the audience. These descriptions can also help you establish your own purpose when you are the writer.

1. *Obvious argument.* The author's purpose is to take a position and to change minds or convince others. The author's point of view and purpose are clearly expressed along with reasons and supporting details that appeal to a wide audience.

2. *Extremist argument.* Authors who hold fast to prejudiced beliefs and stereotypes about various people, causes, or special projects sometimes rely on strongly expressed values and emotional language to appeal to specific audiences who may already share their views.

3. *Hidden argument.* Some texts seem to be written to inform but, on closer reading, actually favor one position over another. Supporting material may be carefully selected to favor a particular view. Also, emotional language, vivid description, or emotional examples can be signs that the author has strong opinions and intends not only to inform but also to convince.

4. *Unconscious argument.* Some authors who try to write objectively are influenced unconsciously by strong personal opinions, and the result is an unconscious intent to change people's minds. Imagine a journalist who strongly opposes war being sent to write an objective article about an active war zone.

5. *Exploratory argument.* In exploratory essays, the author lays out and explains three or more of the major positions on a controversial issue. The reader is invited to view an issue from several perspectives and to understand all of them better. If the author has a position, it may or may not be revealed.

6. *Objective reporting.* The author may report facts and ideas that everyone can accept. The author's own point of view, opinions, or interpretations are deliberately omitted. You might find writing like this in weather reports, some news stories, and government, business, science, and technical reports.

APPLYING THE SIX TYPES OF ARGUMENTATION PURPOSE TO VISUAL ARGUMENT

Even though the descriptions in the previous section apply mainly to written argument, you can easily modify them to help you analyze visual argument as well. Refer to the same six categories to help you recognize the possible intention of the person who created an image. An image may take an obvious argumentation position on an issue, or it may support extremist positions that the viewers already accept. Emotional images that appear on anti-abortion, anti-war, or anti-gay marriage Web sites are such examples. They will be persuasive to you only if you already agree with the positions they depict.

Some images at first may appear to be recording facts without creating issues or controversy, but as you look more closely, you discover unconscious or hidden bias in favor of a particular position, and you find you are looking at an argument. The photograph in Figure 3.2 offers an example. This photo originally appeared in a newspaper as an objective report about President Barack Obama greeting students at Hyde Park Academy in Chicago. Now, look at it again and see if you can detect some signs of hidden or unconscious argument in this picture. Take a closer look at how this figure is presented. How is he positioned in relation to the larger crowd? What do you imagine he is thinking?

Visual argument can also take the form of exploratory argument. In such cases, several images illustrate different visual perspectives on an issue in a way that is similar to an exploratory essay, which in writing identifies and explains several different perspectives on an issue. Examples of visual exploratory argument appear later in this chapter on pages 97 and 109 where, in each case, an issue is

Figure 3.2 *Barack Obama greets students at Hyde Park Academy High School in Chicago.*

Is this photograph an example of objective reporting, or is it hidden argument?

explored visually. An exercise at the end of this chapter invites you to create a visual exploratory argument yourself.

Finally, some images may be mainly objective. Tables of figures, graphs, and other presentations of numbers and additional data qualify as visual argument and may be objective in that they present information and facts everyone would accept. Scientific drawings or photos of procedures that are designed to teach fit into this category as well. Remember, however, that someone selects and presents—essentially edits out as much as includes—visual information, and even in the most ostensibly objective formats, it is always possible for bias and opinion to find its way in just as it does in written material.

ACADEMIC ARGUMENT

Much of what you read in college will be academic writing assigned by your professors and found in textbooks or scholarly journals or books. Any of the types of argumentation just described may appear in academic writing. The ideas in academic writing are often controversial, with authors taking positions on issues and presenting their ideas as either explicit or hidden argument. Academic writing may seem complex and unfamiliar, especially at the beginning of a class: it is new to you, it contains specialized vocabulary, it is dense with many new ideas, and, compared with easier material, it will often contain fewer examples and transitions. Its sentences and paragraphs are often longer as well. Your purpose in

Analyzing Online Argument: Purpose

There is a lot that online argument shares with visual argument. For one thing, Web-based arguments often include visual material, and so serve as another context for visual argument. And as is the case with visual argument, we can also easily find examples of Web-based material that makes obvious or extremist arguments. The list below outlines two key considerations to keep in mind when assessing the purpose behind online argument.

- *Analyzing the purpose behind multimedia argument:* Many Web-based arguments are multimedia in nature, incorporating written, visual, and/or graphic elements together. When you encounter such arguments, bear in mind that its multimedia elements may keep some of the purposes behind a given argument more hidden. The same is true for unconscious argument, where an author may remain unaware of the ways her or his purpose is being shaped both by written and visual material.

- *Analyzing the purpose behind interactive argument:* Online arguments afford readers much greater opportunity to respond to the arguments they encounter. While an author may have one purpose in mind when he or she creates an argument, it is quite possible that this goal will change or evolve as different readers post their own reactions and feedback. The effect of such feedback could easily be felt in relation to an exploratory argument online, in which an author's attempt to lay out a range of differing views on a given issue could be influenced by the views reflected in the responses of different readers. Likewise for objective reporting, in which the interaction between author and audience could easily complicate the question of who or what is truly objective.

Activity

Choose a multimedia or online argument and analyze its purpose.

reading such material is to understand it, analyze it, evaluate it, and, frequently, take a position and write about it.

Your instructor will expect you to use academic style in your college papers. You will engage with complicated issues that invite varying perspectives that seldom take shape as simple pro and con positions. You will learn to take positions on these kinds of issues and to support your ideas with your own reasons and examples as well as with paraphrased, summarized, or quoted material from other writers. Your readers will expect you to document these outside sources so that they can trace the materials you relied on to their origins. The student-written argument essays at the end of each chapter in this book serve as models for the academic writing you will be expected to do in college. Box 3.2 on the next page outlines some strategies you can use to help you complete projects that require reading about issues.

Box 3.2   How to Survey

▶▶▶ Steps for Surveying Books, Articles, and Chapters

Survey a book or an article before you read it to become acquainted with its structure and general qualities, and skim certain parts for the major ideas and a few of the supporting details.

Books. To survey a book (not a novel), follow these six steps in the order given.

1. Read the *title* and focus on what it tells you about the contents of the book.
2. Read the *table of contents.* Notice how the content has been divided and organized into chapters.
3. Skim the *introduction.* Look for background information about the subject and author and for any other information that will help you read the book.
4. Examine the special *features* of the book. Are there headings and subheadings in boldface type that highlight major ideas? Is there a glossary? An index? A bibliography? Are there charts? Other visuals?
5. Read the title and first paragraph of the *first* and *last chapters* to see how the book begins and ends.
6. Read the title and first paragraph of the *other chapters* to get a sense of the flow of ideas.

   This procedure should take about half an hour. It will introduce you to the main issue and approaches in a book, and your reading will then be easier and more focused.

Articles and Chapters. To survey an article or a chapter in a book, follow these six steps in this order.

1. Read the *title* and focus on the information in it.
2. Read the *introduction,* which is usually the first paragraph but can be several paragraphs long. Skim for a claim and any forecasts of what is to come.
3. Read the *last paragraph* and look for the claim.
4. Read the *headings* and *subheadings,* if there are any, to get a sense of the ideas and their sequence. If there are no headings, read the first sentence of each paragraph to accomplish the same goal.
5. Study the *visuals:* pictures, charts, graphs. Read their captions. They often illustrate major ideas or key details.
6. Identify the *key words* that represent the main concepts.

   Surveying an article or chapter takes ten to fifteen minutes. It introduces you to the issue, the claim, and some of the support.

LOOK FOR CLAIMS, SUBCLAIMS, SUPPORT, AND TRANSITIONS

All arguments have the structural components you are familiar with from other kinds of reading and writing. The main difference is their names. The thesis of an argument, which shapes the thinking of the entire text and states what the author finally expects you to accept or believe, is called the *claim*. The main ideas or *subclaims* are assertions, reasons, or supporting arguments that develop the claim. They usually require *support* in the form of facts, opinions, evidence, visual images, and examples. Support makes the claim and subclaims clear, vivid, memorable, and believable. *Transitions* lead the reader from one idea to another and sometimes state the relationships among ideas. There is a constant movement between general and specific material in all texts, including argument texts, and this movement becomes apparent when the ideas are presented in various types of outline form.

UNDERSTAND THE KEY WORDS

When reading material seems difficult, go back and look for words you do not understand. Always identify the key terms, those that represent major concepts. In this book so far, *rhetorical situation, survey, claim,* and *subclaim* are examples of key terms. To find the meaning of difficult words and key terms, first read the context in which you find the word or key term. A word may be defined in a sentence, a paragraph, or several paragraphs. Major concepts in argument are often defined at length, and understanding their meaning will be essential to understanding the entire argument. If the context does not give you enough information, try the glossary, the dictionary, or another book on the subject. Remember that major concepts require longer explanations than a single synonym.

UNDERLINE, ANNOTATE, AND SUMMARIZE IDEAS

As you begin to read, underline and write notes in the margins to help you concentrate and understand. These notes will also help you review and find information later. The key to marking a text is to do it selectively. Do not color an entire paragraph with a highlighter. Instead, underline only the words and phrases that you can later reread and still get a sense of the whole. Use key words. Jot the major ideas in the margins, or summarize them at the ends of sections. Write the big ideas along with your personal reactions on the flyleaves of a book or at the ends of chapters or articles. If you do not own the book, write on self-stick notes and attach them to the book pages. You can also create a computer file for your notes.

Here is an example. This essay about spy drones and privacy has been underlined and annotated. A brief summary has been added at the end to capture the main point. Note that this material is now very easy to understand.

ESSAY #1   ## AS SPY DRONES COME TO THE U.S., WE MUST PROTECT OUR PRIVACY*
Scientific American Editorial Board

Aerial drones on the rise in the U.S.

Before the decade is out, there may be thousands more eyes in the sky. Unmanned aerial vehicles, commonly known as drones, are already a staple of modern warfare. Now they are set to take on a much larger role in the U.S.

Congress set to establish rules for drone use because technology is extremely useful.

Congress has directed the Federal Aviation Administration to set rules by 2015 for how drones may be used in domestic airspace. These rules could open up the skies to unmanned vehicles of all types—from large surveillance drones used by the military to insect-size prototypes being developed in university laboratories. The technology promises to be immensely useful. Public safety agencies can use drones to survey wildfires, conduct search-and-rescue operations, or pursue heavily armed suspects. Farmers will use them to survey their fields; energy companies will fly drones over critical machinery.

Drone technology poses significant risks to privacy.

Still, drones also pose an immense threat to privacy. The proliferation of small, inexpensive aerial vehicles with video downlinks will dramatically alter the cost–benefit ratio of surveillance. No longer will law-enforcement agencies need to consider the expense and risk of operating a helicopter when gathering evidence. Consequently, law-enforcement agencies will have ample opportunity and motivation to deploy drones on open-ended sorties. It is not hard to imagine blanket campaigns that survey entire cities for back-yard marijuana plants or even building code violations. Privacy advocates rightly worry that drones, equipped with high-resolution video cameras, infrared detectors and even facial-recognition software, will let snoops into realms that have long been considered private.

The privacy threat does not just come from law enforcement, either. Paparazzi and private detectives will find drones just as easy to use as the cops. Your neighbor is not allowed to go into your yard without your permission—will he be able to keep a drone hovering just above it?

5   Case law paints a hazy picture of how drones could be employed for surveillance. A 1989 Supreme Court decision ruled that police may use helicopters to peer into semiprivate areas—say, the backyard of a home—without first obtaining a warrant. Such speculative reconnaissance, however, has been naturally limited by the costs of helicopter operations. Will the same law apply to unmanned drones, which are not similarly constrained?

Past Supreme Court decisions provide little guidance about what limits to establish for drones.

A more recent case poses troubling questions about access to the most sacrosanct spaces. In 2001 the Supreme Court ruled that police could not use thermal-imaging technology to gather evidence about the goings-on hidden inside a residence without first obtaining a warrant. The court reasoned that governmental use of "a device that is not in general public use"—a thermal

---

imager—constitutes a search under the Fourth Amendment and therefore requires a judge's approval. Yet if unmanned aerial vehicles become as prevalent as manufacturers hope, one could argue that drones are exempt from that precedent.

Congress should take the lead in creating guidelines for responsible drone use.

Summary: As the prospect of domestic drone use has increased, so too has the need for Congress to create sensible guidelines to protect the privacy of ordinary American citizens.

Already the FAA has permitted a handful of law-enforcement agencies to operate drones on a short-term basis. The limited regulations accompanying those permits (which, thankfully, preclude attaching any weapons to the drones) are insufficient to protect the privacy of citizens. Perhaps this should not be surprising. The FAA is not in the business of privacy protection. Its primary concern is with the safety of domestic airspace.

No federal agency, in fact, can be held accountable if drones are not used responsibly and in a way that respects the Fourth Amendment. As such, <u>Congress should proactively enact laws that confine drones to reasonable, useful purposes.</u> Several sensible ideas were proposed during the last session of Congress, including a bill that would have outlawed drone spying without a warrant and instituted important transparency and accountability measures for their use. But that bill failed to make it out of a subcommittee. <u>The present Congress must be more active than its predecessor in heading off this clear and impending threat to personal privacy.</u>

OUTLINES OR MAPS

If you have read, annotated, and summarized a reading selection and still feel you should understand it better, try writing an outline or a map of the key ideas in it. Both outlines and maps lay out ideas in a visual form and show how they are related to each other. Seeing the organization of ideas improves your understanding and ability to critically evaluate the selection.

Make an Outline

To make an outline, write the claim, the most general idea, at the left-hand margin; indent the subclaims under the claim; and indent the support—the specific facts, opinions, examples, illustrations, other data, and statistics—even further. You may not always need to write an outline. Sometimes you can make a simple mental outline to help you remember the claim and some of the ideas that support and develop it. Here is an outline of the essay "No Escape from 'Helicopter Parents'" (pages 34–35).

OUTLINE OF *"NO ESCAPE FROM 'HELICOPTER PARENTS'"*
  Claim: Helicopter parenting of kids is counterproductive.
    Subclaim: Helicopter parenting has negative effects on both parents and their kids.
      This type of parenting undermines kids' independence.
        Support (examples): Because of such parental oversight, kids are less likely to form healthy relationships, strike off on their own, or develop important job skills.
    Subclaim: This type of parenting is fueled by parental stress and anxiety.
      Support: Helicopter parents practice this type of parenting because they worry about their kids' educational and career opportunities.

Subclaim: This type of parenting undermines the relationship between parents and their kids.
Support: Helicopter parenting leads to confusion over the proper role parents are supposed to play.
Conclusion: "Helicopter parenting is counterproductive"

Make a Map

As an alternative to summaries or outlines, make a map of the ideas in a text. For many students, maps are the preferred way to reduce and reorganize the material they read. To make a map, write the most important idea, the claim, in a circle or on a line, and then attach major subclaims and support to it. Make your map in very brief form. Figure 3.3 is a possible map of the essay "No Escape from 'Helicopter Parents.'" You can be creative with map formats. Use whatever layout will give you a quick picture of the major ideas.

Figure 3.3 *Map of Ideas for "No Escape from 'Helicopter Parents'"*

Source: Nancy Wood.

1. Helicopter parenting has negative effects on both parents and their kids.

2. Helicopter parenting prevents kids from growing into independent, responsible adults.

Helicopter parenting is counterproductive

3. This type of parenting is fueled by parental stress and anxiety.

4. This type of parenting undermines the relationship between parents and their kids.

LO3 Create comprehensive notes for a given reading.

Take Notes and Avoid Plagiarism

From the start, record the information from your reading that you may want to quote, paraphrase, or summarize later when you write your paper. If you have an outline or list of ideas in your computer, type in such material at appropriate spots. If you are keeping paper notes in a folder, write out the passages in full and identify the author and publisher information for later detailed documenting of the source. Write out or type in your own ideas as they occur to you as well.

Copy quoted material exactly as it is written and place it in quotation marks immediately, with the author's name and brief source information at the end. You must add the author's name and the location of the original material (page or paragraph number, title or site, etc.) to paraphrased or summarized material as well. Label your own ideas as "mine," or put them in square brackets [ ]. Here are examples drawn from "As Spy Drones Come to the U.S." (pages 80–81).

▶ Example of a Quote

"Before the decade is out, there may be thousands more eyes in the sky" ("As Spy Drones Come to the U.S." 80).

▶ Example of a Paraphrase

This editorial describes the threat to privacy posed by drone technology ("As Spy Drones Come to the U.S." 80).

▶ Example of a Summary

According to the editorial writers at *Scientific American*, the use of drones domestically is on the rise. As a consequence, the federal government faces new and urgent challenges about how to balance the benefits of drone surveillance with the threats this technology poses to Americans' privacy ("As Spy Drones Come to the U.S." 80–81).

▶ Example of Your Idea

Drone surveillance technology also poses privacy threats when used outside of the U.S.

If you follow this advice on taking notes, you will have no problem with plagiarism. Just in case you are still unclear about what plagiarism is exactly, here is a statement made by the Council of Writing Program Administrators that will help you.

> In an instructional setting, plagiarism occurs when a writer deliberately uses someone else's language, ideas, or other original (not common-knowledge) material without acknowledging its source. This definition applies to texts published in print or online, to manuscripts, and to the work of other student writers.[2]

Plagiarism is regarded as an extremely serious personal and academic violation because it negates the purpose of education, which is to encourage original and analytical thinking in a community in which expression of thought is both respected and protected.

Online research seems to have increased the incidence of plagiarism in student work. Some students find it tempting to copy and paste information from online articles into their own papers without using quotation marks and without documenting the source. Sometimes a student will mix her or his own words with the words of the quoted author and neglect to put the source's words in quotation marks. The result is a strange mix of styles and voices that creates a problem for the reader, who cannot easily sort out the student's words from those of the person being quoted. This, too, is plagiarism.

You can avoid plagiarism by differentiating between your ideas and those of others at all stages of the writing process. This is why you are advised to enclose all direct quotations in quotation marks in your notes, to introduce paraphrases and summaries drawn from other people's works with the names of the authors in your notes, and to keep your own ideas separate from those of others by labeling them or placing them in brackets or a different font. You may safely and responsibly use other people's ideas and words in your paper, but you must always acknowledge that they are theirs.

---

[2]From "Defining and Avoiding Plagiarism: The WPA Statement on Best Practices" (2003). The full statement can be accessed at www.wpacouncil.org/positions/plagiarism.html.

If the passages you have drawn from outside sources are reasonably short, support your own ideas, and you clearly indicate where you found them, then you have done the right thing. If the passages are copied into your paper as though you had written them yourself, then you could receive a poor grade in the course or even be expelled from college. Understand too that you fail to link reading to thinking when you are reading to copy. It is a theft from someone else, but also from yourself. And, of course, you do not learn to improve your own writing when you copy other people's words instead of writing your own.

LO4 Create a plan for revising your own written argument.

Write Your Paper, Read It, Think about It, and Revise It

At some point you will feel that you are ready to read through the material you have gathered and put it in some kind of order so that you can write your paper. Here are some strategies to help you accomplish that.

REFOCUS YOUR ISSUE AND RECONSIDER YOUR AUDIENCE

Read through the materials you have gathered and see if your issue has changed or shifted focus during your reading, thinking, and writing. Select the aspect of your issue that now interests you the most and that you have sufficient materials and ideas to develop. Keep in mind your time constraints and word limitations. Rewrite or refine your claim at this point to make your focus clear and convincing to your audience. You will probably want to adjust or rewrite it once again as you do your final read-through and finish your paper.

Consider whether you can strengthen your argument by doing more reading, probably in sources you have already located. You may also rethink your evaluation of some of the sources you have used. As you reconsider your audience, think about what they already know and what they still need to learn. Review your areas of agreement and disagreement and the amount of common ground you share. What will you need to include in your paper to convince them to consider your point of view?

MAKE AN EXTENDED OUTLINE TO GUIDE YOUR WRITING

A written outline helps many people see the organization of ideas before they begin to write. Other people seem to be able to make a list or even work from a mental outline. Still others "just write" and move ideas around later to create order. There is, however, an implicit outline in most good writing. The outline is often referred to metaphorically as the skeleton or barebones of the paper because it provides the internal structure that holds the paper together. An outline can be simple—a list of words written on a piece of scrap paper—or it can be elaborate, with essentially all major ideas, supporting details, major transitions, and even some of the sections written out in full.

If you have never made outlines, try making one. Outlining requires intensive thinking and decision making. When it is finished, however, you will be able to turn your full attention to writing, and you will never have to stop to figure out what to write about next. Your outline will tell you what to do, and it will ultimately save you time and reduce much of the difficulty and frustration you would experience without it.

WRITE THE FIRST DRAFT

The objective of writing the first draft is to get your ideas in some kind of written form so that you can see them and work with them. Include quoted, paraphrased, and summarized material in your draft as you write. Here is how a professional writer explains the drafting process.

> Writing a first draft should be easy because, in a sense, you can't get it wrong. You are bringing something completely new and strange into the world, something that did not exist before. You have nothing to prove in the first draft, nothing to defend, everything to imagine. And the first draft is yours alone, no one else sees it. You are not writing for an audience. Not yet. You write the draft in order to read what you have written and to determine what you still have to say.[3]

This author advises further that you "not even consider technical problems at this early stage." Nor should you "let your critical self sit at your desk with your creative self. The critic will stifle the writer within." The purpose, he says, is "not to get it right, but to get it written."[4]

Here is another writer, Stephen King, who advises putting aside reference books and dictionaries when concentrating on writing the first draft.

> Put away your dictionary. . . . You think you might have misspelled a word? O.K., so here is your choice: either look it up in the dictionary, thereby making sure you have it right—and breaking your train of thought and the writer's trance in the bargain—or just spell it phonetically and correct it later. Why not? Did you think it was going to go somewhere? And if you need to know the largest city in Brazil and you find you don't have it in your head, why not write in Miami or Cleveland? You can check it . . . but *later*. When you sit down to write, *write*. Don't do anything else except go to the bathroom, and only do that if it absolutely cannot be put off.[5]

You will be able to follow this advice if the materials you have gathered before drafting are available to guide you and keep you on track. If you occasionally get stuck, you can write some phrases, freewrite, or even skip a section that you

---

[3]John Dufresne, "That Crucial First Draft," *Writer*, October 1992, 9.

[4]Ibid., 10–11.

[5]Stephen King, "Everything You Need to Know about Writing Successfully—in Ten Minutes," *The Writer's Handbook*, ed. Sylvia K. Burack (Boston: Writer, 1991), 33.

cannot easily put into words. You will have another chance at your draft later. Right now, work only to capture the flow of ideas, either as they are written on an outline or as they are organized in your mind. You will discover, as you write, that many of the ideas that were only half formed before you began to write will now become clear and complete as you get insight from writing.

BREAK THROUGH WRITER'S BLOCK

Most writers suffer from writer's block from time to time, and there are a number of ways to get going again if you find that you are stuck while writing your first draft.

▶ *Read what you have written so far.* Concentrate on the ideas, think about what you need to write next, and jot down a few notes to remind yourself what you want to do. Then get back to writing.

▶ *Read more about your issue.* If you do not have enough material, take notes on additional sources. Place limits by doing directed reading to meet specific needs.

▶ *Reread your outline, lists, and other idea notes.* Add new ideas that occur to you as you read, and rearrange ideas into new combinations.

▶ *Freewrite, read some more, and freewrite again.* Write fast, in phrases or sentences, on your topic without imposing any structure or order. Go through it later, crossing out what you can't use, changing phrases to sentences, adding material in places, and soon you will find that you are started again.

▶ *Use critical thinking prompts.* Revisit Box 3.1. These prompts will help you think in new ways about your topic and generate new ideas and information as well.

▶ *Talk about your ideas with someone else.* Either talk with someone or ask someone to read the draft as it now is and write their comments on it.

▶ *Give yourself permission to write a less than perfect first draft.* You can paralyze yourself by trying to produce a finished draft on the first try. Lower your expectations for the first draft. Remind yourself that you will need to return later and fine-tune it as well as fix any flaws or omissions.

REVISE THE DRAFT

Resist the temptation to put your paper aside when you have finished drafting and declare it finished. Now is your opportunity to become its first careful reader and to improve it in significant ways. Working with a rough draft is easier than outlining or drafting. It is, in fact, creative and fun to revise because you begin to see your work take shape and become more readable and convincing. It is worthwhile to finish your draft early enough so that you will have several hours to read and revise before you submit it in its final form to a reader.

Look at Your Draft as a Whole

When you have a draft, print it out so that you can see it as a whole. Look at organization first. How does your paper begin? Have you written an introduction that informs your audience about the subject of your paper? What are your main points? Where does each of them begin and end? Have you used enough transitional material to make your ideas stand out? Do you have enough support to make each of your main points believable to your audience? Think about your audience and decide whether you need to add information to make your paper more persuasive. How do you conclude your paper? Is your ending strong and memorable?

If you cannot answer these questions, try making a list or an outline of the most important ideas in it. Apply this test: Can you state the claim or the main point of your paper and list the parts that develop it? Take a good look at these parts, rearrange them if necessary and make them clearer and more complete.

Now, read paragraph by paragraph. Do you make links between the end of one paragraph and the beginning of another so that the ideas in them flow and appear to be clearly related to each other? Is most of each paragraph about one idea? Is that idea developed with sufficient supporting detail?

Check your sentences. Is each a complete thought? Do they all make sense? Rewrite problem sentences or sentence fragments. As a final check, read your entire paper aloud and listen for problems. Correct with pencil as you go along. You can enter corrections into the computer later.

Ask Revision Questions to Help You Locate Other Problems

Ask these seven questions about your draft, which direct your attention both to global revisions for improved clarity and organization and to surface revisions for errors in grammar and usage.

1. *Is it clear?* If you cannot understand your own writing, other people will not be able to either. Be critical of your own understanding as you read your draft. If you encounter confusing passages, stop and analyze why they are confusing and then rewrite them until the words represent what you mean or want to say.

2. *What should I add?* Sometimes in writing the first draft you will write such a sketchy version of an idea that it does not explain your thinking or fully state what you want to say. Add fuller explanations and examples, or do extra research to improve the skimpy or unsubstantiated parts of your paper.

3. *What should I cut?* Extra words, repeated ideas, and unnecessary material often crowd into the first draft. Every writer cuts during revision. Stephen King, who earns millions of dollars each year as a professional writer, describes how he learned to cut the extra words. His teacher was the newspaper editor John Gould, who dealt with King's first feature article, as he describes in this excerpt.

He started in on the feature piece with a large black pen and taught me all I ever needed to know about my craft. I wish I still had the piece—it deserves to be framed, editorial corrections and all—but I can remember pretty well how it looked when he had finished with it. Here is an example:

```
Last night, in the well-loved
gymnasium of Lisbon High School, partisans
and Jay Hills fans alike were stunned by
an athletic performance unequalled in school
history: Bob Ransom, known as "Bullet" Bob
for both his size and accuracy, scored
thirty-seven points. He did it with grace
and speed . . . and he did it with an odd courtesy
as well, committing only two personal fouls
in his knight-like quest for a record which
                                  's  basketball team
has eluded Lisbon thinclads since 1953 . . .
```

When Gould finished marking up my copy in the manner I have indicated above, he looked up and must have seen something on my face. I think he must have thought it was horror, but it was not: it was revelation.

"I only took out the bad parts, you know," he said. "Most of it's pretty good."

"I know," I said, meaning both things: yes, most of it was good, and yes, he had only taken out the bad parts. "I won't do it again."

"If that's true," he said, "you'll never have to work again. You can do *this* for a living." Then he threw back his head and laughed.

And he was right: I *am* doing this for a living, and as long as I can keep on, I don't expect ever to have to work again.[6]

4. ***Are the language and style consistent and appropriate throughout?*** Edit out words that create a conversational or informal tone in your paper. For example:

Change: And as for target shooting, well go purchase a BB gun or a set of darts.[7]
To read: For target shooting, a BB gun or a set of darts serves just as well as a handgun.

Also, edit out cheerleading, slogans, clichés, needless repetition, and exhortations. You are not writing a political speech.

---

[6]King, 30–31.

[7]From a student paper by Blake Decker. Used with permission.

In general, use a formal, rational style in an argument paper unless you have a good reason to do otherwise. Use emotional language and examples that arouse feelings only where appropriate with a particular audience to back up logical argument.

5. ***Is there enough variety?*** Use some variety in the way you write sentences by beginning some with clauses and others with a subject or a verb. Vary the length of your sentences as well. Write not only simple sentences but also compound and complex sentences. You can also vary the length of your paragraphs. The general rule is to begin a new paragraph every time you change the subject. Variety in sentences and paragraphs makes your writing more interesting to read. Do not sacrifice clarity for variety, however.

6. ***Have I used the active voice most of the time?*** The active voice is more direct, energetic, and interesting than the passive voice. Try to use it most of the time. Here is a sentence written in the active voice; it starts with the subject.

> Robotics is an exciting new technology that could enhance nearly every aspect of our lives.

Notice how it loses its directness and punch when it is written in the passive voice.

> Nearly every aspect of our lives could be enhanced by robotics, an exciting new technology.

7. ***Have I avoided sexist language?*** Avoid referring to people in your paper as though they are either all male or all female. However, using such expressions as "he or she" or "himself or herself" sounds inclusive but comes across as awkward. Solve this problem by using plural nouns (*students* instead of *student*) and pronouns (*they* instead of *he or she*). Occasionally, you may need to rewrite a sentence in the passive voice. It is better to write, "The U.S. Constitution is often used as the guide when making new laws," than to write, "He or she often uses the U.S. Constitution as a guide when making new laws."

Avoid the Seven Most Common Errors Students Make

1. Write three or more similar items in a *series,* separated by commas, with the final item connected by *and* or *or.*

   Example: The National Rifle Association, firearms manufacturers, and common citizens are all interested in gun control.[8]

2. Use *parallel construction* for longer, more complicated elements that have a similar function in the sentence.

   Example: Parents who fear for their children's safety at school, passengers who ride on urban public transit systems, clerks who work at convenience stores and gas stations, and police officers who try to carry out their jobs safely are all affected by national policy on gun control.

---

[8]The examples presented here are drawn from a student paper by Blake Decker. I have revised his sentences for the sake of illustration.

3. Keep everything in the same *tense* throughout. Use the present tense to introduce quotations.

   Example: As Sherrill *states,* "The United States is said to be the greatest gun-toting nation in the world." Millions of guns create problems in this country.

4. Observe *sentence boundaries.* Start sentences with a capital letter, and end them with a period or question mark. Make certain they express complete thoughts. Do not punctuate a clause as a sentence. In the following sentence, the "because" clause is incorrectly punctuated as a sentence.

   Example (incorrect): Because criminals, including terrorists, can buy guns easily in this country. There should be a system for checking the background of everyone who purchases a gun.

   The clause is actually a part of the rest of the sentence. Change the period to a comma to correct this common error.

   Example (correct): Because criminals, including terrorists, can buy guns easily in this country, there should be a system for checking the background of everyone who purchases a gun.

5. Make *subjects agree* with *verbs.*

   Example: Restrictions on gun control *interfere* [not *interferes*] with people's rights.

6. Use *clear and appropriate pronoun referents.*

   Example: The *group* [one whole] is strongly in favor of gun control, and little is needed to convince *it* [not *them*] of the importance of this issue.

7. Use *commas* to set off long initial clauses, to separate two independent clauses, and to separate words in a series.

   Example: When one realizes that the authors of the Constitution could not look into the future and imagine current events, one can see how irrational and irresponsible it is to believe that the right to bear arms should in these times still be considered a constitutional right, and according to Smith, the groups that do so "are shortsighted, mistaken, and ignorant."

Check for Final Errors, Add or Adjust the Title, and Submit Your Paper

Just before you submit your paper, check the spelling of every word you are not absolutely sure you know. If spelling is a problem for you, buy a small spelling dictionary or app that contains only words and no meanings. If you use a spell-checker, you should still read your paper one last time since a computer cannot find every kind of error. At this point you should format your paper and correct all the typographical errors that remain. Add a title or adjust your existing title, if necessary. Be sure that the final title provides information that will help the reader understand what your paper is about.

Complete the revision process by reading your paper aloud one more time. Read slowly and listen. You will be surprised by the number of problems that bother your ears that were not noticeable to your eyes. Your paper should be ready now to submit for evaluation.

Practice Your Process by Writing These Papers

LO5 Write examples of summary, summary-analysis, and exploratory essays.

You can practice reading, thinking, and writing about issues by understanding and learning to write the three types of papers that are described next in this chapter: the summary-response paper, the summary-analysis-response paper, and the exploratory paper. These papers can help you think about and develop ideas for papers described in future chapters.

THE SUMMARY-RESPONSE PAPER

A summary-response paper is composed of two parts: (1) the summary shows that you understand what an argument says, and (2) the response shows your reaction to it, including the ideas it generates in your mind.

A summary answers these questions: *What is this about? What did the author say about it?* To write a summary, follow these steps:

a. Survey first. (See instructions on page 78.) Identify the issue, the claim, and some of the subclaims, or ideas that support the claim. This will help you answer the question, *What is this about?*

b. Write a brief list of words or phrases that represent the subclaims or the main points the author makes about the claim. You may be able to do this when you finish surveying. If you cannot, go back and read section by section, or paragraph by paragraph, and make notes on what appear to be the main points. This will help you answer the question, *What did the author say about the claim?*

c. Write a summary in your own words and in complete sentences that includes the author's claim and the main points that support it. Use the words and phrases you have written to guide you.

A response answers these questions: *What are your personal reactions to this essay? How much common ground do you have with the author? What in the essay is new to you? What else does it make you think about? What do you like or dislike about it?*

Here are examples of a summary and a response to "Let's Ban the Cell Phone Ban," which appears on pages 46–47.

▶ Example of a Summary

Summary of "Let's Ban the Cell Phone Ban"

The author focuses on the tendency of college professors to ban all cell phones from their classrooms and asserts that this practice is both extreme and deprives students of a voice in this situation. She challenges the logic professors often use to justify this practice and suggests certain compromise solutions to this problem. Emphasizing the importance of involving students in discussions about classroom policy, Guiterrez makes the case that students should be given a role in deciding how to limit cell phone use within the classroom.

▶ Example of a Response

Response to "Let's Ban the Cell Phone Ban"

I have wondered myself about the fairness of the cell phone ban. Like Guiterrez, I have often felt that students should be given a greater voice in determining the rules that define in-class behavior. However, I wonder if the author is being realistic in expecting professors to accept a larger student role in these matters. Is it really likely that professors would so easily relinquish their own authority? And shouldn't the author's discussion of potential solutions to this problem acknowledge the possibility that professors might refuse to change?

THE SUMMARY-ANALYSIS-RESPONSE PAPER

Add an analysis to a summary-response paper[9] to demonstrate that you understand why a particular argument is effective. Insert the analysis between the summary and your response.

An analysis answers these questions: *How is the essay organized? What and where is the claim? What supports the claim? Is the support adequate and relevant? How does the author establish personal authority? What audience does the author assume? How does the author make the argument, including the support, effective for that audience? What overall qualities in this essay make it an effective (or ineffective) argument?*

▶ Example of an Analysis

Analysis of "Let's Ban the Cell Phone Ban"

The essay opens with the author's description of her own experiences with the cell phone ban. This description leads the author to immediately question the wisdom of this policy, which then forms the basis of her major claim: that students should be given the right to formulate a solution to this problem themselves. The rest of the essay is organized around the author's repeated assertion that students should be treated as adults capable of taking responsibility for these kinds of classroom decisions themselves.

The support includes examples of alternatives to the cell phone ban: having students turn off their phones when they enter class or put their phones in backpacks. These examples are helpful because they help support the author's claim that an outright ban of cell phones is not the only way to address this problem.

The author establishes her authority by citing these specific examples and thus demonstrates her firsthand experience with and knowledge of cell phone bans in classrooms. She assumes an audience who is familiar with classroom life and who perhaps has had doubts about the fairness of cell phone bans. She makes her argument appeal to this audience by using language that emphasizes students' ability to make decisions for themselves. She establishes common ground with her audience throughout by presenting her critique of cell phone bans from the perspective of a person who has experienced them.

---

[9]Thanks to Beth Brunk-Chavez for this assignment.

This is an effective argument because the author establishes common ground not only with students who have experience with cell phone bans, but also with anyone who has experienced difficulties of any kind with a professor in a classroom.

Summary-response and summary-analysis-response papers preserve ideas from your reading, including your own ideas, and often provide original material and even phrasing for future papers that you write on the same subject, such as a Rogerian paper or researched position paper.

THE EXPLORATORY PAPER

In the exploratory paper,[10] the arguer identifies not just one position but as many of the major positions on an issue as possible, both past and present, and explains them through summaries and an analysis of the overall rhetorical situation for the issue. The analysis of the rhetorical situation in these papers explains what caused the issue and what prompted past and present interest and concern with it, identifies who is interested in it and why, and examines the constraints of the inquiry and the various views in the ongoing conversation associated with it. The summaries of the positions not only explain each of the different perspectives on the issue but also provide the usual reasons cited to establish the validity of each perspective. The writer's own opinions are not expressed at all or are withheld until later in the paper.

The war in Iraq created a rhetorical situation because it raised many issues that motivated people all over the world to discuss and argue in an attempt to resolve what were perceived as problems associated with this war. Box 3.3 shows two of the many issues that emerged from this war. Several different perspectives held by individuals and groups who often disagreed with each other are also listed. Notice that the issues that emerged from the Iraq war did not invite simple pro and con positions. This is true of most rhetorical situations that motivate people to argue about issues. In between the either-or, people can and do take a variety of other positions that are not absolute or extreme.

Here are some additional examples. The issue of what to do with convicted criminals invites more perspectives than either putting criminals in jail or putting them to death. Intermediate positions might include sending them to various types of rehabilitation programs, releasing elderly inmates to their families when they are too old or too feeble to be a threat to society, or segregating different types of offenders in correctional institutions. The immigration issue in the United States invites more perspectives than either letting all foreigners in or keeping them all out. Other possibilities include issuing green cards to certain categories of immigrants or providing work permits for immigrant workers for a limited period of time.

There are a number of advantages to writing and reading exploratory papers. When writers and readers view an issue from many perspectives, they acquire a greater depth of understanding of it and the various views taken. Exploratory papers also help establish common ground between writers and readers.

---

[10]I am indebted to the late Professor James Kinneavy of the University of Texas at Austin for the basic notion of the exploratory paper.

Box 3.3	**Examples of Issues and Perspectives That Emerged from the Iraq War**

Issue 1: Why did the United States and its allies start a war in Iraq?

Perspectives:
1. To abolish weapons of mass destruction.
2. To encourage freedom and democracy in Iraq.
3. To destroy international terrorists.
4. To protect foreign oil supplies.
5. To remove a dictator who was perceived as a dangerous threat to the stability in the Middle East.
6. To showcase U.S. military capabilities.

Issue 2: What did the United States and its allies need to do to succeed in this war?

Perspectives:
1. Send more troops.
2. Supply the existing troops with better equipment.
3. Keep a few troops in Iraq indefinitely.
4. Withdraw all troops.
5. Rebuild the parts of Iraq destroyed by the war.
6. Work with the Iraqi government to establish democracy there.

Writers, by restating several opposing positions along with the usual reasons for accepting them, are forced to understand that opposing views have commonalities that permit not only qualified but also multiple perspectives. The reader is interested because the exploratory paper explains several views, which usually include the reader's. The reader is consequently more willing to learn about the other positions on the issue. Exploratory papers can provide mutual understanding and common ground for the next stage in argument, the presentation of the writer's position, and reasons for holding it.

Exploratory papers are a common genre in argument writing. You will encounter them in newspapers, news magazines, other popular magazines of opinion, and scholarly journals. They are easy to recognize because they take a broad view of an issue, and they explain multiple perspectives instead of just one. You will find examples of the exploratory paper at the end of this chapter (page 106).

HOW TO WRITE AN EXPLORATORY PAPER

Your challenge now is to write an exploratory paper of your own. Look at your issue from several angles to decide which position you prefer. If you are later given the assignment to write a position paper on your issue, you will have discovered your own position, and you will also understand some of the other views that you may want to refute. The exploratory paper assignment and the worksheet appear on page 108. To complete it successfully, follow these general suggestions.

1. ***Select an issue, and do some research and reading.*** You will need an issue to write about that invites several different perspectives. You may have identified several issues already. If you do not have an issue, read about a topic that interests you on the Internet or in the library. Take notes on the different perspectives you identify in this material. You might also make copies of the material you locate so that you can quote it later in your paper. (In both cases, document the sources for correct citation later.)

   An example of an issue that invites several perspectives is handgun control: some people believe there should be no restrictions on personal handgun ownership; other people believe possession of handguns should be banned for everyone except police officers and military personnel; a third group believes people have a right to own handguns, but with restrictions, including background checks, special training, and licensing. Notice these are three different positions on this issue, not merely three separate ideas about the issue.

   As you plan the perspectives for your exploratory paper, you can think about perspectives that are for, against, or somewhere else on the spectrum of possibilities; perspectives that represent three (or more) possible approaches or "takes" on an issue; perspectives that describe three (or more) possible ways to solve an issue; perspectives that provide three (or more) ways of interpreting an issue; and so on. These perspectives may be yours or other people's. You may actually find four or five different approaches that different groups of people hold.

2. ***Analyze the rhetorical situation.*** Sketch out answers to the three parts of the rhetorical situation for your issue that are already in place before you begin to write: the exigence, the reading audience, and the constraints. To establish exigence ask, *What happened to arouse interest in this issue in the first place?* To establish audience ask, *Who shares my position on the issue, and who takes other positions?* To establish constraints ask, *What are some of the values, beliefs, and constraining circumstances that cause these groups and individuals to hold their positions?* Or, ask, *What do each of these groups or individuals value, want, and believe about the issue?*

3. ***Write a draft, and include transitions.*** Draw on the ideas for drafting a paper discussed in this chapter. As you write your draft, include transitions to separate and emphasize the different perspectives on your issue. You might use transitions such as "some people believe," "others believe," and "still others believe" "one perspective on this issue is," "another perspective is," and "a final perspective is" or "one way to look at this issue is," "another way is," and "a third way is."

4. ***Work summarized ideas and quotes from your research into your draft.*** In an exploratory paper, you mainly summarize or paraphrase, in your own words, the positions you describe. If you decide to add direct quotations to make these summaries clearer or more interesting, work the quotations smoothly into your draft so that they make sense in context and are easy to read. Tell your reader where the summarized, paraphrased, and quoted material came from by citing original sources fully.

5. ***Revise your paper, and check your citations of source material.*** Follow the suggestions for revision that appear in this chapter. At the end of your paper, list the works quoted in your text by creating a Works Cited page, if you are following MLA style, or a References page, if you are following APA style. To help further, look at the student example of an exploratory paper at the end of this chapter.

LO6 Develop skills for peer review.

Submit Your Paper for Peer Review

If you can, put the draft of your exploratory paper aside for twenty-four hours, then read it critically and make changes to improve it. It helps to read the paper aloud at this point to get an even better idea about what can be improved. Then seek the opinion of other students in a class peer-review session. Peer-review sessions may include only three or four of your fellow students. You may be asked to provide each member of the review group with a photocopy of your paper so that, as you read your paper aloud to them, they can follow along and begin to mark problem areas to discuss later. Or, you may participate in a round-robin reading session, in which group members read all of the papers silently and make brief notes before they discuss the papers one by one. In some cases, your instructor may join the group as an equal member and participate with students in asking questions that call your attention to areas that could be improved. Still another way of conducting peer reviews is for pairs of students to exchange papers to take home and read before the next class. This provides each student with time to read another student's paper more than once, if necessary, to locate areas for improvement.

There are several advantages to submitting your paper for review. No matter how well you write, revise, and edit a paper, another reader is almost always likely to have suggestions that can make your final paper better. Peer groups also make the writing task less isolating and provide immediate feedback from a real audience. They help you become a more sensitive critic of your own and others' work. Most professional writers rely heavily on other people's opinions at various stages of writing. Look at the prefaces of some of the books you are using this semester. Most authors acknowledge the help of several people who have read their manuscript and made suggestions for improvement.

If peer-review groups are not conducted in your writing class, try to find someone else, like a writing center tutor or another student, to read your draft. Most writers need someone to read their work as they continue to refine it.

LO7 Apply the skills of summary, summary-analysis, and exploration to visual argument.

Expressing Multiple Perspectives through Visual Argument

Another way to express multiple perspectives on an issue is through a collection of images that express different perspectives on it. Most images, like those on the next page, need a few words of explanation to make their point. In this case, the title at the top and the four brief captions below the photographs explain the issue—walling off enemies—and various perspectives on how this has been done in four different countries. In the United States, walls are now in place on some parts of the border with Mexico, and more are being planned. Like the walls in China, Berlin, Israel, and Baghdad depicted in Images 1–4, this wall aims to separate people or keep people, such as undocumented immigrants from Mexico and Central America, out.

Walling Off Your Enemies: The Long View

Image 1: The Chinese Perspective

The Great Wall of China was first built between the fifth and third centuries B.C. to protect the northern borders of China. It is about 4,000 miles long at present.

Image 2: The German Perspective

The Berlin Wall, which separated East Berlin from West Berlin for 28 years, fell in 1989, an event that led to the reunification of Germany in 1990.

Image 3: The Israeli Perspective

This wall separates Israelis from Palestinians in the West Bank at the present time.

Image 4: The Iraqi Perspective

In Baghdad, during the Iraq War, Americans put up walls to secure neighborhoods.

These four photographs of walls provide four different perspectives on how governments have coped with perceived enemies by building walls. What do you think about the idea of building walls for protection from enemies? How effective is this solution? What other solutions can you think of that might also work or that might even work better?

Review Questions

1. Briefly describe a process for producing an argument paper that employs reading, thinking, and writing. **(LO1)**

2. What is plagiarism, and what can you do to avoid it? **(LO3)**

3. What are the advantages of outlining your ideas before you write a draft? **(LO4)**

4. Name at least three specific suggestions for revision made in this chapter and describe in detail how you could use each of them. **(LO4)**

5. Describe the exploratory paper along with some of the benefits of writing it. Then, describe exploring a topic visually along with some of the benefits of this form of communicating. **(LO5)**

Exercises and Activities

A. Class Project: Creating Composite Lists of the Reading, Thinking, and Writing Processes of Class Members

This exercise gives you an opportunity to share with your classmates what you do when you read, think about, and write argument. When all class members contribute their strategies to composite class lists, the result is usually a complete description of possible reading and writing processes. Include information, as you go along, about how you think as you read and write.

First, focus on describing what you do when you read and think about argument. Write the title "Reading Argument," and under it write the four headings "Prereading Strategies," "Reading Strategies," "Strategies for Reading Difficult Material," and "Postreading Strategies." Write five minutes to describe your current strategies in each area. Include thinking strategies in your description. Share these strategies with the class, creating master lists on the board.

Second, repeat this activity for writing argument. Write the title "Writing Argument," and under it write the four headings "Prewriting Strategies," "Drafting Strategies," "Strategies to Use When You Get Stuck," and "Postwriting Strategies." Write five minutes to describe your current strategies in each area and include thinking strategies in your description. Class members then contribute to composite lists on the board.

When you have written these lists, complete the following activities and discuss the results with the class.

1. Study the strategies for reading, thinking, and writing that your class has identified. Then,

    a. Discuss the ways in which writing is used as a part of the reading process.
    b. Discuss the ways in which reading is used as part of the writing process.
    c. Discuss how thinking is used as a part of both processes.

2. Turn to the Summary Charts on pages 420–434 and read the descriptions of possible strategies that you could employ at various stages to help you read, think about, and write argument. Discuss strategies you would consider adding to your present reading, thinking, and writing processes.

B. **Class Discussion: Recognizing Written Argument**

This reprinted article by Gina Kolata was published as a news article. Answer the following questions to help you figure out what type of argument is present, if any. Refer back to the description of six types of argumentation purpose on pages 74–75 to help you make your analysis.

1. What is the main issue in this article? It is not directly stated.

2. What are the author's attitudes toward the subject at issue?

3. What supporting material favors the author's point of view? Notice emotional language, vivid description, emotional examples, and the drawing that provide clues to the author's personal point of view.

4. What is the author's intention in this article? To explain? To convince? Or both?

5. What does the author hope you will conclude when you finish reading? Justify your answer with evidence from the article.

BEFORE YOU READ: What do you know about sperm banks, and what is your present opinion of them?

ESSAY #2   **PSST! ASK FOR DONOR 1913***

Gina Kolata

The author is a well-known science journalist for the *New York Times.* She has also published her work in *Science* magazine.

In the old days, nearly two decades ago, when Jeffrey Harrison was selling his sperm to California Cryobank, sperm banks did not tell clients much. Women learned that Donor 150 (Mr. Harrison, who was one of the bank's most-requested donors) was six feet tall, had blue eyes and was interested in philosophy, music and drama.

But they did not learn, for instance, that despite those interests, Mr. Harrison was also "sort of a free spirit," as Danielle, one of his donor-conceived daughters, said after finding him last week.

Mr. Harrison, 50, lives in a recreational vehicle near Los Angeles, eking out a living doing odd jobs and taking care of dogs.

While the women who used his sperm may be perfectly satisfied, women today seem to be looking for a more unquestionably accomplished sort of man. Handsome and brilliant. Talented and charming. Loving and kind. A match one might only dream of finding in the flesh.

5   "Many women see this as another way to give their child a head start in life," says Lori Andrews, a professor at Chicago-Kent College of Law who has studied the sperm bank industry, of the high stakes of sperm selection.

And increasingly, say the banks, women want proof of perfection before buying a dream donor's sperm.

They ask for SAT scores and personality test results. They want baby pictures, pictures of the donor as a teenager, and photos of him as an adult. They want to hear his voice on audio files and they want to read his answers to written questions.

As more and more is added to the profile, its compilation becomes almost a striptease as the veil of anonymity falls away, eventually revealing all but name and address.

The reason for offering clients previously unimaginable degrees of access to information is competition.

10   "It's kind of an arms race," explains William Jaeger, director of Fairfax Cryobank, in Fairfax, Va., which, along with California Cryobank, based in Los Angeles, is among the largest sperm banks in the country.

"One year someone adds a personality profile, the next year someone adds something else," Mr. Jaeger says. "If one of your competitors adds a service, you add a service."

Supplying donors who will be saleable is quite a burden for the banks, which say they accept only about 1 to 2 percent of donor applicants. Often a man's sperm is not good enough, reproductively, or his medical history is problematic. Others are now rejected because their looks or education or even their demeanor is wrong.

"We're somewhat in the position of someone who is arranging a blind date," says Dr. Charles Sims, medical director and a founder of California Cryobank.

So who is Mr. Right for today's woman?
15   He can't be fat.

"We look for a height-weight ratio that is within the norm," Dr. Sims explains.

Being short is negotiable.

"If you have a 5-foot-7 or -8 donor who is a medical student or Ph.D. scientist, that out-weighs the height issue in many situations," Dr. Sims says.

Education matters. California Cryobank only takes men who are in college or who graduated from a four-year college. At the Fairfax bank, "there is a preference for guys with medical and law degrees," Mr. Jaeger says.

20   Some sperm banks reveal more about their depositors than others.

The Fairfax bank, for example, provides adult photos if the donor agrees. The California bank does not, fearing that they could identify the donor years later and cause real problems. The Fairfax bank asks donors if their offspring can contact them when they are 18. The California bank will not do that but will try to discreetly contact a donor and ask if he wants to be identified to an adult child.

"We have felt we have some obligation to anticipate issues that a young man of twenty one, twenty two, or twenty three may not anticipate," Dr. Sims says. "To take an extreme example, let's say we had Bill Clinton as a donor when he was in college. Later he becomes president."

The Fairfax bank also includes "staff impressions" of donors in its dossiers. The staff seems to have favorable impressions of everyone, but some are more favorable than others.

Among the most favorable of all is a man who appears to also be the most-requested donor.

25 "Women sort of fall in love with him," says Joy Bader, director of client services.

The most-requested donor is of Colombian-Italian and Spanish ancestry, is "very attractive, with hazel eyes and dark hair," and, Ms. Bader adds, is "pursuing a Ph.D."

The bank's files have one man, Donor 1913, who fits this description.

Donor 1913, the staff notes in his file, is "extremely attractive," adding in a kind of clinical swoon, "He has a strong modelesque jaw line and sparking hazel eyes. When he smiles, it makes you want to smile as well."

Donor 1913 is an all-around nice guy, they say. "He has a shy, boyish charm," the staff reports, "genuine, outgoing and adventurous."

30 He also answers questions, including, "What is the funniest thing that ever happened to you?"

Donor 1913 relates an incident that occurred when he asked his girlfriend's mother to step on his stomach to demonstrate his strong abdominal muscles.

"As she stepped on top of my stomach, I passed gas," he writes,

Is Don Juan the gas-passer also the most popular donor at Fairfax Cryobank?

Mr. Jaeger, the director, says he'll never tell. He cautions that discussing the most popular donor, whoever it is, might pose a problem—there is already a waiting list for his sperm, and publicity can only make it worse.

"We just can't keep enough of his units on hand," Mr. Jaeger says.

For Discussion:

Does this essay qualify as an argument? Why? Provide evidence for your answer. What does the drawing contribute? If the author had to express her opinion on the subject she writes about, what would it be? What is your opinion?

Arguing Like a Citizen

Issue: "Is sperm donation a business that should be encouraged?"

Take another look at the essay "Ask for Donor 1913." In order to see how the argument made in this piece connects to the issue of citizenship, look at the sample analysis below. In what ways does the discussion here provide you with a starting point for "arguing like a citizen"?

▶▶▶ Thinking Like a Citizen

- Why do I care about this issue?
  As someone who may one day consider starting a family, I feel a direct stake in arguments over sperm donation. Given the cultural pressure these days to create the "perfect" family, I believe it's important to have a candid discussion about the technologies designed

continued

Arguing Like a Citizen (*continued*)

to tailor a family's birth options to their personal specifications. Are these kinds of technologies helpful? Do they raise ethical questions we need to consider more fully?

- Who else cares about this issue?
  In addition to parents or would-be parents, others with a stake in this discussion include the medical professionals in charge of offering these kinds of services. Like the families they serve, these professionals also need to think about the implications of a policy like sperm donation. Should those in charge create certain rules, regulations, or boundaries?

- What different perspectives on this issue might others have?
  Many prospective parents would likely base their views on whether or not a sperm donation helped them achieve their personal goal of choosing the desired attributes for their prospective child. Medical professionals, on the other hand, would need to take a broader view, weighing the medical, social, and ethical effects on society.

▶▶▶ Arguing Like a Citizen

- How does this issue impact or affect my daily life?
  If I decide not to have a family, or if I do and find myself with no direct need to use sperm donation, it could be said that the impact of this issue on my daily life is minimal. Because it raises broader questions about the role technology should play in procreation and childrearing, however, this issue could be said to impact anyone contemplating starting a family in these technologically advanced times. It could, for example, affect my views about what types of fertility treatments are warranted.

- What are the key problems or questions this issue raises for me?
  The key question the issue of sperm donation raises for me concerns the ethics of allowing prospective parents to engineer the procreation process to fit their personal specifications. Is it right for people to control or engineer the birth process to this degree?

▶▶▶ Acting Like a Citizen

- Where could I go in my community to see an example of this debate being waged?
  There are a number of media sources in which this issue might be discussed: medical journals, parenting magazines, fertility Web sites. In addition, there might be any number of local organizations in which this issue might be discussed as well: a local sperm bank, a community medical clinic, a family planning facility.

- What concrete action could I take to change or improve the way this issue is discussed?
  Given how potentially polarizing an issue like this can be, the discussion over sperm donation could well benefit from an effort to frame the debate more in terms of objective, factual information. Finding firm data about the science of sperm donation or information about the particular ways prospective parents have used this technology would help frame the discussion within more objective terms.

Arguing Like a Citizen (*continued*)

Activity

Now use this same framework to analyze the argument in one of the other readings in this chapter. What key issue does the essay address? What larger argument about this issue does it make? Use the questions outlined above to connect this argument to the question of citizenship.

C. **Writing Assignment: The Summary-Response Paper**

Choose an issue that interests you and find three different essays that explore this issue. Using your own words, write a one-page summary-response paper for each of these essays: divide a piece of paper horizontally in half and write a summary on the top half and your response on the bottom half. Refer to the instructions and sample summary on page 91 and the sample response on page 92 to help you.

D. **Class Discussion and Writing Assignment: The Summary-Analysis-Response Paper**

The following essay, "When Texting is Wrong" by Randy Cohen, is an example of the type of argument you might find in a newspaper editorial or opinion column. Read, underline, and annotate the essay. Then briefly discuss answers to the following questions as a class.

1. Who is the author? What are his qualifications? What may have motivated him to write about this subject?

2. What are your own experiences with text messaging? How often do you employ this type of communication? What would you say are its advantages and disadvantages?

3. Finally, write a summary-analysis-response paper. Drawing on the notes you have taken on your reading and discussion of the essay, write a 300- to 500-word paper in which you first summarize the essay, then analyze the essay, and last, respond to the essay. Use the following prompts labeled "Summary," "Analysis," and "Response" to guide your writing.

   ▶ *Summary:* What is this about? What did the author say about it?

   ▶ *Analysis:* Describe the organization of the essay. Include a description of the claim. Describe and evaluate the support. Consider types, quantity, quality, and relevance of the support. Then answer these questions: How does the author establish his authority? What audience does the author assume? How does the author make his writing, including the support, effective for the audience? What overall qualities in this essay make it an effective (or ineffective) argument?

   ▶ *Response:* What are your personal reactions to this essay? How much common ground do you have with the author? What in the essay is new to you? What else does it make you think about? What do you like or dislike about it?

BEFORE YOU READ: What are your own experiences with text messaging? What are the advantages and disadvantages of this particular communications technology?

ESSAY #3 **WHEN TEXTING IS WRONG***

Randy Cohen

Randy Cohen's column, "The Ethicist," regularly appeared in the *New York Times Magazine* from 1999 through 2011.

You're having dinner with your teenage kids, and they text throughout; you hate it; they're fine with it. At the office, managers are uncertain about texting during business meetings: many younger workers accept it; some older workers resist. Those who defend texting regard such encounters as the clash of two legitimate cultures, a conflict of manners not morals. If a community—teenagers, young workers—consents to conduct that does no harm, does that make it O.K., ethically speaking?

The Argument:

Seek consent and do no harm is a useful moral precept, one by which some couples, that amorous community of two, wisely govern their erotic lives, but it does not validate ubiquitous text messaging. When it comes to texting, there is no authentic consent, and there is genuine harm.

Neither teenagers nor young workers authorized a culture of ongoing interruption. No debate was held, no vote was taken around the junior high cafeteria or the employee lounge on the proposition: Shall we stay in constant contact, texting unceasingly? Instead, like most people, both groups merely adapt to the culture they find themselves in, often without questioning or even being consciously aware of its norms. That's acquiescence, not agreement.

Few residents of Williamsburg, Va., in, say, 1740 rallied against the law that restricted voting to property-owning white men. For decades, there was little active local opposition to the sexual segregation in various Persian Gulf states. A more benign example: few of us are French by choice, but most French people act much like other French people, for good and ill. Conformity does not imply consent. It simply attests to the influence of one's neighbors.

5   So it is with incessant texting, a noxious practice that does not merely alter our in-person interactions but damages them. Even a routine conversation demands continuity and the focus of attention: it cannot, without detriment, be disrupted every few moments while someone deals with a text message. More intimate encounters suffer greater harm. In romantic comedy, when someone breaks a tender embrace to take a phone call, that's a sure sign of love gone bad. After any interruption, it takes a while to regain concentration, one reason few of us want our surgeon to text while she's performing a delicate neurological procedure upon us. Here's a sentence you do not want to hear in the operating room or the bedroom: "Now, where was I?"

Various experiments have shown the deleterious effects of interruption, including this study that, unsurprisingly, demonstrates that an interrupted task takes longer to complete and seems more difficult, and that the person doing it feels increased annoyance and anxiety.

Mine is not a Luddite's argument, not broadly anti-technology or even anti-texting. (I'm typing this by electric light on one of those computing machines. New fangled is my favorite kind of fangled.) There are no doubt benefits and pleasures to texting, and your quietly texting while sitting on a park bench or home alone harms nobody. But what is benign in one setting can be toxic in another. (Chainsaws: useful in the forest, dubious at the dinner table. Or, as Dr. Johnson put it in a pre-chainsaw age, "A cow is a very good animal in the field; but we turn her out of a garden.")

Nor am I fretful that relentless texting hurts the texter herself. Critics have voiced a broad range of such concerns: too much texting damages a young person's intelligence, emotional development and thumbs. That may be so, but it is not germane here. When you injure yourself, that is unfortunate; when you injure someone else, you are unethical. (I can thus enjoy reading about a texting teen who fell into a manhole. When a man is tired of cartoon mishaps, he is tired of life. And yes, that teen is fine now.)

Last week, a Massachusetts grand jury indicted a Boston motorman who crashed his trolley into another, injuring 62 people: he was texting on duty. Last month, Patti LuPone berated an audience member who pulled out an electronic device during her show in Las Vegas. (Theaters forbid the audience to text during a performance, a rule routinely flouted. Perhaps stage managers could be issued tranquilizer darts and encouraged to shoot audience members who open any device during a show. At intermission, ushers can drag out the unconscious and confiscate their phones. Or we might institute something I call Patti's Law: Any two-time Tony winner would be empowered to carry a gun onstage and shoot similar offenders.)

10   These are the easy cases, of course: clearly it is unethical to text when doing so risks harming other people. And formal regulation can easily address them; a dozen states and the District of Columbia prohibit texting while driving, for example. But the problem of perpetual texting in more casual settings cannot be solved by legislation. No parent will call the cops if a son or daughter texts at table. Instead, we need new manners to be explicitly introduced at home and at work, one way social customs can evolve to restrain this emerging technology.

Lest casual texting seem a trivial concern, remember that some political observers trace the recent stalemate in the New York Senate to the wrath of power-broker Tom Golisano, who was offended that majority leader Malcolm Smith fiddled with his BlackBerry throughout a meeting between them. When the dust settled, the State Senate had been transformed from merely disheartening to genuinely grotesque. I wouldn't want that on my conscience.

E. Paired Student Activity: Analyzing a Student Exploratory Paper

The following is an example of an exploratory paper written by Prisna Virasin, a student in an argument class. Take a few minutes to read Prisna's paper. Then work in pairs to answer the following questions. Report your answers to the class.

1. What is the issue?

2. Describe the parts of the rhetorical situation that were in place when Prisna started to write. What is the exigence? Who are the groups of people interested in this issue? What are their positions? What are some of the constraints of these groups?

3. What are the perspectives on the issue that the author identifies? Make a list.

4. What transitions does the author use? Underline them.

5. What is the author's perspective? Why does she hold it?

You may want to use Prisna's paper as a model for your own exploratory paper.*

BEFORE YOU READ: What do you know about Barbie dolls?

STUDENT PAPER
#1

Prisna Virasin
Prof. Wood
English 1302
1 March 2013

The Controversy behind Barbie

Explain the issue.

    The Barbie doll was created in 1959 by Ruth Handler, the cofounder of Mattel. Handler created the doll after seeing her daughter, whose nickname was Barbie, and her daughter's friends play with their paper dolls. According to Gaby Wood and Frances Stonor Saunders, Handler realized that little girls wanted a doll "they could aspire to be like, not aspire to look after" (38). This was a revolutionary idea because before the creation of Barbie, the toy store doll selection mainly consisted of baby dolls, which encouraged girls to pretend to be mothers. For Handler, according to Wood and Saunders, Barbie "has always represented the fact that a woman has choices" (39). The "Barbie Dolls" entry on the *History Channel* Web site states, "ninety percent of all American girls in the last forty years have owned at least one Barbie. . . . Each week Mattel sells over 1.5 million dolls—that's two dolls per second."

Describe the rhetorical situation.
▸ Exigence
▸ Interested parties
▸ Constraints

What is the first perspective?

    The fact that Handler created Barbie as a challenge to the ideology that the proper role for women was that of a mother has become ironic in light of the present feminist protest against the Barbie doll. The Barbie protesters have stated that Barbie is responsible for the development of poor body image in girls. They believe that the Barbie's proportions create impossible images of beauty that girls will strive toward. If Barbie were a human, she would be seven feet tall with a thirty-nine-inch chest measurement, twenty-two-inch waist measurement, and thirty-three-inch hip measurement ("Barbie Dolls").

    In addition to protests of the Barbie's physical appearance, there is also the issue of the doll's intellectual image. Barbie detractors have criticized the Barbie lifestyle, which seems to center around clothes, cars, dream homes, and other material possessions. Protests followed the release of the talking Barbie that localized such expressions as "Math is hard" and "Let's go shopping."

---

*See the Appendix to Chapter 12 for the actual MLA format guidelines for student papers.

Parents feared that the first sentence would reinforce the stereotype that girls were less skilled at math than boys were. The second sentence seemed to reinforce the importance of clothes, physical appearance, and material goods. In her article, "Giga-What? Barbie Gets Her Own Computer," Ophira Edut criticizes educational materials based on Barbie for the image they reinforce. Edut states that the Barbie computer is bundled with typing tutor software while the boys' Hot Wheels computer is bundled with adventure games. Also, the Barbie Rapunzel CD-ROM is touted by Mattel to expose girls to fine art and creativity when the only creative function of the program is changing Barbie's clothes and hairstyle interactively on the computer screen.

What is the second perspective?

Supporters of the Barbie doll state that the toy is a fun part of growing up. They refer to the simple fun of playing with Barbie dolls. They believe that Barbie as a figure is a tool in building girls' imaginations. They also maintain that Barbie as a figure is a positive role model because she is able to do almost anything. Barbie was an astronaut before the first woman went into space. Barbie has been a veterinarian, a doctor, a businesswoman, and to top it all off, a presidential candidate.

What is the third perspective?

5   Between the anti-Barbie camp and the pro-Barbie camp, there are the Barbie moderates. The Barbie moderates do not completely agree with how Mattel chooses to portray the "ideal American woman," nor do they view the doll as all evil. They see the positive aspects of the Barbie (the many professions, the ability to foster imaginative play, and the message that girls can choose to be whomever they want) and the negative aspects of the Barbie as a figure (a materialistic nature, a focus on outward appearance, and the vapid blond stereotype). The moderates state that by banning Barbie dolls, we will not be solving the problem of poor body image. They believe that Barbie is a scapegoat—the figure (or doll) to blame for all the negative feelings that children develop about themselves. Although the moderates do not agree with the image of women that Barbie seems to sustain, they also do not believe that this doll (or figure) is the source of the problem.

What is the author's perspective? Why does she hold it?

As a twenty-something female who grew up in America, I am very interested in the Barbie debate. I played with Barbie dolls almost obsessively from first to third grade. I designed clothes for them out of handkerchiefs and tissues and dreamed about becoming a fashion designer. I remember envying the girls who had Barbie Ferraris and dream houses. I looked on in horror as my little sister cut Barbie's hair short and colored it hot pink with a marker. In college, when I was introduced to feminism, I tried to deny any past connection to Barbie. I was ashamed to have ever associated with this figure. I felt sorry for the girls who looked like walking Barbie dolls, always worried about looking perfect. I realize now that I cannot blame thoughts of being fat, short, or out of style on a doll or girls that look like dolls. I agree with the Barbie moderates. As simple as the Barbie looks, it seems that the Barbie issue is more complicated than "Barbie good" or "Barbie bad." The debate encompasses many interesting and controversial issues concerning how we view beauty and how we view ourselves. In my eyes, Barbie is a scapegoat. We, as an entire culture, need to look at our ideas about beauty and what we are teaching children about themselves.

Works Cited

"History of Toys: Barbie Dolls." *History.com.* A&E Television Networks, 2008. Web. 15 Feb. 2008.

Edut, Ophira. "Giga-What? Barbie Gets Her Own Computer." *AdiosBarbie.com,* n.d. Web. 17 Feb. 2008.

Wood, Gaby, and Frances Stonor Saunders. "Dream Doll." *New Statesman* 15 Apr. 2002: 38–40. *Academic Search Complete.* Web. 18 Feb. 2008.

For Discussion:

Did you ever play with a Barbie or G.I. Joe? If not, what were your favorite childhood toys? How did they affect your imagination and self-image? Have they had any lasting effects on you?

F. Writing Assignment: Write an Exploratory Paper

Review "How to Write an Exploratory Paper" (pages 94–95) to help you complete this assignment. Then write a 750- to 900-word exploratory paper. Use the worksheet below to help you plan your exploratory paper. Follow MLA style (see the Appendix to Chapter 12), unless you are advised otherwise.

Worksheet 2	Exploratory Paper

1. Write your issue in a complete sentence. Explain it, and include the information that provides background and makes the issue interesting to your readers.

2. Explain the parts of the rhetorical situation that are already in place as you begin to write. Describe the exigence or context for your issue, including what happened to make people interested in it. Identify the individuals or groups of people interested in this issue, with a brief introduction to their positions. Mention some of the constraints of these groups. For example, what do they think, value, and believe?

3. Describe at least three different positions on your issue, state who holds them, and give some of their reasons for holding them. You may explain more than three positions, if you want or need to do so. Jot down the positions.

   a. Position 1: _____

   b. Position 2: _____

   c. Position 3: _____

4. Explain your personal interest in the issue and the position you favor.

G. Group Work: Analyzing an Argument Essay That Employs Visual Perspectives on the Issue as Support

The following essay was written at a time when some members of Congress were advocating the addition of a flag-burning amendment to the United States Constitution. Read the essay, study the images, and answer the "For Discussion" questions that follow.

BEFORE YOU READ: Is flag burning an issue you feel strongly about? Why or why not?

ESSAY #4   ## FLAG PROTECTION: A BRIEF HISTORY OF RECENT SUPREME COURT DECISIONS*
Congressional Research Service

This excerpt, which provides an historical overview of recent US Supreme Court decisions regarding flag burning, was prepared as part of a report made to Congress in 2006.

Many Members of Congress see continued tension between "free speech" decisions of the Supreme Court, which protect flag desecration as expressive conduct under the First Amendment, and the symbolic importance of the United States flag.

Consequently, every Congress that has convened since those decisions were issued has considered proposals that would permit punishment of those who engage in flag desecration. The 106th Congress narrowly failed to send a constitutional amendment to allow punishment of flag desecration to the States. In the 107th and 108th Congresses, such proposals were passed by the House. This report is divided into two parts. The first gives a brief history of the flag protection issue, from the enactment of the Flag Protection Act in 1968 through current consideration of a constitutional amendment.

The second part briefly summarizes the two decisions of the United States Supreme Court, *Texas* v. *Johnson* and *United States* v. *Eichman*, that struck down the state and federal flag protection statutes as applied in the context punishing expressive conduct.

In 1968, Congress reacted to the numerous public flag burnings in protest of the Vietnam conflict by passing the first federal flag protection act of general applicability. For the next 20 years, the lower courts upheld the constitutionality of this statute and the Supreme Court declined to review these decisions. However, in *Texas* v. *Johnson*, the majority of the Court held that a conviction for flag desecration under a Texas statute was inconsistent with the First Amendment and affirmed a decision of the Texas Court of Criminal Appeals that barred punishment for burning the flag as part of a public demonstration.

Joe Rosenthal, *Marines Raising the American Flag at Iwo Jima*

Leonard Detrick, *Anti-Vietnam War Protesters*

Stephanie Frey, *Daughter Holding Parents' American Flag*

*"Flag Protection: A Brief History of Recent Supreme Court Decisions," Congressional Research Service, Library of Congress.

In response to *Johnson*, Congress passed the federal Flag Protection Act of 1989. But, in reviewing this act in *United States v. Eichman*, the Supreme Court expressly declined the invitation to reconsider *Johnson* and its rejection of the contention that flag-burning, like obscenity or "fighting words," does not enjoy the full protection of the First Amendment as a mode of expression. The only question not addressed in *Johnson*, and therefore the only question the majority felt necessary to address, was "whether the Flag Protection Act is sufficiently distinct from the Texas statute that it may constitutionally be applied to proscribe appellees' expressive conduct." The majority of the Court held that it was not. Congress, recognizing that *Johnson* and *Eichman* had left little hope of an anti-desecration statute being upheld, has considered in each Congress subsequent to these decisions a constitutional amendment to empower Congress to protect the physical integrity of the flag.

For Discussion:

What three perspectives on the flag of the United States are expressed in the three photographs? What three wars do they represent? What effect is created by placing photographs next to each other in this order? How does the historical overview of recent Supreme Court decisions regarding flag burning influence how you read these images?

H. Creative Assignment: Exploring an Issue Visually

Select an issue and create a visual exploratory essay by gathering three or more images that express different perspectives on the issue. As a class, brainstorm together to generate some ideas that will work for this assignment. Here are a few ideas to get you started: modifying your personal image, embracing new media, selecting a major, planning your career, making a major purchase such as a car or computer. Search for images on the Internet or in magazines or newspapers.

PART 2

Understanding the Nature of Argument

The purpose of the next six chapters is to explain the essential component parts of an argument and show how they operate together to convince an audience. Chapter 4 identifies the parts of an argument as explained by Stephen Toulmin in what has come to be known as the Toulmin model. Chapter 5 describes the types of claims and purposes in argument. Chapter 6 describes how support, warrant, and backing combine to provide proof for argument, and also discusses language and style. Chapter 7 alerts you to fallacies or false proofs and provides criteria for judging ethical argument. Chapter 8 teaches the unique characteristics of visual argument and reviews ideas from earlier chapters that apply to visual argument, and Chapter 9 presents Rogerian argument as an alternative strategy to traditional argument. When you finish reading Part Two:

- You will understand and be able to identify the essential parts of an argument.

- You will know the key questions that arguments attempt to answer.

- You will be able to identify types of claims and purposes in argument.

- You will understand how argument employs proof, language, and style to appeal to your reason, your emotions, and your sense of values about people's character.

- You will understand fallacies and the differences between ethical and unethical argument.

- You will know how to analyze and create visual arguments.

- You will know how to write a traditional position paper, a Rogerian argument paper, and an argument analysis paper.

The Essential Parts of an Argument: The Toulmin Model

After studying this chapter, you will be able to:

LO1 Identify and describe the six parts of the Toulmin model of argument.

LO2 Use the Toulmin model to analyze written, visual, and online argument.

Because people have been analyzing argument and writing theories of argument for twenty-five hundred years, there is a considerable tradition of theory to draw on to help with this task. This theoretical background is especially useful because theory describes argument, and once you possess good descriptions, argument will be more familiar and consequently easier for you to read, analyze, and write yourself.

In gaining a theoretical new understanding of argument, you will be adding to what you already know as you gradually build a stronger and larger body of knowledge and comprehension. Eventually, you will achieve "all-at-onceness," a quality Ann E. Berthoff utilizes in her book *The Sense of Learning* to describe the use of many ideas, bits of information, and strategies about reading, writing, and viewing that finally come together so that you are able to practice them unconsciously, simultaneously, and automatically.[1]

For now, however, you are still expanding your knowledge. Your goals in this chapter are to gain a better understanding of the anticipated outcomes of argument and to identify the component parts as they are identified by Stephen Toulmin in his model for argument.

[1] Ann E. Berthoff, *The Sense of Learning* (Portsmouth, NH: Boynton/Cook, 1990), 86–91.

The Outcomes of Argument: Probability versus Certainty

LO1 Identify and describe the six parts of the Toulmin model of argument.

By now you are probably coming to see how closely tied argument is to audience. Whatever the topic, all arguable issues require the possibility of at least two different views; it is in the nature of argument to invite differing perspectives on issues. In practical terms this means always keeping in mind the effects your argument might have on the audience you are aiming to address, as well as the effects, in turn, an audience's response may have on the argument you make. Argument outcomes span a range of possibilities, from achieving a closer agreement with a friendly audience to getting the attention of and even perhaps some consensus from a neutral or hostile audience. Notice that these outcomes of argument are usually not described as establishing "certainty" or "truth" in the same sense that mathematics and science seek to establish certainty and truth. We do not argue about the fact that $2 + 3 = 5$ or that the area of a circle is πr^2. Mathematical proofs seek to establish such truths. Argument seeks to establish what is probably true as well as what might be expedient or desirable on balance for the future. In other words, successful argument depends not only on what we want to say, but on how our listeners or readers respond. Arguers tell you what they think for now along with what they think should be done, given their present information. On that basis, you decide what you think for now, given your present information.

Part of determining what is probable involves understanding the larger context within which a persuader is making an argument: the assumptions and expectations a given audience brings; the views and values that are widely accepted within a given setting. As you can no doubt imagine, the factors that define a given context will change depending on the circumstances. This is why the realm of argument concerns the probably true rather than the definitively true. To understand this realm better, to see more clearly how the outcome of an argument relates to context and audience, it is useful to understand the parts that contribute to the whole argument.

The Parts of an Argument according to the Toulmin Model

Stephen Toulmin, a modern English philosopher, developed a six-part model of argument in his book *The Uses of Argument,* and this model has been useful to many people for explaining the essential parts of an argument.[2] At the time Toulmin wrote his book, his colleagues were logicians who were interested in discovering truth rather than probabilities. Toulmin tells us that his book had a chilly welcome among them. His graduate adviser at Cambridge, he explains, "was deeply pained by the book, and barely spoke to me for twenty years." Another colleague described

---

[2]Stephen Toulmin, *The Uses of Argument* (Cambridge; UK: Cambridge University Press, 1958). I have adapted and added applications of the model to make it more useful for reading and writing.

it as "Toulmin's *anti*-logic book."[3] Given this, Toulmin expected his book to be a failure. His editors, however, assured him that people were buying it, and Toulmin found out who many of these people were when he visited the United States some time later. Professors in speech departments and communication departments all over the United States were using his book to teach students to become better speakers and arguers. If you have ever taken a speech class, you may have already encountered the Toulmin model of argument. As time went by, the model was picked up by English departments to help students improve their reading and writing of argument. The Toulmin model has also been used in schools of law to help students learn to present legal argument. You will find that you can employ the model to help you write essays, reports, letters of application, proposals, legal memos, or any other document intended to convince others. The Toulmin model is also useful in designing or interpreting visual and multimedia argument, such as photos, advertisements, Web sites, TV shows, and movies, and in writing or analyzing persuasive speeches. The Toulmin model is a very natural and practical model because it follows normal human thought processes. You have had experience with all its parts in the everyday arguments you carry on with your friends and family.

The Toulmin model has six parts. The first three parts are present in every argument, including both traditional and consensual argument. They are: (1) the *claim;* (2) the *data,* encompassing subclaims and specific supporting details, which we are calling *support;* and (3) the *warrant.* The other three parts are used as needed to strengthen an argument and adapt it to the needs and beliefs of a particular audience. These parts are: (4) the *backing,* (5) the *rebuttal,* and (6) the *qualifier.* Figure 4.1 shows Toulmin's diagram of these six parts of the model.

To illustrate how these parts work together, let us examine an actual argument. For example, the narrator of a television documentary makes the *claim* that critical thinking is more important now than it was seventy-five years ago. This is followed by *support* that includes pictures of modern scientists launching space shuttles and air traffic controllers directing airplanes to land. These individuals seem intent and busy. It appears to be clear that if they do not think critically, there will be trouble. Then the camera switches to children riding on an old-fashioned school bus of seventy-five years ago. One boy is saying that he wants to grow up and be a farmer like his dad. This youngster is relaxed and bouncing along on the bus. He does not look like he is thinking critically or that he will ever need to do so. The unspoken part of this argument—the assumption that the author of this program hopes the audience will share—is the *warrant.* The author hopes the audience will agree, even though it is not explicitly stated, that farmers of seventy-five years ago did not have to think critically, that modern scientists and engineers do have to think critically, and that critical thinking was not as important then as now. The author wants the audience to look at the two bits of support, the scientist and the farmer's son, and make the leap necessary to accept the claim. The author hopes the audience will think, "That's right, those scientists and that young boy don't seem to share the same demands for critical thinking. Times have changed. Critical thinking is more important now than it was seventy-five years ago."

[3]"Logic and the Criticism of Arguments," in James L. Golden, Goodwin F. Berquist, and William E. Coleman, *The Rhetoric of Western Thought,* 4th ed. (Dubuque, IA: Kendall Hunt, 1989), 375.

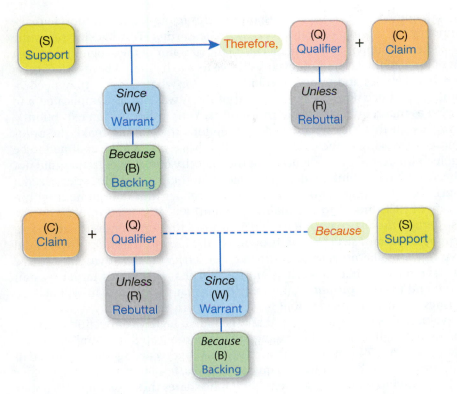

Figure 4.1 *A Diagram of the Toulmin Model of Argument Showing the Six Parts: Claim, Support, Warrant, Backing, Rebuttal, and Qualifier*

Note that an argument can be configured either as "support therefore claim" or as "claim because support."

Those three parts—the *claim,* the *support,* and the *warrant*—are the three parts you will find present in any argument.

If we wanted to evaluate this assumption, we could ask some follow-up questions. First: Is there a logical connection between the author's claim and the support s/he provides? Does juxtaposing images of "scientists" and "farmer's children" logically reinforce a claim about the changing importance of "critical thinking"? If so, how? Second: What are some of the broader assumptions or views that might encourage an audience to accept this logic? What general attitudes toward or assumptions about "farm work" and "scientific work" might cause an audience to make the leap and accept the claim? We will have more to say about each of these types of questions in the pages that follow. For now, it is enough to note that you will find these three parts—the claim, the support, and the warrant—in any argument.

Suppose, at this point, however, that some members of the audience do not accept the claim. An additional three parts of the model are available to make the argument stronger. Here is how these parts could be incorporated into the argument. It might be presented like this: The camera then shifts to an elderly man, who says, "Wait a minute. What makes you assume farmers didn't think? My daddy was a farmer, and he was the best critical thinker I ever knew. He had to think about weather, crops, growing seasons, fertilizer, finances, harvesting, and selling the crops. The thinking he had to do was as sophisticated as that of any modern scientist." This audience member is indicating that he does not share the unstated warrant that farmers of seventy-five years ago had fewer demands on their thinking processes than modern scientists. In response to this rejoinder, the author, to make the argument convincing, provides *backing for the warrant*. This backing takes the form of additional support. The camera cuts to the narrator of the program: "At least two out of three of the farmers of seventy-five years ago had small farms. They grew food for their families and traded or sold the rest for whatever else they needed. The thinking and decision making required of them was not as complicated and demanding as that required by modern scientists. Your father was an exception."

Even though this backing allows for exceptions that should make the argument more convincing to the older man, it still relies on the belief, assumed to be acceptable to the rest of the audience, that the majority of old-time farmers did not have the same critical thinking demands placed on them as modern scientists do.

Notice that this backing takes the form of a smaller unit of argument within the argument. It is linked to the main argument, and it is used to back up the weakest part of the main argument. Furthermore, this smaller argument has a claim-support-warrant structure of its own: (1) the *claim* is that most farmers did not have to think like modern scientists; (2) the *support* is that two out of three did not have to think like modern scientists, and that this man's father was an exception; and (3) the *warrant*, again unstated, is that the older man will believe the statistics and accept the idea that his father was an exception.

To evaluate this warrant, we could ask: Is there a logical connection between working on a "small farm" and engaging in "less complicated thinking"? Are the statistics about "two out of three farmers seventy-five years ago living on small farms" accurate? If the answer to such questions is yes, it is far more likely the older man will be convinced by the argument here. If he shares these assumptions about "small farm work" and "critical thinking," or believes these statistics are accurate, there is a much greater chance he will accept the idea his father was an exception. If he resists this backing for the new warrant by asking, "Hey, where did you get those statistics? They're not like any I ever heard," then another argument would need to be developed to cite the source of the figures and to convince the man of their reliability. As you can see, the requests for backing, for more information to serve as further proof, can go on and on. Let us leave the man defending his father and the narrator, though, and look at what else might appear in this argument.

Suppose the camera now shifts to a modern science professor who wants to challenge the logical connection between "small farms" and "uncritical thinking" by making a rebuttal. She does so by making her own claim: "The critical thinking required seventy-five years ago was demanding and sophisticated. Critical thinkers of the time had to figure out how to get the country out of a severe recession, and they had to develop the technology to win World War II." These opinions are then supported with factual evidence that includes pictures of individuals thinking. As with backing, a rebuttal follows the structure of argument. Once again, there is a clear claim (i.e., critical thinking of seventy-five years ago was demanding and sophisticated) followed by support (i.e., critical thinking addressed complex problems dealing with war and recession), and underwritten by an unstated assumption or warrant (i.e., addressing an economic recession or creating warfare technology requires critical thinking). A handy way to think about a rebuttal, in fact, is as a counterargument: a response to the main argument that relies upon its own claim-support-warrant structure.

After all of these challenges, exceptions, and requests for more information, the author at this point finds it necessary to *qualify* the original claim in order to make it acceptable to more of the audience members. Qualifying involves adding words and phrases to the claim like *sometimes, seems to be, may be,* or *possibly* to make it more acceptable to the audience. In this case, the narrator now restates the qualified claim: "Critical thinking, because of modern science, seems to some people to be more important now than it was seventy-five years ago." Compare this with the original claim that critical thinking *is* more important now than it was seventy-five years ago. Figure 4.2 diagrams this argument according to the Toulmin model. You have probably never systematically used this or any other model to read or write argument. The model can serve as a kind of guide for reading and analyzing arguments, both written and visual, and also for writing or composing them. Authors do not usually use the model as an exact formula, however. Rather, it describes what can be, but is not necessarily always, present in an argument. Consequently, when you read or view argument, you will at times easily recognize parts of the model and at other times you will not. Some arguments, in fact, may not contain one or more of the parts at all, such as a rebuttal, for example. You are not getting it wrong if you read and do not find all of the parts. When you write

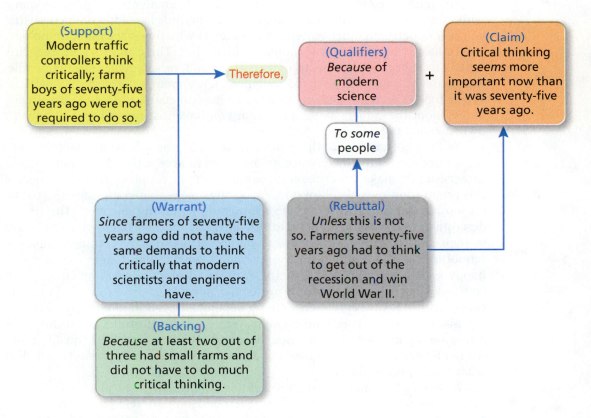

Figure 4.2 *An Example of the Six Elements in the Toulmin Model*

(or create an argument visually), you do not need to make all parts explicit either. The following sections provide some details about each of the six parts that will help you understand them better.

CLAIM

Discover the claim of an argument by asking, "What is the author trying to prove?" Or, plan a claim of your own by asking, "What do I want to prove?" The claim is the main point of the argument. Identifying the claim as soon as possible helps you focus on what the argument is all about.

Synonyms for *claim* are *thesis, proposition, conclusion,* and *main point.* Sometimes an author of an argument in a newspaper or magazine will refer to the "proposition," or an individual arguing on television will ask, "What is your point?" Both are referring to the claim. When someone refers to the claim as the conclusion, do not confuse it with the idea at the end of an argument. The claim can appear at the end, but it can also appear at other places in the argument. The claim is sometimes stated in a sentence or sentences called the *statement of claim.* This sentence can also be called the *thesis statement,* the *purpose sentence,* the *statement of focus,* or the *statement of proposition.*

The terms used in this text to describe the main elements in argument, along with some of their synonyms, appear in Box 4.1. Become familiar with them so that you will understand other writers on the subject who may vary the terminology.

To locate the claim, what should you look for? The claim may be explicitly stated at the beginning of an argument, at the end, or somewhere in the middle. Alternatively, it may not be stated anywhere. It is sometimes *implied,* in which case you will be expected to *infer* it. To infer an implicit claim, use what you already know about the subject along with what you have just read to formulate your own statement of it.

To help illustrate what this looks like, consider the following example. Let's say an author wants to convince an audience to accept the claim that "single-career couples make better parents than dual-career couples." Rather than state this proposition outright, however, the author seeks to accomplish this goal by presenting her audience with two contrasting parenting portraits. The first: a description of a working father and stay-at-home mother, filled with references to their kids' countless play dates, rewarding at-home activities, high grades at school. All of which the author supplements with visual images that depict a happy and rested mother interacting with her contented-seeming children. In contrast, the second description presents a portrait of a two-career family in severe crisis, filled with references to squabbling kids, a house in messy disrepair, a husband and wife barely on speaking terms. To this portrait, the author adds side observations about how overscheduled everybody is, how little "quality time" the family enjoys as a whole. Based on these contrasting family portraits, it is clear what the implied claim is.

Authors often make conscious decisions about where to place a claim and whether to make it explicit or implicit. Their decisions are related to their notions about the audience. A claim at the beginning is straightforward and draws the

Box 4.1	Argument Terminology: Terms Used in This Book and Some of Their Synonyms

▶▶▶ What Terms Are Used in Argument?

TERMS	SYNONYMS	
Claim	thesis	main point
	proposition	macro-argument
	conclusion	controlling idea
Rebuttal	challenge	disagreement
	counterargument	
Statement of claim	thesis statement	statement of focus
	purpose sentence	statement of proposition
Subclaims	reasons	lines of argument
	main ideas	supporting arguments
	micro-arguments	specific issues
	arguments	
Support	evidence	proof
	opinions	premise
	reasons	statistics
	examples	explanations
	facts	information
	data	personal narratives
	grounds	images
Warrants	assumptions	cultural values
	general principles	presuppositions
	widely held values	unstated premises
	commonly accepted beliefs	generally accepted truths
	appeals to human motives	underlying logic

reader in right away. Or an author may decide to lead up to the claim, in which case it may appear either in the middle or at the end.

Delaying the claim pulls the audience in and increases interest and attention. "What is this author after?" the audience wonders, and reads to find out. The end of an essay is the most emphatic and memorable place for a claim. Many authors prefer to put the claim there to give it as much force as possible. There is some risk involved in putting the claim at the end. Students who use this strategy must be careful to insert cues along the way so that readers understand where the argument is headed and do not feel they are being led through a random chain of topics. The unstated claim requires that the reader pay special attention because it is the reader's responsibility to make the inference that the author expects. Because of this effort, the reader may find an inferred claim especially convincing and memorable.

The claim, whether implied or explicitly stated, organizes the entire argument, and everything else in the argument is related to it. The best way to identify it, if it is not obvious or easy to locate, is to complete the following statement as soon as you have finished reading: "This author wants me to believe that . . ." When you have finished that statement, you have the claim. As a writer, you can check your own claim during revision by completing this statement:

I want my audience to agree that . . .

If you can do this, you understand the concept of the claim, and you will be able to recognize the main point in the arguments you read and to use a claim to articulate the main point in any argument you write. You can also use this same type of open statement to determine the claim in a visual or multimedia argument you view or produce.

SUPPORT

Discover the support in an argument by asking, "What additional information does the author supply to convince me of this claim?" Or, if you are the author, ask, "What information do I need to supply to convince my audience?" You can summarize the most essential elements of an argument as a *claim with support*. Aristotle wrote in the *Rhetoric* that the only necessary parts of an argument are the statement of proposition (the claim) and the proof (the support). There has been general agreement about those two essential parts of an argument for more than twenty-three hundred years.

The synonyms that Toulmin uses for *support* are *data* and *grounds,* the British equivalents. In the United States, you will often read arguments in which the author claims to be "grounding" a claim with particular support and *data* is sometimes used as a synonym for *facts and figures.* Other synonyms for support are *proof, evidence,* and *reasons.* Authors also refer to major evidence as *premises.* When you encounter that term in your reading, remember that premises lead to and support a conclusion (a claim). Do not confuse premises with the claim.

Subclaims

At the first level of support are the *subclaims,* which are the supporting arguments or reasons for the claim. Here is an example that illustrates the relationships among an issue area, at the most general level in the example, a specific related issue that represents an idea about the general issue area, a claim that is made in response to the specific related issue, and four subclaims that are used to support the claim. The subclaims are at the most specific level in this example because they represent ideas about the claim.

▶ Issue Area: The Environment

Specific related issue: How serious are the world's environmental problems?

       Claim: The environment is the single-most serious problem the world faces today.

     Subclaims: 1. The rain forests are being destroyed, causing global warming.
              2. Increasing population is depleting resources in some parts of the world.
              3. Many important water sources are being polluted by industry.
              4. The ozone layer, which protects us from harmful sun rays, is being destroyed by chemicals.

Specific Support

The second level of support is the *specific support*. Specific support provides the evidence, opinions, reasoning, examples, and factual information about a claim or subclaim that make it possible for us to accept it. Look back at the claims and subclaims in the example above. If you are to take this claim seriously, you will want some additional specific support to make it convincing.

To locate such support, what should you look for in the argument? One bit of good news: support is always explicitly stated, so you will not have to infer it as you sometimes have to infer the claim. Thus, an understanding of the types of specific support is all you really need to help you recognize it. Let us look at some of the most common types.

Facts

In a court of law, *factual support* (the murder weapon, for example) is laid out on the table. In written argument, it must be described. Factual support can include detailed reports of *observed events* or *places;* specific *examples* of real happenings; references to *events,* either *historical* or *recent;* and *statistical reports*. Factual support is vivid, real, and verifiable. Two people looking at it together would agree on its existence and on what it looks like. They might not agree on what it *means* to each of them—that is, they might interpret it differently. Nevertheless, essentially, they would agree on the facts themselves.

Opinions

When people start interpreting facts and events, opinion enters the picture. Opinions may be the personal opinions of the author or the opinions of experts the author selects to quote. The author can use direct quotations, set off in quotation marks, or summaries or paraphrases of what someone else thinks or reports. Furthermore, opinions may be informed, based on considerable knowledge and excellent judgment, or they may be ill-founded, based on hearsay and gossip. The most convincing opinions are those of experts, whether they are those of the author or of another person. Experts possess superior background, education, and experience on an issue. Contrast in your own mind the opinions of experts with the uninformed opinions of people who are surprised in the streets by reporters and asked to give their opinions. Ill-founded, baseless opinion is boring and rarely convincing. In contrast, informed personal opinions and the opinions of experts can be more interesting and convincing than the facts themselves.

Examples

Examples can be real or made up, long or short. They are used to clarify, to make material more memorable and interesting, and, in argument particularly, to provide proof. Examples that are real, such as instances of actual events or references to particular individuals or places, function in the same way that fact does in an argument. They are convincing because they are grounded in reality. Made-up, or hypothetical examples, are invented by the writer and, like opinions, can only demonstrate what may be the case. Personal experience is one type of example that is frequently used in argument. Writers often go into considerable detail about the experiences that have influenced them to think and behave as they do. Combining personal experience with the opinions and reasoning derived from it is a common way to develop a claim.

Images

Images are also used to support claims and subclaims and make them more vivid and believable to the audience. You have already encountered several examples of images used in this way. Look back at the three images of American flags associated with World War II, the Vietnam War, and the war in Iraq on page 109, and the sperm donor on page 99. Images used as support make abstract ideas more concrete and easier to grasp. They also make them more memorable.

Different authors manage support in different ways, depending on the requirements of the subject, their purpose, and their audience. When the issue is an abstract idea and the audience is informed, the author may present mainly opinions and few, if any, facts or examples. Such arguments include a claim and blocks of logical reasoning organized around subclaims to develop and prove the claim. If you were to outline the argument, you might not need more than two levels, as in the claim and subclaim example on pages 120–121. When the subject requires more specific support or the audience needs more information to be convinced, specific materials at lower levels are required to ground the subclaims in facts, figures, quotations from others, visual images, or author opinions.

The next example expands on the example on page 121 by adding specific support.[4]

▶ Issue Area: The Environment

Specific related issue: How serious are the world's environmental problems?
    Claim: The environment is the single-most serious problem the world
        faces today.

---

[4]The support in the example is drawn from Jeffrey Kluger and Andrea Dorfman, "The Challenges We Face," *Time*, August 26, 2002, A71+.

Subclaim: The rain forests are being destroyed, causing global warming.
  Support: Global warming could cause the oceans to rise, the number of storms to increase, and more droughts. *(opinion)*
Subclaim: Increasing population is depleting resources in some parts of the world.
  Support: One-third of the world does not have enough food and is in danger of starvation. *(fact)*
Subclaim: Many important water sources are being polluted by industry.
  Support: By 2025, two-thirds of the world's population may live in areas where there is a serious water shortage. *(opinion)*
Subclaim: The ozone layer, which protects us from harmful sun rays, is being destroyed by chemicals.
  Support: It was widely reported in the spring of 2013 that the hole in the ozone layer was significantly larger than it had been the previous year. *(fact)*

Quality support helps build common ground between the arguer and the audience. Rantings, unfounded personal opinions that no one else accepts, or feeble reasons like "because I said so" or "because everyone does it" are not effective support. Audiences usually do not believe such statements, they do not share experiences or ideas suggested by them, and they lose common ground with the arguer when they read or hear them.

Common ground is far likelier when an author spends time thinking about what an intended audience does and does not know, and thus what opinions and information an audience would best respond to. In the case of the foregoing environmental discussion, the decision about what support to offer depends on what the intended audience knows about the issue of global warming. For an audience steeped in scientific knowledge, support that relies on anecdote might not be very useful. For an audience conditioned to be skeptical of scientific authority, a careful presentation and explanation of scientific data is probably warranted.

When reading argument, to help you focus on and recognize the support, complete this sentence as soon as you finish:

The author wants me to believe that . . . [the claim] because . . . [list the support].

When you read to revise your own writing, you can complete this statement:

I have convinced my audience to believe [the claim] because [list your support].

WARRANTS

Warrants are the assumptions, general principles, conventions of specific disciplines, widely held values, commonly accepted beliefs, and appeals to human motives that are an important part of any argument.[5] After taking a close look at the claim-support within a given argument, we might ask ourselves a very basic question: How

---

[5]Toulmin's warrants are somewhat similar to Bitzer's constraints in the rhetorical situation. Bitzer, however, extends the concept of constraints to also include the resources available to the writer or producer and the type of text being created, whether written, spoken, or visual. Thus *constraints* is a broader concept than *warrants*.

do we get from here to there? What are the assumptions an author needs her or his audience to share in order for them to be persuaded by this argument? The warrant is where this question gets answered. As the unstated assumption(s) that links a claim to its support, the warrant is what determines whether an audience will accept the argument being made. Even though they can be spelled out as part of the written argument, usually they are not. In many instances, it would be redundant and boring if they were. For example, an argument might go as follows:

Claim: The president of the United States is doing a poor job.
Support: The economy is the worst it has been in ten years.

Toulmin identifies one type of warrant: an assumption that logically compels or guarantees the conclusion being argued for. For the example above, we might define the logical warrant as follows:

If the economy is the worst it has been in ten years, *then* the president is doing a poor job.

Assuming I believe that the economy is in fact the worst it has been in ten years, and assuming I believe the president is doing a poor job when the economy is the worst it has been in ten years, I must agree that the president is doing a poor job. The surest way to identify a logical warrant is to restate the argument's claim-support structure as an "if/then" proposition (shown above). To avoid always presenting the logical warrant as a verbatim restatement of the support and claim, we can also find alternative ways to phrase the same logic. In this case, such a rephrasing might read: When the economy is weak, it is a sign the president is doing a bad job.

To Toulmin's model, however, we might also add a second type of warrant: a contextual warrant. Contextual warrants refer to the broader assumptions, beliefs, or values that influence how an audience will respond to a given argument. For the above example, contextual warrants include: the generally accepted belief that the president is responsible for the economy; the widespread assumption that the economy, as one of the president's chief responsibilities, is also a valid barometer of presidential performance. Note that neither of these assumptions logically compels an audience to accept this argument. If an audience shares these assumptions, however, it is more likely they will find this argument more plausible or compelling.

To sum up: For our purposes, warrants can be divided into two types: *logical* warrants and *contextual* warrants. Logical warrants direct our attention to the assumptions that are internal to a given argument. Contextual warrants, on the other hand, direct our attention to those more general assumptions that frame our understanding of and reaction to a given argument. Each constitutes an important aspect of the warrant overall, and each plays an important role in determining how an audience will respond.

Here is another example, and this one relies on a *value warrant*.

Claim: Businesses have a compelling interest in opposing environmental protection laws.
Support: Obeying environmental protection laws that call for clean air, for example, costs industry money that could otherwise be realized as profit.

Logical Warrant:	Utilizing the "*If, then*" formula, we might state the logical warrant in these terms: "**If** obeying environmental protection laws costs industry money that would otherwise be realized as profit, **then** businesses have a compelling interest in opposing them." If we wanted to cast the warrant in language that did not simply reiterate the terms of the claim-support structure, we might say: "Profits are a higher priority for businesses than environmental concerns when making decisions about their operations."
Contextual Warrants:	The contextual warrant encompasses those broader assumptions that relate to the issue an argument raises, and that influence the views an audience might have about this issue. In this case, examples of a contextual warrant include the widely held belief that profits should stand as the primary measure of a business's success; the common assumption that financial considerations and environmental concerns are typically in tension with each other.

Warrants originate with the arguer. But it is important to remember that the prerogative to respond to and assess warrants rests with the audience. An audience may correctly identify the logic underlying a given claim-support structure, but still disagree with the point being made. An audience may share with the arguer a commonly held belief, and yet use this belief as the basis for drawing a very different conclusion. We can imagine, for example, an audience who shares with an arguer the view that the president is responsible for the economy, and yet who comes to a very different conclusion about whether the economy constitutes a fair measure of presidential performance. Warrants can be shared by the arguer and the audience, or they can be in conflict. Furthermore, if the audience shares the warrants with the arguer, the audience will accept them and the argument is convincing. If the warrants are in conflict and the audience does not accept them (they believe private enterprise, not the president, is responsible for improving the economy), the argument is not convincing to them.

Warrants provide critical links in argument. For instance, they link the support to the claim by enabling an audience to accept particular support *as* proof of or justification for a particular claim. Without the linking warrant, the support may not be convincing. Here is an example.

Claim:	The appeals process for criminals should be shortened . . .
Support:	because the appeals for criminals on death row can cost more than $2 million per criminal.
Expected logical warrant:	If a criminal appeal costs more than $2 million per criminal, then the appeals process should be shortened. (This individual shares the author's warrant, the link is made, and the argument is convincing.)

Alternative logical warrant:	If a criminal appeal costs more than $2 million per criminal, then a remedy other than shortening the appeals process should be found. (This individual supplies an opposing warrant, the link between claim and support is not made, and the argument is not convincing.)
Expected contextual warrants:	Two million dollars is an unreasonably high price to pay for a criminal appeal; the appeals process can be shortened without sacrificing its fairness or effectiveness.
Alternative contextual warrants:	No amount of money is too much to ensure a fair appeals process; shortening the appeals process would detract from its fairness or effectiveness.

Supply your own logical and contextual warrant in the following argument.

Claim:	The government should abolish loan funds for college students . . .
Support:	because many students default on their loans, and the government cannot tolerate these bad debts.
Logical Warrant:	Can you identify the logical warrant underlying this claim-support? Try writing this out using the "if/then" formula outlined earlier. Now try rephrasing this warrant in different terms.
Contextual Warrant:	What are some of the broader assumptions or views that would help an audience accept this argument? What are some of the broader assumptions or views that would make such acceptance less likely?

These examples demonstrate that the warrant links the evidence and the claim by justifying particular evidence as support for a particular claim. Notice also, however, that the warrant attempts to establish a link between the author and the audience as well. Shared warrants result in successful arguments. When the warrant is not shared or when there are conflicting warrants, the audience will question or disagree with the claim.

Besides being related to what people commonly believe, value, want, or accept as background knowledge about a subject, warrants are also culture-bound. Since values, beliefs, and training vary from culture to culture, the warrants associated with them also differ from culture to culture. Tension between Japan and the United States was caused by a Japanese official's claim that American workers are lazy and do not work hard enough. American workers were angry and countered with a rebuttal about how hard they think they work. Japanese and American workers have different work schedules, attitudes, and experience with leisure and work time. Consequently, the part of both arguments that was unstated, the warrant, described hard work in different ways for each culture. The lack of a shared warrant caused the tension. Furthermore, neither side was convinced by the other's argument.

Japanese claim:	American workers are lazy . . .
Support:	because they work only 40 hours a week.
Japanese warrant:	People who work only 40 hours a week are lazy.
American rebuttal:	American workers are hardworking . . .
Support:	because they work 40 hours a week.
American warrant:	People who put in 40 hours a week are industrious and hardworking.

Perhaps now you have begun to appreciate the importance of shared warrants in argument. Shared warrants are crucial to the success of an argument because they are the most significant way to establish common ground between reader and writer in argument. Shared warrants and common ground, as you can imagine, are particularly important in international negotiations. Skillful negotiators analyze warrants to determine whether or not both parties are on common ground. If they are not, communication breaks down and argument fails.

To help you discover the logical warrants that underlie an author's claim, and to assess the validity of this logic, answer the following questions:

What is left out here?
Do I believe that this evidence supports this claim? Why or why not?

To help you compare this logical warrant to the contextual warrants that are shaping your response to this claim, answer the following questions:

What does this author seem to value? Do I share those values?
What is causing the author to say these things? Would I say these things differently? How or why?

As the author of argument, you should consider your audience and whether or not they will accept your warrants. Let's turn now to the other three parts of the Toulmin model that an arguer can use to adapt an argument to a particular audience.

Create-Your-Own-Warrant Exercise

▶ Choose an issue with which you are familiar.

▶ Answer the question, What makes this issue arguable or debatable?

▶ Determine what your own perspective is on this issue.

▶ Write your perspective as an argument (i.e., using the claim-support structure).

▶ Next, write down what you see as the logical warrant for this claim (hint: start by using the "if/then" formula; then try rephrasing this in different terms).

▶ Then, write down what you see as the contextual warrant(s) for this claim.

BACKING

You should have a sense by now that warrants themselves may require their own support to make them more acceptable to an audience, particularly if the audience does not happen to share them with the author. An author may provide backing, or additional evidence and ideas to "back up" a warrant, whenever the audience is in danger of rejecting it. When you are the author, you should provide backing also.

Backing sometimes appears as appeals to generally accepted knowledge and beliefs that are held by most individuals or groups of people who belong to a specific discipline or culture. These beliefs are sometimes spelled out explicitly as backing for a warrant, and at other times they are implied and the audience has to supply them by examining the logic of the argument and making inferences.

Here is an example of backing for a warrant.

Claim:	Immigrants should be allowed to come into the United States . . .
Support:	because immigration has benefited the U.S. economy in the past.
Logical Warrant:	If immigration has benefited the U.S. economy in the past, then immigrants should be allowed to come into the United States.
Contextual Warrants:	Current economic conditions are similar to past conditions; immigration policy should be dictated by economic need.
Backing:	Now, as in the past, immigrants are willing to perform necessary, low-paying jobs that American citizens do not want. Immigrants perform these jobs better than citizens and for less pay. Thus, their inclusion in the workforce is better for the American economy overall.

Look for backing in an argument by identifying the warrant and then by asking whether or not you accept it. If you do not, try to anticipate additional information that would make it more acceptable. Then examine whether the author supplied that or similar additional support. When you are the writer, consider your audience. Will they accept your warrant? Can you strengthen it by supplying additional information or by appealing to common values and beliefs that will help justify your claim?

REBUTTAL

A rebuttal establishes what is wrong, invalid, or unacceptable about an argument and may present counterarguments or new arguments that represent entirely different perspectives or points of view on the issue. To attack the validity of the claim, an author may demonstrate that the support is faulty or that the warrants are faulty or unbelievable. Counterarguments start all over again, with a new set of claims, support, and warrants.

Here is an example of a rebuttal for the argument about immigration:

Rebuttal 1:	Immigrants actually drain more resources in schooling, medical care, and other social services than they contribute in taxes and productivity.
Rebuttal 2:	Modern immigrants are not so willing to perform menial, low-skilled jobs as they were in past generations.

Here is an example of a counterargument for the immigration argument:

Claim:	Laws should be passed to limit immigration . . .
Support:	because we have our own unskilled laborers who need those jobs.
Logical Warrant:	If there are unskilled, native-born laborers who need jobs, laws should be passed to limit immigration.
Contextual Warrants:	Native-born workers are willing to hold these jobs; native-born workers would perform these jobs as well as immigrants; legally curtailing immigration would succeed in motivating or enabling employers to higher native-born workers instead.

Rebuttals can appear as answers to arguments that have already been stated, or the author may anticipate the reader's rebuttal and include answers to possible objections that might be raised. Thus, an author might write a rebuttal to the claim that we should censor television by saying such a practice would violate the First Amendment. Or, if no claim has been made, the arguer could anticipate what the objections to television violence might be (violence breeds violence, children who see violence become frightened, etc.) and refute them, usually early in the essay, before spelling out the reasons for leaving television alone.

Look for a rebuttal or plan for it in your own writing by asking, "What are the other possible views on this issue?" When reading ask, "Are other views represented here along with reasons?" Or, when writing ask, "How can I answer other views?" Phrases that might introduce refutation include *some may disagree, others may think,* or *other commonly held opinions are,* followed by the opposing ideas and your reasons and evidence for rejecting them.

QUALIFIERS

Remember that argument is not expected to demonstrate certainties. Instead, it establishes probabilities. Consequently, the language of certainty (*always, never, the best, the worst,* and so on) promises too much when used in claims or in other parts of the argument. It is not uncommon for an author to make a claim and, while still writing, begin revising and qualifying it to meet the anticipated objections of an audience. Thus words such as *always* and *never* change to *sometimes; is* or *are* change to *may be* or *might; all* changes to *many* or *some; none* changes to *a few;* and *absolutely* changes to *probably* or *possibly.* Qualified language is better for demonstrating probability in argument. Look to see whether the author has stated the claim in other parts of the argument in probable or absolute terms, and then read the entire argument to figure out why or why not. For example, the following is a qualified version of the first claim that all immigrants should be allowed to enter the United States. These qualifications would make the original claim more acceptable to the people who offered the rebuttals and counterargument.

> Immigrants should be allowed to enter the United States only if they can prove that they already have jobs yielding sufficient income to offset social services and that no American citizens are currently available to perform these jobs.

Value of the Toulmin Model

LO2 Use the Toulmin model to analyze written, visual, and online argument.

The Toulmin model has some advantages that make it an excellent model for reading, writing, and viewing argument. Its most essential advantage is that it invites common ground and audience participation in the form of shared warrants, increasing the possibility of interaction between author and audience. By subdividing warrants into two categories, furthermore, we give ourselves an especially useful strategy for analyzing the role different kinds of unstated assumptions play within an argument. As we have seen, the logical warrant works well as a tool for identifying and verifying the internal logic within a claim-support statement. We have also seen, though, that the overall persuasiveness of an argument rests upon more than its internal logic alone. Contextual warrants supplement our analysis of logical warrants by helping us uncover the associated assumptions that help determine whether an audience will find an argument persuasive.

The model works for reading or writing not only in debate and single-perspective argument but also in academic inquiry, negotiation, dialectic, or any other form of argument that requires exchange and attempts to reach agreement. It can even be a useful tool for one-on-one argument or personal decision making.

Writers of argument find the Toulmin model useful as both an invention strategy and a revision strategy. It can be used to help an author come up with the essential parts of an argument in the first place, and later it can be used to check and evaluate the parts of a newly written argument. See page 143 for a writing assignment that uses the Toulmin model as a tool to help the writer think about the parts of a position paper. See page 142 for an example of a student-written position paper with its Toulmin elements labeled in the margins.

Readers of argument find the model useful for analyzing and describing the essential parts of a written argument. Listeners find it just as useful for analyzing and describing the essential parts of an argumentative speech. Viewers find they can use the model to analyze visual argument, whether it appears alone as an argument, independent of text with only a few words of explanation, such as in some paintings, cartoons, photographs, or Web sites; or as support for ideas in a written text, such as photographs, drawings, graphs, and charts that illustrate and explain; or as in video images that support ideas presented on television, in movies,

Figure 4.3 *A Toulmin Analysis of a Cartoon That Makes an Argument*

Claim:	*This job applicant is probably not prepared for this particular job . . .*
Support:	because he has taken tests in high school that rely on answer sheets, and he cannot communicate effectively.
Logical Warrant:	If the knowledge learned and tested in standardized tests is irrelevant to jobs in the real world, it will fail to prepare students for those jobs.
Backing:	Many people believe that standardized tests fail to measure the critical thinking skills and communication skills, especially writing, that are required for success in the workplace.
Rebuttal:	A rebuttal is implied against the position that standardized testing is an adequate test of students' knowledge and job skills. If we wanted a rebuttal that argues against the claim being advanced by this cartoon, we might write: While certain standardized tests fail to impart a measure of useful knowledge, others, in fact, do teach and measure skills that will be effective on the job.
Qualifier:	The job applicant is not prepared for this particular job because he has taken tests in high school that rely on answer sheets, like those used with standardized tests, and he is unable to communicate in the ways this particular employer finds effective.
Contextual Warrants:	Standardized tests detract from people's ability to think critically; one of the key requirements of many jobs is to communicate clearly; standardized tests do not help students develop effective communication skills; a key purpose of standardized tests is to prepare students for future jobs.

This cartoon will be convincing to you if you share the warrant and the backing. If you place a different value on standardized tests than this cartoonist, it will not convince you.

or online. Figure 4.3 provides an example of a Toulmin analysis of a cartoon that makes an argument.

The Toulmin model can be used to write or to analyze both consensual and adversarial arguments. It accommodates all of the various forms of arguments. The model is summarized in a handy chart for quick reference for the use of both readers and writers in the Summary Charts (page 424).

Analyzing Online Argument: Applying the Toulmin Model

The rise of digital culture has dramatically changed the ways we encounter and respond to argument. From online ads to YouTube videos, Web-based arguments come in a variety of different forms, employing an array of different tools to present and support their claims. These changes present challenges to the ways the Toulmin model can be used to analyze argument. Because their claims can take textual, visual, video, or graphic form, online arguments demand an approach more specifically tailored to a multimedia environment. Because they draw upon ideas, information, and evidence from a range of sources, online arguments require closer attention to the credibility of the support they use to advance their claims. And because they provide their audiences with so many opportunities to respond, online arguments invite more scrutiny of the interactive form rebuttals can take. The outline below provides you with a framework for analyzing an online argument in Toulmin terms. How does each set of questions help you tailor a Toulmin analysis to the specific features of online argument? Then take a closer look at the example of online argument that follows. What kind of argument does this digital selection make? And how does the discussion that follows provide you with a model for conducting this kind of analysis yourself?

▶▶▶ Claim

- Through what medium (Web site, social media post, video, etc.) is the claim presented?
- What multimedia elements (textual, visual, video, graphic) are used to convey it?

▶▶▶ Support

- What type of support is offered?
- What form (textual, visual, video, graphic) does this support take?

▶▶▶ Logical Warrant

- What is the logical connection between this claim and support?
- Can you state this connection in an "if/then" form?

▶▶▶ Rebuttal

- What opportunities for audience feedback are included?
- Do these opportunities strengthen or diminish the claim being made?

▶▶▶ Qualifier

- What additional multimedia elements are used to qualify the claim being made?

Analyzing Online Argument: Applying the Toulmin Model (*continued*)

▶▶▶ Contextual Warrants

- What assumptions or associations do people typically bring to this particular medium?
- How do these assumptions or associations influence the claim being made?

GETTING HOME SAFELY IS JUST A CLICK AWAY

 Child Car Safety

SaferCar.gov/TheRightSeat

▶▶▶ Claim

- *Parents and caregivers need to ensure their children are properly buckled up when in the car.*
- The claim is presented in an online public service announcement (PSA) devoted to raising awareness about the importance of child passenger safety.
- The PSA uses written text ("Getting Home Safely Is Just a Click Away") and visual imagery (a picture of ruby red shoes, a picture of a young girl in a car seat) to convey this claim.

▶▶▶ Support

- *Because this child is buckled up safely, she is secure in the knowledge that she will get home safely.*
- The PSA uses its visual imagery to present this support. The image of the smiling girl conveys the Web site's point about traveling safely, while the red slippers capture the idea of returning home.

continued

Analyzing Online Argument: Applying the Toulmin Model (*continued*)

▶▶▶ Logical Warrant

- If parents and caregivers fit children to the proper car seats, their children will arrive home safely.

▶▶▶ Rebuttal

- The PSA provides viewers with links to other child safety resources, such as "campaigns," "marketing tools," and "events/presentations."
- These links are designed to give viewers further information to support the PSA's key claim.
- It also includes a "search" field for viewers to find further connections themselves.

▶▶▶ Qualifier

- The child here can feel confident about her own safety because she has been properly placed within the appropriate car seat.

▶▶▶ Contextual Warrants

- Because they address issues that are in the broader public interest, PSAs are generally regarded as credible or trustworthy sources.
- This Web site builds upon this credibility through its reference to *The Wizard of Oz*, which evokes greater feelings of trust and identification in its audience.

Activity

Choose a multimedia text (Web site, social media post, video, podcast, etc.) that makes a claim about a topical issue. Then use the framework above to analyze this text in Toulmin terms.

Review Questions

1. Name and describe the six parts of the Toulmin model. Which parts, stated or inferred, can be found in any argument? Which parts are used, as needed, to make an argument more convincing to a particular audience? **(LO1)**

2. What are some synonyms for the claim, the support, and the warrant? Consult Box 4.1 (page 119). **(LO1)**

3. What are subclaims? What are some types of specific support? **(LO1)**

4. Define warrants. Why does argument work better when warrants are shared by the arguer and the audience? How does backing strengthen a warrant? **(LO1)**

5. Give some examples of qualifiers. **(LO1)**

6. Describe the difference between logical and contextual warrants. How does each help you evaluate the effectiveness of an argument? **(LO1)**

Exercises and Activities

A. Group Work and Class Discussion: Truth versus Probability

This activity invites you to compare topics that are true and therefore not arguable with topics that are probable and thus open to argument. Think about one other course you are taking this semester and write down one example of something you have learned in that course that is absolutely true or untrue about which you could not argue. Then write one example of something you have learned in that course that is only probably true or untrue and that you therefore see as arguable. Make a class list of these examples. Think carefully about everything you put in the true and untrue columns. These must be topics that no one would argue about because they have been proved to be true or untrue. Here are some key words to help you think about these two types of information.

True: certain, fact, exact statement, right, correct, valid; wrong, incorrect, invalid

Probable: possible, opinion, qualified, reasonable, sound; unreasonable, unsound

You will be learning both types of information in college. Which topics on the probable list might be good topics for argument papers?

B. Group Work and Class Discussion: Using the Toulmin Model to Analyze an Advertisement

Study the advertisement that appears on the next page. Answer the following questions.

1. What is the claim? Complete the sentence, "The author wants me to believe that . . ." Is the claim stated or implied?

2. What is the support? Complete the sentence, "The author wants me to believe that . . . [the claim] because . . . [support]." Look for subclaims (reasons) and specific support (e.g., facts, opinions, examples).

3. What is the logical warrant? Using the "if, then" (support, claim) model, write out what you see as the internal logic underlying this argument. Remember that logical warrants supply the link between support and claim.

4. What are the contextual warrants? What does the author value or believe regarding the claim? Are these values stated or implied? What assumptions does this advertisement invite its viewers to make?

Dr. Jay Grossman is proud of his multidisciplined approach to dentistry – several specialties in one office to help patients avoid the complicated referral process. Dr. Grossman is also proud of his wife and three children. But what Dr. Grossman finds especially rewarding is the few hours he spends each month in a program called "Homeless not Toothless." A program he created to invite Los Angeles' homeless citizens into the practice for free dental care. This passion was not part of the curriculum in dental school. It came from an organization that emphasizes respect for people and commitment to a cause larger than one's self: The United States Navy.

SENSE OF COMMUNITY

– DR. JAY GROSSMAN
UNITED STATES NAVY 1990-1994

5. Is there backing for any of the warrants? Ask, "Does the author supply any additional information or rely on any commonly accepted cultural beliefs and attitudes that would make it easier for me to accept the warrants, whether they are stated or implied? What are they?"

6. Is there a rebuttal? Ask, "Are other views on the issue represented here along with reasons? What are they?"

7. Is there a qualifier? Ask, "Is the claim stated in absolute terms (e.g., always, never, the best, the worst) or in probable terms (e.g., sometimes, probably, possibly)?"

8. Do you find this ad convincing? Why or why not?

C. Group Work and Class Discussion: Using the Toulmin Model to Analyze a Cartoon

Analyze the cartoon below and discuss the answers to the following questions:

a. What is the claim?

b. What is the support?

c. What are the warrants?

d. What is the backing?

e. Are rebuttals or qualifiers present? If so, describe them.

Source: Jeff Staler: © Columbus Dispatch/Dist. by Newspaper Enterprise Association, Inc.

D. Group Work and Class Discussion: Using the Toulmin Model to Analyze an Online Argument

This activity asks you to apply the analytical skills you have honed in previous exercises to arguments you might encounter online. Go online and find an example that presents a contentious or controversial issue being debated. First, answer the same questions as before: (a) What is the claim?, (b) What is the support?, (c) What is the logical warrant?, (d) What are the contextual warrants?, (e) What is the backing?, (f) Are rebuttals or qualifiers present? If so, describe them.

When you are done, return to the question of logical and contextual warrants. Think a bit further about the particular online form in which your argument appears. What is the underlying logic that compels or requires an audience to accept the argument being made? What is the larger context here? Who would you say is the target or intended audience? What assumptions are being made here about who this audience is and what they are looking for? How much of the argument presented here depends on these assumptions being true? How many of these assumptions do you share yourself?

E. Group Work and Class Discussion: Using the Toulmin Model to Read and Analyze a Short Essay

Read the article on pages 139–140. Then answer the questions and discuss your answers with the class. You can expect some disagreement because of your differing backgrounds and experiences. If you disagree on some of these answers, try to figure out what is causing your differences.

a. What is the claim? Is it explicitly stated, or did you have to infer it?

b. What are some examples of support?

c. What are the author's warrants? Does the author supply backing for the warrants? If yes, how?

d. Do you share the author's warrants, or do you have conflicting warrants? If you have conflicting warrants, what are they?

e. Is there a rebuttal in the article? If yes, what is it?

f. Is the claim qualified? How?

g. Do you find this argument convincing? Why or why not?

BEFORE YOU READ: What are your own feelings about college sports? Are you a fan? Do you think the influence of such sports on college life is positive or negative?

ESSAY #1   BUST THE AMATEUR MYTH*

Frank DeFord

The author writes about sports and sports-related issues for a variety of publications, among them *Sports Illustrated* and *The New York Times*. This piece appeared in *The Chronicle of Higher Education* in 2011. It addresses the question of the role big-time athletics should play on college campuses.

The situation in big-time college sports in the United States—essentially football and men's basketball—is not just scandalous. It is immoral.

Many international sports where financial profits are made used to be amateur. Anyway, they were allegedly amateur, but were—as is always the case where money is mixed with forced pro bono performing—corrupted by under-the-table payments and other hanky-panky. Eventually the inability of this deceitful system ever to work was acknowledged by the Olympics and various world athletic federations, and sports such as tennis, track and field, swimming, skiing, rugby, and basketball became honestly professional.

As a consequence, here today in the United States—that bastion of both freedom and capitalism—college football and basketball players are the only athletes in the world who are denied payment for their services in sports where significant sums of money are involved. Especially as the colleges make scores of millions of dollars from box-office and television revenue, when coaches are paid seven-figure contracts, and all sorts of others (including journalists) make handsome salaries on the backs of these young players, it is unconscionable that athletes are not paid—and not just paid token fees but free-market salaries commensurate with what they bring in to the institution they represent.

Why is college sports the only province where "amateurism" is held out as an ideal? Who would suggest that artists, writers, musicians, or dancers should not only work for free but also do so while others profit from their talent? This canard persists only to maintain an indefensible, antiquated system.

5   Colleges protest they can't afford to pay the performers. If so, they should abandon the business of sports—or, anyway, downgrade to Division III or only finance intramurals. Certainly, athletics is a valuable discipline, and a sound mind in a sound body is devoutly to be wished for, but having traveling sports teams is not a requisite for higher education. Either make the economic model work fairly, or get out of the business. To claim that you make millions of dollars but can't pay the performers is sophistry—no less than saying that you are operating a wonderful restaurant except for the incidental fact that you can't pay the cooks and the waiters (although the entrée prices are sky-high and the maitre d' is magnificently recompensed).

Likewise, there is no justification that football and basketball must pay the freight

*"Bust the Amateur Myth" by Frank DeFord from *The Chronicle of Higher Education*, December 11, 2011. Reprinted by permission of the author.

for other so-called "nonrevenue" sports. If football makes the money, the money should go to those who fill up the stadiums and attract the television bounty. In the current situation, a poor football player is not only working for free (and risking concussions and lifelong obesity), but he is, essentially, paying for a volleyball player's scholarship and a swimming coach's salary.

Athletic scholarships should be discontinued—except for the football and basketball players who desire them. The players in the two "revenue sports" would officially be school employees and only, at their option, students. They would have four years of athletic eligibility. Whether or not they wish to attend class and work toward a degree would be their choice. This would eliminate all the fraud attendant to "student" athletes getting into college and staying eligible.

If colleges wanted to provide scholarships for athletes other than football or basketball players, the most talented could earn them—but only in open competition among all students with proficiency in some extracurricular activity. In other words, athletes should be treated no differently than undergraduate actors, artists, musicians, and writers.

If the alumni boosters don't like this they can, for their amusement, start their own leagues that don't tarnish academia. Or they could pay for scholarships for bright and needy high-school students who wish to go to college for an education.

For Discussion:

Do you agree with the author that college athletes should be paid? Why or why not? What would be the effect of treating such athletes as employees?

Arguing Like a Citizen

The essay "Bust the Amateur Myth" makes an impassioned argument about the hypocrisy and corruption of contemporary college athletics. In order to better understand your own position on this issue, as well as the way it connects to the broader question of citizenship, look closely at the sample discussion below.

▶▶▶ Thinking Like a Citizen

- Why do I care about this issue?
  As a fan of college sports, I have a strong desire to watch games that are as entertaining and competitive as possible. As a college student, however, I also feel an obligation to ensure that the rules by which my fellow students participate in these sports are fair and helpful. It is important to me to know that the current college athletic system doesn't infringe upon, or undermine, the traditional academic mission of my school or others like it.

- Who else cares about this issue? What kinds of claims might other stakeholders make?
  Others involved in college athletics might well have views on this issue that differ from my own. College coaches and administrators, for example, might be inclined to focus more on the economic aspects of the current system, basing their support on whether college sports generate much-needed revenue. Likewise, my views might differ from those of the

Arguing Like a Citizen (*continued*)

athletes themselves, who might have to balance their concerns over the academic impact of college sports against the personal benefits their participation might bring.

▶▶▶ Arguing Like a Citizen

- What specific claim about this issue would I make? What kind of support would I present to justify my claim?
  Despite being an avid fan of college sports, I would make the claim that colleges and universities need to treat their student-athletes more like professional employees. To support this claim, I would cite the role student-athletes play in generating income for their schools, while remaining unpaid themselves.

- In making and supporting this claim, what assumptions am I making? What are my warrants?
  The logical warrant connecting my claim to support can be stated this way: If colleges benefit financially from the labor of their student-athletes, then these student-athletes should be treated as employees. The contextual warrant connecting my claim and support is my personal belief that it is inherently unfair for colleges to benefit financially from the unpaid labor of their students.

▶▶▶ Acting Like a Citizen

- Where in my community do I see these differing claims being made?
  The debate over college athletics plays itself out within a number of different arenas. Among lawmakers and educational policy experts, this question plays a role in discussions over how colleges and universities should be funded. In sports circles, it affects fans' interest in and allegiance to different college athletic teams. And on college campuses themselves, this issue could well affect the attitudes students (and student-athletes) have toward faculty, coaches, and other school administrators.

- What concrete action could I take to resolve the issue?
  As a college student concerned about this issue, I could try to raise awareness regarding the unfairness of the current system by: (1) writing a letter to the editor of my college newspaper, (2) joining or forming a campus club dedicated to discussing this issue, and (3) participating in a public demonstration protesting the current system.

Activity

Now that you've seen an example of this discussion, try using the Toulmin model to construct an argument of your own. For the following claim, write a statement that you think would best support it. Then write out a logical and a contextual warrant that links the support and claim together.

Claim: The rules governing the relationship between student-athletes and the schools for which they play should be changed . . .

Support: because . . .

Logical Warrant:

Contextual Warrant:

F. Writing Assignment and Class Project: Writing a Toulmin Analysis and Reporting on It in Class

a. Find a short article, an advertisement, a cartoon, or a letter to the editor and use the Toulmin model to analyze it.

b. Write a 250- to 300-word paper in which you identify and explain the claim, support, warrants, and backing in your example. Provide further information about rebuttals or qualifiers, if they are present.

c. In class, circulate the item among your classmates. Either read your paper or give a two- to three-minute oral report in which you describe the parts of the argument to the class.

A student-written analysis of the cartoon about the price of oranges (page 137) is included below. Reading this student paper should help you write your Toulmin analysis paper. Also, discuss whether you and your classmates agree with this analysis. The Toulmin model is usually not applied in exactly the same way by everyone. There are no absolutely correct answers because different readers' interpretations vary.

STUDENT PAPER

#1

Mohamed T. Diaby Jr.
Prof. Wood
English 1302
12 Feb. 2013

Toulmin Analysis of the "Price of Oranges" Cartoon*

Identifies claim and support.

    The reader has to infer the claim of this cartoon since it is not directly stated. The claim is that the price of oranges will go way up in the United States if they are picked by legal U.S. workers. The support is provided by the shopper, who is considering buying the oranges, and the sign that says they are handpicked by U.S. workers but their price is three for $20 dollars, a prohibitively high price for oranges.

Analyzes warrant.

    The implied warrant is that illegal immigrants will work for lower wages than legal workers will, which keeps the price of oranges low.

Identifies backing.

    The backing is also implied and reinforced by the picture. It suggests that oranges are a staple and are purchased frequently by family shoppers. It also reinforces the common belief that many people will not be able to buy oranges that are handpicked by U.S. workers because they will be too expensive.

Infers rebuttal.

    No direct rebuttal or qualifier appears in this cartoon. I think, however, that this cartoon could be considered as a rebuttal to those who think illegal immigrants should be sent home and no longer allowed to work in the United States. As a rebuttal, this cartoon suggests the consequences of that popular position if it were enforced.

*This paper is modeled on a paper done by Mohamed Diaby Jr. in an argument class.

G. Prewriting: Using the Toulmin Model to Get Ideas for a Position Paper

You have used the Toulmin model in Exercises B through F to read and ana-lyze other people's argument. Now use it to identify the main parts of an argu-ment you will write. You may use the model to help you plan any argument paper. Use the Toulmin model as a prewriting exercise to help you develop ideas for a position paper.

1. Write the claim. All of the rest of your paper will support this claim.

2. Write the support. Write two or three subclaims you will develop in the paper. To help you do this, write the word *because* after the claim, and list reasons that support it. Also jot down ideas for specific support for these subclaims, such as examples, facts, opinions, or visual images that come from your reading of the essays or from your own experience.

3. Write the warrants. Decide whether to spell out the warrants in your paper or to leave them implicit so that the reading audience will have to infer them.

4. Decide on the backing. Assume that your classmates are your audience. They may be reading drafts of your paper. In your judgment, will some of them require backing for any of your warrants because they will not agree with them otherwise? If so, how can you back these warrants? Write out your ideas.

5. Plan rebuttal. Think about the positions others may hold on this issue. You identified some of these positions in your exploratory paper. Write out your strategies for weakening these arguments.

6. Decide whether to qualify the claim to make it more convincing to more people. Write one or more qualifiers that might work.

Read what you have written, and make a note about additional informa-tion you will need to find for your paper. Save what you have written in a folder or in your open computer file. You will use it later when you complete your planning and write your position paper.

H. Group Discussion: Understanding Value Warrants

Often, both the warrants and the backing for warrants come from the systems of values that people hold. The values will not be spelled out in an argument, yet they will still influence the arguer and make an argument more convinc-ing to an audience member who happens to share them. The following essay describes six American value systems. These systems are somewhat oversim-plified, and they do not identify all American value systems nor suggest their relative power. They are useful, however, to help you understand some of the values people may hold. Read the essay and answer the questions for discus-sion at the end.

BEFORE YOU READ: What values are important to you? How would you describe core American values?

ESSAY #2   **AMERICAN VALUE SYSTEMS***

Richard D. Rieke and Malcolm O. Sillars

Rieke and Sillars are speech communication professors whose most recent book is *Argumentation and Critical Decision Making*.

By careful analysis individual values can be discovered in the arguments of ourselves and others. There is a difficulty, however, in attempting to define a whole system of values for a person or a group. And as difficult as that is, each of us, as a participant in argumentation, should have some concept of the broad systems that most frequently bring together certain values. For this purpose, it is useful for you to have an idea of some of the most commonly acknowledged value systems.

You must approach this study with a great deal of care, however, because even though the six basic value systems we are about to define provide a fair view of the standard American value systems, they do not provide convenient pigeonholes into which individuals can be placed. They represent broad social categories. Some individuals (even groups) will be found outside these systems. Many individuals and groups will cross over value systems, picking and choosing from several. Note how certain words appear as value terms in more than one value system. The purpose of this survey is to provide a beginning understanding of standard American values, not a complete catalog.[1]

The Puritan-Pioneer-Peasant Value System

This value system has been identified frequently as the *puritan morality* or the *Protestant ethic*. It also has been miscast frequently because of the excessive emphasis placed, by some of its adherents, on restrictions of personal acts such as smoking and consuming alcohol.[2] Consequently, over the years, this value system has come to stand for a narrow-minded attempt to interfere in other people's business, particularly if those people are having fun. However, large numbers of people who do not share such beliefs follow this value system.

We have taken the liberty of expanding beyond the strong and perhaps too obvious religious implications of the terms *puritan* and *Protestant*. This value system is what most Americans refer to when they speak of the "pioneer spirit," which was not necessarily religious. It also extends, we are convinced, to a strain of values brought to this country by Southern and Eastern European Catholics, Greek Orthodox, and Jews who could hardly be held responsible for John Calvin's theory or even the term *Protestant ethic*. Thus, we have the added word *peasant*, which may not be particularly accurate. Despite the great friction that existed between these foreign-speaking immigrants from other religions and their native Protestant counterparts, they had a great deal in common as do their ideological descendants today. On many occasions after describing the puritan morality we have heard a Jewish student say, "That's the way my father thinks," or had a student of Italian or Polish descent say, "My grandmother talks that way all the time."

5   The Puritan-Pioneer-Peasant value system is rooted in the idea that persons have an obligation to themselves and those around them, and in some cases to their God, to work hard at whatever they do. In this system, people are limited in their abilities and must be prepared to fail. The great benefit is in the striving against an unknowable and frequently hostile universe. They have an obligation to others, must be selfless, and must not waste. Some believe this is the only way to gain happiness and success. Others see it as a means to salvation. In all cases it takes on a moral orientation. Obviously, one might work hard for a summer in order to buy a new car and not be labeled a "puritan." Frequently, in this value system, the instrumental values of selflessness, thrift, and hard work become terminal values where the work has value beyond the other benefits it can bring one. People who come from this value system often have difficulty with retirement, because their meaning in life, indeed their pleasure, came from work.

Likewise, because work, selflessness, and thrift are positive value terms in this value system, laziness, selfishness, and waste are negative value terms. One can see how some adherents to this value system object to smoking, drinking, dancing, or cardplaying. These activities are frivolous; they take one's mind off more serious matters and waste time.

Some of the words that are associated with the Puritan-Pioneer-Peasant value system are:

Positive:	activity, work, thrift, morality, dedication, selflessness, virtue, righteousness, duty, dependability, temperance, sobriety, savings, dignity
Negative:	waste, immorality, dereliction, dissipation, infidelity, theft, vandalism, hunger, poverty, disgrace, vanity

The Enlightenment Value System

America became a nation in the period of the Enlightenment. It happened when a new intellectual era based on the scientific findings of men like Sir Isaac Newton and the philosophical systems of men like John Locke were dominant. The founders of our nation were particularly influenced by such men. The Declaration of Independence is the epitome of an Enlightenment document. In many ways America is an Enlightenment nation, and if Enlightenment is not the predominant value system, it is surely first among equals.

The Enlightenment position stems from the belief that we live in an ordered world in which all activity is governed by laws similar to the laws of physics. These "natural laws" may or may not come from God, depending on the particular orientation of the person examining them; but unlike many adherents to the Puritan value system just discussed, Enlightenment persons theorized that people could discover these laws by themselves. Thus, they may worship God for God's greatness, even acknowledge that God created the universe and natural laws, but they find out about the universe because they have the power of reason. The laws of nature are harmonious, and one can use reason to discover them all. They can also be used to provide for a better life.

10   Because humans are basically good and capable of finding answers, restraints on them must be limited. Occasionally, people

do foolish things and must be restrained by society. However, a person should never be restrained in matters of the mind. Reason must be free. Thus, government is an agreement among individuals to assist the society to protect rights. That government is a democracy. Certain rights are inalienable, and they may not be abridged; "among these are life, liberty and the pursuit of happiness." Arguments for academic freedom, against wiretaps, and for scientific inquiry come from this value system.

Some of the words associated with the Enlightenment value system are:

Positive: freedom, science, nature, rationality, democracy, fact, liberty, individualism, knowledge, intelligence, reason, natural rights, natural laws, progress

Negative: ignorance, inattention, thoughtlessness, error, indecision, irrationality, dictatorship, fascism, book burning, falsehood, regression

The Progressive Value System

Progress was a natural handmaiden of the Enlightenment. If these laws were available and if humans had the tool, reason, to discover them and use them to advantage, then progress would result. Things would continually get better. But although progress is probably a historical spin-off of the Enlightenment, it has become so important on its own that it deserves at times to be seen quite separate from the Enlightenment.

Richard Weaver, in 1953, found that "one would not go far wrong in naming progress" the "god term" of that age. It is, he said, the "expression about which all other expressions are ranked as subordinate. . . . Its force imparts to the others their lesser degrees of force, and fixes the scale by which degrees of comparison are understood."[3]

Today, the unmediated use of the progressive value system is questioned, but progress is still a fundamental value in America. Most arguments against progress are usually arguments about the definition of progress. They are about what "true progress is."

15   Some of the key words of the Progressive value system are:

Positive: practicality, efficiency, change, improvement, science, future, modern, progress, evolution

Negative: old-fashioned,[4] regressive, impossible, backward

The Transcendental Value System

Another historical spin-off of the Enlightenment system was the development of the transcendental movement of the early nineteenth century. It took from the Enlightenment all its optimism about people, freedom, and democracy, but rejected the emphasis on reason. It argued idealistically that there was a faculty higher than reason; let us call it, as many transcendentalists did, intuition. Thus, for the transcendentalist, there is a way of knowing that is better than reason, a way which *transcends* reason. Consequently, what might seem like the obvious solution to problems is not necessarily so. One must look, on important matters at least, to the intuition, to the feelings. Like the Enlightenment thinker, the transcendentalist believes in a unified universe governed by natural laws. Thus, all persons, by following their intuition, will discover these laws, and universal harmony will take place. And, of course, little or no government will be necessary. The original American transcendentalists of the early nineteenth century drew their inspiration from Platonism, German idealism, and Oriental mysticism. The idea was also fairly well limited to the intellectuals. By and large, transcendentalism has been the view of a rather small group of people throughout our history, but at times it has been very important. It has always been somewhat more influential among younger people. James Truslow Adams once wrote that everyone should read Ralph Waldo Emerson at sixteen because his writings were a marvel for the buoyantly optimistic person of that age but that his transcendental writings did not have the same luster at twenty-one.[5] In the late 1960s and early 1970s, Henry David Thoreau's *Walden* was the popular reading of campus rebels. The emphasis of anti-establishment youth on Oriental mysticism, like Zen, should not be ignored either. The rejection of contemporary society and mores symbolized by what others considered "outlandish dress" and "hippie behavior" with its emphasis on emotional response and "do your own thing" indicated the adoption of a transcendental value system. Communal living is reminiscent of the transcendental "Brook Farm" experiments that were attempted in the early nineteenth century and described by Nathaniel Hawthorne in his novel *The Blithedale Romance*.

In all of these movements the emphasis on humanitarian values, the centrality of love for others, and the preference for quiet contemplation over activity has been important. Transcendentalism, however, rejects the common idea of progress. Inner light and knowledge of one's self is more important than material well-being. There is also some tendency to reject physical well-being because it takes one away from intuitive truth.

It should be noted that not everyone who argues for change is a transcendentalist. The transcendental white campus agitators of the late 1960s discovered that, despite all their concern for replacing racism and war with love and peace, their black counterparts were highly pragmatic and rationalistic about objectives and means. Black agitators and demonstrators were never "doing their thing" in the intuitive way of many whites.

It should also be noted that while a full adherence to transcendentalism has been limited to small groups, particularly among intellectuals and youth, many of the ideas are not limited to such persons. One can surely find strains of what we have labeled, for convenience, transcendentalism in the mysticism of some very devout older Roman Catholics, for instance. And perhaps many Americans become transcendental on particular issues, about the value to be derived from hiking in the mountains, for example.

20   Here are some of the terms that are characteristic of the Transcendental value system:

Positive: humanitarian, individualism, respect, intuition, truth, equality, sympathetic, affection, feeling, love, sensitivity, emotion, personal kindness, compassion, brotherhood, friendship, mysticism

Negative: science,[6] reason, mechanical, hate, war, anger, insensitive, coldness, unemotional

The Personal Success Value System

The least social of the major American value systems is the one that moves people toward personal achievement and success. It can be related as a part of the Enlightenment value system, but it is more than that because it involves a highly pragmatic concern for the material happiness of the individual. To call it selfish would be to load the terms against it, although there would be some who accept this value system who would say, "Yes, I'm selfish." "The Lord helps those who help themselves" has always been an acceptable adage by some of the most devout in our nation.

You might note that the Gallup poll . . . is very heavily weighted toward personal values. Even "good family life" rated as the top value can be seen as an item of personal success. This survey includes only a few social values like "helping needy people" and "helping better America," and even those are phrased in personal terms. That is, the respondents were asked "how important you feel each of these is to you." The personal orientation of the survey may represent a bias of the Gallup poll, but we suspect it reflects much of American society. We are personal success–oriented in an individual way which would not be found in some other cultures (e.g., in the Japanese culture).

Here are some of the terms that tend to be characteristic of the Personal Success value system:

Positive: career, family, friends, recreation, economic security, identity, health, individualism, affection, respect, enjoyment, dignity, consideration, fair play, personal

Negative: dullness, routine, hunger, poverty, disgrace, coercion, disease

The Collectivist Value System

Although there are few actual members of various socialist and communist groups in the United States, one cannot ignore the strong attachment among some people for collective action. This is, in part, a product of the influx of social theories from Europe in the nineteenth century. It is also a natural outgrowth of a perceived need to control the excesses of freedom in a mass society. Its legitimacy is not limited to current history, however. There has always been a value placed on cooperative action. The same people today who would condemn welfare payments to unwed mothers would undoubtedly praise their ancestors for barnraising and taking care of the widow in a frontier community. Much rhetoric about our "pioneer ancestors" has to do with their cooperative action. And anticollectivist presidents and evangelists talk about "the team." At the same time, many fervent advocates of collective action in the society argue vehemently for their freedom and independence. Certainly the civil rights

movement constituted a collective action for freedom. Remember the link in Martin Luther King, Jr.'s speech between "freedom" and "brotherhood"?

25   But whether the Collectivist value system is used to defend socialist proposals or promote "law and order," there is no doubt that collectivism is a strong value system in this nation. Like transcendentalism, however, it is probably a value system that, at least in this day, cannot work alone.

Here are some of the terms that tend to characterize the Collectivist value system:

Positive: cooperation, joint action, unity, brotherhood, together, social good, order, humanitarian aid and comfort, equality

Negative: disorganization, selfishness, personal greed, inequality

Clearly, these six do not constitute a complete catalog of all American value systems. Combinations and reordering produce different systems. Two values deserve special attention because they are common in these systems and sometimes operate alone: *nature* and *patriotism*. Since the beginning of our nation the idea has prevailed that the natural is good and there for our use and preservation. Also, since John Winthrop first proclaimed that the New England Puritans would build "a city on the hill" for all the world to see and emulate, the idea has endured that America is a fundamentally great nation, perhaps God-chosen, to lead the world to a better life. This idea may be somewhat tarnished in some quarters today, but there is no doubt that it will revive as it has in the past. Linked to other value systems we have discussed, it will once more be a theme that will draw the adherence of others to arguments.

Notes

1. The following material draws from a wide variety of sources. The following is an illustrative cross-section of sources from a

variety of disciplines: Virgil I. Baker and Ralph T. Eubanks, *Speech in Personal and Public Affairs* (New York: David McKay, 1965), pp. 95–102; Clyde Kluckhohn, "An Anthropologist Looks at the United States," *Mirror for Man* (New York: McGraw-Hill, 1949), pp. 228–261; Stow Persons, *American Minds* (New York: Holt, Rinehart and Winston, 1958); Jurgen Ruesch, "Communication and American Values; A Psychological Approach," in *Communication: The Social Matrix of Psychiatry,* eds. Jurgen Ruesch and Gregory Bateson (New York: W. W. Norton, 1951), pp. 94–134; Edward D. Steele and W. Charles Redding, "The American Value System: Premises for Persuasion," *Western Speech,* 26 (Spring 1962), pp. 83–91; Richard Weaver, "Ultimate Terms in Contemporary Rhetoric," in *The Ethics of Rhetoric*

(Chicago: Henry Regnery, 1953), pp. 211–232; Robin M. Williams, Jr., *American Society,* 3rd ed. (New York: Alfred A. Knopf, 1970), pp. 438–504.

2. It is ironic that the original American Puritans did not have clear injunctions against such activity.

3. Weaver, p. 212.

4. Note that "old-fashioned" is frequently positive when we speak of morality and charm but not when we speak of our taste in music.

5. James Truslow Adams, "Emerson Re-read," in *The Transcendental Revolt,* ed. George F. Whicher (Boston: D. C. Heath, 1949), pp. 31–39.

6. It is interesting to note, however, that one of the major organizations in the United States with transcendental origins, the Christian Science Church, combines transcendentalism with science.

For Discussion:

1. What would you say is the central claim about values that this essay is trying to make? Review the parts of the Toulmin model as they are outlined earlier in this chapter. Using this discussion as your template, conduct your own Toulmin analysis of this essay. Identify the claim: What argument are these authors making about importance of values to argumentation? Find the support: On what basis do they make this claim? What or where is the evidence? Uncover the warrant: Does this evidence logically support the claim being made (logical warrant)? What other assumptions about argument and values do these authors ask you to accept (contextual warrants)?

2. Can you find your own system of values in this article? Of the six value systems described, which of them do you most closely identify with?

3. Look back at the positive words associated with each system of values. Describe a visual image that could be used to depict each system. Use your imagination and describe what you see in your mind that would help readers visualize and understand each of these systems of values.

4. Which value systems do you find operating in the other examples (essays, ads, cartoons) included in this chapter? What value warrants are implicit in each of these selections? Provide reasons for your answers. There are no correct answers. Use your imagination and have some fun with this exercise.

5. When your system of values does not match the system of values implicit in an argument essay, what happens? How does a difference in value systems influence your acceptance of the author's argument?

Types of Claims

After studying this chapter, you will be able to:

LO1 Describe the five different types of claims.

LO2 Identify and analyze how these types of claims operate in written, visual, and online arguments.

Argument theorists categorize claims according to types, and these types suggest the fundamental purposes of given arguments. Becoming aware of these categories and the special characteristics associated with each helps you understand more fully the purposes and special features of the arguments you read and improves your writing of them. When reading, as soon as you identify the type or category of claim in an argument, you can predict and anticipate certain features of that type of argument. This technique also helps you follow the author's line of thought more easily. When writing, knowing the types of claims can provide you with frameworks for developing your purpose and strategy.

When you begin to read argument with the idea of locating the claim and identifying it by type, your ability to identify and understand all the parts of an argument will increase. To accomplish this goal, you first need to learn the strategy described next for analyzing an argument, its key purpose, and its constituent parts.

Five Types of Claims

Virtually all arguments can be categorized according to one of five types of claims. You can identify each argument type by identifying the questions the argument answers. In general, certain types of organization and proof are associated with certain types of claims, as you will see in the following discussion. There are no hard-and-fast rules about using specific organizational strategies or types of proof to develop specific types of claims. Knowing common patterns and tendencies, however, helps readers make predictions about the course of an argument and helps writers plan and write their own arguments.

Here are the five categories of claims, along with the main questions that they answer:

1. *Claims of fact:* Did it happen? Does it exist?
2. *Claims of definition:* What is it? How should we define it?
3. *Claims of cause:* What caused it? What are its effects?
4. *Claims of value:* Is it good or bad? What criteria will help us decide?
5. *Claims of policy:* What should we do about it? What should be our future course of action?

The sections that follow provide additional explanations of the five types of claims, along with the general questions they answer, some examples of actual claims, a list of the types of proof (explained more fully in the next chapter) that are most typically associated with each type of claim, the organizational strategies that one might expect for each type, and a short written argument that illustrates each type as it appears in practice.

CLAIMS OF FACT

When you claim that you turned a paper in on time even though the professor cannot find it, or that you were not exceeding the speed limit when a police officer claims that you were, you are making claims of fact.

> **Questions answered by claims of fact.** Did it happen? Is it true? Does it exist? Is it a fact?
>
> **Examples of claims of fact.** (Note that all of the "facts" in these claims need to be proved as either absolutely or probably true in order to be acceptable to an audience. All of these claims, also, are controversial.) The ozone layer is becoming depleted. Increasing population threatens the environment. American drivers are becoming more responsible. America's military is prepared for any likely crisis. The abominable snowman exists in certain remote areas. Women are not as effective as men in combat. A mass murderer is evil, not insane. The American judicial system operates successfully.
>
> **Types of support associated with claims of fact.** Factual support, as you might guess, is especially appropriate for claims of fact. Such support includes both past and present *facts, statistics, real examples,* and *quotations from reliable authorities. Inductive reasoning,* which cites several examples and then draws

a probable conclusion from them, is also a common type of argument for claims of fact. *Analogies* that establish comparisons and similarities between the subject and something else that is commonly accepted as true are useful. *Signs* that present evidence of a past or present state of affairs are also useful to establish claims of fact. *Expert opinion*, when used to support claims of fact, is usually based on fact.

Possible organizational strategies. *Chronological order*, which traces what has occurred over a period of time, usually in the order in which it occurred, can be used to develop claims of fact. For example, the history of the increase in population might be provided to show how it has happened in time, from then to now. Or, *topical order* may be used. In topical order reasons to support a fact are identified and then developed topic by topic. Thus, reasons might be given for the existence of the abominable snowman, with each one developed at length. This chapter is organized according to topics: the five types of claims.

The claim of fact itself is often stated at or near the beginning of the argument unless there is a psychological advantage for stating it at the end. Most authors make claims of fact clear from the outset, revealing early what they seek to establish.

An example of an argument that contains a claim of fact. The following essay argues that no less than seventy percent of students at community colleges plan to attain a degree at a four-year college or university. The article seeks to establish the fact that conventional assumptions about the students who attend two-year colleges are inaccurate.

BEFORE YOU READ: What is your view of the college admissions process? In your own experience, have you found it to be fair?

ESSAY #1   2-YEAR STUDENTS HAVE LONG HAD 4-YEAR DREAMS*

Stephen J. Handel

Stephen J. Handel is associate vice president for undergraduate admission in the University of California system. He wrote this article for *The Chronicle of Higher Education*.

Facts

Last month the National Student Clearinghouse released a report showing that more than 60 percent of community-college students who transferred to four-year universities ultimately earned bachelor's degrees within six years after transfer. I was pleased to hear these findings but not surprised. New, first-time community-college students have always been ambitious.

---

*"2-Year Students Have Long Had 4-Year Dreams" by Stephen J. Handel, from *The Chronicle of Higher Education*, September 23, 2013. Reproduced by permission.

Claim of Fact

The baccalaureate aspirations and long-term plans of these students should be refreshing to higher-education leaders because they provide a corrective to the persistent public rhetoric insisting that today's students are focusing on developing skills rather than gaining an education. Still, I am disenchanted with those people who so casually dismiss these intentions as unreliable, even profligate, in light of the availability of jobs that require short-term certificates or associate degrees. My argument is not with the proliferation of high-quality pre-baccalaureate credentials; such training is essential for our economy. Rather, it is with the presumption that these students are uninterested in an education every bit as intense as that of undergraduates who enroll initially in four-year institutions.

Statistics

Earning a four-year degree is the pre-eminent educational goal for most incoming community-college students. A 2009 survey by the U.S. Department of Education indicated that more than 80 percent of all new, first-time community-college students sought bachelor's degrees. The desire was especially strong among students from groups traditionally underrepresented in higher education, such as Latinos (85 percent), African-Americans (83 percent), and those in the lowest income quartile (84 percent).

Quotation from Authority

The desire to earn a four-year degree has a long history. Between 1966 and 1999, when the University of California at Los Angeles's Cooperative Institutional Research Program surveyed the educational aspirations of junior-college, and then community-college, students separately from those entering four-year institutions, the proportion of two-year college students whose education goal was a bachelor's degree (or higher) never dropped below 70 percent. Steven G. Brint and Jerome Karabel, in their classic book, *The Diverted Dream* (1989), quote survey results from the 1920s through the 1950s, all of which reported the intentions of two-year college students as largely directed toward a bachelor's degree.

5   Despite their desire to earn a baccalaureate, however, few achieve that goal. Data indicate that only about one-quarter to one-third of students who wish to transfer actually succeed, despite the fact that—as the clearinghouse data reflect—their chances of earning a four-year degree after transfer are good. Perversely, the low number of actual transfers is used to justify the recalibration of student intentions toward pre-baccalaureate credentials. But higher-education observers like Richard Kahlenberg, writing in *The Chronicle*, argue the opposite: "Some look at these numbers and suggest community colleges should downplay the idea of transfer, but it makes more sense to improve and strengthen transfer paths."

Quotation from Authority

Few people seem concerned about the mismatch between what community-college students intend to do and what they actually achieve. A recently published monograph chastises community-college leaders by noting that while community-college "students will readily identify transfer and long-term academic goals, their ultimate goal is on employment. . . . Unfortunately this simple fact is overlooked by most community colleges." Even if we stipulate in the absence of evidence that students are concerned only with jobs, it is unclear how their focus on "transfer and academic goals" undermines that future.

It seems that the wreckage of the recent recession has left us wondering whether the investment in a college degree will continue to signal something other than a labor-market payoff, as reflected in a recent essay, "The Diploma's Vanishing Value," in *The Wall Street Journal*, by Jeffrey J. Selingo, *The Chronicle*'s editor at large.

Inductive Reasoning

In response, there is insistence that the nation fill a growing number of jobs requiring pre-baccalaureate skills. This is accompanied by data showing that individuals earning associate degrees in certain fields will earn more initially than those who obtain baccalaureate degrees.

Embedded in this rhetorical handwringing is a nod to the cost-effectiveness of junior and community colleges, as if those institutions, around for a century, had only recently matured into something more than colleges that other people's kids attended.

Statistics   10   Yet, despite the praise of politicians for the vocational aspects of a community-college credential, they have been unable or unwilling to provide the money to improve completion rates. A recent report from the Century Foundation, *Bridging the Higher Education Divide*, notes that between 1999 and 2009, per-student support at private research institutions went up $14,000, while public community colleges benefited from a per-student increase of just $1.

Of course, the pressure on college students to train for jobs has been around for a long time. Critics have complained since Harvard was founded that college learning yielded very little in the way of marketable skills. For

Historical Analogy

a time in the late 20th century, however, Big Science, the cold war, and billowing middle-class incomes made the baccalaureate degree the accepted passport to Mad Men martinis and split-level suburban homes—assuming, of course, that you were not poor, a member of an ethnic minority group, or a person with a disability. Those folks went to community colleges to train for jobs, right? Then, as now, we comforted ourselves with the notion that such students, assuming they were exceptionally qualified, could transfer to four-year institutions, perhaps even to elite universities. In reality, however, very few were admitted there. Researchers at the University of Southern California and the University of Arizona estimate the number of two-year transfer students attending any one of the country's 179 most elite private and public campuses at fewer than 200, on average.

Claim

In a nation galvanized around college completion, we label tragic those students attending four-year institutions, even nonselective ones, who fail to earn four-year degrees. We seem satisfied, however, with community-college students—working toward an identical goal—who similarly fail.

Liberal Analogy

Conclusion

An enduring contribution of America's community colleges will continue to be the breadth of credentials they offer students of all ages, including occupational certificates, industry-certified training programs, and associate degrees. But let's not forget that many new, first-time community-college students want something more.

Restatement of Claim

They have always wanted more.

For Discussion:

What are some of the cultural stereotypes used to define community colleges and community-college students? In what ways are these stereotypes inaccurate?

CLAIMS OF DEFINITION

When you claim that an athlete who receives compensation for playing a sport is "professional," and therefore loses "amateur" status, or when you argue with a friend whether or not any war can ever be considered a "just" war, you are making a claim of definition.

Questions answered by claims of definition. What is it? What is it like? How should it be classified? How should it be interpreted? How does its usual meaning change in a particular context?

Examples of claims of definition. (Note that here we are looking at definition claims that dominate the argument in the essay as a whole. Definition is also used as a type of support, often at the beginning, to establish the meaning of one or more key terms.) We need to define what constitutes a family before we talk about family values. To determine whether an art exhibition is not art, but pornography, we need to define what we mean by pornography in this context. To determine whether the police were doing their job or were engaging in brutality, we need to establish what we mean by police brutality. To determine whether a person is mentally competent, we need to define what we mean by that designation. If we have established the fact that a young man killed his wife, shall we define this killing as self-defense, a crime of passion, or premeditated murder?

Types of support associated with claims of definition. The main types of support used to prove claims of definition are *references to reliable authorities and accepted sources* that can be used to establish clear definitions and meanings, such as the dictionary or a well-known work. Also useful are *analogies and other comparisons,* especially to other words or situations that are clearly understood and that can consequently be used to shed some light on what is being defined. *Examples, both real and hypothetical,* and *signs* can also be used to clarify or develop definitions.

Possible organizational strategies. *Compare-and-contrast organization* can dominate the development of a claim of definition and serve as the main structure. In this structure, two or more objects are compared and contrasted throughout. For example, in an essay that expands the notion of crime to include white-collar crime, conventional crime would be compared with white-collar crime to prove that they are similar.

Topical organization may also be used. Several special qualities, characteristics, or features of the word or concept are identified and explained as discrete topics. Thus, in an essay defining a criminal as mentally competent, the characteristics of mental competence would be explained as separate topics and applied to the criminal. Another strategy is to *explain the controversy* over the term and *give reasons* for accepting one view over another.

An example of an argument that contains a claim of definition. The following essay argues that the way the U.S. government defines "poverty" needs to be changed. The author argues that the term "poverty" should be dramatically expanded to include millions more Americans whose daily economic struggles clearly qualify them to be defined as poor. Decide whether or not you agree. (Note the sources of the definitions used.)

BEFORE YOU READ: How many people do you think live in poverty in America?

ESSAY #2   **MISMEASURING POVERTY***

Mark Levinson

Mark Levinson is the chief economist of the Service Employees International Union. This article was published in *The American Prospect* in 2012.

Authority

The "facts" about poverty can be deceiving. In her magisterial book *Behind the Beautiful Forevers*, Katherine Boo tells the stories of the inhabitants of a Mumbai slum on the edge of a sewage lake who lack jobs, housing, running water, health care, education, and police protection. It is not unusual to see rats and frogs fried for dinner, feet covered with black fungus, and maggots breeding in wounds wrought by trash-picking. Yet, Boo writes, "almost no one in the slum was considered poor by official Indian benchmarks. . . . [They] were thus part of one of the most stirring success narratives in the modern history of global market capitalism." Some success.

Definition, Statistics

Our government's own count of the poor, while not denying their existence, also minimizes their number—not by undercounting them (though that's a factor, too) but by setting the poverty bar so low that tens of millions of poor Americans are not accounted for. This miscategorization not only paints a picture of a more prosperous America than in fact exists. It also excludes a large number of the poor from assistance that they need and might otherwise obtain.

In fact, the poor are with us today in greater numbers than we have seen since we started keeping track over half a century ago. If we counted them by the standards that most other industrialized democracies employ, their numbers would increase by half[†]—from 46 million to roughly 69 million. To understand how that can be, it is important to grasp the way we define poverty and what that definition has to do with economic hardship.

Definition, Example

The United States measures poverty by a standard developed almost 50 years ago by Mollie Orshansky, a Social Security Administration official. At that time, the typical family spent about one-third of its income on food. Orshansky calculated the costs of an emergency food budget, which would provide adequate nutrition for only a short time, and also a low-cost budget, which would provide adequate nutrition for the entire year. She then multiplied the cost of each budget by three to arrive at two poverty thresholds.

---

*"Mismeasuring Poverty" by Mark Levinson from *The American Prospect*, June 25, 2012. Reprinted with permission.

[†]A previous version of this essay used a different method for measuring these numbers.

Comparisons

5   Orshansky wanted to use the low-cost food budget to compute poverty thresholds. It made sense to base the poverty line on a food budget that would allow adequate nutrition for an entire year. However, President Lyndon Johnson and his Council of Economic Advisers decided to use a figure close to the emergency food budget to set poverty-level income. Since then, the figure has been updated annually for inflation.

The problems with the official measure have long been recognized. Not only are the original thresholds too low, but they are based on outdated assumptions about family expenditures. Food now makes up about one-eighth of an average family's expenditure. At the same time, the costs of housing, child care, and health care have grown. Thus, the official poverty level no longer reflects the true expense of supporting a family at the minimally adequate level. In addition, the current poverty measure is a national standard that does not adjust for variations in the cost of living from state to state and among urban, suburban, and rural areas.

The official poverty standard also fails to accurately tally family resources. When determining whether a family is poor, income is counted before subtracting taxes, resulting in an overestimation of how much families have to spend on basic needs. On the other hand, the method understates the resources of families who receive some types of government assistance because the federal Earned Income Tax Credit (EITC) is not counted, nor are in-kind government benefits such as food stamps and housing assistance.

Last year, the Obama administration released a new measure of poverty called the Supplemental Poverty Measure (SPM), which does not replace the official measure but will be published separately. The SPM is based on an approach recommended in 1995 by the National Academy of Sciences. It adds in-kind aid such as nutritional assistance and subsidized housing and subtracts necessary expenses such as taxes, child care, and other work-related costs as well as out-of-pocket medical expenses. Its thresholds are calculated by ranking households by what they spend on food, clothing, utilities, and shelter and setting the poverty threshold at the 33rd percentile of that ranking.

Statistics

In 2010, according to the official poverty measure, 46.2 million people (15.1 percent of America's population) were poor, while 49.1 million (16 percent) were considered poor using the SPM. There were, however, some important differences between the two measures. Child poverty is lower under the SPM because it takes into account the EITC and food stamps.

Comparison

By contrast, the poverty rate for elderly Americans is higher because, unlike the official measure, SPM subtracts out-of-pocket medical expenses from income.

10   The SPM gives us a more accurate picture of the poor. However, it doesn't fix the fundamental problem with the U.S. poverty threshold, which is, as Shawn Fremstad from the Center for Economic and Policy Research puts it,

Quotation from Authority

"the extent to which it has defined deprivation down over the last several decades because it has not kept pace with changes in typical living standards in the United States." The SPM starts at too low a level, and, as Fremstad points out, it can actually lower poverty thresholds if consumer expenditures on housing, utilities, and food decline—as they have between 2008 and 2010 as a result of the recession and lower housing prices.

Statistics

The poverty line was roughly equal to 50 percent of median income when it was set in the 1960s. It has now declined to about 36 percent. So today's official poor are further behind the average income—in a word, poorer—

Comparisons

than their counterparts were 50 years ago. If we measured the number of Americans who are below 50 percent of the median income, 22.6 percent (69.1 million) are poor—nearly half again as high as the official poverty rate of 15.1 percent.

Most other developed countries use a measure of poverty based on the share of families below 50 percent or 60 percent of median income. Adam Smith explained the rationale for this in *The Wealth of Nations*. He defined the

Quotation from Authority

lack of "necessaries" as the experience of being unable to consume "not only the commodities which are indispensably necessary for the support of life, but whatever the custom of the country renders it indecent for creditable people, even of the lowest order, to be without."

Several organizations have attempted to quantify what a family requires to meet basic needs. The Economic Policy Institute has created Basic Family Budgets for more than 600 localities across the country. Wider Opportunities for Women has developed a Self-Sufficiency Standard for different family types in more than 80 localities in 36 states, and the National Center for Children in Poverty has designed Basic Needs Budgets.

Definition

All of these efforts show that families must have an average income of at least twice the current poverty level to cover basic expenses. More than one-third of Americans—more than 100 million—live beneath that more realistic threshold. These family budgets include only the most essential living expenses and are based on modest assumptions about costs. For example, the budgets assume that family members have access to employer-sponsored health coverage when not covered by public insurance, even though the majority of low-wage workers don't have employer coverage. The budgets do not include money to purchase life or disability insurance or to create a rainy-day fund that would help a family fund a child's education. In short, these budgets indicate what it takes for a family to cover their most fundamental living expenses—enough to get by but not enough to get ahead.

15   In 1964 when the War on Poverty was launched, the Economic Report of the President explained: "By the poor we mean those who are not now maintaining a decent standard of living—those whose basic needs exceed their means to satisfy them."

Claim Based on Definition

There are tens of millions of Americans today "whose basic needs exceed their means to satisfy them" who are not classified as poor and who therefore cannot receive the assistance they need. That is the problem with how we define poverty.

For Discussion:

Why is this author arguing that more Americans should be classified as "poor"? Why does he think this change is necessary? Do you agree? Why or why not?

CLAIMS OF CAUSE

When you claim that staying up late at a party caused you to fail your exam the next day or that your paper is late because the library closed too early, you are making claims of cause.

Questions answered by claims of cause. What caused it? Where or what is its source? Why did it happen? What are the effects? What will probably be the results over the short term? Over the long term?

Examples of claims of cause. The United States champions human rights in foreign countries to further its own economic self-interests. Clear-cutting is the main cause of the destruction of ancient forests. Legalizing marijuana could have beneficial effects for medicine. DNA testing is causing courts to review some of their death penalty decisions. The long-term effect of inadequate funding for AIDS research will be a disastrous worldwide epidemic. A lack of family values can lead to crime. Censorship can have good results by protecting children.

Types of support associated with claims of cause. The argument must establish the probability of a cause-and-effect relationship. The best type of support for this purpose is *factual data,* including *statistics* that are used to prove a cause or an effect. *Analogies,* including *both literal and historical* analogies that parallel cases in history, are also used to show that the cause of one event could also be the cause of another similar event. Another type of support is based on the use of *signs* to establish certain causes or effects. *Induction,* which entails citing several examples as a cause, may be used to invite the inductive leap to a possible effect as the end result. *Deduction* is also used to develop claims of cause. Premises about effects are proposed, and a conclusion about the possible cause is drawn.

Possible organizational strategies. One strategy is to describe *causes and then effects.* Thus clear-cutting would be described as a cause that would lead to the ultimate destruction of the forests, which would be the effect. Or, *effects* may be described and *then the cause or causes.* The effects of censorship may be described before the public efforts that resulted in that censorship. You may also encounter *refutation* of other actual or possible causes or effects.

An example of an argument that contains a claim of cause. The following essay examines the role that new technology plays in encouraging students to cheat. More specifically, the author argues that the professors' reliance upon online teaching tools provides students with greater means and impetus to break the academic rules. The author's conclusions are subjective, and so it is possible that not everyone will agree with this cause-and-effect argument. What do you think?

> **BEFORE YOU READ:** How do you define academic cheating? In your view, is this a straightforward question? On what basis do we draw the line between what does and does not constitute cheating?

ESSAY #3   **HIGH TECH CHEATING ABOUNDS, AND PROFESSORS ARE PARTLY TO BLAME***

Jeffrey Young

Jeffrey Young writes the "College 2.0" column for *The Chronicle of Higher Education.*

Claim of Cause

A casual joke on Twitter recently let slip a dirty little secret of large science and engineering courses: Students routinely cheat on their homework, and professors often look the other way.

Authority

"Grading homework is so fast when they all cheat and use the illegal solutions manual," quipped Douglas Breault Jr., a teaching assistant in mechanical engineering at Tufts University. After all, if every answer is correct, the grader is left with little to do beyond writing an A at the top of the page and circling it. Mr. Breault, a first-year graduate student, ended his tweet by saying, "The profs tell me to ignore it."

Statistics

While most students and professors seem to view cheating on examinations as a serious moral lapse, both groups appear more cavalier about dishonesty on homework. And technology has given students more tools than ever to find answers in unauthorized ways—whether downloading online solution manuals or instant-messaging friends for answers. The latest surveys by the Center for Academic Integrity found that 22 percent of students say they have cheated on a test or exam, but about twice as many—43 percent—have engaged in "unauthorized collaboration" on homework.

Cheating on an engineering problem set could be the perfect crime, in that it can be done without leaving a trace. Students in a large lecture course based on a best-selling textbook can often find the answer online, complete with all the math it took to get there.

5   How can a professor prove that the cheating students did not work things out on their own?

Authority

Enter David E. Pritchard, a physics professor who teaches introductory courses at the Massachusetts Institute of Technology (when he is not in his laboratory devising new ways to use lasers to reveal the curious behavior of supercooled atoms).

*"High-Tech Cheating Abounds and Professors Bear Some Blame," by Jeffrey R. Young from *The Chronicle of Higher Education,* March 28, 2010. © 2010. Reproduced by permission.

Mr. Pritchard did detective work on his students worthy of a *CSI* episode. Because he uses an online homework system in his courses, he realized he could add a detection system to look for unusual behavior patterns. If a student took less than a minute to answer each of several complex questions and got them all right, for instance, the system flagged that as likely cheating. "Since one minute is insufficient time to read the problem and enter the several answers typically required, we infer that the quick-solver group is copying the answer from somewhere," he wrote in a paper last month in the free online journal *Physical Review Special Topics—Physics Education Research*.

Statistics

He and his research team found about 50 percent more cheating than students reported in anonymous surveys over a period of four semesters. In the first year he did his hunting, about 11 percent of homework problems appeared to be copied.

Data

Mr. Pritchard has no interest in becoming a homework cop. What he really wants to do is understand the minds of the offenders. The issue, he says, is far more nuanced than a story of "Top Students Caught Cheating." He told me that the dishonesty reveals flaws in the very way science is taught, and indicates an unhelpful spirit of "us versus them" between professors and students.

10 He believes that the most important part of learning physics comes by doing, and so students who outsource their homework learn little. His studies of his students prove his point. The cheaters generally perform far worse than other students come test time—students who frequently copied their homework scored two letter grades lower on comparable material on the exam.

Why Students Cheat

Here is what surprised me most when talking with people who have tracked college cheaters. Many students simply do not view copying homework answers as wrong—at least not when it is done with technology.

Deduction

That is what Trevor Harding found. He is a professor of materials engineering at California Polytechnic State University at San Luis Obispo who has researched student cheating in engineering.

Data

In surveys, he asked students if they viewed bringing a cheat sheet to an exam as cheating. Most did. Then he asked the same students whether they would consider it cheating to bring a graphing calculator with equations secretly stored on it. Many said no, that was not cheating.

"I call it 'technological detachment phenomenon,'" he told me recently. "As long as there's some technology between me and the action, then I'm not culpable for the action." By that logic, if someone else posted homework solutions online, what is wrong with downloading them?

Statistic

15 The popularity of Web sites full of homework answers seems to confirm his finding. One of them, called Course Hero, boasts a free collection of "over 500,000 textbook solutions." The company set up a group on Facebook, where more than 265,000 people have signed up as "fans."

Data

Drew Mondry, a junior at New England College, who recently transferred from Michigan State, is among them. "The feeling about homework is that it's really just busywork," he told me. (He said he does not cheat on his homework and only signed up as a fan of the Course Hero site because some friends did.) "You just call your friend and say, 'Hey, do you know the answer?'"

In the big science courses he has taken, professors did not put much effort into teaching, so students do not put real effort into learning, he says: "I have yet to meet a professor who really loves teaching an introductory course, and that translates," was how he put it. "If you look bored out of your mind, guess how much I care?"

Some professors seem to believe that since students who cut corners on homework end up bombing exams, students get a kind of built-in punishment for the behavior, says Mr. Pritchard. Poorly performing students might even learn a lesson from their laziness. So the cheating will take care of itself, right? That is the rationalization, anyway.

Definition

Certainly, many professors put a lot of effort into their classes. And, to them, blatant student cheating can feel like a personal insult. Eric Roberts, a computer-science professor at Stanford University who has studied academic cheating, told me about a student in his course who went to a public computer lab, found some other student's homework assignment saved on a machine there, changed the name to his own name, and turned it in as his own work. Except he left the other student's name on one page by mistake. Busted.

20   "This is lazy cheating," Mr. Roberts said. "They're trying to put one over on us. And if they're trying to match wits with us, I'd just as soon win—if that's their game I'll play it."

For Discussion:

How does this essay challenge our commonly held assumptions about academic cheating? How does a cause-and-effect explanation that includes a role played by teachers change the way we typically think about this phenomenon? Do the statistics presented here make an effective case for a teacher role in causing cheating? What are some of the problems you see with this type of support? Does this claim accord with your own personal experiences in the classroom?

CLAIMS OF VALUE

When you claim that sororities and fraternities are the best extracurricular organizations for college students to join or that one college major is better than another, you are making a claim of value.

> *Questions answered by claims of value.* Is it good or bad? How bad? How good? Of what worth is it? Is it moral or immoral? Who thinks so? What do those people value? What values or criteria should I use to determine its goodness or badness? Are my values different from other people's values or from the author's values?

Examples of claims of value. Online technologies are a valuable contribution to the modern classroom. Prayer has a moral function in the public schools. Viewing television is a wasteful activity. Mercy killing is immoral. The contributions of homemakers are as valuable as those of professional women. Animal rights are as important as human rights.

Types of support associated with claims of value. *Appeals to values* are important in developing claims of value. The arguer thus appeals to what the audience is expected to value. A sense of a common, shared system of values between the arguer and the audience is important for the argument to be convincing. These shared values must be established either explicitly or implicitly in the argument. *Motivational appeals* that suggest what the audience wants are also important in establishing claims of value. People place value on the things that they work to achieve.

Other types of support used to establish claims of value include *analogies, both literal and figurative,* that establish links with other good or bad objects or qualities. Also, quotations from *authorities* who are admired help establish both expert criteria and judgments of good or bad, right or wrong. *Induction* is also used by presenting examples to demonstrate that something is good or bad. *Signs* that something is good or bad are sometimes cited. *Definitions* are used to clarify criteria for evaluation.

Possible organizational strategies. *Applied criteria* can develop a claim of value. Criteria for evaluation are established and then applied to the subject that is at issue. For example, in arguing that a particular television series is the best on television, criteria for what makes a superior series are identified and then applied to the series to defend it as best. The audience would have to agree with the criteria to make the argument effective. Or, suppose the claim is made that toxic waste is the worst threat to the environment. A list of criteria for evaluating threats to the environment is established and applied to toxic waste to show that it is the worst of all. Another possibility would be to use *topical organization* by first developing a list of reasons why something is good or bad. Then each of the reasons is examined as a separate topic.

You may also expect that *narrative* structure will sometimes be used to develop a claim of value. Narratives are real or made-up stories that can illustrate values in action, with morals or generalizations noted explicitly or implicitly along the way. An example of a narrative used to support a claim of value is the New Testament parable of the Good Samaritan who helped a fellow traveler. The claim is that helping one another in such circumstances is valued and desirable behavior.

An example of an argument that contains a claim of value. The following editorial engages a different, more light-hearted, debate over values, arguing that the condescension and disdain many cultural elites feel for reality television is misplaced. Pushing back against this attitude, the author makes the case for the value—as well as the pleasure—of watching this kind of pop cultural fare. Notice how the author appeals to values that the audience is also expected to accept.

> **BEFORE YOU READ:** What is your opinion about reality TV? Do you agree with the author that these shows have redeeming social value?

ESSAY #4   # REALITY TV: MORE THAN JUST A GUILTY PLEASURE*

A.K. Simon

The author is a student at The New School. This editorial was posted to the New School Web site Free Press in 2012.

Examples

As part of my concerted attempt to forge a sophisticated New School persona, I name drop Derrida, pepper my speech with terms like "postmodernism," and pretend I read Thomas Pynchon. Part of this incessant charade is concealing my undying love for reality TV because nothing destroys your tenuous claim to coolness faster than admitting you watched a "Toddlers and Tiaras" marathon over the weekend. I know enough to just nod enthusiastically whenever someone makes a reference to "Mad Men." The shameful truth is that I've never seen an episode of "Mad Men" or "30 Rock." I have, however, seen every episode of "The Real Housewives of New York City"—twice.

Claim of Value

Hardly a shocking admission, I know. <u>Plenty of people relegate their love of reality TV to their cache of guilty pleasures, along with their un-ironic love for The Spice Girls and trove of Harry Potter fan fiction.</u> But why does it incur so much guilt? What's wrong with reality TV anyway? Why is it nobler to spend your time watching the umpteenth show about single girls and their problems (They live in New York! They're quirky! So many awkward conversations!) or an hour of Sorkin-bots delivering overwrought sermons about the state of the world?

Narrative

We like to think that what we watch on TV matters more than it actually does. It can't just be entertainment; it has to be a reflection of our values and personalities. It's an identity. If we watch smart and witty shows, then we are smart and witty. If we watch "Mob Wives" and "Hoarders," on the other hand, we're not only insipid but also partially responsible for some staggering societal decline that concerned critics everywhere are attuned to. Who knew a remote could wield so much power? Who knew mediocre television could incite such widespread malaise? Apparently, the latest harbinger of the cultural apocalypse is "Here Comes Honey Boo

---

*"Reality TV: More Than Just a Guilty Pleasure" by A.K. Simon from *The New School Free Press*, September 13, 2012. Reprinted with permission.

Boo," a new show on TLC (the network that brought you such classics as "Extreme Couponing" and "My Strange Addiction") about an outspoken pageant kid and her wacky Southern family. A review in the *Hollywood Reporter* lambasted the show, calling it "heinous," "horrifying," and TLC's latest in a string of "crimes against humanity." According to the article, we have a moral imperative to not watch this show because it represents the "dehumanization and incremental tearing down of the social fabric." Did you get that? Step away from the television, you rube, before you break society.

Appeal to Values, New Definition

In the spirit of this kind of hyperbole, let me declare this: Honey Boo Boo will save the world. She, along with Snooki and The Kardashians, is going to repair our frayed social fabric, fine tune our moral barometer, and restore harmony to a world gone awry. Is it true? Of course not. But it's not any more ridiculous than the claim that this gossamer social fabric is torn every time a Honey Boo Boo comes along. If we're a broken society, it's not because of what we watch on TV. If anything, reality TV gives us insight into the lives of people we'd never know otherwise—adult babies and balloon fetishists, Amish outlaws and Jersey meatheads. It's a guided tour to all the weird and wonderful stories burrowed deep in the fringes of humanity. Even the most vulgar shows serve a purpose; we can cringe at the embarrassing exploits of our fellow human beings and vow never to tread the same path. If all else fails, at least we'll have a couple hours of mindless entertainment. So let's curb the sanctimonious hand-wringing and take the guilt out of this guilty pleasure—even if it means admitting that The Situation is your spirit animal, not Don Draper. The quiet scorn of your classmates will eventually fade, but the relief will last forever.

For Discussion:

According to this author, Americans tend to place too much importance on the effect of what they watch on television. Do you agree? Would we be better off if we regarded such pop culture to be as valuable as any other television entertainment? Why or why not?

CLAIMS OF POLICY

When you claim that all new students should attend orientation or that all students who graduate should participate in graduation ceremonies, you are making claims of policy.

> ***Questions answered by claims of policy.*** What should we do? How should we act? What should future policy be? What concrete course of action should we pursue to solve the problem? (Notice that policy claims focus on the future more than the other types of claims, which tend to deal with the past or present.)

Examples of claims of policy. The criminal should be sent to prison rather than to a mental institution. Everyone should be taught to recognize and report sexual harassment in the workplace. Every person in the United States should have access to health care. Small business loans must be made available to help people reestablish their businesses after a natural disaster. Both filmmakers and recording groups should make objectionable language and subject matter known to prospective consumers. Battered women who take revenge should not be placed in jail. Genetic engineering should be monitored and controlled. Parents should have the right to choose the schools their children attend.

Types of support associated with claims of policy. *Data* and *statistics* are used to support a policy claim, but so are *moral and commonsense appeals* to what people value and want. *Motivational appeals* are especially important for policy claims. The audience needs to become sufficiently motivated to think or even act in a different way. To accomplish this degree of motivation, the arguer must convince the audience that they want to change. *Appeals to values* are also used for motivation. The audience becomes convinced they should follow a policy to achieve important values.

Literal analogies sometimes support policy claims. The arguer establishes what other similar people or groups have done and suggests the same thing can work in this case also. Or, a successful effort is described, and the claim is made that it could work even better on a broader scale. This is another type of literal analogy because it compares a small-scale effort to a large-scale, expanded effort.

Argument from authority is also often used to establish claims of policy. The authorities quoted, however, must be trusted and must have good credibility. Effort is usually made to establish their credentials. *Cause* can be used to establish the origin of the problem, and *definition* can be used to clarify it. Finally, *deduction* can be used to reach a conclusion based on a general principle.

Possible organizational strategies. The *problem–solution* structure is typical of policy claims. The problem is first described in sufficient detail so that the audience will want a solution. Then the solution is spelled out. In addition, the solution suggested is usually shown to be superior to other solutions by anticipating and showing what is wrong with each of the others. In some arguments the problem and solution sections are followed by a *visualization* of how matters will be improved if the proposed solution is accepted and followed. Problem–solution arguments often end with an *action* step that directs the audience to take a particular course of action (vote, buy, etc.).

An example of an argument that contains a claim of policy. The article on pages 167–168 addresses the problem posed by the exponential growth in bottled water. The author describes this problem from different points of view, and outlines the different policy solutions that might best address it. Pay particular attention to how she describes the problem and the potential solutions.

> **BEFORE YOU READ:** Are you a fan of bottled water? What are the advantages and potential costs of this particular product?

ESSAY #5   IS BOTTLED WATER A MORAL ISSUE?*
Rebecca Cho

Rebecca Cho is a frequent contributor to *The Christian Century*.

Value Comparison

Thou shalt not murder. Thou shalt not covet thy neighbor's wife. Thou shalt not . . . drink bottled water?

Claim of Policy

Rooted in the notion that <u>clean drinking water, like air, is a God-given resource that shouldn't be packaged and sold</u>, a fledgling campaign against the bottling of water has sprung up among religious groups.

Comparison

And though the campaign is at a relative trickle and confined mostly to left-leaning religious groups, activists hope to build a broad-based coalition to

Statements of Values

carry the message that access to water should not be restricted to those who can afford it.

Cassandra Carmichael, director of eco-justice programs for the National Council of Churches, said she has noted an increasing number of religious groups that consider the bottling of water a wrongful, "perhaps immoral" act. "We're just beginning to recognize the issue as people of faith," Carmichael said.

5   In October, the National Coalition of American Nuns, a progressive group representing 1,200 U.S. nuns, adopted a resolution asking members to refrain from purchasing bottled water unless necessary.

Likewise, Presbyterians for Restoring Creation, a grassroots group within the Presbyterian Church (U.S.A.), launched a campaign in May urging individuals to sign a pledge against drinking bottled water and to take the message to their churches.

The United Church of Christ, partnering with the National Council of Churches, produced a documentary, Troubled Waters, that looks at the dangers of water privatization around the world, including the bottling of water for sale in poor areas. The documentary aired on ABC television in October.

In the developing world, Carmichael said, water is being sold as a commodity where the resource is scarce. On the rationale that bottling water takes water resources away from the poor, the environmental issue has become an important one for people of faith, Carmichael said. "The moral call for us is not to privatize water. Water should be free for all."

Statistics

Americans consume more bottled water than any other type of beverage except carbonated soft drinks, according to the Beverage Marketing Corporation, a New York-based research organization. In 2005, Americans drank about 7.5 billion gallons of bottled water, a 10.4 percent increase from 2004. The U.S. leads the world in bottled-water consumption.

*"Groups Hope to Make Bottled Water a Moral Issue," by Rebecca U. Cho from *The Christian Century*, January 9, 2007. © 2010. Reproduced by permission.

Problem   10   At the same time, one-third of the world's population lives in water-stressed conditions. That proportion will double by 2025, according to a 2006 United Nations report on water scarcity. Water is scarcest in arid developing countries plagued by drought and pollution, such as South Africa, where agriculture fuels demand.

Sister Mary Ann Coyle, the National Coalition of American Nuns board member who introduced the measure against bottled water, said the fear is that as water becomes a commodity, access to it will no longer remain a right for all people.

Coyle regards drinking bottled water as a sin. She said that in the U.S., people are paying for bottled water when the country's tap water is among the safest in the world.

Claim   "The use of bottled water in the U.S. is more a lifestyle issue than a necessity," Coyle said. "In this country, we should do more to push [avoidance of] bottled water unless we need it."

Claim   But Stephen Kay, spokesperson for the International Bottled Water Association, said targeting bottled water among the hundreds of other products that use water will not lead to long-term solutions in poor areas. Arguing that bottled-water providers are actually a minimal user of ground water, Kay said better solutions would come from determining how to get clean water into areas struggling with access. "It narrows the focus with what I imagine is good intent," he said.

Solution   15   The Coca-Cola Company, a leading provider of bottled water with its Dasani brand, recognizes the serious nature of water issues and is working on several community initiatives in developing countries, said spokesperson Lisa Manley. "From our perspective, water solutions require the efforts of multiple organizations, nonprofits, governments, community organizations and the like," Manley said. "I hope we'd work toward the same purpose of making safe water accessible to all people of the world."

Solution   Nonetheless, Rebecca Barnes-Davies, coordinator of Presbyterians for Restoring Creation, said she hopes that boycotting bottled water would apply pressure on companies marketing it to act responsibly in the U.S. and the rest of the world.

For Discussion:

How effectively does this essay identify bottled water as an environmental or human rights problem? Are you convinced by the evidence the author presents? Do you agree with either of the solutions her essay outlines? How or how not?

Arguing Like a Citizen

Rebecca Cho's essay ("Is Bottled Water a Moral Issue?") raises questions about the ethical and environmental effects of the bottled water industry. In order to better understand the different types of claims this discussion involves, as well as the ways it connects to the question of citizenship, look closely at the sample discussion on the next page.

Arguing Like a Citizen (*continued*)

▶▶▶ Thinking Like a Citizen: Claims of Value

- Why do I care about this issue?
  As someone who regularly drinks bottled water, I am very interested in understanding the effects my individual consumer choices have on the world around me. If it becomes clear that the bottled water industry constitutes a threat to the environment, I would likely decide that the cost of continuing to drink bottled water outweighs the convenience.

- Who else cares about this issue?
  Clearly, an issue like this would be of great interest to anyone concerned about the state of the environment: activists, advocates for different environmental causes. Another key stakeholder in this discussion includes representatives of the bottled water industry itself, whose interest would be in ways to maintain the financial viability of their business.

▶▶▶ Arguing Like a Citizen: Claims of Fact, Definition, and Cause

- What sorts of facts, information, or data most help support my point of view?
  The data I would find most useful are those that provide clear, objective evidence of the bottled water industry's harmful effects. Examples include statistics about the amount of unrecyclable waste this industry produces annually and scientific data documenting a causal connection between such wastes and specific environmental threats like global warming. Such data would enable me to create a definition of the "environmental effects" of the bottled water industry that others would find credible.

- What facts, information, or data most help support others' points of view?
  For industry advocates, the most useful types of information could include statistical studies establishing the purity or healthful properties of bottled water and data about industry plans to dispose of bottled water waste more efficiently and safely. These kinds of information would enable such advocates to advance a definition of the bottled water industry's "environmental effects" that takes these factors into account.

▶▶▶ Acting Like a Citizen: Claims of Policy

- What concrete action could I take to advance my own point of view?
  To advance my own view, I could create a forum (i.e., a campus gathering, a Facebook page) in which my peers could gather to discuss and debate the issue of bottled water consumption. If I wanted to advocate more directly for my view, I might orchestrate a letter-writing campaign to the major bottled water companies, urging them to reconsider their own policies.

Activity

First, choose one of the issues raised in one of the essays in this chapter (i.e., Is the college admissions process fair? Should our established definition of "poverty" be changed? Is the widespread popularity of reality television something we should celebrate?). Then, using the sample discussion above as your guide, discuss the ways you see this issue raising questions of value, fact, definition, cause, and policy.

Analyzing Online Argument: Types of Claims

In our multimedia environment, claims are found in a variety of contexts and come in a variety of forms. But whether they involve issues of fact, definition, cause, value, or policy, there are certain steps you can follow to better understand how such claims work in an online environment:

▶▶▶ Step 1: Find the Claim

- What type of claim is being made (fact, definition, cause, value, or policy)?

▶▶▶ Step 2: Describe the Medium in Which It Is Found

- Through what form is this claim presented (Web site, social media post, online video, email, etc.)?

▶▶▶ Step 3: Identify the Multimedia Features Used to Present It

- What multimedia elements are used to convey this claim (textual, visual, graphic, video)?

Example

To learn how these steps can be put into practice, let's look at a specific example. The screenshot below is excerpted from a White House Web site that addresses the issue of energy conservation. The Web page makes two claims: one of fact, and one of policy. Look over this selection carefully, as well as the discussion that follows. How does this sample provide a model for analyzing claims in a digital context?

▶▶▶ Step 1: Find the Claim

- The key claims here can be stated this way: The President is taking unprecedented action to help create a clean global economy (fact), and this action needs to include every modern energy technology in order to preserve the environment (policy).

Analyzing Online Argument: Types of Claims (*continued*)

▶▶▶ Step 2: Describe the Medium in Which It Is Found

- These claims are showcased in a Web site produced by the White House.

▶▶▶ Step 3: Identify the Features

- The Web site uses both textual and visual elements to convey this claim. The textual elements include the written statements: "The President has taken unprecedented action to build the foundation for a clean energy economy" and "We need an energy strategy for the future—an all-of-the-above strategy for the 21st century that develops every source of American-made energy." These claims are supplemented by the image of the President striding purposefully across a field that depicts solar panels in the background. This image is designed to reinforce viewers' sense of the administration's leadership in taking on this issue.

Activity

Go online and find an example of each of the five types of claims covered in this chapter (fact, definition, cause, value, policy). Then use the three steps outlined above to identify and analyze how each of these claims works.

Value of the Claim Types and the Claim Questions for Reading, Viewing, and Writing Argument

LO2 Identify and analyze how these types of claims operate in written, visual, and online arguments.

Readers and viewers of argument find the list of the five types of claims and the questions that accompany them useful for identifying the claim and the main purpose in an argument: to establish fact, to define, to establish cause, to assign value, or to propose a solution. Claims and claim questions can also help readers identify minor purposes in an argument, those that are developed as subclaims. When a reader is able to discover the overall purpose of an argument, it is much easier to make predictions and to follow the argument.

Viewers of visual argument will discover that images express the same types of purposes as those found in written argument: some images primarily establish facts, others define a term or a problem, and still others establish cause–effect relationships, assign value to a subject, or propose a solution to a problem. Viewers of online argument will make a similar discovery: that the combinations of visual images, written text, and Web-based links can also be analyzed in terms of these five purposes.

Writers of argument find the list of the five types of claims and the questions that accompany them useful for analyzing an issue, writing a claim about it, and identifying both the controlling purpose for a paper and additional ideas that can be developed in the paper. Here is an example of how this can work. The author writes the issue in the form of a question, as in the example "Should high schools be safer places?" Then the author asks the claim questions about this issue and writes a paragraph in response to each of them: Is it a fact that high schools are unsafe places? How should we define *unsafe?* What causes a lack of safety in high schools, and what are the effects? Is a lack of safety good or bad? What criteria could be established to judge the goodness or badness of safety in high schools? What can be done to make high schools safer places? Finally, the author reads the paragraphs and selects the one that is most promising to form the major claim and purpose in the paper. For example, suppose the author decides to write a policy paper, and the claim becomes "Parents, students, teachers, and administrators all need to cooperate to make high schools safer places." To show how that can be done becomes the main purpose of the paper. The information generated by asking the other claim questions, however, can also be used in the paper to provide reasons and evidence. The claim questions, used in this way as part of the prewriting process, can generate considerable information and ideas for a paper.

Review Questions

1. What are the five types of claims? **(LO1)**
2. What are the questions associated with each type? **(LO1)**
3. How do claims typically appear in written argument? That is, do writers limit themselves to a single purpose and claim or not? Discuss. **(LO2)**
4. What events have occurred in the past few months either on campus or on the national or international level that have generated issues? What are some of these issues? **(LO2)**

Exercises and Activities

A. Class Discussion: Predicting Types of Claims

Bring in the front page of a current newspaper or check its "top stories" online. Discuss headlines that suggest controversial topics. Predict from each headline the type of claim that will be made.

B. Group Work: Reading and Analyzing Types of Claims

The class is divided into five groups, and each group is assigned to read the essay on pages 173–175. Prepare for group work by reading the essay. Then, with your group, answer the following questions. Assign a person to report your answers to the class.

1. Which sentence is the claim? Remember that it can appear at the beginning, in the middle, or at the end of the essay. Underline it.

2. What type of claim is it? Decide which of the five types of claims this claim represents.

3. What are one or two examples of support used in the essay? To help you identify support, review the margin labels that identify the support in the five sample readings in the chapter.

4. How would you summarize the argument in the essay in two or three sentences?

5. What is your reaction to the author's position?

BEFORE YOU READ: Do you think an abundance of material possessions contributes more to personal happiness or to unhappiness?

ESSAY #6   **WHEN IT'S ALL TOO MUCH***

Barry Schwartz

The author teaches psychology at Swarthmore College. This article is adapted from his book *The Paradox of Choice: Why More Is Less*, published in 2004.

One day I went to the GAP to buy a pair of jeans. A salesperson asked if she could help. "I want a pair of jeans—32–28," I said. "Do you want them slim fit, easy fit, relaxed fit, baggy or extra-baggy?" she replied. "Do you want them stonewashed, acid-washed or distressed? Do you want them button-fly or zipper-fly? Do you want them faded or regular?"

I was stunned. A moment or two later, I sputtered out something like, "I just want regular jeans. You know, the kind that used to be the only kind."

She pointed me in the right direction. The trouble was that with all these options available to me now, I was no longer sure that "regular" jeans were what I wanted. Perhaps the easy fit or the relaxed fit would be more comfortable. So I tried on all the pants and scrutinized myself in a mirror. Whereas very little was riding on my decision, I was now convinced that one of these options had to be right for me, and I was determined to figure it out.

The jeans I chose turned out to be just fine, but it occurred to me that buying a pair of pants should not be a daylong project. Purchasing jeans was once a five minute affair, now it was a complex decision.

5   Buying jeans is a trivial matter, but it is an example of a much larger issue. When people have no choice, life can be almost unbearable. As the number of choices increases, the autonomy, control and liberation this variety brings can be powerful and positive.

But if the number of choices keeps growing, negative effects start to appear.

---

*Barry Schwartz, "When It's All Too Much," *Parade Magazine*, Jan. 4, 2005. Reprinted by permission of the author.

As choices grow further, the negatives can escalate until we become overloaded. At this point, choice no longer liberates us; it might even be said to tyrannize.

The Explosion of Choices

Modern life has provided a huge array of products to choose from. Just walk into any large supermarket or drugstore looking for hair-care products, and you'll likely be confronted with more than 360 types of shampoo, conditioner and mousse. Need a painkiller? There are 80 options. How about toothpaste? You have 40 types to pick from.

In addition, we now have to make choices in areas of life in which we used to have few or no options. We have to decide which telephone service providers and retirement pension plans are the best for us. Modern cosmetic surgery allows us to change virtually any aspect of our appearance. An explosion of tolerance for "alternative" lifestyles has given us real choices about whether to be monogamous, whether (and when) to marry, whether (and when) to have kids and even whether to have intimate relations with partners of the same or the opposite sex (or both).

More Choices . . . More Happiness?

It seems a simple matter of logic that increased choice improves well-being. But, in fact, the opposite is true. Respected social scientists such as psychologist David G. Myers and political scientist Robert E. Lane tell us that increased choice and increased affluence have, in fact, been accompanied by decreased well-being.

10   The American "happiness quotient" has been going gently but consistently downhill for more than a generation. In the last 30 years—a time of great prosperity—the proportion of the population describing itself as "very happy" has declined. The decline was about 5%. This might not seem like much, but 5% translates into about 14 million Americans.

Not only that, but today, as a society, more Americans than ever are clinically depressed. By some estimates (for example, those of psychologist Martin Seligman in his book *Learned Optimism*), depression in the year 2000 was about 10 times as likely as it was in 1900.

Of course, no one believes that a single factor explains this. But accumulating evidence from psychological research indicates that the explosion of choice plays an important role. It seems that as we become freer to pursue and do whatever we want, we get less and less happy.

The More We Have, the More We Want

Increases in our expectations are partly to blame. The more we are allowed to be the masters of our fates, the more we expect to be. We believe we should be able to find work that is exciting, socially valuable and remunerative. We expect spouses who are sexually, emotionally, and intellectually stimulating. Our children should be beautiful, smart, affectionate, obedient and independent. And everything we buy is supposed to be the best of its kind.

With all the choices available, we may believe we should never have to settle for things that are just "good enough." Those who accept only the best, I call maximizers. In my research, I've found that maximizers are less happy, less optimistic and more depressed. At the very least, maximizing behavior can lead to dissatisfaction—and, sometimes, paralysis.

15   I have a friend who makes going out to dinner a nightmare. He struggles to select a dish and changes his mind repeatedly as his companions sit and stew. And I see my students agonize about which of many paths to follow when they graduate. Many of them

are looking for jobs that will give them everything, and they expect to find them.

Only Ourselves to Blame

We are told we are now in the driver's seat when it comes to what happens in our lives. If we fail, it's our own fault. This might sound only fair, but the pressure we are put under can be enormous—especially in crucial areas of our lives such as medical care.

For example, people in one study were asked whether, if they got cancer, they would want to be in charge of their treatment decisions; 65 percent said yes. Unless, however, they actually had cancer.

Then only 12 percent said yes. People with cancer have experienced the awesome psychological consequences of being responsible for a life-and-death decision, and they don't want that responsibility.

Unattainable expectations, plus a tendency to blame ourselves for our failures, make a lethal combination.

This is the paradox: Here we are, living at the pinnacle of human possibility, awash in material abundance. We get what we say we want, only to discover that it doesn't satisfy us. The success of 21st-century life turns out to be bittersweet. And I believe that a significant contributing factor is the overabundance of choice.

For Discussion:

Are you easily satisfied with what you have, or are you always thinking about trying to accomplish or get more? What would you need in material possessions to make you happy? Has this article changed your opinions on this subject of choice in any way?

C. Group Work and Class Discussion: Analyzing Types of Claims in Visual Argument

Create five groups and have each group look at all of the five images that follow, including the remarks that accompany them. Assign each group one of the images and ask group members to select the best description of it from the list that follows. The images are in a different order from the list of categories. Note: You may need to make an argument for your interpretation because a particular image may serve as an illustration for more than one type of claim. Give reasons for your choices.

a. This visual primarily establishes fact. What is the fact? How convinced are you by this image?

b. This visual shows cause and effect. What is the cause? What is the effect? Do you accept the cause–effect relationship depicted here? Why or why not?

c. This visual is mainly about establishing value. What is being evaluated? Is the value assigned to it positive or negative? Do you agree or disagree? Why or why not?

d. This visual helps define a problem. What is the problem? How does the visual help define it?

e. This visual provides a possible solution for a problem. What is the problem, and what is the solution?

Image 1:
War Casualties

Here is the information that accompanies the opening of a new rehabilitation center in San Antonio, Texas, which this photo depicts. It is "designed to treat the growing number of severely wounded veterans of the Iraq war, some of whom attended the ceremony."

Image 2:
US Border Control

A United States Border Control agent contains people after crossing the Rio Grande River into the United States near McAllen, Texas. (AP)

This Associated Press photograph appeared in an online article of *The New York Post*. The title of the article is "US Border Patrol Launches New Push to Stop Illegal Immigrants from Mexico." What portrait of "border patrol" does this image present? Consider the caption and decide what type of claim it makes. How do you evaluate the use of the term "contain" here? What view of "border control" does this choice of language encourage you to form?

Image 3:
The Rhone Glacier

Retreat A drawing on an 1870 postcard shows the Rhone Glacier sweeping into Gletsch, Switzerland; in 2005 the glacier could hardly be seen.

The small postcard that is superimposed on the larger photograph in this image are both pictures of the same place in Switzerland, only the pictures are taken at different times. What is the issue? Consider the caption above and decide what type of claim is being made.

Image 4:
Go Paperless

What type of claim is established by this ad? What is the claim? How effective is this claim, in your opinion?

Image 5:
Corn Power

Only two words accompany this image (Corn Power), but they should be enough to help you decide what type of claim is being made. What is the issue? What is the claim? What type of claim is it?

D. **Writing Assignment: Analyzing Types of Claims in Online Argument**

How are claims different when presented online? Choose an example of an arguable issue that is being presented online. Then write a 300- to 500-word essay in which you (1) identify and describe the particular type(s) of claims being made and (2) analyze the ways these claims are affected by the features and factors particular to the Web (i.e., audience feedback, interactivity, linked issues, multimedia forms).

E. **Writing Assignment: Argument Using One Type of Claim**

Write a 250- to 300-word paper that is organized around a single type of claim. Use the following claims about campus issues as starter sentences for your paper. Before you write, spend a few minutes with classmates to brainstorm some ideas for each of the papers. If you need more information, go to the Financial Aid Office for topic *a*, the Office of Student Affairs for topics *b* or *d*, to the Registrar's Office for topic *e*, and the Office of Institutional Studies or the Registrar for topic *c*. You might also interview students and faculty or consult the Internet. Use some of the ideas about organizational patterns and support described in this chapter to help you think about and develop your ideas.

a. Is it true? Does it exist? *Claim of fact:* <u>Financial aid for students (is or is not) readily available on our campus.</u>
   Hint: Try a claim with a reasons (or topical order) pattern of organization. Add facts, statistics, and real examples.

b. How should we define it? *Claim of definition:* <u>A dangerous level of alcohol consumption is not defined by everyone in exactly the same way.</u>
   Hint: Explain the controversy over what is considered a dangerous level. Quote an authoritative source that defines the term "dangerous level." Compare definitions of dangerous and not-dangerous levels and use examples and statistics as support.

c. What caused it? What are the effects? *Claim of cause:* <u>Various causes contribute to the student dropout problem in colleges.</u>
   Hint: Describe the major causes for students leaving college before they graduate. Use factual data, including statistics and examples as support. Describe the effects on the students themselves.

d. Is it good or bad? *Claim of value:* <u>Student organizations (do or do not) contribute significant positive value to the college experience.</u>
   Hint: Make a list of the positive values that student organizations provide students, or make a list of negative values that show students should not join these organizations. Apply them to one or more student organizations. Appeal to what most students would value or want.

e. What is the problem and what should we do to solve it? *Claim of policy:* <u>Students do not always know their academic standing in all of their courses during a semester, and measures should (or should not) be taken to correct this lack of information.</u>
   Hint: Try a problem–solution pattern of organization. Use examples, comparisons, quotes from authorities, and appeals to values and motives.

F. Prewriting: Using the Claim Questions to Generate Ideas for a Position Paper

The claim questions can be used to invent ideas for any argument paper you might write. Choose an issue raised by one of the essays in this chapter and formulate a tentative claim about it. Then follow the instructions below to help you generate additional information for your paper.

1. Write your issue in the form of an issue question. *Example:* Is parking a problem on campus?

2. Apply the claim questions to the issue question and write a paragraph in response to each question.
   a. *Fact:* Did it happen? Does it exist?
   b. *Definition:* What is it? How can we define it?
   c. *Cause:* What caused it? What are the effects?
   d. *Value:* Is it good or bad? What criteria will help us decide?
   e. *Policy:* What should we do about it? What should be our future course of action?

3. Read the paragraphs you have written, and select the one that interests you the most and that also seems most promising as the focus for your paper. Now look at your tentative claim and revise it, if necessary, to bring it in line with your new purpose and focus. You may, of course, also use information from the other paragraphs you have written to develop sub-claims and support for your paper. Save what you have written. You will use it later if you plan to write a position paper.

CHAPTER

6

Types of Proof

After studying this chapter, you will be able to:

LO1 Describe and analyze the three categories of traditional proof.

LO2 Explain the characteristics of a logical proof (*logos*) and use them in an argument.

LO3 Explain the characteristics of a proof of credibility (*ethos*) and use them in an argument.

LO4 Explain the characteristics of an emotional proof (*pathos*) and use them in an argument.

LO5 Explain how language and style convey logic (*logos*), credibility (*ethos*), and emotion (*pathos*) in an argument.

LO6 Define the value of using these three types of proof for assessing written, visual, and online argument.

T he claim, the support, and the warrants are the three parts that are present in any argument. This chapter will help you understand the support and warrants that provide proofs for a claim. You will be introduced first to the different types of proof, then to the language and style associated with each of them.

As you begin to work with the proofs, you will discover that they are not uniform patterns that are obvious and easy to recognize. Indeed, slippery and imperfect as they are, they simply represent an attempt to describe what goes on in the real world of argument and in the minds of writers and readers of argument. Understanding them can put you closer to an author, permitting you to better understand how that individual thought about, interpreted, and developed a particular subject. When you switch roles and become the author yourself, your knowledge of what can happen in argument helps you develop your own thoughts and effective arguments.

LO1 Describe and analyze the three categories of traditional proof.

The Traditional Categories of Proof

The traditional categories of proof, like much of our most fundamental argument theory, were first articulated by classical theorists, and they are still useful for describing what goes on in real-world argument today. In the *Rhetoric*, Aristotle said that an arguer must state a claim (or a proposition) and prove it. He also went into detail about the broad categories of proof that can be employed to establish the probability of a claim. Aristotle's categories of proof remain useful because they accurately describe what classical arguers did then and what modern arguers still do today.

Aristotle distinguishes between proofs that can be produced and laid on the table, so to speak—like a murder weapon, fingerprints, or a written contract—and proofs that are invented, and represent the creative thinking and insights of clever and intelligent people.

Aristotle divides this second category of proof into three subcategories: proofs that appeal to logic and reason, proofs that establish the credibility of the source, and proofs that appeal to the emotions. The Greek words used to refer to the proofs are *logos* (logic), *ethos* (credibility), and *pathos* (emotion).

Logical proof appeals to the audience's reason, understanding, and common sense. It is consistent with what people know and believe, and it gives fresh insight and ideas about issues. As proof, it relies mainly on such support as reasoned opinion and factual data as well as on warrants that suggest the soundness and truth of such support. Aristotle declared that logical proof is the most important kind of proof in argument, and most modern theorists agree with him. Richard M. Weaver, a well-known modern rhetorician, for example, says that argument has its primary basis in reasoning and that it appeals primarily to the rational part of humans. Logical proof, he says, provides the "plot" of argument.[1] The other two types of proof are also present and important, however.

Proof that establishes ethos appeals to the audience's impressions, opinions, and judgments about the individual stating the argument. An arguer who demonstrates competence, good character, fair-mindedness, and goodwill toward the audience is more convincing than the arguer who lacks these qualities. Those who project such favorable qualities to an audience have established good *ethos*. Audiences are more likely to trust and believe individuals with good *ethos* than those without it. At times, arguers also need to establish the *ethos* of the experts whom they quote in their arguments. They usually accomplish this purpose by providing information about these authorities so that audiences will appreciate their mastery or expertise and consequently be more willing to accept what they say.

Emotional proof is used to appeal to and arouse the feelings of the audience. The audience's feelings are aroused primarily through emotional language, examples, personal narratives, and vivid descriptions of events that contain

---

[1] Richard M. Weaver, "Language Is Sermonic," in Richard L. Johannesen, ed., *Contemporary Theories of Rhetoric: Selected Readings* (New York: Harper & Row, 1971), 163–79.

emotional elements and that provoke strong feelings in other people. Emotional proof is appropriate in an argument when it is used to develop the claim and when it contributes to the sense of logical conviction and agreement that are argument's intended outcomes. A well-reasoned set of logical proofs contributes to such outcomes. Emotion contributes as well to the strength of the acceptance of a logical conclusion. Imagine, for example, an argument in favor of increasing taxes to build housing for homeless people. The logical argument would describe reasons for these taxes, methods for levying them, and recommendations for spending them. The argument would be strengthened, however, by one or more vivid and emotional examples of homeless people who lead miserable lives.

Visual argument also relies on these same proofs to strengthen its claims; however, visuals are often more powerful than words because they communicate so quickly. Look at the Dow Chemical Company advertisement in Figure 6.1. This ad relies on all three types of proof to make the audience believe the claim that this company is more interested in people all over the world than it is in mere chemistry and chemicals. Examine the ad, read the next paragraph, and answer the questions in the margin next to the ad for yourself.

The producers and authors of the ad expect you to link three elements: the *logical* chemical symbol in the ad; the *emotionally appealing* young Tibetan boy whom they describe as having "one of the best minds on the planet" and the

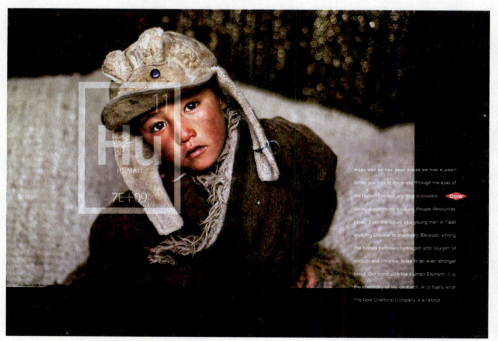

Figure 6.1

Analyze the proofs used in this Dow Chemical Company advertisement. First, look at the ad itself and then, since the words in the ad are too small to read here, read instead the explanation and analysis of this ad in the accompanying paragraphs on this page and the next. Now comment on the use of *logos, ethos,* and *pathos* in this ad. How do they work together to make the claim? How convincing is this ad? Why do you think so?

value statements that help create the company's *ethos*—"When you look at the world through the eyes of the Human Element, anything is possible" and "Our bond with the Human Element. It is the chemistry of life on Earth. And that's what the Dow Chemical Company is all about." Now think about the *warrant*. When you have considered all of the proof, you might state the warrant this way: Of course this boy can learn chemistry and become a successful chemist, if he is given the opportunity and the support. The ad also suggests that because the company values people, Dow Chemical will encourage and possibly provide that support. The *backing* for the warrant assumes that many viewers first looking at the picture of this boy would think that because of his dress and where he lives, he is unlikely to receive a good science education and become a scientist. The proofs and the warrant challenge that initial assumption. The producers and authors of the ad expect the audience to conclude that the company has humanitarian goals and is supportive of disadvantaged people in the world.

The next three sections will introduce you to seven types of logical proof, one type of proof that builds *ethos,* and two types of emotional proof. All are commonly used in argument. The number and variety of logical proofs is greater because logical thinking dominates and provides the "plot" for most argument. However, most arguments rely on a variety of proofs because offering several types of proof usually makes a stronger argument than relying on only one.

Each type of proof will be explained according to the following format so that you can understand each kind as quickly and easily as possible.[2]

Examples: Examples follow a brief general description of each proof.

Claim and support: Describes what to look for, that is, what types of support you can expect to find, and how to find the claim.

Warrant: Identifies what you are expected to assume to make logical connections between the support and the claim. The warrants associated with types of proof suggest specific ways of thinking about support and its function in an argument.

Tests of validity: *Validity* in argument is measured by using your knowledge of the structure of argument and its components and by what you might term a "questioning receptivity" to argumentation. This is another way of describing the critical reading method that requires that you probe whether or not a proof (analogy, statistic, etc.) or argument itself is sound, genuine, effective, authoritative, and believable. You are provided with questions to ask to help you test the reliability and validity of the proof. These questions focus your attention on the support and on the warrant, and on how they do or do not function together as effective proof. The questions can also help you locate the weaknesses in an argument, which will help you plan rebuttal and formulate argument of your own.

---

[2]In this chapter I have drawn on some of Wayne Brockriede and Douglas Ehninger's ideas in "Toulmin on Argument: An Interpretation and Application," *Quarterly Journal of Speech* 46 (1969): 44–53. I have expanded and adapted these authors' analysis of proofs to make it apply to the reading and writing of argument as explained in this book.

Types of Logical Proof: *Logos*

LO2 Explain the characteristics of a logical proof (*logos*) and use them in an argument.

Logical proofs (also called substantive proofs) include facts, reasons, and opinions that are based on reality. Such proofs rely on factual information, statistics, and accounts of actual events, past and present. The support used in logical proof is real and drawn from experience. Logical (or substantive) warrants guarantee the reliability and relevance of this support. Logical proofs represent common ways of thinking about and perceiving relationships among the events and data of the real world and offer those ideas and relationships as support for a line of argument.

A MNEMONIC DEVICE

It is helpful to be able to recall easily the full range of logical proofs either when you are reading argument or when you are developing an argument so that you can use them to your advantage. Figure 6.2 provides a mnemonic device that will help you remember them. It shows the first letter of each proof arranged to make a nonsense word, SICDADS, and a picture to help you remember it. You can run through this mnemonic mentally when you are thinking about ways to develop the ideas in a paper or other format for your argument.

Let us now consider the seven logical proofs in the order provided by the mnemonic SICDADS.

ARGUMENT FROM SIGN

A *specific visible sign* is sometimes used to prove a claim. A sign can be used to prove with certainty: someone breaks out in chickenpox, and the claim, based on that certain sign, is that the person has chickenpox. A sign also can be used to prove the probability of a claim: a race riot, someone argues, is probably a sign of the claim that people think they are treated unfairly. On the other hand, the sign may turn out to be a pseudoproof, the "proof" of a false claim: a child asks, "Why should I believe in Santa Claus?" and the parent answers, "Look at all the toys under the tree that weren't there yesterday." That support is used as a sign for the claim that Santa Claus exists.

Sign
Induction
Cause
Deduction
Analogies (historical, literal, figurative)
Definition
Statistics

"SICDADS" refuted by logical proof.

Figure 6.2 *The Seven Logical Proofs: Their Initials Spell Out SICDADS*

Example of Sign

Here is a hypothetical example of an argument from sign used in an essay. Would you say that the claim based on this sign is a certain or a probable claim?

Claim: The cheers emanating from the thousands of protesters marching in the street is a sign of public unrest.

Support (sign):   There are cheers emanating from the protesters marching in the street.

Warrant: This march indicates that there is public unrest.

Claim and Support

Look for visible clues, symptoms, and occurrences that are explained as obvious and clear signs of a certain belief or state of affairs. Look for the conclusion or claim that is made on the basis of these signs.

Sign Warrants

You are expected to assume that the sign is actually a sign of what the author claims it to be.

Tests of Validity

Is this really a sign of what the author claims it to be? Is there another explanation for the sign?

ARGUMENT FROM INDUCTION

Inductive argument provides a number of examples and draws a claim, in the form of a conclusion, from them. The audience is expected to accept the group of examples as adequate and accurate enough to make the inductive leap to the claim. Inductive argument is also called argument from generalization or argument from example because the claim is a generalization made on the basis of the examples. To help you remember the special features of inductive argument, learn its prefix *in-*, which means "in" or "into," and the root *duc,* which means "lead." *An inductive argument uses examples to lead into a claim or generalization about the examples.*

Examples of Induction

Here is an example of induction. Four different people take their cars to the same car repair shop and are overcharged. The claim is then made that anyone who takes a car to that repair shop will probably be overcharged.

Inductive reasoning is the basis of the scientific method. Most scientific conclusions are reached inductively. When a sufficient number of phenomena are observed repeatedly, a generalization is made to explain them. Here is an example.

Claim (generalization):	The sun always comes up.
Support:	For example, the sun has come up every day of recorded history.
Warrant:	Every day provides a sufficient number of days to make the claim that the sun always comes up.

Consider this third and final example of argument from induction. In the Declaration of Independence (pages 220–222), Thomas Jefferson listed several examples of "repeated injuries" that the king of England was guilty of in dealing with the United States. From these examples, Jefferson drew the conclusion that the United States was justified in declaring the United States free and independent of Great Britain. The warrant is that the repeated injuries gave sufficient reason for the United States to take action and declare independence.

Induction demonstrates probability rather than truth whenever there is the possibility of an example that would prove an exception. For instance, the claim is made that occasional smoking will lead to addiction. But a person is discovered who smokes off and on and never develops cigarette addiction. Yet, an apple always falls from a tree, thereby demonstrating gravity, and the sun always comes up, demonstrating that law of nature. No one has been able to find exceptions to disprove these last two generalizations.

To be effective, inductive argument requires a sufficient number of examples. When a generalization is made on the basis of only one or a few examples, it is called a *hasty generalization*. To claim, for instance, that an office worker should always be able to enter a certain amount of data because he did it once may not be accurate. To make a broad generalization, such as *all* office workers ought to be able to enter a certain amount of data because *one* employee was able to, is called a *sweeping generalization*. An inadequate sample of cases weakens or invalidates an inductive argument.

Claim and Support

Look for a group of examples followed by a generalization (claim) based on the examples, or the generalization (claim) may be stated first and then be followed by several examples.

Inductive Warrants

You are expected to assume that the list of examples is representative and that it shows a definite trend. You are also expected to assume that if you added more examples of the same general type, the conclusion would not change.

Tests of Validity

Is the sample adequate? Would more examples continue to show the trend? Are there examples that show an opposite trend or that provide an exception? (Is a person who smokes occasionally without developing an addiction a single exception?) Can we make the inductive leap from the examples to the generalization to demonstrate that it is probably true?

ARGUMENT FROM CAUSE

Argument from cause places the subject in a *cause-and-effect relationship* to show that it is either the cause of an effect or the effect of a cause. It is very common in argument to explain or to justify a claim with cause-and-effect reasoning.

Historians frequently use argument from cause. When they ask why a certain historical event occurred, they are seeking the cause. Visual and multimedia arguments also can make claims of cause. In advertisements, buying a certain product is often shown to cause beneficial results.

Example of Cause

Claim: The climate is changing worldwide (effect).
Support: Many scientists claim air pollution is the cause.
Warrant: We should believe the scientists.

Claim and Support

Look for examples, events, trends, or people who have caused certain things to happen. Look for the effects. For example, "Video games cause children to become violent." Or, turn it around and look for the effects first and then the causes: "Many children are violent as a result of playing too many violent video games." Look also for clue words such as *cause, effect, resulted in, as a result, as a consequence,* and *because* to indicate that cause-and-effect reasoning is being used.

Causal Warrants

You are expected to assume that the causes really do create the identified effects or that the effects really are the results of the named causes.

Tests of Validity

Are these causes alone sufficient to create these effects? Could these effects result from other causes? Can I think of exceptions to the cause-and-effect outcome?

ARGUMENT FROM DEDUCTION

Deductive argument is also called argument from principle because its warrant is a general principle. Remember that the warrant may or may not be stated explicitly in an argument. Etymology can help you remember the special features of deductive argument. The prefix *de-* means "from" and the root *duc* means "lead." *A deductive argument leads from a general principle,* which is the warrant, applies it to an example or specific case, which is described in the support, and draws a *conclusion,* which is the claim.

Examples of Deduction

Argument deals with matters that are probably rather than certainly true. People do not argue about matters that are certainly true because they already agree about them. Here is an example of a deductive argument based on a general principle that people would agree with and accept as true. Thus, they would not argue about it.

General warrant:	Every person has a unique DNA sequence.
Support (specific case):	The accused is a person.
Claim:	The accused has a unique DNA sequence.

This example might be used as a minor argument to support a claim that someone is guilty of a crime. It would never be the main issue in an argument, however, because it is not arguable.

Most of the deduction you will encounter in argument is arguable because it deals with probabilities rather than with certainties. Here is an example of deductive reasoning. Fictional sleuth Sherlock Holmes used deduction to reach his sometimes astonishing conclusions. Holmes examined the supporting evidences—footprints in this example—and deduced that the man who left them walked with a limp. The general principle, that most uneven footprints are left by people who limp, is an assumption that is important in Holmes's deductive thinking even though it is not stated in the argument. It does not need to be spelled out for readers who are able to supply that warrant themselves as they accept Holmes's conclusion. The Holmes deduction can be summarized as follows: the purpose of this argument is to establish the type of person who left these footprints.

Unstated warrant:	Most uneven footprints are left by people who limp.
Support (specific case):	These footprints are uneven.
Claim:	The person who left these footprints walks with a limp.

Is there any part of that argument that you might challenge as only possibly or probably rather than as certainly true? If so, you can argue about it.

Claim and Support

Identify the claim by answering this question: "On the basis of a general principle (warrant), implied or stated, what does the author expect me to conclude about this specific example or case?"

Deductive Warrants

You are expected to assume that a general principle about a whole category of phenomena (people, places, events, and so forth) has been stated or implied in the argument and that it is accurate and acceptable. You are expected to decide that since the general principle, or warrant, and the support for the specific case are both accurate and acceptable, the conclusion is also acceptable and probably true.

Tests of Validity

Is the warrant sound and believable? Does the warrant apply to the example or case? Is the support for the case accurate? How reliable, then, is the conclusion?

If the reader has a problem with either the warrant or the example in a deductive argument, the conclusion will not be acceptable. Consider Holmes's warrant that uneven footprints are left by people who limp. That may be convincing to some readers but not others. For instance, a reader might reflect that a person who is pretending to limp or is carrying a heavy suitcase could also leave uneven footprints. This reader would then question the warrant and decide that the proof is not even probably true.

Here is another example of a deductive argument that would not be equally successful with all audiences.

> *Unstated warrant:* Families cannot be happy when the mother works outside the home.
> *Support (specific case):* The mother in this family works outside the home.
> *Claim:* This is an unhappy family.

For readers who come from happy homes with working mothers, the warrant in this example would seem faulty.

In the next example of a deductive argument, the support could be a problem for some readers who might have trouble accepting it because they think children's stories are not literary and do not have deep symbolic levels of meaning. Another reader might disagree and argue for the opposite point of view, providing examples of children's stories that have such literary qualities and thus refute the other readers' claim. Whether or not a reader accepts the conclusion depends entirely on whether the reader also accepts the warrant and support.

> *Warrant:* All literary stories have deep symbolic levels of meaning.
> *Support (specific case):* This children's story has deep symbolic levels of meaning.
> *Claim:* Children's stories are literary stories.

All parts of a deductive argument need to be well grounded, accurate, and acceptable to an audience for it to be convincing.

Induction and Deduction Sometimes Work Together

A number of examples are cited and a generalization is made based on those examples—this is the inductive part of the argument. The generalization can then be utilized as the starting point for a deductive argument, one in which it serves as the warrant, that part of the argument that the audience needs to accept. This generalization is combined with a specific case, and a claim is made that is based on applying the generalization to the specific case. Here is a hypothetical example that shows how this can be structured. Imagine an essay in which a student, based on interviews with his fellow classmates, makes the argument that standardized tests should no longer be used to evaluate his academic performance.

Induction: Recall that the warrants are implied by the arguer and assumed by the audience.

> *Examples:* Suppose the author's interviews revealed that seven students in this classroom believe that standardized tests should no longer be used to evaluate academic performance.
> *Claim (generalization):* Standardized testing should not be used to evaluate student performance in college classrooms.

Warrants:	The opinions of those seven students is a sufficient number for the instructor to change the curriculum. Student opinion can change an instructor's teaching policy.

Deduction: Now the claim of the inductive argument becomes the warrant or general principle that is the starting place for the deductive argument.

General warrant:	Evaluation of student performance should be based on academic work other than standardized test scores.
Specific case:	The author objects to standardized testing.
Claim:	Therefore, the author's academic evaluation should be based on criteria other than standardized testing.

Tests of Validity

Examine the two inductive warrants: Are those seven students enough to create a change in an instructor's evaluation policy? Can student opinion change an instructor's policy in a class? If you answer no to both those questions, then you will not accept the general warrant in the deductive argument either because it is based on the unacceptable warrants in the inductive argument: Students don't set policy for evaluating student performance, and even if they did, seven students would not be a large enough number to make this change. Both the inductive and the deductive arguments can be shown to be invalid because they are based on faulty warrants.

ARGUMENT FROM HISTORICAL, LITERAL, OR FIGURATIVE ANALOGY

Historical and literal analogies explore similarities and differences between items in the same general category, and *figurative analogies* do the same, only with items in very different categories. In drawing analogies, we show how something we may not know much about is like something we know in greater detail. *In other words, we interpret what we do not know in light of what we do know.* We then supply the warrant that what happened in one case will happen in the other, we draw conclusions, and we make a claim based on the comparisons in the analogy.

Historical Analogies

These explain what is going on *now* in terms of what went on in similar cases *in the past.* Future outcomes are also often projected from past cases. The idea is that what happened in the past will probably repeat itself in the present. Also, the two events are so similar that the result of the former will surely be the result of the latter.

Example of a Historical Analogy

The following example compares a present event with a past event.

Claim:	People will lose faith in the war in Afghanistan.
Support:	People lost faith in the Vietnam War.
Warrant:	The two wars are similar.

Literal Analogies

These compare two items in the same category: two school systems, two governments, two religions, two individuals. Outcomes are described as in historical analogies—that is, what happened in one case will happen in the other because of the similarities or the differences.

Example of a Literal Analogy

Two similar items (spending policies) are compared in this example.

> *Claim:*   The state should spend more money on education.
> *Support:*   Another state spent more money with good results.
> *Warrant:* The two states are similar, and the results of one will be the results of the other.

Figurative Analogies

These compare items from two different categories, as in metaphor, but the points of comparison in a figurative analogy are usually spelled out in more detail than they are in a metaphor. Many figurative analogies appeal to emotion rather than to reason. Figurative analogies are effective as logical proof only when they are used to identify *real qualities* that are shared by both items and that can then be applied to help prove the claim logically. When the items in a figurative analogy are compared either to add ornament or to stir up an emotional response, the analogy functions as emotional proof. It engages the emotions rather than reason.

Examples of Figurative Analogies

Here are some examples of figurative analogies used as logical proof. To prove that reading a difficult book should take time, Francis Bacon compares that activity with taking the time to chew and digest a large meal. The qualities of the two activities, rather than the activities themselves, are compared. Since these qualities are not spelled out, the audience must infer that both take time and that understanding, like digestion, benefits and becomes a permanent part of the individual. Here is this argument laid out so that you can see how it works.

> *Claim:*   Reading a difficult book should take time.
> *Support:*   Digesting a large meal takes time.
> *Warrant:* Reading and eating are sufficiently alike that they can be compared.

In another example of a figurative analogy used as logical proof, the human fossil record is compared to an apple tree in early winter that has only a few apples on it. The quality that the fossil record and the tree have in common, which the reader must infer, is that both tree and fossil record have a complicated system of branches and limbs. Also, the few apples on the tree are like the few available fossils. At one time there were many of both. The qualities compared in these two instances improve a rational understanding of the fossil record.

Here is a third example of a figurative analogy. This analogy comes from an ad sponsored by the Sierra Club, a group that works to protect the environment. Two pictures are placed side by side. The first is of the Statue of Liberty, which is 305 feet high, and the second is of a giant sequoia tree, which is 275 feet high. A question is posed: "Would you destroy the Statue of Liberty for scrap metal?" We are expected to reason by analogy and compare destroying the Statue of Liberty for scrap metal with destroying the tree for lumber or sawdust. The individual who created this ad hopes this analogy will encourage people to want to protect the trees as much as they want to protect the Statue of Liberty. Would you say that this figurative analogy appeals mainly to emotion or to reason?

Claim and Support

Look for examples of items, events, people, and periods of time that are being compared. Whether these items are drawn from the past or the present, as in the case of historical or literal analogies, they must be drawn from the same category: two types of disease, two types of school systems, two types of government, and so on. Look for the clue words *compare, contrast, like, similar to,* and *different from* to signal that comparisons are being made.

In the case of figurative analogies, look for two items being compared that are from totally different categories. Identify the qualities that they have in common. Look for the clue words *like, as, parallel, similar to,* or *compare.* Discover claims that are made as a result of comparing similarities or differences.

Comparison Warrants

You are expected to assume that the items being compared are similar as described and that what happens in one case will probably occur in the other. For figurative analogies, you are expected to assume that the qualities of the two items are similar and significant enough so that reference to one will help explain the other and will serve as convincing proof.

Tests of Validity

Are the two items similar as claimed? Can I think of ways they are not similar or of other qualities they share that would change the claim? Are the outcomes likely to be the same in both cases? Why or why not?

For figurative analogies: Are the qualities of these two items similar, significant, and real enough to help prove a logical argument? Or are they so dissimilar, so far-fetched, or so trivial that the comparison does not prove anything? Does the analogy serve as an ornament, an emotional appeal, or a logical proof?

ARGUMENT FROM DEFINITION

Definition is extremely important in argument. It is difficult to argue about any subject unless there is general agreement about the meanings of the *key terms,* especially when they are part of the claim. Sometimes an entire argument is based on the audience's acceptance of a certain meaning of a key term, which is often in the form of an if–then statement. If the audience accepts the definition, the arguer says, then the claim should be accepted "by definition."

Examples of Definition

An argument against gay marriage can be laid out as deduction, in the manner shown in the example below. Notice that *if* marriage is defined as a union between a man and a woman, *then* by definition two men or two women cannot marry.

Warrant:	Marriage is defined as the union of a man and a woman.
Support (specific case):	Two people of the same sex are not a man and a woman.
Claim:	Two people of the same sex cannot marry.

For the audience to accept gay marriage, they would have to change their definition of marriage to include a marriage between two men or two women. If that were done, there would no longer be an argument on this subject.

Claim and Support

Look for all definitions or explanations of words or concepts. These may be a sentence, several paragraphs, or an entire essay in length. Notice if the definition is used simply to define a word or if it is used as part of the proof in the argument. Look for a claim that you are expected to accept as a result of the definition.

Definition Warrants

You are expected to assume that the definition describes the fundamental properties and qualities of the term accurately so that it can be used to prove the claim.

Tests of Validity

Is this an accurate and complete definition? Is it convincing in this context? Are there exceptions or other definitions for this term that would make the final claim less reliable?

ARGUMENT FROM STATISTICS

Like other forms of logical proof, statistics describe relationships among data, people, occurrences, and events in the real world, only they do so in quantitative terms.

Modern readers have considerable faith in numbers and statistics. They seem more "true" than other types of support to many people. It is more convincing to some, for example, to make the claim that we should end draft registration because it costs $27.5 million per year than simply to claim that we should end it because we no longer need it.

Read statistical proofs carefully to determine where they come from and how reliable, accurate, and relevant they are. Always note whether the original figures have been altered or interpreted in some way. Figures are often rounded off or stated in different terms, such as percentages or plots on a graph. They are also sometimes compared to other material that is familiar to the audience to make them more interesting or memorable.[3] In addition, the use of various types of graphs or charts makes data and statistics visual and easier to grasp and remember.

Example of Statistics

Here is an example of a use of misleading statistics in an article titled "Can a 15-Year-Old Be a 'Woman without a Spouse'?"[4]

Claim: A majority of American women now live without a spouse.
Support: It is reported that 51 percent of American women live without a spouse.
Warrant: This 51 percent represents a majority.

This article critiques a previous article in a newspaper that reports, "For what experts say is probably the first time, more American women [in 2005] are living without a husband than with one." This was such a striking statistic that the original article appeared on the front page of the newspaper. The subsequent critique of the article pointed out that teenagers, ages fifteen to seventeen, were included in the report, and that 90 percent of that group (6 million) were still living with their parents. One reader pointed out that it was dishonest to include fifteen-year-old women as "women living without a spouse" in the survey because some states do not even permit people to marry at age fifteen. By removing high school age women (ages fifteen to seventeen) from this group, the figure dropped, leaving 48 percent of American women living without a spouse. By eliminating all teenagers and counting only women twenty years or older, the figure dropped to 47 percent, and neither adjusted figure could be presented as a "new majority." Sources for the statistics were the Census Bureau data and the Census Bureau's 2005 American Community Survey. Both are reliable sources. The problem with the report was the inclusion of individuals in it who did not belong, which falsely elevated the figures.

Claim and Support

Look for numbers and data, in both their original and their converted form, graphs and charts of figures, and interpretations of them, including comparisons. Look for a claim based on the data.

---

[3]James Wood, *Speaking Effectively* (New York: Random House, 1988), 121–27.
[4]*New York Times*, February 11, 2007, Op-Ed, 12. Byron Calame, the author of the article, is a public editor, that is, the in-house editor who serves as the readers' representative. He receives complaints about writing or interpretations in articles, checks facts, and critiques accounts in the *New York Times* for fairness and accuracy.

Statistical Warrants

You are expected to assume that the data have been gathered and reported accurately by competent people, that they are representative and complete unless stated otherwise, and that they have been interpreted fairly and truthfully.

Tests of Validity

Where did these statistics come from? To what dates do the statistics apply? How reliable is the source? How accurate are they? How are they presented? Have they been rounded off, changed, or converted? How has the change affected their accuracy? Do they prove what they are supposed to prove? Have they been interpreted fairly, or are they exaggerated or skewed? Has enough backing been provided to prove their reliability? With what are they compared, and how does this comparison contribute to their final significance? Is any significant information left out?

Tests of Validity for Statistics Presented as Graphs

Statistics are sometimes presented in graph form. The tests of validity in this case include these: Where did the information come from? What information is included in the sample? How was it gathered? Is anything significant left out or ignored because it did not fit? Are the charts and graphs labeled accurately? Are there any exaggerations?

LO3 Explain the characteristics of a proof of credibility (*ethos*) and use them in an argument.

Proof That Builds Credibility: *Ethos*

The materials provided in argument that help the audience gain a favorable impression of the arguer, the group the arguer represents, or the authorities and experts the arguer cites help create *ethos*, or the credibility of the author. The author may build credibility by referring to experience and credentials that establish his or her own expertise or the expertise of people who are quoted.

ARGUMENT FROM AUTHORITY

We are usually inclined to accept the opinions and factual evidence of people who are authorities and experts in their fields.

Examples of Authority

In an article that claims California will have another earthquake, the author describes and provides the credentials for several professors of geology from the major universities in Southern California as well as scientists from the U.S. Geological Survey Office before quoting their opinions as support.

> *Claim:* California will have an earthquake.
> *Support:* Professors and scientists say so.
> *Warrant:* These experts are reliable.

Authors themselves sometimes establish their own credentials by making references to various types of past experience that qualify them to write about their subject. They also sometimes assert the *ethos* of the group they represent, in statements like "the great Republican Party," or they establish the group's *ethos* by citing their accomplishments.

Claim and Support

Look for all references to the author's credentials, whether made by the author or by an editor. Look for references to the author's training, education, professional position, background, and experience. Notice, also, references to the audience's concerns, beliefs, and values that demonstrate the author's effort to establish common ground and to show fairness and goodwill toward the audience. Look for references to groups the author may represent, and notice how they are described. Look for direct or paraphrased quotations from experts. Differentiate between facts and statements of opinion. Look for credential statements about these experts. Look for claims that are made more valid because of this expert opinion.

Authoritative Warrants

You are expected to assume that the information provided about the author, the group, or the expert is accurate, that these authorities are honorable, fair, reliable, knowledgeable, and experienced, and that they exhibit goodwill toward the audience.

Tests of Validity

Is there enough information to establish the true character and experience of the author? Is this information complete and accurate? Is there enough information about the group to believe what the author says about it? Are the credentials of the experts good enough to make their contributions reliable? Also, are the credentials relevant to the issue? (A star athlete may not be the best judge of soft drinks or fast food.) If a source is quoted, is the source reliable? Argument based on authority is as good as the authorities themselves.

Types of Emotional Proof: *Pathos*

LO4 Explain the characteristics of an emotional proof (*pathos*) and use them in an argument.

Some argument theorists would say that there should be no appeals to emotion or attempts to arouse the emotions of the audience in argument. The idea is that an argument should appeal only to reason. Emotion, they claim, clouds reasoning and judgment and gets the argument off course. Richard M. Weaver, quoted earlier in this chapter, would disagree. Weaver points out that people are not just austerely unemotional logic machines who are interested only in deduction, induction, and cause-and-effect reasoning. People also use language to communicate feelings, values, and motives.[5]

---

[5]Weaver elaborates on some of the distinctions between logic and emotion in "Language Is Sermonic."

Furthermore, when we consider that the source of much argument lies in the dramatic, emotionally laden occurrences of everyday life, we realize how impossible it is to eliminate all emotion from argument. As you read the many argument essays in this book, study the emotional material that professional writers use. Try to develop a sense of when emotion contributes to argument in effective and appropriate ways and when it does not. In general, emotional proofs are appropriate in argument when the subject itself is emotional and when it creates strong feelings in both the writer and the reader. For writers of argument, emotion leads to positions on issues, influences the tone of the writing, and informs some of the interpretations. For readers, emotion leads to a stronger engagement with the issue and influences the final outcomes. Emotional proof is appropriate when the occasion justifies it and when it strengthens logical conviction. It is inappropriate when it merely gives vent to feelings, serves as an ornament, or distracts the audience from the logical conclusion of the argument. Types of emotional proof focus on *motivation*, what all people want, and on *values*, what we consider good or bad, favorable or unfavorable, acceptable or unacceptable.

MOTIVATIONAL PROOFS

Some proofs appeal explicitly to what all audiences are supposed to want, such as food, drink, warmth and shelter, sex, security, belongingness, self-esteem, creativity, or self-expression. Authors also sometimes appeal to (or through) the opposites of these needs and values, relying on hunger, cold, fear, self-doubt, boredom, or other types of dissatisfaction to motivate people to change their behavior and restore themselves to a more positive state of being. Advertisements aimed at convincing young people that they should avoid taking illegal drugs often show the negative effects of drugs to appeal to people's fears. The purpose of motivational proof is to urge the audience to take prescribed steps to meet an identified need.

Examples of Motivational Proofs

Advertisements and speeches by political candidates provide obvious examples of motivational proof. Drink a certain beer or buy a brand of blue jeans, and you will be irresistible to others. Similarly, support a particular candidate, and you will personally gain job security and safe neighborhoods.

> *Claim:* You should support this candidate.
> *Support:* This candidate can help you get job security and safe neighborhoods.
> *Warrant:* You want job security and safe neighborhoods.

Claim and Support

To find the claim, look for what you are asked to believe or do to get what you want.

Motivational Warrants

Look for references to items or qualities that you might need, want, or fear.

Tests of Validity

What am I supposed to need or fear? Do I really need it or fear it? What am I supposed to do? Will doing what is recommended satisfy the need in the ways described?

VALUE PROOFS

Some proofs appeal to what all audiences are expected to value, such as fairness, reliability, honesty, loyalty, industry, patriotism, courage, integrity, conviction, faithfulness, dependability, creativity, freedom, equality, and devotion to duty.

Examples of Value Proofs

Here is an example that claims that a school curriculum can contribute to the values of equality and acceptance if it is multicultural.

> *Claim:*   The curriculum should be multicultural.
> *Support:* A multicultural curriculum will contribute to equality and acceptance.
> *Warrant:* You value equality and acceptance.

Claim and Support

Look for value statements that are generally accepted by everyone because they have been proved elsewhere many times. Examples include "Freedom of speech is our constitutional right," "There should be no freedom without responsibility," and "Individuals who have the courage of conviction are to be trusted." Look for slogans that display such values as "Honest Abe," "The home of the free and the brave," and "Honesty is the best policy." Or, look for narratives and examples that display values, such as the story of an industrious, thrifty, and ambitious mother who is unemployed. When the values are not directly stated, ask, "What values or beliefs are causing the author to say this?" Look for a claim that shows what will result if the recommended values are accepted.

Value Warrants

You are expected to assume that you share the author's values and that they are as important as the author says they are.

Tests of Validity

What are the values expressed or implicit in this argument? Do I share these values with the author? If not, how do we differ? What effect do these differences have on my final acceptance of the claim?

A MNEMONIC DEVICE

The mnemonic VAM (for *value, authority,* and *motivation*) may help you remember and use the proofs involving *ethos* and *pathos*.

LO5 Explain how language and style convey logic (*logos*), credibility (*ethos*), and emotion (*pathos*) in an argument.

Logos, *Ethos*, and *Pathos* Communicated through Language and Style

You can learn to recognize logic, *ethos*, and emotion in argument not only by the use of proofs but also by the language and style associated with each of these types of appeal. Actually, you will not often encounter pure examples of one of these styles, but instead you will encounter a mix, with one of the styles predominating. The same is true of writing. You may plan to write in a logical style, but emotion and *ethos* seep in and actually help you create a richer and more varied style for your argument.

LANGUAGE THAT APPEALS TO LOGIC

The language of logical argument, which is the language associated with reason, is sometimes called rational style. Words that carry mainly denotative meaning are favored in rational style over connotative and emotionally loaded language. The denotative meaning of a word is the commonly held meaning found in the dictionary. It is the meaning most people would agree on because to denote is to name or indicate specifically. Examples of words that have predominantly denotative meanings and that are emotionally neutral include *introduction, fact, information, question,* and *literal meaning.* Most people would agree on the meanings of those words and could produce synonyms. Words with strong connotative meaning may have many extra, unique, symbolic, or personal meanings and associations attached to them that vary from person to person. Examples of words with connotative meaning include *rock star, politician, mugger, family values,* and *human rights.* Asked to define such words, different people would provide meanings and examples that would not be exactly alike or match the denotative meanings of these words in a dictionary.

For support, rational style relies on opinion in the form of reasons, literal or historical analogies, explanations, and definitions and also on factual data, quotations, and citations from experts and authorities. Furthermore, the reader is usually not required to make as many inferences as for other, less formal styles of writing. Most parts of the argument are spelled out explicitly for the sake of agreement and better adherence of minds.

Slogans that elicit emotional responses, such as "America is the greatest country," "The American people want change," or "Now is the time for healing," are generally omitted in rational style. Slogans of this type substitute for logical thinking. Readers think better and draw better conclusions when provided with well-reasoned opinion, quotations from authorities, and facts.

For example, in the opening paragraph of an essay titled "The Lost Art of Political Argument," Christopher Lasch uses rational style to argue in favor of argument and debate.

> Let us begin with a simple proposition: What democracy requires is public debate, not information. Of course it needs information too, but the kind of

information it needs can be generated only by vigorous popular debate. We do not know what we need to know until we ask the right questions, and we can identify the right questions only by subjecting our own ideas about the world to the test of public controversy. Information, usually seen as the precondition of debate, is better understood as its by-product. When we get into arguments that focus and fully engage our attention, we become avid seekers of relevant information. Otherwise, we take in information passively—if we take it in at all.[6]

Rational style, as you can see in this excerpt, evokes mainly a cognitive, rational response from its readers.

LANGUAGE THAT DEVELOPS *ETHOS*

Authors who seek to establish their own credentials and good character use language to provide a fair-minded view of reality that is restrained and accurate rather than exaggerated or overly opinionated. When language is used to create positive *ethos,* an audience will trust the author as a credible source of information and opinion.

Language that develops *ethos* has several specific characteristics. To begin with, the writer exhibits a consistent awareness of the audience's background and values by adopting a vocabulary level that is appropriate for the topic and the audience. The writer does not either talk down to or overwhelm the audience, use technical jargon for an audience unfamiliar with it, or use slang or colloquial language unless the context specifically calls for that. Rap music, for example, invites a different vocabulary level than a scholarly paper does.

Writers intent on establishing *ethos* are sensitive to different audiences and what they will admire, trust, and accept. They try to use language precisely and to say exactly what they mean. They project an honest desire to communicate by avoiding ranting, filler material that gets off the subject, or anything that the audience would perceive as offensive or repugnant.

As you have probably already realized, an author can destroy *ethos* and alter an audience's favorable impression by changing the language. A student who uses colloquial, everyday expressions in a formal essay written for a professor, a commencement speaker who shouts obscenities at the audience, a father who uses formal, abstract language to talk to his five-year-old—all have made inappropriate language choices for their particular audiences, thereby damaging their *ethos* with those audiences.

When you read argument, notice how an author uses language to build connections and trust as well as to establish reliability with the audience. When you write argument, use language that will help the audience regard you as sincere and trustworthy. Appropriate language is essential when you write a college paper. The use of slang, slogans, and street language and expressions in otherwise formal writing damages your credibility as a serious thinker. Writing errors, including

---

[6]Christopher Lasch, "The Lost Art of Political Argument," *Harper's,* September 1990, 17.

mistakes in spelling, punctuation, and grammar, also destroy *ethos* because they indicate a lack of concern and goodwill for your readers.

Here is an example of language that builds effective *ethos* with an audience. These excerpts come from Martin Luther King Jr.'s "Letter from Birmingham Jail" (pages 313–325). King was jailed because of his involvement in the civil rights movement in Birmingham, Alabama, and he had been criticized publicly for his participation by eight fellow clergymen of that city. He wrote this letter to those clergymen. Notice that he deliberately uses language that is sincere and honest and that establishes his credibility as a trustworthy and responsible human being with values his audience is likely to share. He does not come across as a troublemaker or a man who is angry at the system, as one might find with someone who has been jailed for participating in civil rights demonstrations. Rather, he comes across as thoughtfully conscious of his actions and ethically bound to participate as he is.

My Dear Fellow Clergymen:

While confined here in the Birmingham city jail, I came across your recent statement calling my present activities "unwise and untimely." . . . Since I feel that you are men of genuine good will and that your criticisms are sincerely set forth, I want to try to answer your statement in what I hope will be patient and reasonable terms.

I think I should indicate why I am here in Birmingham, since you have been influenced by the view which argues against "outsiders coming in." . . . I, along with several members of my staff, am here because I was invited here. I am here because I have organizational ties here.

But more basically, I am in Birmingham because injustice is here. Just as the prophets of the eighth century B.C. left their villages and carried their "thus saith the Lord" far beyond the boundaries of their home towns, and just as the Apostle Paul left his village of Tarsus and carried the gospel of Jesus Christ to the far corners of the Greco-Roman world, so am I compelled to carry the gospel of freedom beyond my own home town. Like Paul, I must constantly respond to the Macedonian call for aid.

Moreover, I am cognizant of the interrelatedness of all communities and states. I cannot sit idly by in Atlanta and not be concerned about what happens in Birmingham. Injustice anywhere is a threat to justice everywhere. We are caught in an inescapable network of mutuality, tied in a single garment of destiny. Whatever affects one directly, affects all indirectly. Never again can we afford to live with the narrow, provincial "outside agitator" idea. Anyone who lives inside the United States can never be considered an outsider anywhere within its bounds.

Highlight the language in these passages that you think King used to establish good *ethos* with the eight clergymen. Notice how King deliberately uses language to project sincerity and goodwill toward this audience. He also selects examples and appeals to values that are compatible with their interests and values. King's letter is a classic example of argument that establishes effective *ethos* with a particular audience.

LANGUAGE THAT APPEALS TO EMOTION

References to values and motives summon feelings about what people regard as good and bad and about what they want, and authors use the language associated with emotional style in a variety of ways to express and evoke feelings about these matters. The following paragraphs describe a few special techniques that are characteristic of emotional style. Examples of each are drawn from the essay in Chapter 5 titled "When It's All Too Much," on pages 173–175.

Emotionally loaded language evokes connotative meanings and causes the audience to experience feelings and associations at a personal level that are not described in dictionaries. Here is an example: "I was stunned. A moment or two later, I sputtered out something like, 'I just want regular jeans. You know, the kind that used to be the only kind.'" Underline the words and phrases in the sentence that draw forth your emotions.

Emotional examples engage the emotions, as in this example: "For example, people in one study were asked whether, if they got cancer, they would want to be in charge of their treatment decisions; 65 percent said yes. Unless, however, they actually had cancer. Then only 12 percent said yes. People with cancer have experienced awesome psychological consequences of being responsible for a life-and-death decision, and they don't want that responsibility." Most readers can understand this type of consideration.

Vivid description of an emotional scene creates an emotional reader response, as in this example: "I have a friend who makes going out to dinner a nightmare. He struggles to select a dish and changes his mind repeatedly as his companions sit and stew. And I see my students agonize over which of many paths to follow when they graduate. Many of them are looking for jobs that will give them everything, and they expect to find them." Notice how this description brings you into the scene, causing you to better understand the point the author is making about his own students.

Emotional tone, created by emotional language and examples, indicates that the author has a strong feeling about the subject and wants the audience to share that feeling. Here is an example: "Here we are, living at the pinnacle of human possibility, awash in material abundance. We get what we want, only to discover that it does not satisfy us."

Figurative analogies contribute to emotion in an argument, particularly when two emotional subjects are compared and the resulting effect appeals more to emotion than to reason. For example, the author sums up his argument in the following way: "The success of 21st-century life turns out to be bittersweet." The comparison of modern life and a "bittersweet" edible is supposed to have an emotional effect on the reader.

Emotional style is the easiest of all the styles to recognize because it uses charged language and is often close to our own experiences. Do not become distracted by emotional material or use it excessively in your own arguments. Remember, in argument, logic is the plot and emotion and *ethos* add support. Box 6.1 provides a summary of the characteristics of language used to appeal to reason, to establish *ethos,* and to appeal to emotion.

Box 6.1   A Summary of Language and Style in Argument

▶▶▶ How Do You Make Appeals in Argument?

TO APPEAL TO LOGIC	TO DEVELOP *ETHOS*	TO APPEAL TO EMOTION
Style		
Theoretical abstract language	Language appropriate to audience and subject	Vivid, concrete language
Denotative meanings		Emotionally loaded language
Reasons	Restrained, sincere, fair-minded presentation	Connotative meanings
Literal and historical analogies	Appropriate level of vocabulary	Emotional examples
Explanations	Correct grammar	Vivid descriptions
Definitions		Narratives of emotional events
Factual data and statistics		Emotional tone
Quotations		Figurative analogies
Citations from experts and authorities		
Informed opinion		
Effect		
Evokes a cognitive, rational response	Demonstrates author's reliability, competence, and respect for the audience's ideas and values through reliable and appropriate use of support and general accuracy	Evokes an emotional response

Analyzing Online Argument: The Use of Proofs

In our multimedia environment, proofs come in a variety of forms. Here is a set of steps you can follow to identify and analyze logical, emotional, and *ethos*-based proofs in an online context:

▶▶▶ Step 1: Find an Online Argument and Identify the Proofs

- Which proofs are evident: *logos, pathos,* or *ethos*?

Analyzing Online Argument: The Use of Proofs (*continued*)

▶▶▶ Step 2: Describe the Medium in Which the Proofs Are Found

- Are you examining a Web site, social media post, online video, email, or some other form of online argument?

▶▶▶ Step 3: Identify the Multimedia Features Used to Present the Proofs

- What multimedia elements are used to convey the proofs?

Example

To learn how these steps can be put into practice, let's look at a specific example. The screenshot below comes from a Web site for the Centers for Disease Control and Prevention, a federal government agency tasked with monitoring and ensuring the health and safety of the American public. Look over this selection carefully, as well as the discussion that follows. How does this sample provide a model for analyzing proofs in a digital context?

CDC Home

CDC Centers for Disease Control and Prevention
CDC 24/7: Saving Lives. Protecting People.™

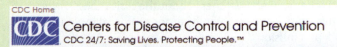

A-Z Index A B C D E F G H I J K L M N O P Q R S T U V W X Y Z #

Drinking Water

For Specific Groups

Public

Public Health & Medical Professionals

Outbreak Response

Drinking Water Advisories

Publications, Data, & Statistics

Drinking water comes from a variety of sources including public water systems, private wells, or bottled water. Ensuring safe and healthy drinking water may be as simple as turning on the tap from an EPA-regulated public water system. Other water sources may need a water filter, a check on water fluoridation, or an inspection to ensure a septic tank is not too close to a private well. It is important to know where drinking water comes from, how it's been treated, and if it's safe to drink.

continued

Analyzing Online Argument: The Use of Proofs (*continued*)

▶▶▶ Step 1: Find an Online Argument and Identify the Proofs

- This Web site employs logical, emotional, and *ethos*-based proofs. The key logical proof involves the cause-and-effect relationship between the CDC's call to verify the quality of water sources on the one hand, and ensuring public health and safety on the other. The emotional proofs here revolve around the image of the young girl drinking from a water fountain, a visual designed to evoke viewer interest and sympathy. The *ethos*-based proofs can be found in the information about the CDC's mission and goals.

▶▶▶ Step 2: Describe the Medium in Which the Proofs Are Found

- The Web site is the homepage for the Center for Disease Control and Prevention, a federal government agency tasked with ensuring public health and safety.

▶▶▶ Step 3: Identify the Multimedia Features Used to Present the Proofs

- A number of the Web site's textual elements are used to present its cause-and-effect proof. Among them is the statement "Ensuring safe and healthy drinking water may be as simple as turning on the tap from an EPA-regulated public water system." The Web site uses visual imagery to present its emotional proof. The key example of this is the image of the young girl at the drinking fountain, which raises viewer awareness about the seriousness of this issue. The Web site uses its interactive features to establish its *ethos* proofs, allowing viewers to learn more about the CDC's work and mission.

Activity

Go online and find examples of arguments that employ each of these proofs. Then use the steps outlined above to analyze how each of these arguments uses its proof.

LO6 Define the value of using these three types of proof for assessing written, visual, and online argument.

Value of the Proofs for Reading, Viewing, and Writing Argument

Analyzing the proofs in an argument focuses a reader's attention on the author's reasoning, use of supporting detail, and warrants. These are the elements in an argument that convince an audience. Applying the tests of validity to the proofs can also help a reader recognize faulty reasoning, which can sometimes reveal a manipulative or immoral purpose in the argument. You will learn more about faulty reasoning in the next chapter. It is not convincing once you figure out how it works.

Viewers of argument, just like readers, should first establish whether a visual image or a Web-based text presents a position on a subject that is open to different interpretations and vantages or serves restrictively as support for a particular position, and then make an attempt to state the claim and analyze the proofs that support it. Look for the ways in which the creator of the image or text appeals to your reason, to your sense of fairness and goodwill, and to your emotions. Warrants and backing will also be present in visual and multimedia arguments. Analyze them to gain further insight into the image as argument. You can also apply the tests of validity to visual argument, just as you would with written argument.

Writers of argument can use the proofs to help them think of ways to develop a claim. By running through the list of proofs and asking relevant questions—What do I need to define? Should I use statistics? Can I generalize from some examples? What caused this? To what can I compare this? Whom should I quote? To what audience values and motives can I appeal?—authors invent and structure ideas and locate material to be used at the concrete, specific level in a paper. The specific material is what makes a paper convincing. Also, thinking about the proofs makes authors more consciously aware of their own warrants and helps them decide whether to make the warrants explicit in the argument or whether to leave them implicit so that the audience has to supply them. Finally, an awareness of proofs can help writers avoid inadequate or irrelevant proof and faulty reasoning in their writing.

The exercises and activities for this chapter will provide you with practice in using the proofs to invent support and warrants for a position paper. The proofs and the tests for validity are summarized for readers, viewers, and writers in the Summary Charts on pages 428–433.

Review Questions

1. Describe logical proofs. Name the seven types of logical proof. (Use the mnemonic SICDADS to help you remember them.) **(LO2)**

2. Describe proofs that build *ethos,* or credibility. Name one type of proof that builds *ethowt.* **(LO3)**

3. Describe emotional proofs. Name two types of emotional support and explain why they appeal to the emotions. **(LO4)**

4. Describe some of the features of the language and style associated with the three types of proof. **(LO5)**

5. How does visual argument employ the proofs? Give an example. **(LO6)**

Exercises and Activities

A. **Class Discussion: Analyzing *Logos, Pathos,* and *Ethos* in an Advertisement**

Study the advertisement on the next page (Image 1), and identify the logical proofs, the emotional proofs, and the proofs that establish *ethos.* Use the mnemonics SICDADS and VAM to help you remember the proofs. Which type of proof is strongest in this public service announcement, in your opinion? How effective is this message overall? Why do you think so?

Image 1:
Underage Drinking

Underage Drinking

At MADD, we know that our hopes for a safer future are riding on tomorrow's drivers. By getting today's youth off to a good start, we are taking a giant step toward fulfilling our vision of a nation without drunk driving. That's why we're focused on tackling underage drinking, a problem that threatens the safety of our kids and endangers entire communities, now and down the road.

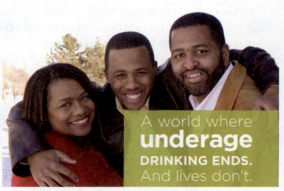

A world where **underage** DRINKING ENDS. And lives don't.

B. Class Discussion: Analyzing the Proofs in an Essay

Underline the material in each paragraph that helps you answer the questions in the margin.

BEFORE YOU READ: What are your present opinions about illegal immigration and undocumented workers in the United States?

ESSAY #1   # STOP CALLING PEOPLE "ALIENS"*

Careen Shannon

Careen Shannon is a lawyer and writer who lives in New York City. This article appeared on Salon.com in 2013.

What kind of context is being established?

The use of the word "illegal" to describe non-citizens who are present in the United States without authorization is finally beginning to die a much-deserved death, at least in the mainstream press. The announcement by the Associated Press on April 2, 2013, that it would no longer use the word "illegal" to describe a person, only a status or an action, was soon followed by a number of other major newspapers, including the *New York Times*—which announced on April 23, 2013, that while it would not ban use of the term "illegal immigrant," it would encourage editors and reporters to consider alternatives. Other news organizations, including the *Miami Herald*, had long since replaced the term "illegal immigrant" with "undocumented immigrant." (Of course, even the word "undocumented" is imprecise. Non-citizens present in the United States without lawful immigration status possess all manner of documents—just not the right ones.)

Despite this trend, the term "alien" remains not only in popular use, but also in the federal statute, the Immigration and Nationality Act, that regulates immigration to the United States. The text of the recently introduced comprehensive immigration reform bill authored by a bipartisan "Gang of Eight" U.S. senators does nothing to upset this long-standing practice. Like the Japanese word "gaijin," the word "alien" serves to exclude those upon whom it is bestowed. Some might argue that the fact that the word is embedded in our very law would seem to belie any suggestion of stigma associated with the word. After all, *Black's Law Dictionary* defines "alien" rather dispassionately as "[a] person who resides within the borders of a country but is not a citizen or subject of that country." So what if the "regular" dictionary also says that "alien" means "strange" or "repugnant" or "in science fiction, a being in or from outer space and not native to the Earth; extraterrestrial"? That has nothing to do with immigration, or how we treat immigrants, does it?

Actually, it does. There is a well-developed body of scholarship on the racist roots of U.S. immigration laws and how the term "alien"—and, even more perniciously, "illegal alien"—has been used to define and exclude those foreign nationals who are viewed as unwelcome, whether because of race, religion, language, culture, poverty, or some combination of the above. There is little doubt that, as professor Kevin R. Johnson, dean of the University of California at Davis School of Law, has put it, "[t]he concept of the alien has . . . subtle social consequences. . . . [I]t helps to reinforce and strengthen nativist sentiment toward members of new immigrant groups, which in turn influences U.S. responses to immigration and human rights issues." And sometimes, the social consequences are not so subtle: witness Arizona's notorious immigration enforcement law (S.B. 1070), which requires law enforcement officers making lawful stops to check the immigration status of any person reasonably suspected of being an "alien" who is unlawfully present in the United States.

All of this still begs the question: Why "alien"? How did the specific term "alien"—which means not just non-citizen or non-national but, in a certain sense, non-person—become an accepted legal definition, and colloquial description, of the immigrant under U.S. law? Would using a different word change the public's attitude toward immigrants? And what does outer space have to do with it?

Etymology of Alien as Foreigner

5 The word "alien" is thought to have entered the English language sometime between 1300 and 1350 from the Latin (with a stop along the way at Middle French). The Latin word "alienus" derived from the earlier "alius," meaning "other" or "else." So an "alien" is, essentially, someone who comes from somewhere else.

According to the *Oxford English Dictionary* (*OED*), use of the word "alien" in the way most closely approximating its usage in U.S. immigration jurisprudence—as a noun, meaning "[a] person belonging to another family, race, or nation; a stranger, a foreigner," especially "[o]ne who is a subject of another country than that in which he resides"—first appears in the written English language in 1330. In 1384, the Wycliffe Bible, a translation of the Latin Vulgate Bible into Middle English, also used the word "alyenys" (aliens) as a noun. A later usage—"All Alienys ai banyst hale"—is from a history of Scotland from 1425 (and means something like "all aliens are banished to a remote place"). The *OED* cites the first legal usage as dating from 1522, when a law passed under Henry VIII provided, "No Stranger, being Alien borne . . . shall take, retaine or keep into his or their seruices any maner of Journyman."

Fast-forward to early American jurisprudence, and the U.S. Constitution gives Congress the power "[t]o establish an uniform Rule of Naturalization." The Naturalization Act of 1790—the first American law touching at all on the subject of immigration—provided the first such set of rules, allowing Congress to naturalize "any Alien being a free White person," so long as such person met certain residence requirements, established that he or she was a person of good moral character, and took an oath or affirmation to support the Constitution of the United States. And thus was the word "alien" enshrined in U.S. immigration law.

Aliens as Other

Describe the analogy. Why is it used here?

Notwithstanding the fact that "alien" is embodied in our law as a term of art, and that its first dictionary definition simply means "foreigner," not only does its second definition as "strange" or "repugnant" give the word a certain stench, its third definition as "extraterrestrial" enhances its dehumanizing effect. When I was called "E.T." in Japan many years ago, I could laugh it off because I knew that I would be returning to the United States once my graduate fellowship was complete. It did not have any long-lasting effect on how I perceived myself as a human being. For immigrants to the United States, whether they are here without authorization or have immigrated through statutorily sanctioned channels, the lingering after-effects of the designation are undoubtedly harder to shake off.

What do these analogies prove?

Among many American indigenous peoples, the word a group or tribe uses to refer to itself often means something like "human being." For example, students of anthropology invariably learn about anthropologist Napoleon Chagnon's encounters with the Yanomami (or Yanomamö) people, an isolated Amazonian tribe who live in the remote rain forest of southern Venezuela and northern Brazil. The word "Yanomami" means "human being" in the tribe's language and was adopted by Chagnon to refer both to the culture and the people, though he may not have initially known what the word actually meant to the Yanomami themselves. Another example: While Europeans adopted the term "Eskimo" to refer to the indigenous peoples in Alaska, northern Canada and Greenland without realizing that it was actually a (possibly pejorative) description accorded them by neighboring ethnic groups, the so-called Eskimos called themselves "Inuit," which simply means "people."

Describe the deductive reasoning in this paragraph.

10   Conversely, the words for "foreigner" in many languages reflect the users' perception that the person referred to is most decidedly different in

some fundamental way. For example, the Cantonese word used to refer to Europeans (i.e., white people) is "gwai lo" (or "gwei lo"), which means "ghost person," and is sometimes translated into English as "foreign devil." The predecessor word to "gaijin" in Japanese was "nanbanjin," literally "southern barbarian people," referring to the Portuguese—the first Europeans to visit Japan—who arrived in ships sailing from the south. In Europe, the Vikings were considered savages or barbarians by those whom they invaded—the word "barbarian" deriving from the Greek "barbaros" ("foreign, strange, ignorant") and "barbaroi" ("all that are not Greek"). Calling people from foreign lands by names that reflect one's own prejudices appears to be a consistent trait across cultures, and there is no dearth of examples of how human beings tend to adopt dehumanizing appellations for those perceived as "other."

Describe the inductive reasoning in this paragraph.

Discomfort with the "other" is also revealed in the problematic issue of cross-racial eyewitness identification, which numerous empirical studies have demonstrated are notoriously unreliable. Attributing such misidentifications to deliberate racism, however, may miss the point. The cause can just as easily be something less malevolent but equally unsettling: sheer unfamiliarity with one another's faces, notwithstanding the fact that people of different races often live side-by-side (at least in large urban areas) in this country, and see each other in movies and on television on a daily basis. In 2001, John Rutledge, an attorney now in private practice in Nevada, hypothesized as much, based on his unique experience of having been one of the few Caucasian students in the predominantly African-American student body at Howard University School of Law, and citing a number of psychological studies to support his personal conclusion that prior to matriculating at Howard, he was quite simply unfamiliar with the physiognomic variety of African-American faces. It seems he may have been on to something, as a more recent study found that exposing Caucasian subjects to African-American faces significantly improved their ability to differentiate them.

Describe the cause-effect argument in this paragraph. What idea does it establish?

Aliens as Extraterrestrials

What does outer space have to do with any of this? As it turns out, the use of the word "alien" to refer to creatures from outer space is much more recent than one might imagine. The earliest references in the OED Online date from stories in a pulp science fiction magazine, *Wonder Stories*, in 1929 (the "alien intelligence") and 1932 (the "alien ship"). In both cases, the word is used as an adjective, not a noun. But science fiction also contains some uses of "alien" as a noun to refer to extraterrestrials dating from the same general period. In 1935, Earl Binder wrote of a "Robot Alien" in *Wonder Stories*. In 1931, Nat Schachner & Arthur Leo Zagat wrote about "ten-foot tall aliens" in *Venus Mines*. And in 1912, Edgar Rice Burroughs (best known for his Tarzan stories) has a Martian character in "A Princess of Mars" call earthling John Carter "an alien." Still, in the scheme of things, the use of "alien" to refer to extraterrestrial creatures is really quite recent.

So what does this all mean? Well, it turns out that we had already been calling foreigners aliens for centuries before we started using the word to refer

What kind of logical proof is being offered here and in the next paragraph? What is the warrant?

to extraterrestrials. So it's not that we think foreigners resemble Martians, *it's that we think Martians resemble foreigners.* Put another way: It is not the case that, the first time we saw a foreigner, he reminded us of a Martian. Rather, when we in the English-speaking world first conceived of the possibility—or at least first started writing about the notion—that there might be Martians (green skin and all that), we imagined them to be akin to foreigners. This actually has interesting sociological implications. Could this account, for example, for why people who insist they are not racist often do so by saying something like, "I don't care if you're black, white, green or purple . . ."?

Why is it important to recognize that we appear to have named extra-terrestrials after foreigners, rather than the other way around? Because it shows just how very much we fear what is different. It also suggests that until we demystify foreigners—perhaps by remembering that apart from Native Americans, we are all descendants of immigrants, i.e., foreigners, in this country—we will just, at best, find a new euphemism to name that which makes us uncomfortable.

The Importance of the Power to Name

15   "Gaijin" is now considered to be politically incorrect. In at least some circles, so is "alien." Do we care?

What generalization about language does the author draw from her college practices?

Another personal anecdote: As a college student—and an English major, no less—I insisted on spelling woman as "womon" and women as "womyn" in all of my papers. I would include an introductory paragraph or footnote in every paper explaining the political and etymological reasons (something along the lines of "woman" deriving from the Old English "wifman," a compound of "wif" [female] and "man" [human being], therefore essentially defining man as the norm, and woman as the exception). I also consistently wrote "s/he" instead of "he" as a generic singular pronoun. But that's not the best part. The best part is that no professor ever objected to these grammatical choices I made—or even mentioned them. Granted, this was at Oberlin College, in the 1970s. In few other times or places could such a feat have been accomplished with a straight face, much less with a decent grade point average. Readers will note that I have long since abandoned the practice. But was the instinct entirely misplaced? I think not. Even if my college-era feminist linguistic choices were based, in part, on a kind of politically correct folk etymology, there was a real point to be made: Language has power. Changes in how language is used can lead to changes in how power is wielded.

How does quoting Cumming contribute to the *ethos* of the writer

Linguists talk about euphemism (starting with the Greek root "eu," "good") and dysphemism (from the Greek root "dus," "bad") as, in the words of Susanna Cumming, formerly a professor of linguistics at the University of California at Santa Barbara, "terms [that] give us ways of talking about the evaluative content of language: that part which doesn't describe a thing in the world, but rather expresses the speaker's attitude towards it." "Euphemism" can thus be defined as "making something sound better," and "dysphemism" as "making something sound worse." As Professor

Cumming has put it, "A euphemism is used as an alternative to a dispreferred expression, in order to avoid possible loss of face: either one's own face or, through giving offence, that of the audience, or of some third party."

What is the general principle this example is designed to illustrate?

For example, think about the following words: the N-word, negro, colored, black, African-American. How do these words make you feel? Do you think that your race might make a real difference in how you react when you hear or read these words? What about the following: imbecile, insane, retarded, mentally ill, mentally challenged, developmentally disabled? How about deformed, crippled, handicapped, differently abled? It's almost as if there should be a line, a fill-in-the-blank, at the end of all of those strings of words. After all, we're bound to come up with new terms soon, aren't we? These changes "arise through a process called pejorization: a neutral or even euphemistic word for a 'bad' thing comes to be seen as a 'bad' word (which then needs to be replaced with another euphemism)." In each of the examples provided above, "a formerly neutral term becomes dysphemistic and has to be replaced."

What motives and values are appealed to in this paragraph?

Let's bring this closer to home. Be honest, now: Which of the following is closer to what comes to mind when you hear the term "illegal alien" or "undocumented alien"—a German graduate student who has overstayed her visa, or a Mexican laborer who has illegally crossed our southern border? I think it's a safe bet that, whatever your political persuasion, you were more likely to think of the Mexican. Many have argued for replacing "alien" (or "illegal alien") with some other term. ("What about immigrant, undocumented immigrant . . . or human being?" asks Kevin Johnson, reasonably enough.) Among those who work in the area of international human rights law on issues of global migration, the somewhat bureaucratic term "irregular migrant" has become chic in recent years. Are we just taking political correctness to a ridiculous extreme?

Underline examples of emotionally loaded language.

20   Again, I think not. The power inherent in the ability to ascribe names is real, as is the impact on the named. Nowadays, it is socially unacceptable for a white man to call a black man "boy," but for years this was accepted practice in polite society—and, it is now commonly understood, not only reflected white society's racism but served to perpetuate the oppression of African-American men. Calling a grown woman a "girl" has a similarly belittling effect, and the fact that the practice has not yet been universally repudiated tells us something important about the continued inequality of women in American society. As Professor Catherine MacKinnon of the University of Michigan Law School has written, "Social inequality is substantially created and enforced—that is, *done*—through words and images." Referring to immigrants as "aliens," when "alien" is commonly understood to be derogatory (whether because it means foreign, or strange, or brings images of extraterrestrial space creatures to mind), not only reflects immigrants' place in American society, but in a very real way it enforces it. Laurie Berg, an Australian legal scholar, agrees, and has said, "[T]hese characterisations matter . . . [T]he labels which attach to . . . migrants . . . also function to delineate the precise capacity in which they are accorded rights."

Analyze how definition is used in this argument.

In her seminal book, *Language and Woman's Place*, linguist Robin Lakoff declared that "[l]inguistic imbalances are worthy of study because they bring into sharper focus real-world imbalances and inequalities. They are clues that some external situation needs changing . . ." While she was specifically discussing terms she considered demeaning to women, her point is equally relevant to terms that are demeaning to immigrants.

We can agree to stop using the word "alien" to refer to immigrants, agree that it is demeaning and causes real damage to the individuals concerned. However, a new euphemism alone won't solve the problem. While the term "irregular migrant" might seem to be less demeaning than "illegal alien" or "undocumented alien"—better, then, than any phrase that includes the word "alien"—the term still implies that there is something not-regular, not "normal," about the people concerned. To the extent that "irregular migrant" or some other term (other, that is, than "human being") replaces "alien" in popular, legal and academic discourse, it will only temporarily paper over the truth about such migrants' place in society.

What cause-effect reasoning is used here? How does it contribute to the conclusion?

Robin Lakoff has also said that "linguistic and social change go hand in hand: one cannot, purely by changing language use, change social status." It is, however, sometimes difficult to tease out what is cause and what is effect. Does social change create language change, or does language change create social change? According to Lakoff, "[A]t best, language change influences changes in attitudes slowly and indirectly, and these changes in attitudes will not be reflected in social change unless society is receptive already." But as a member of a community of lawyers, scholars, advocates and others who work with, and care deeply about the plight of, immigrants in this country, I feel that we have a duty to do what we can to make society receptive already. So let's stop calling non-citizens aliens. Let's just call them people.

For Discussion:

What is the issue? What is the author's position on the issue? Read the title and the final paragraph of the essay. Then state the claim of the essay. What logical proofs does the author use to prove her claim? Which is most effective? Why? How does she engage your emotions? How does she build *ethos*? Are these strategies convincing?

Arguing Like a Citizen

In her essay "Stop Calling People 'Aliens,'" Careen Shannon uses *logos, ethos,* and *pathos*-based proofs to make her argument about the need to change the language typically used to discuss illegal immigration. In order to better understand how these proofs work, as well as the ways they connect to the question of citizenship, look closely at the sample discussion below.

Arguing Like a Citizen (*continued*)

▶▶▶ Thinking Like a Citizen

- Why do I care about this issue?
  The question of how we discuss illegal immigration matters to me because I believe it's important that political discussions present issues in the most accurate and objective way. If this (or any) debate is tainted by inflammatory language, it becomes much more difficult to make informed decisions about this issue as a citizen and a voter.

- Who else cares about this issue?
  Another constituency with a clear stake in this discussion are those immigrant residents in the United States who are undocumented. For this group, discussions over the proper terminology to use in the immigration debate have both a practical impact (What should the policy regarding illegal immigration be?) and an emotional impact (What language is acceptable to describe people who are undocumented in the United States?).

▶▶▶ Arguing Like a Citizen

- What proofs would I find persuasive?
  Logos: As someone interested in improving the accuracy and objectivity of political debate, I would be greatly persuaded by the logical argument that changing the terminology around this discussion would increase the opportunity for voters to make reasoned, informed decisions.
  Ethos: In a similar vein, I would also be persuaded by arguments that supported this argument with: (1) personal testimony that establishes the writer's authority to speak on this subject and (2) data, statistics, or studies that prove how effective this shift in language would be.
  Pathos: Recognizing that this issue raises questions about dignity and fairness, I would also be persuaded by an argument that uses personal testimonials about the struggles of undocumented people themselves as proof.

▶▶▶ Acting Like a Citizen

- What concrete actions could I take to make these proofs more effective?
  Logos: To help enhance the accuracy or objectivity of the immigration discussion, I could contact my state and local officials and urge them to employ different language in their own public discussion of this issue.
  Ethos: To help enhance the authority or credibility of this argument, I could interview various experts and stakeholders in this debate (academics, policymakers, advocates), asking them for their suggestions about the proper language to use in discussing illegal immigration.

continued

Arguing Like a Citizen (*continued*)

Pathos: To increase the emotional appeal of this argument, I might create a venue (i.e., Web site, campus meeting, etc.) that allows people who have had firsthand experience with the immigration system to share their own personal stories.

Activity

Choose an issue that is of particular interest or importance within your community. First, describe this issue. What are the key questions associated with it? What are the main disagreements different people have about it? What individuals or groups do these discussions involve? Next, put yourself in the role of someone involved in this discussion. What position or perspective would you advance? And what plan of action would you advocate for implementing your perspective in your community? Create language in support of your position using each of the three types of support: *logos, ethos,* and *pathos.* And finally, when you are finished, write an assessment of the types of support you felt were most effective, and say why.

C. Group Work and Discussion: Analyzing an Essay and Supporting Images

Read Essay #2, below, and then study Images 2 and 3 on page 218, which illustrate some of the assertions in the essay.

BEFORE YOU READ: What images or associations come to mind when you hear the word poverty? How do you define this term?

ESSAY #2   POVERTY IN AMERICA: CONSEQUENCES FOR INDIVIDUALS AND THE ECONOMY

This excerpt is part of the testimony presented by the government General Accountability Office to the U.S. House of Representatives Ways and Means Committee in 2007.

Approximately 13 percent of the total population live below the poverty line, as defined by the Census Bureau. Poverty imposes costs on the nation in terms of both programmatic outlays and productivity losses that can affect the economy as a whole. To better understand the potential range of effects of poverty, GAO was asked to examine (1) what the economic research tells us about the relationship between poverty and adverse social conditions, such as poor health outcomes, crime, and labor force attachment, and (2) what links economic research has found between poverty and economic growth. To answer these questions, GAO reviewed the economic literature by academic experts, think tanks, and government agencies, and reviewed additional literature by searching various databases for peer-reviewed economic journals, specialty journals, and books. We also provided our draft report for review by experts on this topic.

Economic research suggests that individuals living in poverty face an increased risk of adverse outcomes, such as poor health and criminal activity, both of which may lead to reduced participation in the labor market. While the mechanisms by which poverty affects health are complex, some research suggests that adverse health outcomes can be due, in part, to limited access to health care as well as greater exposure to environmental hazards and engaging in risky behaviors. For example, some research has shown that increased availability of health insurance such as Medicaid for low-income mothers led to a decrease in infant mortality. Additionally, exposure to higher levels of air pollution from living in urban areas close to highways can lead to acute health conditions. Data suggest that engaging in risky behaviors, such as tobacco and alcohol use, a sedentary life-style, and a low consumption of nutritional foods, can account for some health disparities between lower and upper income groups. The economic research we reviewed also points to links between poverty and crime. For example, one study indicated that higher levels of unemployment are associated with higher levels of property crime. The relationship between poverty and adverse outcomes for individuals is complex, in part because most variables, like health status, can be both a cause and a result of poverty. These adverse outcomes affect individuals in many ways, including limiting their development of the skills, abilities, knowledge, and habits necessary to fully participate in the labor force.

Research shows that poverty can negatively affect economic growth by affecting the accumulation of human capital and rates of crime and social unrest. Economic theory has long suggested that human capital—that is, the education, work experience, training, and health of the workforce—is considered one of the fundamental drivers of economic growth. The conditions associated with poverty can work against this human capital development by limiting individuals' ability to remain healthy and develop skills, in turn decreasing the potential to contribute talents, ideas, and even labor to the economy. An educated labor force, for example, is better at learning, creating and implementing new technologies. Economic theory suggests that when poverty affects a significant portion of the population, these effects can extend to the society at large and produce slower rates of growth. Although historically research has focused mainly on the extent to which economic growth alleviates poverty, some recent empirical studies have begun to demonstrate that higher rates of poverty are associated with lower rates of growth in the economy as a whole. For example, areas with higher poverty rates experience, on average, slower per capita income growth rates than low-poverty areas.

For Discussion:

What are some of the consequences of poverty? Why should government officials be concerned with this problem? What authorities are cited to make this argument about poverty? What is the effect? What statistics could be added to make this argument even more effective?

Examine two images that support the ideas in Essay #2. Images 2 and 3 are relevant to the Congressional testimony on poverty you just read. Photographs like these, which portray poverty in America, frequently appear as visual support when foundations or other groups seek money to alleviate economic misfortune

Image 2:
Tenements in Holyoke, Massachusetts

Why does this photograph qualify as a visual argument? What claim does it make?

Image 3:
Little Girl on Bed in Rundown Bedroom

This photo did not appear as part of an essay about poverty in America, but it could still be read as a commentary on this issue. How does this photograph qualify as a visual argument about poverty in America? What details stand out as evidence or proof? Do you think it would be an appropriate supplement to the GAO Congressional testimony? How or how not?

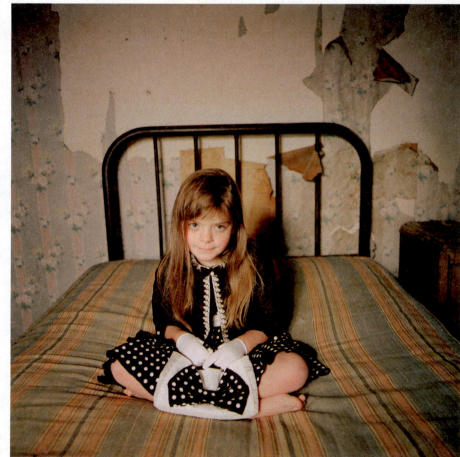

described in the testimony. In adding visual proof to support an argument, an author needs to make an appropriate choice. With that in mind, look at the images and answer the questions that follow.

1. How would you characterize the type of visual proof that predominates in Images 2 and 3? Is it logical, emotional, or does it establish someone's *ethos*?

2. Which of these visual proofs do you think provides the most appropriate support for the information presented in the Congressional testimony, Image 2 or Image 3?

3. Consider the rhetorical situation for this testimony. Who is presenting this testimony? Who is the audience?

4. How might a display of these images create a stronger message?

D. Writing Assignment: Logical and Emotional Proofs in Online Argument

1. Study the CDC Web site in "Analyzing Online Argument: The Use of Proofs" (page 205). Then answer the following questions:

   ▶ What is the issue this Web site addresses?

   ▶ What argument about this issue is being made here?

   ▶ In what ways does this Web site rely on logical proofs? Can you identify them?

   ▶ In what ways does this Web site rely on emotional proofs? Can you identify them?

2. Write a 300- to 400-word essay that describes the logical and emotional proofs that appear in the CDC Web site.

E. Writing Assignment: Proofs and Style in the Declaration of Independence

The Declaration of Independence, a classic argument, was written by Thomas Jefferson in 1776 to explain why the American colonies wanted to separate from Great Britain. It established America as independent states, and thus it is a revolutionary document with a revolutionary purpose.

1. Read the Declaration of Independence. To understand it better, divide it into its three major component parts. Draw a line at the end of part 1, which explains the general principles behind the revolutionary action. Then draw a line at the end of part 2, which lists the reasons for the action. Finally, identify the purpose of the third and last brief part of the document.

2. The document presents an argument with the value warrants stated in part 1, the support in part 2, and the conclusion in part 3. Summarize the ideas in each part of the argument.

3. Test the argument by questioning the warrants and the support. Do you agree with them? If you accept them, you accept the conclusion.

4. Identify some of the proofs in the document, and comment on their soundness and effectiveness.

5. Describe the predominant style in the document, and give examples that support your answer.

6. Write a 250-word paper in which you explain the insights you now have about the structure, proofs, and style of the Declaration of Independence.

BEFORE YOU READ: What do you remember about the writing of the Declaration of Independence?

ESSAY #3   # THE DECLARATION OF INDEPENDENCE
Thomas Jefferson

The Declaration of Independence was approved by Congress on July 2, 1776, and published two days later.

When in the course of human events, it becomes necessary for one people to dissolve the political bands which have connected them with another, and to assume among the Powers of the earth, the separate and equal station to which the Laws of Nature and of Nature's God entitle them, a decent respect to the opinions of mankind requires that they should declare the causes which impel them to the separation.

We hold these truths to be self-evident, that all men are created equal, that they are endowed by their Creator with certain unalienable Rights, that among these are Life, Liberty and the pursuit of Happiness.

That to secure these rights, Governments are instituted among Men, deriving their just powers from the consent of the governed.

That whenever any Form of Government becomes destructive of these ends, it is the Right of the People to alter or to abolish it, and to institute a new Government, laying its foundation on such principles and organizing its powers in such form, as to them shall seem most likely to effect their Safety and Happiness. Prudence, indeed, will dictate that Governments long established should not be changed for light and transient causes; and accordingly all experience hath shown that mankind are more disposed to suffer, while evils are sufferable, than to right themselves by abolishing the forms to which they are accustomed. But when a long train of abuses and usurpations pursuing invariably the same Object evinces a design to reduce them under absolute Despotism, it is their right, it is their duty, to throw off such government, and to provide new Guards for their future security.

5   Such has been the patient sufferance of these Colonies, and such is now the necessity which constrains them to alter their former Systems of Government. The history of the present King of Great Britain is a history of repeated injuries and usurpations, all having in direct object the establishment of an absolute Tyranny over these States. To prove this, let Facts be submitted to a candid world.

He has refused his Assent to Laws, the most wholesome and necessary for the public good.

He has forbidden his Governors to pass Laws of immediate and pressing importance, unless suspended in their operation till his Assent should be obtained; and when so suspended, he has utterly neglected to attend to them.

He has refused to pass over Laws for the accommodation of large districts of people, unless those people would relinquish the right of Representation in the Legislature, a right inestimable to them and formidable to tyrants only.

He has called together legislative bodies at places unusual, uncomfortable, and distant from the depository of their Public Records, for the sole purpose of fatiguing them into compliance with his measures.

10 He has dissolved Representative Houses repeatedly, for opposing with manly firmness his invasions on the rights of the people.

He has refused for a long time, after such dissolutions, to cause others to be elected; whereby the Legislative Powers, incapable of Annihilation, have returned to the People at large for their exercise; the State remaining in the meantime exposed to all the dangers of invasion from without, and convulsions within.

He has endeavored to prevent the population of these States; for that purpose obstructing the Laws for Naturalization of Foreigners; refusing to pass others to encourage their migration hither, and raising the conditions of new Appropriations of Lands.

He has obstructed the Administration of Justice, by refusing his Assent to Laws for establishing Judiciary Powers.

He has made Judges dependent on his Will alone, for the tenure of their offices, and the amount and payment of their salaries.

15 He has erected a multitude of New Offices, and sent hither swarms of Officers to harass our People, and eat out their substance.

He has kept among us, in time of peace, Standing Armies without the consent of our legislatures.

He has affected to render the Military independent of and superior to the Civil Power.

He has combined with others to subject us to jurisdictions foreign to our constitution, and unacknowledged by our laws; giving his Assent to their acts of pretended Legislation:

For quartering large bodies of armed troops among us:

20 For protecting them, by a mock Trial, from Punishment for any Murders which they should commit on the inhabitants of these States:

For cutting off our Trade with all parts of the world:

For imposing Taxes on us without our Consent:

For depriving us in many cases of the benefits of Trial by Jury:

For transporting us beyond Seas to be tried for pretended offenses:

25 For abolishing the free System of English Laws in a neighboring Province, establishing therein an Arbitrary government, and enlarging its Boundaries so as to render it at once an example and fit instrument for introducing the same absolute rule into these Colonies:

For taking away our Charters, abolishing our most valuable Laws, and altering fundamentally the Forms of our Governments:

For suspending our own Legislatures, and declaring themselves invested with Power to legislate for us in all cases whatsoever.

He has abdicated Government here, by declaring us out of his Protection and waging War against us.

He has plundered our seas, ravaged our Coasts, burnt our towns, and destroyed the Lives of our people.

30 He is at this time transporting large Armies of foreign Mercenaries to complete the works of death, desolation and tyranny, already begun with circumstances of Cruelty & perfidy scarcely paralleled in the most barbarous ages, and totally unworthy the Head of a civilized nation.

He has constrained our fellow Citizens taken Captive on the high Seas to bear Arms against their Country, to become the executioners of their friends and Brethren, or to fall themselves by their Hands.

He has excited domestic insurrections amongst us, and has endeavored to bring on the inhabitants of our frontiers, the merciless Indian Savages, whose known rule of warfare is an undistinguished destruction of all ages, sexes and conditions.

In every stage of these Oppressions We have Petitioned for Redress in the most humble terms: Our repeated Petitions have been answered only by repeated injury. A Prince, whose character is thus marked by every act which may define a Tyrant, is unfit to be the ruler of a free people.

Nor have We been wanting in attention to our British brethren. We have warned them from time to time of attempts by their legislature to extend an unwarrantable jurisdiction over us. We have reminded them of the circumstances of our emigration and settlement here. We have appealed to their native justice and magnanimity, and we have conjured them by the ties of our common kindred to disavow these usurpations, which would inevitably interrupt our connections and correspondence. They too have been deaf to the voice of justice and of consanguinity. We must, therefore, acquiesce in the necessity, which denounces our Separation, and hold them, as we hold the rest of mankind, Enemies in War, in Peace Friends.

35   We, therefore, the Representatives of the *United States of America*, in General Congress, Assembled, appealing to the Supreme Judge of the world for the rectitude of our intentions, do, in the Name, and by authority of the good People of these Colonies, solemnly publish and declare, That these United Colonies are, and of Right ought to be Free and Independent States; that they are Absolved from all Allegiance to the British Crown, and that all political connection between them and the State of Great Britain, is and ought to be totally dissolved; and that as Free and Independent States, they have full power to levy War, conclude Peace, contract Alliances, establish Commerce, and to do all other Acts and Things which independent States may of right do. And for the support of this Declaration, with a firm reliance on the protection of Divine Providence, we mutually pledge to each other our Lives, our Fortunes and our sacred Honor.

For Discussion:

Describe the rhetorical situation for the Declaration of Independence. Why is it usually described as a "revolutionary document"? What are the four "self-evident" truths mentioned in this document? Do all people have equal claim to the rights described here, or can you think of constraining circumstances when certain individuals might be denied these rights? Do individuals pursue these rights, or do governments guarantee them? What is the difference? Discuss.

F. Prewriting: Using the Proofs to Generate Ideas for a Position Paper

You have analyzed other authors' use of proofs in the preceding exercises. Now think about how you can use the proofs in your own writing. Use the mnemonics SICDADS and VAM to help you consider the proofs and ask the following questions. Write out answers for those that are most promising.

1. *Signs:* What symptoms or signs will demonstrate that this is so?

2. *Induction:* What examples can I use and what conclusions can I draw from them? Are they convincing enough to help the reader make the "inductive leap"?

3. *Cause:* What has caused this? Why is this happening? Think of explanations and examples of both cause and effect.

4. *Deduction:* What concluding statements do I want to make? What general principles and examples (or cases) are they based on?

5. *Analogies:* How can I show that what happened in one case will probably happen again in another case? Can I use a literal analogy to compare items in the same general category? Can I use a figurative analogy to compare items from different categories? Can I demonstrate that history repeats itself by citing a historical analogy?

6. *Definition:* What words or concepts will I need to define?

7. *Statistics:* What statistics can I use? Would they be more convincing in graph form?

8. *Values:* To what values can I appeal? Should I spell them out or leave them implicit? Will narratives and emotional language make my appeals to values stronger?

9. *Authority:* Whom should I quote? What can I use from my own background and experience to establish my own expertise? How can I use language to create common ground and establish *ethos*?

10. *Motives:* What does my audience need and want in regard to this topic? How can I appeal to those needs? Will emotional language help?

11. *Visual proof:* Could I strengthen my paper with visual proof, if that is part of the assignment? What could I use?

The Fallacies and Ethical Argument

After studying this chapter, you will be able to:

LO1 Identify and describe the different types of logical fallacies in argument.

LO2 Identify and describe the different types of fallacies that affect *ethos* or character in argument.

LO3 Identify and describe the different types of emotional fallacies in argument.

LO4 Describe the characteristics of ethical argument, and use them in creating your own argument.

In an advertisement for a health club, an attractive, muscular man is embracing a beautiful, slim woman. Both are dressed in exercise clothing. The caption reads, "Studies show diets don't work. This picture shows exercise does." No further evidence is provided. You do not have to be an expert in argument theory to sense that something is wrong with this proof.

There are encounters in arguments, as in the case of the advertisement just described, in which a reader will find material that may appear at first to be a proof but really is not a proof at all—it is a *pseudoproof*, or what is commonly called a *fallacy*. Fallacies lead an audience astray, they distort and distract, they represent inadequate reasoning or nonreasoning, and they either exaggerate or oversimplify a claim instead of proving it.

The author of the advertisement in the opening example expects the reader to accept a number of unstated warrants that most people would reject were they explicitly stated: (1) the studies about dieting are a reasonable sample to show that dieting does not change the shape of your body; (2) the best way to take up effective exercise and develop a well-shaped body is to join an exercise club; and (3) if you improve the shape of your body, you will find romance on the floor of the exercise club. The visual support is the picture of the two attractive people who are embracing in their exercise clothes. The final claim, based on those warrants and that support, of course, is that you should join the exercise club.

Suppose you encounter the exercise club advertisement at a time when you feel overweight, out of shape, and unloved. You might be tempted to believe the argument because the warrants and the support reflect what you would wish to believe or want to be so. Fallacies can seem convincing when they appear to support what an audience already believes or wants to believe.

Warrants that few people would find convincing can create the common ground necessary for successful argument if they hold an emotional appeal to someone's deep prejudices, unreasonable biases, or irrational beliefs or wishes. You may have encountered Web sites like those supported by hate groups, for example, that present support and warrants that you would never find acceptable. As you analyze the reasoning on these sites, you discover that it is extremist and that it supports only one narrow view. The support is often distorted, insufficient, unreliable, exaggerated, or oversimplified. Furthermore, the warrants are untrue, and emotional material is used to stir up excessive feelings rather than to prove a rational point. You can also often identify a number of specific fallacies on such sites.

When you are tempted to believe an argument that does not seem logical to you or seems to have something wrong with it, consider why you are tempted to believe it. If fallacies and unacceptable reasoning are weakening the claim or proving the argument false, analyze it and expose these problems.

You will encounter fallacies in advertisements or other visual media, letters to the editor, some forms of journalism such as blogs, and other argument writing that you find both in print and online. Avoid quoting sources that contain fallacies, and avoid fallacies in your own writing. Fallacies in your writing, whether created by you or by the authors you choose to quote, weaken your argument and damage your *ethos*. Recognize fallacies by asking, "Is this material even relevant? Is it adequate? Do I agree? Does it support the claim?" Learning the common types of fallacies will also help you recognize and avoid them. Described here are the most common ones, in the same categories we have used for genuine proofs: logic, character (*ethos*), and emotion.

Fallacies in Logic

LO1 Identify and describe the different types of logical fallacies in argument.

Fallacies pose as logical proof, but you will see that they are really pseudoproofs that prove nothing at all. You may have trouble remembering all of their names; many people do. Concentrate instead on the fallacious thinking characterized by each of them, such as introducing irrelevant material; exaggerating; providing wrong, unfair, inadequate, or even no support; harboring unacceptable warrants; drawing inappropriate conclusions; and oversimplifying the choices.

Begging the Question

No support is provided by the arguer who begs the question, and the claim is simply restated, over and over again, in one form or another. For example, "Capital punishment deters crime because it keeps criminals from committing murder" simply restates the same idea in other words. Have you ever encountered people who claim something is true because they say it is true? If the individual is a recognized authority on the issue, then such a claim may be accurate and relevant. Imagine, however, a politician who claims that a work of art is immoral because he thinks it is. No criteria for judging the morality or immorality of art are provided. We are simply asked to accept the subjective opinion of someone who may know very little about art. This individual is begging the question.

Red Herring

A red herring provides irrelevant and misleading support that pulls the audience away from the real argument. For example, "I don't believe we should elect this candidate because she would have to put her kids in day care" is a red herring; qualifications to hold office have nothing to do with household arrangements. Whether or not Barry Bonds is a great baseball player and well-liked by fans is a red herring in a legal case that must judge whether he is innocent or guilty of having taken performance-enhancing drugs.

Non Sequitur

Non sequitur is Latin for "it does not follow." In this type of fallacy, the conclusion does not follow from the evidence and the warrant. Here are some examples: the professor in the Hawaiian shirt and gold chains must be an easy grader; the self-consciously beautiful woman who has applied for a job as an administrative assistant would not do the job well; that man with the powerful new laptop must be highly skilled in the use of computer technology. The warrants for these three examples are that the professor's clothes indicate how he will grade, beautiful women cannot be good administrative assistants, and owning powerful equipment implies the ability to use it. You can probably sense the problems with these warrants. They are so difficult for most people to accept that none of these examples come across as convincing arguments.

Straw Man

A straw man involves attributing an argument to an opponent that the opponent never made and then refuting it in a devastating way. The arguer sets up an idea, refutes it, and appears to win, even though the idea may be unrelated to the issue being discussed. For example, a political candidate might set up a straw man by claiming that his opponent has said he is too old to do the job, when in fact the opponent has never mentioned age as an issue. Then the candidate refutes the age issue by detailing the advantages of age and appears to win the argument, even though this is not an issue at all. In fact, by refuting this false issue, the candidate may give the impression that he could refute any other arguments put forth by the opposition as well. The use of a straw man suggests competence where it might not actually exist.

Stacked Evidence

Stacking evidence to represent only one side of an issue that clearly has two sides gives a distorted impression of the issue. For example, to prove that social networking enhances and improves social bonds, the only evidence given is that Facebook helps us reconnect with long-lost friends, Twitter allows us to send out endless updates about our experiences and activities, and texting provides us with a way to stay instantaneously in touch. Examples where social networking leads to misunderstanding, miscommunication, or a loss of intimacy are never mentioned.

Manufactured Evidence

Using fake evidence to prove a claim will discredit an entire argument and ruin the reputation of the individual who makes it up. A famous example occurred in 2004 when a South Korean scientist announced he had created human embryos through cloning, a development that would enable him to extract embryonic stem cells from them for use in further research on therapeutic cloning. This research held great promise for curing certain diseases and injuries. The results were published in *Science,* widely accepted as the most credible scientific journal. A few months later, the announced research results were exposed as intentional fabrications. Because he had used fake or false evidence, the scientist had to step down from his official positions and *Science* retracted his papers.

Unreliable or Insufficient Evidence

Evidence should be verifiable, which means you should be able to look it up in another source and find the same information. There should also be enough evidence, and major information that could change the way one interprets the evidence should not be omitted. DNA evidence is often used in criminal cases to prove guilt. However, it is also increasingly being used to exonerate criminals who were wrongly accused of crimes in the first place and who have been in prison for many years in spite of their innocence. In these cases, the evidence used to convict them was insufficient or unreliable, and new DNA evidence proves that it was unreliable.

Exaggerated or Oversimplified Evidence

Here is an example of what can happen when exaggerated evidence is used. In 2010 a renowned researcher of primate behavior at Harvard University was forced to issue a public retraction of some of his findings because other scientists were not able to replicate his results when conducting the same experiments. Skepticism among other scientists about these results, combined with the researcher's public disavowal of his own findings, has led many in the academic world to doubt the validity of all his research, even work completely unrelated to the experiments in question, and has also resulted in a decision by Harvard University to place him on academic leave.

Oversimplifying evidence can also discredit an argument. For example, to argue that handguns should be sold to "good" people and not to criminals oversimplifies. It is difficult to accept a conclusion based on evidence of this sort because it has no actual content.

Distorted Statistics

Statistics can be manipulated or changed so that they appear to support a claim when, actually, they do not. For example, the owner of a company argues that salaries in the company are good since the average salary is $40,000. What is left out is that one individual makes $120,000, while four others make only $20,000 each. Presenting the average salary to suggest an equitable pay scale distorts the truth.

Either-Or

Some arguments are oversimplified by the arguer and presented as black-or-white, either-or choices when there are other alternatives. Some examples are "This country can either have a strong defense program or a strong social welfare program," "We can develop either a strong space program or an urban development program," "A woman can either be a mother or have a career," and "A man can either go to graduate school or become a company man." No alternative, middle-ground, or compromise positions are acknowledged.

Post Hoc

Post hoc is short for *post hoc, ergo propter hoc,* a Latin phrase that translates as "after this, therefore because of this." To put it more simply, *post hoc* is the fallacy of faulty cause. For example, it is fallacious to claim in an advertisement that people will be more attractive and more popular if they drink a certain brand of soda. Look at other advertisements on television or in magazines, and you will easily find other examples of *post hoc,* the claim that one thing causes another when there is actually no causal relationship between them. Think about the outdoor healthy virility of the Marlboro man, for example, and the suggestion that he got that way by smoking cigarettes. Another example is the person who finds romance by serving a particular spaghetti sauce or using a specific cologne.

Hasty Generalization

Sometimes arguers "jump to conclusions" by basing a conclusion on too few examples. For example, someone may conclude that the U.S. government is hopelessly flawed because the president and the Congress cannot reach agreement on a particular piece of legislation, or that since there are episodes of school violence across the country, all schools are inherently violent and dangerous. Hasty generalizations often contribute to stereotyping.

LO2 Identify and describe the different types of fallacies that affect *ethos* or character in argument.

Fallacies That Affect Character or *Ethos*

Fallacies that are aimed at attacking character or at using character instead of evidence for proof are misleading and can damage *ethos.*

Ad Hominem

Ad hominem means "to the man" in Latin. An *ad hominem* argument attacks a person's character rather than a person's ideas or policies. The press is notorious for such attacks during political campaigns, and so are some of the candidates themselves. The "character issue," for example, may receive more attention than more serious, substantive issues. Such *ad hominem* discussion scrutinizes negative information that is provided about the candidates' personal lives rather than about their ideas or the issues that concern them. The purpose of *ad hominem* argument is to discredit. Take another example of an *ad hominem* dispute, but in this case the beliefs or ethical qualities of a person are exposed to negative attack. For example, piety is said to have no validity because of the careless personal and financial habits of a television evangelist. This *ad hominem* argument directs attention away from the issue (here, bad actions) and toward the person as bad. Thus we become prejudiced and biased against an individual personally, or an institution generally, instead of evaluating facts or ideas when *ad hominem* exchange predominates.

Guilt by Association

The fallacy of guilt by association suggests that people's character can be judged by examining the character of their associates. For example, an employee in a company that defrauds the government is declared dishonest because of his employment with the company, even though he may have known nothing of the fraud. Or, an observer is thrown into jail along with some political protesters simply because she was in the wrong place at the wrong time. Political figures are often judged as morally defective if they associate with people with questionable values and reputations. It is assumed that these individuals are members of these groups and guilty by association.

Using Authority Instead of Evidence

This is a variation of begging the question. The arguer relies on personal authority to prove a point rather than on evidence. For example, a salesman tells you to buy the used car because he is honest and trustworthy and he knows your neighbor.

Emotional Fallacies

LO3 Identify and describe the different types of emotional fallacies in argument.

Irrelevant, unrelated, and distracting emotional materials are often introduced into argument to try to convince the audience. Here are some examples.

Bandwagon Appeal

The bandwagon fallacy centers on the claim that everyone is doing something, so you should too. For example, everyone is making their own YouTube videos, so you should also jump on the bandwagon and do it. Political and other public opinion polls are sometimes used to promote the bandwagon appeal. The suggestion is that since a majority of the people polled hold a certain opinion, you should adopt it as well.

When you feel yourself being influenced by what everyone else seems to be doing, decide whether basing your action on the bandwagon appeal is what you really want to do. Maybe you are about to jump on the bandwagon and eat more vegetables, which would be okay, but if you are about to drink too much alcohol because everyone else is doing it, then maybe you need to get off that bandwagon.

Slippery Slope

The slippery-slope fallacy is a scare tactic that suggests that if we allow one thing to happen, we will immediately be sliding down a slippery slope to disaster. This fallacy is sometimes introduced into environmental and social issues. If we allow loggers to cut a few trees, we will soon lose all the forests. Or if gay marriage is legalized, the entire institution of marriage will be threatened.

Creating False Needs

Emotional proofs, as you have learned, appeal to what people value and think they need. Sometimes an arguer will create a false sense of need where none exists or will unrealistically heighten an existing need in order to make the argument more convincing. Advertising provides excellent examples. The housewife is told she needs a shining kitchen floor with a high gloss that only a certain wax can provide. Parents are reminded that they want smart, successful children, so they should buy a tablet for each of them. The ad for the health club described at the beginning of this chapter that promises both weight loss and romance creates a false need for people who may be only vaguely concerned about their weight and the possibilities of romance before reading this ad.

Distorted Emotional Appeal

Irrelevant and unrelated emotional examples or stories that are unrelated to the subject are sometimes used to try to prove a point. For example, providing horrible details about the suffering of a terminally ill patient to prove that assisted suicide should be legal can be irrelevant and unrelated to the claim. This is particularly true when the patient's suffering can be relieved in other ways, such as with drug therapies. Faulty analogies, like comparing governments to hungry wolves, distorted visuals, like showing how happy people can become by doing abdominal exercises, extreme slogans, like those printed on placards in public demonstrations, and hate language aimed at particular groups of people represent misuse and distortion of emotional appeal. On close scrutiny, they can be exposed as ineffective proof.

These examples of fallacies provide you with a good sense of what constitutes fallacious reasoning. Armed with this list and with the tests of validity for genuine proofs listed under "Tests of Validity" in the Summary Charts (pages 428–433), you now have what you need to evaluate the strength and validity of the proofs in an argument. This information will help you make evaluations, form rebuttals to challenge weak arguments, and create arguments of your own that rely on genuine proofs instead of fallacies. We now leave unethical argument with its fallacies and faulty evidence and turn to the subject of ethics and morality in argument.

Analyzing Online Argument: Identifying Fallacies

Our fast-paced, 24/7, multimedia world is particularly susceptible to fallacious argument. From misleading ads to Photoshopped news photos, mudslinging political campaigns to factually incorrect Web sites, our digital world is awash with arguments that commit one or another kind of fallacy. The steps below provide a guideline for identifying and analyzing fallacies online.

▶▶▶ Step 1: Find the Fallacy

- What type of fallacy is presented (i.e., logical, character, or emotional)?
- What specific form does it take (i.e., hasty generalization, faulty causality, either-or, etc.)?

▶▶▶ Step 2: Describe the Multimedia Features Used to Present It

- Through what medium is it presented (Web site, social media post, online video, email, etc.)?
- What multimedia elements does it include?

▶▶▶ Step 3: Identify the Flaws

- What flaw or mistake does this fallacy involve?

To put this analysis into practice, let's look at a specific example. The screenshot below comes from the Web site for The Anti-Vaccination Action Group, an organization that argues against the

continued

Analyzing Online Argument: Identifying Fallacies (*continued*)

need to vaccinate young children. Take a look at this selection as well as the sample step-by-step analysis that follows. What argument does this Web site make? What fallacy does it commit? And what roles do different multimedia elements play?

▶▶▶ Step 1: Find the Fallacy

- In making a cause-and-effect argument about the medical risks that vaccination poses to children, this site commits a logical fallacy, specifically the fallacy of the hasty generalization.

▶▶▶ Step 2: Describe the Multimedia Features Used to Present It

- This site uses a combination of textual and visual elements to make its argument.
- The photo of the baby receiving a vaccination and the cartoon image of the mother defending herself against an onslaught of vaccination needles make a blanket argument about the danger posed by all vaccines, regardless of the disease they are designed to prevent. These visual elements dovetail with the written elements here, reinforcing the site's stated mission to "dispel the myths about vaccine safety."

▶▶▶ Step 3: Identify the Flaws

- As noted above, this site commits the fallacy of the hasty generalization. Rather than make a more narrowly focused argument that identifies the specific risks posed by specific types of vaccines, this site uses its visual imagery to create a cartoonish version of the vaccine debate. And rather than include links to medical studies or statistics that might support its claim, the site relies on its blanket generalization about "vaccination" as its sole support.

Activity

Go online and find an example of a fallacy. First, identify in which of the three categories (logical, character, emotional) it belongs. Next, describe the particular fallacy it commits (i.e., stacked evidence, either-or, *post hoc*, etc.). Then use the three steps outlined above to analyze this fallacy in greater depth.

LO4
Describe the characteristics of ethical argument, and use them in creating your own argument.

Ethics and Morality in Argument

A person's ability to argue persuasively has been recognized as a potentially powerful influence over other people for centuries. Thus the classical argument theorists, Aristotle, Cicero, and Quintilian, all recognized that citizens should be schooled in argumentation so that they could argue for the causes that would benefit society. They also argued that society needed moral arguers because, without them, immoral arguers would gain too much power. Plato criticized arguers who used their persuasive powers to manipulate people to achieve their own selfish ends.

Ethical arguers must have the courage and willingness to argue logically and honestly from a strong sense of personal integrity and values. They should also have a strong sense of responsibility and feel obliged to advocate for the changes in their community that they believe are necessary or right. Consequently, the emotional and motivational appeals ethical arguers use should be consistent with value systems that will benefit not just one individual but all of society. To learn how to better distinguish between ethical and unethical appeals, look at the "Arguing Like a Citizen" section below.

Arguing Like a Citizen

Hannah Sternberg's essay, "Conservative Feminism Is Not an Oxymoron" (pages 238–239), makes the argument that conservative politics and support for women's rights are not incompatible. In order to check this argument for potential fallacies, as well as to better understand how this general issue connects to the question of citizenship, look closely at the sample discussion below.

▶▶▶ Thinking Like a Citizen

- Why do I care about this issue?
  Feminism is one of the most controversial topics in today's culture, one that is connected to some of our society's most important and topical debates. As such, it is also an issue that tends to divide people, not only politically but also emotionally. Because it raises such strong feelings and is so susceptible to misunderstanding, I feel it is especially important that debates over feminism avoid fallacies at all costs.

- Who else cares about this issue?
  Because it is so wide-ranging an issue, it could be said that the subject of feminism is of concern to everyone. More specifically, those interested in civil and gender rights or who have an active interest in cultural politics would find this discussion especially relevant.

▶▶▶ Arguing Like a Citizen

- What potential fallacies might an argument like this commit?
  There are logical, character, and emotional fallacies to which discussions of feminism are vulnerable. Among the logical fallacies are either-or thinking (i.e., feminism is either all good or all bad) and faulty causality (i.e., supporting or opposing feminism will lead to a terrible outcome). Among the fallacies of character are ad hominem (i.e., attacking the character, background, or intentions of feminists). Among the emotional fallacies are slippery slope (i.e., a specific, individual feminist idea or proposal will inevitably lead to a chain of undesirable outcomes) and distorted emotional appeals (i.e., presenting a cartoonish or caricatured version of feminism).

continued

Arguing Like a Citizen (*continued*)

▶▶▶ Acting Like a Citizen

- What concrete action could I take to avoid these fallacies?
  In general terms, the most effective way to avoid the types of fallacies outlined above is to foster discussions of feminist-related issues that highlight the common ground that differing or opposed political parties might actually share. In more specific terms, this might involve enrolling in a class with classmates whose views on a particular feminist-related issue are different from my own, or attending a forum (campus talk, public event, etc.) that brings together spokespeople with whom I disagree.

Activity

Choose an issue that you feel is of particular importance within your community. First, conduct some basic research into this issue. What does the issue involve? What key questions or problems does it raise? Who are the different stakeholders, the individuals and/or groups, who care most about this issue? And how do their perspectives on this issue differ? Next, take a closer look at the appeals or proofs each side or set of stakeholders uses to support its point of view. What types of fallacies do you detect? Which of these fallacies would you consider to be the *least* ethical? Why? And what, in your view, is the *most* ethical set of appeals on which to argue this particular issue?

Unethical individuals who argue mainly to manipulate public opinion often use unethical tactics to influence and gain adherence to their points of view. Such tactics include opinion polls that push for particular points of view, exaggerated or manipulated statistics, manufactured evidence, outright lies, and deliberately fallacious reasoning. Language can also be manipulated to change audience perceptions. For example, a recent government report on hunger was criticized for substituting the terms "low food security" and "very low food security" for the word *hunger*. It would seem that some people thought that changing the word *hunger,* with its strong negative connotations, to vague multiword terms with weaker connotations might subtly minimize the sting of the problems of poverty and starvation in the country.

It is important that you learn to recognize the differences between ethical and unethical argument. You can begin by asking the questions that follow and then searching for information that will help you answer them. Discussing these questions with others will help you achieve a sense of whether an argument is ethical or unethical. Gathering additional information about the issue and the arguer can also help. Read reviews, editorials, commentaries, and look up biographical information about the author online. Inform yourself about the author's affiliations and background to help you discover his or her true purpose and motives, point of view, and values. Look for additional information on these matters, whether stated explicitly or implicitly, in the argument itself. Gather information on the rhetorical situation and understand some of the perspectives and positions held by others.

Ask These Questions to Help You Determine Whether an Argument Is Ethical or Unethical:

1. Has the arguer made an adequate effort to understand the issue and its consequences? Does the arguer also understand the positions held by other people?

2. Is the arguer just and fair-minded? Is the support fair, accurate, and convincing? Can I accept the warrants? Should the claim be qualified, if it is not already?

3. Does the arguer sincerely believe that the position he or she is proposing is in the best interests both of the audience and of the larger society?

4. Is the position being proposed actually in the best interests of the audience and the larger society? Who is benefited and who is burdened or hurt?

5. Does the arguer seem to be manipulating the audience by hiding the real purpose of the argument, by using inappropriate emotional appeals, by manu-facturing evidence, by using inaccurate evidence, or by telling lies?

6. Is the arguer changing the definition of words or substituting unusual words for commonly used words to cloud people's perceptions of the issue?

7. Is the arguer recasting or rewording an issue to reduce its threat when it actually represents a significant threat?

8. Do the images distort or exaggerate, or do they present the individual or situation accurately? Do they function as reliable support that enhances the argument, or are they irrelevant, inaccurate, or insulting so that they weaken the argument?

Use this list of criteria to judge the ethical and moral qualities of the argumentation you read or view and let them also guide you when you write. You will be more convincing to your audience.

Review Questions

1. What are fallacies? Why are they also described as pseudoproofs? Under what circumstances might you be tempted to believe a fallacy? **(LO1, LO2, LO3)**

2. What are some of the qualities that characterize fallacious thinking? **(LO1, LO2, LO3)**

3. Name at least two fallacies in logic, two that affect *ethos,* and two emotional fallacies. **(LO1, LO2, LO3)**

4. What is the difference between *ethos* and ethics in argument? **(LO4)**

5. Describe some of the qualities of ethical argument. **(LO4)**

Exercises and Activities

A. Class Discussion: Analyzing Advertisements

Look at the two reprinted advertisements below. The first comes from the Web site for Axe deodorant; the second is from a political Web site with a right-leaning political and social viewpoint. These ads are either selling products or promoting ideas. Study each one carefully and then answer the questions provided here.

1. What is being promoted in each visual?

2. How would you state the claim communicated by each?

3. What reasons and evidence are used to support the claim?

4. Characterize the language used in each visual. For example, does any of the language establish the *ethos* of the advertiser, or appeal to logic or to emotion? Provide some examples.

5. Describe the most obvious fallacies in each of these visuals.

6. How does each visual fit the forum in which it appears in terms of subject matter and values?

Image 1:

A Deodorant Ad

Source: Reproduced with kind permission of Unilever PLC and group companies.

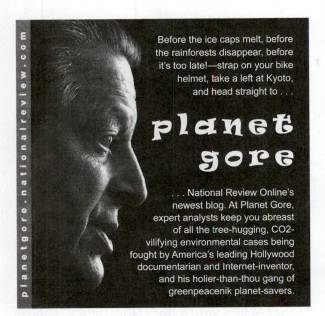

Before the ice caps melt, before the rainforests disappear, before it's too late!—strap on your bike helmet, take a left at Kyoto, and head straight to . . .

planet gore

. . . National Review Online's newest blog. At Planet Gore, expert analysts keep you abreast of all the tree-hugging, CO2-vilifying environmental cases being fought by America's leading Hollywood documentarian and Internet-inventor, and his holier-than-thou gang of greenpeacenik planet-savers.

Image 2:
A Political Web Site

B. Class Discussion: Bring a Fallacy to Class

Review the fallacies in this chapter. Then find an example of a fallacy and either bring it to class or describe it to the class. Explain why it is a fallacy. Look at advertisements that appear in print, on television, or online; listen to political speeches and political commentary; visit Web sites, blogs, or simply listen to your friends and family.

C. Group Work and Discussion: Analyzing Fallacies in Online Argument

Because the Web allows virtually anybody the chance to present her or his opinion on essentially any issue, online arguments are especially susceptible to fallacies of logic (*logos*), character (*ethos*), and emotion (*pathos*). Find an example of an online argument that, in your view, relies upon one or more fallacious appeals. First, analyze it. What type of fallacies do you detect? What, specifically, makes each of them flawed or faulty? Then, rewrite this argument using appeals that you feel are more valid. In what ways do these changes make the argument stronger?

D. Group Work and Discussion: Analyzing Fallacies in Written Argument

The argument on pages 238–239 is written by an author who holds strong opinions about the subject. As you read the essay, focus on those specific statements with which you cannot agree. Then try to figure out why you do not agree. Is the evidence weak or irrelevant? Are there fallacies in its structure? Expose the weaknesses in this argument. After making an assessment, discuss your findings with the class.

BEFORE YOU READ: What do you associate with feminism?

ESSAY #1   CONSERVATIVE FEMINISM IS NOT AN OXYMORON*
Hannah Sternberg

The essay below appeared in The Foundry, a Web site created by the conservative political organization The Heritage Foundation.

Hillary Clinton will be feted this Friday at a "world summit" event hosted by Tina Brown, the editor in chief of *Newsweek*. This week Brown relaunched the magazine with a cover story featuring Hillary as one of the "150 Women Who Shake the World." Clinton and other public figures such as Christiane Amanpour and Nancy Pelosi as well as pop culture icons like Mia Farrow and Susan Sarandon own the message on strong women. They embody the identification of so-called "women's issues" with left-leaning politics. But conservatives don't have to relinquish the banner of feminism to liberal ideology.

The primary (and most literal) dictionary definition of feminism is "the theory of the political, economic, and social equality of the sexes." However, in popular ideology it has unquestionably been superseded by its secondary, connotative definition, "organized activity on behalf of women's rights and interests." "Interest" has been broadly interpreted to mean virtually any liberal agenda. This has led to the frequent claim that for a woman to be conservative, she betrays her sex; there is no such thing as a conservative feminist. Such a political philosophy belittles women. It assumes that women lack the intellectual capacity to choose their own views; their opinions on everything from abortion to the economy must be prefabricated by the liberal thought machine. It is also a distasteful blow to the idea of individual self-determination: *what* a person is, is more important to liberals than *who* a person is. Individuality is undermined by group identification. The political movement that purports to defend "equal rights" for women begins by asserting that the female half of the population is born into their ideology and is not permitted to deviate from it. Liberal hypocrisy on feminism is rife in a number of highly visible positions:

Abortion

Liberals claim that pro-life activists are paternalistic because, by combating abortion, they are depriving women of the right to choose for themselves whether to terminate a pregnancy. Yet many of these same liberals oppose the establishment of Pregnancy Resource Centers, pro-life institutions that educate women on the other ways, besides abortion, to cope with unexpected pregnancy, including support services for the pregnancy period itself, as well as information on the alternatives of adoption or parenting. Similarly, many liberals oppose measures to require women to view an ultrasound before having an abortion

*"Conservative Feminism Is Not an Oxymoron" by Hannah Sternberg from *The Foundry*, March 11, 2011. Reprinted with permission.

because it might persuade them to change their minds. Liberals are so convinced that abortion is the best choice for women experiencing unexpected pregnancy that they would like to prevent those women from learning about any other options or being exposed to the full reality of the procedure. Who's paternalistic now?

School Choice

Liberals oppose school choice, claiming that it siphons much-needed funds from the public school system. But school choice simply means that money funds the child instead of funding the school. In addition to being fiscally incorrect (many school choice programs, such as the DC Opportunity Scholarship Program, not only cost less per-pupil than surrounding public schools but are funded on a structure specifically designed to avoid decreasing the funds to public schools), this anti-school choice position is a shocking insult to parents. The liberal position on school choice is clear; mothers cannot be trusted to choose their own children's education.

The Defense of Freedom and Human Rights

5 Liberal feminist groups are vitriolic in condemning the wars in Iraq and Afghanistan, which liberated millions of women from the atrocities of the Taliban and other Islamist regimes. They support organizations such as the U.N., which recently seated Iran—a flagrant violator of basic rights for women—on its Commission on the Status of Women, and they support its resolutions against Israel, the only country in the Middle East that recognizes full equal rights for women. Liberals justify their support in the name of multiculturalism—the relative equality of every society, even if they legalize the honor killing of rape victims by their own family members and institutionalize spousal abuse. Liberals find multiculturalism far more of an enlightened idea than the American tradition of promoting universal democratic principles, which they view as "intellectual colonialism." What constitutes this "intellectual colonialism" that is such a threat to progressive multiculturalism? It's the spread of the unique ideas upon which America was founded: ideas hailed as universal and immutable truths, stemming from that first declaration "that all men are created equal, that they are endowed by their Creator with certain unalienable Rights, that among these are Life, Liberty and the pursuit of Happiness." What could be more empowering than the simple declaration that all people, women and men, are entitled to the respect of their basic human dignity?

But these truths are a threat to the liberal interpretation of feminism, which claims that men and women are *not* born equal, but that women (and other gender- or race-based groups) are born into a pre-destined ideology, while other "majority" groups (most of the time, white men) are born into collective guilt for their fathers' transgressions. These truths are also a threat to the progressive concept of multiculturalism, which claims that moral relativism is the only truth, and that America's founding principles are merely "values," applicable only in a particular time and place.

Yet if the last idea is true, what defense does progressivism offer for the basic human dignity of women everywhere?

For Discussion:

What do you see that weakens this argument? How could the author have made it a stronger argument?

E. Class Discussion: Recognizing Ethical Argument

Read the historical material and look at the two photographs that accompany "The Gettysburg Address," read the text of the address, and be prepared to state your views on why the speech and the images are good examples of ethical argument.

Rhetorical Situation

Lincoln gave his most famous speech, "The Gettysburg Address," during the U.S. Civil War when the issue facing the country was national unity.

For three days in early July 1863, the forces of the Union and the Confederacy engaged in an intensely fought battle around Gettysburg, Pennsylvania. According to official estimates, by the time this battle had concluded, over 50,000 Union and Confederate soldiers lay dead, with another 30,000 soldiers wounded. Because it stemmed the northward advance of the Confederate forces, causing General Robert E. Lee and his army to retreat south to Virginia, the Battle of Gettysburg is widely regarded as one of the key turning points in the Civil War.

Several months after this battle, President Lincoln traveled to Gettysburg to commemorate the site as a national cemetery. Rather than make a lengthy, formal address, President Lincoln chose to deliver a surprisingly short two-minute speech in which he cast the enormous military sacrifice as a testament to the enduring power of American democracy.

THE GETTYSBURG ADDRESS

Gettysburg, Pennsylvania, November 19, 1863

On June 1, 1865, Senator Charles Sumner commented on what is now considered the most famous speech by President Abraham Lincoln. In his eulogy on the slain president, he called it a "monumental act." He said Lincoln was mistaken that "the world will little note, nor long remember what we say here." Rather, the Bostonian remarked, "The world noted at once what he said, and will never cease to remember it. The battle itself was less important than the speech."

Four score and seven years ago our fathers brought forth on this continent, a new nation, conceived in Liberty, and dedicated to the proposition that all men are created equal.

Now we are engaged in a great civil war, testing whether that nation, or any nation so conceived and so dedicated, can long endure. We are met on a great battle-field of that war. We have come to dedicate a portion of that field, as a final resting place for those who here gave their lives that that nation might live. It is altogether fitting and proper that we should do this.

But, in a larger sense, we can not dedicate—we can not consecrate—we can not hallow—this ground. The brave men, living and dead, who struggled here, have consecrated it, far above our poor power to add or detract. The world will little note, nor long remember what we say here, but it can never forget what they did here. It is for us the living, rather, to be dedicated here to the unfinished work which they who fought here have thus far so nobly advanced. It is rather for us to be here dedicated to the great task remaining before us—that from these honored dead we take increased devotion to that cause for which they gave the last full measure of devotion—that we here highly resolve that these dead shall not have died in vain—that this nation, under God, shall have a new birth of freedom—and the government of the people, by the people, for the people, shall not perish from the earth.[1]

Image 1:

President Lincoln among the crowd at Gettysburg.

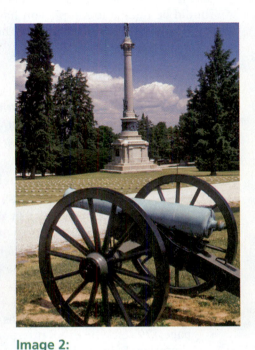

Image 2:

The Soldiers' National Monument that stands in the center of the National Cemetery at Gettysburg, Pennsylvania.

For Discussion:

Lincoln was shot on April 14, 1865, and he died the next day. The Civil War ended May 26, 1865. What qualities make "The Gettysburg Address" an ethical argument? Describe the values in the address that help define it as an ethical argument. What are some of the most famous phrases in the address, and why are they still important? Describe how the address served the best interests of the audience and the larger society in 1863 and continues to serve in our society today. Comment on the images. How does Image 1 help establish the rhetorical situation for the address? What is the effect of including an old photograph instead of a modern one? Image 2 is a photograph of a monument. Describe the qualities of a monument that make it an effective visual argument.

[1] *AbrahamLincolnOnline.org,* 1995–2008. Speeches. April 2008, showcase.netins.net/web/creative/lincoln/gettysburg .htm.

F. **Writing Assignment: A Position Paper**

This assignment invites you to review and experiment with some of the strategies for planning and writing an argument paper that you have learned. For this assignment, you will write a position paper in which you will select a topic, take a position on it, do some reading, make a claim, and prove it. Your claim should be related to a topic you have chosen yourself or have selected from essays you have read in this book. The paper should be about 1,000 words long, typed, and double-spaced.

Planning and Prewriting

Complete some or all of the prewriting activities listed here so that you will have plenty of material to draw on when you draft your paper.

1. Select an issue and test it. Phrase it as a question and apply the twelve tests in Box 1.3 on page 39.

2. Write an issue proposal to help you focus your issue and plan your research. See Exercise I on page 40.

3. Locate three or four sources that are related to your topic and write summary-response papers for each of them. See Exercise C on page 103.

4. Write an exploratory paper to help you understand the topic. See Exercise F and Worksheet 2 on page 108.

5. Use the Toulmin model to help you find the elements for the paper; see Exercise G, page 143. Use the claim questions to refine and focus your claim and generate further ideas for subclaims and support; see Exercise F, page 179. Use the proof questions to develop convincing proofs for your claim; see Exercise F, page 222.

6. Use the following evaluation questions to improve your support and eliminate fallacies. You can ask these questions both before you write and after you draft your paper, as part of the revision process. They will help you focus on the quantity and quality of your support. Correct or eliminate any items that might weaken your argument.

   a. Do I have enough support to be convincing? What can I add?
   b. Is my support reliable and convincing? How can I make it more so?
   c. Is anything exaggerated or oversimplified? How can I be more accurate?
   d. Do I rely too much on my own authority ("This is true because I say so") instead of giving support? Can I add support and the opinions of additional authorities to be more convincing?
   e. Am I weakening this argument with too much emotional appeal? Should any of it be eliminated?
   f. Have I used any fallacies as proof? (Check especially for hasty generalizations and *post hoc* or faulty cause, probably the two most common fallacies. Look for other fallacies. If you find any, either clarify and rewrite to make them acceptable or eliminate them.)

Writing a List or an Outline

Use one of the patterns listed here to organize your ideas and develop the claim.

▶ If you are writing a fact paper that answers the question "What happened?" consider using a chronological pattern. Use transitions such as *first, then,* and *next.* You can begin your paper with present events and use flashbacks to explain what occurred in the past, or you can simply explain things in the past to present order in which they occurred.

▶ If you are writing a definition paper that answers the question "What is it?" consider using comparison to establish meaning by showing what the item or idea you are defining is like and what it is not like. You can achieve similar clarity by presenting examples of several meanings for the item or idea and then settle on the best of these meanings for your conclusion.

▶ If you are writing a cause paper that answers the question "What caused it?" consider using a cause-and-effect or effect-and-cause pattern of organization. Cause and effect explains how certain causes result in certain effects, and effect and cause describes the effects first and then explains what caused them.

▶ If you are writing a value paper that answers the question "Is it good or bad?" consider a claim-plus-reasons pattern. Complete the sentence "It is (good or bad) because . . ." and add reasons and evidence.

▶ If you are writing a policy paper that answers the question "What should we do?" consider using the problem–solution pattern of organization. Describe the problem first, and then describe one or more solutions.

Drafting, Revising, and Final Editing

Use your extended list or outline to help you write a draft, revise the draft, and prepare the final copy. Work quoted material into your draft as you write. Use MLA documentation to cite in-text references and to create a Works Cited page, unless you are advised otherwise.

Read the example position paper that is reproduced on the following pages. The question is "What should be done with young offenders?" This paper was written by Kelly Dickerson, a student in an argument class. The type of claim, the elements of the Toulmin model, and the proofs are identified in the margin.

Notice also how Kelly worked quoted material into her paper for ease of reading. Quotations flow with the rest of the text, and they are clear. Furthermore, the introductions for the quotations, along with the in-text citations, show the reader where to find the originals, if there is interest in locating them. Use this paper as a model to help you integrate quotations into your own paper and prepare a Works Cited page.*

---

*See the Appendix to Chapter 12 for the actual MLA format guidelines for student papers.

STUDENT PAPER
#1

Kelly Dickerson
Professor Wood
English 1302
25 October 2013

Minor Problems?

Support: Definition

Every time Americans tune in to local news broadcasts or read daily papers, they are likely to be shocked at the increasing number of serious crimes committed by youths who are only sixteen or seventeen years old, or even younger. It is sometimes difficult to imagine these youngsters behaving like hardened criminals, but statistics continually prove that their crimes are often just as brutal as those committed by their adult counterparts. Inevitably, people begin questioning how successful the juvenile justice system is in reforming these youths. Increasingly, violent juveniles are being tried and sentenced as adults in our legal system. Some of them, after the death sentence was reinstated in the United States in 1976, were even sentenced to death, at least until 2005 (Wallis).

Support: Authority

Warrant: The penalty was appropriate but is no longer an option.
Support: Facts

At that time the Supreme Court made it illegal to sentence anyone to death for crimes committed before the age of 18. Specifically, in 2005, the Supreme Court ruled that no one could be sentenced to death for crimes they had committed while they were 16 or 17 years old. A similar ruling in 1988 removed the death penalty as an option for individuals committing crimes when they were 15 years old or younger (Wallis).

Support: Cause

What causes juveniles to commit serious crimes like murder, rape, robbery, physical assault, or illegal drug involvement? People hold different perspectives on this issue. Aristotle describes youths as "passionate, quick to anger, and apt to give way to it . . . their angry passions get the better of them." Aristotle wrote 2,400 years ago, and modern descriptions of youth are not that different from his. Wallis quotes attorney Steven Presson who states, "We've been arguing for decades that kids don't have the same moral culpability that adults have." Daniel Weinberger explains in "A Brain Too Young for Good Judgment" that the 15-year-old student who shot his fellow students at Santana High School has, because of his age, an immature brain. The prefrontal cortex, the part of the brain that is used for judgment and suppressing impulsive behavior, is not fully formed at that age. The difference between earlier times, including

Support: Quotes from authorities

Aristotle's ancient Greece, and now, according to Weinberger, is that we live in a culture that romanticizes gunplay. In modern society, "if a gun is put in the control of the prefrontal cortex of a hurt and vengeful 15-year-old, and it is pointed at a human target, it will very likely go off."

Support: Effect

Support: Example

Not all 15-year-olds commit such deadly crimes, but those who do should be held accountable. Examples of teen crime are vivid and terrifying. William Glaberson writes about Omar Ahmed Khadr, a 15-year-old Al Qaeda recruit who threw a grenade that killed a U.S. soldier in 2002. Khadr has been imprisoned in Guantánamo Bay, Cuba, for the past five years, and even though international law does not require special treatment for criminals under 18 years old, he is likely to be given less than a life term. Prosecutors in his case, however, claim that he was trained in terrorist activities by his family and should be held to adult standards. Other child fighters in Africa and other countries do not hesitate to kill when they have been trained to do so. Child killers are a more and more common occurrence around the world.

Warrant: The examples prove these individuals should be held accountable.

5   Despite the staggering increase in serious crimes committed by young offenders, the punishment that juveniles receive has traditionally almost never fit the severity of the crimes. Since the system views children as not being fully developed, physically or mentally, it has prevented them from being held accountable for their wrongdoing. With the recent lifting of the death penalty for juveniles, punishment may become even more lenient.

Subclaim: The punishment does not always fit the crime.

When "children" commit horribly vicious crimes and are routinely treated as victims of society who are too delicate to receive the punishments they deserve, they get the message that crime "pays" because there are no serious consequences for their actions. When the system lacks an element of fear, there is nothing to deter youthful offenders from committing future crimes. Assigning adult sentences to youths who commit serious crimes is absolutely just if the punishment is to fit the crime.

Warrant: The punishment should fit the crime.

Warrant: Adult sentences are a deterrent to crime.

Most pro-rehabilitation advocates argue that juvenile criminals are completely different from their adult counterparts and should therefore be treated differently in the justice system. I agree that rehabilitation efforts may be very important in decreasing the amount of juvenile crime, particularly repeat crime. However, I believe that these measures should be directed toward youths who have committed minor offenses. Nando, the young man Feuer describes in "Out of Jail, Into Temptation: A Day in a Life," would be a good candidate for a rehabilitation program. Sending him back to his former neighborhood without job training or money will almost certainly cause him to regress to his former way of life.

Rebuttal: Agree on minor crimes

Support: Examples from authorities

Rebuttal, cont.:
Disagree for serious
crimes

Warrant: Cost to
society should
determine
punishment

Policy claim

Conversely, I feel that juveniles like the ones who shoot their classmates or indulge in terrorist activities, those who are convicted of serious crimes—including murder, rape, robbery, physical assault, and illegal drug involvement—should be tried as adults. Their actions are obviously more serious than those who commit misdemeanor offenses, and they almost always result in greater direct harm to society. A message has to be sent that we will no longer tolerate brutal crimes simply because of the age of the criminal. These youths must be held completely accountable for their crimes, suffering harsh consequences and ultimately realizing that they are no longer protected by the law. The cost to society is the same regardless of the age of the criminal. What comfort does it give to the family of a slain or injured victim that the person who killed or maimed their loved one was a minor? Parents of children shot and killed at school by teenage killers suffer no less because their child was shot by a young offender. Instead of treating the person who shot a fellow student like a victim of society, this person should be treated like any other person who victimizes society and causes pain to individuals and communities.

Works Cited

Aristotle. *Rhetoric* II. 12. Trans. Lane Cooper. New York: Appleton-Century-Crofts, 1932. Print.

Feuer, Alan. "Out of Jail, Into Temptation: A Day in a Life." *New York Times* 28 Feb. 2000. Print.

Glaberson, William. "A Legal Debate in Guantánamo on Boy Fighters." *International Herald-Tribune* 2 June 2007. Print.

Wallis, Claudia. "Too Young to Die." *Time* 14 Mar. 2005: 40. Print.

Weinberger, Daniel R. "A Brain Too Young for Good Judgment." *New York Times* 10 Mar. 2001: A27. Print.

Visual Argument

After studying this chapter, you will be able to:

LO1 Describe the features particular to visual argument.

LO2 Use the Toulmin model and the list of fallacies to critique visual argument.

LO3 Create written arguments that incorporate visual elements.

LO4 Create stand-alone visual arguments.

I n a world where we are inundated with visual material—from magazine covers to movies, billboards to YouTube videos—you may very well feel that you spend more time *viewing* argument than you do reading and writing it. Even though it relies far more on pictures, graphics, and images than words to convey its message, visual material does nonetheless express its own perspective on argument.

When understood as an example of argument, in fact, images frequently take on additional meaning. An image can often be perceived as a visual argument in that it makes a claim about an issue and supports it, just as written argument does. This chapter advances the view that the same tools of analysis you use to analyze written argument can be successfully applied to analyze visual argument. Visual argument, however, also has certain special characteristics that make it unique. Those characteristics are the subject of this chapter, which teaches you not only to analyze visual argument but also to create it yourself. Instruction and examples appear in the "Exercises and Activities" section at the end of the chapter.

Recognizing Visual Argument

You will need to discover, first, whether you are looking at an argument. You discover this by asking, *Is the visual about an issue that has not been resolved or settled?* and *Does this issue potentially inspire two or more different views?* If your answer to both of these questions is yes, then attempt to describe the issue and the perspective being developed. Next, use two types of information for further analysis. First, analyze the special features of visual argument that are explained later in this chapter to get a sense of how the argument works and how effective it is. Second, apply argument theory to understand the material better as an argument.

Just like written argument, visual argument can be straightforward, with an obvious purpose and claim; covert, with a hidden claim that you may need to infer; or even unconscious, with the artist advocating a point of view without being fully aware of it. Furthermore, argument expressed through pictures can represent either commonly held or extreme points of view and can present one or several different views on an issue.

You will encounter visual argument both online and in print in a variety of forms, including advertisements, photographs, drawings, illustrations, paintings, sculptures, cartoons, diagrams, flowcharts, various types of graphs, visual demonstrations, tables of numbers, or even maps. Marketers use visual argument on Web sites and billboards, on signs, and in packaging and other marketing materials such as brochures or various other types of promotional materials. All this visual material can be (and increasingly is) employed to further an argument and convince you of a particular point of view.

Notice how many of these venues for visual argument are a part of the modern media, a particularly potent context for visual argument. Reflect on the amount of time you spend each day taking in or sending information via new media, and you may be surprised how much your life is affected. Whenever you encounter visual argument in the media or anywhere else, make a point of identifying its purpose because it always has one.

Now let us look at some of the special features of visual argument that make it particularly effective for advancing arguments.

LO1 Describe the features particular to visual argument.

Why Visual Argument Is Convincing: Eight Special Features

The following special features of visual argument demonstrate how it works and why it is convincing. However, not all visual argument demonstrates all of the special features described in this list, and sometimes these features combine or overlap with one another. They are separated and described here for purposes of instruction. Becoming aware of them will help you look at visuals as potential argument and also understand how images achieve their persuasive effect with an audience.

1. *Visual argument is immediate and tangible and pulls you into the picture.* Visual argument works on a different level of perception than written argument. To use a new media word, it has velocity. It communicates fast and evokes a rich, dense, and immediate response from a viewer. For example, if you are watching a movie or an online video, you may have the experience of sharing or even taking part in the action yourself. At the least, you will react in some immediate way to what you are seeing. If the image is fixed in a photograph, you may experience its immediacy and timelessness. A moment has been captured and preserved forever. Look at the photograph in Figure 8.1. It has been characterized as the most famous picture from the Vietnam War.

2. *Visual argument often establishes common ground and invites viewer identification through shared values and points of view.* Visual argument usually establishes common ground, including a sense of personal identification and shared values with the characters, the action, or the scene, and it does so more quickly than words in print. All viewers, however, may not experience the same degree of common ground or the same type of identification.

Look at the photograph in Figure 8.2 taken by American Douglas Martin. This is a picture of Dorothy Counts, an African American girl who enrolled in a newly desegregated high school in Charlotte, North Carolina, during the civil rights movement. Escorted by the individuals on either side of her, she makes her way to her first day of school. Dorothy is being taunted by white students in the background who wanted to keep their school segregated.

Dorothy Counts, now Dot Counts Scoggins, still lives in Charlotte, North Carolina. In 2007 the Charlotte-Mecklenburg Schools community celebrated both

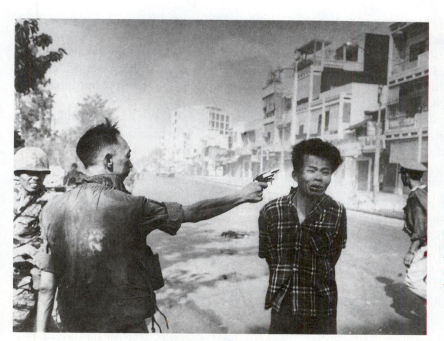

Street Execution of a Vietcong Prisoner, 1968

Figure 8.1 *Visual argument is immediate and tangible and pulls you into the picture.*

In this photograph an officer in the South Vietnamese army is shooting a suspected member of the Vietcong, an armed rebel force supported by North Vietnam, and the photographer has captured the moment when the bullet enters this man's head and kills him. This picture provoked strong antiwar arguments in its time, and it continues to invite responses to issues associated with war. What pulls you into this picture? What issue does it raise for you? What position do you take on the issue?

Figure 8.2 *Visual argument often establishes common ground and invites viewer identification through shared values and points of view.*

This photograph won The Associated Press, World Press Photo of the Year Award in 1957 and remains one of the most famous pictures from the civil rights era. With whom do you identify and experience the greatest amount of common ground in this picture? Do you identify with Dorothy as she moves toward her first experiences in her new school? Do you identify with either of the individuals escorting her? Do you have anything in common with the white students in the background? What values are embedded in this image? What issue does the picture raise for you, and what position would you take on it?

Dorothy Counts Entering a Newly Desegregated School, 1957

the 40th anniversary of the desegregation of the school system and the 50th anniversary of the difficult days that the young Dorothy Counts (she was 15 in 1957) spent in Harding High School in an effort to help desegregate public schools. The school district also invited a couple of the students who were screaming at her and making faces in this picture to the ceremony. They were present, and they apologized, after all these years.[1]

Attitudes and values have changed radically in the years since this photograph was taken. The picture demonstrates the potential power and influence of visual argument. It memorializes an event that has now become a part of history and that vividly illustrates how dramatically views on school segregation have changed throughout the United States.

    3. *Visual argument often evokes an emotional response.* Visual argument operates more directly on the emotions than written argument because images communicate more immediately than words. Because of this, visual images often invite a different, sometimes more powerful, form of critical attention. Look, for example, at the picture presented in Figure 8.3. This image, which appeared in October 2010, was one of many news stories detailing the devastation wrought by the floods in Pakistan. Notice how powerfully this picture conveys the effects of

[1]From information supplied by Professor Andy Brown and student Kristina Wolfe, of the University of North Carolina at Charlotte, and Dave Morris, long-time resident of Charlotte.

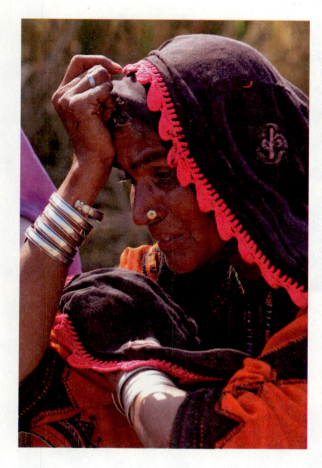

Figure 8.3 *Visual argument often evokes an emotional response.*

A Pakistani flood survivor is pictured in a flood-affected area of southern Pakistan. The floods have devastated this woman's village, and she now waits for aid to be delivered to her community. Would you characterize your response to this picture as primarily rational or emotional? What in this image prompts your response? Describe your response.

this natural disaster, eliciting a far more emotionally charged response than would a written statistical report.

4. *Visual argument often relies on the juxtaposition of materials from very different categories, inviting the viewer to make new links and associations.* In placing objects, people, or actions that are not usually associated with each other in a common context, a photographer invites the viewer to establish new associations and to reach new conclusions. Figure 8.4 is a photograph of an anti–Vietnam War demonstrator at a march in 1968. He is offering flowers that symbolize peace to troops that have been called in to protect the area.

5. *Visual argument often employs icons to prompt an immediate response from a viewer.* Icons are images that people have seen so often that they respond to them immediately and in predictable ways—a fact upon which people who include iconic references in visual argument rely. The American eagle, for example, is more than a bird to most US citizens. It symbolizes the nation and the values associated with a democratic form of government. Icons appear on computer screens and on the cash registers at McDonald's to prompt quicker responses than the words or numbers they replace. The photograph on the next page (see Figure 8.5) of Marines raising the US flag on Iwo Jima toward the end of

Figure 8.4 *Visual argument often relies on the juxtaposition of materials from very different categories, inviting the viewer to make new links and associations.*

The juxtaposition of flowers and soldiers in the context of an antiwar demonstration invites the viewer to respond directly to how these different things appear together. What associations do you have with flowers and soldiers? Think of them separately and then together. How would you state the claim in this picture? Would you accept or argue against this claim?

A Vietnam War Protester Offering Flowers to Troops During an Antiwar Demonstration, 1968

Figure 8.5 *Visual argument often employs icons to prompt an immediate response from a viewer.*

What does this photograph, taken toward the end of World War II, communicate to you? What is its purpose? What is the effect of not seeing the faces of the men? Describe the composition, including the focal point of the picture and the arrangement of the different parts. What feelings does it evoke? Why has it become a national icon?

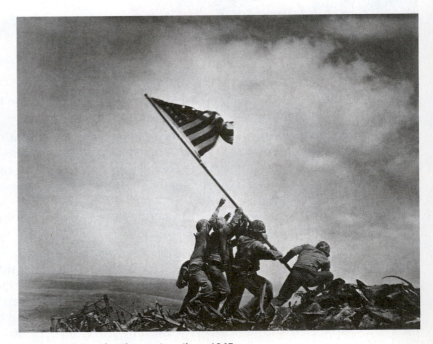

Marines Raising the Flag on Iwo Jima, 1945

World War II has been printed so many times, including on postage stamps, that it has become a national icon. It has also inspired a famous statue in Arlington Cemetery in Washington, D.C.

    6. *Visual argument often employs symbols.* You have seen how icons invite viewers to respond with the commonly held, established meanings and feelings, or even to add to those that are usually associated with them. Icons are symbolic since most people look beyond their literal meaning and add the extra meanings they have come to represent. However, of the many symbols used in argument, few are so familiar that they can be classified as icons. Look at the color photograph of the split tree in Figure 8.6. This photograph appears in *The Border: Life on the Line* by Douglas Kent Hall. The caption under the picture is "Near El Paso, Texas." El Paso is located on the Texas–Mexico border. This particular tree is a symbol, but not an icon.

    7. *Visual argument is selective.* Whenever you look at a visual argument, it is important to think not only about what is included in the picture but also about what is omitted from it. If you could stand back and see more of the entire scene, of which the picture itself is only a small part, your perception of the picture might change a great deal. In any such framed image, you are allowed to see only what the photographer sees or wants you to see. You can infer what else is there or imagine what else is going on outside the frame of the picture. The power of images often resides in this "edited" quality, but it is also a limit that the viewer must keep in mind. Look at the photographs in Figure 8.7 of different people participating in the recent debate about health care reform. Notice that each picture provides emotional proof (*pathos*).

Tree Located on the Texas–Mexico Border

Figure 8.6 *Visual argument often employs symbols.*

This quotation by Graham Greene can be found in the front of the book in which this picture appears: "How can life on the border be other than reckless? You are pulled by different ties of love and hate." Consider the location of this tree and that it was included in a book describing life on the United States–Mexico border. What symbolic meaning would you assign to it in this border context? How would you describe this meaning? What claim do you infer from looking at this picture? How might someone refute that claim? What type of proof is the tree in this context?

Each of these images depicts a recent gathering regarding health care reform. How do the two images compare? In what ways do they encourage viewers to form opposing views about the health care reform initiative? In the first, President Barack Obama greets Minnie Small, 84, of Silver Spring, Maryland, after a national teleconference town hall meeting at the Holiday Park Multipurpose Senior Center. The second shows a group of protesters demonstrating against Obamacare. How would the first picture be different had the photographer decided to photograph the entire scene in this room, with everyone in the room receiving equal attention? What is the effect of moving in on one individual to the exclusion of everyone else? How does this compare to the group shot of protesters presented in the second picture? What claim does each of these images seem to be making?

8. *Visual argument invites [varied] interpretations from viewers.* No two people looking at a visual argument will interpret it in exactly the same way because individual viewers bring information and associations from their own past experience and use it to fill in some of the meaning suggested by the picture. Readers do that too, of course, particularly when they infer a claim or supply the warrants in a written argument. When viewers, like readers, draw on their backgrounds to fill out the meaning of a visual argument, they become vested in its message since some of the meaning now belongs to them. As a result, these viewers are more likely to accept the argument.

Look, for example, at the two images on page 273. Image 1 shows a detail from Michelangelo's scenes of the Creation, which appear on the ceiling of the Sistine Chapel in Rome. Here God is passing life to human beings by stretching out His life-giving finger to the lifeless, limp finger of Adam. Now look at the picture in Image 2. This picture depicts a group of refugees reaching for food in the midst of the civil war in Syria. One viewer, looking at this picture, says the photographer is claiming, "People need to act to assist those who are caught in war-torn areas." Another puts the claim differently: "Aid to people in war-torn areas inevitably leads to conflict and struggle over scarce resources." A third viewer has a different idea: "Refugees in war-torn areas need to be offered more than just corn." How would you interpret the meaning of this picture? How would you argue in favor of your interpretation?

Now look at Figure 8.8, which is a visual argument that invites individual interpretations. This is a photograph of animal rights activists in France who have

Figure 8.8 *Visual argument invites unique interpretations from viewers.*

Animal Fur Protest

A group of naked animal rights activists hold billboards denouncing the breeding and use of animals for fur production. This photo was taken in April 2013. The claim of this argument is clear from the writing on these activists' signs: "Only My Skin"; "No Fur"; "Bare Skin, Not Skinned." What is not clear, and therefore open to interpretation, is the significance of the support for the claim. Why do you think these individuals chose to stage their protest in this way? Why are these people nearly nude, and why are they standing on a beach? What is the meaning of this support? What warrants are you expected to supply that will link this support to the claim? You are expected to make some inferences to understand this argument, and not everyone may make the same inferences.

created a tableau with several naked people standing on a beach holding signs. Members of the group Coalition to Abolish the Fur Trade, these demonstrators aim their protest at companies that participate in the fur trade. There is no correct interpretation of how the argument in Figure 8.8 is supposed to persuade a viewer to agree with the activists. Your guess may turn out to be as good as the next person's.

Analyzing Online Argument: Visuals

Here is a set of steps you can use to analyze the visuals in online argument. As you look over this list, think about the ways these steps can be used to conduct a form of visual analysis suitable to the Web.

▶▶▶ Step 1: Identify the Key Visual Images on a Web Site

- What types of visual images does this selection include? Describe them.
- What message or claim does each image advance?
- How do these messages or claims contribute to the overall message of the site?

continued

Analyzing Online Argument: Visuals (*continued*)

▶▶▶ Step 2: Compare Visuals to Other Multimedia Elements

- What other elements (textual, graphic) does this site include?
- How do these elements relate to the visual imagery?
- How do these elements reinforce the visual claims being made?

▶▶▶ Step 3: Link Visuals to Related Images

- What links to related sites does this selection provide?
- What additional images do these links include?
- Do these images reinforce or extend the original visual argument? How?

An Example Analysis: Let's Move Web Site

To see how these steps can be put into practice, consider the example below. This selection features a screenshot from the government Web site Let's Move, a program dedicated to promoting healthy activities and lifestyle among America's youth. How does this sample analysis provide you with a guide for undertaking this work yourself?

▶▶▶ Step 1: Identify the Key Visual Images on a Web Site

- This Web site includes two key visual images. The first depicts President Barack Obama and Vice President Joe Biden demonstrating active movement. The second, included above this photo, features the phrase "Let's Move" annotated with the icons of an apple and the silhouette of an active child. Taken together, these images convey the message that young people need to lead active lifestyles, one that includes exercise and healthy eating.

Analyzing Online Argument: Visuals (*continued*)

▶▶▶ Step 2: Compare Visuals to Other Multimedia Elements

- The message conveyed by these visuals is reinforced and extended by the written elements this Web site includes. In many ways, the imagery here provides visual confirmation of such statements as: "America's move to raise a healthier generation of kids" and "active schools go back to school." Each of these statements reinforces the main visual claim being made that an active lifestyle is essential to the health and well-being of young people.

▶▶▶ Step 3: Link Visuals to Related Images

- This screenshot is one of many that the Let's Move Web site includes. Among the other images are those that depict the president and first lady engaging in physical exercise and healthy eating. In addition, the Web site extends its visual argument by including links to sources that provide further information about the Let's Move program, and about ways to become more directly involved.

Activity

Go online and find an example of a visual argument. Then use the steps outlined above to analyze the ways this example uses visual imagery to advance its claim.

Using Argument Theory to Critique Visual Argument

LO2 Use the Toulmin model and the list of fallacies to critique visual argument.

Consider the rhetorical situation to gain insight into the context for the argument, including the type of visual argument you are examining, the intended viewers, the artist's background and motivation, the possible constraints of all parties, and the exigence or outside motivation for the argument. Apply the Toulmin model to discover the claim, support, warrants, backing for the warrants, and the presence of a rebuttal or a qualifier.

Learn more about the claim and purpose for the argument by asking the claim questions. Establish which type of claim tends to predominate: a fact claim establishes what happened; a definition claim defines and clarifies what it is; a cause claim looks for causes and sometimes shows effects; a value claim looks at whether it is good or bad; and a policy claim establishes what we should do about it.

Then analyze the proofs. Which are present, *logos*, *ethos*, and/or *pathos*, and which type of proof predominates in the argument? What is the effect of the proofs? Then look at specific types of proof, including signs, induction, cause, deduction, analogies, definition, statistics, values, authority, and motives. How do those that are present further the argument? Refer to the tests of validity for each of the proofs you identify to judge their effectiveness.

Also, look for fallacies and consider the effect they have on the overall argument. Look for visual fallacies in particular. For example, ask if the image may have been selected or changed to represent a particular point of view. Ask whether a photo, Web site image, or film clip represents a unique or an exaggerated way of viewing a subject, or whether it is an accurate picture of what really exists or happened. Consider the photographs taken of disasters, such as major floods or volcanic eruptions: they usually depict the worst, most extreme results of the disaster. You can at least wonder how representative these pictures are of what actually has happened.

Remember, too, that computers can be used to augment or change images. Tabloid newspapers and satirical Web sites sometimes create humorous composite images by Photoshopping one person's head on another person's body. Examine whether there is any evidence that a visual has been changed, doctored, or recreated in any way so that what you see as present in the image is a consequence of manipulation rather than insightful framing. Take time to look at visuals carefully. This helps you understand what is really going on in them and make some judgments about their accuracy and value.

Bias in Visual Argument

You will encounter bias in visual argument just as you do in written argument. All argument, by definition, shows bias for a particular point of view or a particular position. When you spot a visual argument that strikes you as biased, identify the source and type of bias being expressed. Here are examples of two images, each of which provides a biased take on the role our digital culture is playing in our lives. Figure 8.9 is an icon that raises fears about the risks to privacy posed by online technologies. More specifically, it suggests that users of such technologies are in danger of having their personal information stolen, and consequently need to take steps to protect this information. Figure 8.10 offers its own take on this issue, suggesting that our constant exposure to and reliance upon online technologies can be exhausting and overwhelming.

Figure 8.9

This photo depicts a Facebook privacy setting. How do you interpret this visual icon? What argument does it seem to be making about privacy and identity online? How would you describe the bias in this photo?

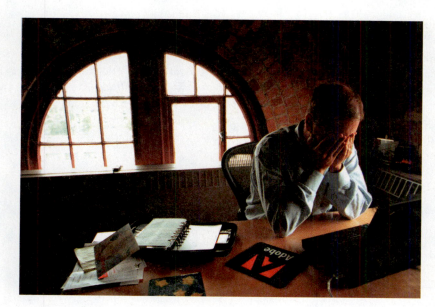

Figure 8.10

How would you describe the biased point of view toward digital technologies in this picture?

Watching for fallacies, visual distortions, exaggerations, Photoshop changes in original images that have been applied to make them more persuasive and outright or even less obvious bias in visual argument will help you make fair and objective critiques. In addition, ask these questions to make ethical evaluations of images: Does the arguer understand the issue and its consequences? Is the position proposed in the best interests of the audience? Is the arguer honest and fair-minded? Or, in contrast, is the arguer unethical and manipulative? Try to put your own prejudices and favorite ideas aside while you make these objective judgments.

Sample Analysis of a Visual Argument

The following analysis of the political cartoon in Figure 8.11 draws on both the special features of visual argument and argument theory.

SPECIAL FEATURES OF VISUAL ARGUMENT EMPLOYED IN THE CARTOON

Visual argument pulls the viewer in, creates common ground, evokes an emotional response, uses juxtaposition, employs icons, uses symbols, is selective, and invites a unique interpretation from the viewer.

1. I am pulled into this picture by the striking image of police officers surrounding a seemingly innocent diner at a restaurant. Furthermore, common ground is established through the presence of such recognizable, everyday items as a tablecloth, utensils, and wine glasses.

Figure 8.11 *A political cartoon making a visual argument.*

2. The juxtaposition of an ordinary eating scene and police raid causes me to associate restaurant dining with the issue of crime, and thereby invites me to begin thinking about whether there are rules about how and what we eat that we are not supposed to break.

3. The diner with a napkin tucked in his shirt and the table set with utensils and tablecloth have been depicted so often in ads and other media that they can be considered icons. Thus, they communicate quickly and forcefully.

4. Cartoonist Larry Wright has selected what he wants to feature in this picture: the stereotypical depiction of a fancy restaurant, the police officers with guns, and the key phrase "trans fats." As a result, the focus is on conventional dining habits, and the prevailing rules about what we are and are not supposed to eat.

5. I interpret this picture by remembering all the different occasions when I have eaten in restaurants, and I wonder whether I should stop eating so much of this food in order to preserve my health. On the other hand, I also wonder whether the current warnings about the unhealthy effects of certain foods are perhaps overblown, as suggested by the overreaction of the police in this picture.

ARGUMENT THEORY USED FOR ANALYSIS OF THE CARTOON

Useful theory includes applying the rhetorical situation (TRACE), the Toulmin model, the claim questions, and the types of proof, including *logos*, *ethos*, and *pathos*; identifying fallacies; bias; and determining whether or not the argument is convincing and ethical.

Rhetorical Situation

Text: Political cartoon with an argumentation intent.

Reader/viewer: People who eat out at restaurants or who consume food high in trans fats.

Author/artist: Larry Wright, a cartoonist for Wright/Cagle cartoons.

Constraints: Some viewers may be suspicious of public warnings about food health because such warnings seem to change so routinely; the artist seems to share this attitude by suggesting that our current concerns about trans fats might be overblown.

Exigence: The FDA's recent issuing of warnings about the dangers of trans fats.

Toulmin Model

Claim: Individual consumers should have the right to make their own decisions about the relative health consequences of what they eat.

Support: The overreaction of the police in trying to prevent the "crime" of eating trans fats denies this right.

Warrant: The police do not have the right to enforce rules about our personal eating habits.

Type of Claim: This is a policy claim. It suggests that the government should stop trying to get people to eat healthy food.

Types of Proof (logos, ethos, pathos)

Cause: Excessive worrying about food health can lead to an infringement of individual choice.

Analogies: The choice of where and what to eat is analogous to other individual rights.

Value: We value individual freedom of choice.

Motivation: Everyone should enjoy the same prerogative to choose what they eat, free from government interference or coercion.

Fallacies: The police response is exaggerated and oversimplified for this occasion.

Bias: It is biased in favor of individual freedom of choice and against excessive government interference.

Ethical Evaluation

Best interests of society? Yes, because preserving individual freedoms benefits every member of society.

Ethical? Perhaps. It depends on whether we think individual freedom of choice is a more important consideration than public health.

We have described visual argument, explained why it is convincing, and illustrated how you can analyze it by examining its special features and applying argument theory. Let us change the focus now to present some ideas that will help you create visual arguments of your own. Visual argument can be used to provide support for a written argument, or it can stand alone as an independent argument. We now examine both possibilities.

LO3 Create written arguments that incorporate visual elements.

Add Visual Argument to Support Written Argument

You may, at times, decide to add pictures, photographs, drawings, flowcharts, graphs, or other images to your papers as support for your claim. You can see from studying the images presented so far in this chapter that visual argument, when compared to written argument, is immediate and concrete, can appeal powerfully to the emotions, and can enhance an argument's message by making it convincing in ways that words alone cannot do. When an image is used as support, be certain that it functions as support for the specific claim or subclaim you are presenting.

Include images in your argument writing by adding clip art from the Internet or by using various types of printed visual material drawn from books, magazines, and newspapers. Downloaded images from the Internet can be pasted into your paper electronically. You can also use Photoshop to juxtapose or combine images that will invite your viewer to think about your claim in a new way. Printed images or drawings can be photocopied and pasted into your paper. Of course, if you prefer, draw your own diagrams, flowcharts, or sketches to add visual support for the claim. Also, decide whether or not to add a line or two of explanation under each visual to explain its relationship to the written text. You will need to do that if the relationship between the ideas in the text and the visual support is not immediately clear to the reader. Document all visual sources to show where you obtained them.

When you have quantities of numerical data, experimental results, or complex plans that are too cumbersome to describe in the written body of your paper, present it visually. Graphs, charts, tables, and flowcharts are valuable for condensing such material, often making it more easily accessible to the audience.

There are many different types of graphs, but the most commonly used are line, bar, and circle (or pie) graphs. These three kinds of graphs can be generated through common word processing or spreadsheet programs such as Microsoft Word or Excel for insertion in a paper.

Bar graphs in particular are used when you want to compare measurements of some kind. The numbers used in the measurements are often large, and the bar graph offers a picture that makes the numbers easily understandable in relation to one another. Figure 8.12 provides an example of a bar graph that shows the estimated number of new HIV infections in the United States between 2008 and 2010. The graph divides the number of new infections into different categories of race, gender, and sexuality.

Line graphs are most often used to show a change in a measurement over time. Some of the different measurements associated with line graphs are temperature, height and weight, test scores, population changes, and profits or deficits. Figure 8.13 shows the changes in global temperature over a 120-year period. *Circle graphs* are ordinarily used to show how something is divided. Figure 8.14 shows a circle graph that sums the percentage of the different types of federal government expenditures during a single year.

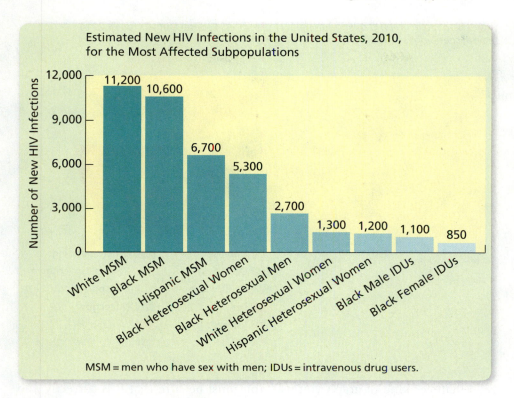

Estimated New HIV Infections in the United States, 2010, for the Most Affected Subpopulations

MSM = men who have sex with men; IDUs = intravenous drug users.

Figure 8.12 *Bar graph comparing large numbers*

Source: Centers for Disease Control and Prevention.

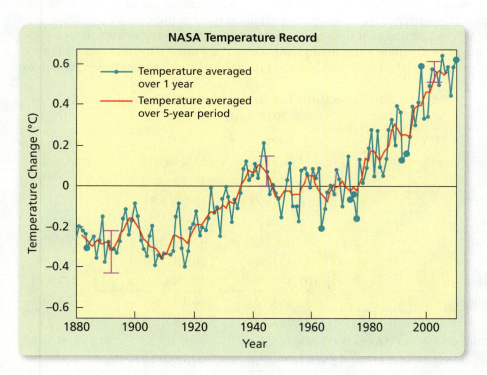

Figure 8.13 *Line graph showing change over time*

Figure 8.14 *Circle graph showing how federal spending is divided into sectors*

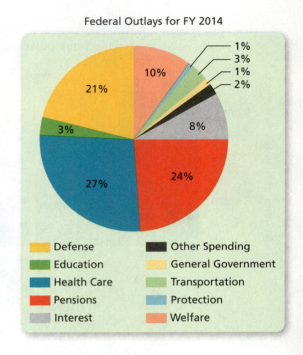

Federal Outlays for FY 2014

Defense
Education
Health Care
Pensions
Interest
Other Spending
General Government
Transportation
Protection
Welfare

Whatever kind of graph you use, you must be sure that it is correctly and clearly titled and labeled, that the units of measurement are noted, and that you report the source of the statistical information used in the graph.

When you find that the statistical information you want to include in a paper is too detailed and lengthy for a graph, a chart or a table is usually recommended. For example, Figure 8.15 provides the projected figures for population growth for

Figure 8.15
Table presenting comparison data

Population Projections for Selected Countries and World: 2006, 2025, and 2050

COUNTRY	2006	2025	2050
Bangladesh	147,365,352	204,538,715	278,855,405
Brazil	188,078,227	217,825,222	228,426,737
China	1,313,873,713	1,453,123,817	1,424,161,848
India	1,111,713,810	1,448,821,234	1,807,878,574
Iraq	26,783,383	40,418,381	56,360,778
Japan	127,463,611	120,001,048	88,886,568
Mexico	107,448,525	130,188,682	147,807,650
Nigeria	131,858,731	206,165,846	356,523,587
Russia	142,068,484	128,180,386	108,187,353
United States of America	288,444,215	348,666,188	420,080,587
World	6,528,088,562	7,863,750,137	n.a.

ten major countries as well as for the world as a whole. It appears in a paper that argues in favor of zero population growth.

Create Visual Arguments That Stand Alone

We have suggested ways to use visual materials as illustrations that support ideas in written arguments. Many visual arguments are, however, quite independent of written text and stand alone as persuasive arguments themselves without the benefit of accompanying verbal explanations. Creating visual arguments of this type requires imagination, creativity, and critical thought. Like other types of argument, you will find visual arguments that stand alone all around you. Look at book covers, bulletin boards and displays, posters, t-shirts, and even your fellow students. Some of your classmates may dress and arrange their hair so that they are walking visual arguments. Figure 8.16 (below) provides two examples.

You can use the same types of images and equipment for all visual argument. These include single or composite images, moving images, photographs, drawings, paintings, or even three-dimensional installations with objects placed in juxtaposition to make a claim. For example, a stack of books and a light bulb could make the claim that reading helps people think and generate ideas. Experiment with stock photography from the Internet, Photoshop or Paint Shop Pro, cameras and camcorders, poster board and markers, scissors and paste.

For visual argument, as with other types of argument, you will need to make a claim about an issue that generates more than one perspective. Select an issue that is important to you and that you can make important to your audience. Reflect on all of the elements in the rhetorical situation as you would in creating a verbal argument. These include the materials and methods you will use; the characteristics and interests of your viewers; your own resources and interests; the

(a)

(b)

Figure 8.16 *Clothing can make an argument. (a) Singer, songwriter, and activist Bono, member of the rock group U2, makes a statement with his jacket. (b) A supporter of same-sex marriage and his message.*

constraints, including values, that either pull you and your viewers together or push you apart; and your exigence or motivation for working with this issue in the first place. Use the Toulmin model to set up the main parts of your argument: you will need a claim, support, and warrants that you and your audience can share. Consider also how you can use *logos*, *ethos*, and *pathos* to create a persuasive and convincing argument.

Think through the eight special features of visual argument and how you will employ some of them to make your argument more convincing. You will want to create images that:

▶ Communicate quickly and have immediate and tangible effects on viewers.

▶ Invite viewer identification and establish common ground through shared values.

▶ Engage the emotions of the viewers.

▶ Juxtapose materials from different categories so that the viewer will make new links and associations.

▶ Employ familiar icons that prompt immediate responses from viewers.

▶ Present visual symbols that viewers can easily interpret.

▶ Include only materials that viewers should focus on and omit everything else.

▶ Invite unique interpretations from viewers through visual subtleties that do not mean the same things to all people.

Figure 8.17 *Visual argument that uses words to extend its meaning*

Arguing Like a Citizen

The photo in Figure 8.17 makes a visual argument about the issue of homelessness. In order to better understand how visual arguments work, as well as the ways they connect to the question of citizenship, look closely at the discussion below.

▶▶▶ Thinking Like a Citizen

- Why do I care about this issue?
  In my view, the issue of homelessness is one of the greatest moral challenges confronting our nation. Homelessness affects people from all walks of life, but its costs are particularly high for children and families. Because it leaves so many of our society's most vulnerable in such a dangerous position, homelessness raises in a particularly vivid way the question of civic responsibility: What obligation do we have to relieve the suffering of our fellow citizens?

▶▶▶ Arguing Like a Citizen

- What response to homelessness would I advocate?
  I would argue that Americans need to approach homelessness as more than a social or political issue, but as a moral issue as well. In advocating for specific policies to address homelessness, I would make the additional claim that supporting such measures is an ethical obligation.

▶▶▶ Acting Like a Citizen

- What concrete actions could I take to help resolve this issue?
  The concrete actions I might take to help address homelessness include (1) donating to or volunteering at a food pantry or homeless shelter; (2) writing a letter to my local or state representative urging action on this issue; and (3) participating in a campus event to raise money for a local pantry or shelter.

Activity

Choose another visual that makes its own argument about homelessness. What particular visual elements does it include? And what specific claims about this issue do these elements make? Then, using the sample discussion above as your guide, analyze the ways this visual argument connects to the question of citizenship. How is this visual's treatment of the homeless issue important to you? What key questions does it raise? And what concrete action would you take to help resolve this issue?

Consider adding a few words to your visual argument to enhance or extend its meaning. For an example, take a look at the image in Figure 8.17 on page 266. Clearly the photographer here is deeply concerned with the plight of the homeless, particularly homeless children, and uses the image here to convey this view. Notice how the inclusion of the single word "please" adds a powerful dimension of meaning to the picture. Rather than a photoline describing the picture, this term instead creates common ground by reminding viewers of the young children they know (or have) themselves. By juxtaposing the word "please" with the image of a dirt-covered young boy, the picture adds emotional appeal to its critique of homelessness. By adding this word, the photo invites a more complex and personal interpretation from a viewer than the picture alone could provide. Not all people would state the claim this picture makes in exactly the same way. How would you state it?

Review Questions

1. Where are you likely to encounter visual argument? How do you recognize it? **(LO1)**

2. What are the eight special features of visual argument that make it convincing? **(LO1)**

3. What information about argument theory might you employ to help you analyze visual argument? **(LO2)**

4. Describe some ways that you might use visual argument as support for a written argument. **(LO3)**

5. What ideas from this chapter might help you create an effective visual argument that stands alone? **(LO4)**

Exercises and Activities

A. **Group Work and Class Discussion: Analyzing Visual Argument**

In small groups, view the five photographs on the following pages from the perspective of argument, analyze them, and discuss them as a class. Here are some general questions to guide your discussion. Additional "For Discussion" questions accompany each image.

1. Is this a visual argument? Why do you think so?

2. What was occurring and in what context that prompted the photographer to take the photograph?

3. What is it about? What is the claim? What are the implied values or point of view?

4. Does it engage your emotions? What is your emotional reaction?

5. Does it establish common ground? Do you identify with anyone or anything in it?

6. What other special features of visual argument make it effective?

   ▶ Is it immediate and tangible? How does it pull you into the picture?

   ▶ What is included? Left out? Changed? Distorted? Exaggerated?

   ▶ Does it rely on juxtaposition? How? To what effect?

   ▶ Does it use icons? To what effect?

   ▶ Does it use symbols? To what effect?

   ▶ Would everyone interpret it in the same way? What is your interpretation?

7. What do you conclude about the purpose, meaning, and effectiveness of this image?

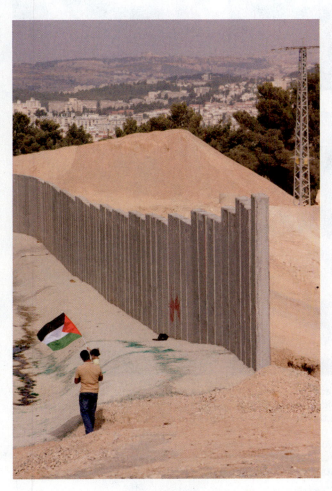

Image 1:

West Bank Barrier

This photograph appeared over the caption "Father and daughter waving a Palestinian flag stand near the Israeli separation barrier being constructed in the West Bank. This barrier, projected to be 436 miles long when completed, has been controversial since 2002 when the Israeli government decided to build a wall to protect its citizens from Palestinian suicide bombers."

For Discussion: Here is an excerpt from the poem "The Mending Wall" by Robert Frost. Two men are repairing the rock wall between their farms. One of them makes the statement, "Something there is that doesn't love a wall." His neighbor has a conflicting view. He says, "Good fences make good neighbors." Apply each of these statements to the West Bank barrier. Which makes better sense in this context? What do you conclude about the final value of this barrier?

Image 2:

Drawing National Boundaries

The first of these photos captures a scene from a march in Los Angeles protesting against current policies regarding illegal immigration. The second photo depicts a supporter of tighter immigration control attending a rally in Washington, D.C.

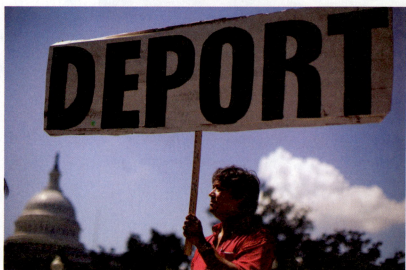

For Discussion: Each photo makes a different claim. Describe them along with the support provided for each. What warrants are implicit in each photo? What backing, in the form of pervasive cultural values in the United States and Mexico, enhance the persuasive strength of these photos? Some people in the United States advocate building a strong barrier along the U.S.–Mexican border to keep Mexican workers and others from crossing over illegally; other people reject this idea. State your position on this issue along with your reasons for holding it.

Image 3:
Coming Home to a Destroyed Neighborhood

This photo is captioned, "Affluent Lebanese drive down the street to look at a destroyed neighborhood, August 15, 2006, in southern Beirut, Lebanon." During the summer of 2006, Hezbollah in Lebanon fired rockets into northern Israel, and Israel retaliated by bombing Hezbollah headquarters, airports, and major highways in Beirut, Lebanon. This photograph was taken the first day of the ceasefire. It shows four young women who have borrowed a car and a driver to return to their neighborhood. It is a candid shot, and the photographer, Spencer Platt, won the World Press Photo Award in 2007 for it.[2]

For Discussion: According to the photographer, many people look at this picture and ask if it is actually taken in the Middle East. What about it invites that reaction? Compare it with war zone photographs that you have seen of Syria or Afghanistan. What special characteristics of visual argument are present in this photo? Which predominate? State the claim. How would others in your class state the claim?

Image 4:
LeBron James

This picture, taken by sports photographer Christian Petersen, depicts basketball superstar Lebron James in action in Game 3 of the 2013 NBA Finals against the San Antonio Spurs.

For Discussion: What pulls you into this picture? When viewed from the perspective of argument, what claim does this photograph make? Photographers sometimes say that they have to capture a particular moment to get a good picture. How does that observation apply to this picture? What other special features of visual argument are apparent here?

[2]Miki Johnson, "Spencer Platt Wins World Press Photo Award," PopPhoto.com, February 9, 2007, http://www.popphoto.com/photographynewswire/3794/spencer-platt-wins-world-press-photo-award.html.

Image 5:
At Home Outdoors

The individuals in this picture are aboriginal people of Balgo in the Great Sandy Desert of northwest Australia. Otherwise known as indigenous Australians, they are descended from the first known inhabitants of Australia. Traditionally, they spend their time outdoors. The house in this photograph is provided by the government, presumably to improve their lives, and it is used mostly for storage. This picture first appeared in *National Geographic* magazine in 1991.

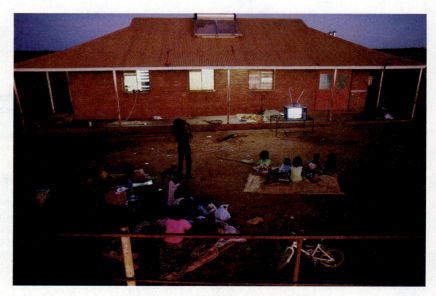

For Discussion: What are the people in this photograph doing? Describe the cultural values shown in this photograph. Are there any conflicts in values? What does the photograph suggest about attempts by governments or organizations to impose new cultural customs or values on groups of people? How would you state the claim made by this picture? Comment on the use of juxtaposition here. What, if any, added content is related to the time of day indicated in the photograph?

B. Group Work, Class Discussion, and Writing Assignment: Analyzing Multiple Perspectives on an Issue Expressed through a Collection of Visual Arguments

1. Review "Expressing Multiple Perspectives through Visual Argument" along with the collections of related images on pages 97 and 109.

2. Look at the three images on pages 273 and 274, understand the context for each of them, and answer the questions for discussion on page 274 that accompany them.

3. Write a title for the images that communicates what they have in common and what issue they address when viewed as a group of images that makes an argument.

4. Write an essay in which you describe the four different perspectives on the issue expressed by the photographs; write in detail about how each is related to and contributes to the development of the idea in your title. Draw a conclusion about this set of images that expresses your final assessment of them.

Image 1:
Adam and God

This image is a reproduction of a work of art. It was painted on the ceiling of the Sistine Chapel in Rome by Michelangelo in 1511, where it can be viewed today; it depicts the creation of Adam.

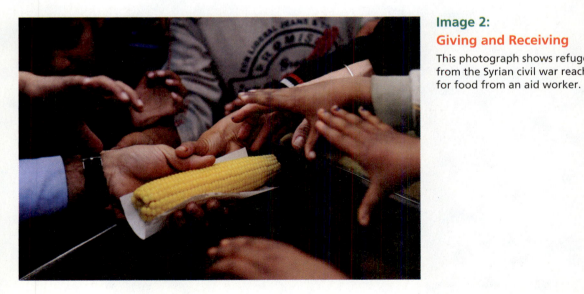

Image 2:
Giving and Receiving

This photograph shows refugees from the Syrian civil war reaching for food from an aid worker.

Image 3:
Robot with a Grappler

This photo ran in the *New York Times* in 2002 over the caption, "A robot with a grappler holding a wounded Palestinian yesterday on a highway in Megiddo, Israel, 12 miles southeast of Haifa. Israeli Radio said the man was a suicide bomber whose explosives detonated prematurely."

For Discussion: Compare the hands in each of the three images on page 273 and above. How are they similar? How are they different? Discuss how juxtaposition is used in each of these photographs. What is the effect? What additional associations form in your mind as you look at each of these three photographs? What is your personal interpretation of each of them? That is, what does each communicate to you? How effective are each of these images as arguments? How effective are they as a collection of images that makes an argument?

C. Individual Work and Class Discussion: Analyzing a Cartoon

To help you with this exercise, follow the model for the analysis of a cartoon provided on pages 259–261 of this chapter, which employs both the special features of visual argument and argument theory as tools for analysis. Look at the cartoon, answer the questions that follow it on the next page, and discuss your answers with the class.

Questions about the Special Features of Visual Argument

1. What pulls you into this cartoon? What do you notice first? What can you say about the composition that draws you into it?

2. Do you experience common ground with anyone in the image? Are any values expressed that you share?

3. Does this cartoon arouse your emotions? What is your emotional reaction?

4. Does the cartoon rely on juxtaposition? What is placed in juxtaposition, and what is the effect?

5. Do any icons appear in this cartoon? If yes, describe them. What do they contribute?

6. Do any symbols appear in this cartoon? If yes, describe them and consider what they contribute.

7. Is the image selective? What is included, what is left out, and what is the effect?

8. How would you interpret this cartoon? What do you think the cartoonist's purpose is, what is the final effect, and what do you conclude about it?

Questions from Argument Theory

1. Describe the rhetorical situation: What type of text is this? Who are the intended viewers? Who is the cartoonist? What constraints of the viewers and the cartoonist can you infer? What is the exigence for this cartoon?

2. Apply the Toulmin model: What is the claim? What is the support? What is the warrant? What is the backing? Is there a rebuttal? Is there a qualifier?

3. What would you say is the type of claim made in this cartoon: fact, definition, cause, value, or policy?

4. What types of proof are employed? Comment on the use of *logos*, *ethos*, and *pathos*.

5. Are there any fallacies in this cartoon? If yes, describe them.

6. What is your ethical evaluation of this cartoon? Is its claim in the best interests of society? Why or why not?

D. Writing Assignment: Locating a Visual Argument and Analyzing It

Find a visual argument online or in printed magazines, newspapers, or books. Write an analysis of the visual argument. Why do you think the item you have selected is a visual argument? Identify the issue. Point out the special features of visual argument that make it convincing. State your interpretation of the claim, even if you have to infer it. Point out the support and the warrants and describe the backing. State why you do or do not find the argument convincing.

E. Creating a Stand-Alone Visual Argument and Writing an Analysis of It

This assignment requires you to create a visual argument, to write a paper in which you analyze it, and then to present and explain it to the class.

a. Identify an issue that you can make an argument about using visual material. You may choose an issue from one of the visual arguments that appear in this chapter, or you may select an issue of your own.

b. Make a claim about the issue.

c. Create a visual argument. Draw on the suggestions made in this chapter (pages 265–268).

d. Include just enough writing on your visual argument to help viewers understand your claim.

e. Write a paper, about 250–350 words long, that explains and interprets your visual argument. Consider the following to include in your analysis or add other information. Your goal is to describe what you have expressed in your visual argument and explain to your viewers just how you created it to accomplish this goal.

　　1. Explain the rhetorical situation: What is the context for your issue and your visual argument?

　　2. Write a Toulmin analysis of your visual argument. Here is an example of a possible Toulmin analysis of the student-made collage on page 278 about artworks:

Issue:	Has art become too expensive?
Claim:	Art is too expensive.
Support:	The examples of art pasted on the dollar sign are expensive.
Warrant:	I cannot afford those artworks.
Backing:	Most people viewing this collage know how expensive these famous artworks are.
Inferred rebuttal:	I have money to buy less expensive artworks, and I think they are just as enjoyable to own.

　　3. Identify the type of claim, and describe how you have used *logos*, *ethos*, and *pathos*.

　　4. Describe your own interpretation of your argument. Why did you put it together as you did?

f. Share your visual argument with the class. Include the ideas in your written analysis. Ask for other interpretations from class members.

g. *Examples:* Two student-made visual arguments appear on page 278. The first is a collage, the second is a sculpture. The second example is accompanied by a short analysis that explains what the student accomplished from her point of view.

STUDENT VISUAL ARGUMENT 1

Untitled

Elisabeth Elsberg, a student in a first-year writing class, created this collage from print images that were cut and pasted onto a painted background.

For Discussion: To work with audiences, icons must be immediately recognizable to most people. What parts of this artwork would you classify as iconic? Are they clearly iconic? How does this student use juxtaposition? Comment on the use of selectivity in this piece. What has been selected? What has been left out? How do you interpret this visual argument? How would you state its claim?

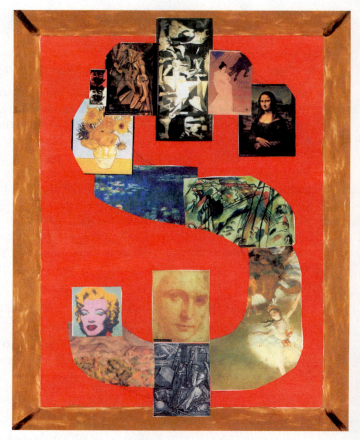

STUDENT VISUAL ARGUMENT 2

Never Again

Karen Hernandez, the student who made this visual argument, created the figures out of clay. She then installed the clay figures on a platform that displays photographs from the Holocaust, with a title that expresses the claim: "Never Again."

ANALYTICAL ESSAY OF STUDENT VISUAL ARGUMENT 2

*NEVER AGAIN**

Karen Hernandez

The artist was a student attending the University of Texas at Arlington when she made the sculpture and wrote this essay about it. The graphic novel *Maus* by Art Spiegelman provided the inspiration for this argument. *Maus* had been a reading assignment in her writing class. It tells the story of Spiegelman's parents' experiences during the Holocaust.

In 1938 Hitler and the Nazi government began a reign of terror and death that would leave over ten million people dead through pogroms and in prison camps. The book *Maus* tells one survivor's story, and I have tried to speak with this work of art of the horror that these people endured, just as the author of the book does. The skeletal figures of my piece are made of clay because it creates the closest appearance to human bones, and the figures are skeletal because this is the way many of the survivors looked when they were rescued from the camps. I have also left them in various sizes and shapes just as real people are; however, my figures are left incomplete (no hands or feet) because this is how the Germans viewed them, as less than human beings.

Even though the figures are skeletal, they have taken on an almost lifelike quality of expression in the way some heads are bowed, while others are held up. Some of the figures lean as if in pain or fatigue, and others seem to look at those standing nearby or into space. The longer I look at them, the more human they become to me, and I hope I have been able to impart this to the viewer as well.

I have also included, on the box below, pictures of victims and survivors of the Holocaust so that the observer will know that this work is more than just the artist's imagination, and that these horrors really did occur. I also chose to place the title across the front of the piece so that, like the group who first used it in the Holocaust museum, I might impart to the viewer the reminder that those who died during this terrible time of death and horror will not have done so in vain, and they will be remembered. Something like this will happen NEVER AGAIN.

For Discussion:

What do you find most striking about this visual argument? What pulls you in as you look at this photograph of it? How is juxtaposition used, and what is the effect? Are the words written on the front of the visual argument sufficient to suggest the claim it is making? How does the analytical essay help you further understand this visual argument?

---

*"Never Again" by Karen Hernandez.

Worksheet 3 | Visual Argument Development

1. Write an issue question to focus your issue (example: *How can the unemployed be put back to work?*).

2. Write a claim that answers your issue question (example: *The government should create green-collar jobs to help the unemployed and the environment.*).

3. Check the type of visual argument you will create (check more than one, if necessary):

   _____ stand-alone argument   _____ photograph

   _____ support for my essay   _____ drawing

   _____ composite image   _____ painting

   _____ single image   _____ collage of images

   _____ still image   _____ graphic story (comics)

   _____ moving image   _____ three-dimensional installation

   _____ all original   _____ PowerPoint

   _____ images from print sources   _____ sculpture

   _____ images from Internet   _____ video

4. Check the materials you will need:

   _____ computer   _____ video camera

   _____ Paint Shop Pro   _____ poster board

   _____ Photoshop   _____ colored markers

   _____ PowerPoint   _____ scissors and paste

   _____ magazines   _____ paints

   _____ newspapers   _____ other art supplies

   _____ still camera   _____ objects for installation

5. Which of the eight special features of visual argument will be evident in my work?

6. What words should I add to make it clear to my audience?

Rogerian Argument and Common Ground

After studying this chapter, you will be able to:

LO1 Define the purpose and key aspects of Rogerian argument.

LO2 Create your own examples of Rogerian argument.

LO3 Apply the principles of Rogerian argument to academic writing.

Traditional argument, which has its origin in classical sources, is the form of argument that predominates in American culture. It is what you are used to when you listen to people argue on television or when you read arguments in blogs, periodicals, or books. In traditional argument, the arguer states a claim and proves it by drawing on various types of proofs, including reasoning and evidence. The object is to convince an audience that the claim is valid and that the arguer is right. In this traditional model, the arguer uses the rebuttal to demonstrate how the opposition is wrong and to state why the audience should reject that position. Thus, the emphasis is on winning the argument. Debate, with participants on both sides trying to win by convincing a third-party judge, is one form of traditional argument, as is courtroom argument and all other single-perspective argument in which one person argues to convince one or more people of a particular point of view.

As you know from your own experience, traditional argument does not always achieve its aims with the audience. Indeed, in certain situations when strongly held opinions or entire value systems are challenged, traditional argument may not be effective at all. The audience might simply stop listening or walk away. When that happens, it is useful to have another argumentation strategy to turn to, one that might work better in cases in which there seems to be a standoff or a lack of common ground among the arguing parties.

Rogerian argument, so called because it evolved from techniques originally applied by psychotherapist Carl Rogers, is a technique that is particularly useful for reducing conflict and establishing common ground between people who hold divergent positions and who may at times express hostility toward each other. Common ground often seems impossible to achieve in such situations, but two opposing parties can almost always find something to agree on if they try hard enough.

To achieve the goal of establishing common ground, Rogerian argument also employs rebuttal differently. Instead of using rebuttal to show how the opposition is wrong, as in traditional argument, Rogerian argument requires that the arguer spend at least some time at the beginning of the argument not only explaining how the opposition's position is right but also identifying situations in which it might be valid. The arguer cannot do this successfully without finding some common ground with the opposition. It is almost impossible to show how any part of another individual's opposing position is valid if you disagree with it totally.

To illustrate, imagine an argument between two individuals who are seeking common ground on methods for reducing gun-related violence. One of these individuals advocates that private citizens arm themselves with handguns as a deterrent to shooters. Another believes that the availability of handguns is the problem and advocates that private gun ownership be abolished. Common ground exists between the two parties because of their common concern for personal safety. To use Rogerian argument in this situation, the anti-handgun party would restate the pro-handgun party's position and would emphasize the common concern they both have for protecting their safety, before they search together for a solution on which they can agree.[1]

You may find Rogerian argument frustrating at first, especially if you favor contentious debate in situations in which your ideas and values seem to be under threat. Because Rogerian argument emphasizes making connections with the opposition and reducing hostility in such situations, you will need to curb your instincts to launch your argument by letting the opposition know how wrong you think they are. You can learn to use Rogerian argument, even if it is not your preferred or most natural style of arguing, in situations where traditional argument is no longer effective. It is a useful strategy when other strategies are failing. Let us look at a couple of examples.

LO1 Define the purpose and key aspects of Rogerian argument.

Achieving Common Ground in Rogerian Argument

In 2005, Cal Thomas, a politically conservative newspaper columnist, and Bob Beckel, a liberal political analyst and consultant, began coauthoring their popular column "Common Ground" that appears in the newspaper *USA Today*. In 2007,

---

[1]I am indebted to Jenny Edbauer for this example.

they published *Common Ground: How to Stop the Partisan War That Is Destroying America,* and in it Cal Thomas describes their collaboration.

> We're a good example of how common ground can work. Before we knew each other, we only knew "about" each other. I saw you [Beckel] as a liberal Democrat with "evil" ideas and positions conservatives associate with that label. You saw me as a conservative Republican with similar "evil" ideas and suspect friends. When we got to know each other and talked about politics, as well as personal and family challenges, we stopped seeing each other in stereotype and came first to respect and then (shock, shock) even to admire each other. The politics became less important than the relationship. And, most surprising of all, we found ourselves in agreement about quite a number of things, though we occasionally still differ on the best ways to achieve our common goals.[2]

Their purpose in writing the book, they make clear, is to encourage U.S. politicians to follow their example and make it a rule to seek common ground as part of the political process for resolving difficult and divisive issues. Indeed, Thomas and Beckel claim they are presenting "a plan that makes polarization the issue and common ground the solution." They "believe the time is right to challenge polarization and for common ground to become the next dominant strategic force in national politics."[3] To support this idea, they argue that the public prefers this approach: "Surveys conducted over several years have found that Americans believe even the most partisan issues—from abortion to the Iraq war—can be resolved with an honest commitment by elected leaders in Washington to finding consensus."[4]

Rogerian argument, with its emphasis on finding common ground and reaching consensus, can sometimes help people who differ strongly in their views find a bedrock of values and ideas that they can all hold in common. As a result, divided individuals are often able to resolve at least some of their differences. The process of seeking political common ground that Thomas and Beckel believe is beginning to occur in political discussions, and that they hope will occur more often, includes listening, understanding, and accepting points of view different from one's own, recognizing that both positions have some merit, and finally finding a way to resolve some of the differences. This process is at the heart of Rogerian argument strategy.

Let us look at another real-life example of building common ground between disagreeing parties with each side demonstrating an understanding of the other's point of view. Environmentalists, who typically want to protect the environment at all costs, often find themselves in opposition to individuals who make their living by exploiting the environment. Loggers, ranchers, mill owners, and other industrialists, for example, can fall into this second category. Individuals from both groups, stereotyped as "nature haters" and "eco-freaks" by the press, met in Idaho to discuss efforts for protecting endangered wildlife in the area. The environmentalists went to the meeting with some trepidation, but "as they joked and sparred over steak and beer, they discovered that neither side lived up to its stereotype. 'We found that we didn't hate each other,' said Alex Irby, a manager at

---

[2]Cal Thomas and Bob Beckel, *Common Ground: How to Stop the Partisan War That Is Destroying America* (New York: HarperCollins, 2007), 257.

[3]Thomas and Beckel, 12.

[4]Thomas and Beckel, 10.

the Konkolville sawmill. 'Turns out, we all like to do a lot of the same things. We love the outdoors.'" Timothy Egan, who wrote about the details of the meeting for the *New York Times Magazine*, makes this comment: "Loggers in the back country sitting down with environmentalists is an astonishing change." One can infer that the common ground established in this meeting was brought about by each side describing to the other the value they placed on the environment and on outdoor activity in general. In such an exchange, both parties perceived that they had been heard, and further dialogue was then possible.

As you can see from both of these examples, understanding the rhetorical situation in general and the audience in particular by analyzing the thoughts and values of the parties involved is of critical importance in Rogerian argument. As you read the rest of this chapter, including the examples of Rogerian arguments written by students at the end of the chapter, pay particular attention to how Rogerian arguers analyze their audiences' dissenting opinions and values and then respond to them as part of their overall strategy.

LO2 Create your own examples of Rogerian argument.

Rogerian Argument as Strategy

Carl Rogers was a psychotherapist who was well known for the empathetic listening techniques he used in psychological counseling. Here is how he describes the importance of listening:

> I like to be heard. A number of times in my life I have felt myself bursting with insoluble problems, or going round and round in tormented circles, or during one period, overcome by feelings of worthlessness and despair. I think I have been more fortunate than most in finding at these times individuals who have been able to hear me and thus to rescue me from the chaos of my feelings. I have been able to find individuals who have been able to hear my meanings a little more deeply than I have known them. These individuals have heard me without judging me, diagnosing me, appraising me, evaluating me. They have just listened and clarified and responded to me at all levels at which I was communicating. I can testify that when you are in psychological distress and someone really hears you without passing judgment on you, without trying to take responsibility for you, without trying to mold you, it feels damn good. At these times it has released the tension in me. It has permitted me to bring out the frightening feeling, the guilt, the despair, and the confusions that have been a part of my experience. When I have been listened to and when I have been heard, I am able to reperceive my world in a new way and to go on. It is astonishing how elements which seem insoluble become soluble when someone listens, how confusions which seem irremediable turn into relatively clear flowing streams when one is heard. I have deeply appreciated the times that I have experienced this sensitive, empathic, concentrated listening.[5]

Rogers later became interested in how listening techniques could be used to improve communication in other difficult, emotionally charged situations. Richard Young and his colleagues Alton Becker and Kenneth Pike built on Rogers's ideas to formulate Rogerian argument, a method for helping people in difficult situations

---

[5]Carl R. Rogers, *A Way of Being,* Boston: Houghton Mifflin, 1980, 12–13. I thank Barbara Ciarello for calling this to my attention.

make connections, create common ground, and understand one another. The object was to avoid undue conflict or, even worse, a mutual standoff.[6]

According to Young, Becker, and Pike, written Rogerian argument reduces the reader's sense of threat and conflict with the writer so that alternatives can be considered. Four goals are met with this strategy.

Goal 1. Writers let readers know they have been understood. To accomplish this purpose, the writer restates the opponent's position in summary form by using dispassionate, neutral language. The writer demonstrates that the reader has been heard and that the writer understands the issue exactly as the reader does. The loggers and the environmentalists listened and understood one another in the example cited earlier.

Goal 2. Writers show how readers' positions are valid in certain contexts and under certain conditions. The writer demonstrates to the reader that at least part of the reader's position is both valid and acceptable and thereby makes it easier for the reader to reciprocate and accept part of the writer's position. Both the loggers and the environmentalists discovered validity in each other's positions since neither group wanted to destroy wildlife.

Goal 3. Writers help readers understand that both of them share the same values, types of experience, attitudes, and perceptions and are thus similar in significant ways. The loggers and environmentalists made it clear to each other that they shared a love of the outdoors, held some of the same values, and enjoyed the same types of experiences.

Goal 4. Writers propose solutions made up of elements from both sides that can be agreed to by both parties. At this point, environmentalists discovered that loggers were quite willing to pursue ways to preserve wildlife.

The most important feature of Rogerian argument is listening empathetically and nonjudgmentally. Rogers perceived that people usually listen judgmentally and evaluatively. They are eager to jump in, point out what is right or wrong, and make corrections or refutations, whereas Rogerian listening requires that insight into the other's position precede evaluation. Thus, a writer of Rogerian argument takes the reader's place, and this is achieved by requiring that the writer provide neutral summaries of the reader's position that show sympathetic understanding of it and its context. In doing this, the writer encourages a continued and open exchange of ideas with the reader. In Rogers's words, the writer "listens with" as opposed to "evaluating about."

In real life, Rogerian argument is used frequently, particularly in business and perhaps increasingly in politics, where agreement is indispensable. Some people in business claim they could not get anything done if they did not use Rogerian strategies on a daily basis. William L. Ury, one of the founders of the Program on Negotiation at Harvard Law School, claims that in business now, the best way to compete is to cooperate. Cooperation is necessary because of the numerous mergers and cooperative ventures between companies. Many companies now work with the same markets and the same customers, and they cannot compete, as in former times, without weakening themselves as much as their competitors.[7]

---

[6]Richard Young, Alton Becker, and Kenneth Pike, *Rhetoric: Discovery and Change* (New York: Harcourt, Brace, and World, 1970), 7–8, 274–90.

[7]William L. Ury, "Getting Past No . . . to Yes! The Art of Negotiation." Workshop, Dallas, October 12, 1999.

Box 9.1	Traditional and Rogerian Argument Compared

▶▶▶ What Is Rogerian Argument?

	TRADITIONAL ARGUMENT	ROGERIAN ARGUMENT
Basic strategy	Writer states the claim and gives reasons to prove it. Writer refutes the opponent by showing what is wrong or invalid.	The writer states opponent's claim to demonstrate understanding and shows how it is valid.
Ethos	Writer establishes own character by demonstrating fair-mindedness, competence, and goodwill.	Writer builds opponent's *ethos* and enhances own character through empathy.
Logos	Writer appeals to reason to establish a claim and refute the opponent's claim.	Writer proceeds in an explanatory fashion to analyze the conditions under which the position of either side is valid.
Pathos	Writer arouses emotions with evocative language to strengthen the claim.	Writer uses descriptive, dispassionate language to cool emotions on both sides.
Goal	Writer seeks to change opponent's mind and thereby win the argument.	The writer creates cooperation, the possibility that both sides might change, and a mutually advantageous outcome.

Box 9.1 contrasts Rogerian argument, as explained by Young, Becker, and Pike, with the traditional model of argument.

Analyzing Online Argument: Rogerian Argument

While the emergence of the Web has fostered greater public engagement with issues, it has also, in many cases, led to greater polarization. Extreme viewpoints of those who evince no interest in hearing, let alone accepting, other views are found everywhere on the Web. As a result, some online arguments try to seek common ground. The steps outlined below provide you with a guide for using the principles of Rogerian analysis to find common ground in online arguments.

▶▶▶ Identify the Differences

- What, if anything, is polarizing about this online argument?
- What key multimedia elements are used to present a polarizing viewpoint, if any?

Analyzing Online Argument:
Rogerian Argument (*continued*)

▶▶▶ Restate This Position in Neutral Terms

- How can you restate this multimedia argument in a more objective way?

▶▶▶ Uncover the Common Values

- What assumptions, views, and values might this arguer share with those on the other side of this argument?

▶▶▶ Propose a Solution

- What changes would you make to this multimedia text, if any, to create common ground?

The Web site below offers an example of how these steps for creating common ground can be put into practice. Look closely at this image and the sample analysis that follows.

Immigration

continued

Analyzing Online Argument: Rogerian Argument (*continued*)

▶▶▶ Identify the Differences

Excerpted from the official White House Web site, this selection uses a combination of visual and textual elements to create common ground around the controversial issue of immigration reform. More specifically, it makes an argument designed to reconcile concerns over fairness and security that typically divide pro- and anti-immigration groups.

▶▶▶ Restate This Position in Neutral Terms

The selection seeks to accomplish this goal first by employing language that emphasizes the importance of collaboration and compromise. For example: "Together, we can create a fair, effective and common sense immigration system that lives up to our heritage as a nation of laws and a nation of immigrants." This same emphasis is reinforced through the links included, which bring together all of the key issues (i.e. "security," "enforcement," "citizenship") over which discussions about illegal immigration most often become polarized. By presenting them as a set of related concerns that this "comprehensive reform plan" will address, the Web site succeeds in conveying to viewers its desire to overcome the differences that typically prevent the creation of common ground. This message of inclusion is also conveyed visually, in the form of the U.S. map, which draws a connection between vibrant immigration and national economic health.

▶▶▶ Uncover the Common Values

Through these various multimedia elements, this Web site succeeds in uncovering the potential common ground that might bring the sides involved in the debate over illegal immigration closer together. Such common ground includes: an acknowledgment that illegal immigration is not a threat to the economic health of the United States; an agreement that sensible immigration reform needs to incorporate concerns over national security; a commitment that immigration reform will also respect the rule of law.

▶▶▶ Propose a Solution

With these shared values clearly communicated, it is easy to imagine a viewer willing to seriously consider the immigration reform plan presented here. Such a viewer would likely be swayed by the argument that immigration can be managed with the requisite attention to fairness, security, and economic health.

Activity

Now use these same steps to analyze an online argument of your own. Choose an example of an online argument that, in your view, is especially polarizing. What does this argument look like? What views does it pit against each other? Moreover, what is it about these views that makes this issue so polarizing? Use the steps outlined above to create a model for how these differences might be bridged.

Writing Rogerian Argument

To write Rogerian argument, according to Young, Becker, and Pike, the writer proceeds in phases rather than following set organizational patterns or argumentation strategies. These phases are as follows:

1. The writer introduces the issue and shows that the opponent's position is understood by restating it.

2. The writer shows in which contexts and under what conditions the opponent's position may be valid. Note that the opponent is never made to feel completely wrong.

3. The writer then states his or her own position, including the contexts in which it is valid.

4. The writer states how the opponent's position would benefit if the opponent were to adopt elements of the writer's position. An attempt is finally made to show that the two positions complement each other and that each supplies what the other lacks.

Rogerian Argument in Academic Writing

LO3 Apply the principles of Rogerian argument to academic writing.

Rogerian argument as described by Young, Becker, and Pike is rarely, if ever, written exactly according to their format. You can learn more about Rogerian argument, however, by using their format as practice. The "Exercises and Activities" section of this chapter provides two examples of Rogerian argument papers written by students who followed Young, Becker, and Pike's formulations. You also will be invited to write a Rogerian argument paper using this format.

As you read professionally written argument, however, you are much more likely to find elements or variations of Rogerian argument rather than arguments that include all of the parts of the Young, Becker, and Pike model. Here are some variations of Rogerian argument that you may encounter in your academic reading.

1. *Report on past research at the beginning of an academic argument.* Authors of academic argument, as a matter of convention, often begin with a review of what previous writers have contributed to the subject. They identify the writers by name and summarize their contributions before identifying and developing their own contribution to the subject. Thus an ongoing chain of conversation is established that acknowledges what has gone before the new material that is the actual subject of the article.

2. *Research proposal.* Research proposals that request funds and resources from granting agencies typically begin with a positive summary of the contributions of past researchers. Only after this former work has been acknowledged does the researcher explain how the new proposed research will build on what has gone before.[8]

---

[8]I am indebted to Mary Stanley for alerting me to this use of Rogerian argument.

3. ***Rogerian response paper.*** This paper is written in response to an essay written by another person with whom the author disagrees. The author of a response paper typically rejects the position that the author of the other essay presents but hopes to create common ground and understanding with that person to keep a dialogue on the issue going. The goal is to make a connection with the author of the other essay and thus create a context of understanding so that both authors can continue exploring the issue. Such papers usually begin with a restatement of the other author's position along with an acknowledgment of what is valuable about that position before the author goes on to present a different view of the matter.

As you read arguments written by other authors, look for elements of Rogerian argument. The three examples just cited by no means exhaust the possibilities.

Using Rogerian Principles to Argue Like a Citizen

One criticism sometimes leveled at Rogerian argument when it is first encountered is that it can be perceived to be manipulative. Though it can be used in this way, it is not inherent to this form of argumentation. People who use Rogerian argument in unethical ways to manipulate other people may exhibit a condescending attitude or fake sincerity. They may also use some of the same tactics that unethical arguers use in traditional argument: for example, hiding the real purpose of the argument by misrepresenting the issue; using inappropriate emotional appeals, including emotionally loaded language; manufacturing evidence; or the use of inaccurate evidence, exaggerations, or lies.

Individuals who practice ethical Rogerian argument, on the other hand, make a genuine attempt to understand an issue and its consequences from a range of different perspectives. Participants in Rogerian argument have to sincerely believe that the position they propose is in the best interests of both parties and, possibly, the larger society as well. They need to be able to answer the questions, *Who are benefited by what I want?* and *Who are burdened or hurt?* and to scrupulously consider the consequences of their answers to those questions. They need to listen and hear nonjudgmentally; they need to seek genuine agreement with at least part of the opponent's position; and they need to develop some unconditional positive regard for the individuals with whom they are engaged and show that regard in all that they say. In other words, participants in Rogerian argument need to think, argue, and act like a citizen.

In order to test out this premise, return for a moment to the online issue you analyzed above. Now that you have seen how Rogerian argument can help overcome the polarization we so often see in the online media, look at the sample analysis below to see how this same framework can help you connect such a common ground argument to citizenship.

▶▶▶ Thinking Like a Citizen

• Why do I care about this issue?
  This issue is important to me because it concerns one of our national values in which I believe most deeply: the right of all immigrants, regardless of their circumstances or

Using Rogerian Principles to Argue Like a Citizen (*continued*)

background, to seek a new home in the United States. I am keenly aware that America was founded as an immigrant nation and, as a result, I feel strongly that we should support immigration laws that honor this tradition. As an American citizen, however, I also find myself in sympathy with the point often made by those in favor of tighter restrictions on immigration, especially illegal immigration: the need for everyone to respect the rule of law.

▶▶▶ Arguing Like a Citizen

- What argument can I make that supports my view but also creates the possibility of common ground?
  In light of my views on this issue, I think the most effective argument is one that acknowledges the rights of immigrants while simultaneously recognizing the importance of obeying the law. Such an argument might read like this: Existing law needs to be changed to allow more immigrants the chance to enter the United States legally, as well as to strengthen penalties for those who attempt to enter the country illegally.

▶▶▶ Acting Like a Citizen

- What concrete action can I take to create greater common ground on this issue?
  To help garner public acceptance of this argument, I could undertake any one of the following measures: (1) write a letter in support of this approach to my local or state representative, (2) participate in a public discussion with opponents of immigration reform, and (3) solicit firsthand stories about the challenges and struggles faced by newly arrived immigrants and post them online.

Activity

Choose a polarizing issue and, following the steps above, use the principles of Rogerian argument to explain your position on the issue so that those who disagree will find it more acceptable.

Review Questions

1. What are the four goals of Rogerian argument, and how do they differ from those of traditional argument? **(LO1)**

2. What are some of the advantages and disadvantages of Rogerian argument? **(LO1)**

3. In what type of argumentation situation do you think you might find Rogerian argument more productive than traditional argument? Describe an issue, along with the rhetorical situation, that might prompt you to resort to Rogerian argument. **(LO2)**

4. In what type of argumentation situation do you think you might find traditional argument more productive than Rogerian argument? Describe an issue, along with the rhetorical situation, that might prompt you to use traditional argument instead of Rogerian argument. **(LO2)**

5. What difficulties, if any, do you personally contemplate in using Rogerian argument? How do you feel about using this strategy? **(LO2)**

Exercises and Activities

A. Class Discussion: Understanding Rogerian Argument as a Strategy

The selection below was written by Mike Rose, a professor of Education at UCLA. Read the passage, analyze the Rogerian strategy, and answer the questions at the end.

> **BEFORE YOU READ:** What are your views on the value of education? Do you know of anyone who holds a different view? What is it?

ESSAY #1   **HEAL THE ACADEMIC–VOCATIONAL SCHISM***
Mike Rose

Mike Rose is a professor in the Graduate School of Education and Information Studies at the University of California, Los Angeles, and the author most recently of *Back to School: Why Everyone Deserves a Second Chance at Education*.

Since the passage of the Carl D. Perkins Vocational Education and Technology Act of 1990, educators have made a concerted effort to enrich vocational curricula with academic content. Today colleges have seen a new burst of energy around "contextualized learning," the attempt to make subject matter more relevant and comprehensible by teaching it in the context of another subject—for example, teaching mathematics through fashion or automotive technology.

Much has been achieved, but attempts to integrate the academic and the vocational curricula will be limited or subverted unless we deal with the cultural and institutional factors that created the academic–vocational divide itself.

For a long time in the West, intellectual elites have tended to distinguish between physical work and technical skill—labor, the mechanical arts, crafts and trades—on the one hand, and deliberative and philosophical

---

*"Heal the Academic–Vocational Schism" by Mike Rose from *The Chronicle of Higher Education*, September 10, 2012. Reproduced by permission.

activity on the other. The latter emerges from leisure or, at least, from a degree of distance from the world of work and commerce. The distinction carries with it judgments about intellectual acuity and virtue.

This difference runs through America's cultural history, although it seems at odds with the country's strong orientation toward practicality. It was evident after the Revolutionary War, when mechanics were portrayed in editorials as illiterate and incapable of participating in government, and it contributed to the structure of curriculum tracking in the 20th century's comprehensive high schools.

5   At the postsecondary level a longstanding tension persists between liberal study and professional or occupational education. Is the goal of college to immerse students in the sciences and humanities for the students' intellectual growth and edification, or to prepare them for work and public service?

With the increase in occupational majors since the 1960s, the vocational function is clearly ascendant, yet you don't have to work in a two- or four-year college very long to sense the status distinctions among disciplines, with those in the liberal tradition, seen as intellectually "pure" pursuits—mathematics, philosophy—having more symbolic weight than education or business or, to be sure, the trades.

Such tension plays out when arts and sciences faculty are brought together with faculty in occupational programs. The way subject areas and disciplines are organized in school and college leads future faculty to view knowledge in bounded and status-laden ways. And there is no place in a historian's training, let's say, where she is assisted in talking across disciplines with a biologist, let alone to a person in medical technology or the construction trades.

Those separations are powerfully reinforced when people join an institution. The academic–vocational divide has resulted in separate departments, separate faculties, separate budgets, separate turf and power dynamics. Now egos and paychecks enter the mix. These multiple separations lead to all sorts of political conflicts and self-protective behaviors that work against curricular integration. And it certainly doesn't help that efforts at integration are often framed such that the academic side will bring the intellectual heft to the vocational courses, a laying on of culture.

If the conflicts are mild, curricular integration still faces limits. From what I've seen, the work of integration tends to stay at the technical, structural level: Where in carpentry or nursing is math used, and how can we teach it in that context? This is a reasonable focus—the specific work that needs to be done.

10   But one could also imagine discussing how carpentry and nursing are mathematical activities. Or how the math being learned can transfer to other domains. Or how thinking mathematically opens up a way to understand the world: carpentry and nursing, but also employment and the economy, social issues, the structure of the physical environment. Educators tend to teach mathematics in vocational settings in the most practical, applied terms, and to locate further mathematical topics as the domain of liberal study.

The academic–vocational divide also leads us to think about vocational students in limited ways. They are narrowly job-oriented, hands-on, not particularly intellectual. That characterization is reinforced by loose talk about learning styles. It is true that a significant number of vocational students did not have an easy time in school and can barely tolerate the standard lecture-based, textbook-oriented classroom. It is a grind for them when, in pursuit of a degree beyond an occupational certificate, they must take general-education courses.

But dissatisfaction with the standard curriculum does not necessarily indicate a lack of interest in liberal-arts topics. Countless people, young and not so young, come alive intellectually when the setting is changed, from museum-based educational programs to staging Shakespeare in prison. And the change in curriculum and setting doesn't have to be that exceptional. I think of a welding student in his 40s, a tough, goal-oriented guy, who excitedly told me about a field trip in his art-history class, and his amazement and pleasure that he was able to identify architectural structures by period and knew something about them.

If we sell our students short, we have done the same with the vocational curriculum. Despite all that John Dewey tried to teach us, we often underestimate the rich conceptual content of occupations. A powerful feature of contextualized learning is that it forces us to articulate the conceptual dimensions of the vocational course of study.

Likewise, occupations have a history and sociology and politics that can be examined. And they give rise to ethical, aesthetic, and philosophical questions: Students confront traditions and standards, and have to make decisions about the right action; they make aesthetic judgments; they are moved to reflect on the power of the tools and processes they use, and what deep knowledge will enable them to do; and they begin to identify with and define themselves by the quality of their work.

15   As I noted, faculty on the liberal-studies side of the academic–vocational divide aren't primed by their training to see all of this, and, sadly, vocational education itself has fostered this restrictive understanding. The authors of an overview from the National Center for Research in Vocational Education conclude that, historically, "vocational teachers emphasized job-specific skills to the almost complete exclusion of theoretical content." Indeed, as a profession, vocational education has further restricted the education of its students by excluding from its curriculum the study of the economics, politics, and sociology of work.

The assumptions about work, intelligence, and achievement that underlie a curriculum are as important as the content of the curriculum itself. A lot of historical debris has kept us from bridging the academic–vocational divide—now is the time to start sweeping it away.

For Discussion:

What is the issue in this passage? What different attitudes toward education are identified? What are their differences? How does Rose create common ground between these attitudes? How does Rose use Rogerian strategy? Summarize the different attitudes showcased here and describe the Rogerian elements in the passage.

B. Writing Assignment: Write a Rogerian Response

Select the essay in this chapter or elsewhere with which you disagree the most and write a Rogerian response to it. Use either essay or personal letter format. Your paper should be from 300 to 500 words long.

Prewriting

Write a brief summary of the position taken by the author of the essay you have selected. Then write a brief summary of your position. Make certain you understand both positions clearly.

Writing

Do all of the following in your paper:

1. State the opposition's position as presented in the article and describe in what instances this position might work or be acceptable. As you write, imagine that the individual who wrote the article or letter will be reading your response. Write so that that person will feel "heard."

2. Write a clear transition to your position on the issue.

3. State how your position would also work or be acceptable.

4. Try to reconcile the two positions.

C. Class Discussion: Creating Images for Visual Rogerian Argument

Creating images to support visual arguments, or creating stand-alone Rogerian visual arguments, can be challenging because two different positions need to be portrayed as equal and potentially correct. Further, the idea of consensual agreement needs to be part of the picture as well. Images 1, 2, and 3 can be used as images to represent Rogerian argument. No detailed captions appear with these images. They speak for themselves. Look at each of them, and then answer the "For Discussion" questions.

Image 1:
Hands across the World

Image 2:
Sports Handshake

Image 3:
**Bipartisanship
and What It Can Achieve**

For Discussion: What do these three images have in common? In what argumentation contexts and for what types of issues would each be appropriate? To answer these questions, study the icons used in each visual. What do they communicate about the broader context of each argument? Do you have any ideas for visual argument that communicate the methods and goals of Rogerian argument? Use your imagination, and describe your ideas for the class.

D. Group Activity: Creating Your Own Rogerian Web Site

First, choose an issue that seems especially controversial or polarizing. What does the debate around this issue typically look like? What are the different views that are expressed, and how are they different? Next, use the principles of Rogerian argument to create a hypothetical Web site in which these differences might be resolved. How would this Web site present the issue at hand? How would it speak to the stakeholders in this debate who hold such differing or opposing views? What specific features would most effectively help achieve this goal?

E. Writing Assignment: Rogerian Argument

You are now going to write a Rogerian argument of around 1,000 words on an issue of your choice. There are several ways to set up this assignment. Read through the following options, select one that appeals to you, and proceed with the rest of the instructions for the assignment. The basic instructions in option 1 apply to all four options. Examples for options 1, 2, and 3 are provided at the end of this exercise.

Option 1. If you wrote an exploratory paper, write a Rogerian argument in response to the position you discovered that is most unlike the position you favor. You may have already articulated this opposing position in your exploratory paper. Move this position to the beginning of your Rogerian argument paper, and rewrite it until you believe you have fairly and dispassionately represented that other point of view. People who hold that view need to be able to agree that you have heard and understood them.

Look for common ground with that other view. Use that common ground to describe contexts and conditions in which the opponent's position might be valid. Do not show what is wrong with this other position.

Now write a transition that changes the subject to your position. Describe your position, and show the contexts in which it is valid.

Finally, reconcile the two positions. Show how they can complement each other, how one supplies what the other lacks, and how everyone would benefit if elements of both were finally accepted.

Option 2. Select any issue that you understand from at least two opposing points of view. You should feel strongly about your point of view, and you should have strong negative feelings about opposing viewpoints. Write a Rogerian argument in response to an opposing viewpoint.

Option 3. Recall the last time you were in an argument in which there was a stalemate and no one seemed to win. Write a letter to the individual with whom you were arguing. Use Rogerian strategy.

Option 4. Team up with a classmate who disagrees with you on a specific issue. Take turns articulating your partner's position until that person feels "heard" and understood. Then write a Rogerian argument in response to that position.

Prewriting

Write a one-paragraph summary of the opposing position and a one-paragraph summary of your position. Refer to these summaries when you write your paper.

Writing

Write your paper, making sure you do all of the following:

1. Introduce the issue and restate the opposing position to show you understand it.

2. Show in which contexts and under what conditions the opposing position may be valid. State it so that it is acceptable to the opposition.

3. Write a clear transition that moves the reader from the position you have just explained to the position that you favor and will now defend.

4. State your own position and describe the context in which it is valid.

5. Show how the opposing position would be strengthened by adding elements of your position. Then try to reconcile the two positions.

Examples

The following are two examples of Rogerian argument written by students.

Example 1 *(Option 1).* "Human Cloning: Is It a Viable Option?" was written by a student in an argument class who had also written an exploratory paper on this subject. The student conducted research for the paper, and items from her annotated bibliography appear on pages 347–349. In writing this paper, the student began with the position she had researched that was most unlike her own and rewrote it until she thought it would satisfy the individuals who hold that position. Notice that she was able to use the research for her other paper to add support for this paper as well. The marginal annotations make it easier for you to distinguish the parts of her paper.

Following the student's paper is a Rogerian argument evaluation sheet that has been filled out to show how her argument conforms to the recommended parts of a Rogerian argument. The requirements for the Rogerian argument paper are described in the left column, and the right column shows how well this paper met those requirements. When you have finished reading the paper in Example 2, see if you can identify and describe the parts of this paper well enough to complete an evaluation sheet like the sample. This analysis will help you understand how to write your own Rogerian argument.

STUDENT PAPER

#1

Angela A. Boatwright
Professor Thorne
English 1302
30 April 2014

Human Cloning: Is It a Viable Option?*

Introduction to issue and summary of rhetorical situation.

Well, hello Dolly! Although research in animal or human cloning is not new, the technology has never had as much potential as it does today. Interest in what is and is not considered ethical in cloning research has surfaced since the historic announcement in Scotland of the existence of a cloned sheep named Dolly. Scientists were able to create a cloned sheep by taking the genes from a six-year-old sheep and putting them into an enucleated egg from another sheep. This egg was then implanted in the womb of yet another sheep, resulting in the birth of an identical twin that is six years younger than its sister (Bailey). This is the first known asexual reproduction of a mammal. It seems a reasonable assumption that a human clone is the next logical step down this technological pathway.

Explanation of opposing position to create common ground.

Those who support unregulated human cloning experimentation justify their position by citing the medical gains and potential benefits the technology has to offer. They believe that the possible benefits of this technology far outweigh the risks and, furthermore, that it is an ethical practice because of its potential benefits. Some of these benefits include the generation of skin grafts for burn victims and bone marrow for patients undergoing cancer chemotherapy (Butler and Wadman 8). Cloning also shows promise for treating infertility and could become an option either for infertile couples or for people who have genetic defects and fear passing these defects on to their offspring.

Supporters of cloning believe that the arguments against cloning are vague and speculative and that they simply do not justify a ban. It is not the technology that frightens people so much as it is a lack of understanding. When people picture the result of an attempt at human cloning, they see images of Frankenstein or an army of Hitlers. Researchers believe that given time to digest the information, the public will one day regard cloning with the same openness and sense of normalcy that it now regards blood transfusions and organ transplants. They also reason that a ban on cloning could drive the technology underground, leading to a greater potential for unsafe, unregulated, and exploitative misuse.

Description of context in which opposing position is valid.

Everyone would probably agree that technological advances have changed our lives in positive ways, and cloning research is not likely to be an exception. The fear held by cloning supporters, that the sensationalism created by this issue has clouded the judgment of the public and lawmakers who support a ban on cloning, is certainly a valid concern. Although it is not clear that human cloning will offer any great benefits to humanity, no one has yet made a persuasive case that it would do any real harm either

*"Human Cloning: Is It a Viable Option?" by Angela Boatwright.

(Macklin 64). It would be an injustice to completely abandon the possibilities that could enhance the lives of so many people based solely on hypothetical applications of a technology that may never be realized. Each disease we are able to eradicate is another huge step for humankind.

Transition to author's view.

5   I agree that we should do everything in our power to improve the longevity and quality of life of all people, but I do not believe it should be at the expense of the dignity of human life. Many people who oppose cloning view it as an "invasion of personality." Even Dr. Ian Wilmut and his colleagues, the creators of Dolly, hold the position that cloning of humans would be unethical (64). He points out that it took 277 attempts to produce one live lamb. Of the 277 "reconstructed" embryos, 29 were implanted into recipient ewes, and 3 out of 5 lambs showed developmental abnormalities and died soon after birth. He believes similar tests with humans would not be acceptable.

Explanation of author's view.

Those of us who advocate anticloning measures believe that the potential abuse of such power could have disastrous consequences. The fear of the creation of human clones for the sole purpose of harvesting them for "spare parts" is too great to ignore. Another concern is that cloning will lead to efforts to breed individuals with perceived exceptional genetic qualities, eliminating the diversity that makes the human race what it is. There is a widespread belief that parents might create unrealistic expectations for cloned children, believing they no longer have the potential limitations of their genetic ancestors (Pence 135). Cloning is really a major step toward regarding our children as acceptable only if they conform to the choices of our will (Carey).

Many of us are also bound by the religious ideas we have been brought up with, telling us that only God has the right to create life. It is sinful to think of removing that sovereign right from an omnipotent God and placing it in the hands of mere mortals. Like the majority of Americans, I believe that human cloning experimentation should be banned before it can become an out-of-control reality.

Personal example to introduce idea of reconciliation of the two opposing positions.

I am fortunate to be the mother of a wonderful and beautiful baby girl. If I had been given the opportunity to choose her characteristics, would I have elected to change my child? I absolutely would not. I would not trade any of her personal traits for something "better." I love her just as God gave her to me. Yet with absolute certainty, I can admit that if she developed a life-threatening ailment, I would not hesitate for a second to utilize any cloning technology available to cure her. This is not to say I would sacrifice another life for hers, only that I would employ any and all resources available short of that alternative.

Reconciliation of positions.

If we can agree that human life should always be held in the highest esteem, we have the basis for reconciling our positions. Cloning should not be used to pick and choose the type of people who are allowed to exist, but we should explore the potential medical benefits of cloning technology research. Many of the medical procedures we take for granted every day were once as controversial as cloning is at this very moment. Most of these procedures became successful at the cost of testing on live beings, but with their consent. We must never allow human beings to be the subjects of experimentation without their knowledge or permission. We may not impose conditions on human beings that they might not have consented to if allowed to make the decision for themselves.

10   A moratorium might be a better solution than an outright ban. A moratorium would authorize a temporary delay of human cloning research and allow us the time to sort out the details and ensure that an educated decision is made. It is easier to make an intelligent decision when there is not a feeling of impending doom hanging over our heads. "In a democratic society we don't usually pass laws outlawing something before there is actual or probable evidence of harm" (Macklin 64). This statement can serve as a guide for future policy on human cloning.

Works Cited

Bailey, Ronald. "The Twin Paradox: What Exactly Is Wrong with Cloning People?" *Reason* May 1997. *Reasononline*. Web. 12 Mar. 2014.

Butler, Declan, and Meredith Wadman. "Calls for Cloning Ban Sell Science Short." *Nature* 6 Mar. 1997: 8–9. Print.

Carey, John. "Human Clones: It's Decision Time." *Business Week* 10 Aug. 1998: 32. Print.

Macklin, Ruth. "Human Cloning? Don't Just Say No." *U.S. News & World Report* 10 Mar. 1997: 64+. Print.

Pence, Gregory E. *Who's Afraid of Human Cloning?* Lanham: Rowman, 1998. Print.

Wilmut, Ian. "Roslin Institute Experiments: Creation of Dolly the Sheep." *Congressional Digest* Feb. 1998: 41+. Print.

For Discussion:

Describe a rhetorical situation in which it would be better to write this paper using Rogerian strategy than it would be to write it as a position paper, using traditional argument. Describe the readers, constraints, and, in particular, the exigence as you imagine the rhetorical situation for this paper.

Evaluation Sheet for Rogerian Argument Paper

REQUIREMENTS OF ROGERIAN ARGUMENT	WHAT THE AUTHOR DID
1. Introduce the issue and state the opposing position to show that you understand it.	1. Introduced the issue in paragraph 1 and presented the opposing view accompanied by good reasons in paragraphs 2 and 3.
2. Show how the opposition might be right.	2. Showed the contexts in which the other position might be valid in paragraph 4.
3. Write a clear transition from the opposing position to your position.	3. Wrote a transition in the first sentence of paragraph 5 to move from opposing to own position.
4. Give your position and show how you might be right.	4. Presented own position in paragraphs 5, 6, and 7.
5. Reconcile the two positions.	5. Reconciled the two views in paragraphs 8, 9, and 10.

Example 2 *(Option 2).* "Dear Boss" was written by a student who worked parttime while going to college and needed to change her working hours and some of her responsibilities. She had already spoken to her boss about making some changes but ended up with more responsibility instead of less. She was worried that her boss might think she was selfish and unconcerned about the welfare of the company. She was also worried that working too many hours would endanger her scholarship. It was very important to her that she reach a resolution to her problem. She decided to use Rogerian strategy to come to a better resolution of her dilemma with her boss. (After reading "Dear Boss," complete an evaluation using the sheet on page 300.)

STUDENT PAPER
#2

Elizabeth Nabhan
Professor Wood
English 1302
30 April 2014

Dear Boss*

Dear Boss,

   I am writing to you in response to our recent conversation regarding my responsibilities as an employee of Smith and Smith. You indicated to me that you felt I had a surplus of free time at work and suggested that I was obviously capable of handling a greater workload. Shortly thereafter, you delegated to me several new tasks that are to be performed on a regular basis. I understand that you believe I should pick up the additional workload to ensure that I am performing at a maximum level of output on a day-to-day basis. Also, you think I would complete the tasks more effectively than the individuals previously assigned to them.

   I understand your reasoning that I should maintain a high level of output on a daily basis. As an employee of the company, it is my obligation to be productive for the duration of my workday. Not producing enough work results in idle time that, in turn, results in a loss to the company. It is intrinsic to the very nature of my role as a corporate auditor to ensure that the company does not engage in wasteful expenditures. If I worked nonstop every workday I would maximize my rate of efficiency and save the company the cost of hiring an additional employee. Furthermore, I accept your opinion that I am the employee who could most efficiently handle the new tasks you would like me to take on. My knowledge and experience with the required tasks puts me at an advantage over the employees previously delegated this work. Because of this, I would be able to complete the tasks much more quickly than other employees who would likely require more research time. Your perspective is fundamentally valid. However, I would like to introduce several factors that I believe may also bear consideration. In doing so,

---

*"Dear Boss" by Elizabeth Nabhan.

I believe it will be possible to reach a satisfactory conclusion regarding the issue of my workload and responsibilities.

According to the terms of my employment, I am required to complete a minimum of twenty hours per week. It was mutually agreed that any time I am not enrolled in school, I am free to work up to forty hours per week. The period during which I had an unusually ample amount of "down time" occurred during the summer months when I was not enrolled in school. As a result, I did briefly have an increased number of work hours. During this interim period I could have easily increased my workload, but I was not assigned any new tasks. In fact, additional duties were not assigned to me until after I commenced the fall semester. My hours are now reduced by nearly one-half, and, as a result, my idle time has diminished significantly. An increased workload now will limit the time I spend on each project and could result in a decrease in the quality of the work I complete.

I do not think there is any great concern as to whether the employees originally assigned to my newest tasks are able to complete them satisfactorily. These employees were hired based on their skills for completing the tasks at hand, and none of these tasks could be considered as falling outside of the scope of their regular duties. Furthermore, I believe it would be counterproductive to reassign their tasks to me, as it would essentially undermine these other employees' expertise. This type of situation can often lead to a decrease in morale, which would in turn affect each employee's total output. Finally, I would like to reconsider the belief that idle time on my part results in decreased productivity. During my free time I am in a position to assist other staff members as necessary. I also utilize this time to observe subordinate employees, which is consistent with my role as the corporate auditor.

5   Our individual points of view share the common purpose of doing what is best for the company as a whole. Therefore, I believe it is possible to accomplish this goal via compromise. According to your perspective, I should take on additional responsibilities to fill gaps in my productivity while relieving less-qualified employees. From my point of view, I feel that my time is already effectively spent. I suggest the following steps be taken in order to ensure that each of our needs are met: First, my reduced hours must be taken into consideration when assigning me work. When I am in a position to take on additional duties, I feel I should be assigned those most compatible with my job description. More general tasks should be delegated to other employees. To alleviate your hesitation regarding their ability to perform these, I accept the responsibility of overseer and will offer them any help they may need. In doing so, I will apply my own expertise to more specific tasks without overburdening myself in such a way as to reduce my overall efficiency. Additionally, this will allow other employees the opportunity to sharpen their skills, while remaining under my observation. I propose this delegation of duties be put into effect under a probationary period, during which time we can observe the success of the program, and, if needed, redelegate tasks. Thank you for your consideration.

Sincerely,
Elizabeth Nabhan

For Discussion:

What is the issue? What is the boss's position? What is the student's position? If you were the boss, how would you respond to this letter?

F. Class Project: Combining Strategies in a Class Debate with Attempts to Reconcile the Opposing Positions

This activity provides the opportunity to combine elements of traditional and Rogerian argument theory.

Debate is a traditional forum for argument, and a common model for debate is to have two people on each side of the issue present their views and a judge who declares a winner. Your class can set up a debate in which everyone participates. For this class debate, however, we will use a somewhat different strategy that involves not only stating the opposing viewpoints but also working to find some common ground between the two opposing positions to achieve more productive argument and to avoid a standoff with no agreement and no resolution of the issue.

We draw on *social judgment theory* to help organize the debate. Social judgment theorists, who study the positions that individuals take on issues, plot positions on a continuum that ranges from extremely positive to extremely negative. They then describe these positions in terms of latitudes of acceptance. Individuals at the extremes of the continuum have narrow latitudes of acceptance and can usually tolerate only positions that are very close to their own. Somewhere in the middle is a latitude of noncommitment. People in this area, who are not strongly involved with the issue, have comparatively wide latitudes of acceptance and can tolerate a wide range of positions. The object of this debate is to increase everyone's latitudes of acceptance so that productive argument can take place.

Preparing for the Debates

1. *Select an Issue*

   The class can either nominate possible issues from the following list of topics and articles in this book or make recommendations of their own. They can then vote on which one of them is to be the topic for debate. The issue should be written in statement form, as in the list, so that individuals can either agree or disagree with it.

   Resolved: Traditional families are best, with the mother taking care of the children and the father working to support the family.
   Resolved: Dating services in America and arranged marriages in other countries are the best ways of finding a suitable husband or wife.
   Resolved: Relying on egg donors and sperm banks can be the best way to conceive brilliant and successful children.
   Resolved: The grading system conventionally used in elementary and high school should be abolished.

Resolved: The United States should build a fence along the United States–Mexico border to control illegal immigration.

Resolved: Wars are inevitable.

Or: Brainstorm campus or current events issues and then vote on which one to debate.

2. *Create Three Groups*

The class will divide into three groups. Two groups are encouraged to take strong affirmative and negative positions and to argue from those points of view, presenting pro and con arguments, with presumably narrow latitudes of acceptance. A third group with a wider latitude of acceptance will take the middle-ground positions and present suggestions for resolving some of the conflict. This group will look for common ground in the extreme positions, try to resolve conflict, and work to achieve better understanding and perhaps even a change of views in the opposing groups.

Group 1 is the affirmative group that is in favor of the subject for debate. Group 2 is the negative group that is against it. Group 3 is the moderate group that will attempt to resolve the conflict. The groups should be equal in size. To achieve this equality, some students may have to argue for positions that they do not in fact actually hold.

3. *Do Background Reading and Writing*

All three groups should do some background reading on the subject for debate. The negative and affirmative teams will read to get ideas for their arguments and to develop ideas for refutation. The moderates should read to understand the opposing positions. Students in groups 1 and 2 will write 250-word papers outside of class that present some arguments to support their positions. After they have listened to the debate, the moderates will write 250-word papers that make an effort to resolve the conflict.

Conducting the Debate

Day One

1. *Begin with the opening papers (10 minutes).* Two students from the affirmative group and two from the negative group agree to start the debate by reading their papers. The first affirmative, first negative, second affirmative, and second negative read papers in that order.

2. *Others join in (20 minutes).* Students may now raise their hands to be recognized by the instructor to give additional arguments from their papers. Each person should stand to speak. The speakers should represent each side in turn. The class should decide whether everyone should first be allowed to speak before anyone is permitted to speak a second time. The instructor should cut off speakers who are going on too long.

3. *Caucus and closing remarks (15 minutes).* The affirmative and negative groups caucus for 5 minutes to prepare their closing arguments. Each group selects a spokesperson who then presents the group's final, strongest arguments in a 2-minute closing presentation.

4. *Moderates prepare responses.* The moderates write 250-word responses outside of class that answer the following question: Now that you have heard both sides, how would you resolve the conflict?

Day Two

1. *Moderates read (20 minutes).* All moderates read their papers. Each paper should take about 2 minutes to read.

2. *Analyze outcomes (30 minutes).* The class should now discuss the outcomes of the debate by addressing the following questions:

   a. What, in general, were some of the outcomes?
   b. Who changed their opinions? Which opinions? Why?
   c. Who did not change? Why?
   d. What are some of the outcomes of the attempts to reduce conflict and establish common ground?
   e. What strategies have you learned from participating in this debate that can help you in real-life arguments?
   f. Did you detect any fallacies that weakened the arguments?

Review and Synthesis of Argument Strategies

After studying this chapter, you will be able to:

LO1 Use key points about argument and argument theory to analyze two texts and write an argument analysis.

The purpose of this chapter is to provide you with the opportunity to review and synthesize what you have learned about reading, writing, and viewing argument. Your task here is to apply argument theory as you read and analyze two letters. The first, "A Call for Unity: A Letter from Eight White Clergymen," was published in a Birmingham, Alabama, newspaper in April 1963. The second, "A Letter from Birmingham Jail," was written shortly thereafter by Martin Luther King Jr. in response to the clergymen's letter.

As you read the two letters, assess the rhetorical situation from visual as well as textual material, notice the positions both parties take on the issue, and identify the claims, support, warrants, and backing for the warrants in each letter. Look for and analyze fallacies and refutation. As part of a final evaluation, decide whether each letter is primarily ethical or unethical. Consider that you must formulate reasons and evidence for your final evaluation. Plan to make some notes on these matters as you read.

Then, in the "Exercises and Activities" section that follows these example arguments, you are asked to apply your understanding to write an argument analysis paper. In this paper, you will explain the results of your reading and analysis. You will not be criticizing or showing what is wrong with the letters; you will not be arguing with the ideas or attempting to refute them. Instead, your purpose will be to explain the argumentation methods that these authors use to make their arguments. You will rely on information about argument theory that you have learned in earlier chapters in this book to help you make your evaluations and write a thorough analysis paper. A side benefit of this assignment is that you will learn to write a type of paper that is sometimes required in other classes.

Reading for the Argument Analysis Paper

LO1 Use key points about argument and argument theory to analyze two texts and write an argument analysis.

Use the following information to help you read and analyze the letters:

1. The rhetorical situation for the letters is detailed in pages 308–310. Read this section first to help you situate these letters in their historical context.

2. Focus topics that identify relevant argument theory are listed along with directed questions in pages 310–311. Page numbers for each topic are provided, if you need to review. When you finish reading the two letters, you should be able to answer the questions that accompany each of the topics. A group work and discussion exercise to help you understand and work with these topics is provided on pages 325–326.

3. Questions appear in the margins of the letters that will direct your attention to various argumentation techniques and methods that the clergymen and King employ. Answer these questions as you read. Your answers will help you understand the letters, respond to the questions that accompany the topics, and gather the information you will need to write your paper. Underline the information in the letters that answers the questions in the margins. Write your own insights and thoughts in the margins. These activities will help you generate plenty of material for your paper.

Writing the Argument Analysis Paper

The complete assignment for the argument analysis paper appears at the end of this chapter on page 326. You may want to read it now so that you will know what you will finally be asked to do. Here are some ideas to help you write this paper.

1. Create a structure for your essay, even if it is little more than a list of your main points. Or, if you prefer, make an outline. Place your ideas in an order that makes sense to you. Since you will be comparing and contrasting the two letters in this paper, you may want to write first about the clergymen's letter and then about King's letter and draw conclusions about both of them last. Or, as an alternative, set up topics, such as *emotional proof* or *writing style,* and then describe how each author, in turn, employs each technique in their letters.

2. You will be asked to explain the rhetorical situation. Be sure to place each letter in historical context and to describe the audiences each one addresses. Then explain the issue from both points of view and summarize the authors' positions. Be sure to include enough detail to help your reader understand the ideas in each letter and how each is organized. Make a brief outline of each letter to guide your summary writing.

3. You will be asked to state the claims and describe the support in both letters. The following example, written about claim and support in "Stop Calling People 'Aliens,'" provides one way to do this. The following sentence not only states the claim but also lists the types of support the author, Careen Shannon, uses. More information about the support can be provided in the paragraphs that follow.

> In her essay "Stop Calling People 'Aliens,'" Careen Shannon uses all three kinds of proof—*logos, ethos,* and *pathos*—to support her claim that the language used to describe undocumented workers is both inappropriate and harmful, and plays a dangerous role in shaping public attitudes toward both immigrants and immigration policy.

4. Include summarized, paraphrased, or quoted material from the letters to provide evidence to support your main points. Here is an example, again using Shannon, which illustrates how a summary and a direct quote could provide support.

> Shannon uses an analogy to suggest the harmful effects that inappropriate language can have. "Like the Japanese word 'gaijin,' " she writes, "the word 'alien' serves to exclude those upon whom it is bestowed" (210). Even when such language has been officially sanctioned as acceptable, Shannon continues, the harm it causes is enough to invalidate its legitimacy. "So what," she says, "if the 'regular' dictionary also says that 'alien' means 'strange' or 'repugnant' or 'in science fiction, a being in or from outer space and not native to the Earth; extraterrestrial'? That has nothing to do with immigration, or how we treat immigrants, does it?" (210).

Place page numbers in parentheses at the end of each summarized, paraphrased, or quoted passage to show where you found it in this textbook, as in the example above.

5. Write a conclusion in which you evaluate these letters. Are they ethical or unethical? Is one more effective and convincing than the other? Why? Write a final evaluative claim about the letters that is based on the ideas and evidence in your paper. At this point, decide whether you want to leave your claim at the end of your paper or to move it to an earlier position in your paper. Where would it be most effective?

6. Read your draft, revise it, and submit it.

Rhetorical Situation for "A Call to Unity: A Letter from Eight White Clergymen" and "Letter from Birmingham Jail"

Birmingham, Alabama, was a very strange place in 1963. Black people were allowed to sit only in certain parts of buses and restaurants, they were required to drink from separate water fountains, and they were not allowed in white churches, schools, or various other public places. The Reverend Martin Luther King Jr. was a well-known minister in the black Baptist church and a leader in the civil rights

Dr. Martin Luther King Jr. was jailed more than once during the civil rights movement. In this 1960 photo, police in Atlanta, Georgia, are taking him to court in handcuffs for participating in a sit-in at a segregated lunch counter in a department store. He was sentenced in this instance to four months of hard labor and was released on bail pending appeal only after Bobby Kennedy[1] phoned the judge.

For Discussion: What special features of visual argument are apparent in this photograph?

movement at that time. The purpose of the movement was to end segregation and discrimination and to obtain equal rights and access for African Americans in the United States, but especially in the South.

Dr. King and others carefully prepared for demonstrations that would take place in Birmingham in the spring of 1963. The demonstrators began by "sitting in" at lunch counters that had never served blacks before and by picketing stores. Twenty people were arrested the first day on charges of trespassing. The civil rights leaders then applied for permits to picket and stage protests against the injustices of discrimination and segregation. They were refused permission, but they demonstrated and picketed anyway. Dr. King was served with an injunction granted by a circuit judge. It said civil rights leaders could not protest, demonstrate, boycott, or sit in at any facilities. King and other leaders decided that this was an unfair and unjust application of the law, and they decided to break the law by ignoring the injunction.

---

[1]Bobby Kennedy, brother of President John F. Kennedy, was the U.S. Attorney General at this time.

King himself decided to march on Good Friday, and he expected to go to jail. (As the photograph and caption document, Dr. King had long been aware that nonviolent civil disobedience required acceptance of any consequent punishments so as to create the tension of protest.) Indeed, before he had walked half a mile, he was arrested and jailed, along with fifty other people. King stayed in jail for eight days. During that time, he wrote his famous letter. It was written in response to a letter signed by eight white clergymen that had been published in a local newspaper.

After King left jail, there were further protests and some violence. Thousands of people demonstrated, and thousands were jailed. Finally, black and white leaders began to negotiate, and some final terms were announced on May 10, 1963. All lunch counters, restrooms, fitting rooms, and drinking fountains in downtown stores were to be desegregated within ninety days; blacks were to be hired in clerical and sales jobs in stores within sixty days. The many people arrested during the demonstrations were to be released on low bail, and permanent lines of communication were to be established between black and white leaders. The demonstrations ended then, and the city settled down and began to implement the agreements.[2]

Focus Topics to Help You Analyze the Letters

Answer the questions that accompany the eight focus topics listed. Use the questions in the margins of the letters to help you locate the information you need to address the questions as well as suggestions posted under each topic.

1. *Rhetorical situation (pages 43–46).* Consider each of these points.
   a. What is the *exigence* for these two letters? What caused the authors to write them? What was the problem? Was it a new or recurring problem?
   b. Who is the *audience* for the clergymen's letter? For King's letter? What is the nature of these audiences? Can they be convinced? What are the expected outcomes?
   c. What are the *constraints*? Speculate about the beliefs, attitudes, habits, and traditions that were in place that limited both the white clergymen and King. How did these constraining circumstances influence the audience for both letters at that time?
   d. Think about the *authors* of both letters. Who are they? Speculate about their backgrounds, experience, affiliations, and values. What motivated them to write?
   e. What kind of *text* is each letter? What effect do its special qualities and features have on the audience?

---

[2]This account is drawn from Lee E. Bains Jr., "Birmingham, 1963: Confrontation over Civil Rights," in *Birmingham, Alabama, 1956–1963: The Black Struggle for Civil Rights*, ed. David J. Garrow (Brooklyn: Carlson, 1989), 175–83.

f. Think about *yourself as the reader*. What is your position on the issue? What constraints affect the way you read about it? Do you perceive common ground with either the clergymen or King, or both? Describe it. Are you influenced by these letters? How?

2. *Organization and claims (pages 151–166)*. Divide each letter into its main parts. What is the subject of each part? Why have the parts been placed in this particular order? What is the relationship between them? What is the main claim in each letter? What types of claims are they? What are some of the subclaims? What types of claims are they?

3. *Logical proofs and style (pages 185–196 and 200–201)*. Analyze the use of logical proof in each of the letters. Provide examples. Describe their effect on the audience. Provide an example of the language of rational style in one of the letters.

4. *Emotional proofs and style (pages 197–199 and 203)*. Analyze the use of emotional proof in each of the letters. Provide examples. Describe their effect on the audience. Provide an example of the language of emotional style in one of the letters.

5. *Proofs and style that establish* ethos *(pages 196–197 and 201–202)*. Analyze the use of proofs that establish *ethos* or credibility in the letters. Provide examples. Describe their effect on the audience. Provide an example of language that establishes *ethos* in one of the letters.

6. *Warrants and backing (pages 123–128)*. Identify the warrants (both logical and contextual) in each of the letters. What appeals to community values provide backing for the warrants? How much common ground do you think exists between the authors of the letters? How much common ground do you share with the authors? As a result, which letter do you find more convincing? Why?

7. *Fallacious thinking and rebuttals (pages 224–230 and 128–129)*. Provide examples of reasoning that is considered fallacious or wrongheaded by the opposing parties in each of the letters. What rebuttals are made in response to these? How effective are they?

8. *Ethical or unethical (pages 232–235)*. Do the clergymen and King both make an adequate effort to understand the issue and its consequences? Does each also understand the position held by the other? Is their support fair, accurate, and/or convincing? Can you, as the reader, accept their warrants? Can you accept the references to community values that serve as backing for these warrants? Should the claims be qualified, if they are not already? Do the clergymen and King sincerely believe their positions are in the best interests of the people in Birmingham as well as of the larger society? Do you agree with them? Who is benefited and who is burdened by their positions? Do you find evidence that either the clergymen or King are trying to manipulate the audience by hiding their real purpose, using inappropriate emotional appeals, manufacturing evidence, using inaccurate evidence, or telling lies? Do either of the arguers change the usual definitions of words to cloud perceptions, or do they minimize issues to trivialize them? What do you conclude about the ethical and unethical qualities of the letters?

ESSAY #1

A CALL FOR UNITY: A LETTER FROM EIGHT WHITE CLERGYMEN*

The eight white Alabama clergymen who wrote this letter to the editor of a Birmingham, Alabama, newspaper represent various religious denominations.

April 12, 1963

What is the issue?

We the undersigned clergymen are among those who, in January, issued "An Appeal for Law and Order and Common Sense," in dealing with racial problems in Alabama. We expressed understanding that honest convictions in racial matters could properly be pursued in the courts, but urged that decisions of those courts should in the meantime be peacefully obeyed.

What is the clergymen's position?

What is the claim?

Since that time there had been some evidence of increased forebearance and a willingness to face facts. Responsible citizens have undertaken to work on various problems which cause racial friction and unrest. In Birmingham, recent public events have given indication that we all have opportunity for a new constructive and realistic approach to racial problems.

What type of claim is it?

What are the rebuttals?

However, we are now confronted by a series of demonstrations by some of our Negro citizens, directed and led in part by outsiders. We recognize the natural impatience of people who feel that their hopes are slow in being realized. But we are convinced that these demonstrations are unwise and untimely.

How do the authors build *ethos*?

We agree rather with certain local Negro leadership which has called for honest and open negotiation of racial issues in our area. And we believe this kind of facing of issues can best be accomplished by citizens of our own metropolitan area, white and Negro, meeting with their knowledge and experience of the local situation. All of us need to face that responsibility and find proper channels for its accomplishment.

How do they appeal to logic?

5   Just as we formerly pointed out that "hatred and violence have no sanction in our religious and political traditions," we also point out that such actions as incite to hatred and violence, however technically peaceful those actions may be, have not contributed to the resolution of our local problems. We do not believe that these days of new hope are days when extreme measures are justified in Birmingham.

How do they appeal to emotion?

We commend the community as a whole, and the local news media and law enforcement officials in particular, on the calm manner in which these demonstrations have been handled. We urge the public to continue to show restraint should the demonstrations continue, and the law enforcement officials to remain calm and continue to protect our city from violence.

What are the warrants?

Describe the predominant style.

We further strongly urge our own Negro community to withdraw support from these demonstrations, and to unite locally in working peacefully for a better Birmingham. When rights are consistently denied, a cause should be pressed in the courts and in negotiations among local leaders, and not in the streets. We appeal to both our white and Negro citizenry to observe the principles of law and order and common sense.

(Signed)

C.C.J. Carpenter, D.D., L.L.D., Bishop of Alabama; Joseph A. Durick, D.D., Auxiliary Bishop, Diocese of Mobile-Birmingham; Rabbi Milton L. Grafman, Temple Emanu-El, Birmingham, Alabama; Bishop Paul Hardin, Bishop of the Alabama–West Florida Conference of the Methodist Church; Bishop Nolan B. Harmon, Bishop of the North Alabama Conference of the Methodist Church; George M. Murray, D.D., L.L.D., Bishop Coadjutor, Episcopal Diocese of Alabama; Edward V. Ramage, Moderator, Synod of the Alabama Presbyterian Church in the United States; Earl Stallings, Pastor, First Baptist Church, Birmingham

ESSAY #2   LETTER FROM BIRMINGHAM JAIL*

Martin Luther King Jr.

Martin Luther King Jr. was a Baptist minister who preached nonviolence and equal justice. He was a pivotal leader in the civil rights movement of the 1960s.

April 16, 1963

My Dear Fellow Clergymen:

What is the issue? What is King's position?

Identify and describe the Rogerian elements and efforts to establish common ground throughout this letter.

While confined here in the Birmingham city jail, I came across your recent statement calling my present activities "unwise and untimely." Seldom do I pause to answer criticism of my work and ideas. If I sought to answer all the criticisms that cross my desk, my secretaries would have little time for anything other than such correspondence in the course of the day, and I would have no time for constructive work. But since I feel that you are men of genuine good will and that your criticisms are sincerely set forth, I want to try to answer your statement in what I hope will be patient and reasonable terms.

I think I should indicate why I am here in Birmingham, since you have been influenced by the view which argues against "outsiders coming in." I have the honor of serving as president of the Southern Christian Leadership Conference, an organization operating in every southern state, with head-quarters in Atlanta, Georgia. We have some eighty-five affiliated organizations across the South, and one of them is the Alabama Christian Movement for Human Rights. Frequently we share staff, educational and financial resources with our affiliates. Several months ago, the affiliate here in Birmingham asked us to be on call to engage in a nonviolent direct-action program if such were deemed necessary. We readily consented, and when the hour came we lived up to our promise. So I, along with several members of my staff, am here because I was invited here. I am here because I have organizational ties here.

How does King build *ethos*?

What is the effect of the comparison with Paul?

Draw a line at the end of the introduction.

Draw a line at the end of each of the other major sections of material. Label the subject of each section in the margin.

What is the subject of this first section?

What is the claim?

What type of claim is it?

Is it qualified?

Identify and analyze the effect of the emotional appeals.

What are some of the values expressed in this argument?

But more basically, I am in Birmingham because injustice is here. Just as the prophets of the eighth century B.C. left their villages and carried their "thus saith the Lord" far beyond the boundaries of their home towns, and just as the Apostle Paul left his village of Tarsus and carried the gospel of Jesus Christ to the far corners of the Greco-Roman world, so am I compelled to carry the gospel of freedom beyond my own home town. Like Paul, I must constantly respond to the Macedonian call for aid.

Moreover, I am cognizant of the interrelatedness of all communities and states. I cannot sit idly by in Atlanta and not be concerned about what happens in Birmingham. Injustice anywhere is a threat to justice everywhere. We are caught in an inescapable network of mutuality, tied in a single garment of destiny. Whatever affects one directly, affects all indirectly. Never again can we afford to live with the narrow, provincial "outside agitator" idea. Anyone who lives inside the United States can never be considered an outsider anywhere within its bounds.

5   You deplore the demonstrations taking place in Birmingham. But your statement, I am sorry to say, fails to express a similar concern for the conditions that brought about the demonstrations. I am sure that none of you would want to rest content with the superficial kind of social analysis that deals merely with effects and does not grapple with underlying causes. It is unfortunate that demonstrations are taking place in Birmingham, but it is even more unfortunate that the city's white power structure left the Negro community with no alternative.

In any nonviolent campaign there are four basic steps: collection of the facts to determine whether injustices exist; negotiation; self-purification; and direct action. We have gone through all these steps in Birmingham. There can be no gain-saying the fact that racial injustice engulfs this community. Birmingham is probably the most thoroughly segregated city in the United States. Its ugly record of brutality is widely known. Negroes have experienced grossly unjust treatment in the courts. There have been more unsolved bombings of Negro homes and churches in Birmingham than in any other city in the nation. These are the hard, brutal facts of the case. On the basis of these conditions, Negro leaders sought to negotiate with the city fathers. But the latter consistently refused to engage in good-faith negotiation.

Then, last September, came the opportunity to talk with leaders of Birmingham's economic community. In the course of the negotiations, certain promises were made by the merchants—for example, to remove the stores' humiliating racial signs. On the basis of these promises, the Reverend Fred Shuttlesworth and the leaders of the Alabama Christian Movement for Human Rights agreed to a moratorium on all demonstrations. As the weeks and months went by, we realized that we were the victims of a broken promise. A few signs, briefly removed, returned; the others remained.

As in so many past experiences, our hopes had been blasted, and the shadow of deep disappointment settled upon us. We had no alternative except to prepare for direct action, whereby we would present our very bodies as a means of laying our case before the conscience of the local and the national community. Mindful of the difficulties involved, we decided to

Identify and describe
the rebuttals.

undertake a process of self-purification. We began a series of workshops on
nonviolence, and we repeatedly asked ourselves: "Are you able to accept
blows without retaliating?" "Are you able to endure the ordeal of jail?"
We decided to schedule our direct-action program for the Easter season,
realizing that except for Christmas, this is the main shopping period of the
year. Knowing that a strong economic-withdrawal program would be the
by-product of direct action, we felt that this would be the best time to bring
pressure to bear on the merchants for the needed change.

Then it occurred to us that Birmingham's mayoral election was coming up
in March, and we speedily decided to postpone action until after election day.
When we discovered that the Commissioner of Public Safety, Eugene "Bull"
Connor, had piled up enough votes to be in the runoff, we decided again
to postpone action until the day after the runoff so that the demonstrations
could not be used to cloud the issues. Like many others, we waited to see
Mr. Connor defeated, and to this end we endured postponement after
postponement. Having aided in this community need, we felt that our direct-
action program could be delayed no longer.

10   You may well ask: "Why direct action? Why sit-ins, marches and so
forth? Isn't negotiation a better path?" You are quite right in calling for
negotiation. Indeed, this is the very purpose of direct action. Nonviolent
direct action seeks to create such a crisis and foster such a tension that a
community which has constantly refused to negotiate is forced to confront
the issue. It seeks so to dramatize the issue that it can no longer be ignored.
My citing the creation of tension as part of the work of the nonviolent-
resister may sound rather shocking. But I must confess that I am not afraid
of the word "tension." I have earnestly opposed violent tension, but there
is a type of constructive, nonviolent tension which is necessary for growth.

What is the effect of
the comparison with
Socrates?

Just as Socrates felt that it was necessary to create a tension in the mind so
that individuals could rise from the bondage of myths and half-truths to the
unfettered realm of creative analysis and objective appraisal, so must we
see the need for nonviolent gadflies to create the kind of tension in society
that will help men rise from the dark depths of prejudice and racism to the
majestic heights of understanding and brotherhood.

What is King's
planned argumenta-
tion strategy?

The purpose of our direct-action program is to create a situation so crisis-
packed that it will inevitably open the door to negotiation. I therefore concur
with you in your call for negotiation. Too long has our beloved Southland
been bogged down in a tragic effort to live in monologue rather than dialogue.

One of the basic points in your statement is that the action that I and my
associates have taken in Birmingham is untimely. Some have asked: "Why
didn't you give the new city administration time to act?" The only answer
that I can give to this query is that the new Birmingham administration must
be prodded about as much as the outgoing one, before it will act. We are
sadly mistaken if we feel that the election of Albert Boutwell as mayor will
bring the millennium to Birmingham. While Mr. Boutwell is a much more

Why does King refer
to history?

gentle person than Mr. Connor, they are both segregationists, dedicated to
the maintenance of the status quo. I have hope that Mr. Boutwell will be
reasonable enough to see the futility of massive resistance to desegregation.

Why does he refer to Niebuhr?

Identify and analyze the emotional proof.

To what human motives and values does King appeal?

Identify emotional language, examples, and vivid description.

What is the effect of the emotional proof?

What is the predominant type of proof in the first section of the letter?

But he will not see this without pressure from devotees of civil rights. My friends, I must say to you that we have not made a single gain in civil rights without determined legal and nonviolent pressure. Lamentably, it is a historical fact that privileged groups seldom give up their privileges voluntarily. Individuals may see the moral light and voluntarily give up their unjust posture; but, as Reinhold Niebuhr has reminded us, groups tend to be more immoral than individuals.

We know through painful experience that freedom is never voluntarily given up by the oppressor; it must be demanded by the oppressed. Frankly, I have yet to engage in a direct-action campaign that was "well-timed" in the view of those who have not suffered unduly from the disease of segregation. For years now I have heard the word "Wait!" It rings in the ear of every Negro with piercing familiarity. This "Wait" has almost always meant "Never." We must come to see, with one of our distinguished jurists, that "justice too long delayed is justice denied."

We have waited for more than 340 years for our constitutional and God-given rights. The nations of Asia and Africa are moving with jetlike speed toward gaining political independence, but we still creep at horse-and-buggy pace toward gaining a cup of coffee at a lunch counter. Perhaps it is easy for those who have never felt the stinging darts of segregation to say, "Wait." But when you have seen vicious mobs lynch your mothers and fathers at will and drown your sisters and brothers at whim; when you have seen hate-filled policemen curse, kick and even kill your black brothers and sisters; when you see the vast majority of your twenty million Negro brothers smothering in an airtight cage of poverty in the midst of an affluent society; when you suddenly find your tongue twisted and your speech stammering as you seek to explain to your six-year-old daughter why she can't go to the public amusement park that has just been advertised on television, and see tears welling up in her eyes when she is told that Fun-town is closed to colored children, and see ominous clouds of inferiority beginning to form in her little mental sky, and see her beginning to distort her personality by developing an unconscious bitterness toward white people; when you have to concoct an answer for a five-year-old son who is asking, "Daddy, why do white people treat colored people so mean?" when you take a cross-country drive and find it necessary to sleep night after night in the uncomfortable corners of your automobile because no motel will accept you; when you are humiliated day in and day out by nagging signs reading "white" and "colored" when your first name becomes "nigger," your middle name becomes "boy" (however old you are) and your last name becomes "John," and your wife and mother are never given the respected title "Mrs." when you are harried by day and haunted by night by the fact that you are a Negro, living constantly at tiptoe stance, never quite knowing what to expect next, and are plagued with inner fears and outer resentments; when you are forever fighting a degenerating sense of "nobodiness"—then you will understand why we find it difficult to wait. There comes a time when the cup of endurance runs over, and men are no longer willing to be plunged into the abyss of despair. I hope, sirs, you can understand our legitimate and unavoidable impatience.

Draw a line where the subject changes. What is the subject of the second section?

How and why does King use definition?

How does he support the definition?

What is the effect of the support?

Explain the example of just and unjust laws.

How does King further elaborate on this idea?

15   You express a great deal of anxiety over our willingness to break laws. This is certainly a legitimate concern. Since we so diligently urge people to obey the Supreme Court's decision of 1954 outlawing segregation in the public schools, at first glance it may seem rather paradoxical for us consciously to break laws. One may well ask: "How can you advocate breaking some laws and obeying others?" The answer lies in the fact that there are two types of laws: just and unjust. I would be the first to advocate obeying just laws. Conversely, one has a moral responsibility to disobey unjust laws. I would agree with St. Augustine that "an unjust law is no law at all."

Now, what is the difference between the two? How does one determine whether a law is just or unjust? A just law is a man-made code that squares with the moral law or the law of God. An unjust law is a code that is out of harmony with the moral law. To put it in the terms of St. Thomas Aquinas: An unjust law is a human law that is not rooted in eternal law and natural law. Any law that uplifts human personality is just. Any law that degrades human personality is unjust. All segregation statutes are unjust because segregation distorts the soul and damages the personality. It gives the segregator a false sense of superiority and the segregated a false sense of inferiority. Segregation, to use the terminology of the Jewish philosopher Martin Buber, substitutes an "I-it" relationship for an "I-thou" relationship and ends up relegating persons to the status of things. Hence segregation is not only politically, economically, and sociologically unsound, it is morally wrong and sinful. Paul Tillich has said that sin is separation. Is not segregation an existential expression of man's tragic separation, his awful estrangement, his terrible sinfulness? Thus it is that I can urge men to obey the 1954 decision of the Supreme Court, for it is morally right; and I can urge them to disobey segregation ordinances, for they are morally wrong.

Let us consider a more concrete example of just and unjust laws. An unjust law is a code that a numerical or power majority group compels a minority group to obey but does not make binding on itself. This is *difference* made legal. By the same token, a just law is a code that a majority compels a minority to follow and that it is willing to follow itself. This is *sameness* made legal.

Let me give another explanation. A law is unjust if it is inflicted on a minority that, as a result of being denied the right to vote, had no part in enacting or devising the law. Who can say that the legislature of Alabama which set up the state's segregation laws was democratically elected? Throughout Alabama all sorts of devious methods are used to prevent Negroes from becoming registered voters, and there are some counties in which, even though Negroes constitute a majority of the population, not a single Negro is registered. Can any law enactment under such circumstances be considered democratically structured?

Sometimes a law is just on its face and unjust in its application. For instance, I have been arrested on a charge of parading without a permit. Now, there is nothing wrong in having an ordinance which requires a permit for a parade. But such an ordinance becomes unjust when it is used to maintain segregation and to deny citizens the First-Amendment privilege of peaceful assembly and protest.

20   I hope you are able to see the distinction I am trying to point out. In no sense do I advocate evading or defying the law, as would the rabid segregationist. That would lead to anarchy. One who breaks an unjust law must do so openly, lovingly, and with a willingness to accept the penalty. I submit that an individual who breaks a law that conscience tells him is unjust, and who willingly accepts the penalty of imprisonment in order to arouse the conscience of the community over its injustice, is in reality expressing the highest respect for law.

Analyze the deductive reasoning in this paragraph.

Of course, there is nothing new about this kind of civil disobedience. It was evidenced sublimely in the refusal of Shadrach, Meshach and Abednego to obey the laws of Nebuchadnezzar, on the ground that a higher moral law was at stake. It was practiced superbly by the early Christians, who were willing to face hungry lions and the excruciating pain of chopping blocks rather than submit to certain unjust laws of the Roman Empire. To a degree, academic freedom is a reality today because Socrates practiced civil disobedience. In our own nation, the Boston Tea Party represented a massive act of civil disobedience.

Identify and describe the effect of the historical analogies.

We should never forget that everything Adolf Hitler did in Germany was "legal" and everything the Hungarian freedom fighters did in Hungary was "illegal." It was "illegal" to aid and comfort a Jew in Hitler's Germany. Even so, I am sure that, had I lived in Germany at the time, I would have aided and comforted my Jewish brothers. If today I lived in a Communist country where certain principles dear to the Christian faith are suppressed, I would openly advocate disobeying that country's antireligious laws.

What type of proof predominates in the second part of the letter?

Draw a line where the subject changes. What is the subject of the third section?

I must make two honest confessions to you, my Christian and Jewish brothers. First, I must confess that over the past few years I have been gravely disappointed with the white moderate. I have almost reached the regrettable conclusion that the Negro's great stumbling block in his stride toward freedom is not the White Citizen's Councilor or the Ku Klux Klanner, but the white moderate, who is more devoted to "order" than to justice; who prefers a negative peace which is the absence of tension to a positive peace which is the presence of justice; who constantly says: "I agree with you in the goal you seek, but I cannot agree with your methods of direct action" who paternalistically believes he can set the timetable for another man's freedom; who lives by a mythical concept of time and who constantly advises the Negro to wait for a "more convenient season." Shallow understanding from people of good will is more frustrating than absolute misunderstanding from people of ill will. Lukewarm acceptance is much more bewildering than outright rejection.

What are King's warrants in this passage?

I had hoped that the white moderate would understand that law and order exist for the purpose of establishing justice and that when they fail in this purpose they become the dangerously structured dams that block the flow of social progress. I had hoped that the white moderate would understand that the present tension in the South is a necessary phase of the transition from an obnoxious negative peace, in which the Negro passively accepted his unjust plight, to a substantive and positive peace, in which all men will respect the dignity and worth of human personality. Actually, we who

How do King's warrants differ from the clergymen's?

How and why does King use definition here?

engage in nonviolent direct action are not the creators of tension. We merely bring to the surface the hidden tension that is already alive. We bring it out in the open, where it can be seen and dealt with. Like a boil that can never be cured so long as it is covered up but must be opened with all its ugliness to the natural medicines of air and light, injustice must be exposed, with all the tension its exposure creates, to the light of human conscience and the air of national opinion before it can be cured.

25   In your statements you assert that our actions, even though peaceful, must be condemned because they precipitate violence. But is this a logical assertion? Isn't this like condemning a robbed man because his possession of money precipitated the evil act of robbery? Isn't this like condemning Socrates because his unswerving commitment to truth and his philosophical inquiries precipitated the act by the misguided populace in which they made him drink hemlock? Isn't this like condemning Jesus because his unique God-consciousness and never-ceasing devotion to God's will precipitated the evil act of crucifixion? We must come to see that, as the federal courts have consistently affirmed, it is wrong to urge an individual to cease his efforts to gain his basic constitutional rights because the quest may precipitate violence. Society must protect the robbed and punish the robber.

I had also hoped that the white moderate would reject the myth concerning time in relation to the struggle for freedom. I have just received a letter from a white brother in Texas. He writes: "All Christians know that the colored people will receive equal rights eventually, but it is possible that you are in too great a religious hurry. It has taken Christianity almost two thousand years to accomplish what it has. The teachings of Christ take time to come to earth." Such an attitude stems from a tragic misconception of time, from the strangely irrational notion that there is something in the very flow of time that will inevitably cure all ills. Actually, time itself is neutral; it can be used either destructively or constructively. More and more I feel that the people of ill will have used time much more effectively than have the people of good will. We will have to repent in this generation not merely for the hateful words and actions of the bad people but for the appalling silence of the good people. Human progress never rolls in on wheels of inevitability; it comes through the tireless efforts of men willing to be coworkers with God, and without this hard work, time itself becomes an ally of the forces of social stagnation. We must use time creatively, in the knowledge that the time is always right to do right. Now is the time to make real the promise of democracy and transform our pending national elegy into a creative psalm of brotherhood. Now is the time to lift our national policy from the quicksand of racial injustice to the solid rock of human dignity.

You speak of our activity in Birmingham as extreme. At first I was rather disappointed that fellow clergymen would see my nonviolent efforts as those of an extremist. I began thinking about the fact that I stand in the middle of two opposing forces in the Negro community. One is a force of complacency, made up in part of Negroes who, as a result of long years of oppression, are so drained of self-respect and a sense of "somebodiness" that they have adjusted to segregation; and in part of a few middle-class Negroes who,

Identify and describe the effects of the analogies in these paragraphs.

What is the fallacious thinking King complains of here?

Summarize King's reasoning about time.

Describe the two opposing forces.

because of a degree of academic and economic security and because in some ways they profit by segregation, have become insensitive to the problems of the masses. The other force is one of bitterness and hatred, and it comes perilously close to advocating violence. It is expressed in the various black nationalist groups that are springing up across the nation, the largest and best-known being Elijah Muhammad's Muslim movement. Nourished by the Negro's frustration over the continued existence of racial discrimination, this movement is made up of people who have lost faith in America, who have absolutely repudiated Christianity, and who have concluded that the white man is an incorrigible "devil."

How and why does King attempt to reconcile the opposing forces?

I have tried to stand between these two forces, saying that we need emulate neither the "do-nothingism" of the complacent nor the hatred and despair of the black nationalist. For there is the more excellent way of love and nonviolent protest. I am grateful to God that, through the influence of the Negro church, the way of nonviolence became an integral part of our struggle.

Identify and describe the causal proof.

If this philosophy had not emerged, by now many streets of the South would, I am convinced, be flowing with blood. And I am further convinced that if our white brothers dismiss as "rabble-rousers" and "outside agitators" those of us who employ nonviolent direct action, and if they refuse to support our nonviolent efforts, millions of Negroes will, out of frustration and despair, seek solace and security in black-nationalist ideologies—a development that would inevitably lead to a frightening racial nightmare.

Summarize King's reasoning about the effects of oppression.

30 Oppressed people cannot remain oppressed forever. The yearning for freedom eventually manifests itself, and that is what has happened to the American Negro. Something within has reminded him of his birthright of freedom, and something without has reminded him that it can be gained. Consciously or unconsciously, he has been caught up by the *Zeitgeist*, and with his black brothers of Africa and his brown and yellow brothers of Asia, South America and the Caribbean, the United States Negro is moving with a sense of great urgency toward the promised land of racial justice. If one recognizes this vital urge that has engulfed the Negro community, one should readily understand why public demonstrations are taking place. The Negro has many pent-up resentments and latent frustrations, and he must release them. So let him march; let him make prayer pilgrimages to the city hall; let him go on freedom rides—and try to understand why he must do so. If his repressed emotions are not released in nonviolent ways, they will seek expression through violence; this is not a threat but a fact of history. So I have not said to my people: "Get rid of your discontent." Rather, I have tried to say that this normal and healthy discontent can be channeled into the creative outlet of nonviolent direct action. And now this approach is being termed extremist.

What is the effect of these comparisons?

But though I was initially disappointed at being categorized as an extremist, as I continued to think about the matter I gradually gained a measure of satisfaction from the label. Was not Jesus an extremist for love: "Love your enemies, bless them that curse you, do good to them that hate you, and pray for them which despitefully use you, and prosecute you." Was not Amos an extremist for justice: "Let justice roll down like waters and righteousness like an everflowing stream." Was not Paul an extremist for the Christian gospel: "I bear in my body the marks of the Lord Jesus." Was not Martin Luther an extremist: "Here I stand; I cannot do otherwise, so help me God." And John Bunyan: "I will stay in jail to the end of my days before I make a butchery of my conscience." And Abraham Lincoln: "This nation cannot survive half slave and half free." And Thomas Jefferson: "We hold these truths to be self-evident, that all men are created equal. . . ." So the question is not whether we will be extremists, but what kind of extremists we will be. Will we be extremists for hate or for love? Will we be extremists for the preservation of injustice or for the extension of justice? In that dramatic scene on Calvary's hill three men were crucified. We must never forget that all three were crucified for the same crime—the crime of extremism. Two were extremists for immorality, and thus fell below their environment. The other, Jesus Christ, was an extremist for love, truth and goodness, and thereby rose above his environment. Perhaps the South, the nation and the world are in dire need of creative extremists.

Summarize King's description of the oppressor race.

I had hoped that the white moderate would see this need. Perhaps I was too optimistic; perhaps I expected too much. I suppose I should have realized that few members of the oppressor race can understand the deep groans and passionate yearnings of the oppressed race, and still fewer have the vision to see that injustice must be rooted out by strong, persistent and determined action. I am thankful, however, that some of our white brothers in the South have grasped the meaning of this social revolution and committed themselves to it. They are still all too few in quantity, but they are big in quality. Some—such as Ralph McGill, Lillian Smith, Harry Golden, James McBride Dabbs, Ann Braden and Sarah Patton Boyle—have written about our struggle in eloquent and prophetic terms. Others have marched with us down nameless streets of the South. They have languished in filthy, roach-infested jails, suffering the abuse and brutality of policemen who view them as "dirty nigger-lovers." Unlike so many of their moderate brothers and sisters, they have recognized the urgency of the moment and sensed the need for powerful "action" antidotes to combat the disease of segregation.

What types of proof are used in this third section?

Draw a line where the subject changes. What is the subject of the fourth section?

Reconsider the rhetorical situations: What went before? What will come later?

Let me take note of my other major disappointment. I have been so greatly disappointed with the white church and its leadership. Of course, there are some notable exceptions. I am not unmindful of the fact that each of you has taken some significant stands on this issue. I commend you, Reverend Stallings, for your Christian stand on this past Sunday, in welcoming Negroes to your worship service on a non-segregated basis. I commend the Catholic leaders of this state for integrating Spring Hill College several years ago.

But despite these notable exceptions, I must honestly reiterate that I have been disappointed with the church. I do not say this as one of those negative critics who can always find something wrong with the church. I say this as a minister of the gospel, who loves the church; who was nurtured in its bosom; who has been sustained by its spiritual blessings and who will remain true to it as long as the cord of life shall lengthen.

35   When I was suddenly catapulted into the leadership of the bus protest in Montgomery, Alabama, a few years ago, I felt we would be supported by the white church. I felt that the white ministers, priests and rabbis of the South would be among our strongest allies. Instead, some have been outright opponents, refusing to understand the freedom movement and misrepresenting its leaders; all too many others have been more cautious than courageous and have remained silent behind the anesthetizing security of stained-glass windows.

How does King build *ethos* in this fourth section?

In spite of my shattered dreams, I came to Birmingham with the hope that the white religious leadership of this community would see the justice of our cause and, with deep moral concern, would serve as the channel through which our just grievances could reach the power structure. I had hoped that each of you would understand. But again I have been disappointed.

What common ground did King hope would be clear? How was he disappointed?

I have heard numerous southern religious leaders admonish their worshipers to comply with a desegregation decision because it is the law, but I have longed to hear white ministers declare: "Follow this decree because integration is morally right and because the Negro is your brother." In the midst of blatant injustices inflicted upon the Negro, I have watched white churchmen stand on the sideline and mouth pious irrelevancies and sanctimonious trivialities. In the midst of a mighty struggle to rid our nation of racial and economic injustice, I have heard many ministers say: "Those are social issues, with which the gospel has no real concern." And I have watched many churches commit themselves to a completely other-worldly religion which makes a strange, unBiblical distinction between body and soul, between the sacred and the secular.

How and why does King use vivid description?

I have travelled the length and breadth of Alabama, Mississippi and all the other southern states. On sweltering summer days and crisp autumn mornings I have looked at the South's beautiful churches with their lofty spires pointing heavenward. I have beheld the impressive outlines of her massive religious-education buildings. Over and over I have found myself asking: "What kind of people worship here? Who is their God? Where were their voices when the lips of Governor Barnett dripped with words of inter-position and nullification? Where were they when Governor Wallace gave a clarion call for defiance and hatred? Where were their voices of support when bruised and weary Negro men and women decided to rise from the dark dungeons of complacency to the bright hills of creative protest?"

Yes, these questions are still in my mind. In deep disappointment I have wept over the laxity of the church. But be assured that my tears have been tears of love. There can be no deep disappointment where there is not deep love. Yes, I love the church. How could I do otherwise? I am in the rather unique position of being the son, the grandson and the great-grandson of preachers. Yes, I see the church as the body of Christ. But, oh! How we have blemished and scarred that body through social neglect and through fear of being nonconformists.

40   There was a time when the church was very powerful—in the time when the early Christians rejoiced at being deemed worthy to suffer for what they believed. In those days the church was not merely a thermometer that recorded the ideas and principles of popular opinion; it was a thermostat that transformed

What is the effect of the historical analogy?

the mores of society. Whenever the early Christians entered a town, the people in power became disturbed and immediately sought to convict the Christians for being "disturbers of the peace" and "outside agitators." But the Christians pressed on, in the conviction that they were "a colony of heaven," called to obey God rather than man. Small in number, they were big in commitment. They were too God-intoxicated to be "astronomically intimidated." By their effort and example they brought an end to such ancient evils as infanticide and gladiatorial contests.

Things are different now. So often the contemporary church is a weak, ineffectual voice with an uncertain sound. So often it is an arch-defender of the status quo. Far from being disturbed by the presence of the church, the power structure of the average community is consoled by the church's silent—and often even vocal—sanction of things as they are.

But the judgment of God is upon the church as never before. If today's church does not recapture the sacrificial spirit of the early church, it will lose its authenticity, forfeit the loyalty of millions, and be dismissed as an irrelevant social club with no meaning for the twentieth century. Every day I meet young people whose disappointment with the church has turned into outright disgust.

How does King contrast organized religion and the inner church? What is the effect?

Perhaps I have once again been too optimistic. Is organized religion too inextricably bound to the status quo to save our nation and the world? Perhaps I must turn my faith to the inner spiritual church, the church within the church, as the true *ekklesia* and the hope of the world. But again I am thankful to God that some noble souls from the ranks of organized religion have broken loose from the paralyzing chains of conformity and joined us as active partners in the struggle for freedom. They have left their secure congregations and walked the streets of Albany, Georgia, with us. They have gone down the highways of the South on tortuous rides for freedom. Yes, they have gone to jail with us. Some have been dismissed from their churches, have lost the support of their bishops and fellow ministers. But they have acted in the faith that right defeated is stronger than evil triumphant. Their witness has been the spiritual salt that has preserved the true meaning of the gospel in these troubled times. They have carved a tunnel of hope through the dark mountain of disappointment.

Why does King use historical analogies here?

I hope the church as a whole will meet the challenge of this decisive hour. But even if the church does not come to the aid of justice, I have no despair about the future. I have no fear about the outcome of our struggle in Birmingham, even if our motives are at present misunderstood. We will reach the goal of freedom in Birmingham and all over the nation, because the goal of America is freedom. Abused and scorned though we may be, our destiny is tied up with America's destiny. Before the pilgrims landed at Plymouth, we were here. Before the pen of Jefferson etched the majestic words of the Declaration of Independence across the pages of history, we were here. For more than two centuries our forebears labored in this country without wages; they made cotton king; they built the homes of their masters while suffering gross injustice and shameful humiliation—and yet out of a bottomless vitality they continued to thrive and develop. If the inexpressible cruelties of slavery could not stop us, the opposition we now face will surely fail. We will win

What types of proof are used in the fourth section?

Draw a line where the subject changes. What is the subject of the fifth section?

our freedom because the sacred heritage of our nation and the eternal will of God are embodied in our echoing demands.

45   Before closing I feel impelled to mention one other point in your statement that has troubled me profoundly. You warmly commended the Birmingham police force for keeping "order" and "preventing violence." I doubt that you would have so warmly commended the police force if you had seen its dogs sinking their teeth into unarmed, nonviolent Negroes. I doubt that you would so quickly commend the policemen if you were to observe their ugly and inhumane treatment of Negroes here in the city jail; if you were to watch them push and curse old Negro women and young Negro girls; if you were to see them slap and kick old Negro men and young boys; if you were to observe them, as they did on two occasions, refuse to give us food because we wanted to sing our grace together. I cannot join you in your praise of the Birmingham police department.

What is the predominant type of proof in this fifth section?

It is true that the police have exercised a degree of discipline in handling the demonstrators. In this sense they have conducted themselves rather "nonviolently" in public. But for what purpose? To preserve the evil system of segregation. Over the past few years I have consistently preached that nonviolence demands that the means we use must be as pure as the ends we seek. I have tried to make clear that it is wrong to use immoral means to attain moral ends. But now I must affirm that it is just as wrong, or perhaps even more so, to use moral means to preserve immoral ends. Perhaps Mr. Connor and his policemen have been rather nonviolent in public, as was Chief Pritchett in Albany, Georgia, but they have used the moral means of nonviolence to maintain the immoral end of racial injustice. As T. S. Eliot has said: "The last temptation is the greatest treason: To do the right deed for the wrong reason."

Provide some examples.

Describe the effect.

I wish you had commended the Negro sit-inners and the demonstrators of Birmingham for their sublime courage, their willingness to suffer and their amazing discipline in the midst of great provocation. One day the South will recognize its real heroes. They will be the James Merediths, with the noble sense of purpose that enables them to face jeering and hostile mobs, and with the agonizing loneliness that characterizes the life of the pioneer. They will be old, oppressed, battered Negro women, symbolized in a seventy-two-year-old woman in Montgomery, Alabama, who rose up with a sense of dignity and with her people decided not to ride segregated buses, and who responded with ungrammatical profundity to one who inquired about her weariness: "My feets is tired, but my soul is at rest." They will be the young high school and college students, the young ministers of the gospel and a host of their elders, courageously and nonviolently sitting in at lunch counters and willingly going to jail for conscience's sake. One day the South will know that when these disinherited children of God sat down at lunch counters, they were in reality standing up for what is best in the American dream and for the most sacred values in our Judaeo-Christian heritage, thereby bringing our nation back to those great wells of democracy which were dug deep by the founding fathers in their formulation of the Constitution and the Declaration of Independence.

Draw a line to set off the conclusion. What is the concluding idea?

What is King's purpose in this conclusion?

Do you find the two letters convincing? Why or why not?

Are the clergymen's and King's arguments moral or immoral according to your values and standards?

Never before have I written so long a letter. I'm afraid it is much too long to take your precious time. I can assure you that it would have been much shorter if I had been writing from a comfortable desk, but what else can one do when he is alone in a narrow jail cell, other than write long letters, think long thoughts and pray long prayers?

If I have said anything in this letter that overstates the truth and indicates an unreasonable impatience, I beg you to forgive me. If I have said anything that understates the truth and indicates my having a patience that allows me to settle for anything less than brotherhood, I beg God to forgive me.

50   I hope this letter finds you strong in the faith. I also hope that circumstances will soon make it possible for me to meet each of you, not as an integrationist or a civil-rights leader but as a fellow clergyman and a Christian brother. Let us all hope that the dark clouds of racial prejudice will soon pass away and the deep fog of misunderstanding will be lifted from our fear-drenched communities, and in some not too distant tomorrow the radiant stars of love and brotherhood will shine over our great nation with all their scintillating beauty.

Yours for the cause of Peace and Brotherhood,
Martin Luther King, Jr.

Review Questions

1. Describe the argument analysis paper. **(LO1)**
2. What is the purpose of this paper? **(LO1)**
3. What rhetorical strategies will help you accomplish this purpose? How are these strategies different from those employed in other types of argument papers? **(LO1)**
4. Describe the rhetorical situation for the letters by the eight white clergymen and Dr. Martin Luther King Jr. **(LO1)**
5. What are the focus topics? Provide three examples of them. **(LO1)**

Exercises and Activities

A. Group Work and Discussion: Understanding the Focus Topics

Divide the class into eight groups, and assign each group one of the eight focus topics listed on pages 310–311. Here are the topics: rhetorical situation; organization and claims; logical proofs and style; emotional proofs and style; proofs and style that establish *ethos*; warrants and backing; fallacious thinking and rebuttals; and ethical or unethical qualities. Utilize the questions that accompany each focus item on the list. To prepare for the group work, all students will read the two letters outside of class and make notes individually on the focus topic assigned to their group. The brief questions in the margins of the letters will facilitate this reading and note taking. In class, the groups will meet briefly to consolidate their views on their topic. Each of the groups will then make a brief oral report on their topic, and other class members will discuss the results and take some notes. These notes will be used as prewriting materials for the argument analysis paper.

B. **Writing Assignment: An Argument Analysis Paper**

Write an argument analysis paper of at least 1,000 words in which you analyze the two letters by the clergymen and King. Put the letters in historical context by describing the rhetorical situation, with particular emphasis on the exigence, the audiences, and the constraints. Explain the issue from both points of view. Summarize the positions taken on the issue in both letters. State the claims in both letters. Describe and evaluate the support, warrants, and backing in both. Identify any fallacies and describe how the authors use rebuttal. Finally, evaluate the ethical or unethical qualities that appear in these letters and write a conclusion in which you make a claim about the relative effectiveness of the two letters. Which letter is more effective? Why? Have your own views been modified or changed? How?

Writing a Researched Argument

The purpose of the next three chapters is to teach you to write an argument paper that derives from and reflects your own perspective and that incorporates research materials from outside sources. Since other professors or even employers may ask you to produce such papers, this instruction should be useful to you not only now but also in the future. When you finish studying Part Three:

- You will know how to write your claim and determine the main argumentation purpose of your research paper.

- You will know how to analyze your audience and predict how it might change.

- You will know how to think about your claim and gather material from your own background and experience to support it.

- You will know how to organize and conduct library and online research to support your claim further.

- You will know a variety of possible ways to organize the ideas for your paper.

- You will know how to incorporate research materials into your paper, document them properly, and prepare the final copy.

The Research Paper: Planning, Research, and Invention

After studying this chapter, you will be able to:

LO1 Identify an arguable issue.

LO2 Write a clear research claim.

LO3 Create a coherent research plan.

LO4 Analyze your audience.

LO5 Locate a variety of sources.

LO6 Evaluate sources.

LO7 Organize and present sources in an accepted bibliographic form.

LO8 Take and organize effective notes.

This chapter presents the information you will need to help you plan, research, and write a researched position paper. Many of the procedures for the researched position paper can be elaborate because a research paper is more complicated than the other papers you have written. As you read this chapter, you can expect to encounter a good deal of information and material. All of this information, including the assignments in the "Exercises and Activities" at the end of the chapter, is included for one purpose: to help you plan and write a successful and well-researched argument paper. Stay on top of these assignments, and you will be pleased with the final results.

Identifying an Issue

To get you started, consider following the suggestions below. They will ease you into this assignment, help you think, and make you feel knowledgeable and confident.

1. *Decide on an issue and write an issue proposal.* An issue may be assigned by the instructor, or it can be left entirely up to you. If you are choosing an issue yourself, coming across one as you read the newspaper, watch television, or surf online, think about the unresolved questions it raises. Work to find an issue that captures your attention and interest, and that you are certain is arguable. Then write an issue proposal to focus the issue and help you think about what more you need to learn.

2. *Do some initial reading.* If you are not familiar enough with your issue, locate one or more sources about it and begin to do some background reading. Read enough material to form an idea of the various positions that people are likely to take on this issue

3. *Write an exploratory paper.* You can list and explain three or more perspectives on your issue or write an exploratory paper in which you explain multiple perspectives. This process of exploring the different views on or approaches to the issue will help you find an original and interesting perspective of your own, as it also deepens your understanding of the perspectives others take on it.

Developing Your Claim

Whether or not you write an issue proposal and an exploratory paper, you will want to write your claim for your position paper as early in the process as possible. Your claim is important because it provides purpose, control, and direction for everything else that you include in your paper. Try freewriting about your issue. You can also write your issue as a question, and then freewrite a response to give yourself a better sense of the purpose and claim for your paper. Ask the following questions to clarify and develop your claim. Some tentative answers to these questions now can help you stay on track and avoid problems with the development of your paper later.

IS THE CLAIM NARROW AND FOCUSED?

You may have started with a broad issue area, such as technology or education, that suggests many specific related issues. If you participated in mapping sessions in class, you discovered a number of the specific related issues in your issue area. Mapping and freewriting can help you narrow your issue. However, you may now need to narrow your issue even further by focusing on one aspect of it. Here is an example:

Issue area: The environment

> *Specific related issue:*
> What problems are associated with nuclear energy?

Aspects of that issue:
What should be done with nuclear waste?
How hazardous is nuclear energy, and how can we control the hazards?
What are the alternatives to nuclear energy?

In selecting a narrowed issue to write about, you may want to focus on only one of the three aspects of the nuclear energy problem. You might, for instance, decide to make this claim: *Solar power is better than nuclear energy.* Later, as you write, you may need to narrow this topic even further and revise your claim: *Solar power is better than nuclear energy for certain specified purposes.* Any topic can turn out to be too broad or complicated when you begin to write about it.

You could also change your focus or perspective to narrow your claim. You may, for example, begin to research the claim you have made in response to your issue but discover along the way that the real issue is something else. As a result, you decide to change your claim. For example, suppose you decide to write a policy paper about freedom of speech. Your claim is, *Freedom of speech should be protected in all situations.* As you read and research, however, you discover that an issue for many people is a narrower one related to freedom of speech, specifically as it relates to violent video games and children's behavior. In fact, you encounter an article that claims that video game violence should be censored even if doing so violates free speech rights. You decide to refocus your paper and write a value paper that claims, *Video game violence is harmful and not subject to the protection of free-speech rights.*

CAN YOU LEARN ENOUGH TO COVER THE CLAIM FULLY?

If the information for an effective paper is unavailable or too complicated, write another claim, one that you know more about and can research more successfully. You could also decide to narrow the claim further to an aspect that you understand and can develop.

WHAT ARE THE VARIOUS PERSPECTIVES ON YOUR ISSUE?

Make certain that the issue you have selected invites two or more perspectives. If you have written an exploratory paper on this issue, you already know what several views are. If you have not written such a paper, explore your issue by writing several claims that represent a number of points of view, and then select the one you want to prove. For example:

Solar power is better than nuclear energy.
Solar power is worse than nuclear energy.
Solar power has some advantages and some disadvantages when compared with nuclear energy.
Solar power is better than nuclear energy for certain specified purposes.

HOW CAN YOU MAKE YOUR CLAIM BOTH INTERESTING AND COMPELLING TO YOURSELF AND YOUR AUDIENCE?

Develop a fresh perspective on your issue when writing your claim. Suppose you are writing a policy paper that claims public education should be changed. However, you get bored with it. You keep running into old reasons that everyone already knows. Then you discover new aspects of the issue that you could cover with more original ideas and material. You learn that some people think parents should be able to choose their children's school, and you learn that competition among schools might lead to improvement. You also learn that contractors can take over schools and manage them in order to improve them. You refocus your issue and your perspective. Your new fact claim is, *Competition among schools, like competition in business, leads to improvement.* The issue and your claim now have new interest for you and your audience because you are looking at them in a whole new way.

Developing a Research Plan

LO3 Create a coherent research plan.

A research plan will guide your future thinking and research and help you maintain the focus and direction you have already established. Even though you may not know very much about your issue or your claim at this point, writing out what you do know and what you want to learn can be valuable. Add some ideas to the plan for beginning research and getting started on a first draft. Box 11.1 provides an example.

Box 11.1	A Research Plan Helps You Get Started

▶▶▶ A Research Plan

Value Claim Plus Reasons
Video game violence is harmful and should not be subject to the protection of free speech rights because:

Video game violence and violence in life seem to be related.

Children do not always differentiate between video images and reality.

Parents do not supervise their children's screen time.

Even though free speech is a constitutional right, it should not be invoked to protect what is harmful to society.

Research Needs
I need to find out how free speech is usually defined. Does it include all freedom of expression, including forms of video game violence? Also, I will need to find the latest studies on video game violence and violent behavior, particularly in children. Will I find that there is a

continued

Box 11.1   *continued*

cause–effect relationship? Even though I want to focus mainly on value and show that violent video games are bad, I will also need to include definition and cause in this paper.

Plan for First Draft
I will define video game violence and free speech. I need to do some background reading on censorship and freedom of speech and summarize some of this information for my readers. My strongest material will probably be on the relationship between violent video games and violence in real life. I think now I will begin with that and end with the idea that the Constitution should not be invoked to protect harmful elements like video game violence. I am going to write for an audience that either has children or cares about the welfare of children. I will use examples from an article I found about how children imitate the games they play on their digital devices.

You now have the beginning of an argument paper: a claim, some reasons, and some ideas to explore further. Your claim may change, and your reasons will probably change as you think, read, and do research. Before going further, however, you need to think more about the audience. The nature of your audience can have a major influence on how you will finally write the argument paper.

LO4 Analyze your audience.

Understanding the Audience

In order for the writer of argument to reach an audience, create common ground, and bring about change, two essential requirements need to be met. First, the audience must be willing to listen and perhaps be willing to also change. Second, the author must be willing to study, understand, and appeal to the audience. Such analysis will enable the author to relate to the audience's present opinions, values, and motives and to show as often as possible that the author shares them in ways that reveal or highlight the common ground essential for effective argument. Thus, both audience and author need to cooperate to a certain degree for argument to achieve any outcomes at all.

Three strategies will help you begin the process of understanding and appealing to your audience:

1. *Assess the Audience's Size and Familiarity.* Audiences come in all sizes and may or may not include people you know. Audiences often include specific, known groups such as family members, classmates, work associates, or members of an organization to which you belong. You may also, at times, write for a large, unfamiliar audience composed of local, national, or international members. Of course, some audiences are mixed, with people you know and people you do not know. Your techniques will vary for building common ground with large and small, familiar and unfamiliar audiences, but the aim of your argumentation will not change.

2. ***Determine What You and the Audience Have in Common.*** You may or may not consider yourself a member of your audience, depending on how closely you identify with them and share their views. For example, if you are a member of a union, you probably identify and agree with its official positions, particularly on work-related issues. If you work with management, you are likely to hold other views about work-related issues. The methods you use to achieve common ground with each of these audiences will be somewhat different, depending on whether you consider yourself a member of the group or not.

3. ***Determine the Audience's Initial Position and How It Might Change.*** Remember that there are several possible initial audience positions and several ways in which they might change. For example, a friendly audience might read your argument, confirm their original belief, and strengthen their commitment. An audience that mildly agrees or mildly opposes your position may finally agree with you, become interested in the issue for the first time, or tentatively accept your views, at least for now. A neutral audience may become less neutral and may even decide to accept your position, and a hostile audience might be willing to consider some of your views, or agree to compromise, agree to disagree, or actually change and agree with you.

ASKING QUESTIONS ABOUT A FAMILIAR AUDIENCE

The following list presents thirteen questions to ask about a familiar audience. You do not have to answer every question about every audience. You may need to add a question or two, depending on your audience. Answer questions that are suggested by the particular rhetorical situation for your argument:

1. Describe the audience in general. Who are its members? What do you have in common with them?

2. What are some of the demographics of the group? Consider size, age, gender, nationality, education, and professional status.

3. What are some of their organizational affiliations? Consider political parties, religion, social and living groups, and economic status.

4. What are their interests? Include outside interests, reading material, and perhaps majors.

5. What is their present position on your issue? What audience outcomes can you anticipate?

6. Will they interpret the issue in the same way you have?

7. How significant is your issue to the audience? Will it touch their lives or remain theoretical for them?

8. Are there any obstacles that will prevent your audience from accepting your claim as soon as you state it?

9. How involved are audience members in the ongoing conversation about the issue? Will they require background and definitions? Are they knowledgeable enough to contemplate policy change?

10. What is the attitude of your audience toward you?

11. What beliefs and values do you and your audience share?

12. What motivates your audience? What are the members' goals and aims?

13. What argument style will work best with your audience?

USING INFORMATION ABOUT YOUR AUDIENCE

When you complete the analysis of your audience, examine all the information you have gathered and consciously decide which audience characteristics to appeal to in your paper. Look at the cartoon below. In this humorous example, the speaker thinks he has assessed what concerns motivate his audience. Suppose that you are the student who is planning to write a paper about the value of providing jury training in order for jurors to make competent judgments. Your audience is your argument class. You decide that the general questions about the makeup of the group suggest that you have a fairly typical college audience. Its members are varied enough in their background and experience so that you know they will not all share common opinions on all matters. They do have in common, however, their status as college students. Furthermore, all of you belong to the same group, so you can assume some common values and goals. All of them, you assume, want to be

Image 1:
The Results of a Careful Audience Analysis

"I'll tell you what this election is about. It's about homework, and pitiful allowances, and having to clean your room. It's also about candy, and ice cream, and staying up late."

For Discussion: Describe the appeals this speaker makes to this audience. Why might they be effective?

SOURCE: © 1996 The New Yorker Collection, Robert Weber from cartoonbank.com. All Rights Reserved.

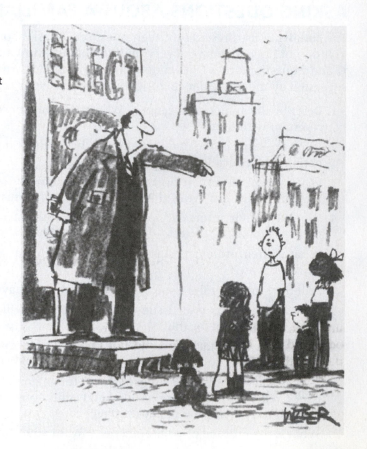

successful, to graduate, and to improve themselves and society; you can appeal to these common motives. All or most of them read the news online or watch local news programs, so they will have common background on the rhetorical situation for your issue. You have asked about their present views on jury training, and you know that many are neutral. Your strategy will be to break through this neutrality and provoke commitment for change.

You decide, furthermore, that you may have to focus the issue for them because they are not likely to see it your way without help. They should also, you decide, know enough to contemplate policy change. You can appeal to their potential common experience as jurors and their need for physical safety, fairness, and good judgment in dealing with criminals. You can further assume that your audience values competence, expertise, and reasonableness, all important outcomes of the training system you intend to advocate.

Get Organized for Research

To prepare for your research, begin by writing what you already know and think about your issue, and by reading broadly to both expand your background information and refine your research. The following suggestions will aid you in reading efficiently to meet these prerequisites for your paper.

▶ **Link your research to your research plan.** As you read, expand on the brief outline you wrote using the research plan worksheet. You do not need to make the plan elaborate, but you will need some kind of list or outline to help you decide on tentative content and a possible order for your ideas. Each piece of research material that you gather and each creative idea should be related to an item on your list or outline. Change the outline when necessary. Once you begin research, you may find you need to narrow your topic and write on only one aspect of it, add additional reasons as support, or even change the pattern of organization. Stay flexible and adjust your outline or list as you go along so that it continues to focus and guide your research.

▶ **Think about your audience.** Write out what your audience needs as background. Also, consider what reasons and evidence they might find particularly convincing.

▶ **Think of some search keywords.** Make a list of keywords associated with your issue that will help you locate sources on library and online search engines. For example, if you are writing about college entrance tests, you could enter terms such as *testing, standardized testing, college entrance tests, standardized college entrance tests,* or *tests and college admission.* To focus your search more specifically, enter a less broad term such as *new SAT.* Keyword searches will help you find both relevant and irrelevant information. Refine and narrow sources by trying different combinations of keywords and, as you proceed, by using terms that are less broad.

▶ **List the types of research materials you will seek.** Jot down where you can find them as well. Books and articles will be high on your list, but you may also want to use other sources, such as personal interviews, speeches, Web sites, television programs, radio programs, advertisements, song lyrics, graphs, photographs, drawings or paintings, maps, letters, or any other types of material that would help you write an argument that is convincing to your audience.

Locating Sources for Research

Begin your research by becoming acquainted with the general layout of your library. Explore the library's online catalog, which indexes all its holdings; find out where the books, magazines, and journals are located; and then find the microforms, the government documents, the reference books, and the media section that houses video and audio materials. In addition, learn where the copy center or copy machines are located. Then find the reference desk and the reference librarians who will help you whenever you are stuck or need advice.

USE THE LIBRARY'S ONLINE CATALOG

Most libraries store information about all of their holdings, including all books and periodicals (magazines, journals, and newspapers), in an online index. Note that the periodicals are indexed in the online catalog and not the articles themselves.

Any computer with access to the Internet will allow you to search your library's online catalog. Search for a book by entering the author's name, the title, or the subject, and look for a particular magazine or journal by entering the title or the subject. Online catalogs also permit you to search by keyword. The keyword search is a powerful and effective research tool that can help you find mainly books but also other materials relevant to your topic, such as reference books, government documents, and various magazines and newspapers that have been reduced in size and preserved on microfilm.

Start with a keyword that represents your topic, such as *clear-cutting*, and the computer will display all titles of the books and other holdings in the library that contain that word. Read the titles as they appear on the screen and identify those that might be useful. When you have found a title that looks promising, move to the screen that shows a more complete description of that book. There you will find all of the other subject headings under which that book is listed in the index. Use those subject headings, or keywords extracted from them, to expand your search. For instance, you might move from your first keyword, *clear-cutting*, to a new keyword, *erosion*, in order to access more varied material. Online catalogs are user-friendly and will tell you on the screen how to use them. Follow the directions exactly, and ask for help if you get frustrated.

FIND A LIBRARY BOOK

To locate the actual books or other research materials you think you want to use, copy the *call number* listed with the title in the online catalog. Copy it exactly; find out where the source is located by consulting a directory. If you cannot find it, look at the other books and resources in the area. They will often be on the same or a similar subject. Some libraries allow you to click on the call number of a book in the online catalog to find a list of the volumes that are shelved in close proximity. Books often contain bibliographies, or lists of related books and articles, which can lead you to additional sources.

FIND ARTICLES IN LIBRARY SUBSCRIPTION DATABASES

Most libraries subscribe to huge licensed online databases that allow you, with a single command, to search through articles from a large number of different print periodicals for information on your topic. All of these databases provide full publishing information about the articles they index, including the author, title, and date and place of publication. Some databases also provide either abstracts or full-text versions of the articles themselves. Also, most of these databases allow the user to forward either article information or an entire article to one's email account to be read later.

Verify which database services your library subscribes to before you begin. Here are a few of the most common ones:

Academic Search Complete describes itself as the "world's largest scholarly, multi-discipline, full text database," with peer-reviewed articles from more than four thousand periodical titles;

CQResearcher provides full-text articles on topics of current interest that include a wide range of issues;

LexisNexis Academic indexes six thousand international titles, including national and international newspapers, provides full text, and is updated hourly; and

EBSCO host allows you to search multiple databases at the same time.

Some databases specialize in particular areas of research and list journals, magazines, newspapers, books, and other media related to that area. Check each database you use to see how far back in time it goes. Some cover only the last twenty to twenty-five years, while others go back one hundred years or more.

Use databases by typing in subjects or keywords and executing a search. A list of associated articles in periodicals and scholarly journals will be displayed on the screen, with the most current appearing first. Read the title and, if there is one, the brief annotation of what the article is about to help you decide which articles to locate and read.

FIND PRINTED JOURNAL OR MAGAZINE ARTICLES

If the database does not provide you with the full text of an article, you will have to find it in the printed periodical in which it first appeared. Look up the name of the periodical, including the volume number, issue number or month, and year, in the online catalog and copy the call number. Then look for it in the same way you would a book. You can learn additional information about the magazine or journal itself, including who publishes it and why, the types of material it publishes, and its overall quality by visiting its Web site and reading about it. Scholarly journals, for example, are often described as "refereed," which means the articles in them are read by several expert reviewers before they are accepted for publication and appear in print. As a general rule, such articles are very reliable sources.

FIND NEWSPAPER ARTICLES

The databases we have just described will lead you to newspaper articles as well as journal and magazine articles, and many of them are full text. When they are not, you may be able to find the newspaper in which the article appeared online or in the microfilm section of the library. When you encounter the abbreviations *mic, mf, cm,* or *mfc* as part of the catalog information for a book or magazine, you will need to find these sources in the microfilm section of the library.

FIND REFERENCE MATERIALS AND GOVERNMENT DOCUMENTS

Two other areas of the library can be useful for research. The reference area contains a variety of volumes that provide factual, historical, and biographical information. Government documents contain data and other forms of information that are useful for argument. Indexes, such as the *Public Affairs Information Bulletin,* which your library may have online, show you the types of factual information you can expect to find in documents published by the government. Your librarian will help you locate the actual documents themselves.

MAKE APPROPRIATE USE OF THE WEB

Since the Web, unlike library databases, is free and available to everyone, not all of the materials found are quality sources. Unlike the sources indexed in library databases that have also appeared in print, not all of the Internet material goes through a publisher or editor. In fact, anyone familiar with computers can set up a Web site and put articles or other documents on it. To maintain your own credibility with your audience, a good rule of thumb is that no source from the Internet or in print should be used unless it has gone through a submission process and has been selected for publication by an editor of a reputable publication. While finding sources from well-known magazines and journals or professional organizations is generally safe, selecting sources from second-rate publications or from individuals lacking credentials reflects negatively on your credibility. Consequently, it is wise to use online articles and information sparingly, unless directed otherwise by your instructor. Your paper will benefit from your use of a variety of sources.

Use a browser such as Safari, Firefox, or Internet Explorer to gain access to the Web. You can then surf the Internet to find information for your paper by using search engines such as *Google, Google Scholar,* or *Yahoo.*

VARY KEYWORD SEARCHES

Some search engines allow you to use operators like *and*, *or*, and *not* to combine your search terms in a more focused way so that the results can be more relevant. By using specific keywords and their grammatical variations and synonyms along with these operators, you can find more particular information. Some of the search engines take you directly to your subject, and others first present a directory of categories that are generated by the authors of the Web sites. They include subject guides (lists of categories like *science* and *education*) that can lead you to good general information about your issue as well as sites that serve as good starting points by offering lots of links.

USE *WIKIPEDIA*, BLOGS, EMAIL, AND SOCIAL MEDIA WITH CAUTION

Wikipedia, a free, online encyclopedia that is open to anyone who has information to contribute, can be a good source of background information when you begin to think about your topic. Some of the entries, for example, are accompanied by useful bibliographies that can lead you to additional sources. Be cautious, however, about quoting *Wikipedia* in your paper. Some schools have policies that discourage the use of *Wikipedia* as a source for a scholarly paper because the entries have not been refereed by panels of experts and because anyone can write or edit material on this site at any time. Ask about the policy at your school. If you do use *Wikipedia* as a source, use it in a limited way just as you would any encyclopedia, to provide a few basic facts or definitions. Do cite it as a source for any information you use from it that is not general knowledge. It should not be the only source you cite for that information, however.

Blogs are online journals that may be written by anyone who wants to do this type of writing on the Internet. Blogs can be personal, opinionated, and idiosyncratic. Explain exactly why you are quoting a blog. For example, you might quote a sampling of opinions on an issue from a few blogs. If you do, make your sources of information clear, explain how they contribute to your paper, and say why you have used them. Follow this same general advice for material you quote from email, texts, or social networking sites such as Twitter or Facebook.

Evaluating Sources

LO6 Evaluate sources.

It is essential that you evaluate every source you use in your paper, whether it is a print or an online source. Here is a list of suggestions to help you do this.

ANALYZE WEB ADDRESS EXTENSIONS

Web sites have a variety of purposes. A site may be created to sell a product, persuade the reader to vote for a political candidate, provide entertainment, or offer educational information. Understanding how to read a Web address can provide valuable clues to help you determine the purpose of a site. The following examples demonstrate the most common Web site extensions:

◗ The *.gov* extension means the Web site was created by a government agency. An example is *irs.gov*.

◗ The *.edu* extension means an educational institution produced the Web site. An example is *stanford.edu*.

◗ The *.mil* extension means the site is produced by the military. An example is *army.mil*.

◗ The *.com* extension means the Web site has a commercial purpose. An example is *honda.com*. The most common Web extension on the Internet is *.com*.

◗ The *.org* extension means the Web site was produced by a nonprofit organization. An example is *npr.org*.

ANALYZE THE RHETORICAL SITUATIONS OF YOUR SOURCES

This will help you gain even more insight into them. Think of TRACE:

◗ *Text.* Consider the *text*: Analyze its point of view on the issue, compare it with other sources on the same subject, analyze the values implicit in it, look at the types of support it contains, and examine its conclusions.

◗ *Reader.* Ask, Who is the intended *reader*? Notice where (in what city or nation or which institution) the publication is from and when (the date of publication). Is the source intended for a particular category of readers or a universal audience? Would you classify yourself as one of the intended readers?

◗ *Author.* Learn more about the *author*. Look for biographical information online or in the published work.

◗ *Constraints.* Think about the *constraints* that may have influenced the author to write about an issue in a certain way. Also, think about the constraints that might influence you as you read it.

◗ *Exigence.* Try to understand the author's motivation or *exigence* for writing on the issue.

EVALUATE THE CREDIBILITY OF YOUR SOURCES

To help you determine the credibility of all sources, but particularly online sources, ask the following questions.

1. *Is the source associated with an organization that is recognized in the field?* For example, a government Web site such as www.census.gov, which contains information about economic or population trends, is credible because government sites are nationally recognized for such information.

2. *Is the source listed under a reputable domain?* Look at what comes after "www" in the URL. For example, information found at www.stanford.edu has some credibility because it is associated with a university. Universities are generally considered reliable sources of information.

3. *Is the source published in a journal that is peer-reviewed?* Check the journal's Web site or look at a print copy. The journal will usually advertise this on its front page. For example, *Modern Language Notes*, published by Johns Hopkins University Press, is credible because everything written in it has been reviewed by a panel of experts to ensure that the work meets a high standard of scholarship. Articles in such sources also meet the standards for academic writing, which makes them valuable potential sources for your research.

4. *Is the source directed mainly to extremists?* You will recognize such sources by their emotional language, extreme examples, and implicit value systems associated with extremist rather than mainstream groups. Learn what you can about such groups and try to determine whether or not they have a wide appeal. Your goal should be to find information with sufficiently wide appeal so that it might be acceptable to a universal audience.

5. *Is the evidence in the source stacked to represent one point of view?* Again, an unusual amount of emotional language, carefully selected or stacked evidence, and quotations from biased sources and authorities characterize this material. You can attack the obvious bias in this material, if you want to refute it.

6. *Is the source current?* Check to see when a Web site was published and last updated. Many topics are time sensitive. A Web site that discusses US anti-terrorism policies but is dated before September 11, 2001, might have limited value unless you are examining the history of American foreign policy in this area.

7. *Is the source sloppily edited, undocumented, or unreasonable?* Material that is poorly edited, infrequently updated, or old may be untrustworthy. Other red flags are inflammatory language and no identified author. Sweeping generalizations made without evidence, undocumented statistics, or unreasonable arguments indicate questionable sources for research.

8. *Is the source moral, immoral, ethical, or unethical, according to your values?* This is the bottom-line question that will help you differentiate credible from noncredible sources for research.

Creating a Bibliography

LO7 Organize and present sources in accepted bibliographic form.

The bibliography is the alphabetically arranged (by author's last name) list of evaluated sources you have decided are credible, related to your issue, and potentially valuable to your research. You will begin by reading them. You may not use all of them, and some of them may lead you to other sources that you will add later. You will either enter these items directly into a computer, or write them on note cards to be typed later.

For every source, create a file that includes the following basic bibliographic information: *who* is the author, *what* is the title, *where* was the source published, *when* was it published, *which* medium of publication is it, *when* did I access it, and *why* would I use it? For each source, add a note to suggest why you might use it in your paper. You will need this information later when you assemble the bibliography or list of works cited in your paper, so write or type all of it out accurately. You will not want to have to find a source again later. Here are some examples in MLA style.

▶ *Bibliographical information for a book* must include the author, the title italicized (underlined in handwritten notes), the place of publication, publisher, date of publication, and medium of publication. To help you, add the call number so that you can find it later in the library.

Example:

Stock, Gregory. *Redesigning Humans: Our Inevitable Genetic Future*. Boston: Houghton, 2002. Print.
  [Call number, QH 438.7 S764]

▶ *Bibliographical information for a printed article* must include the author's name (if there is one), title of the article (in quotation marks), name of the publication (italicized), volume. Issue numbers (for scholarly journals), date of publication, page numbers, and medium of publication. Add the call number or a location.

Example:

Sandel, Michael J. "The Case Against Perfection: What's Wrong with Designer Children, Bionic Athletes, and Genetic Engineering." *Atlantic Monthly* Apr. 2004: 51–62. Print.
  [photocopied article; in research file folder]

▶ *Bibliographical information for online material accessed on the Web or in a database* must include as many of the following elements as are available or needed for the type of source: author's (editor's, etc.) name; title of article (in quotation marks); title of the journal or book (italicized); volume. Issue numbers (for a scholarly journal) and date of publication (or last update); page or paragraph numbers (if numbered, N. pag. when unpaged) for articles; name of the Web site or database (italicized); sponsor, owner, or publisher of the site (or N.p. if not available), date of sponsorship, publication, or update (use n.d. when unavailable); medium; access or use date; and the address (URL) of the service or site when an author-title search does not locate the source.

Example:

Hayden, Thomas. "The Irrelevant Man." *US News & World Report* 3 May 2004. *Academic Search Complete*. Web. 15 May 2014.

ADD ANNOTATIONS TO YOUR BIBLIOGRAPHY

Your instructor may ask you to create an annotated bibliography to help you organize the research for your paper. An annotated bibliography is an alphabetical listing of all of the sources you might use in your paper, with notes or annotations that explain, describe, or critically evaluate the material. That is, your written assessment accompanies each listing. These can include a summary of the argument and authority of the source; a description of the contents and a brief, critical evaluation; and an interpretation of how you could use the material in your paper.

Taking and Organizing Your Notes

You may want to create a file where you will enter your own ideas as well as the various types of reading notes you want to record, including material you *quote* word for word, the material you *paraphrase* or rephrase in your own words, and the material you *summarize*. Here is an example of what each type of source use looks like:

Quoting Material

In his essay "A Defense of Grade Deflation," Princeton student Will Harrel writes, "Grade deflation discourages people from gaming the system and taking 'easy' courses in which everybody gets an A. Coupled with the new pass/D/fail policy changes, these effects now encourage students to take courses that excite them, not just ones that promise A's" (11).

Paraphrasing Material

In his essay "A Defense of Grade Deflation," Princeton student Will Harrel defends this practice, claiming that it improves student motivation and fosters greater student interest in the courses they take (11).

Summarizing Material

In his essay "A Defense of Grade Deflation," Princeton student Will Harrel makes the case for the superiority of this practice over conventional grading practices (11).

On the other hand, you may prefer to keep such materials in a research notebook, in a paper folder, or on note cards. A combination of these possibilities may work best for you. The cardinal principle in whatever note-taking system you use is to clearly indicate on every note which ideas and language belong to other authors and which of them are your own. Add the author's name and the page number to all quoted, paraphrased, or summarized material; place direct quotations in quotation marks; and set off your own ideas and comments in square brackets [ ], place them in a different font or color in your computer files, or label them "mine."

Arrange your notes as you go along and enter them under appropriate headings in a computer file or on the list or outline that you have prepared to guide your research, or on note cards. Add additional headings to this plan when you need them. One way to accomplish this on a computer is to open two windows or document pages side by side. One window displays the headings from your research plan that may become major sections in your paper, and the other window displays an online article you are reading and noting. Copy and paste quoted material from the article and drop it into your outline. Get in the habit of *always* enclosing such material in quotation marks, and then add the name of the author at the end. Add the page number as well, if you can. Many online sources do not have page (or paragraph) numbers. You do not need at this point to add the title, place, or date of publication of each source since that information is available in your bibliography by author name. If you are using more than one book by the same author, write both the author's name and a short version of the title at the end of the citation.

When you are taking notes, you can omit words in a direct quotation to make it shorter and more to the point; indicate where words have been omitted with three spaced periods, known as an *ellipsis*. If the omitted material occurs at the end of a sentence, add a period immediately after the last quoted word, followed by the three spaced periods. Add the page number after the closing quotation mark.

If your research leads you to a new source and you want to use it, add full information about it to your bibliography. Every source you quote should be represented in your bibliography. Conversely, you should not have any items in your eventual Works Cited list that you do not quote, paraphrase, or summarize in your paper.

Clearly distinguish paraphrased and summarized material from your own ideas, just as you would quoted material. Introduce each paraphrase or summary that you enter into your document with a phrase that attributes it to its original author. "According to Scott . . . " or "Jones points out . . . " will make it clear who is responsible for the material that follows, even if it has been reworded and does not appear in quotation marks. Add a page number at the end, if it is from a paged source.

Review Questions

1. What are the claim questions, and how can they be used to establish the purposes in your position paper? **(LO2)**

2. What is the purpose of the research plan? What types of information are included in it? **(LO3)**

3. What are a few items described in this chapter that you consider particularly important in conducting an audience analysis? **(LO4)**

4. Name some of the characteristics of a credible source. **(LO6)**

5. What is a bibliography? What is an annotated bibliography? How might writing an annotated bibliography help you research and write your paper? **(LO7)**

Exercises and Activities

A. The Researched Position Paper: Creating Peer Writing Groups

Do an analysis of the small group of four or five individuals in your class who will serve as readers and critics of your paper from now until you hand it in. Your aim is to get an idea of how your audience regards your issue before you write, and to help your audience become interested in your paper. Do this as a group project, with each group member in turn interviewing the others and jotting down answers to the questions in Worksheet 4.

Worksheet 4   Audience Analysis

1. Describe your issue. What is your audience's present position on this issue? Describe some other perspectives on your issue, and ask for reactions to those ideas. State your claim and ask if there is anyone who cannot accept it as stated. If there is, ask why.

2. How significant is your issue to the audience? If it is not considered significant, describe why it is significant to you.

3. How involved are audience members in the ongoing conversation about the issue? What do they already know about it?

4. How will you build common ground? What beliefs and values do you and your audience share about your issue?

5. What argument style will work best with them? A direct adversarial style? Or a consensual style? Why?

6. Write what you have learned from this analysis to help you plan your appeal to this audience. Include values and motives in your discussion.

B. Pairs of Students: Becoming Familiar with the Library

Visit the library with a classmate or with your entire class and learn how to access the online catalog, the subscription databases of periodical articles, and the Web. Find out how to print full-text articles in the library or send them to your email address at home. Arrange for passwords, if those are required. Then learn to locate the following: books and bound periodicals in the stacks; current periodicals; microfilm or microfiche, including how to use the viewers; and government documents. Finally, locate the reference desk and the reference librarians, who are always willing to help you with a research project.

C. The Researched Position Paper: Conducting Research

Follow the steps delineated in the research worksheet below.

Worksheet 5   Research

1. Locate a variety of sources on your issue and make evaluative judgments about each of them.

2. Gather ten to twelve of your most reliable sources. Include books, print and online articles, and other potential sources. Create a bibliography. Add annotations.

3. Survey and skim for specific information. Take notes.

4. Read critically to understand, and read creatively for original ideas. Take notes.

D. Writing Assignment: Researched Position Paper: Annotated Bibliography

a. *Collect ten quality sources about your issue.* Make certain that your sources express several different perspectives or ways of thinking about your issue. Copy all the publisher's information needed to cite your sources in MLA or APA format, and assemble your bibliography in alphabetical order.

b. Survey, skim, and read selected parts of each source.

c. Write a summary, a response, and an indication of how you might use each source in your paper after each item.

E. The Researched Position Paper: Adding Visual Materials to the Annotated Bibliography

If the assignment calls for it, add related images, graphs, or charts to your bibliography to use later in your paper. Add publisher's information needed to cite your sources in MLA and APA format just as you would an essay or book. Here is an example of an image that might be used in a paper about cloning humans. Publisher's information in MLA format follows the description of the image. It would now be ready to move into your paper.

Image 2:
What's Wrong with Cloning Humans?

This image accompanied a 2009 article in *The Guardian* newspaper examining the dangers of human cloning.

Use at beginning of paper to help readers visualize what human cloning might look like should it ever become a reality.

SOURCE: "Cloned" babies, photograph from Ian Sample, "What's Wrong with Cloning Humans?" *The Guardian*, Apr. 2009; Web; 17 Mar. 2014.

STUDENT PAPER
#1

Angela A. Boatwright
Professor Thorne
English 1302
15 March 2014

Human Cloning: An Annotated Bibliography

Online journal
(appeared earlier
in print)

Bailey, Ronald. "The Twin Paradox: What Exactly Is Wrong with Cloning People?" *Reason* May 1997. *Reasononline*. Web. 12 Mar. 2014.

This article explains simply, in nonscientific terms, exactly what was done to clone Dolly the sheep. The author briefly explains the legislation that has resulted from the first asexual reproduction of a mammal. Bailey explains what a clone would be and discusses the reasons why human clones could in no way be exact copies of their predecessors. Clones would have different personalities and would be as different as identical twins. He doesn't feel it is unethical to clone humans because they would be treated with the same moral status as any identical twins or triplets. He states that as long as we treat cloned individuals as we would treat any other human being, all other ethical problems we have concerning cloning would essentially disappear.

This article answers the questions I had regarding exactly what a clone would be like in relation to the "original model." It reinforces the belief I had that clones would be different people because of different social influences and environmental factors that have so much to do with the personality of an individual.

I will use information about Dolly and the uniqueness of clones in my discussion about the feasibility of cloning people.

Web site (online
publication)

U.S. Dept. of Energy Office of Science. "Cloning Fact Sheet." *Genomics.* energy .gov. Human Genome Project Information, 23 July 2008. Web. 14 Feb. 2014.

According to this government Web site, which is maintained by the Human Genome Project, both scientists and physicians at present advise against cloning humans. When the first cloned animal, Dolly, died in 2003, she had developed both arthritis and cancer. Since that time, animal cloning has been very difficult. Only one or two tries out of one hundred are successful with animals. Also, many cloned animals are born with "large offspring syndrome" and other birth defects. They often die prematurely. There is fear that cloning humans could lead to similar problems. For these reasons, human cloning at this time is considered unethical and dangerous.

This Web site also provides links to anti-cloning legislation information and answers many other questions about all types of cloning issues. It is a credible Web site.

I will draw some information from this Web site to use in the introduction to my paper; and I will also use the information about the dangers of human cloning in my conclusion.

Magazine article
(print)

Mann, Charles C. "The First Cloning Superpower." *Wired* (Jan. 2003): 116+.
Print.

The author has interviewed a number of scientists in China who are
working on therapeutic cloning techniques that employ stem cell research
with the ultimate end of growing human replacement organs and tissues.
China does not have as many regulations against experimenting with human
stem cells as do the United States and other Western countries. China allows
almost complete freedom to scientists in this field, disallowing only human
reproductive cloning experiments. This means that scientists can experiment
with embryonic stem cells to clone spare human parts, to regenerate damaged
nerve and other tissue, and to find cures for diseases that have had no
cures in the past. The author gives several examples of Chinese scientists
who received their education in the United States but could not conduct
stem cell research there because of bans on such research, and who have
now returned to China where they have the freedom and access to funding
and materials to conduct such research. The Chinese government hopes to
win a Nobel Prize for China's work with therapeutic cloning.

While the United States debates the morality of this technology, China,
with a different set of values, pursues it. Stem cell research and therapeutic
cloning will be carried on in other parts of the world as well, even while
being banned in the United States. This science is not likely to go away,
and it is potentially extremely valuable to humans.

I will use this article to develop my section on the feasibility of therapeutic cloning.

Book (print)

Pence, Gregory E. *Who's Afraid of Human Cloning?* Lanham: Rowman, 1998. Print.

This is a comprehensive source of information on cloning. The book
provides a complete overview, including discussions on the misconceptions,
ethics, regulations, and arguments regarding human cloning. This author
is most definitely an advocate of human cloning technology. He feels the
discussion of this issue to date has been horribly one-sided. He states that
never in the history of modern science has the world seen such an instant,
overwhelming condemnation of an application to humanity of a scientific
breakthrough. His aim is to correct this problem of a one-sided debate over
the issue.

I will probably cite this book because of the wealth of information it
contains. Although the author advocates human cloning, his book is a
fairly good source of material for arguing against human cloning.

I will use ideas from this book in my introduction to show how some
people are in favor of cloning and how some are not. I will also make
the distinction between cloning humans and therapeutic cloning, both
of which are controversial.

Article in print and
online (accessed
on database)

Wilson, Jim. "Cloning Humans." *Popular Mechanics* June 2002: 42–44.
Academic Search Complete. Web. 11 Mar. 2014.

This article discusses the technological progress of cloning and the
"inevitability" that humans will soon be cloned. Wilson begins by showing
that cloning humans is not different from the procedure used for in vitro

fertilization (IVF). For IVF, a human conception (the union of a male sperm and female egg) takes place in a glass lab dish, grows into an embryo, and is then implanted in a human uterus. Human clones will go through the same process, Wilson tells us. The difference between IVF and cloned embryos is that the genetic blueprint for IVF cases comes from two parents, whereas clones require only one. Wilson traces the potential for human cloning back to 1997 and shows that while the world marveled at the cloning of Dolly the sheep, the scientific community marveled that researchers from Duke University Medical Center had learned that cloning humans would be simpler than cloning sheep.

Once this discovery was made, Italian researcher Severino Antinori argued that the genetic pattern of sterile males could be passed on via clones. Antinori, who successfully performed IVF for a woman 62 years of age, presented his findings at the International Cloning Consortium in Rome in 2001. His case was taken quite seriously by the scientific community, and since then a number of cloning projects have emerged. The formation of the first human-cloning company, Clonaid, was announced by founder Claude Vorilhon. Clonaid's chief scientist, Brigitte Boisselier, is a chemist who perfected the process of forcing DNA-inoculated cells to divide successfully. Thanks to Boisselier, this cloning process is no less successful than that of standard fertility techniques. The market for this process is fertility clinics.

This article shows how the technology for cloning may be used in a way that is more insidious than many may have previously thought. Combining cloning with fertility treatment to allow couples and individuals to pass along their genetic traits may be a way for cloning to become silently mainstreamed.

I will use this material at the end of my paper to suggest what could happen if this technology is not carefully monitored.

F. The Researched Position Paper: Evaluating Your Research

Look back over your bibliography and the other research and ideas you have gathered and complete the worksheet below. Make certain all of the information you want to use is complete and that you have the information you need to cite all sources. Add, correct, or eliminate any material that might weaken your argument.

Worksheet 6	Research Evaluation

Examine the research you have done so far.

a. Do I have enough information to be convincing? What can I add?

b. Is my information reliable and convincing? How can I make it more so?

c. Is anything exaggerated or oversimplified? How can I be more accurate?

d. Do I rely too much on my own authority ("This is true because I say it is") instead of giving support? Can I add opinions of other authorities to be more convincing?

e. Am I weakening this argument with too much emotional material? Should any of it be eliminated?

G. The Researched Position Paper: Inventing Ideas

Read through the list of invention strategies in Worksheet 7, which follows on this page. The list is a composite of approaches. Some of them will be "hot spots" for you. That is, they will immediately suggest profitable activity for developing your paper. Check those strategies that you want to use at this point and complete them.

Worksheet 7	Invention

Your claim: _____

Begin to develop your claim by using some of the following invention strategies. If you cannot generate information and ideas, do some background reading and then return to these strategies.

1. Freewrite for five minutes.
2. Brainstorm additional ideas and details in brief phrases for another five minutes.
3. Make a list or map that shows the parts of your paper.
4. Explain to someone in your class or group what you expect to accomplish in your paper, or talk into a tape recorder about it.
5. Write your insights in a computer file, a journal, or on sheets of paper filed in a folder.
6. Mentally visualize and write a description of a scene related to your claim.
7. Make a research plan. Write your claim plus three to five reasons. Add ideas for research and a draft plan.
8. Think about possible organizational patterns to shape your paper. What might work best—a claim with reasons, problem–solution, cause and effect, compare and contrast, chronology or narrative, or a combination of two or more patterns?

The Research Paper: Using Sources, Writing, and Revising

After studying this chapter, you will be able to:

LO1 Plan and organize your researched argument.

LO2 Incorporate research into your first draft.

LO3 Revise and prepare your final research draft.

LO4 Present your research orally to your class.

In this chapter, you will learn to write a research paper in which you take a position on your issue, organize your research material and notes, and write a research paper that is convincing to your audience. The instruction in this chapter includes organizing and outlining the paper, incorporating research into your first draft, and revising and preparing the final copy.

Organizing Your Argument

Before you begin drafting, you should think about your claim. What type of claim are you planning to make? What method of organization and types of support are best suited to this claim? Once you have some preliminary ideas about your argument, you can outline it and organize your notes.

Matching Patterns and Support to Claims

Some of the organizational patterns are particularly appropriate for specific types of claims. Table 12.1 (below) suggests patterns you might want to consider as promising for particular argumentation purposes. You could, of course, combine more than one pattern to develop a paper. For example, you may begin with a narrative of what happened, then describe its causes and effects, and finally propose a solution for dealing with the problems created by the effects.

When you use organizational patterns to help you think, these same patterns can function to organize your ideas into a complete argument. However, the patterns may be too constraining if you start with one and try to fill it in with your material. If you prefer to work with ideas first, without the conscious constraints of a pattern to guide you, at some point patterns of argumentation must be

Table 12.1 **Appropriate Patterns for Developing Types of Claims (in Descending Order of Suitability)**

CLAIMS OF FACT	CLAIMS OF DEFINITION	CLAIMS OF CAUSE	CLAIMS OF VALUE	CLAIMS OF POLICY
Claim with reasons	Deduction	Cause and effect	Applied criteria	Problem–solution
Induction	Claim with reasons	Claim with reasons	Cause and effect	Applied criteria
Chronology or narrative	Compare and contrast	Rogerian argument	Claim with reasons	Cause and effect
Cause and effect	Rogerian argument	Deduction	Chronology or narrative	Claim with reasons
Rogerian argument	Exploration	Exploration	Rogerian argument	Rogerian argument
Exploration	Induction		Induction	Exploration
			Deduction	
			Compare and contrast	
			Exploration	

considered. When you are finished, or nearly finished, organizing your research and ideas, move out of the creative mode and into the critical mode to analyze what you have done. You may find that you have arranged your ideas according to one or more of the patterns without being consciously aware of it. This is a common discovery. Now use what you know about the patterns to improve and sharpen the divisions among your ideas and to clarify these ideas with transitions. You will ultimately improve the readability of your paper by making it conform more closely to one or more specific patterns of organization.

Some proofs and support work better than others to establish different types of claims.[1] Table 12.2 offers suggestions, not rules, for you to consider. Remember that a variety of types of proof and a generous amount of specific support create the best, most convincing argument papers.

Table 12.2 **Proofs and Support That Are Particularly Appropriate for Developing Specific Types of Claims**

CLAIMS OF FACT	CLAIMS OF DEFINITION	CLAIMS OF CAUSE	CLAIMS OF VALUE	CLAIMS OF POLICY
Facts	Reliable authorities	Facts	Value proofs	Facts
Statistics	Accepted sources	Statistics	Motivational proofs	Motivational proofs
Real examples	Analogies with the familiar	Historical analogies	Literal analogies	Value proofs
Quotations from reliable authorities	Examples (real or made up)	Literal analogies	Figurative analogies	Literal analogies
Induction	Signs	Signs	Quotations from reliable authorities	Reliable authorities
Literal and historical analogies		Induction	Induction	Deduction
Signs		Deduction	Signs	Definition
Informed opinion		Quotations from reliable authorities	Definition	Statistics
			Cause	Cause

---

[1] I am indebted to Wayne E. Brockriede and Douglas Ehninger for some of the suggestions in Table 12.2. They identify some types of proof as appropriate for different sorts of claims in their article "Toulmin on Argument: An Interpretation and Application." *Quarterly Journal of Speech* 46 (1960): 44–53.

Outlining Your Paper and Cross-Referencing Your Notes

An outline is a useful tool to guide your writing, helping you work through your own ideas and relate them to material from outside sources. Think of your outline as a guide that will help you write later. At the very least, indicate on your outline the major ideas, in the order you intend to write about them, and add the ideas and research you will use for support and development. Read your original ideas and research notes, and check to make certain that all are cross-referenced in some way to the outline. Identify the places where you need more information and research. Work with your outline until it flows logically and makes sense. Pay attention to the parts, the order of the parts, and the relationships among the parts.

The following sample outline is an outline of the student-written researched position paper that appears in the Appendix to this chapter, on pages 373–382. It is the sort of outline one might take to a peer-editing group to discuss and receive suggestions for the actual writing of the paper.

Sample Outline	Working Title: "The Big Barbie Controversy"

▶▶▶ Strategy for Paper

Summarize positions in exploratory paper in introductory paragraphs and describe personal interest in Barbie to create my own *ethos*; establish and apply criteria for judging Barbie doll as both good as a role model for building girls' self-esteem and bad for that purpose; conclude by stating that Barbie is neither good nor bad and should not be the focus of this issue; instead, parents and community are responsible for helping children build self-esteem. Value claim at the end.

▶▶▶ Introduction (Summary of Positions in Exploratory Paper and Background History)

▶ My childhood interest in Barbie—loved her. My sister's disinterest.

▶ Feminism—how changed my view; new respect for sister.

▶ New commonsense view: Barbie just a doll with marketable appeal.

▶ History of Barbie doll: new concept in 1959; offers choices to girls; evidence of success.

▶▶▶ Is Barbie Good for Girls' Confidence and Self-Esteem?

▶ A powerful icon; evidence of doll's popularity.

▶ Criteria for showing Barbie is good for girls: Barbie is everywhere; people all over the world play with these dolls; it is fun to play with Barbie; Barbie stimulates imagination and is a good role model because she can take on many roles.

Sample Outline   *continued*

▶▶▶ Is Barbie Bad for Girls' Confidence and Self-Esteem?

▶ Criteria for showing Barbie is bad for girls: she creates a poor body image; encourages eating disorders; encourages stereotypes; is a negative role model.

▶▶▶ Refutation: Does Barbie Have to Be Either Good or Bad?

▶ Refute those who say all bad: anorexia older than Barbie; cannot protect children from everything that might be a negative influence.

▶ Refute those who say all good: people who played with Barbie still self-critical and have limited insight into themselves.

▶▶▶ Conclusion

It is not Barbie's responsibility to create a self-image in children.

▶▶▶ Claim

Adults and society are responsible for children's self-images. Barbie is being used as a scapegoat.

Note that this outline is worked out in detail in some areas but not in others. The ideas in it so far, however, belong to the author. The peer group that critiques it at this stage would be able to help the author decide whether she has gathered enough source material to write a credible paper or whether she needs to read and take more notes. When your own research seems to be complete, and you have on file the notes you intend to include in the paper, they can now be cross-referenced to your outline and placed in the order in which you will use them in the paper. You are ready to write the draft next. Most of the material in the paper will be your own insights, observations, ideas, and examples. The researched material will be incorporated into the paper to add information, interest, clarity, and credibility.

Incorporating Research into Your First Draft

LO2 Incorporate research into your first draft.

Your objective is to create a smooth document that can be read easily while, at the same time, demonstrating to your readers exactly which materials are yours and which are drawn from outside sources. Here are some suggestions to help you accomplish this.

1. *Use quoted material sparingly.* You want to have the controlling voice in your paper. No more than 20 percent of your paper should be made up of direct quotations of other people's words. When you do quote, select material that is interesting, vivid, and best stated in the quoted words.

2. *Paraphrase or summarize when you do not know enough to use your own explanations.* Use your own words to rephrase or summarize other people's explanations and ideas so that yours is the dominant voice in your paper.

3. *Begin and end your paper with your own words instead of a quotation, paraphrase, or summary of other people's ideas.* The beginning and end are emphatic places in a paper. Put *your* best ideas there, not someone else's.

4. *Introduce each quotation, paraphrase, or summary in your paper so that your readers will know who wrote the original material.* Make it clear where your words and ideas leave off and where someone else's begin. Introduce each quotation, paraphrase, or summary with the name of the person you are quoting or otherwise citing. Consider adding a description of that person's credentials to establish his or her *ethos* and authority.

5. *Integrate every quotation into your paper so that it flows with the rest of the text and makes sense to the reader.* Work in the quotations so that they make sense in context.

6. *If your author quotes someone else and you want to use that quote in your own paper, introduce the quotation by indicating who originated it.* Make clear you are quoting someone your source quoted.

7. *Cite the source of the quotation, paraphrase, or summary in parentheses at the end of it.* Further instructions for writing in-text parenthetical citations are given in the Appendix to this chapter.

Write all quotations, paraphrases, and summaries into your first draft so that your entire paper will be in place for smooth reading.

CLEARLY IDENTIFY WORDS AND IDEAS FROM ALL SOURCES TO AVOID PLAGIARISM

Whenever you use quoted, paraphrased, and summarized material from other sources in your paper, you must indicate where your words leave off and someone else's begin, and you must identify the original source for all borrowed material.

Sometimes students mix their words in with the words of the author they are quoting and, as a result, the reader cannot easily sort out the students' words from those of the person being quoted. This is a form of plagiarism. Plagiarism is a very serious offense. Be sure to carefully document your sources using the guidelines given in the Appendix to this chapter.

DOCUMENT YOUR SOURCES

Some of the main features of source acknowledgment are explained in the Appendix to this chapter on pages 362–402. Use this section as a reference guide when you are working borrowed material into your paper and when you are preparing the final list of the works you have used. These methods will inform your reader about exactly what material in your paper is yours, what belongs to other people, and where you found the material in your research.

As you incorporate borrowed material from other sources, you will need to follow a system and a set of conventions that has been prescribed for this purpose. Two such systems are described later in the chapter: MLA style, which is recommended by the Modern Language Association for papers written in the humanities, is explained first. MLA documentation style provides advice on how to acknowledge the work of other individuals in your paper itself and how to give full information about these sources in a list of "Works Cited" at the end of your paper. Following the discussion of MLA style is a researched position paper in MLA style format (pages 363–383). It was written by a student, and you can use it as an example when you write your own paper. Study the annotations in the margins of this paper. They demonstrate how quoted and summarized material can be incorporated into papers and acknowledged according to MLA style. Answer the questions that accompany this paper (page 383) to further develop your expertise in using MLA style.

The second documentation style is APA style, recommended by the American Psychological Association for papers written in education and the social sciences. APA documentation calls for a somewhat different system from MLA. Information is provided for citing sources in the text of an APA-style paper and listing these sources on a "References" page at the end. A student paper written in APA style provides an illustration of this documentation format (pages 392–401).

Other documentation styles, not described in this text, include CSE style, which is recommended by the Council of Science Editors for scientific papers, including natural sciences, chemistry, geography, and geology; and Chicago style, the style recommended by the University of Chicago Press. Chicago style is followed throughout this book. If an instructor asks you to use CSE or Chicago style in a paper, consult the Internet or a published manual for guidelines. No matter which system you use while writing a paper, be consistent, and never mix styles.

Making Revisions and Preparing the Final Copy

LO3 Revise and prepare your final research draft.

It may take several tries, but you will eventually get a version of your paper that you are ready to show to other readers. Seek the help of your peer editing group, a tutor, your instructor, or other readers once again, when you have improved your paper as much as possible on your own. When you arrive at this point, you will think your paper is pretty good. However, a new reader will always find ways to improve your paper. This is the time, then, to put aside pride and let others take a final look at what you have written. A fresh set of eyes (and ears) usually adds to the careful refining you are trying to accomplish. During this final revision process, you and your readers can also use the Toulmin model to help you identify and revise the major elements in your paper.

1. Find your claim. Is it clear? Is it well positioned?

2. Check the quantity and quality of your support. Is there enough? Is it relevant? Is it authoritative and accurate?

3. Check your warrants. Are they likely to be acceptable to your audience?

4. Think about backing for your warrants. Should you explain backing for your warrants to make them stronger and more acceptable to your audience?

5. Focus on your rebuttal, if you have one. Does it effectively address the opposing arguments?

6. Consider a qualifier. Ask yourself: Would a qualified claim make your argument stronger?

Once you have reviewed these questions, it is time to prepare the final copy using MLA or APA format. See the Appendix to this chapter for further details on formatting.

Finally, spell-check your paper, and proofread it one last time. Correct all of the errors that you can find. Errors in a research paper damage your *ethos* with your readers. Careless errors communicate that you do not really value your own work or your audience. When your paper is as error-free as you can make it, it is ready for submission.

LO4 Present your research orally to your class.

Present Your Paper Orally to the Class

Your instructor may ask you to present the results of your research to the class in the form of oral argument. Like written and visual argument, oral argument possesses special features that make it uniquely effective for presenting arguments. Listed below are a few of these advantages.

1. *Oral argument is immediate.* When the speaker and the audience are together in the same physical location, face to face, the potential for effective argument is greatly enhanced. This is true of all forms of oral argument, whether spoken, chanted, or sung. The physical presence of an effective speaker intensifies what is said, and the audience is thus more likely to pay attention and be influenced. Furthermore, a good speaker is always aware of the audience and can adapt both words and delivery to keep listeners' attention and influence them in desired ways. At times, the effectiveness of oral argument can be enhanced by the use of multimedia tools such as PowerPoint, slide shows, and video.

2. *Oral argument employs physical as well as verbal strategies.* Speakers are able to influence perception in ways that writers cannot. For example, speakers can use physical gestures, vocal inflections, facial expressions, eye contact, physical setting, dress, and physical appearance in effective and dramatic ways to strengthen delivery and make their words more powerfully convincing.

3. *Oral argument usually employs a less formal style than written argument and can be easier to respond to and understand.* When compared with written argument, oral argument usually has fewer main points, more support of all kinds, and more obvious transitions to help the listener move from one idea to another.

Such informality results in an enhanced rapport and the establishment of more common ground between the speaker and the audience. The informality of spoken argument, when compared with written argument, is often more inviting to an audience and makes it easier for listeners to pay attention, believe the speaker, and become convinced.

Analyze oral argument just as you would written, visual, or multimedia argument. That is, when listening to oral argument, you can recognize and understand the rhetorical situation; analyze the use of *logos*, *ethos*, and *pathos*; identify and expose fallacies; apply the Toulmin model; and make ethical judgments, just as you would when reading an essay or viewing a visual argument. Apply these methods of analysis when you create oral argument. Exercise B on pages 360–361 explains how to prepare your researched position paper for oral presentation in class.

Review Questions

1. What steps can you take to avoid plagiarism when you are incorporating research materials into your draft and when you are preparing the final copy? **(LO2)**

2. What is the purpose of the "Works Cited" page (MLA) and the "References" page (APA)? **(LO2)**

3. What are some of the special features of oral argument? **(LO3)**

Exercises and Activities

A. Writing Assignment: The Researched Position Paper

1. *Write a list, outline, or partial manuscript that will serve as a plan for your paper, and bring it to class.* Refer to the example on pages 354–355 in this chapter. In peer editing groups of three or four students, explain to the group what your paper is about, and how you plan to organize and develop it. Suggestions from the others can help with ideas and organization, as well as adding research. Decide whether or not to add images or graphics as support.

2. *Create a class peer critique sheet.* The peer critique sheet provides a guide for critiques and revision. Make a list of all of the special requirements for a researched position paper: a title, a clear claim, adequate support, clear organization, accurate documentation, and so on. Select five to ten items from this list that you believe are essential elements to consider during revision. Organize them on a peer critique sheet. Use these sheets in your peer editing group to critique individual student papers and make good recommendations for revision.

3. *Write a draft of your paper, revise it, and bring it to class.* At this point, it is useful to have one or more people read your paper and give you ideas for improving it. Your readers may use the peer critique sheets created

in Exercise A2 above, either writing their comments on them or on the papers. This can be accomplished in one of the following ways:

a. *Groups in class*: The members of your peer group should first read all of the papers written by your group and make a few notes about each of them on the peer critique sheets or on the papers. As an alternative, the authors can read their papers aloud, with each paper discussed in turn. Members of the group should offer observations and recommendations for improvement to each author, and as the discussion progresses, they may continue to add suggestions to the peer critique sheets, which should be given to the authors at the end of the session.

b. *Individuals outside of class*: Exchange papers with a classmate and critique each other's work outside of class. Before the next class period, read the paper you have been assigned carefully and make as many useful suggestions as you can on the paper itself and on the peer critique sheet. When you return to class, talk through your suggestions with the author. Then listen to that individual's ideas for improving your paper.

4. *Make final revisions, and then prepare the final copy.* Your researched position paper should be a length specified by your instructor. It should be double-spaced and should use a specified number of outside sources. Use MLA or APA format throughout. The student paper on pages 373–382 demonstrates general format, in-text citations, and "Works Cited" requirements for MLA style. The student paper on pages 392–401 does the same for APA style. Notice that, in these papers, the ideas that control them are the authors' original ideas and opinions and the quoted and paraphrased material is used to provide support.

5. *Write a one-page Toulmin analysis of your paper.* Submit it with your final paper.

6. *Write a submission letter to your instructor.* Submit a letter to your instructor with your final paper, and in it describe what you like about your paper and what still dissatisfies you. Identify problems or passages on which you would like some feedback.

B. Class Project: Conducting a Class Symposium and Presenting Your Research

Adapt your researched position paper to create a five-minute oral presentation of the research you have completed. Follow these instructions:

1. Work with your written manuscript to change it into an oral report. Underline and number the most important ideas. Since oral argument usually has fewer main ideas than written argument, limit yourself to three to five main ideas so that you can explain them in the time you have.

2. Think about your audience. How much background information about your topic will you have to present or possibly add at the beginning of your speech to help your audience understand it?

3. Remember, also, that your listeners have only one chance to understand the main ideas. Add some obvious transitions to clarify your main ideas

and make them stand out. These might include, for example, explaining your main points in your introduction, numbering them as you explain them, and restating and summarizing them at the end of your speech.

4. You will not read your speech, but you will probably want some speaking notes to refer to as you speak. Accomplish this by writing a 250-word abstract of your researched position paper. State the claim, the main points made about it, some of the evidence, and your conclusion. Now go back and underline the points in the abstract that you want to talk about and number these in the margin. While you are speaking, you might need to glance at your abstract from time to time to remind yourself of the next point, and, if you find that you are stuck, you can read a sentence or two. Writing the abstract in sentences will also help you get the phrasing right so that you will speak more fluently.

5. Organize members of your class in groups around the same or related topics. The best group size is five to seven students with a moderator. The moderator will call on the students in your group to present your abstracts of your research papers.

6. Practice your speech and time it. If anything in the speech seems to be unclear or awkward, make revisions. Work with the speech until it fits within the time frame of five minutes.

7. Consider what multimedia tools you might want to use to make your presentation more forceful and memorable. You may want to provide images, graphs, or charts. Or, you may want to include visuals in a Power-Point presentation or slide show. Here are the rules for using visuals during an oral presentation: (a) make it large enough for your audience to read easily, and (b) do not put it in front of your audience until you are ready to discuss it.

8. Practice the speech several times until you can give it fluently.

9. When you give your speech, use eye contact and experiment with some gestures. Above all, concentrate on communicating with your audience.

10. Answer questions from the class. Participate in a brief class discussion of the ideas presented by your group.

C. Analyzing a Student's Researched Position Paper

An example of a researched position paper, written in MLA style, appears in the Appendix to this chapter on pages 373–382. Take a few minutes to read this paper along with the labels in the margins. Then work in pairs to answer the questions that follow the paper on page 383. If you have difficulty answering the questions about quotations and in-text page references or the list of "Works Cited," refer to pages 363–372 for help. Report your answers to the questions to the class.

How to Document Sources Using MLA and APA Style

LO1 Cite and document sources in MLA style.

LO2 Cite and document sources in APA style.

The following material will demonstrate, first, how to use in-text citations to show your readers exactly what material you have included in your paper from outside sources and, second, how to prepare a final list of sources with publication details at the end of your paper. This list is called either Works Cited, if you are following MLA style, or References, if you are following APA style. In-text citations are structured to make clear to the reader who is to be credited with the words or ideas and where in the Works Cited or References list to find the full documentation of that source.

The first section of this appendix discusses MLA documentation. If you need information on APA style, turn to page 384. For additional detail on how to use MLA style, consult the *MLA Handbook for Writers of Research Papers* (7th ed., 2009), published by the Modern Language Association; for APA style, consult the *Publication Manual of the American Psychological Association* (6th ed., 2009) and the *APA Style Guide to Electronic References* (6th ed., 2012), both published by the American Psychological Association.

MLA: How to Cite Sources in the Body of the Text

LO1 Cite and document sources in MLA style.

The MLA system of documentation asks that you show where you originally found a direct quotation or the information for a paraphrase or a summary by inserting a brief parenthetical citation at the end of the borrowed material in your written text. The typical in-text parenthetical citation contains the author's last name and the page number: (Jones 5). However, if you include the author's name in the text, then you do not need to include it in the citation. If you include a book or journal title because no author is available, place the title in italics (for a book) or quotation marks (for an article). All sources that you cite in the text of your paper must also appear in the Works Cited list. Here are examples of common types of in-text citations.

1. *A direct quotation with the author mentioned in the text* If you introduce the author's name in the body of the text before you quote directly, then there is no need to include the name in the parenthetical citation.

> Although various critics have accused Arnold Schoenberg's musical compositions of being "atonal," Alex Ross points out that the composer was "simply offering a tonality of a less familiar kind" (176).

2. *A direct quotation with the author not mentioned in the text*

> Although various critics have accused Arnold Schoenberg's musical compositions of being "atonal," others argue that the composer was "simply offering a tonality of a less familiar kind" (Ross 176).

3. *A paraphrase or summary with the author mentioned in the text*

> According to Calvin Tomkins, the rebuilding and expansion of the New York Museum of Modern Art proves that modern art has not reached its end (72).

4. *A paraphrase or summary with the author not mentioned in the text*

> If the rebuilding and expansion of the New York Museum of Modern Art is any indication, claims that modern art has reached its end may soon be proven wrong (Tomkins 72).

5. *Two or more authors* If two or three authors have written the material you have borrowed, include all of their last names in either the introductory wording or the citation.

> Pimentel and Teixeira remind us, "Virtual reality is all about illusion" (7).

> "Virtual reality is all about illusion" (Pimentel and Teixeira 7).

For more than three authors, use only the first author's last name and add *et al.* to the citation. (*Et al.* is an abbreviation of the Latin *et alii,* meaning "and others." It is not italicized in your paper.)

> "Television is not primarily a medium of entertainment in all societies" (Comstock et al. 25).

6. *Two books by the same author* To indicate which book you are citing, either include the name of the book in the introductory material or add a shortened title to the parenthetical information to differentiate between the books. For example, if you are using *Simulation and Its Discontents* (2009) and *Alone Together: Why We Expect More From Technology and Less From Each Other* (2012), both by Sherry Turkle, document as follows:

> Sherry Turkle notes that we can become dazzled by the possibilities of digital culture: "immersed in simulation, we feel exhilarated by possibility" (*Simulation and Its Discontents* 7). She elaborates this point by claiming that "technology proposes itself as the architect of our intimacies" (*Alone Together* 1).

If the author is not mentioned in the text, include the author's name followed by a comma before the shortened title of the work: (Turkle, *Alone Together* 30).

7. *A corporate or group author* Sometimes written materials are attributed to a corporate or group author (e.g., a corporation, company, association, or organization) rather than to an individual author. In this case, use the name of the corporation or group, preferably in the wording that precedes the quotation.

> The RAND Corporation observes that "when the No Child Left Behind Act was passed into law in January 2002, it heralded the beginning of one of the most expansive efforts to reform public education" (7).

If the corporate author is not mentioned in the text, include the corporate author's name as part of the citation before the page number.

> (RAND Corporation 7)

8. *An unknown author* When no author is listed for either a book or an article, use the title or the first words of an abbreviated title in your citation.

> *Article:* ("Creativity and Television" 14)
>
> *Book:* (*World Almanac* 397)

9. *A work reprinted in a book or journal* If you quote an article, poem, story, or any other work that is reprinted not in its original but in another compilation, cite the author you are quoting in the text and the page number. The author or editor of the compilation is not cited in the parenthetical citation, but is fully cited in the Works Cited. Thus, a quotation that includes words from the essay by Mike Rose on pages 292–294 of this book by Nancy V. Wood and James S. Miller would be cited in the text as (Rose 292–94).[1]

10. *Short quotations versus block quotations* Short quotations do not exceed four lines of text. For short quotations, place quotation marks around the quoted material, insert the citation information in parentheses, and place the period outside it.

---

[1]Note that inclusive page ranges in MLA style ellide the hundred- or thousand-place numeral for the closing page in the range, as long as it is clear which pages are being cited. For example, 199–203 would not be ellided.

> According to Nate Stulman, "many college students now opt to communicate visually, using photo-sharing sites like Instagram instead of relying on the word-based communication tools like Twitter. Why bother using words at all when an image works just as well?" (268).

Quotations that exceed four lines of text should be blocked. To block a quotation, you should eliminate the quotation marks and indent each line 1 inch (or ten spaces) from the left margin, including the first line if you quote all or part of a single paragraph (that is, do not set a paragraph indent). If you quote two or more full paragraphs, indent the first line of each paragraph an additional ¼ inch (or three spaces), as in the example below. Place the period at the end of the text, followed by the parenthetical citation. Use double-spacing, as you do throughout your paper. It is good writing style to provide a brief introduction to a long quote and to finish the quote with a concluding thought.

> Nate Stulman describes some of the more popular forms of online communication among the students at his school:
>> You might expect that most college students would rely on tools like Twitter to communicate because they are so easy and efficient. For proof, we need only to look at how many public figures—from celebrities to politicians—keep their followers updated on their latest thoughts and actions by sending out Tweets. Given this, you might think that college students would follow suit. However, a quick survey of my classmates reveals that many consider communicating via Twitter to be too much work, and feel that sites like Instagram allow them to say everything they want to say through a single image. (268)
> These experiences may be typical of students at other colleges as well.

11. *Ellipsis points and quoted material* Occasionally, you will want to delete material from the original source either to make your document shorter or to make the writing that includes the quote more readable. If you do so, indicate by inserting ellipsis points to signal that you have removed words. The following example shows how to use ellipsis points to indicate you have omitted words in the middle of a sentence.

> "If there were a wider appreciation for motherhood in society, women might . . . hold their heads high when going to the boss and asking for a reduced hour work schedule" (Hewlett 308).

When deleting the ending of a sentence in a short quotation, indicate that deletion by using three spaced points and a fourth after the parenthetical citation. The fourth point serves as the period to the sentence.

> "A weakness of mass entertainment is its impersonality . . ." (Jones 226).

When there is no parenthetical citation (for example, within a large block quotation), then the sentence is completed by placing the period before the ellipsis.

12. *Tables* Place tables as close as possible to the text they explain or illustrate. At the top, place with the word *Table* and assign an arabic numeral. On a new line, give it a caption capitalized headline style. Provide source information immediately below the table. Notes, if any, follow, numbered with lowercase letters (*a, b, c,* etc.). Double-space throughout (for a small table) and align as shown. Indent the second or more lines in the caption and source line two spaces; indent the first line of notes five spaces.

The following table shows calories used in common physical activities at both moderate and vigorous levels.

Table 1

Calories Used per Hour in Common Physical Activities

Moderate Physical Activity	Approximate Calories/ 30 Minutes for a 154 lb Person	Approximate Calories/ Hr for a 154 lb Person
Hiking	185	370
Light gardening/yard work	165	330
Dancing	165	330
Golf (walking and carrying clubs)	165	330
Bicycling (<10 mph)	145	290
Walking (3.5 mph)	140	280
Weight lifting (general light workout)	110	220
Stretching	90	180

Source: United States. Dept. of Health and Human Serv., Centers for Disease Control; Healthy Weight Statistics, 17 Aug. 2011; Web; 17 Mar. 2014.

13. *Graphs, artwork, photographs, and other illustrations* Graphs, artwork, photographs, and other illustrations are labeled Fig., the abbreviation for *Figure*, followed by an arabic numeral; the caption (see format below) is followed on the same line by any source information.

Fig. 1. Quarterly earnings according to region.

14. *Poetry and song lyrics* Quote three lines or less of poetry in your text by using quotation marks and a slash with spaces on each side [/] to separate the lines. The parenthetical citation should contain the line numbers.

In his poem "The Discovery," Paul Laurence Dunbar populates his poem with mythic characters: "These are the days of elfs and fays: / Who says that with the dreams of myth / These imps and elves disport themselves?" (1–3).

For more than three lines, indent the quotation 1 inch (or ten spaces) from the left margin.

> Mythic figures populate Dunbar's poem:
>
> > These are the days of elfs and fays:
> > Who says that with the dreams of myth,
> > These imps and elves disport themselves?
> > Ah no, along the paths of song
> > Do all the tiny folk belong.
> >
> > Round all our homes,
> > Kobolds and gnomes do daily cling,
> > Then nightly fling their lanterns out.
> > And shout on shout, they join the rout,
> > And sing, and sing, within the sweet enchanted ring. (1–10)

15. *Electronic sources* Cite electronic sources in the text just as you would print sources. Introduce the quotation with the author's name, or cite the author's last name (or a short title, if there is no author) with a page or paragraph number in parentheses at the end. If the source has no page or paragraph numbers, or if you are citing or quoting from the whole source as a single document, place only the author's name in the parentheses. Here is an example of a quotation from an online journal that numbers paragraphs rather than pages.

> "Rose represents the unnamed multitude of women who were placed in the same circumstances but whose stories were never told" (Mason, par. 8).

If you use the author's name in the body of the text introducing the quotation, then place only the paragraph number in the citation.

> According to Mason, "Rose represents the unnamed multitude of women who were placed in the same circumstances but whose stories were never told" (par. 8).

Some online sources do not provide page or paragraph numbers. There are two ways to cite such sources. If you place the author's name in the text, there is no parenthetical citation at the end.

> Carlos Oliveira phrases the question about media and reality this way: "Take, for instance, the alteration of our reality through the mass media. Do the media create reality? Or do they alter or destroy it?"

If you do not mention the author in the text, place only the author's name in the citation.

> "Take, for instance, the alteration of our reality through the mass media. Do the media create reality? Or do they alter or destroy it?" (Oliveira).

Also, some online sources are a single page, which may or may not be numbered. When your source is a single page, include any page number in the Works Cited entry but use the no-page-number model in your text. For example, look at the quotation from Rachel Sa in paragraph 15 of the MLA student research paper titled "The Big Barbie Controversy" on page 380. No page number is included in the text since this is a single-page source. Now turn to page 382 and look at the Works Cited entry for Sa. Notice that the page number is included here.

MLA: How to Cite Sources in the Works Cited List

Attach to the draft a list of all the works you have quoted, paraphrased, or summarized in your paper along with full publication information for each source. This list is titled Works Cited, and it begins on a new page, which is numbered consecutively. Included below is the MLA format for citing print, electronic, and nonprint sources.

How to List Print Books

1. *A book by one author*

Lepore, Jill. *Book of Ages: The Life and Opinions of Jane Franklin.* New York: Knopf, 2013. Print.

2. *A book by two or three authors*

Chayes, Antonia H., and Martha Minow. *Imagine Coexistence: Restoring Humanity after Violent Ethnic Conflict.* San Francisco: Jossey, 2003. Print.

3. *A book by more than three authors*

Stewart, Charles J., et al. *Persuasion and Social Movements.* 3rd ed. Prospect Heights: Waveland, 1994. Print.

4. *Two or more books by the same author*

Solove, Daniel. *Nothing to Hide: The False Tradeoff Between Privacy and Security.* New Haven: Yale UP, 2013. Print.

---. *Understanding Privacy.* Cambridge: Harvard UP, 2010. Print.

5. *A book by a corporate or group author*

Harvard Business School Press. *The Results-Driven Manager: Winning Negotiations That Preserve Relationships: A Time-Saving Guide.* Boston: Harvard Business School P, 2004. Print.

6. *A book with no author named*

The World Almanac and Book of Facts. New York: World Almanac, 2013. Print.

7. *A republished book*

Locke, John. *An Essay Concerning Human Understanding.* 1690. New York: Dover, 1959. Print.

8. *A translation*

Virilio, Paul. *Ground Zero.* Trans. Chris Turner. London: Verso, 2002. Print.

9. *A second or subsequent edition*

Wood, Nancy V., and James S. Miller. *Perspectives on Argument.* 8th ed. New York: Pearson, 2015. Print.

10. *Proceedings from a conference or symposium*

Medhurst, Martin J., and H. W. Brands, eds. *Presidential Rhetoric: Critical Reflections on the Cold War Linking Rhetoric and History.* Texas A&M Conf. on Presidential Rhetoric, 5–8 Mar. 1998. College Station: Texas A&M UP, 2000. Print.

11. *An introduction, preface, foreword, or afterword*

Rajchman, John. Introduction. *Pure Immanence.* By Gilles Deleuze. Trans. Anne Boyman. New
    York: Zone, 2001. 7–23. Print.

12. *A government document*

United States. FBI. Dept. of Justice. *National Instant Criminal Background Check System.*
    Washington, DC: GPO, 2004. Print.

How to List Print Articles

13. *An article from a magazine*

Filkins, Dexter. "The Shadow Commander." *New Yorker* 23 Sept. 2013: 54–62. Print.

14. *An article from a newspaper*

Rutenberg, Jim, and Micheline Maynard. "TV News That Looks Local, Even If It's Not." *New
    York Times* 2 June 2003: C1+. Print.

15. *An article in a periodical with no author listed*

"Metamorphosis." *New Yorker* 5 Nov. 2001: 10. Print.

16. *An article in a journal*

Mountford, Roxanne. "The Rhetoric of Disaster and the Imperative of Writing." *Rhetoric
    Society Quarterly* 31.1 (2001): 41–48. Print.

17. *An edited collection of articles or an anthology*

Handa, Carolyn, ed. *Visual Rhetoric in a Digital World.* Boston: Bedford, 2004. Print.

18. *An article in an edited collection or an anthology*

Stroupe, Craig. "Visualizing English: Recognizing the Hybrid Literacy of Visual and Verbal
    Authorship on the Web." *Visual Rhetoric in a Digital World.* Ed. Carolyn Handa. Boston:
    Bedford, 2004. 13–37. Print.

19. *A cross-reference to an edited collection or an anthology* To avoid duplicating
information when citing more than one source from a collection or anthology, set
up a cross-reference in the Works Cited list. Cite the whole anthology or collection
as you would any source. For the entire collection, the editor is the author.

Handa, Carolyn, ed. *Visual Rhetoric in a Digital World.* Boston: Bedford, 2004. Print.

Stroupe, Craig. "Visualizing English: Recognizing the Hybrid Literacy of Visual and Verbal
    Authorship on the Web." Handa 13–37.

20. *A reprinted article in an edited volume or collection* The following entry
cites a chapter from Gunther Kress's book *Literacy in the New Media Age* reprinted
in the collection by Handa.

Kress, Gunther. "Multimodality, Multimedia, and Genre." *Literacy in the New Media Age.*
    London: Routledge, 2003. 106–21. Rpt. in *Visual Rhetoric in a Digital World.* Ed. Carolyn
    Handa. Boston: Bedford, 2004. 38–54. Print.

21. *A signed article in a reference work* Omit page numbers for reference
works that arrange entries alphabetically.

Davidson, W. S., II. "Crime." *Encyclopedia of Psychology.* Ed. Raymond J. Corsini. 4 vols. New
    York: Wiley, 1984. Print.

22. *An unsigned article in a reference work*

"Quindlen, Anna." *Current Biography Yearbook.* Ed. Judith Graham. New York: Wilson, 1993. Print.

23. *A review*

Ottenhoff, John. "It's Complicated." Rev. of *The Moment of Complexity: Emerging Network Culture,* by Mark C. Taylor. *Christian Century* 119.21 (2002): 56–59. Print.

24. *A letter to the editor*

Cooper, Martin. Letter. *Business Week* 17 May 2004: 18. Print.

25. *An editorial*

"Curbing Antibiotics on Farm Taking Too Long." Editorial. *USA Today* 27 Oct. 2013: 21A. Print.

26. *A published interview*

Yellen, Janet. Interview by Robert Kutner. *American Prospect* 7 (Sept. 2013): 12–15. Print.

27. *A personal interview*

Wick, Audrey. Personal interview. 27 Dec. 2013.

28. *A lecture, speech, or address*

King, Martin Luther, Jr. "I Have a Dream." March on Washington. Lincoln Memorial, Washington, DC. 28 Aug. 1963. Address.

How to List Electronic Sources

Entries for Internet sources consist of six basic divisions: the author's name, title of the document, print publication information (where applicable), electronic publication information, medium, and date of access. URLs are required only when it would be difficult for a reader to locate the source without it.

29. *Individual Web page*

Lepi, Katie. "Where in the World Do the Most Young People Use Technology?" *Edudemic.* Edudemic, 20 Oct. 2013. Web. 4 Nov. 2013.

30. *An entire Internet site*

CNN.com. Cable News Network, 2013. Web. 24 May 2013.

31. *A home page for a course*

Stern, David. Heidegger. Course home page. Fall 2000. Dept. of Philosophy, U of Iowa. Web. 15 June 2008. <http://www.uiowa.edu/c026036/>.

32. *A personal Web page*

Blakesley, David. Home page. 18 Sept. 2003. Web. 22 Nov. 2008.

33. *An online book*

Mussey, R. D. *An Essay on the Influence of Tobacco Upon Life and Health.* Boston: Perkins and Marvin, 1836. *Project Gutenberg.* Project Gutenberg Online Book Catalog, 2006. Web. 31 Mar. 2014.

34. *A part of an online book*

Mussey, R. D. "Cases Illustrative of the Effects of Tobacco." *An Essay on the Influence of Tobacco Upon Life and Health.* Boston: Perkins and Marvin, 1836. *Project Gutenberg.* Project Gutenberg Online Book Catalog, 2006. Web. 31 Mar. 2014.

35. *An article in an online newspaper*

Webb, Cynthia L. "The Penguin That Ate Microsoft." *Washington Post.* Washington Post, 27 May 2004. Web. 28 May 2008.

36. *An article in an online magazine*

Reiss, Spencer. "The Wired 40." *Wired* July 2006. Conde Nast Digital, 2009. Web. 6 Aug. 2013.

37. *An article in an online scholarly journal*

Josien, Laurent, and Britton Broderick. "Cheating in Higher Education: The Case of Multi-methods Cheaters." *Academy of Educational Leadership Journal* 17.2 (2013): 93+. *Educators Reference Complete.* Web. 4 Nov. 2013.

38. *A review*

Gray, Donna. Rev. of *Psychic Navigator,* by John Holland. *BookReview.com.* 18 Oct. 2004. Web. 20 Oct. 2008.

39. *A publication on a CD-ROM or DVD-ROM*

Leston, Robert. "Drops of Cruelty: Controlling the Mechanisms of Rhetorical History." *Proceedings of the Southwest/Texas Popular and American Culture Associations: Years 2000–2003.* Ed. Leslie Fife. Emporia: SW/TX PCA/ACA P, 2003. 681–91. CD-ROM.

40. *A work from a library subscription database*

Goldwasser, Joan. "Watch Your Balance." *Kiplinger's Personal Finance* 58.3 (2004): 96. *LexisNexis Academic.* Web. 22 June 2008.

Wishart, Jocelyn. "Academic Orientation and Parental Involvement in Education during High School." *Sociology of Education* 74.3 (2001): 210–30. *JSTOR.* Web. 27 Oct. 2008.

41. *A television or radio program*

Rehm, Diane. *The Diane Rehm Show. With E. L. Doctorow.* American University Radio, 24 May 2004. Web. 12 June 2008.

42. *An advertisement*

Lanvin. Advertisement. *Haut Fashion.* Web. 17 June 2008.

43. *A cartoon or comic strip*

Adams, Scott. "Dilbert." Comic strip. *Dilbert.com.* United Feature Syn., 27 Sept. 2004. Web. 20 Oct. 2013.

44. *An email*

Harris, Omar. "Re: Artist Statement." Message to the author. 25 Apr. 2014. Email.

45. *A blog post*

Hunt, Sharon. "Rolling on the Beach." *Gastronomica.* Google, 8 June 2013. Web. 12 June 2013.

46. *A Facebook post*

The White House. "The Affordable Health Care Act." *Facebook.* 20 Sept. 2013. Web. 21 Sept. 2013.

47. *A Twitter post*

Obama, Barack (BO). "The way business is done in Washington has to change."
  —President Obama on the #shutdown. 19 Oct. 2013. 3:58 p.m. Tweet.

48. *A YouTube video*

Wesch, Michael. "A Vision of Students Today." *YouTube*. YouTube, 12 Oct. 2007. Web.
  23 Oct. 2013.

How to List Other Nonprint Sources

49. *Sound clip or recording*

Roosevelt, Franklin, D. "The Only Thing We Have to Fear Is Fear Itself." 4 Mar. 1933. *Great
  Speeches of the Twentieth Century.* CD. 2007.

50. *A film or video recording*

Rabbit-Proof Fence. Dir. Phillip Noyce. Miramax, 2002. Film.

51. *A painting, sculpture, or photograph*

Klee, Paul. *Red Balloon.* 1922. Oil on gauze mounted on board. Guggenheim Museum,
  New York.

52. *A map or chart*

Oregon. Map. Chicago: Rand, 2000. Print.

New York City Transit. Map. *Mta.info.* Metropolitan Transportation Authority, 2007. Web.
  3 July 2007.

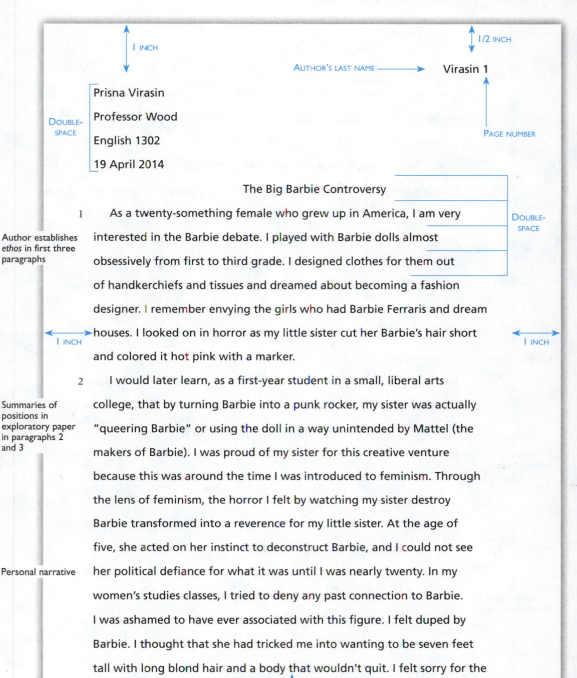

Prisna Virasin

Professor Wood

English 1302

19 April 2014

Virasin 1

The Big Barbie Controversy

1   As a twenty-something female who grew up in America, I am very interested in the Barbie debate. I played with Barbie dolls almost obsessively from first to third grade. I designed clothes for them out of handkerchiefs and tissues and dreamed about becoming a fashion designer. I remember envying the girls who had Barbie Ferraris and dream houses. I looked on in horror as my little sister cut her Barbie's hair short and colored it hot pink with a marker.

2   I would later learn, as a first-year student in a small, liberal arts college, that by turning Barbie into a punk rocker, my sister was actually "queering Barbie" or using the doll in a way unintended by Mattel (the makers of Barbie). I was proud of my sister for this creative venture because this was around the time I was introduced to feminism. Through the lens of feminism, the horror I felt by watching my sister destroy Barbie transformed into a reverence for my little sister. At the age of five, she acted on her instinct to deconstruct Barbie, and I could not see her political defiance for what it was until I was nearly twenty. In my women's studies classes, I tried to deny any past connection to Barbie. I was ashamed to have ever associated with this figure. I felt duped by Barbie. I thought that she had tricked me into wanting to be seven feet tall with long blond hair and a body that wouldn't quit. I felt sorry for the

(continued)

Annotations (left margin):
- Author establishes *ethos* in first three paragraphs
- Summaries of positions in exploratory paper in paragraphs 2 and 3
- Personal narrative

Annotations (layout labels):
- 1 INCH
- 1/2 INCH
- AUTHOR'S LAST NAME
- PAGE NUMBER
- DOUBLE-SPACE
- DOUBLE-SPACE
- 1 INCH
- 1 INCH
- 1 INCH

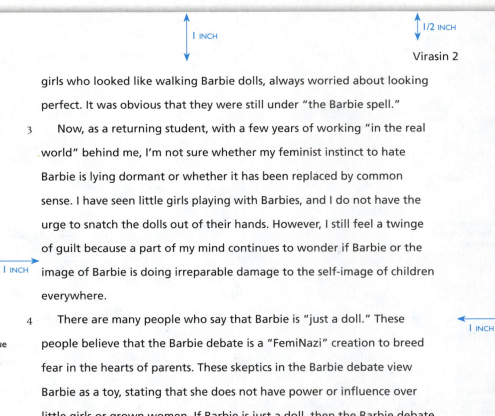

Virasin 2

girls who looked like walking Barbie dolls, always worried about looking

perfect. It was obvious that they were still under "the Barbie spell."

3   Now, as a returning student, with a few years of working "in the real

world" behind me, I'm not sure whether my feminist instinct to hate

Barbie is lying dormant or whether it has been replaced by common

sense. I have seen little girls playing with Barbies, and I do not have the

urge to snatch the dolls out of their hands. However, I still feel a twinge

of guilt because a part of my mind continues to wonder if Barbie or the

image of Barbie is doing irreparable damage to the self-image of children

everywhere.

4   There are many people who say that Barbie is "just a doll." These

Focus on issue   people believe that the Barbie debate is a "FemiNazi" creation to breed

fear in the hearts of parents. These skeptics in the Barbie debate view

Barbie as a toy, stating that she does not have power or influence over

little girls or grown women. If Barbie is just a doll, then the Barbie debate

Transition to   is indeed without foundation. In reviewing Barbie's history, I found that
Barbie's history

she was created to make a difference in girls' lives and has succeeded in

becoming a very marketable product.

5   The Barbie doll was created in 1959 by Ruth Handler, the cofounder

of Mattel. Handler created the doll after seeing her daughter, whose

nickname was Barbie, and her daughter's friends play with their paper

Quotation: authors   dolls. According to Gaby Wood and Frances Stonor Saunders, Handler
identified in text

realized that little girls wanted a doll "they could aspire to be like, not

aspire to look after" (38). This was a revolutionary idea because before

the creation of Barbie, the toy store doll selection mainly consisted

(continued)

Virasin 3

of baby dolls, which encouraged little girls to pretend to be mothers. Ruth Handler states that Barbie "has always represented the fact that a woman has choices" (39). In 1959, Mattel sold 350,000 Barbie dolls. In 2004, according to the "Barbie Dolls" discussion on the History Channel Web site, "ninety percent of all American girls in the last forty years have owned at least one Barbie." This Web site provides additional evidence of Barbie's continued popularity: "If every Barbie doll ever manufactured were laid end-to-end, they would circle the earth three-and-one-half times." The Barbie doll and other Barbie products average sales of 1.9 billion dollars a year.

6   Barbie is also marketed internationally, in more than 140 countries. Stephanie Deutsch, who has written a book about collecting Barbie dolls and who is a collector herself, says, "It is fascinating to see how Barbie dolls from other countries reflect the ideals of foreign societies," and she goes on to describe the "wild and sexy" dolls of Brazil, and the Barbie dolls strapped to candles for little girls in Greece to carry in religious processions (5). In 1968, Barbie dolls were first provided with the mechanism to talk. Besides English, some Barbie dolls spoke Spanish, and others spoke French, German, or Japanese. One of Barbie's friends spoke with a British accent (34).

7   I believe that Barbie's influence lies in her pervasiveness. She is everywhere, and therefore she is on the minds of many people. I don't think that Barbie is "just a doll." With the overarching product placement, marketing force, and popularity of the Barbie doll, she is undeniably a powerful icon of American society.

Margin annotations:
1 INCH
1/2 INCH
Online source mentioned in text; no page number available
1 INCH
1 INCH
Transition to why Barbie's good
1 INCH

(continued)

Virasin 4

8   Avid Barbie fans span many different age groups. There are three-
to six-year-olds who play with Barbie dolls, wear Barbie brand clothes,
and sleep on Barbie brand beds with matching sheet sets. Barbie doll
collectors have met for over twenty years to celebrate all things Barbie.
Special collection Barbies are auctioned for thousands of dollars.
Supporters of Barbie state that, apart from being a national icon, Barbie
is just a fun part of growing up. They refer to the simple fun of playing
with Barbie dolls. They believe that Barbie is a tool in building girls'

Fig. 1. *A President 2000 Barbie.*

imaginations. They also maintain that Barbie
is a positive role model because she is able to
do almost anything. Barbie was an astronaut
before the first woman went into space. Barbie
is a veterinarian, a doctor, a businesswoman,
and to top it all off, a presidential candidate.
Figure 1 shows the Barbie that was dressed to
run for President of the United States in 2000.
Included in the package are a blue campaign
suit, a red ball gown, campaign material, and
an Internet Web site. In her article about growing up with Barbie, Patricia
reminisces:

        What always fascinated me about Barbie was that she could be—
    and was—anything I wanted her to be. By extension, I felt the same
    was true for me. That's the real magic of Barbie. Deciding which
    career she ought to pursue on any given day fired my imagination
    far more than pushing a baby-size doll around in a carriage ever did.

Criteria for goodness

Appeals to motives and values

Quote longer than four lines

(continued)

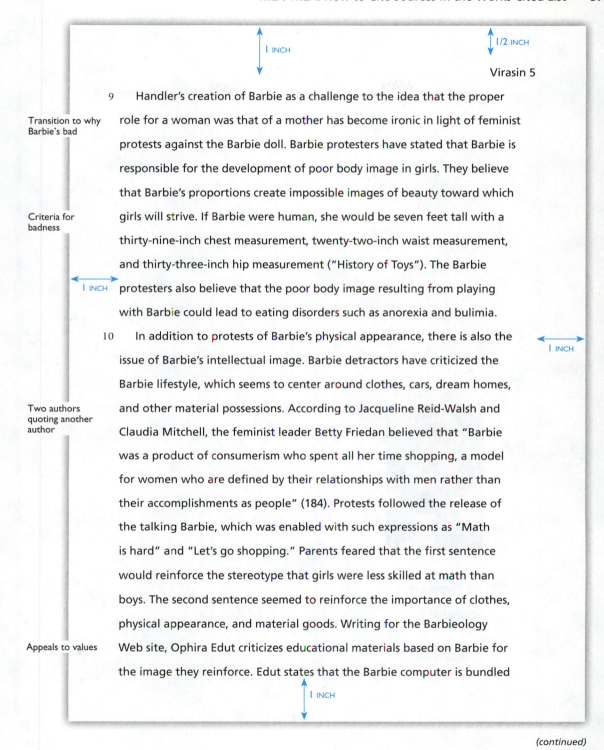

1 INCH

1/2 INCH

Virasin 5

Transition to why
Barbie's bad

9　　Handler's creation of Barbie as a challenge to the idea that the proper
role for a woman was that of a mother has become ironic in light of feminist
protests against the Barbie doll. Barbie protesters have stated that Barbie is
responsible for the development of poor body image in girls. They believe
that Barbie's proportions create impossible images of beauty toward which

Criteria for
badness

girls will strive. If Barbie were human, she would be seven feet tall with a
thirty-nine-inch chest measurement, twenty-two-inch waist measurement,
and thirty-three-inch hip measurement ("History of Toys"). The Barbie

1 INCH

protesters also believe that the poor body image resulting from playing
with Barbie could lead to eating disorders such as anorexia and bulimia.

10　　In addition to protests of Barbie's physical appearance, there is also the
issue of Barbie's intellectual image. Barbie detractors have criticized the

1 INCH

Barbie lifestyle, which seems to center around clothes, cars, dream homes,
and other material possessions. According to Jacqueline Reid-Walsh and

Two authors
quoting another
author

Claudia Mitchell, the feminist leader Betty Friedan believed that "Barbie
was a product of consumerism who spent all her time shopping, a model
for women who are defined by their relationships with men rather than
their accomplishments as people" (184). Protests followed the release of
the talking Barbie, which was enabled with such expressions as "Math
is hard" and "Let's go shopping." Parents feared that the first sentence
would reinforce the stereotype that girls were less skilled at math than
boys. The second sentence seemed to reinforce the importance of clothes,
physical appearance, and material goods. Writing for the Barbieology

Appeals to values

Web site, Ophira Edut criticizes educational materials based on Barbie for
the image they reinforce. Edut states that the Barbie computer is bundled

1 INCH

(continued)

↕ 1 INCH

↕ 1/2 INCH

Virasin 6

with typing tutor software, while the boy's Hot Wheels (a kind of tricycle) computer is bundled with adventure games. Also, the Barbie Rapunzel CD-ROM is touted by Mattel to expose girls to fine art and creativity, when the only creative function of the program is the option of changing Barbie's clothes and hairstyle interactively on the computer screen.

11   Some people have questioned whether or not Barbie is a suitable American icon. They challenge Barbie's ability to represent the all-American woman positively. In 2004, Mattel announced the release of a new California Barbie doll that would more accurately reflect the times ("It's Splittsville"). This Barbie has broken up with Ken, who is now "just a friend," and has taken up with Blaine, an Australian surfer. California Barbie uses modern "instant messaging to stay connected to her game. Her ears can be pierced. Her car has a working CD player" (Verdon 18A).

← 1 INCH

1 INCH →

Summary of an article

Fig. 2. *Jenna Debryn shows off her Razanne doll, a modest Muslim alternative to Barbie.*

Source: Reed Saxon/ AP Wide World Photos. Web.

12   Still, a television advertisement following the release of the Cali Girl Barbie shows she has not changed that much from the old Barbie. In this ad, Barbie says she is "born to shop," and she can "never have too much stuff" or "too many friends."

According to Seth M. Siegel, the government of Iran has banned Barbie, and police officers are confiscating Barbie dolls from toy stores all over that country. The Iranian government believes that Barbie is "un-Islamic" because of the way she represents Western immorality. She dresses provocatively and has a close relationship with a man who is not her

↕ 1 INCH

(continued)

Virasin 7

husband. For many Iranians, Barbie has become a symbol of American women in a very negative sense (22–24). As an alternative, little Muslim girls are encouraged to play with the Razanne doll that better reflects Muslim culture and values. Figure 2 provides a picture of a Muslim girl, who lives in the United States, and her Razanne doll.

13   Does the Barbie debate boil down to whether Barbie is good or bad? I believe that if she has the power to convey all of the positivity that Barbie fans believe she embodies, then the same power can be used to contaminate the world with all of the negativity that the Barbie protesters warn us against. She is a pervasive image in American society, but that does not necessarily mean that we have to label her as either good or bad. As a feminist, I am willing to concede that women are neither all good nor all bad. As a female image, Barbie plays the dual role quite well. We can make Barbie into whatever we want. She can be an astronaut or a punk rocker or a punk-rock astronaut. I believe that Barbie supporters have made her into a goddess, while Barbie protesters have turned her into a demon. In both cases, I believe she has become a scapegoat.

14   In addressing the issue that Barbie causes poor body image that could lead to eating disorders, the obvious statement that I can make is that eating disorders were around long before Barbie was created. Also, because of Barbie's immense popularity, if the doll truly caused eating disorders, eating disorders would have reached epidemic proportions. In actuality, only about five percent of women suffer from eating disorders. Barbie supporters also ask why male action dolls are not protested against when they have similar unattainable proportions.

Transition to refutation

Refutation of those who say Barbie's all bad

(continued)

Virasin 8

15   By banning Barbie, we will not be solving the problem of poor body image. Also, Barbie's image is so pervasive that it would be almost

No need to cite a page number for a one-page source

impossible to shelter children from her. In a satirical editorial by Rachel Sa, she muses on the absurdity of sheltering children from all things Barbie: "Maybe the safest thing is to just keep your little girls in their bedrooms. Yes! Just keep them shut away until all of that icky stuff disappears or until they grow up—surely by then they will have figured out how to deal with it all on their own."

16   If one were to believe the argument made by Barbie supporters that Barbie creates positive self-image in girls, and combine this belief with

Refutation of those who say Barbie's all good

the fact that Barbie is very pervasive in the United States, it should follow that American females who have played with Barbie would have nearly eradicated any thoughts of negative self-image. Theoretically then, at least ninety percent of American women would have conquered self-critical thoughts about their physical or intellectual state as a result of their contact with Barbie. However, women know that these self-critical thoughts are a part of many women's daily lives, and even the most ardent Barbie fanatic has "bad hair days" or "fat days."

17   It is not the responsibility of the Barbie doll to create positive or negative self-images in children. The ability to influence children falls

The real issue

mainly on the shoulders of all adults in the communities in which these children live. This includes the global community in which we now find ourselves living. The issue of self-image should be addressed by all cultures early on and continuously in children's lives. Only by positively reinforcing unconditional acceptance of children's physical appearance are we going

(continued)

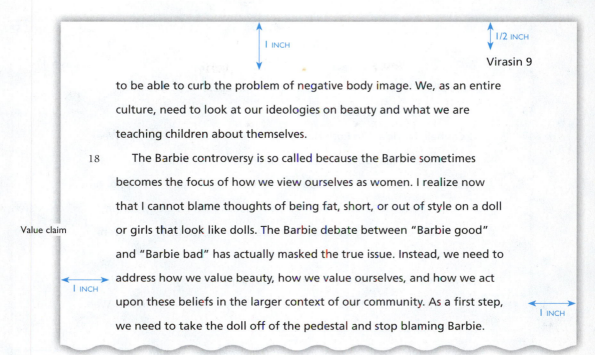

1 INCH

1/2 INCH

Virasin 9

to be able to curb the problem of negative body image. We, as an entire culture, need to look at our ideologies on beauty and what we are teaching children about themselves.

18   The Barbie controversy is so called because the Barbie sometimes becomes the focus of how we view ourselves as women. I realize now that I cannot blame thoughts of being fat, short, or out of style on a doll or girls that look like dolls. The Barbie debate between "Barbie good" and "Barbie bad" has actually masked the true issue. Instead, we need to address how we value beauty, how we value ourselves, and how we act upon these beliefs in the larger context of our community. As a first step, we need to take the doll off of the pedestal and stop blaming Barbie.

Value claim

1 INCH

1 INCH

Virasin 10

Works Cited

"History of Toys: Barbie Dolls." *History.com*. A&E Television Networks, 2008. Web. 15 Apr. 2014.

California Barbie. Advertisement. The WB Network, 18 Mar. 2004. Television.

Deutsch, Stephanie. *Barbie: The First Thirty Years.* 2nd ed. Paducah: Collector, 2003. Print.

Edut, Ophira. "Giga-What? Barbie Gets Her Own Computer." *AdiosBarbie.com*, n.d. Web. 3 Apr. 2014. <http://www.adiosbarbie.com /bology/bology_computer_html>.

The Works Cited follows the text, but always on a new page, numbered consecutively. Center the title, double-space, and use a hanging indent, as shown.

5 SPACES

In MLA style, divide a URL only after a slash; never add a hyphen or other mark.

1 INCH

(continued)

Virasin 11

"It's Splitsville for Barbie and Ken." *CNN.com*. Cable News Network,

    12 Feb. 2004. Web. 15 Apr. 2014.

O'Connell, Patricia. "To Ruth Handler: A 21 Barbie Salute." *BusinessWeek*

    Online 1 May 2002. *Academic Search Complete*. Web. 11 Apr. 2014.

Reid-Walsh, Jacqueline, and Claudia Mitchell. "Just a Doll? Liberating

    Accounts of Barbie-Play." *Review of Education/Pedagogy/Cultural*

    Studies 22.2 Aug. 2000: 175–90. *Academic Search Complete*. Web.

    3 Apr. 2014.

Sa, Rachel. "Blame It on Barbie: How Was I Supposed to Know She Was

    Warping Our Minds?" *Toronto Sun* 4 May 2002: 15. *LexisNexis*. Web.

    3 Apr. 2014.

Seigel, Seth M. "Sell the West as a Brand." *Brandweek* 10 June 2002:

    22–24. *Academic Search Complete*. Web. 3 Apr. 2014.

Verdon, Joan. "Barbie Says, Bye-Bye Doll." *Fort Worth Star-Telegram* 13

    Feb. 2004: 1A+. Print.

Wood, Gaby, and Frances Stonor Saunders. "Dream Doll." *New Statesman*

    15 Apr. 2002: 38–40. *Academic Search Complete*. Web. 3 Apr. 2014.

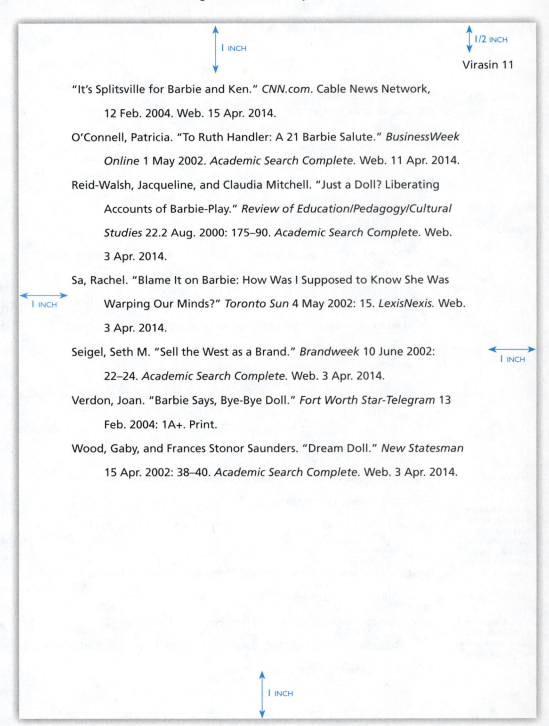

Questions on the Researched Position Paper, MLA Style

1. Where does the author put her claim: at the beginning, middle, or end of the paper? What is her claim? What type of claim is it? Why do you think she placed it where it is?

2. How does this author use the ideas from her exploratory paper at the beginning of her paper? What is accomplished by this strategy?

3. What types of proofs and support does this student use in her paper? Comment on the images. What do these images accomplish?

4. What warrants does the author expect you to accept?

5. What major ideas does the author refute in this paper?

6. What organizational pattern does the author use to organize some of the major parts of her paper?

7. Identify and underline the transitional sentences. Read some of them aloud in class.

8. Find an example of a quotation that is introduced with the author's or organization's name in the text, followed by a page reference in parentheses.

9. Find an example of two authors who quote another author.

10. Find an example of a quotation that is identified at the end of a sentence by the author and page number because the author is not mentioned in the text.

11. Locate an example of an online quotation that is identified by the title in the text but that has no available page number to place at the end of the quotation.

12. Find an example of a summarized article that is introduced with the author's name and concludes with page references.

13. Find a long quotation and explain how and why it is punctuated as it is.

14. Roughly what percentage of this paper is made up of quotations from other people's writings and what percentage is the author's own writing?

15. Read the "Works Cited" page and identify the different types of sources this author used.

T he APA portion of this appendix is divided into two sections: (1) how to cite sources in the body of the text, and (2) how to cite sources in the References list.

LO2 Cite and document sources in APA style.

APA: How to Cite Sources in the Body of the Text

As in MLA style, the APA system of documentation asks that you show where you originally found a direct quotation or the information for a paraphrase or a summary by inserting a brief parenthetical citation at the end of the borrowed material in your written text.

1. *A direct quotation with the author mentioned in the text* If you introduce the author's name in the body of the text before you quote directly, then there is no need to include the name in the parentheses.

Although various critics have accused Arnold Schoenberg's musical compositions of being "atonal," Alex Ross (2001) points out that the composer was "simply offering a tonality of a less familiar kind" (p. 176).

2. *A direct quotation with the author not mentioned in the text*

Although various critics have accused Arnold Schoenberg's musical compositions of being "atonal," others argue that the composer was "simply offering a tonality of a less familiar kind" (Ross, 2001, p. 176).

3. *A paraphrase or summary with the author mentioned in the text*

According to Calvin Tomkins (2001), the rebuilding and expansion of the New York Museum of Modern Art proves that modern art has not reached its end (p. 72).

4. *A paraphrase or summary with the author not mentioned in the text*

If the rebuilding and expansion of the New York Museum of Modern Art is any indication, claims that modern art has reached its end may soon be proven wrong (Tomkins, 2001, p. 72).

5. *Two or more authors*

Pimentel and Teixeira (1993) remind us, "Virtual reality is all about illusion" (p. 7).

"Virtual reality is all about illusion" (Pimentel & Teixeira, 1993, p. 7).

If a work has three, four, or five authors, list all of the authors' last names for the first reference, then use only the first author's last name and the abbreviated term *et al.* (but not italicized) for subsequent references. If a work has six or more authors, use only the first author's last name and *et al.* for all references.

"Television is not primarily a medium of entertainment in all societies" (Comstock et al., 1978, p. 25).

6. *Two books by the same author* To indicate which book you are citing, use the publication dates to distinguish between the books. For example, if you are using *Simulation and Its Discontents* (2009) and *Alone Together: Why We Expect More*

From Technology and Less From Each Other (2012), both by Sherry Turkle, document as follows:

> Sherry Turkle notes that we can become dazzled by the possibilities of digital culture: "immersed in simulation, we feel exhilarated by possibility" (2009, p. 7). She elaborates this point by claiming that "technology proposes itself as the architect of our intimacies" (2012, p. 1).

7. *A corporate or group author*

> The RAND Corporation (2004) observes that "when the No Child Left Behind Act was passed into law in January 2002, it heralded the beginning of one of the most expansive efforts to reform public education" (p. 7).

Otherwise, mention the corporate author in the citation after the quotation.

> (RAND Corporation, 2004, p. 7)

8. *An unknown author*

> *Article:* ("Creativity and Television," 1973, p. 14)

> *Book:* (*World Almanac*, 2003, p. 397)

9. *A work reprinted in a book or journal* If you quote an article, poem, story, or any other work that is reprinted from its original publication, cite the author of the work you are quoting, not the author or editor who reprinted it, but use the date of the reprint.

10. *Short quotations versus block quotations* Quotations should not be formatted as block quotations unless they exceed forty words. For short quotations, place quotation marks around the quoted material, insert the citation information, and place the period outside of the parentheses.

> Author Benjamin Cheever (1999) says he uses his computer to "write and read letters, and if it did not involve the elimination of envelopes and a certain parallel loosening of style, the process would be similar to the one that once involved lambskins and sharpened feathers" (p. 7).

Quotations that exceed forty words are blocked. It is good writing style to provide a brief introduction to a long quote and to finish the quote with a concluding thought.

> Author Benjamin Cheever (1999) contrasts his use of the computer with that of individuals who spend a lot of time on the Internet.
>> The news bulges with stories about dispensing therapy on the Net, doing business on the Net, trolling for unsuspecting sexual prey on the Net. Not on this computer. Most of what I do on the electronic superhighway is write and read letters, and if it did not involve the elimination of envelopes and a certain parallel loosening of style, the process would be similar to the one that once involved lambskins and sharpened feathers. (p. 7)
>
> Cheever has essentially substituted his computer and its word processing program for his old typewriter.

11. *Ellipsis points and quoted material* Occasionally, you will want to delete material from the original source either to make your document shorter or more readable. Always indicate that you have removed words by inserting ellipsis points.

> "If there were a wider appreciation for motherhood in society, women might . . . hold their heads high when going to the boss and asking for a reduced hour work schedule" (Hewlett, 2002, p. 308).

12. *Tables* Tables should be placed as closely as possible to the text they explain or illustrate.

The following table shows calories used in common physical activities at both moderate and vigorous levels.

Table 1

Calories Used per Hour in Common Physical Activities

Moderate Physical Activity	Approximate Calories/ 30 Minutes for a 154 lb Person	Approximate Calories/ Hr for a 154 lb Person
Hiking	185	370
Light gardening/yard work	165	330
Dancing	165	330
Golf (walking and carrying clubs)	165	330
Bicycling (<10 mph)	145	290
Walking (3.5 mph)	140	280
Weight lifting (general light workout)	110	220
Stretching	90	180

Note. From "Healthy Weight Statistics," Centers for Disease Control (CDC, 2011).

13. *Graphs, artworks, photographs, and other illustrations* Graphs, artworks, photographs, and other illustrations should be placed close to the text they illustrate.

Figure 1. Quarterly earnings according to region.

14. *Electronic sources* If a page number is available in an electronic source, cite as you would a print source. Some electronic journals number paragraphs rather than providing page numbers. If this is the case, then include the author's name, the year, and the page or paragraph number (if available) in parentheses, just as you would for a print source. If paragraph numbers are available, use the symbol ¶ or use the abbreviation *para.* (not italicized) to show you are citing a paragraph number.

> "Rose represents the unnamed multitude of women who were placed in the same circumstances but whose stories were never told" (Mason, 2003, ¶ 8).

If no page or paragraph number is provided, cite a heading in the work and direct the reader to the paragraph in that section by number:

> (Regelin, 2002, Management plan section, para. 4)

If no author is listed, cite a short title, headline style, and place it in quotes.

> ("Wolf in Alaska," 2003)

APA: How to Cite Sources in the References List

Attach to the draft a list of all the works you have quoted, paraphrased, or summarized in your paper along with full publication information for each source. This list is titled References, and it begins on a new page, which is numbered consecutively. Included below are examples of APA format for citing print, electronic, and nonprint sources.

How to List Print Books

1. *A book by one author*

Lepore, J. (2013). *Book of ages: The life and opinions of Jane Franklin.* New York, NY: Knopf.

2. *A book by two to six authors*

Chayes, A. H., & Minow, M. (2003). *Imagine coexistence: Restoring humanity after violent ethnic conflict.* San Francisco, CA: Jossey-Bass.

Comstock, G., Chaffee, S., Katzman, N., McCombs, M., & Roberts, D. (1978). *Television and human behavior.* New York, NY: Columbia University Press.

3. *A book by more than six authors* When a book has more than six authors, list the first six names, just as in the example above that lists five, followed by *et al.*

4. *Two or more books by the same author* Alphabetize the titles by publication date, with the earliest date first.

Solove, D. (2010). *Understanding privacy.* Cambridge, MA: Harvard University Press.

Solove, D. (2013). *Nothing to hide: The false tradeoff between privacy and security.* New Haven, CT: Yale University Press.

5. *A book by a corporate or group author* When the author and the publisher are the same, as they are in the following example, use the word *Author* (not italicized) as the name of the publisher.

Harvard Business School Press. (2004). *The results-driven manager: Winning negotiations that preserve relationships.* Boston, MA: Author.

6. *A book with no author named*

The world almanac and book of facts. (2013). New York, NY: World Almanac Books.

7. *A republished book*

Locke, J. (1959). *An essay concerning human understanding.* New York, NY: Dover. (Original work published 1690)

8. *A translation*

Virilio, P. (2002). *Ground zero* (C. Turner, Trans.). London, UK: Verso.

9. *A second or subsequent edition*

Bovee, C. L., & Thill, J. V. (2000). *Business communication today* (6th ed.). Upper Saddle River, NJ: Prentice Hall.

10. *Proceedings from a conference or symposium* Treat the title of the conference or symposium as a proper noun.

Gray, W. D. (Ed.). (2004). *Proceedings of the Twenty-Fifth Annual Conference of the Cognitive Science Society.* Mahwah, NJ: Erlbaum.

11. *An introduction, preface, foreword, or afterword*

Rajchman, J. (2001). Introduction. In G. Deleuze, *Pure immanence* (A. Boyman, Trans.) (pp. 7–23). New York, NY: Zone.

12. *A government document*

Federal Bureau of Investigation. U.S. Department of Justice. (2004). *National instant criminal background check system.* Washington, DC: U.S. Government Printing Office.

How to List Print Articles

List all the pages on which the article is printed, whether they are successive or interrupted by other pages. Insert *p.* or *pp.* only for newspaper articles and articles or chapters in books. Omit *p.* or *pp.* for journal and magazine articles, unless there is no volume number.

13. *An article from a magazine*

Filkins, D. (2013, September 23). The shadow commander. *The New Yorker,* pp. 54–62.

If a volume number is available, insert it in italics after the comma following the magazine title: *Natural History, 96,* 12–15.

14. *An article from a newspaper*

Rutenberg, J., & Maynard, M. (2003, June 2). TV news that looks local, even if it's not. *The New York Times,* p. C1.

15. *An article in a periodical with no author listed*

Metamorphosis. (2001, November 5). *The New Yorker,* p. 10.

16. *An article in a journal with continuous pagination in each volume*

Hanlon, J. (2004). It is possible to give money to the poor. *Development and Change, 35,* 375–384.

17. *An article in a journal*

Kruse, C. R. (2001). The movement and the media: Framing the debate over animal experimentation. *Political Communication, 18*(1), 67–88.

18. *An edited collection of articles or an anthology*

Johnson, V. D., & Lyne, B. (Eds.). (2002). *Walkin' the talk: An anthology of African American literature.* Upper Saddle River, NJ: Prentice-Hall.

19. *An article in an edited collection or an anthology*

Willis, C. (2002). Heaven defend me from political or highly educated women! Packaging the new woman for mass consumption. In A. Richardson & C. Willis (Eds.), *The new woman in fact and in fiction: Fin-de-siècle feminisms* (pp. 53–65). New York, NY: Palgrave Macmillan.

20. *A reprinted article in an edited volume or collection*

Kress, G. (2004). Multimodality, multimedia, and genre. In C. Handa (Ed.), *Visual rhetoric in a digital world* (pp. 106–121). Boston, MA: Bedford/St. Martin's. (Original work published 2003)

21. *A signed article in a reference work*

Davidson, W. S., II. (1984). Crime. In R. J. Corsini (Ed.), *Encyclopedia of psychology* (Vol. 1, pp. 310–312). New York, NY: Wiley.

22. *An unsigned article in a reference work*

Quindlen, Anna. (1993). In J. Graham (Ed.), *Current biography yearbook* (pp. 477–481). New York, NY: Wilson.

23. *A review*

Ottenhoff, J. (2002). It's complicated. [Review of the book *The moment of complexity*]. *Christian Century, 119*(21), 56–59.

24. *A letter to the editor*

Cooper, M. (2004, May 17). [Letter to the editor]. *Business Week,* p. 18.

25. *An editorial*

Curbing antibiotics on farm taking too long. (2013, October 27). [Editorial]. *USA Today*, p. 21A.

26. *A published interview*

Kutner, R. (2013, September). [Interview with J. Yellen]. *American Prospect, 7*, 12–15.

27. *A personal interview* You would not cite this in the References list. Cite it in the text instead.

Audrey Wick (personal communication, December 27, 2013) holds a different perspective.

28. *A lecture, speech, or address*

King, M. L., Jr. (1963, August 28). I have a dream. Speech delivered at the Lincoln Memorial, Washington, DC.

How to List Electronic Sources

29. *An entire Internet site* Do not list entire Web sites in the References but instead mention them in the body of the paper.

CNN has one of the most comprehensive news sites on the Internet (www.cnn.com).

30. *A document from a professional Web site*

Herman, P. (n.d.). Events. *Milton-L Home Page.* Retrieved January 15, 2003, from http://www.richmond.edu/~creamer/milton/events.html

31. *A home page for a course*

Stern, D. (2000). Heidegger. Retrieved from http://www.uiowa.edu/~c026036/

32. *A personal homepage*

Blakesley, D. (2003, September 18). Home page. Retrieved from http://web.ics.purdue.edu/~blakesle/

33. *An online book*

Mussey, R. D. (1836). *An essay on the influence of tobacco upon life and health.* Retrieved from http://www.gutenberg.org/dirs/1/9/6/6/19667/19667.txt

34. *A part of an online book*

Mussey, R. D. (1836). Cases illustrative of the effects of tobacco. *An essay on the influence of tobacco upon life and health.* Retrieved from http://www.gutenberg.org/dirs/1/9/6/6/19667/19667.txt

35. *An article in an online newspaper*

Webb, C. L. (2004, May 27). The penguin that ate Microsoft. *The Washington Post.* Retrieved from http://www.washingtonpost.com

36. *An article in an online magazine*

Reiss, S. (2006, July). The wired 40. *Wired, 14*(07). Retrieved from http://www.wired.com

37. *An article in an online scholarly journal* If an article or book has a digital object identifier (DOI), use the DOI in the format in which the source lists it.

Gregory, J., & Salmon, G. (2013, October 31). Professional development for online university teaching. *Distance Education, 34*(3), 256–270. doi:10.1080/01587919.2013.835771

If there is no DOI, then provide a retrieval statement with the Web home page of the journal, even if you accessed the article through a subscription database.

Wishart, J. (2001). Academic orientation and parental involvement in education during high school. *Sociology of Education, 74,* 210–230. Retrieved from http://soe.sagepub.com

38. *A review*

Gray, D. (2004). [Review of the book *Psychic Navigator*]. BookReview.com. Retrieved from http://www.bookreview.com

39. *A publication on a CD-ROM or DVD-ROM*

Leston, R. (2002). Drops of cruelty: Controlling the mechanisms of rhetorical history. *Proceedings of the Southwest/Texas Popular and American Culture Associations: Years 2000–2003.* Ed. Leslie Fife. [CD-ROM]. (681–691). Emporia, KS: SW/TX PCA/ACA Press, 2003.

40. *Email* You would not cite this in the References list. Cite it instead in the text, as in this example.

Byron Hawks (personal communication, October 4, 2013) suggests a different approach.

41. *Blog post*

Hunt, S. (2013, June 8). Rolling on the beach [Blog post]. Retrieved from http://www.gastronomica.org/rolling-on-the-beach/

42. *Twitter post*

Obama, B. [BO]. (2013, October 19). The way business is done in Washington has to change: https://twitter.com/BarackObama/status/391639514713563136

43. *Facebook post*

The White House. [ca. 2013]. Affordable Health Care Act [Facebook page]. Retrieved September 20, 2013, from https://www.facebook.com/WhiteHouse

44. *A television or radio program*

Rehm, D. (Executive producer & host). (2004, May 24). *The Diane Rehm Show* with E. L. Doctorow [Radio broadcast]. Washington, DC: American University Radio.

How to List Other Nonprint Sources

45. *Sound clip or recording*

Roosevelt, F. (Speaker). (2007). The only thing we have to fear is fear itself [CD].

46. *Film*

Noyce, P. (Director). (2002). *Rabbit-proof fence* [Motion picture]. United States: Miramax Films.

47. *DVD* Place the type of medium in square brackets.

Pearson Composition/Professional Development (Producer). (2009). *Trends and Teaching* [DVD]. Pearson.

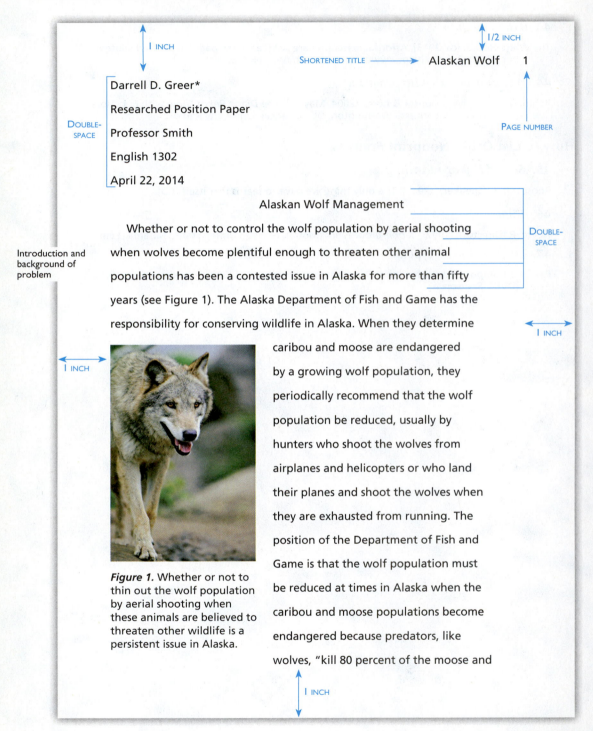

1 INCH

1/2 INCH

SHORTENED TITLE ⟶   Alaskan Wolf   1

Darrell D. Greer*

Researched Position Paper

DOUBLE-SPACE

Professor Smith

PAGE NUMBER

English 1302

April 22, 2014

Alaskan Wolf Management

Whether or not to control the wolf population by aerial shooting

DOUBLE-SPACE

Introduction and background of problem

when wolves become plentiful enough to threaten other animal

populations has been a contested issue in Alaska for more than fifty

years (see Figure 1). The Alaska Department of Fish and Game has the

responsibility for conserving wildlife in Alaska. When they determine

1 INCH

caribou and moose are endangered

by a growing wolf population, they

periodically recommend that the wolf

population be reduced, usually by

hunters who shoot the wolves from

airplanes and helicopters or who land

their planes and shoot the wolves when

they are exhausted from running. The

position of the Department of Fish and

Game is that the wolf population must

be reduced at times in Alaska when the

caribou and moose populations become

endangered because predators, like

wolves, "kill 80 percent of the moose and

Figure 1. Whether or not to thin out the wolf population by aerial shooting when these animals are believed to threaten other wildlife is a persistent issue in Alaska.

1 INCH

(continued)

*APA guidelines call for a separate title page, which includes a running head for publication, the full title, and the author's name and institutional affiliation (see the *Publication Manual of the American Psychological Association*, 6th ed., 2010). Your professor, however, may ask you to present your identifying information as shown here.

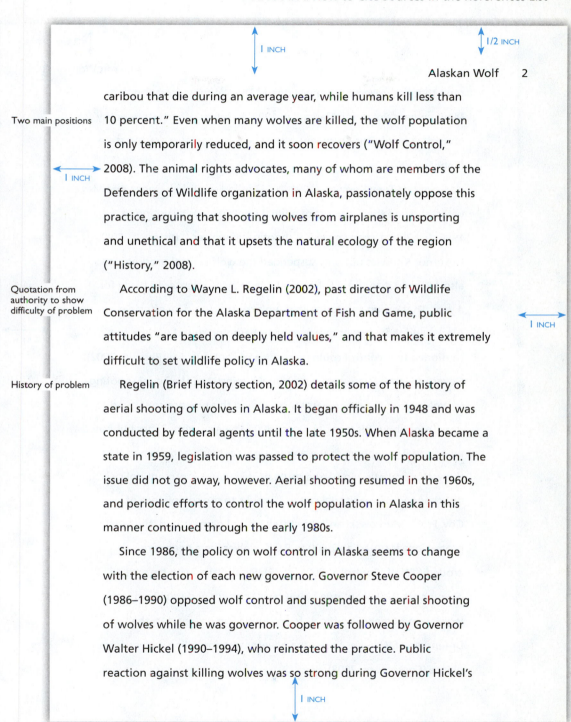

Alaskan Wolf   2

Two main positions

caribou that die during an average year, while humans kill less than 10 percent." Even when many wolves are killed, the wolf population is only temporarily reduced, and it soon recovers ("Wolf Control," 2008). The animal rights advocates, many of whom are members of the Defenders of Wildlife organization in Alaska, passionately oppose this practice, arguing that shooting wolves from airplanes is unsporting and unethical and that it upsets the natural ecology of the region ("History," 2008).

Quotation from authority to show difficulty of problem

According to Wayne L. Regelin (2002), past director of Wildlife Conservation for the Alaska Department of Fish and Game, public attitudes "are based on deeply held values," and that makes it extremely difficult to set wildlife policy in Alaska.

History of problem

Regelin (Brief History section, 2002) details some of the history of aerial shooting of wolves in Alaska. It began officially in 1948 and was conducted by federal agents until the late 1950s. When Alaska became a state in 1959, legislation was passed to protect the wolf population. The issue did not go away, however. Aerial shooting resumed in the 1960s, and periodic efforts to control the wolf population in Alaska in this manner continued through the early 1980s.

Since 1986, the policy on wolf control in Alaska seems to change with the election of each new governor. Governor Steve Cooper (1986–1990) opposed wolf control and suspended the aerial shooting of wolves while he was governor. Cooper was followed by Governor Walter Hickel (1990–1994), who reinstated the practice. Public reaction against killing wolves was so strong during Governor Hickel's

1 INCH

1/2 INCH

1 INCH

1 INCH

1 INCH

(continued)

term that the governor commissioned "The Wolf Conservation and Management Policy for Alaska," in 1993, to set an official state policy on wolf control. This document is still the guiding policy for the state (Regelin, 2002).

Governor Tony Knowles (1994–2002) followed Hickel. Under Knowles, voters showed their support of animal rights groups by voting in 1996 and 2000 to ban the aerial shooting of wolves ("History," 2008). Governor Knowles not only suspended the wolf control program, he also assigned it to the U.S. National Academy of Sciences to study for a year. That group concluded that wolf control could be effective in Alaska and that current practices were based on sound science, but cautioned that control could be costly and controversial (Regelin, 2002). Governor Frank Murkowski (2002–2006), reinstated the aerial shooting of wolves, and the controversy surrounding this practice continued to rage throughout his term. In March 2004 *The New York Times* published an editorial in support of the animal rights activists and warned that the wolf population in Alaska could be wiped out if present policy is not changed. This editorial states: "Thanks to the compliance of Gov. Frank Murkowski and the state's official game board, the legal protections for Alaska's 7,000 to 9,000 wolves have been seriously eroded ("Wolf 'Control,'" 2004, p. 12). Sarah Palin, who became governor in 2006, continued Murkowski's policy and proposed legislation to make it difficult for conservation groups, like the Defenders of Wildlife, to sue the government for killing wolves from planes (Cockerham, 2008).

(continued)

Alaskan Wolf   4

Comparison

The situations in 1993 and 2008 have a lot in common. In the early 1990s Alaska witnessed a decline in the populations of caribou and moose in the Fortymile, Delta, and Nelchina Basin areas. This decline in the caribou and moose populations was due mainly to the increase of the wolf populations in these three areas. Robert Stephenson of the Alaska Department of Fish and Game claimed at that time, "Wolf packs will kill one caribou every two days or so, and one moose every three to ten days" (Keszler, 1993, p. 65). The Delta caribou herd alone declined from about eleven thousand in 1989 to fewer than four thousand just four years later ("Alaska Wolf," 1993). With statistics such as these, the size of the caribou and moose populations in Alaska was clearly a problem that needed ongoing attention.

Now, as then, a rapid decline in caribou and moose populations can be devastating to the state. Not only are they a valuable resource for Alaska in terms of nonresident hunting and tourist sightseeing, but for many remote residents, caribou and moose are the main source of food.

Quotations worked into text suggest the unique character of the problem in Alaska.

The way of life for many Alaskans is one that the average American cannot begin to understand. Max Peterson, the executive director of the International Association of Wildlife Agencies, says that in Alaska, "people interact as another predator in the ecosystem," and as a result, "the interest in Alaska by people outside Alaska certainly is greater than their knowledge of Alaska" (Keszler, 1993, p. 67). Ted Williams (1993) clarifies the lifestyle that many rural Alaskans lead:

Genuine subsistence is the most environmentally benign of all possible lifestyles. Subsisters do not—indeed cannot—deplete

(continued)

Alaskan Wolf   5

A long quotation of more than forty words is indented and written in block form. No quotation marks are necessary for indented quotations. The page number is indicated at the end, and the author is mentioned in the text.

fish and wildlife because if they do, they will subsist no more. But even in the remotest native villages, Alaska as trackless wilderness where people blend with nature is just an old dream. Many villagers are now on social welfare programs and are therefore cash dependent. (p. 49)

Failing to protect existing caribou and moose populations can lower the subsistence level for some Alaskans, even more than it is at present.

The biologists of the state of Alaska commonly believe that wolf populations are nowhere close to being endangered, and that the current wolf control programs will sustain future wolf populations ("Wolf Control," 2008). The total wolf population in Alaska at present is estimated to be between 7,700–11,200. According to the Division of Wildlife Conservation in Alaska, the wolf population has never been endangered, and the future of the wolf in Alaska is secure ("Wolf in Alaska," 2008). In 2008 five wolf control programs are in place in about 9.4 percent of the total area of Alaska. Aerial shooting that is designed to protect other animal populations is permitted in these areas. "In these areas, wolf numbers will be temporarily reduced, but wolves will not be permanently eliminated from any area" ("Wolf Control," 2008). In the past five years, gunners in airplanes who carry state permits have killed more than 700 wolves (Cockerham, 2008).

Statistics and quotations from authorities to strengthen the solution preferred by this author

In 1993, when Governor Walter Hickel and the Alaska Department of Fish and Game announced the new "Wolf Conservation and Management Policy for Alaska" that allowed for the aerial shooting of wolves, the

(continued)

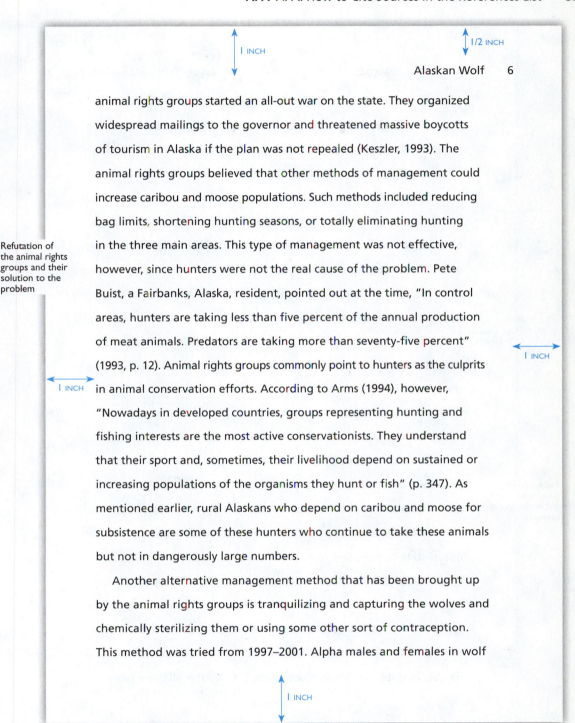

Alaskan Wolf   6

animal rights groups started an all-out war on the state. They organized

widespread mailings to the governor and threatened massive boycotts

of tourism in Alaska if the plan was not repealed (Keszler, 1993). The

animal rights groups believed that other methods of management could

increase caribou and moose populations. Such methods included reducing

bag limits, shortening hunting seasons, or totally eliminating hunting

in the three main areas. This type of management was not effective,

however, since hunters were not the real cause of the problem. Pete

Buist, a Fairbanks, Alaska, resident, pointed out at the time, "In control

areas, hunters are taking less than five percent of the annual production

of meat animals. Predators are taking more than seventy-five percent"

(1993, p. 12). Animal rights groups commonly point to hunters as the culprits

in animal conservation efforts. According to Arms (1994), however,

"Nowadays in developed countries, groups representing hunting and

fishing interests are the most active conservationists. They understand

that their sport and, sometimes, their livelihood depend on sustained or

increasing populations of the organisms they hunt or fish" (p. 347). As

mentioned earlier, rural Alaskans who depend on caribou and moose for

subsistence are some of these hunters who continue to take these animals

but not in dangerously large numbers.

Another alternative management method that has been brought up

by the animal rights groups is tranquilizing and capturing the wolves and

chemically sterilizing them or using some other sort of contraception.

This method was tried from 1997–2001. Alpha males and females in wolf

Refutation of the animal rights groups and their solution to the problem

I INCH · 1/2 INCH · I INCH · I INCH · I INCH

(continued)

1/2 INCH

1 INCH

packs in control areas were sterilized. During these years the caribou population experienced an increase from 22,000 to 38,000. Whether or not the wolf sterilization program caused this increase in the caribou population is still being studied. Even if it is finally judged to be the main cause of the increase in caribou, the sterilization program has been accounted unfeasible for implementation throughout Alaska because of its scope and cost (Regelin, 2002). In the long run, sterilization is less effective than killing wolves for another reason. It would take too long to be effective in reducing an existing wolf population. Sterilization only deals with the wolf numbers in the future, not with existing numbers, which would remain the same for the present. Existing wolves in the immediate future could devastate the caribou and moose populations in the meantime.

1 INCH

1 INCH

Refutation of other solutions and evaluation of evidence

In the U.S. Constitution, the management of fish and wildlife is left up to the individual states. When Alaska made the professional decision that the best way to control its wolf population was by aerial shootings, the animal rights groups picked only that part of a larger plan to attack. In media reports, activists "portrayed the plan simply as a mass extermination of wolves designed to increase game numbers for out-of-state hunters and wildlife watchers" (Keszler, 1993, p. 39). The Defenders of Wildlife claim now that Governor Palin's proposed bill, which makes it difficult for conservation groups to sue the government for killing wolves, will take "science and public input out of the process"; the current wildlife director counters that people will still be able to state their views (Cockerham, 2008). After all these years,

1 INCH

(continued)

1 INCH

1/2 INCH

Alaskan Wolf   8

the issue of wolf population control in Alaska is still far from settled. In August 2008 the citizens of Alaska will vote for the third time on whether or not to ban aerial hunting of wolves. The 1996 and 2000 propositions of Governor Knowles's term passed by 58.5 percent and 53 percent of the votes, respectively. Each proposition either banned or limited the killing of wolves ("History," 2008).

    Animal rights commercials in 1993 showed "visions of helicopter gunships slaughtering wolves by the hundreds" (Keszler, 1993, p. 39). Since then other images of wolves in distress have been distributed to influence public opinion on this issue (Regelin, 2002). What is not always clear to the public, however, is that the aerial shooting of wolves is just one small part of the plan that also includes protecting the wolves themselves when their numbers become too low. The animal rights groups have not focused on those parts of the wolf plan that deal with restrictions to help the wolves in areas where their populations are sparse. The Alaska Department of Fish and Game, Division of Wildlife Conservation in Alaska, makes it clear that the long-term conservation of wolves is a major goal. Furthermore, when wolves are killing other important animal populations, they must be reduced ("Wolf Control," 2008).

    The professional wildlife biologists at the Alaska Department of Fish and Game have taken a lot of heat from the animal rights media reports on their decision to go ahead with the original plan to manage wolf populations through aerial shootings and other methods not mentioned by the media. Governor Hickle in 1991 and Governor Palin in 2008 were both besieged with requests from animal rights activists to

1 INCH

1 INCH

1 INCH

Establishment of the *ethos* of conservationists in Alaska to make their plan acceptable

(continued)

1/2 INCH

1 INCH

Author has identified a problem, evaluated several solutions, and arrived at this solution as the best possible one. This is a value argument because it claims that one of several considered solutions is the best.

discontinue aerial hunting of wolves. The biologists of the state of Alaska have devoted their lives to the preservation of wildlife. They know Alaska and Alaska's wildlife better than anyone else. After researching and trying other methods, they believe the best solution to their problem is aerial shootings. Their main concern is to protect the wildlife population as a whole, not just to wage a "war on wolves." While the animal rightists are sitting in their offices wondering which animals to save, the biologists at the Alaska Department of Fish and Game are in the field researching the range conditions and overall population conditions to manage the wildlife community as a whole.

1 INCH

Problem–solution and policy are also strong features in this argument.

Value claim in last sentence

The resolution of the Alaskan wolf management issue needs to be left to the experts. As inhumane and immoral as it might seem to many citizens, the aerial shooting of wolves is periodically the best solution for game management in Alaska.

1 INCH

1 INCH

(continued)

Alaskan Wolf   10

References

Alaska wolf update. (1993, August). *American Hunter,* 6.

Arms, K. (1994). *Environmental science* (2nd ed.). Fort Worth, TX: Harcourt
Brace.

Buist, P. (1993, September). [Letter to the editor]. *American Hunter,* p. 12.

Cockerham, S. (2008, January 30). Palin wants to shoot down wolf
lawsuits. *Anchorage Daily News.* Retrieved from http://www.adn.com/

History of wolf control in Alaska. (2008). Retrieved from Defenders of
Wildlife Web site: http://www.defenders.org

Keszler, E. (1993, May). Wolves and big game: Searching for balance in
Alaska. *American Hunter,* pp. 38–39, 65–67.

Regelin, W. L. (2002, March). *Wolf management in Alaska with an historic
perspective.* Retrieved from http://www.wc.adfg.state.ak.us
/index.cfm?adfg=wolf.wolf_mgt

Williams, T. (1993, May–June). Alaska's war on the wolves. *Audubon,*
pp. 44–47, 49–50.

Wolf control in Alaska. (2003, December 29). Retrieved from Alaska
Department of Fish and Game—Division of Wildlife
Conservation Web site: http://www.wildlife.alaska.gov/index
.cfm?adfg=wolf.control

Wolf "control" in Alaska. (2004, March 14). [Editorial]. *New York Times,*
p. A12.

The wolf in Alaska. (2008). Retrieved from Alaska Department of
Fish and Game—Division of Wildlife Conservation Web site:
http://www.wildlife.alaska.gov

In APA format, break long URLs after a double slash or before a period or a single slash. Never add a hyphen.

Questions on the Researched Position Paper, APA Style

1. Where does the author place his claim? What type of claim is it? Why do you think he placed it where it is?

2. What are the two conflicting positions on wolf management described in this paper? How much common ground would you say there is between the two positions?

3. What are some of the types of proofs and support that this student uses in his paper? Comment on the use of *logos*, *ethos*, and *pathos* in general, as well as on specific types of proofs, including the image of the wolf.

4. What warrants are held by the conservationists? What warrants are held by the animal rights advocates? What warrants does this author expect you to accept?

5. What major ideas does this author refute in this paper?

6. What organizational pattern do you detect in this paper?

7. Find an example of a summary of information from a document on an Internet site with no available author.

8. Find an example of a quotation that is longer than forty words.

9. Roughly what percentage of this paper is made up of quotations from other people's writings, and what percentage is the author's own writing?

10. Read the "References" list and identify the different types of sources this author used.

4

Further Applications: Argument and Literature

C hapter 13 suggests some ways to apply argument theory to reading and writing about literature. When you finish reading Part Four:

- You will know how to apply argument theory to literary works.

- You will know how to analyze arguments made by literary works.

- You will know how to analyze arguments made by characters in literary works.

- You will know how to write your own arguments about literary works.

Argument and Literature

After studying this chapter, you will be able to:

LO1 Analyze arguments made by literary works and the characters in literary works.

LO2 Write arguments about literary works.

The purpose of this chapter is to help you apply argumentation theory when you read imaginative literature and when you write papers about literature, including poetry, short stories, plays, and novels. Any theory that is applied to literature can help you look at it in completely new ways, and so it is with argument theory. In particular, argument theory is useful for speculating about the ideas and themes in literature, especially when there is no general agreement about what these ideas are exactly. It can also provide insight into literary characters, especially into how they argue and interact with one another. Finally, argument theory can help you write papers about literature and argue in favor of your own understandings and insights.

Argument can be found everywhere. Creative writers, along with the imaginative characters they create, are as given to argument as any other people. In fact, literature often raises issues, takes positions on them, and even changes people's views about them. Literature can be convincing because it invites readers to identify with the characters, which creates empathy and common ground, and because it almost always employs effective emotional tone, vivid language, and compelling examples. Literature has high interest appeal as well. Argument achieved through literary narrative can be one of the most convincing forms of argument.

Finding and Analyzing Arguments in Literature

LO1 Analyze arguments made by literary works and the characters in literary works.

When you apply argument theory to the reading of literature, you will be "inside the text," so to speak, analyzing what is there and working to understand it. Your focus may be on the main argument made by the text, or it may be on one or more of the characters and the arguments they make. Let us consider first how to analyze the main argument.

WHAT IS AT ISSUE? WHAT IS THE CLAIM?

To use argument theory to read a literary text and analyze the main argument, focus on the issues raised in the work, the perspectives that are expressed, and the claims that are made. The claims may be explicit, overt, and openly expressed, or they may be implicit, covert, and merely suggested, so that you will need to infer them yourself. There may also be conflicting claims in a single work that seem at times to contradict each other. The Toulmin model is useful for analyzing and understanding the main line of argument in a literary work.

For example, here is a poem by Robert Herrick (1591–1674) that makes an explicit argument.

To the Virgins, to Make Much of Time

Gather ye rosebuds while ye may,
  Old Time is still a-flying;
And this same flower that smiles today,
  Tomorrow will be dying.

The glorious lamp of heaven, the sun,
  The higher he's a-getting,
The sooner will his race be run,
  And nearer he's to setting.

That age is best which is the first,
  When youth and blood are warmer;
But being spent, the worse, and worst
  Times still succeed the former.

Then be not coy, but use your time,
  And while ye may, go marry:
For having lost but once your prime,
  You may forever tarry.

In applying the Toulmin model to this poem, most readers would agree that a policy claim is stated in the first line and restated in different language in the last stanza. There would not be much disagreement, furthermore, that one way to state this claim is: "Young people should marry in their prime and not later." Alternatively, the poet's first line, "Gather ye rosebuds while ye may," taken metaphorically to mean that one should take advantage of good things when they are before you and available, serves as well to express the claim of this poem. The support is supplied in the form of reasons: time is flying, and it is better to marry when one is young than when one is old. The warrant that connects the support to the claim is that people will want to marry in the first place. Individuals who accept this warrant may be persuaded that they should, indeed, seize the day and wait no longer.

The claims in imaginative literature are not always this easy to identify. In many cases, it is necessary to ask questions to uncover what is at issue and to formulate the claim. Here are some questions to help you make these determinations.

1. *What is most of this work about?* The answer will help you identify the subject of the work.

2. *Can the subject be regarded as controversial?* That is, would it invite more than one perspective? This question will help you discover the issues.

3. *What positions are taken on the issue, and who takes them?* This question will help you discover both explicit and implicit claims along with who is making them: the author, a narrator, or various characters in the text.

4. *If the claim is not stated, what evidence can I use from the text to help me state it myself?* Draw on such evidence to help you make the claim explicit.

5. *Will everyone agree that this is a viable claim, or will I need to make a case for it?* Paper topics often come from disagreements over how to state the main argument in a literary work.

In her poem "The Mother," Gwendolyn Brooks begins, "Abortions will not let you forget." She continues by saying that she has never forgotten her "killed children," and she ends the poem:

> oh, what shall I say, how is the truth to be said?
> You were born, you had body, you died.
> It is just that you never giggled or planned or cried.
> Believe me, I loved you all.
> Believe me, I knew you, though faintly, and I loved,
> I loved you all.

One could argue that the claim of the poem is in the first sentence, "Abortions will not let you forget," a claim of fact in the poet's experience. However, by the time one has read the entire poem, one can also infer and make a case for a value claim, that abortions cause the mothers who seek them considerable psychological pain and that, as with any experience of death, an absence is born or created that is difficult for them to endure as time goes on. There is sufficient evidence in the poem to make an argument for that second claim as well.

Other literary texts express conflicting claims about an issue. In poet Robert Frost's "Mending Wall," two claims are made about the issue concerning the value of fences. The two claims are "Something there is that doesn't love a wall" and "Good fences make good neighbors." These claims contradict each other. Furthermore, careful readers have pointed out that convincing arguments are made for both of these positions in the poem. In the case of "Mending Wall," the poem tends to start an argument rather than deliver one.[1] Once again, paper topics come out of such disagreements and can provide you with material for lively writing. You can always take a position yourself on any argument started by a literary work.

In other literary texts, arguments are made entirely through metaphor, as in Frost's poem "Birches," in which swinging on birch trees becomes a way of escaping from the cares of life, or in another Frost poem, "The Road Not Taken," in which the two roads in the poem become metaphors for two possible life choices. Metaphors are comparisons of items from two different categories. They work like figurative analogies since they invite readers to make unique mental connections and to expand their perspective on a subject in new and original ways. The meanings of metaphors in a literary work are often difficult to pin down exactly. Thus, they become the subject of controversy and are often open to a variety of interpretations. The disputed meaning of a key metaphor in a literary work can become a fruitful paper topic.

CHARACTERS MAKING ARGUMENTS

The second way to employ argument theory to analyze literature is to apply it to specific arguments that are made by characters within a literary text. Also enlightening is to consider how these individual characters' arguments contribute to the main argument of the text. Focusing on the rhetorical situation and the modes of appeal, identifying fallacies, and applying the Toulmin model all help with this type of analysis.

It is useful to identify the type of argument. For example, a character may argue internally with himself, as Hamlet does when he asks, "To be or not to be, that is the question" in Shakespeare's *Hamlet*. A character may also argue with an imaginary audience, like the woman who constructs an imaginary argument with her child's counselor in the short story "I Stand Here Ironing" by Tillie Olsen. Two individuals may argue one on one, both trying to convince the other, as in the poem "Myth" by Muriel Rukeyser; or the character may make a single-perspective argument to convince a mass audience, as Marc Antony does in his speech that begins "Friends, Romans, countrymen, lend me your ears" in Shakespeare's *Julius Caesar*. The characters may argue in front of a third-party judge, as they do in the play *Inherit the Wind*. Identifying the type of argument will help you understand the rhetorical situation in which it takes place. It will focus your attention on who is arguing, with whom these characters are arguing, and to what end.

A famous literary argument is Satan's persuasion of Eve in John Milton's seventeenth-century epic *Paradise Lost*. The story is familiar. Adam and Eve have been placed in the Garden of Eden by God and have been told they may eat anything in the garden except the fruit from the tree of knowledge. The rhetorical situation can be narrated like this: Satan is the arguer. He sneaks into the garden, inhabits the serpent, and in that guise tempts Eve, his audience, to eat the forbidden fruit. This is a one-on-one argument with Satan trying to convince Eve. The

---

[1]Tim Morris provided me with some of the examples and insights in this chapter, such as this one, as well as with some of the literary examples in "The Reader."

exigence of Satan's argument is that he needs to get a foothold on earth so that he can spend more time there and less time in Hell, a very unpleasant place in this poem. Satan's constraints are that he must get Eve alone because he is afraid he cannot persuade Adam; Eve is a bit vain, as he has discovered, and there are good angels around who could also frustrate his plan. Thus, he decides to hide in the serpent. Satan's persuasive argument, full of fallacies as it is, is successful with Eve. She eats the fruit, she persuades Adam to eat it also, and, as a result, they are expelled from the garden (paradise) forever.

In the poem, we witness the entire persuasive process that involves Satan and Eve, from the audience analysis carried on by Satan as he hides in the garden, watching Eve and analyzing her weaknesses, to the final changes in Eve's thoughts and actions brought about by Satan's argumentative speeches. As part of this process, we overhear Satan's initial planning of his argument, and as he schemes and plans, we observe that there is a vast difference between his private feelings and beliefs and the roles he adopts to establish *ethos* with Eve. Satan is not an ethical arguer; he is an immoral manipulator. We also watch Satan deliberately plant a highly emotional version of the temptation in Eve's mind in the form of a dream. The remembered pleasure and emotional appeal of this dream will help make the later logical argument even more readily acceptable to Eve.

When Satan-in-the-serpent delivers the speeches in Book 9 of the poem that finally convince Eve that she should eat the apple, he employs *ethos*, *pathos*, and *logos* to strengthen his argument. He flatters Eve; he appeals to her desire to be more powerful; he refutes what God has told her with fallacious reasoning; he uses induction to show that he ate the fruit and did not die and, therefore, Eve will not die either; he points to himself as a sign of the intelligence and power that can come from eating the fruit; and he uses a deductive argument that can be summarized as follows:

> Eve should know evil in order to recognize good.
> Eating the fruit will help Eve know evil.
> Therefore, Eve should eat the fruit in order to recognize good.

There are other examples of logical and emotional appeal in this argument that are not detailed here. Furthermore, if the Toulmin model is also employed to analyze Satan's argument, his purpose and strategy become even clearer, particularly as we examine some of his warrants. One of these, for example, is that humans want to become gods. Satan himself envies God and assumes that humans will also.

Another unique feature of the argument in *Paradise Lost* is that we are allowed to witness the argument outcomes. Not only do we observe Eve's outward actions, but we are also a party to her inner thoughts following Satan's speech. We see her eat the fruit. We learn from her private musings how her reasoning, her emotional state, and the credibility she places in the serpent have been changed by Satan's speeches. We have a full explanation of what has convinced Eve to disobey God and why the argument has been successful.

If you become interested in analyzing the argument in *Paradise Lost*, you might also like to know that Satan makes no fewer than twenty public addresses in the poem and that his audiences range in size from the single listener Eve to the multitudes of the fallen angels. Furthermore, Adam, Eve, God, the Son, and some of the angels in the poem make arguments of their own that can be profitably analyzed with argument theory.

Consider this list of questions to analyze the arguments of fictional characters in literature. Any one of these questions could help you discover a claim for a paper on a literary work. You would develop your claim by drawing examples from the literary work itself to illustrate your argument.

1. What is at issue in the literary work?

2. Who is the character taking a position on this issue, and what is the character's position on the issue?

3. What is the rhetorical situation for the argument?

4. What is the claim made by the character? Is it stated overtly? Is it implied? Write it yourself as a statement, and identify its type.

5. How does the character establish credibility? What logical and emotional proofs does the character use?

6. What type of language predominates: language that appeals to reason, language that appeals to emotion, or language that establishes credibility? Describe the language.

7. What are the warrants?

8. How does the character establish common ground? Through warrants? Through Rogerian argument? What else?

9. Are rebuttals used? How effective are they?

10. Are there fallacies? How do they distort the argument?

11. What are the outcomes of the argument? Is it convincing? To whom? What happens as a result?

12. Is the argument moral or immoral by the standards established in the text itself? How would you evaluate the argument according to your own standards and values?

13. How does the argument made by the character contribute to the main argument of the text?

Writing Arguments about Literature

LO2 Write arguments about literary works.

Argument theory can also be used to help you formulate your own argument about your insights and understanding of a literary text. At this point, you will move "outside the text," and you will begin by identifying an issue about the text on which there is no general agreement. You will then take a position on that issue, state your position in a claim, and present evidence from the text to prove it. Argument theory can be extremely beneficial in writing scholarly argument of this type. The Toulmin model will help you the most. It can help you identify an issue to write about in the first place, and it can also help you set up the elements of your argument.

Your first challenge will be to move from reading the piece of literature to writing about it. First, you will need to find an issue to write about. To help you find an issue, ask, *What is unclear about this text that I think I can explain?* or *What is left out by the author that I think I can explain?* Focus on the main argument of the text, on the characters themselves, on what the narrator says about the characters, or on the meaning of metaphors to help you discover possible issues to write about. In addition, issues may emerge in class discussion, or issues may come from the questions in your literature anthology. If all else fails, write a summary of a literary text along with your reaction to it. Then read your reaction and circle the most promising idea in it. It should be an idea that you think you can make a claim about and defend with evidence from the text.

Consider some examples of issues that appear in literary texts. In Henry James's novel *The Turn of the Screw*, there is an unresolved question about whether the ghosts are real or not. One student actually went through the novel and highlighted in one color all of the evidence that suggests they are real and then highlighted in another color all of the evidence that suggests they are imaginary. According to this student, the quantity of evidence for both explanations was roughly comparable in the novel. If you decided to write about that issue, you could argue for either position and find many people who would agree with you. Your instructor would evaluate your paper on the quality of its argument rather than on whether you had resolved the controversy or not. Some literary controversies cannot be finally resolved any more than many issues in life can be finally resolved.

Look at another example of a literary issue. At the end of Ernest Hemingway's short story "The Short Happy Life of Francis Macomber," a wounded and enraged buffalo charges the main character, who is on an African safari. His wife shoots, but the bullet kills her husband instead of the buffalo. The "great white hunter" who is leading this expedition assumes the wife meant to kill her husband instead of the buffalo, and there is plenty of evidence in the story to suggest that this might have been her intent. However, it is equally possible to argue that she was really shooting at the buffalo and hit her husband by mistake. You could write a paper in which you argue for either position, as long as you provide evidence from the story to support your position. In other words, you could make either position convincing.

Here are some questions to help you make a claim about a literary work and write a convincing argument to support it:

1. What is an issue raised by this text that needs clarification?

2. What are the different perspectives that can be taken on this issue?

3. Which perspective will I take?

4. What support from the text will I use to defend my position?

5. What warrants are implicit in my argument, and will they be acceptable to the person who will evaluate this paper? Should I make the backing explicit to strengthen the warrants?

6. Would my paper be more convincing if I include a rebuttal of the opposing positions?

7. Will my claim be more acceptable to my audience if I qualify it?

Once you have read and thought about a literary text, and you have answered these questions, you will write your paper just like you would write any other position paper in which your aim is to state what you think and provide evidence to support it.

Review Questions

1. How can argument theory be used in the study of literature? Name and describe the three approaches described in this chapter. **(LO1)**

2. What are some of the questions a reader can ask to arrive at a claim in a work of literature? What are some of the ways in which claims are expressed in literature? **(LO1)**

3. Describe the argument theory you would employ to help you analyze an argument that a character makes in a literary work. **(LO1)**

4. What are some of the suggestions made in this chapter to help you find a topic for a position paper you might write about an issue in literature? **(LO2)**

5. What is your main responsibility as a writer when you argue on one side or the other of a literary issue? **(LO2)**

Exercises and Activities

A. **Writing Assignment: Analyzing Arguments in Poems**

The two poems on the following pages present arguments.

1. Read the poems; then freewrite for five minutes on each of them to capture your original thoughts and reactions.

2. Discuss the answers to the "For Discussion" questions that appear at the end of each poem.

3. Describe the rhetorical situation for each poem: Describe the text. Who is the author? What audience does the author seem to have in mind, and how closely do you match that imagined audience? What are the author's constraints regarding the issue? What are your constraints? What is the exigence for the poem?

4. Write a 350- to 400-word paper on one of the poems that explains the issue, the claim (or claims) made in the poem, the support, the expected warrants, and your final reaction to the claim(s), including the degree of common ground you share either with the author or with another character in the poem.

POEM #1   **TOTALLY LIKE WHATEVER, YOU KNOW?***

Taylor Mali

Mali is a contemporary poet who is well known for his oral performances of his poetry.

In case you hadn't noticed,
it has somehow become uncool
to sound like you know what you're talking about?
Or believe strongly in what you're saying?
5   Invisible question marks and parenthetical (you know?)'s
have been attaching themselves to the ends of our sentences?
Even when those sentences aren't, like, questions? You know?

Declarative sentences—so-called
because they used to, like, DECLARE things to be true
10   as opposed to other things which were, like, not—
have been infected by a totally hip
and tragically cool interrogative tone? You know?
Like, don't think I'm uncool just because I've noticed this;
this is just like the word on the street, you know?
15   It's like what I've heard?
I have nothing personally invested in my own opinions, okay?
I'm just inviting you to join me in my uncertainty?

What has happened to our conviction?
Where are the limbs out on which we once walked?
20   Have they been, like, chopped down
with the rest of the rain forest?
Or do we have, like, nothing to say?
Has society become so, like, totally . . .
I mean absolutely . . . You know?
25   That we've just gotten to the point where it's just, like . . .
whatever!

And so actually our disarticulation . . . ness
is just a clever sort of . . . thing
to disguise the fact that we've become
30   the most aggressively inarticulate generation
to come along since . . .
you know, a long, long time ago!

I entreat you, I implore you, I exhort you,
I challenge you: To speak with conviction.

35   To say what you believe in a manner that bespeaks
the determination with which you believe it.

Because contrary to the wisdom of the bumper sticker,
it is not enough these days to simply QUESTION AUTHORITY.
You have to speak with it, too.

For Discussion:

What is the issue that is addressed in this poem? What is the author's position on the issue? What is the claim, and what type of claim is it? What is the organizational pattern in the poem? What support is presented for the claim? What warrants does the author hope you will share with him? How much common ground do you have with this author? What is your own experience with this issue? What is your personal response to the author's claim?

POEM #2   ## MENDING WALL*

Robert Frost

Frost is a well-known American poet who often wrote about people and settings in New England. He wrote this poem in 1914.

Something there is that doesn't love a wall,
That sends the frozen-ground-swell under it,
And spills the upper boulders in the sun;
And makes gaps even two can pass abreast.
5   The work of hunters is another thing:
I have come after them and made repair
Where they have left not one stone on a stone,
But they would have the rabbit out of hiding,
To please the yelping dogs. The gaps I mean,
10   No one has seen them made or heard them made,
But at spring mending-time we find them there.
I let my neighbor know beyond the hill;
And on a day we meet to walk the line
And set the wall between us once again.
15   We keep the wall between us as we go.
To each the boulders that have fallen to each.
And some are loaves and some so nearly balls
We have to use a spell to make them balance:
"Stay where you are until our backs are turned!"
20   We wear our fingers rough with handling them.
Oh, just another kind of outdoor game.
One on a side. It comes to little more:
There where it is we do not need the wall:
He is all pine and I am apple orchard.

25   My apple trees will never get across
            And eat the cones under his pines, I tell him.
            He only says, "Good fences make good neighbors."
            Spring is the mischief in me, and I wonder
            If I could put a notion in his head:
30   "Why do they make good neighbors? Isn't it
            Where there are cows? But here there are no cows.
            Before I built a wall I'd ask to know
            What I was walling in or walling out,
            And to whom I was like to give offense.
35   Something there is that doesn't love a wall,
            That wants it down." I could say "Elves" to him,
            But it's not elves exactly, and I'd rather
            He said it for himself. I see him there
            Bringing a stone grasped firmly by the top
40   In each hand, like an old-stone savage armed.
            He moves in darkness as it seems to me,

            Not of woods only and the shade of trees.
            He will not go behind his father's saying,
            And he likes having thought of it so well
45   He says again, "Good fences make good neighbors."

For Discussion:

What is the issue in this poem? Describe the perspectives that are presented on this issue. State the conflicting claims. Who makes these claims? How are the individuals who make them characterized in the poem? Is the conflict of views resolved? Can you imagine an argument that finds common ground being employed to resolve the conflict? Why or why not? With whom do you identify in this poem and share the most common ground? Why?

B. Writing Assignment: An Argument about a Literary Work

The purpose of this assignment is to discover an issue, make a claim, and write about your interpretation of a story. Edgar Allen Poe is well known for exploring the issues of guilt and punishment in his fiction. Poe's story presents these issues in a particularly complex way. In order to determine exactly what claim Poe is making about these issues, undertake the following steps:

1. When you have finished reading the story, freewrite for five minutes to capture your original thoughts and reactions.

2. As a class, discuss answers to the following questions:

   a. What is this story about? What issues are raised by this story?
   b. What is the perspective of the narrator in this story? What makes it difficult to identify with this perspective?

    c. Write a claim made by this story; then help list a few of these claims on the board. Which of these claims could be supported with evidence from the text? Which would you like to write about? Write your claim. Read with the class some of these claims.

3. Answer the next four questions to plan your paper.

    a. What evidence from the text can you use to support your claim (examples, quotations, etc.)? Underline it.

    b. What warrants are implicit in your argument? Will they be acceptable to the person who reads your paper, or should you provide backing?

    c. Would your paper be more convincing if you included a rebuttal? What would it be?

    d. Will your claim be more acceptable if you qualify it? How would you do that?

4. Write a 500-word position paper defending the claim you have made about this story.

STORY #1   **THE CASK OF AMONTILLADO**
Edgar Allen Poe

Edgar Allen Poe (1809–1849) is a well-known author of American Gothic fiction and poetry.

The thousand injuries of Fortunato I had borne as I best could, but when he ventured upon insult I vowed revenge. You, who so well know the nature of my soul, will not suppose, however, that gave utterance to a threat. At length I would be avenged; this was a point definitely, settled—but the very definitiveness with which it was resolved precluded the idea of risk. I must not only punish but punish with impunity. A wrong is unredressed when retribution overtakes its redresser. It is equally unredressed when the avenger fails to make himself felt as such to him who has done the wrong.

It must be understood that neither by word nor deed had I given Fortunato cause to doubt my good will. I continued, as was my wont, to smile in his face, and he did not perceive that my smile *now* was at the thought of his immolation.

He had a weak point—this Fortunato—although in other regards he was a man to be respected and even feared. He prided himself on his connoisseurship in wine. Few Italians have the true virtuoso spirit. For the most part their enthusiasm is adopted to suit the time and opportunity, to practice imposture upon the British and Austrian millionaires. In painting and gemmary, Fortunato, like his countrymen, was a quack, but in the matter of old wines he was sincere. In this respect I did not differ from him materially;—I was skilful in the Italian vintages myself, and bought largely whenever I could.

It was about dusk, one evening during the supreme madness of the carnival season, that I encountered my friend. He accosted me with excessive warmth, for he had been drinking much. The man wore motley. He had on a tight-fitting parti-striped dress, and his head was surmounted by the conical cap and bells. I was so pleased to see him that I thought I should never have done wringing his hand.

5   I said to him —"My dear Fortunato, you are luckily met. How remarkably well you are looking to-day. But I have received a pipe of what passes for Amontillado, and I have my doubts."

"How?" said he. "Amontillado, A pipe? Impossible! And in the middle of the carnival!"

"I have my doubts," I replied; "and I was silly enough to pay the full Amontillado price without consulting you in the matter. You were not to be found, and I was fearful of losing a bargain."

"Amontillado!"

"I have my doubts."

10   "Amontillado!"

"And I must satisfy them."

"Amontillado!"

"As you are engaged, I am on my way to Luchresi. If any one has a critical turn it is he. He will tell me —"

"Luchresi cannot tell Amontillado from Sherry."

15   "And yet some fools will have it that his taste is a match for your own.

"Come, let us go."

"Whither?"

"To your vaults."

"My friend, no; I will not impose upon your good nature. I perceive you have an engagement. Luchresi—"

20   "I have no engagement; —come."

"My friend, no. It is not the engagement, but the severe cold with which I perceive you are afflicted. The vaults are insufferably damp. They are encrusted with nitre."

"Let us go, nevertheless. The cold is merely nothing. Amontillado! You have been imposed upon. And as for Luchresi, he cannot distinguish Sherry from Amontillado."

Thus speaking, Fortunato possessed himself of my arm; and putting on a mask of black silk and drawing a roquelaire closely about my person, I suffered him to hurry me to my palazzo.

There were no attendants at home; they had absconded to make merry in honour of the time. I had told them that I should not return until the morning, and had given them explicit orders not to stir from the house. These orders were sufficient, I well knew, to insure their immediate disappearance, one and all, as soon as my back was turned.

25   I took from their sconces two flambeaux, and giving one to Fortunato, bowed him through several suites of rooms to the archway that led into the vaults. I passed down a long and winding staircase, requesting him to be cautious as he followed. We came at length to the foot of the descent, and stood together upon the damp ground of the catacombs of the Montresors.

The gait of my friend was unsteady, and the bells upon his cap jingled as he strode.

"The pipe," he said.

"It is farther on," said I; "but observe the white web-work which gleams from these cavern walls."

He turned towards me, and looked into my eyes with two filmy orbs that distilled the rheum of intoxication.

30   "Nitre?" he asked, at length.

"Nitre," I replied. "How long have you had that cough?"

"Ugh! ugh! ugh! —ugh! ugh! ugh! —ugh! ugh! ugh! —ugh! ugh! ugh! —ugh! ugh! ugh!"

My poor friend found it impossible to reply for many minutes.

"It is nothing," he said, at last.

35   "Come," I said, with decision, "we will go back; your health is precious. You are rich, respected, admired, beloved; you are happy, as once I was. You are a man to be missed. For me it is no matter. We will go back; you will be ill, and I cannot be responsible. Besides, there is Luchresi —"

"Enough," he said; "the cough's a mere nothing; it will not kill me. I shall not die of a cough."

"True —true," I replied; "and, indeed, I had no intention of alarming you unnecessarily —but you should use all proper caution. A draught of this Medoc will defend us from the damps."

Here I knocked off the neck of a bottle which I drew from a long row of its fellows that lay upon the mould.

"Drink," I said, presenting him the wine.

40   He raised it to his lips with a leer. He paused and nodded to me familiarly, while his bells jingled.

"I drink," he said, "to the buried that repose around us."

"And I to your long life."

He again took my arm, and we proceeded.

"These vaults," he said, "are extensive."

45   "The Montresors," I replied, "were a great and numerous family."

"I forget your arms."

"A huge human foot d'or, in a field azure; the foot crushes a serpent rampant whose fangs are imbedded in the heel."

"And the motto?"

"*Nemo me impune lacessit.*"*

50   "Good!" he said.

The wine sparkled in his eyes and the bells jingled. My own fancy grew warm with the Medoc. We had passed through long walls of piled skeletons, with casks and puncheons intermingling, into the inmost recesses of the catacombs. I paused again, and this time I made bold to seize Fortunato by an arm above the elbow.

*No one attacks me with impunity.

"The nitre!" I said; "see, it increases. It hangs like moss upon the vaults. We are below the river's bed. The drops of moisture trickle among the bones. Come, we will go back ere it is too late. Your cough —"

"It is nothing," he said; "let us go on. But first, another draught of the Medoc."

I broke and reached him a flagon of De Grave. He emptied it at a breath. His eyes flashed with a fierce light. He laughed and threw the bottle upwards with a gesticulation I did not understand.

55   I looked at him in surprise. He repeated the movement —a grotesque one.

"You do not comprehend?" he said.

"Not I," I replied.

"Then you are not of the brotherhood."

"How?"

60   "You are not of the masons."

"Yes, yes," I said; "yes, yes."

"You? Impossible! A mason?"

"A mason," I replied.

"A sign," he said, "a sign."

65   "It is this," I answered, producing from beneath the folds of my roquelaire a trowel.

"You jest," he exclaimed, recoiling a few paces. "But let us proceed to the Amontillado."

"Be it so," I said, replacing the tool beneath the cloak and again offering him my arm. He leaned upon it heavily. We continued our route in search of the Amontillado. We passed through a range of low arches, descended, passed on, and descending again, arrived at a deep crypt, in which the foulness of the air caused our flambeaux rather to glow than flame.

At the most remote end of the crypt there appeared another less spacious. Its walls had been lined with human remains, piled to the vault overhead, in the fashion of the great catacombs of Paris. Three sides of this interior crypt were still ornamented in this manner. From the fourth side the bones had been thrown down, and lay promiscuously upon the earth, forming at one point a mound of some size. Within the wall thus exposed by the displacing of the bones, we perceived a still interior crypt or recess, in depth about four feet, in width three, in height six or seven. It seemed to have been constructed for no especial use within itself, but formed merely the interval between two of the colossal supports of the roof of the catacombs, and was backed by one of their circumscribing walls of solid granite.

It was in vain that Fortunato, uplifting his dull torch, endeavoured to pry into the depth of the recess. Its termination the feeble light did not enable us to see.

70   "Proceed," I said; "herein is the Amontillado. As for Luchresi —"

"He is an ignoramus," interrupted my friend, as he stepped unsteadily forward, while I followed immediately at his heels. In an instant he had reached the extremity of the niche, and finding his progress arrested by the rock, stood stupidly bewildered. A moment more and I had fettered him to the granite. In its surface were two iron staples, distant from each other about two feet, horizontally. From one of these depended a short chain, from the other a padlock. Throwing the links about his waist, it was but the work of a few seconds to secure it. He was too much astounded to resist. Withdrawing the key I stepped back from the recess.

"Pass your hand," I said, "over the wall; you cannot help feeling the nitre. Indeed, it is very damp. Once more let me implore you to return. No? Then I must positively leave you. But I must first render you all the little attentions in my power."

"The Amontillado!" ejaculated my friend, not yet recovered from his astonishment.

"True," I replied; "the Amontillado."

75   As I said these words I busied myself among the pile of bones of which I have before spoken. Throwing them aside, I soon uncovered a quantity of building stone and mortar. With these materials and with the aid of my trowel, I began vigorously to wall up the entrance of the niche.

I had scarcely laid the first tier of the masonry when I discovered that the intoxication of Fortunato had in a great measure worn off. The earliest indication I had of this was a low moaning cry from the depth of the recess. It was not the cry of a drunken man. There was then a long and obstinate silence. I laid the second tier, and the third, and the fourth; and then I heard the furious vibrations of the chain. The noise lasted for several minutes, during which, that I might hearken to it with the more satisfaction, I ceased my labors and sat down upon the bones. When at last the clanking subsided, I resumed the trowel, and finished without interruption the fifth, the sixth, and the seventh tier. The wall was now nearly upon a level with my breast. I again paused, and holding the flambeaux over the mason-work, threw a few feeble rays upon the figure within.

A succession of loud and shrill screams, bursting suddenly from the throat of the chained form, seemed to thrust me violently back. For a brief moment I hesitated, I trembled. Unsheathing my rapier, I began to grope with it about the recess; but the thought of an instant reassured me. I placed my hand upon the solid fabric of the catacombs, and felt satisfied. I reapproached the wall; I replied to the yells of him who clamored. I re-echoed, I aided, I surpassed them in volume and in strength. I did this, and the clamorer grew still.

It was now midnight, and my task was drawing to a close. I had completed the eighth, the ninth and the tenth tier. I had finished a portion of the last and the eleventh; there remained but a single stone to be fitted and plastered in. I struggled with its weight; I placed it partially in its destined position. But now there came from out the niche a low laugh that erected the hairs upon my head. It was succeeded by a sad voice, which I had difficulty in recognizing as that of the noble Fortunato. The voice said—

"Ha! ha! ha! —he! he! he! —a very good joke, indeed —an excellent jest. We will have many a rich laugh about it at the palazzo —he! he! he! —over our wine —he! he! he!"

80   "The Amontillado!" I said.

"He! he! he! —he! he! he! —yes, the Amontillado. But is it not getting late? Will not they be awaiting us at the palazzo, the Lady Fortunato and the rest? Let us be gone."

"Yes," I said, "let us be gone."

"For the love of God, Montresor!"

"Yes," I said, "for the love of God!"

85   But to these words I hearkened in vain for a reply. I grew impatient. I called aloud —

"Fortunato!"

No answer. I called again —

"Fortunato!"

No answer still. I thrust a torch through the remaining aperture and let it fall within. There came forth in return only a jingling of the bells. My heart grew sick; it was the dampness of the catacombs that made it so. I hastened to make an end of my labor. I forced the last stone into its position; I plastered it up. Against the new masonry I re-erected the old rampart of bones. For the half of a century no mortal has disturbed them. *In pace requiescat!***

For Discussion:

How is crime and punishment depicted in this story? How does this depiction differ from the way you would define the relationship between crime and punishment?

**Rest in peace!

Summary Charts

TRACE

THE RHETORICAL SITUATION

FOR YOU AS THE READER

Text. What kind of text is it? What are its special qualities and features? What is it about?

Reader. Are you one of the readers the writer anticipated? Do you share common ground with the author and other audience members? Are you open to change?

Author. Who is the author? How is the author influenced by background, experience, education, affiliations, or values? What is the author's motivation to write?

Constraints.* What beliefs, attitudes, habits, affiliations, or traditions will influence the way you and the author view the argument?

Exigence. What caused the argument, and do you perceive it as a defect or problem?

FOR THE TARGETED READER AT THE TIME THE TEXT WAS WRITTEN

Text. What kind of text is it? Is it unique to its time?

Reader. Who were the targeted readers? What qualities did they have as the original audience? Were they convinced? How are they different from other or modern readers?

Author. Who is the author? What influenced the author? Why was the author motivated to write?

Constraints.* What beliefs, attitudes, habits, affiliations, or traditions influenced the author's and the readers' views in this argument?

Exigence. What happened to cause the argument? Why was it a problem? Has it recurred?

FOR YOU AS THE WRITER

Text. What is the assignment? What should your completed paper look like?

Reader. Who are your readers? Where do they stand on the issue? How can you establish common ground? Can they change?

Author. What is your argumentation strategy? What is your purpose and your perspective? How will you make your paper convincing?

Constraints.* How are your training, background, affiliations, and values either in harmony or in conflict with your audience? Will they drive you apart or help build common ground?

Exigence. What is motivating you to write on this issue? Why is it compelling to you?

*Do not confuse constraints with warrants. Constraints are a broader concept. See page 123.

The Process

Be selective and flexible in using the strategies, and remember that there is no best order. You will backtrack and repeat.

WHEN YOU ARE THE READER

Prereading Strategies

▶ **Read the title and first paragraph; consult your background.** Identify the issue. Free-associate and write words and phrases that the issue brings to mind.

▶ **Evaluate and improve your background.** Do you know enough? If not, read or discuss to get background. Look up a key word or two.

▶ **Survey the material.** Locate the claim (the main assertion) and some of the subclaims (the ideas that support it); notice how they are organized. Do not slow down and read.

▶ **Write out your present position on the issue.**

▶ **Make some predictions, and write one big question.** Jot down two or three ideas that you think the author may discuss, and write one question you would like to have answered.

Reading Strategies

▶ **Pick up a pencil, underline, and annotate the ideas that seem important.** Write a brief summary.

▶ **Identify** and **read** the information in the **introduction, body,** and **conclusion.**

▶ **Look for the claim, subclaims, and support.** Box the transitions to highlight relationships between ideas and changes of subject.

▶ **Find the key words** that represent major concepts, and jot down meanings as needed.

▶ **Analyze the rhetorical situation.** Remember TRACE: Text, Reader, Author, Constraints, Exigence.

▶ **Analyze argument strategies.**

▶ **Read with an open mind, and analyze the common ground** between you and the author.

Strategies for Reading Difficult Material

▶ **Read all the way through once** without stopping.

▶ **Write a list** of what you understand and what you do not understand.

▶ **Identify words and concepts** you do not understand, look them up, and analyze how they are used in context.

WHEN YOU ARE THE WRITER

Prewriting Strategies

▶ **Get organized to write.** Set up a place with materials. Be motivated.

▶ **Understand the writing assignment,** and **schedule time.** Break a complicated writing task into manageable parts, and set aside time to write.

▶ **Identify an issue, and do some initial reading.** Use the twelve tests to make certain you have an arguable issue (Box 1.3).

▶ **Analyze the rhetorical situation,** particularly the exigence, the audience, and the constraints.

▶ **Focus** on your issue and **freewrite.**

▶ **Brainstorm, make lists, and map ideas.**

▶ **Talk it through** with a friend, your instructor, or members of a peer-editing group.

▶ **Keep a journal, notebook, or folder of ideas.**

▶ **Mentally visualize** the major concepts.

▶ **Do some** directed **reading and thinking.**

▶ **Use argument strategies.**

▶ **Use reading strategies.**

▶ **Use critical thinking prompts.**

▶ Plan and conduct **library research.**

▶ Make an **expanded list or outline** to guide your writing.

▶ **Talk it through again.**

Drafting Strategies

▶ **Write the first draft.** Put your ideas on paper so that you can work with them. Use your outline and notes to help you. Either write and rewrite as you go or write the draft quickly with the knowledge that you can reread and rewrite later.

Strategies to Use When You Get Stuck

▶ **Read more and take more notes.**

▶ **Read your outline, rearrange parts, and add information to it.**

▶ **Freewrite** on the issue, **read some more,** and then **freewrite** some more.

▶ **Talk about your ideas** with someone else.

▶ **Lower your expectations for your first draft.** At this point, the writing does not have to be perfect.

The Process (*continued*)

WHEN YOU ARE THE READER

▶ **Reread the material,** and add to your list of what you can and cannot understand.

▶ **Reread again** if you need to do so.

▶ **Discuss the material** with someone who has also read the material for further clarification and understanding.

Postreading Strategies

▶ **Monitor your comprehension.** Insist on understanding. Check the accuracy of your **predictions,** and answer your question.

▶ **Analyze the organization,** and write a **simplified outline,** a **map, or a summary to help you understand and remember.**

▶ **Write a response** to help you think.

▶ **Compare your present position** with your position before you began to read.

▶ **Evaluate the argument.** Decide whether it is ethical or unethical and convincing or not convincing.

WHEN YOU ARE THE WRITER

Postwriting Strategies

▶ **Read your draft critically** and also **have someone else read it.** Put it aside for 24 hours, if you can, to develop a better perspective for reading and improving.

▶ **Rewrite and revise.** Make changes and additions until you think the paper is ready for others to read. Move sections, cross out material, add other material, and rephrase for clarity, as necessary.

▶ **Check your paper** for final mechanical and spelling errors, **write the final title,** and **type or print the paper.**

The Toulmin Model

WHEN YOU ARE THE READER

1. *What is the claim?* What is this author trying to prove? Look for the claim at the beginning or at the end, or infer it.

2. *What is the support?* What information does the author use to convince you of the claim? Look for reasons, explanations, facts, opinions, personal narratives, and examples.

3. *What are the warrants?* What assumptions, general principles, values, beliefs, and appeals to human motives are implicit in the argument? How do they link the claim and the support? Do you share the author's values? Does the support develop the claim? Are the warrants stated, or must they be inferred?

4. *Is backing supplied for the warrants?* See whether additional support or appeals to widely accepted values and belief systems are provided to make the warrants more acceptable to the reader.

5. *Is there a rebuttal?* Are other perspectives on the issue stated in the argument? Are they refuted? Are counterarguments given?

6. *Has the claim been qualified?* Look for qualifying words such as *sometimes*, *probably*, *most*, and *possibly*. Decide what is probably the best position to take on the issue, for now.

WHEN YOU ARE THE WRITER

1. *What is my claim?* Decide on the type of claim and the subclaims. Decide where to put the claim in your paper.

2. *What support will I use?* Invent reasons, opinions, and examples. Research and quote authorities and facts. Consider using personal narratives.

3. *What are my warrants?* Write out the warrants. Do they strengthen the argument by linking the support to the claim? Do you believe them yourself? Will the audience share them or reject them?

4. *What backing for the warrants should I provide?* Add polls, studies, reports, expert opinion, or facts to make your warrants convincing. Refer to generally accepted values and widely held belief systems to strengthen the warrants.

5. *How should I handle rebuttal?* Include other perspectives and point out what is wrong with them. Make counterarguments.

6. *Will I need to qualify my claim?* Decide whether you can strengthen your claim by adding qualifying words such as *usually*, *often*, or *probably*.

Types of Claims

CLAIMS OF FACT

What happened? Is it true? Does it exist? Is it a fact?

Examples:

Increasing population threatens the environment.

Video games promote violence.

Women are not as effective as men in combat.

READERS

- Look for claims that state facts.
- Look for facts, statistics, real examples, and quotations from reliable authorities.
- Anticipate induction, analogies, and signs.
- Look for chronological or topical organization or a claim plus reasons.

WRITERS

- State the claim as a fact, even though it is controversial.
- Use factual evidence and expert opinion.
- Use induction, historical and literal analogies, and signs.
- Consider arranging your material as a claim with reasons.

CLAIMS OF DEFINITION

What is it? What is it like? How should it be classified? How should it be interpreted? How does its usual meaning change in a particular context?

Examples:

We need to define what constitutes a family before we discuss family values.

A definition will demonstrate that the riots were an instance of civil disobedience.

Waterboarding can be defined as a form of torture.

READERS

- Look for a claim that contains or is followed by a definition.
- Look for reliable authorities and sources for definitions.
- Look for comparisons and examples.
- Look for compare-and-contrast, topical, or deductive organization.

WRITERS

- State your claim, and define the key terms.
- Quote authorities, or go to dictionaries, encyclopedias, or other reliable sources for definitions.
- If you are comparing to help define, use compare-and-contrast organization.
- Use vivid description and narrative.
- Use deductive organization.

CLAIMS OF CAUSE

What caused it? Where did it come from? Why did it happen? What are the effects? What probably will be the results on both a short-term and a long-term basis?

Examples:

Clear-cutting is the main cause of the destruction of ancient forests.

Censorship can result in limits on freedom of speech.

The American people's distrust of government has been caused by the behavior of Congress.

(continued)

Types of Claims *(continued)*

READERS

▸ Look for a claim that states or implies cause or effect.

▸ Look for facts and statistics, comparisons such as historical analogies, signs, induction, deduction, and causal arguments.

▸ Look for cause-and-effect or effect-and-cause organization.

WRITERS

▸ Make a claim that states or implies cause or effect.

▸ Use facts and statistics.

▸ Apply Burke's pentad to focus the main cause.

▸ Use historical analogies, signs, induction, and deduction.

▸ Consider using cause-and-effect or effect-and-cause organization.

CLAIMS OF VALUE

Is it good or bad? How good? How bad? Of what worth is it? Is it moral or immoral? Who thinks so? What do those people value? What values or criteria should I use to determine its goodness or badness? Are my values different from other people's or the author's?

Examples:

Online technologies are a valuable addition to modern education.

School prayer has a moral function in the public schools.

Animal rights are as important as human rights.

READERS

▸ Look for claims that make a value statement.

▸ Look for value proofs, motivational proofs, literal and figurative analogies, quotations from authorities, signs, and definitions.

▸ Expect emotional language.

▸ Look for applied criteria, topical, and narrative patterns of organization.

WRITERS

▸ State your claim as a judgment or value statement.

▸ Analyze your audience's needs and values, and appeal to them.

▸ Use literal and figurative analogies, quotations from authorities, signs, and definitions.

▸ Use emotional language appropriately.

▸ Consider the applied criteria, claim with reasons, or narrative organizational patterns.

CLAIMS OF POLICY

What should we do? How should we act? What should future policy be? How can we solve this problem? What course of action should we pursue?

Examples:

The criminal should be sent to prison rather than to a mental hospital.

Sex education should be part of the public school curriculum.

Battered women who take revenge should not be placed in jail.

READERS

▸ **Look for claims** that state that something **should be done.**

▸ Look for statistical data, motivational appeals, literal analogies, and argument from authority.

▸ Anticipate the problem–solution pattern of organization.

WRITERS

▸ **State the claim as something that should be done.**

▸ Use statistical data, motivational appeals, analogies, and authorities as proof.

▸ Use emotional language appropriately.

▸ Consider the problem–solution pattern of organization.

Rogerian Argument: Seeking Common Ground

TRADITIONAL ARGUMENT VERSUS ROGERIAN ARGUMENT

ELEMENT	TRADITIONAL ARGUMENT	ROGERIAN ARGUMENT
Basic strategy	Writer states claims and gives reasons to prove it.	Writer states opponent's claim to show understanding that it is valid.
Ethos	Writer establishes own character by demonstrating competence.	Writer builds own and opponent's *ethos* through empathy.
Logos	Writer appeals to reason to establish a claim.	Writer analyzes the conditions under which both claims are valid.
Pathos	Writer arouses emotions to bolster claim.	Writer uses dispassionate language to cool emotions on both sides.
Goal	Writer seeks to change opponent's mind and win argument.	Writer works toward cooperation and a mutually beneficial outcome.

GOALS OF ROGERIAN ARGUMENT

1. To let readers know they have been understood.
2. To show how readers' positions are valid in certain contexts and under certain conditions.
3. To help readers understand that they and the writer share similar values, types of experience, attitudes, and perceptions.
4. To propose solutions made up of elements from both sides that can be agreed to by both parties.

STEPS FOR WRITING ROGERIAN ARGUMENT

1. Introduce the issue and show that the opponent's position is understood by restating it.
2. Demonstrate in which contexts and under what conditions the opponent's position may be valid.
3. State your own position, including the contexts in which it is valid.
4. State how the opponent's position would benefit if the opponent were to adopt elements of the writer's position.
5. Show how the two positions complement each other and how each supplies what the other lacks.

Types of Proof and Tests of Validity

LOGICAL PROOFS

Do not confuse proofs with support. A proof represents a complete line of argument that includes a claim, support, and warrant. A proof demonstrates a particular way of thinking about and developing the main claim of the argument. The logical proofs have been arranged according to the mnemonic SICDADS: Sign, Induction, Cause, Deduction, Analogies, Definition, Statistics.

WHEN YOU ARE THE READER

Look for clues, symptoms, and occurrences that are explained as signs or symptoms that something is so.

Look for a conclusion or claim based on examples or cases.

Sign

Pointing out the symptoms or signs that something is so.

Example:

Claim: The child has chickenpox.

Support: The child has spots.

Warrant: Those spots are a sign of chickenpox.

Test of Validity: Ask whether this is really a sign of what the author claims, or is there another explanation.

Induction

Drawing a conclusion (claim) from a number of representative cases or examples.

Example:

Claim: Everyone liked that movie.

Support: I know three people who liked it.

Warrant: Three examples are enough.

Tests of Validity: Ask whether there are enough examples, or is this a "hasty" conclusion or claim. Try to think of an exception that would change the conclusion or claim. See if you can make the "inductive leap" from the examples to the conclusion or claim and accept it as probably true.

WHEN YOU ARE THE WRITER

Think of symptoms or signs that you can use to demonstrate that something is so.

Give some examples and draw a conclusion/claim based on them; *or* make the claim and back it up with a series of examples.

Cause

Look for examples, trends, people, or events that are cited as causes for the claim. Look for effects of the claim.

Placing the claim in a cause-and-effect relationship to show that it is either the cause of an effect or an effect of a cause.

Example:

Warrant: Depression in a group of people has increased.

Support: This group of people has also increased its use of the Internet.

Claim/conclusion: The Internet may be causing depression.

Tests of Validity: Ask whether these causes alone are sufficient to create these effects, or is it that these effects result from other causes. Try to think of exceptions to the cause-and-effect outcome.

Make a claim, and ask what caused it.

What was done?

Where was it done?

Who did it?

How was it done?

Why did it happen?

Deduction

Locate or infer the general principle (warrant).

Apply it to the example or case.

Draw a conclusion or claim.

Applying a general principle (warrant) to an example or a case and drawing a conclusion.

Example:

Warrant: Most uneven footprints are left by people who limp.

Support: These footprints are uneven.

Claim: The person who left these footprints walks with a limp.

Test of Validity: Ask whether the general principle (warrant) and the support are probably true, because then the claim is also probably true.

Make a general statement.

Apply it to an example or a case.

Draw a conclusion.

Decide whether to make the general statement (warrant) explicit or implicit.

(continued)

Types of Proof and Tests of Validity *(continued)*

LOGICAL PROOFS

WHEN YOU ARE THE READER

Analogies: Literal, Historical, and Figurative

Interpreting what we do not understand by comparing it with something we do. Literal and historical analogies compare similar items, and figurative analogies compare items from radically different categories.

Example of historical analogy:

Claim: Many people will die of AIDS.

Support: Many people died of the Black Death.

Warrant: AIDS and the Black Death are similar.

Example of literal analogy:

Claim: The state should spend more money on education.

Support: Another state spent more money with good results.

Warrant: The two states are similar, and the results of one will be the results of the other.

Example of figurative analogy:

Claim: Reading a difficult book should take time.

Support: Digesting a large meal takes time.

Warrant: Reading and eating are sufficiently alike that they can be compared.

Tests for Validity: For literal analogies, ask whether the cases are so similar that the results of one will be the results of the other. For historical analogies, ask whether history will repeat itself. For figurative analogies, ask whether the qualities of the items being compared are real enough to provide logical support or are they so dissimilar that they do not prove anything.

WHEN YOU ARE THE WRITER

Literal and historical analogy:

Think of items in the same category that can be compared. Show that what happened in one case will also happen in the other. Or, demonstrate that history repeats itself.

Figurative analogy:

Think of comparisons with items from other categories. Try to compare items that have similar qualities, characteristics, or outcomes.

Literal and historical analogy:

Look for items, events, people, or periods of time that are being compared.

Figurative analogy:

Look for extended metaphors or items being compared that are from totally different categories.

Definition

Look for definitions of key words or concepts.

Definitions can be short (a word or sentence) or long (several paragraphs or an entire essay).

Notice whether the reader is supposed to accept the claim "by definition" because it has been placed in an established category.

Describing the fundamental properties and qualities of a term or placing an item in a category and proving it "by definition."

Example:

Warrant: Family values characterize the good citizen.

Support: Radical feminists lack family values.

Claim: Radical feminists are not good citizens.

Tests of Validity: Ask whether the definition is accurate and reliable, or are there exceptions or other definitions that would make it less reliable. Ask whether the item belongs in the category in which it has been placed.

Define the key terms and concepts in your claim.

Define all other terms that you and your reader must agree on for the argument to work.

Place some ideas or items in established categories and argue that they are so "by definition."

Statistics

Look for numbers, data, and tables of figures along with interpretations of them.

Using figures or data to prove a claim.

Example:

Claim: We should end draft registration.

Support: It costs $27.5 million per year.

Warrant: This is too much; it proves we should end it.

Tests of Validity: Ask where the statistics came from, to what dates they apply, and whether they are fair and accurate. Ask whether they have been exaggerated or skewed. Ask whether they prove what they are supposed to prove.

Find data, statistics, and tables of figures to use as evidence to back up your claim.

Make clear where you find the statistics, and add your interpretations and those of experts.

(continued)

431

Types of Proof and Tests of Validity *(continued)*

PROOF TO ESTABLISH *ETHOS*

WHEN YOU ARE THE READER

Look for references to the author's credentials, background, and training. Look for credential statements about quoted authorities.

Look for references to items or qualities you might need or want and advice on how to get them.

Look for emotional language, description, and tone.

WHEN YOU ARE THE WRITER

Refer to your own experience and background to establish expertise.

Quote the best and most reliable authorities.

Establish common ground and respect by using appropriate language and tone.

Think about what the members of your audience need, and show how your ideas will help them meet these needs.

Use emotional language and tone where appropriate.

Authority

Quoting established authorities or experts or establishing one's own authority and credibility.

Example:

Claim: California will have an earthquake.

Support: Professors and scientists say so.

Warrant: These experts are reliable.

Tests of Validity: Ask whether the experts, including both outside authorities and the author, are really experts. Remember that argument from authority is only as good as the authorities themselves.

EMOTIONAL PROOFS

Motives

Appealing to what all audiences are supposed to need, such as food, drink, warmth, shelter, sex, security, belonging, self-esteem, creativity, and self-expression. Urging audiences to take steps to meet their needs.

Example:

Claim: You should support this candidate.

Support: The candidate can help you get job security and safe neighborhoods.

Warrant: You want job security and safe neighborhoods.

Tests of Validity: Ask whether you really need what the author assumes you need. Ask whether doing what is recommended will satisfy the need as described.

Values

Appealing to what all audiences are supposed to value, such as reliability, honesty, loyalty, industry, patriotism, courage, conviction, faithfulness, dependability, creativity, integrity, freedom, equality, devotion to duty, and acceptance by others.

Example:

Claim: The curriculum should be multicultural.

Support: A multicultural curriculum will contribute to equality and acceptance.

Warrant: You value equality and acceptance.

Tests of Validity: Ask whether you share the author's values. Ask about the effect that differences in values will have on the argument.

Look for examples or narratives that display values.

Infer values (warrants) that are not explicitly stated.

Look for emotional language and tone.

Appeal to your audience's values through warrants, explicit value statements, and narratives that illustrate values.

Use emotional language and tone where appropriate.

Types of Fallacies

FALLACIES IN LOGIC (*LOGOS*)

Arguments that rely on flawed, inconsistent, or contradictory logic

Begging the Question: no support provided by the arguer. The claim is simply restated, over and over again, in one form or another.

Red Herring: irrelevant and misleading support that pulls the audience away from the real argument.

Non Sequitur: conclusion that does not follow from the evidence and the warrant.

Straw Man: falsely attributing an argument to an opponent in order to refute it.

Stacked Evidence: representing only one side of an issue that clearly has two sides.

Manufactured Evidence: using fake evidence to prove a claim.

Either-Or: an oversimplified argument that presents an either-or choice when there are other alternatives.

Post Hoc: "after this, therefore because of this," a claim that asserts a faulty cause.

Hasty Generalization: a claim that bases its conclusion on too few examples.

FALLACIES THAT AFFECT CHARACTER (*ETHOS*)

Arguments that attack the character of an arguer rather than provide evidence for proof

Ad Hominem: attacking a person's character rather than a person's ideas or policies.

Guilt by Association: suggesting that people's characters can be judged by examining the characters of their associates.

Using Authority Instead of Evidence: relying on personal authority to prove a point rather than evidence.

EMOTIONAL FALLACIES (*PATHOS*)

Arguments that rely on irrelevant, unrelated, and distracting emotion to make their point

Bandwagon Appeal: an argument that says everyone is doing something, so you should, too.

Slippery Slope: suggesting that if we allow one thing to happen, we will immediately be sliding down a slippery slope to disaster.

Creating False Needs: creating a false sense of need where none exists.

Distorted Emotional Appeal: using irrelevant or unrelated emotional examples to prove a point.

PART 5

The Reader

Introduction to The Reader
Reading and Writing About Issue Areas

The Reader contains seven sections that introduce you to broad issue areas that engage modern society: families and personal relationships; technology; school and education; race, culture, and identity; the environment; immigration; and war and peace. Essays are then organized under specific related issues in each broad category. The Reader contains essays that explore some of the individual perspectives and positions people have taken in regard to these issues. You may expand your information and understanding of these issues by doing additional research and reading in other reliable sources on the Internet, in the library, or elsewhere. Web sites that provide a starting point for further online research appear in the introduction to each issue area of The Reader.

Purpose of The Reader

The Reader serves three main purposes:

1. It introduces you to big issue areas and a few specific related issues. It also helps you build background and provides you with information to quote in your papers.

2. It provides you with models of different types of arguments and thus gives you a better idea of how argument works in general. It provides you with examples and strategies for improving your own written arguments. (See Table 1.)

3. It helps you invent arguments of your own by providing you with essays that function as springboards for your own thoughts and reactions.

Table 1   **Examples of Argument Strategies in Reader Articles**

STRATEGY	EXAMPLES
Argument papers	**Exploratory:** Morozov, 469; Mead (paragraphs 1–3), 581. **Rogerian:** Jain, 456; James, 576. **Position:** Yemma, 462; Steinberg, 473.
Claims	**Fact:** Jaschik, 493; Carey, 496; Kelley, 561. **Definition:** Pederson, 441; Weiss, 452; Kirschenbaum, 476; Cottom, 491. **Cause:** Moosa, 449; Carr, 466. **Value:** McWilliams, 533. **Policy:** Perez, 500; Soper, 503; Reid/Paul, 559. **Qualified claim:** Carter, 550; Goldberg, 565.
Language and style	**Language that appeals to logic:** Pederson, 441. **Language that appeals to emotion:** Soper, 503. **Language that develops *ethos*:** Jain, 456; Viertel, 535.
Organizational patterns	**Claim plus reasons:** Ali, 442; Steinberg, 473; Mead, 581. **Chronological or narrative:** Kurzweil, 479; Dilday, 515. **Compare and contrast:** Kirschenbaum, 476; Goldberg, 565. **Problem–solution:** Silver, 498; Soper, 503.
Proofs: *Ethos*	**Self as authority:** Pederson, 441; Jain, 456; Dilday, 515. **Quoted authorities:** Lozada, 525.
Proofs: *Logos*	**Sign:** Soper, 503; Watzman, 591. **Induction:** Dilday, 515; Mead (see paragraphs 4–8), 581. **Cause:** Mead, 581. **Deduction:** Smith, 517; James, 576. **Analogy:** Cooper, 556; Kelley, 561; Goldberg, 565. **Definition:** Cooper, 556; Mead, 581.
Proofs: *Pathos*	**Motives:** Kurzweil, 479. **Values:** Ali, 442; Halper, 523.
Adaptation to rhetorical situation	Pederson, 441; Hassler, 455; Watzman, 591.
Support	**Examples:** Ali, 442; Jain, 456; Kurzweil, 479; Orenstein, 482. **Facts:** Price, 543; Kelley, 561. **Narration:** Jain, 456; Orenstein, 482; Kondo, 518. **Personal examples and narratives:** Pederson, 441; Halper, 523; Pierce, 588. **Images:** Orenstein, 482; Price, 543.
Warrants	Smith, 517; Kondo, 518.
Backing for warrants	Halper, 523.

How to Use The Reader

1. Select an issue area that is compelling for you. Understand why it is compelling. Assess your background on it. Anticipate ways to build common ground with those who oppose you.

2. Survey it: Read the titles and summaries of the articles in the table of contents, read the introductory material and "The Rhetorical Situation" at the beginning of the issue area, and read the introductions to the articles.

3. Select the specific related issue that interests you the most.

4. Read the articles about the related issue, and jot down the claim and some of the major support and warrants for each article.

5. Make a map or write a list of all of the smaller issues that you think are related to the issue you have read about. Discover the aspect of the issue that interests you the most. This will be your issue.

6. Understand the perspectives presented by the articles in The Reader on your issue. You may also want to do outside research. Write an exploratory paper in which you explain at least three perspectives on your issue.

7. Take a position on your issue, and phrase it as a question.

8. State your claim, clarify your purpose, and plan and write an argument paper that presents your position on the issue.

QUESTIONS TO HELP YOU READ CRITICALLY AND ANALYTICALLY

1. What is at issue?
2. What is the claim? What type of claim is it?
3. What is the support?
4. What are the warrants?
5. What are the weaknesses in the argument, and how can I refute them?
6. What are some other perspectives on the issue?
7. Where do I stand now in regard to this issue?

QUESTIONS TO HELP YOU READ CREATIVELY AND MOVE FROM READING TO WRITING

1. What is my exigence for writing about this topic?
2. What is my general position compared to the author's?
3. With which specific ideas do I agree or disagree?
4. Do the essays confirm what I think, or do they cause me to change my mind?
5. What original or related ideas occur to me as I read?

6. What original perspective can I take?

7. What type of claim do I want to make?

8. What can I quote, paraphrase, or summarize in my paper?

SECTION 1
Families and Personal Relationships

The Issues

A. **What Is the Status of the Traditional American Family? How Is the Family Being Redefined?**

According to older, and increasingly outmoded, stereotypes, the "traditional family" is a unit composed of a man and a woman—the man acting as the breadwinner and the woman as the homemaker—plus children. In different ways, the articles in this section challenge and rethink this definition. In her essay, Sarah Yoest Pederson offers a different perspective on same-sex parenting and therefore on the concept of family itself. Lorraine Ali's essay, "The Curious Lives of Surrogates," meanwhile, considers why some mothers and fathers have chosen to redefine their relationship to traditional notions of family. And finally, Tauriq Moosa ("We Need to Have a Frank Discussion About Marriage") calls for a radical reevaluation of the ways we think about marriage and commitment in the modern age.

B. **What Causes Personal Relationships to Succeed or Fail?**

The articles in this section take a close look at how relationships are constructed in today's world and considers what makes them either successful or difficult to establish and sustain. In "Unmasking the Neurobiology of Love," therapist Robert Weiss explores the physiological basis of romantic love. In "Digital Dating," Christine Hassler looks at the role online technology has played in changing the social mores of courtship. The next two articles expand our idea of personal relationships by considering the role of arranged marriages for contemporary young people in America (Anita Jain) and by exploring evolving attitudes toward love, sex, and marriage among the so-called Millennial generation (John Yemma).

Exploring Online Argument

The following Web sites present interesting perspectives on families and personal relationships.

All Family Resources™	Family Equality Council
Children and Family Research Center	Coalition for Marriage and Families
Harvard Family Research Project	MarriageEqualityUSA
National Marriage Project	American Association for Family and Marriage Therapy
National Fatherhood Initiative	CYFERnet (Children, Youth, and Families Educational and Research Network)
Relationship Web	AdoptUSKids
National Association of Mothers' Centers	

The Rhetorical Situation

The organization of families and the nature and quality of human relationships have always been a source of controversy. The world's religions, along with different social customs and traditions, provide both the constraints and some of the warrants for the positions that many individuals take on issues associated with families and personal relationships. This is particularly true in the case of marriage as a social and religious institution. Much of the controversy centers around the ideal—or, from some perspectives, the myth—of the happy, healthy American nuclear family consisting of one man, one woman, and an unspecified number of children.

In Shakespeare's day, marriages were arranged, largely by the bride and groom's families, on the grounds that elders were more knowledgeable about relationships and that families were the best resource for ensuring a comfortable, stable, and financially healthy marriage. Numerous cultures across the globe rely on arranged marriages, and many members of those cultures, both here and abroad, continue to negotiate their way between traditional customs and emerging concepts of romance, dating, and marriage. Finally, many kinds of nontraditional families—single-parent or same-sex–parent families, blended families created by remarriage, multigenerational families, grandparent-led families, adoptive families, and even commuter families—are not necessarily new in America, but are receiving more attention, both positive and negative, from politicians, psychologists, and community activists.

While multiple models for family structure have, to some extent, always existed, romantic and familial relations probably have undergone a more radical change in the twentieth and twenty-first centuries. Some people think that the women's movement in the second half of the twentieth century changed what women and men expect from one another, although that process probably began much earlier. Nevertheless, such events as women's acquisition of the right to vote (1920), the entrance of women into the workforce during World War II, and the eventually unsuccessful fight in the 1970s for the Equal Rights Amendment pushed both men and women to reevaluate their social roles. Social customs and the law have begun to reflect some of these changes. The legal status of single-sex marriage in the United States remains unresolved. On the other hand, the Family and Medical Leave Act of 1993 allows an employee of either gender to take up to twelve weeks of unpaid leave from work to care for a new baby, a newly adopted child, or a sick spouse, child, or parent; thus, the definition of family acknowledged in this legislation is broad.

The science of romance has also been a subject of much attention. While Romeo and Juliet may have fallen in love at first sight, for ordinary humans, factors ranging from hormone production to smell help to bring human beings together. Not merely the sexual drive but romance itself is influenced by the body's chemistry, for Mother Nature wants humans not only to reproduce but also to stick together and raise their offspring to maturity, a process that takes at least eighteen years. Even that most idealized symbol of romantic love, the kiss, not only unleashes a chemical cocktail that releases stress and promotes social bonding, but it also communicates information about the genetic compatibility of two people as potential mates. Some modern young people embrace science as a way to find a life partner, while others turn to the Internet, and still others return to traditional methods such as arranged marriage or engaging a matchmaker.

A. What Is the Status of the Traditional American Family? How Is the Family Being Redefined?

> **BEFORE YOU READ:** Think of a childhood book or story that you remember fondly or know well. How does that narrative describe children's relations to parents or other adults in the family?

A FAMILY OF A DIFFERENT FEATHER*

Sarah Yoest Pederson

Sarah Yoest Pederson is Op-Ed editor for the *Fort Worth Star-Telegram*.

There are books on the most-challenged list that probably won't surprise you—works with sexually explicit language, stories that contain violence. But that last year's most-challenged book was the children's story *And Tango Makes Three* makes me a bit sad. We could have used it at our house last fall.

I'm a mom of two, one of whom is a voracious reader. She's also 5, and a lot of books that she might be ready for intellectually aren't really appropriate for her emotionally. *Tango* is. And it would have been a godsend a year ago, when the debate about same-sex couples hit home.

The Princess had a classmate—let's call him Sam—who happens to have two moms. My husband and I had talked about that and decided that the best way to respond, if Her Highness ever raised the topic, was something simple: "Well, honey, there are lots of ways to be a family. We happen to think our way works best for us. [Sam's] moms feel like theirs works best for them."

Dodging the Larger Issue? Maybe. But c'mon—kids that age are egocentric little things. Other peoples' sexuality isn't something they're going to spend a lot of time on. . . . "Hey, Mom," came the voice from the back seat. "How can [Sam] have two moms and no dad? Doesn't every baby have to have a dad?"

5   I took a deep breath and started in.

"Well, you're right—God takes a seed from the mom and a seed from the dad to make a baby. But with [Sam's] family, the dad isn't there now. There are all kinds of ways to be a family. Daddy and I think our way is best for our family. [Sam's] moms probably think their way is best for their family."

She didn't spend much time chewing on that, picking out the unanswered questions in the deliberately vague answer. "Oh," she said. "I get it." She paused. "Can I open my presents as soon as we get home?" And that was that.

Little Tango "was the very first penguin in the zoo to have two daddies," the book says. In classrooms all across this country, there are kids in Tango's boat. And straight parents would be well-served to read the book and figure out how they'll respond when the issue is raised in their home. Of course, to do that, they'd have to be able to find it. I tried six large bookstores; finally, at the seventh, I got the only copy they had.

There are lots of ways to be a family. And there are lots of ways to lead a family. You can choose to acknowledge differences and to show respect for love and kindness, as *Tango* does, or you can choose to act like a bird of a different feather.

10   It's called an ostrich.

BEFORE YOU READ: What assumptions or associations do you bring to the role of surrogate parenting? In what ways does this role challenge the ways family is traditionally defined?

THE CURIOUS LIVES OF SURROGATES*

Lorraine Ali

Lorraine Ali is a contributing editor for *Newsweek* who has written extensively about culture and the arts since joining the magazine in 2000.

Jennifer Cantor, a 34-year-old surgical nurse from Huntsville, Ala., loves being pregnant. Not *having* children, necessarily—she has one, an 8-year-old daughter named Dahlia, and has no plans for another—but just the experience of

---

growing a human being beneath her heart. She was fascinated with the idea of it when she was a child, spending an entire two-week vacation, at the age of 11, with a pillow stuffed under her shirt. She's built perfectly for it: six feet tall, fit and slender but broad-hipped. Which is why she found herself two weeks ago in a birthing room in a hospital in Huntsville, swollen with two six-pound boys she had been carrying for eight months. Also in the room was Kerry Smith and his wife, Lisa, running her hands over the little lumps beneath the taut skin of Cantor's belly. "That's an elbow," said Cantor, who knew how the babies were lying in her womb. "Here's a foot." Lisa smiled proudly at her husband. She is, after all, the twins' mother.

It is an act of love, but also a financial transaction, that brings people together like this. For Kerry and for Lisa—who had a hysterectomy at the age of 20 and could never bear her own children—the benefits are obvious: Ethan and Jonathan, healthy six-pound, 12-ounce boys born by C-section on March 20. But what about Cantor? She was paid, of course; the Smiths declined to discuss the exact amount, but typically, surrogacy agreements in the United States involve payments of $20,000 to $25,000 to the woman who bears the child. She enjoyed the somewhat naughty pleasure of telling strangers who asked about her pregnancy, "Oh, they aren't mine," which invariably invoked the question, "Did you have sex with the father?" (In case anyone is wondering, Lisa's eggs were fertilized in vitro with Kerry's sperm before they were implanted on about day five.) But what kind of woman would carry a child to term, only to hand him over moments after birth? Surrogates challenge our most basic ideas about motherhood, and call into question what we've always thought of as an unbreakable bond between mother and child. It's no wonder many conservative Christians decry the practice

as tampering with the miracle of life, while far-left feminists liken gestational carriers to prostitutes who degrade themselves by renting out their bodies. Some medical ethicists describe the process of arranging surrogacy as "baby brokering," while rumors circulate that self-obsessed, shallow New Yorkers have their babies by surrogate to avoid stretch marks. Much of Europe bans the practice, and 12 states, including New York, New Jersey and Michigan, refuse to recognize surrogacy contracts. But in the past five years, four states—Texas, Illinois, Utah and Florida—have passed laws legalizing surrogacy, and Minnesota is considering doing the same. More than a dozen states, including Pennsylvania, Massachusetts and, most notably, California, specifically legalize and regulate the practice.

Today, a greater acceptance of the practice, and advances in science, find more women than ever before having babies for those who cannot. In the course of reporting this story, we discovered that many of these women are military wives who have taken on surrogacy to supplement the family income, some while their husbands are serving overseas. Several agencies reported a significant increase in the number of wives of soldiers and naval personnel applying to be surrogates since the invasion of Iraq in 2003. At the high end, industry experts estimate there were about 1,000 surrogate births in the United States last year, while the Society for Assisted Reproductive Technology (SART)—the only organization that makes an effort to track surrogate births—counted about 260 in 2006, a 30 percent increase over three years. But the number is surely much higher than this—in just five of the agencies *NEWSWEEK* spoke to, there were 400 surrogate births in 2007. The numbers vary because at least 15 percent of clinics—and there are dozens of them across the United States—don't report numbers to SART. Private agreements made outside an agency aren't counted, and the figures do not factor in pregnancies in which one of the intended parents does not provide the egg—for example, where the baby will be raised by a gay male couple. Even though the cost to the intended parents, including medical and legal bills, runs from $40,000 to $120,000, the demand for qualified surrogates is well ahead of supply.

Another reason for the rise in surrogacies is that technology has made them safer and more likely to succeed. Clinics such as Genetics & IVF Institute in Virginia, where Cantor and the Smiths underwent their IVF cycles, now boast a 70 to 90 percent pregnancy success rate—up 40 percent in the past decade. Rather than just putting an egg into a petri dish with thousands of sperm and hoping for a match, embryologists can inject a single sperm directly into the egg. The great majority of clinics can now test embryos for genetic diseases before implantation. It's revolutionizing the way clinics treat patients. Ric Ross, lab director at La Jolla IVF in San Diego, says these advances have helped "drop IVF miscarriage rates by 85 percent."

5   IVF has been around only since the 1970s, but the idea of one woman bearing a baby for another is as old as civilization. Surrogacy was regulated in the Code of Hammurabi, dating from 1800 B.C., and appears several times in the Hebrew Bible. In the 16th chapter of Genesis, the infertile Sarah gives her servant, Hagar, to her husband, Abraham, to bear a child for them. Later, Jacob fathers children by the maids of his wives Leah and Rachel, who raise them as their own. It is also possible to view the story of Jesus' birth as a case of surrogacy, mediated not by a lawyer but an angel, though in that instance the birth mother did raise the baby.

The most celebrated case of late, though, resulted in the legal and ethical morass known as the "Baby M" affair. Mary Beth Whitehead, age 29 in 1986, gave birth to a girl she had agreed to carry for an infertile couple. But Whitehead was also the baby's biological mother and tried to keep her after the birth, leading to a two-year custody battle. (In the end, she was denied custody but awarded visitation rights.) As a result, surrogacy agreements now almost always stipulate that the woman who carries the baby cannot also donate the egg.

But even as surrogacy is becoming less of a "Jerry Springer" spectacle and more of a viable family option for those who can afford it, the culture still stereotypes surrogates as either hicks or opportunists whose ethics could use some fine-tuning. Even pop culture has bought into the caricature. In the upcoming feature film "Baby Mama," a single businesswoman (Tina Fey) is told by a doctor she is infertile. She hires a working-class gal (Amy Poehler) to be her surrogate. The client is a savvy, smart and well-to-do health-store-chain exec while Poehler is an unemployed, deceitful wild child who wants easy money.

When Fey's character refers to her surrogate as "white trash," we're supposed to laugh. "I just don't understand how they can think that," says surrogate Gina Scanlon of the stereotypes that influenced the film. Scanlon, 40, is a married mother of three who lives in Pittsburgh. Scanlon is also a working artist and illustrator who gave birth to twin girls for a gay New Jersey couple 18 months ago. The couple—a college professor and a certified public accountant—chose Scanlon because she was "emotionally stable," with a husband and children of her own. Unlike egg donors, who are usually in their 20s, healthy women as old as 40 can serve as surrogates; Scanlon two weeks ago underwent an embryo transfer and is now pregnant again for a new set of intended parents. "Poor or desperate women wouldn't qualify [with surrogacy agencies]," she says. As for the implication that surrogates are in it only for the money, she notes that there are many easier jobs than carrying a baby 24 hours a day, seven days a week.

(And most jobs don't run the risk of making you throw up for weeks at a time, or keep you from drinking if you feel like it.) "If you broke it down by the hour," Scanlon says wryly, "it would barely be minimum wage. I mean, have [these detractors] ever met a gestational carrier?" And even if they have, how would they know?

Very little is understood about the world of the surrogate. That's why we talked to dozens of women across America who are, or have been, gestational carriers. What we found is surprising and defies stereotyping. The experiences of this vast group of women—including a single mom from Murrietta, Calif., a military spouse from Glen Burnie, Md., and a small-business owner from Dallas—range from the wonderful and life-affirming to the heart-rending. One surrogate, Scanlon, is the godmother of the twins she bore, while another still struggles because she has little contact with the baby she once carried. Some resent being told what to eat or drink; others feel more responsible bearing someone else's child than they did with their own. Their motivations are varied: one upper-middle-class carrier in California said that as a child she watched a family member suffer with infertility and wished she could help. A working-class surrogate from Idaho said it was the only way her family could afford things they never could before, like a $6,000 trip to Disney World. But all were agreed that the grueling IVF treatments, morning sickness, bed rest, C-sections and stretch marks were worth it once they saw their intended parent hold the child, or children (multiples are common with IVF), for the first time. "Being a surrogate is like giving an organ transplant to someone," says Jennifer Cantor, "only before you die, and you actually get to see their joy."

10   That sense of empowerment and self-worth is one of the greatest rewards surrogate mothers experience. "I felt like, 'What else am I going to do with my life that means so much?'" says Amber Boersma, 30, of Wausau, Wis. She is blond, outgoing and six months pregnant with twins for a couple on the East Coast who could not bear children on their own due to a hysterectomy. Boersma, married to a pharmaceutical rep, is a stay-at-home mom with a 6-year-old girl and 4-year-old boy, and a college graduate with a communications degree. "Some people can be successful in a major career, but I thought I do not want to go through this life meaning nothing, and I want to do something substantial for someone else. I want to make a difference."

Then there's the money. Military wife Gernisha Myers, 24, says she was looking through the local San Diego PennySaver circular for a job when she saw the listing: "Surrogate Mothers Wanted! Up to $20,000 Compensation!" The full-time mother of two thought it would be a great way to make money from home, and it would give her that sense of purpose she'd lacked since she left her job as an X-ray technician in Phoenix. In 2004, Myers and her husband, Tim, a petty officer third class in the Navy, were transferred from Arizona to California. Ever since, she missed bringing home a paycheck, helping other people—and being pregnant. She loved the feel of her belly with a baby inside, and the natural high that comes from "all those rushing hormones." So last fall she signed with one of the many surrogacy agencies near the 32nd Street Naval Station, where her husband is assigned. Her grandmother was not pleased with Myers's decision. "She said, 'Gernisha! We just do not do that in this family,'" recalls Myers. "My uncle even said he was disgusted. But you know what? I'm OK with it because I know I am doing something good for somebody else. I am giving another couple what they could never have on their own—a family."

Like Myers, military wives are largely young stay-at-home moms who've completed their own families before they hit 28.

IVF clinics and surrogate agencies in Texas and California say military spouses make up 50 percent of their carriers. "In the military, we have that mentality of going to extremes, fighting for your country, risking your life," says Jennifer Hansen, 25, a paralegal who's married to Army Sgt. Chase Hansen. They live in Lincoln, Neb., and have two young kids, and Chase has been deployed to Iraq for two of the past five years. "I think that being married to someone in the military embeds those values in you. I feel I'm taking a risk now, in less of a way than he is, but still a risk with my life and body to help someone." Surrogate agencies target the population by dropping leaflets in the mailboxes of military housing complexes, such as those around San Diego's Camp Pendleton, and placing ads in on-base publications such as the *Military Times* and *Military Spouse*. Now surrogate agencies say they are solicited by ad reps from these publications. Military wives who do decide to become surrogates can earn more with one pregnancy than their husbands' annual base pay (which ranges for new enlistees from $16,080 to $28,900). "Military wives can't sink their teeth into a career because they have to move around so much," says Melissa Brisman of New Jersey, a lawyer who specializes in reproductive and family issues, and heads the largest surrogacy firm on the East Coast. "But they still want to contribute, do something positive. And being a carrier only takes a year—that gives them enough time between postings."

Dawne Dill, 32, was a high-school English teacher before she married her husband, Travis, a Navy chief, and settled in Maryland. She's now a full-time mother with two boys of her own, and is carrying twins for a European couple who prefer to remain anonymous. Dill is due in May. The attraction of surrogacy for her, apart from wanting to feel useful, was that the money could help pay for an occupational-therapy gym for her older son, who is autistic. "We're thinking of building the gym in our basement so he can get to it whenever he needs," says Dill. She worried that having an autistic child might disqualify her as a surrogate, but fortunately the agency was unconcerned. "They said because I was not genetically related to the twins, that it was just not an issue, and my IPs [intended parents] never brought it up to me personally. I assume they're OK with it, but maybe think it's too touchy of a subject to discuss openly with me," says Dill. As a prepartum gift, the couple sent Dawne and her husband to the Super Bowl.

Military wives are attractive candidates because of their health insurance, Tricare, which is provided by three different companies—Humana, TriWest and Health Net Federal Services—and has some of the most comprehensive coverage for surrogates in the industry. Fertility agencies know this, and may offer a potential surrogate with this health plan an extra $5,000. Last year military officials asked for a provision in the 2008 defense authorization bill to cut off coverage for any medical procedures related to surrogate pregnancy. They were unsuccessful—there are no real data on how much the government spends on these cases. Tricare suggests that surrogate mothers who receive payment for their pregnancy should declare the amount they're receiving, which can then be deducted from their coverage. But since paid carriers have no incentive to say anything, most don't. "I was told by multiple people—congressional staff, doctors and even ordinary taxpayers—that they overheard conversations of women bragging about how easy it was to use Tricare coverage to finance surrogacy and delivery costs and make money on the side," says Navy Capt. Patricia Buss, who recently left the Defense Department and now holds a senior position with Health Net Federal Services. The subject of Tricare surrogacy coverage is becoming a hot topic throughout the military world; on Web sites such as militarySOS.com, bloggers with sign-on names such as "Ms. Ordinance" and "ProudArmyWife" fiercely debate the subject.

15   Surrogacy is not just an American debate—it is global. Thanks to reproductive science, Gernisha Myers, who is African-American, is now 18 weeks pregnant with the twins of Karin and Lars, a white couple who live in Germany. They are one of many international couples who turned to America to solve their infertility issues because surrogacy is not allowed in their own country. Couples have come to the United States from many countries, including Iceland, Canada, France, Japan, Saudi Arabia, Israel, Australia, Spain and Dubai, in recent years. Although some couples are now turning to India for cheaper fertility solutions—yes, even surrogacy is being outsourced at a tenth of the price—the trend has yet to diminish America's draw as a baby mecca.

Karin and Lars picked Myers after they read her agency profile. Myers says that the psychological screening is one of the most grueling, invasive and odd parts of the process. "The [questionnaire] asked some weird questions, like 'Do you think about killing people sometimes?' Or 'Would you want to be a mountain ranger if you could?' Or 'Do you find yourself happier than most?' But when they asked 'Are you afraid you're going to get attached to the babies?' I said, 'In a way, yes, even though I know they're not mine.' They said, 'Believe it or not, some GCs [gestational carriers] never feel any kind of bond.' I found that hard to believe back then, but now I know what they're talking about. I don't feel that motherly bond. I feel more like a caring babysitter."

Myers's psychological detachment has a lot to do with the fact that, like most carriers today, she's in no way biologically related to the baby inside her—the legacy of the "Baby M" case. The most recent significant case involving a surrogacy dispute, *Johnson v. Calvert* in 1993, was resolved in favor of the intended parents, and against a surrogate who wanted to keep the baby. John Weltman, president of Circle Surrogacy in Boston, says that parents who work with a reputable agency have a "99 percent chance of getting a baby and a 100 percent chance of keeping it." But up until just about two years ago, Weltman says every single intended parent asked, "Will she [the carrier] try and keep the baby?" Now, he says, a third of his clients don't even mention it.

That doesn't mean that it's gotten any easier for the surrogate to give up the baby. Most gestational carriers say it is still the hardest part of the job, and some have a rougher time than others. Gina Scanlon recalls the days after the birth of her first pair of surrogate twins: "When you go home it's so quiet," she says. "The crash comes. It's not the baby blues. It's not postpartum depression. It's that the performance is over. I was practically a celebrity during the pregnancy—someone was always asking me questions. After I had them, no one was calling. Now nobody cares. You're out. You're done. It's the most vain thing. I felt guilty and selfish and egotistical."

Stephanie Scott also found that life after surrogacy was not what she expected, especially since everything hummed along so nicely when she was pregnant. Seven and a half months in, she was feeling great—all except for those damn nesting urges. The stay-at-home mom tried to stay out of the baby stores and avoid those sweet pink onesies and baby booties shaped like tiny ballet slippers—but it was near impossible to resist. Her mind-set should have served as a warning. Although she knew the baby in her swollen belly belonged to a couple on the East Coast, she hadn't prepared herself for that biological surge that keeps stores like Babies 'R' Us in business. "I showed up to the delivery room with six months' worth of baby clothes," admits Scott, 28. "They ended up being my gift to the baby's intended parents. Sort of like a baby shower in reverse. I know, it's weird." But that was nothing compared to the childbirth: "When she was born, they handed her to me for a second," she says. "I couldn't look, so I closed my eyes tight, counted 10 fingers and 10 toes, then gave her away. I cried for a month straight. I was devastated."

20   The baby Scott gave birth to is now 3, and photos of the toddler come twice a year, on the child's birthday and Christmas. Scott says she thinks things would have been different had she been counseled more by the agency on attachment issues, but it was a small and less than professional operation (and there are plenty of those in the unregulated world of surrogacy agencies). It's one of the reasons Scott opened her own business in Dallas, Simple Surrogacy. "I would never just throw a girl out there like that. Surrogates need to know what lies ahead."

Any comprehensive road map of surrogacy should include not just potential attachment but an entire pull-down sheet on the second most difficult area of terrain: the relationship between surrogate and intended parent. The intentions and expectations of both parties are supposed to be ironed out ahead of time through a series of agency questionnaires and meetings. What kind of bond do they seek with one another—distant, friendly, close? Do they agree on difficult moral issues, like abortion and selective termination? And what requests do the IPs have of potential carriers? The parties are then matched by the agency, just as singles would be through a dating service. And the intended parents— or parent—are as diverse as the surrogates: gay, straight, single, married, young and old. Much of the time it works, even though it does often resemble an experiment in cross-cultural studies. "In what other world would you find a conservative military wife forming a close bond with a gay couple from Paris?" says Hilary Hanafin, chief psychologist for the oldest agency in the country, Center for Surrogate Parenting. And a good match doesn't necessarily equal a tight

connection like that of Jennifer Cantor's and Lisa Smith's. Christina Slason, 29, who delivered a boy in January for same-sex partners from Mexico City, felt as the couple did—that a close relationship was not necessary. "We agreed that we would keep in touch, but neither of us felt the need to really bond," says Slason, a mother of three who lives in San Diego with her husband, Joseph, a Navy corpsman. "We were there to have a baby, nothing more. We were all clear on that."

But things are not always that clear. For Joseph, a single father from Massachusetts who asked to be identified only by his first name for privacy reasons, the process of finding a suitable surrogate on his own was frustrating, particularly when the first match got cold feet and pulled out. Intended parents Tamara and Joe Bove were troubled when the carrier for their triplets refused to go on bed rest even when a doctor advised her the babies' lives would be at risk if she did not: "She had delivered monstrously large twins vaginally before, even though one of them was breech. So she was kind of surprised that this could happen to her and just wouldn't cooperate." Tamara was plagued with worry. "Our plan was to keep in touch even after the babies were born, but then she stopped listening to the doctors. But you still have to keep acting like everything is fine because she's in control until the babies are born." (Despite Tamara's worries, the triplets were born healthy at 31 weeks via a C-section.)

Control, not surprisingly, is a sore point. A favorite pastime among surrogates—most of whom join support groups at the request of their agencies—is sharing stories of the most bizarre IP requests they've heard. One military surrogate was told if her husband was deployed anywhere in Asia, she was not to have sex with him when he returned for fear that he was unfaithful and carrying an STD.

Jennifer Hansen, the surrogate from Nebraska, says she had a few requests from her intended parents that were odd to her "as a Midwestern girl." Hansen says she's been asked not to pump her own gas. "They believe it leads to miscarriage," she says. "I've also been asked to change my cleaning supplies to all green, natural products. I'm a Clorox girl, and have no idea where to even buy these products. So they just box them up and send them to me from California." What most surrogates don't realize, according to Margaret Little, a professor of philosophy at Georgetown University and fellow at the Kennedy School of Ethics, is that the contracts governing their conduct during the pregnancy are not enforceable. She does have to surrender the baby once he's born, but cannot be forced to have (or not have) an abortion, or to obey restrictions on what she can eat, drink or do. The intended parents' only recourse is to withhold payment; they cannot police her conduct. "Surrogacy raises important red flags," Little says, "because you are selling use of the body, and historically when that's happened, that hasn't been good for women."

25   On the other hand, other agencies reported that some concerned surrogates

have pumped and shipped their breast milk to the intended parents weeks after the birth out of fear that the newborn will not build a strong immune system without it.

As for Jennifer Cantor, resting at home last week after delivering Jonathan and Ethan, she intends to stay in touch with the family whose lives are now inextricably bound up with hers. Before returning to their home in Georgia, Lisa and Kerry brought the twins for a visit with the stranger who bore them, and with Cantor's daughter, Dahlia, whose relationship to them doesn't even have a word in the language yet. Lisa described her babies as "the true meaning of life . . . absolutely perfect." Next time they're hoping for girls. They're also hoping to find someone like Cantor—who, however, does not plan to be a surrogate again, much as she enjoyed it. She is relieved that she can sit normally and put her arms around Dahlia again, without a big belly in between them. She was happy that she had been able to fulfill her dream of bearing a child for someone else. "It was exactly," she said last week, "the experience I imagined it would be."

BEFORE YOU READ: Are the social norms around marriage changing? In your view, are these changes for the better?

WE NEED TO HAVE A FRANK DISCUSSION ABOUT MARRIAGE*

Tauriq Moosa

Tauriq Moosa is a regular contributor for *The Guardian*. He is also a tutor in bioethics at the University of Cape Town in South Africa. This essay appeared in the online version of *The Guardian* in 2014.

When a formerly happy couple calls it quits, who gets the Farmville money in the divorce settlement?

Technology permeates nearly every inch of life today, including love and marriage. The Internet provides ways for singles to

---

meet, gadgets and devices present opportunities and challenges to married couples, and increasingly social media plays a key role in the break-up of previously happy unions.

In addition to facilitating the love and marriage dance, technology—in the form of both gadgets and data—is becoming a contentious element in the process of splitting up. Questions like who gets the iPad in a divorce are now more complicated, running into issues like: who has cloud access to the family data, who owns the virtual assets in Farmville and how to split up Facebook friends.

Internet's "Love Story" Turns into "Defending Your Life"

People have been using sites like eHarmony and Match.com to meet up for over a decade now. But just as the Internet can grant love in a lasting online connection, it can take it away in a nasty status update, a gossipy text, or an indiscreet picture posting.

5   Social media sites like Facebook and Twitter have ballooned in popularity with everyone and their mother, brother, sister and even their grandma joining in on the fun.

With so many people sharing so much on a site many perceived to be private, these online places became fertile flirting ground. Earlier this year, a survey revealed the extent of this misbehavior, saying one-third of divorce cases in England implicated Facebook. The 5,000 people polled cited three reasons for listing the social network in divorce petitions—sending inappropriate messages to the opposite sex, posting negative comments about exes on the social network, and friends disclosing a spouse's behavior.

In March, the American Academy of Matrimonial Lawyers found 80 percent of divorce cases included social media posts, mostly from Facebook, as evidence in the past five years.

There are even tools for those trying to hide their bad behavior, a telling sign that there is a problem. Apps like "iWipe" erase all evidence of "digital lipstick," by deleting stored data and preventing the tracking of its members' activities on the site. The app is created by a dating site, whose slogan "Life is short. Have an affair," underscores its mission to help users shield data from suspecting spouses.

And once couples file the divorce papers, social media continues to play a paramount role as couples, and now their attorneys, sift through these feeds to bolster their claims of infidelity in divorce cases and parental deficits in custody disputes.

10   The situation is at the point where divorcing couples are being ordered to share their Facebook passwords and other online accounts, underscoring their importance in family court cases.

For example, a Connecticut judge issued the order in response to the husband's revelation his wife wrote incriminating posts on Facebook about her feelings towards the children and her ability to care for them on the couple's shared computer. Wife Courtney Gallion was also ordered to hand over passwords for her eHarmony and Match.com accounts.

Some may see the judge's order in the Gallion case as court-sanctioned hacking, but others see it as a reasonable request for a relevant piece of a family court puzzle. Regardless of the viewpoint, the reality is as people increasingly welcome technology to bind their families together, there will be a reckoning when there is a decision to split apart.

Divvying Up the Digital Assets

In the case of a divorce, what happens to this virtual property a couple has acquired together?

Splitting up today means couples need to consider what to do with items beyond pots, pans, pictures, music collections, and other testaments to a life once shared. It extends to technology devices like smartphones, tablets, laptops, Xbox, and more complicated and intangible items like iTunes and Flickr accounts, Twitter followers, and even gaming avatars and virtual goods.

15   The process is simpler if each person in a couple kept things separately—simply unfriend the hostile in-laws and others who side with the ex and reset privacy settings. Also, if you didn't mingle your iTunes account with a spouse and continued to maintain your own file sharing system, for example, it is a little clearer.

But, for couples who have merged all their technology, share social media accounts and maybe even store it all conveniently in one giant, familial cloud, then the situation is murkier. In a contentious divorce, details on how to divide digital goods like a shared photo site or an extensive movie streaming library will increasingly be addressed in divorce agreements and separation plans.

Beyond this, another technologically thorny issue facing divorcing families is how to settle virtual assets, which are non-physical objects that Internet users buy for use in online communities and games.

In Farmville, Second Life and other online games, people spend money to buy enhanced goods and features like pets, coins, avatar clothing and weapons, and virtual farm real estate for these and other online activities. In some games, players trade and sell these goods and can convert them back to real-world currency, often for a profit.

These kinds of activities raise questions in divorce settlements because if the virtual goods were purchased during a marriage, they may be considered community property, and in the vast virtual world, the worth of these assets varies. Attorney Anita Ramasastry, a Justia columnist, points out in a recent article that the 2010 sale of Club Neverdie, in the multiplayer Entropia Universe, the first virtual world with a real-cash economy, can give a glimpse into the

kind of dollar amounts these virtual assets can reach. In 2005, player Jon "Neverdie" Jacobs bought an asteroid for $100,000, and later sold the virtual nightclub for over $600,000, reportedly the highest price ever paid for a virtual asset.

20   In explaining why someone would pay such a startling amount for a virtual property, Ramasastry wrote, "Because Club Neverdie had become a go-to spot for players visiting its nightclub, stadium, and mall. As a result, Jacobs was making around $200,000 in actual cash every year from players' purchasing virtual goods and services."

Alternately, the dilemma could extend beyond gaming. For example, late last year, the S(edition) website debuted, offering original, downloadable art from renowned artists, who produce original creations to be displayed on phones, tablets, televisions and computers.

So far, artists like Michael Craig-Martin, Wim Wenders and Shepard Fairey, who created President Obama's "Hope" poster, have signed on to the digital platform, which allows consumers to purchase a less expensive version from their favorite artists. Still, the limited edition mobile works cost between $6 and $600, so an authenticated collection could end up being a considerable marital property whose ownership could come into play during a split.

As the importance of virtual property and digital goods continues to rise, corresponding property and matrimonial laws will need to evolve to discuss them. Today's personal relationships are so intertwined with technology—online sites can spark a match, social media can cement the bond or present temptations that dissolve it, and digital evidence is growing in divorce filings. In light of these trends, it can't be too surprising that the role technology plays in creating new bonds and property interests will continue to challenge courts and lawyers as they decide how to divide them when love goes sour.

B. What Causes Personal Relationships to Succeed or Fail?

> **BEFORE YOU READ:** Take a moment to reflect upon the title here. Is there anything jarring, even contradictory, about defining love as a "neurobiological" phenomenon?

UNMASKING THE NEUROBIOLOGY OF LOVE*

Robert Weiss

Robert Weiss is the founding director of The Sexual Recovery Institute. This article appeared online in *The Huffington Post* in 2013.

Romantic love has always been one of mankind's greatest mysteries—difficult to define, yet equally difficult to miss when it happens. For centuries poets, philosophers, and more than a few stray troubadours have endlessly pondered the nature of this ever-so-ephemeral emotion, providing us with a few moderately useful nuggets of wisdom like:

> Love is a portion of the soul itself.
>   (Victor Hugo)
>
> Love is the beauty of the soul.
>   (St. Augustine)
>
> Love is like oxygen. (The Sweet)

In case you're wondering, The Sweet was a shiny-jumpsuit-wearing 1970s British pop band. There's a great picture of them online "at the height of their career."

Silliness aside, there is no denying that love is a natural function, as essential to us human beings as breathing, eating, and sleeping. But still, we really have no idea what it really is or how and why it occurs. Certainly love is within us. We feel it, we enjoy it, and we ache both for it and from it. We chase it, we crave it, and sometimes we think we can't live without it. Nevertheless, we seem to know very little about it . . . until very recently.

Spoiler Alert!

If you'd prefer that love remain life's great mystery, stop reading now. Buy your sweetheart a box of chocolates, pipe some Usher into your bedroom, and skip the remainder of this article.

5   For the rest of you . . .

Love Is a State of Mind

Thanks to increasing insight into our own neurobiology, we now know unequivocally that love lives not in our hearts but in our brains.

---

*Robert Weiss, "Unmasking the Neurobiology of Love," *Huffington Post*, April 11, 2013. Used by permission of the author.

In fact, and somewhat amazingly, we even know where in the brain this exhilarating emotion resides. Essentially, when any part of the human brain is activated (by a thought, a movement, a drug, an external stimulus, etc.) we can track that activation with functional magnetic resonance imaging (fMRI) scans. (These scans measure, among other things, increased blood flow to activated regions of the brain.) Using this technology, monitoring and mapping things like sexual arousal and romantic love has become a relatively straightforward endeavor. Unsurprisingly, a whole lot of scientists have decided to hop on this particular research bandwagon, producing uniformly similar results. In one study, researchers tracked the brain activity of ten women and five men who said they were "intensely in love" and had been for anywhere from one to seventeen months. The researchers monitored the brains of these individuals as they viewed photographs of their beloved, and photographs of a familiar but not beloved person. The results very clearly showed that:

- Intense romantic love is associated with activation of dopamine-releasing regions in the brain, such as the striatum, which is part of the brain's "pleasure center." Dopamine release is the neurochemical process that evokes within all of us strong feelings of enjoyment, satisfaction, contentment, and the like.

- Intense romantic love also activates regions of the brain associated with motivation to acquire a reward, primarily the insula, which "gives value" to all pleasurable, life-sustaining activities (thereby ensuring that we continue to engage in them).

Based on these findings, the research team concluded that romantic love is in essence a goal-oriented motivation state rather than a specific emotion. In other words, individuals who are "in love" feel strongly motivated to be with their beloved because being with that person causes a high level of emotional (read neurobiological) reward. So, basically, we want to be with the person we love because it feels good. No surprises there, but then scientific folks tend to like to prove things that the rest of us already know—so now we all know for certain that love exists, and that it can even be measured and analyzed. It's a real thing.

Another study took things a step further, linking sexual desire to romantic love. This research analyzed the results from twenty separate fMRI trials, each of which examined brain activity while subjects were engaged in tasks like viewing pornographic photos, photos of their significant others, and non-pornographic photos of familiar but not beloved people and/or strangers. After pooling this data, the authors of the study were able to "map" exactly where and how both sexual desire and romantic love stimulate the brain. As it turns out, sexual desire and romantic love both activate the striatum (the brain's pleasure center), yet only romantic love (and not porn use) also activates the insula (the part of the brain that organizes and makes sense of our emotions and social connections). Thus, the striatum is responsible for sexual desire and initial attraction, and the insula is responsible for transforming (giving value) to that desire, and turning it (potentially) into love. In other words, love is co-created by and "lives within" the striatum and the insula—inside our heads.

"Love Is the Drug"

Perhaps unwittingly, Roxy Music, another (better dressed) '70s band from across the pond, was scientifically on target when it recorded its hit almost 40 years ago.

The striatum and the insula, where love resides, are also the parts of the brain most directly associated with the formation and maintenance of addictive disorders. "Love is the drug, got a hook in me . . ." Indeed. The same process of anticipation, craving, and reward upon connection that occurs with the pursuit of intense romantic love also occurs in a very similar way with substance and behavioral addictions. As Concordia University Professor Jim Pfaus, co-author of the study linking sexual desire and love, states, "Love is actually a habit that is formed from sexual desire as that desire is rewarded. It works the same way in the brain as when people become addicted to drugs."

10   This is not to say that the experience of love is in any way pathological or that everyone who falls in love is "addicted" to the object of his/her affection. To qualify as an addiction we need to see not only obsession and compulsion, but also directly related and repeated negative life consequences. And thank goodness most people who fall in love don't experience those unwanted consequences. For most of us, the process of falling in love is healthy, joyful, and life affirming (not to mention necessary for the survival of our species—read, procreation). So even though the feeling of being in love might show up in the brain looking like some form of emotional crack cocaine, in reality love doesn't necessarily lead people down the merry path of addiction the way that crack nearly always does. Rather, the early focused intensity of romantic love helps to push us forward into the more intimate challenges of a long-term meaningful relationship. In other words, the "rush" of early love encourages us to become temporarily obsessed and therefore to stay around the other person long enough to form the attachment bonds necessary for sustained love and intimacy (also securing the safety of any newborn progeny that might come out of this love). So while the beginning stages of a relationship—the period of time when how the other person walks, talks, eats, and thinks is the subject of endless fantasies and late-night phone calls—may look and feel like addiction, this particular neurochemical cascade is in reality a temporary, transitory state that exists to lead us into long-term intimate relationships. True love—lasting, meaningful attachment—is built over time in the brain, as the insula assigns increasing value to our connection with that very special someone.

So now that you know what love really is, I strongly suggest to those already in a meaningful relationship that you do something—right this very instant—to let your spouse or partner know how deeply you value them, because valuing another human being and caring about how they feel underlies the true nature of lasting romantic love. Science proves it! And for you singles out there, just know that the season we are now entering—commonly known as spring—is all about nature providing us with sensual triggers that lead toward romantic love. As the trees turn green and the blooming flowers rise out of the ground, so too does our desire to meet and mate. It's natural, meaningful, and important—and, oh yeah, it's also all in our heads.

> **BEFORE YOU READ:** Is dating easier when it is conducted online? What are the advantages and disadvantages of this approach?

DIGITAL DATING: DESPERATION OR NECESSITY?*

Christine Hassler

A former Hollywood agent, Christine Hassler is the author of the book, *Twenty-Something, Twenty-Everything*.

"I always thought dating online was for desperate, older people, but now that I'm finding I can't meet anybody, I'm actually considering it myself! Am I crazy or pathetic for considering it? And I'm afraid to tell my friends. Should I keep it a secret to hide my shame? I just think I'm going to feel like a loser if I tell people that I met someone online."

Online Dating-Phobic, 26, Atlanta

Dear Online Dating-Phobic,

It's a bit scary, but true: human connections are either replaced or initiated by internet connections. We now live in a different age of emails instead of letters, text messages instead of phone calls, and Facebook "friending" and "poking" are seen as a real relationship bond. Everything we do from finding a job to finding a friend seems to have an online component, so no need to be ashamed for wanting to broaden your circle, for friendship or dating, by taking advantage of the myriad of possibilities brought to you by the world wide web—just don't rely on it completely.

The stigma against online dating, particularly for twenty-somethings, is really intriguing, especially because you are the generation that founded social networking sites like Facebook and Myspace. You are looking for a person to date, someone to be in your life and no one else's, so who cares what your friends think? And they are probably doing it too!

Think about it this way: what do you gain by trying online dating, and what do you lose by not trying it? By not attempting it, you get to remain safe behind your concept of regular dating, which by your own admission has become undesirable. Or you can try online dating and open yourself up to the possibilities. Just be cautious. Be smart and careful about what information you post, who you give your personal contact information to, and where and when you meet someone for the first time (I recommend afternoon coffee in a very public place).

5   Also, online dating isn't only for pathetic or older people, so you can let that go. Here's some insight from Adam Sachs, co-founder of the group dating site Ignighter.com: "I can see how young people would look at the conventional online dating sites and think that going on one of those dates would make them feel like a loser or desperate. I was once like that too! There's nothing organic about creating your own blind date. And there's nothing fun about it either. What's natural and fun is meeting new people in the company of your social circle. That's why we created Ignighter.com. It's a group-to-group dating

---

*Used by permission of Christine Hassler.

site, a way for you and your friends to meet another group of friends in an environment that is safer, less awkward, and more fun."

Another upside to online dating is often you get to know a person better than when meeting them face-to-face when judgments about superficial things may get in the way. I'm not saying to give up meeting friends of friends, or talking to a person who catches your eye; use online dating as just another tool rather than an end-of-the-line solution. You never know where or when sparks will fly with someone, so if meeting Mr. or Ms. Right is a priority, start researching dating sites. But please, no embellishing profiles or glamour shot photos. If you want to attract your "soul-match," be who you are on and off line.

BEFORE YOU READ: What kinds of social and cultural traditions define courtship and marriage in your own family history?

IS ARRANGED MARRIAGE REALLY ANY WORSE THAN CRAIGSLIST?*

Anita Jain

Anita Jain is currently a technology and telecommunications reporter for *Crain's New York Business.*

Recently, I was cc'd on an e-mail addressed to my father. It read, "We liked the girl's profile. The boy is in good state job in Mississippi and cannot come to New York. The girl must relocate to Mississippi." The message was signed by Mr. Ramesh Gupta, "the boy's father."

That wasn't as bad as the time I logged on to my computer at home in Fort Greene and got a message that asked, forgoing any preamble, what the date, time, and location of my birth were. Presumably sent to determine how astrologically harmonious a match a Hindu suitor I'd be, the e-mail was dismayingly abrupt. But I did take heart in the fact that it was addressed only to me.

I've been fielding such messages—or, rather, my father has—more and more these days, having crossed the unmarriageable threshold for an Indian woman, 30, two years ago. My parents, in a very earnest bid to secure my eternal happiness, have been trying to marry me off to, well, just about anyone lately. In my childhood home near Sacramento, my father is up at night on arranged-marriage Web sites. And the result—strange e-mails from boys' fathers and stranger dates with those boys themselves—has become so much a part of my dating life that I've lost sight of how bizarre it once seemed.

Many women, Indian or not, whose parents have had a long, healthy marriage hope we will, too, while fearing that perhaps we've made everything irreparably worse by expecting too much. Our prospective husbands have to be rich and socially conscious, hip but down-to-earth.

5   For some Indians, the conundrum is exacerbated by the fact that our parents had no choice for a partner; the only choice was how hard they'd work to be happy.

---

*Anita Jain, "Is Arranged Marriage Really Any Worse Than Craigslist?" *New York Magazine.* Reprinted with permission.

For Discussion: This photograph functions in many ways as a form of autobiography. What can you tell about Anita Jain as a person from the iconographic details in the photograph (e.g., clothing, flowers, pictures, furniture, etc.)?

For Writing: Think of this image as evidence for the claim made by the article that follows it. What is the article's principal claim? How does the image function as evidence for the main essay's argument from the writer's personal *ethos*?

Context: The caption to this photograph reads: The author in her Fort Greene apartment. This casually posed photograph shows the author of the article at home in her urban apartment. The image shows a combination of Indian and American, and traditional and modern influences on the writer's *ethos*.

My father saw my mother once before they got married. He loves to shock Americans by recounting how he lost sight of her at a bazaar the day after their wedding and lamented to himself that he would never find her again, as he'd forgotten what she looked like. So while we, as modern Indian women, eschew the idea of marrying without love, the idea that we're being too picky tends to nag even more than it otherwise would.

Still, for years, I didn't want to get married the way my brother did. He'd met his wife through a newspaper ad my parents had taken out. He's very happily married, with a baby daughter, but he also never had a girlfriend before his wedding day. I was precocious when it came to affairs of the heart, having enjoyed my first kiss with cute Matt from the football squad at 14.

Perhaps it was that same spirit of romantic adventurism that led me, shortly after college, to go on the first of these "introductions," though I agreed to my parents' setup mainly with an eye toward turning it into a story for friends.

At the time, I was working as a journalist in Singapore. Vikram, "in entertainment," took me to the best restaurant in town, an Indonesian place with a view of the skyscrapers. Before long, though, I gathered that he was of a type: someone who prided himself on being modern and open-minded but who in fact had horribly crusty notions passed down from his Indian parents. I was taken aback when he told me about an Indian girl he'd liked. "I thought maybe she was the one, but then I found out she had a Muslim boyfriend in college," he said. I lodged my protest against him and arranged marriage by getting ragingly intoxicated and blowing smoke rings in his face. Childish? Maybe, but I didn't want to be marriageable back then. Indeed, I rarely thought of marriage at the time.

But for Indians, there's no way to escape thinking about marriage, eventually. It wouldn't be a stretch to say that *shaadi*, the word for marriage in many Indian languages, is the first word a child understands after *mummy* and *papa*. To an Indian, marriage is a matter of karmic destiny. There are many happy unions in the pantheon of Hindu gods—Shiva and Parvati, Krishna and Radha.[1] [. . .]

10 The pressure on me to find a husband started very early. A few days after my 1st birthday, within months of my family's arrival in the U.S., I fell out the window of a three-story building in Baltimore. My father recalls my mother's greatest concern, after learning that I hadn't been gravely injured: "What boy will marry her when he finds out?" she cried, begging my father to never mention my broken arm—from which I've enjoyed a full recovery—to prospective suitors out of fear my dowry would be prohibitively higher. (A middle-class family can easily spend $100,000 these days on a dowry in India.) Much savvier in the ways of his new country, my father laughed it off. "But there is no dowry in America!"

Fulfilling his parental duty, my father placed matrimonial ads for me every couple of years during my twenties in such immigrant newspapers as *India Abroad*. They read something like, "Match for Jain girl, Harvard-educated journalist, 25, fair, slim." [. . .]

Depending on whether my father was in a magnanimous mood, he would add "caste no bar," which meant suitors didn't have to belong to Jainism, an offshoot of Hinduism with the world's most severe dietary restrictions. [. . .]

This desultory casting around to see what was out there has become much more urgent now that I'm in my thirties, and in their quest, my parents have discovered a dizzying array of Web sites: *shaadi.com*, *indiamatrimony.com*, etc. Within these sites are sub-sites for Indian regions, like *punjabi-matrimony.com*. You might be surprised at

who you'd find on them: the guy in the next cubicle, your freshman-year roommate at NYU, maybe even the cute girl you tried to pick up at a Lower East Side bar last night.

Far from being a novel approach to matrimony, these sites are a natural extension of how things have been done in India for decades. Even since well before the explosion of the country's famously vibrant press in the fifties, Indians were coupling up via matrimonial ads in national papers ("Match sought for Bengali Brahmin, wheatish complexion," etc.).

15 My father took to the Web sites like a freshly divorced 42-year-old who's just discovered Craigslist. He uploaded my profile on several, indicating that only men living in New York City need apply (*nota bene*, Mr. Ramesh Gupta). Unfortunately, in the world of shaadi.com, this means most of the men live in New Jersey, while working in IT departments all around New York.

My father also *wrote* my profile. This may be why dates are surprised to discover I enjoy a glass of wine or two with dinner, and another couple afterward, even though the profile says, "I never drink." And he writes back to those who appear aboveboard. This is no small task, as anyone who's done any online dating can attest. As my father puts it, wagging his head, "You get a lot of useless types."

Like most Indians of their generation, my parents believe there are only two legitimate professions: doctor and engineer (not medicine and engineering, but doctor and engineer). . . . The problem is that while he wants doctor or engineer, my heart beats for the diametric opposite. Take the aging but rakish foreign correspondent I was smitten with last year. Nearing 50, he'd just seen his marriage fall apart, and he mourned its passing by plastering his body with fresh tattoos and picking bar fights. I found it terribly sexy that he rode a Harley, perhaps less so that his apartment was decorated with Wonder Woman paraphernalia. He was on a downward spiral, but perhaps my parents might appreciate that he'd won a Pulitzer earlier in his career?

The relationship didn't go anywhere, as my father might have warned me if I'd told him about such things. I will admit to needing a little romantic assistance. Since moving here a few years ago, I'd hardly describe my dating life as successful. There was Sadakat, the half-Finnish, half-Pakistani barrister from London who slept most of the day and worked most of the night writing a book on criminal justice. Circumscribed within this schedule, our dates would begin at midnight. Once I fell asleep on the bar during the middle of one.

Then there were the ones who simply never called again. The boy from Minnesota who imported women's leather clothing from Brazil, the Cockney songwriter, the French dot-com millionaire. Perhaps I didn't want to marry these men, but I certainly wanted to see them again. I began to feel baffled by Western norms of dating, what one Indian friend calls "dating for dating's sake." [. . .]

20   Given such escapades, it may come as no surprise that I've started to look at my father's efforts with a touch less disdain. At least the messages aren't as mixed, right? Sometimes they're quite clear. One of the first setups I agreed to took place a year ago. The man—I'll call him Vivek—worked in IT in New Jersey and had lived there all his life. He took the train into the city to meet me at a Starbucks. He was wearing pants that ended two inches before his ankles. We spoke briefly about his work before he asked, "What are you looking for in a husband?" Since this question always leaves me flummoxed—especially when it's asked by somebody in high-waters within the first few minutes of conversation—I mumbled something along the lines of,

"I don't know, a connection, I guess. What are you looking for?" Vivek responded, "Just two things. Someone who's vegetarian and doesn't smoke. That shouldn't be so hard to find, don't you think?"

It's a common online-dating complaint that people are nothing like their profiles. I've found they can be nothing but them. And in their tone-deafness, some of these men resemble the parents spurring them on. One Sunday, I was woken by a call at 9 A.M. A woman with a heavy Indian accent asked for Anita. I have a raspy voice at the best of times, but after a night of "social" smoking, my register is on par with Clint Eastwood's. So when I croaked, "This is she," the perplexed lady responded, "She or he?" before asking, "What are your qualifications?" I said I had a B.A. "B.A. only?" she responded. "What are the boy's qualifications?" I flung back in an androgynous voice. She smirked: "He is M.D. in Kentucky *only*." Still bleary-eyed, but with enough presence of mind to use the deferential term for an elder, I grumbled, "Auntie, I will speak to the boy only." Neither she, nor he, called back. [. . .]

My father's screening method is hardly foolproof. Once, he was particularly taken with a suitor who claimed to be a brain surgeon at Johns Hopkins and friends with a famous Bollywood actress, Madhuri Dixit.[2] I was suspicious, but I agreed to speak to the fellow. Within seconds, his shaky command of English and yokel line of questioning—"You are liking dancing? I am too much liking dancing"—told me this man was as much a brain surgeon as I was Madhuri Dixit. I refused to talk to him again, even though my father persisted in thinking I was bullheaded. "Don't you think we would make sure his story checked out before marrying you off?" he said.

Sometimes, though, you get close, really close. A year ago, I was put in touch with a McKinsey consultant in Bombay whom

I'll call Sameer. I liked the fact that he was Indian-American but had returned to India to work. We had great conversations on the phone—among other things, he had interesting views on how people our age were becoming more sexually liberated in Indian cities—and I began envisioning myself kept in the finest silk saris. My father kept telling me he wanted it all "wrapped up" by February—it was only Christmas! Sameer had sent a picture, and while he wasn't Shahrukh Khan, he wasn't bad.[3]

Back for a break in New York, Sameer kindly came to see me in Brooklyn. We went to a French bistro, where he leaned over the table and said, "You know, your father really shouldn't send out those photos of you. They don't do justice to your beauty." Sameer was generous, good-natured, engaging, seemingly besotted with me, on an expat[riate] salary—and also on the Atkins diet to lose 50 pounds. *My* Bombay dreams went up in smoke.

25   In this, I guess I am like every other woman in New York, complaining a man is too ambitious or not ambitious enough, too eager or not eager enough. But they are picky, too. These men, in their bid to fit in on Wall Street or on the golf course, would like a wife who is eminently presentable—to their boss, friends, and family. They would like a woman to be sophisticated enough to have a martini, and not a Diet Coke, at an office party, but, God forbid, not "sophisticated" enough to have three. Sometimes I worry that I'm a bit too sophisticated for most Indian men.

That's not to say I haven't come to appreciate what Indian men have to offer, which is a type of seriousness, a clarity of intent. I've never heard from an Indian man the New York beg-off phrase "I don't think I'm ready for a relationship right now. I have a lot of things going on in my life."

Indian men also seem to share my belief that Westerners have made the progression toward marriage unnecessarily agonizing. Neal, a 35-year-old Indian lawyer I know, thinks it's absurd how a couple in America can date for years and still not know if they want to get married. "I think I would only need a couple of months to get to know a girl before I married her," he says.

In more traditional arranged marriages—which are still very much alive and well in India—couples may get only one or two meetings before their wedding day. In America, and in big Indian cities, a couple may get a few months before they are expected to walk down the aisle, or around the fire, as they do seven times, in keeping with Hindu custom. By now, I certainly think that would be enough time for me.

Other Indian women I know seem to be coming to the same conclusion. My friend Divya works the overnight shift at the BBC in London and stays out clubbing on her nights off. Imagine my surprise when I discovered she was on keralamatrimony.com, courtesy of her mother, who took the liberty of listing Divya's hobbies as shopping and movies. (I was under the impression her hobbies were more along the lines of trance music and international politics.) Though she's long favored pub-going blokes, Divya, like me, doesn't discount the possibility that the urologist from Trivandrum or the IT guy could just be the one—an idea patently unthinkable to us in our twenties.

30   It's become second nature for women like us to straddle the two dating worlds. When I go out on a first date with an Indian man, I find myself saying things I would never utter to an American. Like, "I would expect my husband to fully share domestic chores." Undeniably, there's

a lack of mystery to Indian-style dating because both parties are fully aware of what the endgame should be. But with that also comes a certain relief.

With other forms of dating the options seem limitless. The long kiss in the bar with someone I've never met before could have been just that, an exchange that has a value and meaning of its own that can't be quantified. Ditto for the one-night stand. (Try explaining that one to my parents.) The not-knowing-where-something-is-headed can be wildly exciting. It can also be a tad soul-crushing. Just ask any single woman in New York.

Indians of my mother's generation—in fact, my mother herself—like to say of arranged marriage, "It's not that there isn't love. It's just that it comes after the marriage." I'm still not sure I buy it. But after a decade of Juan Carloses and short-lived affairs with married men and Craigslist flirtations and emotionally bankrupt boyfriends and, oddly, the most painful of all, the guys who just never call, it no longer seems like the most outlandish possibility.

Some of my single friends in New York say they're still not convinced marriage is what they really want. I'm not sure I buy that, either. And no modern woman wants to close the door on any of her options—no matter how traditional—too hastily.

My friend Radhika, an unmarried 37-year-old photographer, used to hate going to her cousins' weddings, where the aunties never asked her about the famines in Africa or the political conflict in Cambodia she'd covered. Instead it was, "Why aren't you married? What are your intentions?" As much as she dreaded this,

they've stopped asking, and for Radhika, that's even worse. "It's like they've written me off," she says.

35   On a recent trip to India, I was made to eat dinner at the children's table—they sent out for Domino's pizza and Pepsis—because as an unmarried woman, I didn't quite fit in with the adults. As much as I resented my exile, I realized that maybe I didn't want to be eating vegetable curry and drinking rum with the grown-ups. Maybe that would have meant they'd given up on me, that they'd stopped viewing me as a not-yet-married girl but as an unmarriageable woman who'd ruined her youth by being too choosy and strong-headed.

This way, the aunties can still swing by the kids' table as I'm sucking on a Pepsi and chucking a young cousin on the chin, and ask me, "When are you getting married? What are your intentions?" And I can say, "Auntie, do you have a boy in mind?"

Editor's Notes

1. The god Krishna and Radha are legendary Hindu lovers. So are Shiva and Parvati, although they did not have an easy life together. Shiva was originally married to Sati, but her father did not approve of the marriage and ignored him. Humiliated, Sati threw herself into the sacrificial fire. Shiva was so inconsolable that the gods decided to revive Sati. Reborn as Parvati, she danced in front of Shiva and drew him back from his ascetic life into marriage.

2. "Bollywood" is the term applied to the Hindu-language film industry in India; the parallels with Hollywood are obvious. Madhuri Dixit is an award-winning actress and an icon of the Bollywood film industry.

3. Shahrukh Khan is a famous Bollywood actor.

> **BEFORE YOU READ:** In your view, what attitudes toward relationships define the Millenial generation? Do you think these attitudes represent a dramatic shift from the past?

MILLENNIAL GENERATION: WHAT'S LOVE GOT TO DO WITH IT?*

John Yemma

The author is the editor for *The Christian Science Monitor*, where this article appeared in 2012.

It is a truth universally acknowledged that a happily married man writing about courtship must be in need of a serious talking to. Nothing so lacks credibility, especially with younger readers. Oh, sure, he may on occasion text his wife a sweet nothing using "r" as a verb to show how with-it he is. He may throw caution to the wind and attempt to dance "the robot" at a nephew's wedding. But he almost always will put air quotes around such not-really-modern-anymore fads to signal his actual distance from them.

For those reasons and more, it is probably best for me to send you directly to Eilene Zimmerman's fascinating and thorough exploration of modern dating.

Depending on your vintage and values, your view of 2012 courtship may range from quiet approval to mild alarm. There is, for instance, a definite standoffishness about marriage in the Millennial Generation (also known as Generation Y, meaning those born in the 1980s and early '90s). But even if young people are waiting longer before saying their vows than any previous generation, they aren't necessarily anti-marriage. What they most want, it appears, is to get marriage right.

"They've seen a lot of divorce in their parents' generation," Eilene told me the other day. "They've been through difficult holidays. But they're really into family and marriage. They actually want to move to the suburbs and raise a family one day—just not now."

5   Many have struggled through a bleak job market while carrying big college debt, so they are naturally cautious. Even the dreaded subject of sex is not what you may think in an age of ubiquitous contraception and noncommittal "hookups": Despite a casual attitude toward intimacy, risky behavior is not something this well-warned generation embraces. In some ways, says Eilene, Gen-Y is like the famed GI generation that fought in World War II and built the postwar world. By midcentury, in other words, this may be a fairly conservative cohort.

Eilene is an Gen-Xer. I'm a baby boomer. Talking about generations is unavoidable in trying to understand society. The drawback, of course, is that as with every other way humans categorize themselves—race, gender, religion, class—there are tremendous variations within the categories. Music, dress, slang, and hairstyles may characterize an age group, but those are superficialities. Individuals within Gen-Y are carving out distinct paths when it comes to tricky issues like intimate relations. That was true even of us boomers, not all of whom went to San Francisco with flowers in our hair.

In the not too distant future, Millennials themselves may wonder about the dating scene for the next demographic cohort, Generation Z (aka, Digital Natives). They, too, will have to use air quotes when it comes to current mores.

Society is a large and interesting blend of ages, communities, families, and individuals. But when it comes to affairs of the heart, most people are looking for the same

---

thing: deep and abiding commitment. The StoryCorps project has assembled a collection of long-running love stories in a book titled "All There Is." The collection echoes the testimonials from elderly couples that were sprinkled throughout the 1989 date movie "When Harry Met Sally"—how we met, what we mean to each other, the relationship two people build throughout a lifetime. One of the "All There Is" couples mentioned six nice things that one couple learned to say to each other throughout their marriage: You look great. Can I help? Let's eat out. I was wrong. I am sorry. I love you.

From neolithic times to the digital age, those have been words to live by.

10   So, Honey, if u r reading this, u look great. Happy Valentine's Day. Let's eat out tonight. I promise not to dance the robot.

Questions to Help You Think and Write About Family and Personal Relationships

1. How have the opinions of Ali, Pederson, and Moosa influenced your views on the traditional family? What were your views before reading these essays? What are your views now?

2. Define the cultural images or ideals of "motherhood" and "fatherhood" and analyze ways in which today's fathers either are or are not becoming more like mothers. Conversely, are today's mothers more like fathers? You can choose to focus on a real-life situation or on a fictional representation of family in literature or film.

3. Using Lorraine Ali's essay "The Curious Lives of Surrogates" as a starting point, consider what you think would be the right time to start a family. What do you need to achieve and what goals do you need to meet before making your own family and why?

4. In "Unmasking the Neurobiology of Love," Robert Weiss argues that romance should be understood as an essentially physiological phenomenon. Choose a film or a fictional work that challenges this view. What alternative portrait of romance does it present? Do you find it to be a more appealing or persuasive depiction than the one offered by Weiss? Why or why not?

5. Hassler suggests that online dating offers certain advantages for people just getting to know each other. Describe a popular social situation or event familiar from your school or town and analyze how it allows individuals to get to know one another, either through digital technology or some other means.

6. Anita Jain, as a modern young woman with traditional parents, has experienced both the pros and cons of having family manage or even arrange a young person's dating and possible marriage. What are the advantages and disadvantages of involving family in such decisions? What, in the end, do you think is the best way to find a romantic partner or spouse?

7. **Arguing Like a Citizen:** John Yemma tracks the growing trend among young people away from an interest in or concern for romantic love. Choose an example of a cultural organization in your community (i.e., campus counseling center; online dating service) that you think either exemplifies or challenges

this trend. Then conduct some first-hand research into the particular ways this organization teaches young people to approach personal relationships. What attitudes toward love and relationships does this organization promote? How do these messages compare to the attitudes Yemma profiles in his article? Do you find these messages to be helpful? Why or why not?

SECTION 2
Modern Technology

The Issues

A. How Are Online Technologies Changing the Way We Live?

People are always divided about technology, and digital technologies are no exception. The essays by Nicholas Carr and Scott Steinberg offer contrasting views of the intellectual and educational benefits of Web-based activities. Evgeny Morozov, one of the most outspoken critics of the digital revolution, weighs in on this question, wondering aloud whether the proliferation of so-called "smart" technologies is actually making us dumber. And finally, Matthew Kirschenbaum takes a different line of argument, looking at the ways that computers can foster intense, sustained acts of reading and writing.

B. How Is Technology Changing Our Definition of What It Means to Be Human?

As the first decade of the twenty-first century moves forward, technologies for human engineering are becoming not only possible but commonplace. Ray Kurzweil, an important inventor and an enthusiastic promoter of biological and computer science, gives us his vision of the decades to come. Peggy Orenstein reports on *in vitro* fertilization as an increasingly common choice for Americans seeking to have children; she describes the human faces, fears, and aspirations behind the science and explores ethical issues involved in the choice to use an egg donor. Lastly, Kathleen Craig raises questions about the relationship between "real-world" and our virtual identity by chronicling the ways people use avatars and online gaming as a means to make money.

Exploring Online Argument

The following Web sites present interesting perspectives on modern technology.

Institute for the Future of the Book	Berkman Center for Internet and Society
Web 2.0: The Machine Is Us/ing Us (YouTube)	Protect Your Privacy Online (government site)
Lawrence Lessig's blog	Douglass Rushkoff's blog
Stanford Center for Internet and Society (CIS)	E Learning and Digital Cultures
Electronic Frontier Foundation	Frontline: Digital Nation
Creative Commons	Big Think: Are Digital Tools Making Us Less Creative?
Facebook	TED Talk: Life in the Digital Now
YouTube	*Wikipedia*
Open Content Alliance	

The Rhetorical Situation

Several essays in this section of The Reader engage the many debates that have accompanied the rise of digital culture over the last several years. The original dream of the Web was to supply people with the tools and the space to communicate, collaborate, and innovate in unprecedented new ways. Devices such as laptops and smartphones now connect us to a vast universe of information and ideas at the touch of a button. Social media sites such as Facebook, YouTube, and Twitter provide vehicles for connecting with each other virtually every moment of every day. These new technologies have fostered individual creativity and led to the rise of a whole new amateur culture; they have allowed individuals to publish their own writing, showcase their own skills, and broadcast themselves.

On the other hand, the rise of the Web has also led to significant challenges. While these new technologies have fostered creativity, they have also blurred the line around the ownership of intellectual property. And while the participatory spirit of such sites as Wikipedia has dramatically expanded the pool of information available online, many worry that this expansion has come at the expense of true knowledge. Some universities, in fact, have gone so far as to ban Wikipedia as a source for student essays. Others level the same criticism against search behemoths like Google, worrying that their one-click search tools are undermining our ability to evaluate information critically. And finally there are the social consequences of our digital culture. Privacy advocates are growing more concerned about the extent to which our online behavior can be tracked by the government or corporations. Many parents voice concern about the types of interactions their children engage in through social media.

Other essays in The Reader, meanwhile, focus on the potential benefits and ethical drawbacks of using bioengineering to improve human life. Ray Kurzweil looks forward to a time, not too far in the future, when tiny robots can enter the body to trigger reactions ranging from an attack on cancer cells to turning off an enzyme that destroys "good" cholesterol. He thinks that with science, we can soon extend and improve the lives of many people. The ethical dilemmas posed by genetic engineering become most pronounced in the creation of human life. Efforts to "perfect" the human species by ruling out genetic defects from the beginning may be hubris in the face of nature and, for many religions, a usurpation of divine authority. On the other hand, new technologies such as *in vitro* fertilization (IVF) are giving parents expanded options for creating a loving family. Genetic engineering has already become a factor of everyday life.

A. How Are Online Technologies Changing the Way We Live?

BEFORE YOU READ: Countless commentators have heralded the advantages of the digital age. Where do you stand on this question? In your view, has the "information revolution" wrought by the digital technologies changed our lives for the better? How or how not?

IS GOOGLE MAKING US STUPID?*

Nicholas Carr

Nicholas Carr writes about technology, culture, and economics. His books have been translated into twenty languages. In addition to his most recent bestsellers, *The Shallows* and *What the Internet Is Doing to Our Brains*, Carr is the author of two earlier books, *The Big Switch* (2008) and *Does IT Matter?* (2004).

"Dave, stop. Stop, will you? Stop, Dave. Will you stop, Dave?" So the supercomputer HAL pleads with the implacable astronaut Dave Bowman in a famous and weirdly poignant scene toward the end of Stanley Kubrick's *2001: A Space Odyssey*. Bowman, having nearly been sent to a deep-space death by the malfunctioning machine, is calmly, coldly disconnecting the memory circuits that control its artificial "brain." "Dave, my mind is going," HAL says, forlornly. "I can feel it. I can feel it."

I can feel it, too. Over the past few years I've had an uncomfortable sense that someone, or something, has been tinkering with my brain, remapping the neural circuitry, reprogramming the memory. My mind isn't going—so far as I can tell—but it's changing.

I'm not thinking the way I used to think. I can feel it most strongly when I'm reading. Immersing myself in a book or a lengthy article used to be easy. My mind would get caught up in the narrative or the turns of the argument, and I'd spend hours strolling through long stretches of prose. That's rarely the case anymore. Now my concentration often starts to drift after two or three pages. I get fidgety, lose the thread, begin looking for something else to do. I feel as if I'm always dragging my wayward brain back to the text. The deep reading that used to come naturally has become a struggle.

I think I know what's going on. For more than a decade now, I've been spending a lot of time online, searching and surfing and sometimes adding to the great databases of

---

*Nicholas Carr, "Is Google Making Us Stupid?" *The Atlantic Monthly*. Reprinted with permission of the author.

the Internet. The Web has been a godsend to me as a writer. Research that once required days in the stacks or periodical rooms of libraries can now be done in minutes. A few Google searches, some quick clicks on hyperlinks, and I've got the telltale fact or pithy quote I was after. Even when I'm not working, I'm as likely as not to be foraging in the Web's info-thickets, reading and writing e-mails, scanning headlines and blog posts, watching videos and listening to podcasts, or just tripping from link to link to link. (Unlike footnotes, to which they're sometimes likened, hyperlinks don't merely point to related works: they propel you toward them.)

For me, as for others, the Net is becoming a universal medium, the conduit for most of the information that flows through my eyes and ears and into my mind. The advantages of having immediate access to such an incredibly rich store of information are many, and they've been widely described and duly applauded. "The perfect recall of silicon memory," *Wired*'s Clive Thompson has written, "can be an enormous boon to thinking." But that boon comes at a price. As the media theorist Marshall McLuhan pointed out in the 1960s, media are not just passive channels of information. They supply the stuff of thought, but they also shape the process of thought. And what the Net seems to be doing is chipping away my capacity for concentration and contemplation. My mind now expects to take in information the way the Net distributes it: in a swiftly moving stream of particles. Once I was a scuba diver in the sea of words. Now I zip along the surface like a guy on a Jet Ski.

5   I'm not the only one. When I mention my troubles with reading to friends and acquaintances—literary types, most of them—many say they're having similar experiences. The more they use the Web, the more they have to fight to stay focused on long pieces of writing. Some of the bloggers I follow have also begun mentioning the phenomenon. Scott Karp, who writes a blog about online media, recently confessed that he has stopped reading books altogether. "I was a lit major in college, and used to be [a] voracious book reader," he wrote. "What happened?" He speculates on the answer: "What if I do all my reading on the web not so much because the way I read has changed, i.e., I'm just seeking convenience, but because the way I THINK has changed?"

Bruce Friedman, who blogs regularly about the use of computers in medicine, also has described how the Internet has altered his mental habits. "I now have almost totally lost the ability to read and absorb a longish article on the web or in print," he wrote earlier this year. A pathologist who has long been on the faculty of the University of Michigan Medical School, Friedman elaborated on his comment in a telephone conversation with me. His thinking, he said, has taken on a "staccato" quality, reflecting the way he quickly scans short passages of text from many sources online. "I can't read *War and Peace* anymore," he admitted. "I've lost the ability to do that. Even a blog post of more than three or four paragraphs is too much to absorb. I skim it."

Anecdotes alone don't prove much. And we still await the long-term neurological and psychological experiments that will provide a definitive picture of how Internet use affects cognition. But a recently published study of online research habits, conducted by scholars from University College London, suggests that we may well be in the midst of a sea change in the way we read and think. As part of the five-year research program, the scholars examined computer logs documenting the behavior of visitors to two popular research sites, one operated by the British Library and one by a U.K. educational consortium, that provide access to journal articles, e-books, and other sources of written information. They found that people using the sites exhibited "a form of skimming activity," hopping from one source to another and rarely returning to any source they'd already visited. They typically read no more than one or two pages of an article or book before they would "bounce" out to another site. Sometimes they'd save a long article, but there's no evidence that they ever went back and actually read it. The authors of the study report:

> It is clear that users are not reading online in the traditional sense; indeed there are signs that new forms of "reading" are emerging as users "power browse" horizontally through titles, contents pages and abstracts going for quick wins. It almost seems that they go online to avoid reading in the traditional sense.

Thanks to the ubiquity of text on the Internet, not to mention the popularity of text-messaging on cell phones, we may well be reading more today than we did in the 1970s or 1980s, when television was our medium of choice. But it's a different kind of reading, and behind it lies a different kind of thinking—perhaps even a new sense of the self. "We are not only *what* we read," says Maryanne Wolf, a developmental psychologist at Tufts University and the author of *Proust and the Squid: The Story and Science of the Reading Brain.* "We are *how* we read." Wolf worries that the style of reading promoted by the Net, a style that puts "efficiency" and "immediacy" above all else, may be weakening our capacity for the kind of deep reading that emerged when an earlier technology, the printing press, made long and complex works of prose commonplace. When we read online, she says, we tend to become "mere decoders of information." Our ability to interpret text, to make the rich mental connections that form when we read deeply and without distraction, remains largely disengaged.

Reading, explains Wolf, is not an instinctive skill for human beings. It's not etched into our genes the way speech is. We have to teach our minds how to translate the symbolic characters we see into the language we understand. And the media or other technologies we use in learning and practicing the craft of reading play an important part in shaping the neural circuits inside our brains. Experiments demonstrate that readers of ideograms, such as the Chinese, develop a mental circuitry for reading that is very different from the circuitry found in those of us whose written language employs an alphabet. The variations extend across many regions of the brain, including those that govern such essential cognitive functions as memory and the interpretation of visual and auditory stimuli. We can expect as well that the circuits woven by our use of the Net will be different from those woven by our reading of books and other printed works.

10   Sometime in 1882, Friedrich Nietzsche bought a typewriter—a Malling-Hansen Writing Ball, to be precise. His vision was failing, and keeping his eyes focused on a page had become exhausting and painful, often bringing on crushing headaches. He had been forced to curtail his writing, and he feared that he would soon have to give it up. The typewriter rescued him, at least for a time. Once he had mastered touch-typing, he was able to write with his eyes closed, using only the tips of his fingers. Words could once again flow from his mind to the page.

But the machine had a subtler effect on his work. One of Nietzsche's friends, a composer, noticed a change in the style of his writing. His already terse prose had become even tighter, more telegraphic. "Perhaps you will through this instrument even take to a new idiom," the friend wrote in a letter, noting that, in his own work, his "'thoughts' in music and language often depend on the quality of pen and paper."

> **BEFORE YOU READ:** What kind of experience do you have with "smart" technology? Do you find such devices to useful? Are there any downsides to this type of technology?

ARE SMART GADGETS MAKING US DUMB?*

Evgeny Morozov

Evgeny Morozov writes frequently about the social, economic, and political implications of digital technology. His work has appeared in such publications as *The New York Times*, *Slate*, and *The Wall Street Journal*. He is the author of the book, *To Save Everything, Click Here: The Folly of Technological Solutionism*. This piece was published in *The Wall Street Journal* in 2013.

Would you like all of your Facebook friends to sift through your trash? A group of designers from Britain and Germany think that you might. Meet BinCam: a "smart" trash bin that aims to revolutionize the recycling process.

BinCam looks just like your average trash bin, but with a twist: Its upper lid is equipped with a smartphone that snaps a photo every time the lid is shut. The photo is then uploaded to Mechanical Turk, the Amazon-run service that lets freelancers perform laborious tasks for money. In this case, they analyze the photo and decide if your recycling habits conform with the gospel of green living. Eventually, the photo appears on your Facebook page.

You are also assigned points, as in a game, based on how well you are meeting the recycling challenge. The household that earns the most points "wins." In the words of its young techie creators, BinCam is designed "to increase individuals' awareness of their food waste and recycling behavior," in the hope of changing their habits.

BinCam has been made possible by the convergence of two trends that will profoundly reshape the world around us. First, thanks to the proliferation of cheap, powerful sensors, the most commonplace objects can finally understand what we do with them—from umbrellas that know it's going to rain to shoes that know they're wearing out—and alert us to potential problems and programmed priorities. These objects are no longer just dumb, passive matter. With some help from crowdsourcing or artificial intelligence, they can be taught to distinguish between responsible and irresponsible behavior (between recycling and throwing stuff away, for example) and then punish or reward us accordingly—in real time.

5   And because our personal identities are now so firmly pegged to our profiles on social networks such as Facebook and Google our every interaction with such objects can be made "social"—that is, visible to our friends. This visibility, in turn, allows designers to tap into peer pressure: Recycle and impress your friends, or don't recycle and risk incurring their wrath.

These two features are the essential ingredients of a new breed of so-called smart technologies, which are taking aim at their dumber alternatives. Some of these technologies are already catching on and seem relatively harmless, even if not particularly revolutionary: smart watches that pulsate when you get a new Facebook poke; smart scales that share your weight with your Twitter followers, helping you to stick to a diet; or smart pill bottles that ping you and your doctor to say how much of your prescribed medication remains.

But many smart technologies are heading in another, more disturbing direction. A number of thinkers in Silicon Valley see these technologies as a way not just to give consumers new products that they want but to push them to behave better. Sometimes this will be a nudge; sometimes it will be a shove. But the central idea is clear: social engineering disguised as product engineering.

In 2010, Google Chief Financial Officer Patrick Pichette told an Australian news program that his company "is really an engineering company, with all these computer scientists that see the world as a completely broken place." Just last week in Singapore, he restated Google's notion that the world is a "broken" place whose problems, from traffic jams to inconvenient shopping experiences to excessive energy use, can be solved by technology. The futurist and game designer Jane McGonigal, a favorite of the TED crowd, also likes to talk about how "reality is broken" but can be fixed by making the real world more like a videogame, with points for doing good. From smart cars to smart glasses, "smart" is Silicon Valley's shorthand for transforming present-day social reality and the hapless souls who inhabit it.

But there is reason to worry about this approaching revolution. As smart technologies become more intrusive, they risk undermining our autonomy by suppressing behaviors that someone somewhere has deemed undesirable. Smart forks inform us that we are eating too fast. Smart toothbrushes urge us to spend more time brushing our teeth. Smart sensors in our cars

can tell if we drive too fast or brake too suddenly.

10   These devices can give us useful feedback, but they can also share everything they know about our habits with institutions whose interests are not identical with our own. Insurance companies already offer significant discounts to drivers who agree to install smart sensors in order to monitor their driving habits. How long will it be before customers can't get auto insurance without surrendering to such surveillance? And how long will it be before the self-tracking of our health (weight, diet, steps taken in a day) graduates from being a recreational novelty to a virtual requirement? How can we avoid completely surrendering to the new technology? The key is learning to differentiate between "good smart" and "bad smart."

Devices that are "good smart" leave us in complete control of the situation and seek to enhance our decision-making by providing more information. For example: An Internet-jacked kettle that alerts us when the national power grid is overloaded (a prototype has been developed by U.K. engineer Chris Adams) doesn't prevent us from boiling yet another cup of tea, but it does add an extra ethical dimension to that choice. Likewise, a grocery cart that can scan the bar codes of products we put into it, informing us of their nutritional benefits and country of origin, enhances—rather than impoverishes—our autonomy (a prototype has been developed by a group of designers at the Open University, also in the U.K.).

Technologies that are "bad smart," by contrast, make certain choices and behaviors impossible. Smart gadgets in the latest generation of cars—breathalyzers that can check if we are sober, steering sensors that verify if we are drowsy, facial recognition technologies that confirm we are who we say we are—seek to limit, not to expand, what we can do. This may be an acceptable price to pay in situations where lives are at stake, such as driving, but we must resist any attempt to universalize this logic. The "smart bench"—an art project by designers JooYoun Paek and David Jimison that aims to illustrate the dangers of living in a city that is too smart—cleverly makes this point. Equipped with a timer and sensors, the bench starts tilting after a set time, creating an incline that eventually dumps its occupant. This might appeal to some American mayors, but it is the kind of smart technology that degrades the culture of urbanism—and our dignity.

Projects like BinCam fall somewhere between good smart and bad smart, depending on how they're executed. The bin doesn't force us to recycle, but by appealing to our base instincts—Must earn gold bars and rewards! Must compete with other households! Must win and impress friends!—it fails to treat us as autonomous human beings, capable of weighing the options by ourselves. It allows the Mechanical Turk or Facebook to do our thinking for us.

The most worrisome smart-technology projects start from the assumption that designers know precisely how we should behave, so the only problem is finding the right incentive. A truly smart trash bin, by contrast, would make us reflect on our recycling habits and contribute to conscious deliberation—say, by letting us benchmark our usual recycling behavior against other people in our demographic, instead of trying to shame us with point deductions and peer pressure.

15   There are many contexts in which smart technologies are unambiguously useful and even lifesaving. Smart belts that monitor the balance of the elderly and smart carpets that detect falls seem to fall in this category. The problem with many smart technologies is that their designers, in the quest to root out the imperfections of the human condition, seldom stop to ask how much frustration, failure and regret is required for happiness and achievement to retain any meaning.

It's great when the things around us run smoothly, but it's even better when they don't do so by default. That, after all, is how we gain the space to make decisions—many of them undoubtedly wrongheaded—and, through trial and error, to mature into responsible adults, tolerant of compromise and complexity.

Will those autonomous spaces be preserved in a world replete with smart technologies? Or will that world, to borrow a metaphor from the legal philosopher Ian Kerr, resemble Autopia—a popular Disneyland attraction in which kids drive specially designed little cars that run through an enclosed track? Well, "drive" may not be the right word. Though the kids sit in the driver's seat and even steer the car sideways, a hidden rail underneath always guides them back to the middle. The Disney carts are impossible to crash. Their so-called "drivers" are not permitted to make any mistakes. Isn't it telling that one of today's most eagerly anticipated technologies is a self-driving car, now on its way to being rolled out by Google?

To grasp the intellectual poverty that awaits us in a smart world, look no further than recent blueprints for a "smart kitchen"—an odd but persistent goal of today's computer scientists, most recently in designs from the University of Washington and Kyoto Sangyo University in Japan.

Once we step into this magic space, we are surrounded by video cameras that recognize whatever ingredients we hold in our hands. Tiny countertop robots inform us that, say, arugula doesn't go with boiled carrots or that lemon grass tastes awful with chocolate milk. This kitchen might be smart, but it's also a place where every mistake, every deviation from the master plan, is frowned upon. It's a world that looks more like a Taylorist factory than a place for culinary innovation. Rest assured that lasagna and sushi weren't invented by a committee armed with formulas or with "big data" about recent consumer wants.

20   Creative experimentation propels our culture forward. That our stories of innovation tend to glorify the breakthroughs and edit out all the experimental mistakes doesn't mean that mistakes play a trivial role. As any artist or scientist knows, without some protected, even sacred space for mistakes, innovation would cease.

With "smart" technology in the ascendant, it will be hard to resist the allure of a frictionless, problem-free future. When Eric Schmidt, Google's executive chairman, says that "people will spend less time trying to get technology to work . . . because it will just be seamless," he is not wrong: This is the future we're headed toward. But not all of us will want to go there.

A more humane smart-design paradigm would happily acknowledge that the task of technology is not to liberate us from problem-solving. Rather, we need to enroll smart technology in helping us with problem-solving. What we want is not a life where friction and frustrations have been carefully designed out, but a life where we can overcome the frictions and frustrations that stand in our way.

Truly smart technologies will remind us that we are not mere automatons who assist big data in asking and answering questions. Unless designers of smart technologies take stock of the complexity and richness of the lived human experience—with its gaps, challenges and conflicts—their inventions will be destined for the SmartBin of history.

Reading Images: Today's Technology

For Discussion: This cartoon implies that our machines rule our lives. Can you think of some concrete evidence to support this claim?

For Writing: This cartoon also makes a particular claim about the influence of technology on families and personal relationships. What is that claim, and what evidence for it is provided by the image itself?

Context: Dick Locher has been an editorial cartoonist at the *Chicago Tribune* since 1973, and in 1983 he won the Pulitzer Prize. His work focuses on life's absurdities and on politics.

BEFORE YOU READ: What sort of information do you typically go online to find? Are there any offline sources of information you regularly consult for answers to questions?

HOW VIDEO GAMES CAN MAKE YOU SMARTER*

Scott Steinberg

Scott Steinberg is the head of technology at video game consulting firm TechSavvy Global, as well as the founder of *GameExec* magazine and Game Industry TV. The creator and host of online video series *Game Theory*, he frequently appears as an on-air technology analyst for ABC, CBS, NBC, FOX, and CNN. This article appeared on CNN.com in 2011.

Critics often accuse video games of making players lazy, inept and socially awkward. Contrary to popular belief, though, many build, not burn brain cells by requiring extensive problem solving, teamwork and dynamic decision-making skills.

Also capable of building players' confidence and helping them see the world from multiple viewpoints, games can be powerful learning tools.

At minimum, they readily encourage fans to fall on their face then pick themselves up and try again, promoting hands-on learning without the fear of ridicule or embarrassment.

Following are four ways that video games can actually help make you smarter. The next time some cretin demands you drop the controller, consider citing all as you strike a wounded pose and educate the poor Neanderthal.

Hands-on Experience

5 More interactive and absorbing than passive forms of entertainment like movies and TV, video games promote higher levels of engagement because observers are actively and enthusiastically involved with on-screen activity.

It's a point author James Paul Gee emphasizes in "What Video Games Have to Teach Us About Learning and Literacy," which argues that digital diversions promote more substantive learning. As he once told UK newspaper *The Guardian*, "good video games . . . are complex designed systems that players have to learn to engage with reflectively and strategically." Many children can pass biology and physics tests, he points out, but few can apply that knowledge to solve real-world problems.

Job Training

Businesses and universities are increasingly turning to interactive simulations and virtual worlds as training tools to educate employees.

From Cisco to NASA, the U.S. Army to IBM, numerous corporations, government organizations and colleges have all employed interactive learning solutions.

Consider Loyalist College in Ontario, which offered students a simulation of U.S./Canada border crossings where they played the role of guards, and actually saw the rate of successful test scores jump from 56% to 95%. Or the Hilton Garden Inn, which built a custom 3-D hospitality training game for the PlayStation Portable, reasoning that it's more informative and reasonable for staffers to experiment by interacting with virtual customers.

Contextual Learning

10 Video games may soon save lives as well.

According to Dr. Jeffrey Taekman, the director of Duke University's Human Simulation and Patient Safety Center, "serious games and virtual environments are the future of education."

Besides offering medical students the ability to practice on patients (which is much safer in the digital world), simulations offer health care providers several upsides. Chief among them, he says, are the abilities to make choices, see results and apply information immediately.

Beyond allowing for greater scalability and group collaboration than traditional classrooms, every decision made in a virtual world, he continues, can be tracked and benchmarked against best practices, then standardized or archived for others' review. "The traditional textbook will soon become passé," he suggests. "Gaming platforms will offer an interactive way for students to learn and apply information in context."

Teamwork and Collaboration

Massively multiplayer games such as "World of Warcraft," "EVE Online" and "City of Heroes" may seem like idle fantasy and sci-fi escapes.

15 But many require active teamwork and high-level project management to do well. Collaborative elements often take the form of loose alliances disguised as in-game guilds, factions or virtual corporations where players join forces to complete objectives such as seizing territory or battling otherwise unstoppable opponents.

As Georgia Tech professor and Persuasive Games founder Ian Bogost explains, these titles frequently require advanced mastery of resource allocation and practical leadership techniques.

Requiring direct management and informed decision-making at multiple levels, group heads quickly learn to delegate responsibility, direct personnel and steer allies toward a common goal. Actively promoting teamwork between seemingly disparate individuals located states or entire countries apart, he says, all ironically offer preparation for a job in today's increasingly virtual workforce.

So, beware. Your superhero-obsessed buddy or Harry Potter-loving child may be tomorrow's next genius inventor or corporate mogul in disguise.

Reading Images: Ways of Reading

Image 1:
Girl Reading

Image 2:
Diverse et Artificiose Machine (1588)

Image 3:
The Multitasking Generation

Context: These images offer different ideas about the nature of reading raised in the next reading by Matthew Kirschenbaum. The first image, from the NEA report *To Read or Not to Read*, reveals the ideal of reading held by the authors of that report. The second, an image from a Renaissance book, shows a reader working his way through parallel passages in many works, comparing the passages rather than reading a single book from cover to cover. Image 3 is a portrait of a girl multitasking that gives several views of digital reading.

For Discussion: These three images reflect different approaches to text, which require different acts of attention and imply different purposes. What argument does each of these images make about the true purpose of reading?

For Writing: Using these three images as a starting point, construct your own definition of what constitutes an act of "reading" in the digital age. Which image fits best your own way of reading, whether a book or some other piece of writing?

> **BEFORE YOU READ:** Think about the ways in which you use your computer on a daily basis. Which activities would you generally characterize as "reading," and which activities as "writing"?

HOW READING IS BEING REIMAGINED*

Matthew Kirschenbaum

Matthew Kirschenbaum is an associate professor of English and the associate director of the Maryland Institute for Technology in the Humanities at the University of Maryland at College Park.

There is no doubt that it is time for a serious conversation about reading, not least because books themselves are changing.

Google, in cooperation with several dozen research libraries worldwide, is digitizing books at the rate of 3,000 a day. The noncommercial Open Content Alliance is scanning at a more modest pace but gaining ground, especially among institutions who chafe at some of the restrictions imposed by *Google* and its competitors. *LibraryThing*, an online book catalog that allows readers to list their books and find other readers with (sometimes uncannily) similar tastes, has almost 300,000 users who have collectively tagged some 20 million books. *Newsweek* ran a cover story on "The Future of Reading" in their November 26 [2007] issue. And on Monday, the same day that the National Endowment for the Arts released *To Read or Not to Read: A Question of National Consequence*, the follow-up to its controversial 2004 *Reading at Risk: A Survey of Literary Reading in America* report, Amazon.com launched Kindle, an e-book reader device that the *Newsweek* story describes as the "iPod of reading."

My purpose is not to debunk the NEA's most recent report, which synthesizes a number of studies to conclude that Americans—especially younger ones—are reading less, that they are reading "less well," and that these trends have disturbing implications for culture, civics, and even the national economy. The data are significant to anyone who cares about reading and its place in a 21st-century society, and deserve to be treated seriously. But clearly the report comes to us at a moment when reading and conversations about reading are in a state of flux. It's worth taking a moment to account for this broader context. High-profile projects like *Google*'s and new devices like Kindle suggest what I call the remaking of reading, meaning that reading is being both reimagined and re-engineered, made over creatively as well as technologically.

Historically, we've placed very different values on different kinds of reading. The reading of novels and other "literary" works—precisely the core concern of the earlier NEA report—has not always enjoyed the pride of place it has in the current cultural canon. When Cervantes sent poor, mad Don Quixote on his delirious adventures at the beginning of the 17th century, there existed a popular prejudice surrounding the reading of chivalric romances. Until well into the 19th century, novel-reading was regarded in Europe as a pastime fit mostly for women and the indolent—and

*Used by permission of Matthew Kirschenbaum.

a potentially dangerous one, since women, especially, could not be trusted to distinguish fiction from reality. But both the 2004 and the current report are curiously devoid of historical awareness, as though there is but a single, idealized model of reading from which we have strayed.

5   *To Read or Not to Read* deploys its own self-consistent iconography to tell us what reading is. In the pages of the report we find images of an adolescent male bent over a book, a female student sitting alone reading against a row of school lockers, and a white-collar worker studying a form. These still lives of the literate represent reading as self-evident—we know it when we see it. Yet they fail to acknowledge that such images have coexisted for centuries with other kinds of reading that have their own iconography and accoutrements: Medieval and early modern portraits of scholars and scribes at work at their desks show them adorned with many books (not just one), some of them bound and splayed on exotic devices for keeping them open and in view; Thomas Jefferson famously designed a lazy susan to rotate books in and out of his visual field. That kind of reading values comparison and cross-checking as much as focus and immersion—lateral reading as much as reading for depth.

That is the model of reading that seems compatible with the Web and other new electronic media. Yet it also raises fundamental questions about what it means to read, and what it means to have read something. When can we claim a book to have been read? What is the dividing line between reading and skimming? Must we consume a book in its entirety—start to finish, cover to cover—to say we have read it? Pierre Bayard, a literature professor in France, recently made a stir with a naughty little volume called *How to Talk about Books You Haven't Read*. When I read it (well, most of it), the book provoked the most intense author envy I have ever felt—not because I too secretly enjoy perpetuating literary frauds, but because Bayard speaks to a dilemma that will be familiar to every literate person: namely, that there are far more books in the world (50 million or 60 million by the estimates I've seen) than any of us will ever have time to read. Reading, Bayard says, is as much about mastering a system of relationships among texts and ideas as it is about reading any one text in great depth. He quotes the extreme case of the fictional librarian in Robert Musil's *The Man without Qualities* (a book Bayard admits to having only skimmed): The librarian resolutely reads no books whatsoever for fear that undue attention to any one of them will compromise the integrity of his relation to them all.

The structure of *To Read or Not to Read* presents itself as tacit acknowledgment that not all of its own text will likely be read by any one reader, since it is clearly designed to be "not read" in at least some of the ways that accord with Bayard's observations. The report is accompanied by an Executive Summary, a condensed version of the major findings. Its internal organization is carefully laid out, with summary points at the head of each chapter, topic sentences, extensive notes, sidebars, and sections labeled as conclusions.

The authors of the report would doubtlessly insist that the kind of person who reads (or doesn't read) books by French intellectuals writing about books they haven't read (or have only skimmed) is not the kind of reader who has them much worried. It's the people, especially the young ones, who are simply not reading at all that are cause for alarm. But the new report also places extreme emphasis on what it repeatedly terms "voluntary" reading. Reading that one does for work or for school doesn't "count" in this regard. While one can appreciate the motivations here—the NEA is interested in people who read because they choose to, not because they have to—it seems oddly retrograde. How many of us who count ourselves as avid readers are able to maintain clear boundaries between work and leisure anymore?

Likewise, while the authors of the report repeatedly emphasize that they include online reading in their data, the report sounds most clumsy and out of touch when referring to new media. The authors of the report tend to homogenize "the computer" without acknowledging the diversity of activity—and the diversity of reading—that takes place on its screen. Our screens are spaces where new forms like blogs and e-mail and chats commingle with remediations of older forms, like newspapers and magazines—or even poems, stories, and novels. Reading your friend's blog is not likely a replacement for reading Proust, but some blogs have been a venue for extraordinary writing, and we are not going to talk responsibly or well about what it means to read online until we stop conflating genre with value.

10   The report also fails to acknowledge the extent to which reading and writing have become commingled in electronic venues. The staccato rhythms of a real-time chat session are emblematic in this regard: Reading and writing all but collapse into a single unified activity. But there is a spectrum of writing online, just as there is a spectrum of reading, and more and more applications blur the line between the two. Many electronic book interfaces allow users to annotate their texts, for example; some allow users to share those notes and annotations with others (CommentPress, from the Institute for the Future of the Book, is

exemplary in this regard, as is Zotero, from the Center for History and New Media at George Mason University). Alph, a project directed by Nancy Kaplan at the University of Baltimore, is developing new online reading interfaces for children; the ability to leave notes and marks behind for these young readers' peers is a signature design feature. Book Glutton, a Web service still in beta mode, provides adult users with a shared electronic library; readers write notes for other readers in the margins of the books, and this virtual marginalia persists over time, accreting in Talmudic fashion.[1] Moreover, readers can choose to chat in real time with other readers perusing the same chapter that is on their screens.

What kind of activity is taking place here? What are the new metrics of screen literacy? I don't have that data, it's not my field, but anecdotally my instinct is that computer users are capable of projecting the same aura of deep concentration and immersion as the stereotypical bookworm. Walk into your favorite coffee shop and watch the people in front of their screens. Rather than bug-eyed, frenzied jittering, you are more likely to see calm, meditative engagement—and hear the occasional click of fingers on keyboards as the readers write.

Editor's Notes

1. The Talmud is a record of rabbinic discussions pertaining to Jewish law, ethics, customs, and history. The Talmud is perhaps second in authority only to the Jewish Bible (Old Testament). Here Kirschbaum refers to the cumulative and encyclopedic nature of the Talmud.

B. How Is Technology Changing Our Definition of What It Means to Be Human?

> **BEFORE YOU READ:** Kurzweil talks about a number of technologies that, in the near future, will let us control our bodies and biological predispositions. At this point in time, what do you think is the most amazing or interesting way in which science is letting us control our bodies?

OUR BODIES, OUR TECHNOLOGIES*

Ray Kurzweil

Ray Kurzweil has been described as "the restless genius" by *The Wall Street Journal*. He invented the first flat-bed scanner, pioneered omni-font optical character recognition, the first print-to-speech reading machine for the blind, the first text-to-speech synthesizer, and the first music synthesizer capable of recreating orchestral instruments. This essay is an abridged version of Kurzweil's Cambridge Forum Lecture.

In the 2020s, we'll see nanobots, blood-cell-sized devices that can go inside the body and brain to perform therapeutic functions. But what happens when we have billions of nanobots inside the capillaries of our brains, non-invasively, widely distributed, expanding human intelligence, or providing full-immersion virtual reality? It turns out that information technology is increasingly encompassing everything of value. It's not just computers, it's not just electronic gadgets. It now includes the field of biology. We're beginning to understand how life processes, disease, aging, are manifested as information processes and gaining the tools to actually manipulate those processes. It's true of all of our creations of intellectual and cultural endeavors, our music, movies are all facilitated by information technology, and are distributed, and represented as information.

Evolutionary processes work through indirection. Evolution creates a capability, and then it uses that capability to evolve the next stage. That's why the next stage goes more quickly, and that's why the fruits of an evolutionary process grow exponentially. The first paradigm shift in biological evolution, the evolution of cells, and in particular DNA (actually, RNA came first)—the

evolution of essentially a computer system or an information processing backbone that would allow evolution to record the results of its experiments—took billions of years. Once DNA and RNA were in place, the next stage, the Cambrian explosion, when all the body plans of the animals were evolved, went a hundred times faster. Then those body plans were used by evolution to concentrate on higher cognitive functions. Biological evolution kept accelerating in this manner. *Homo sapiens*, our species, evolved in only a few hundred thousand years, the blink of an eye in evolutionary terms.

Then again working through indirection, biological evolution used one of its creations, the first technology-creating species to usher in the next stage of evolution, which was technology. The enabling factors for technology were a higher cognitive function with an opposable appendage, so we could manipulate and change the environment to reflect our models of what could be. The first stages of technology evolution—fire, the wheel, stone tools—only took a few tens of thousands of years.

Technological evolution also accelerated. Half a millennium ago the printing press took a century to be adopted, half a century ago the first computers were designed pen

---

*Used by permission of Ray Kurzweil.

on paper. Now computers are designed in only a few weeks' time by computer designers sitting at computers, using advanced computer-assisted design software. When I was at MIT [Massachusetts Institute of Technology] in the mid-1960s, a computer that took about the size of this room cost millions of dollars yet was less powerful than the computer in your cell phone today.

5   One of the profound implications is that we are understanding our biology as information processes. We have 23,000 little software programs inside us called genes. These evolved in a different era. One of those programs, called the fat insulin receptor gene, says, basically, hold onto every calorie because the next hunting season might not work out so well. We'd like to change that program now. We have a new technology that has just emerged in the last couple years called RNA interference, in which we put fragments of RNA inside the cell, as a drug, to inhibit selected genes. It can actually turn genes off by blocking the messenger RNA expressing that gene. When the fat insulin receptor was turned off in mice, the mice ate ravenously and remained slim. They didn't get diabetes, didn't get heart disease, they lived 20 percent longer, they got the benefit of caloric restriction without the restriction.

Every major disease and every major aging process has different genes that are used in the expression of these disease and aging processes. Being able to actually select when we turn them off is one powerful methodology. We also have the ability to turn enzymes off. Torcetrapib, a drug that's now in FDA Phase 3 trials, turns off a key enzyme that destroys the good cholesterol, HDL, in the blood. If you inhibit that enzyme, HDL levels soar and atherosclerosis slows down or stops.

There are thousands of these developments in the pipeline. The new paradigm of rational drug design involves actually understanding the information processes underlying biology, the exact sequence of steps that leads up to a process like atherosclerosis, which causes heart attacks, or cancer, or

insulin resistance, and providing very precise tools to intervene. Our ability to do this is also growing at an escalating rate.

Another exponential process is miniaturization. We're showing the feasibility of actually constructing things at the molecular level that can perform useful functions. One of the biggest applications of this, again, will be in biology, where we will be able to go inside the human body and go beyond the limitations of biology. Rob Freitas has designed a nanorobotic red blood cell, which is a relatively simple device, it just stores oxygen and lets it out. A conservative analysis of these robotic respirocytes shows that if you were to replace ten percent of your red blood cells with these robotic versions you could do an Olympic sprint for 15 minutes without taking a breath, or sit at the bottom of your pool for four hours. It will be interesting to see what we do with these in our Olympic contests. Presumably we'll ban them, but then we'll have the specter of high school students routinely outperforming the Olympic athletes.

A robotic white blood cell is also being designed. A little more complicated, it downloads software from the Internet to combat specific pathogens. If it sounds very futuristic to download information to a device inside your body to perform a health function, I'll point out that we're already doing that. There are about a dozen neural implants either FDA-approved or approved for human testing. One implant that is FDA-approved for actual clinical use replaces the biological neurons destroyed by Parkinson's disease. The neurons in the vicinity of this implant then receive signals from the computer that's inside the patient's brain. This hybrid of biological and non-biological intelligence works perfectly well. The latest version of this device allows the patient to download new software to the neural implant in his brain from outside his body.

10   These are devices that today require surgery to be implanted, but when we get to the 2020s, we will ultimately have the "killer app" of nanotechnology, nanobots, which are blood cell-sized devices that can go inside the body

and brain to perform therapeutic functions, as well as advance the capabilities of our bodies and brains. If *that* sounds futuristic, I'll point out that we already have blood cell-sized devices that are nano-engineered, working to perform therapeutic functions in animals. For example, one scientist cured type I diabetes in rats with this type of nano-engineered device. And some of these are now approaching human trials. The 2020s really will be the "golden era" of nanotechnology.

It is a mainstream view now among informed observers that by the 2020s we will have sufficient computer processing to emulate the human brain. The current controversy, or I would say, the more interesting question is, will we have the software or methods of human intelligence? To achieve the methods, the algorithms of human intelligence, there is underway a grand project to reverse-engineer the brain. And there, not surprisingly, we are also making exponential progress. If you follow the trends in reverse brain engineering it's a reasonable conclusion that we will have reverse-engineered the several hundred regions of the brain by the 2020s.

By early in the next decade, computers won't look like today's notebooks and PDAs, they will disappear, integrated into our clothing and environment. Images will be written to our retinas for our eyeglasses and contact lenses, we'll have full-immersion virtual reality. We'll be interacting with virtual personalities; we can see early harbingers of this already. We'll have effective language translation. If we go out to 2029, there will be many turns of the screw in terms of this exponential progression of information technology. There will be about thirty doublings in the next 25 years. That's a factor of a billion in capacity and price performance over today's technology, which is already quite formidable.

By 2029, we will have completed reverse engineering of the brain, we will understand how human intelligence works, and that will give us new insight into ourselves. Non-biological intelligence will combine the suppleness and subtlety of our pattern-recognition capabilities with ways computers have already demonstrated their superiority. Every time you use *Google* you can see the power of non-biological intelligence. Machines can remember things very accurately. They can share their knowledge instantly. We can share our knowledge, too, but at the slow bandwidth of language.

This will not be an alien invasion of intelligent machines coming from over the horizon to compete with us, it's emerging from within our civilization, it's extending the power of our civilization. Even today we routinely do intellectual feats that would be impossible without our technology. In fact our whole economic infrastructure couldn't manage without the intelligent software that's underlying it.

15 The most interesting application of computerized nanobots will be to interact with our biological neurons. We've already shown the feasibility of using electronics and biological neurons to interact non-invasively. We could have billions of nanobots inside the capillaries of our brains, non-invasively, widely distributed, expanding human intelligence, or providing full immersion virtual reality encompassing all of the senses from within the nervous system. Right now we have a hundred trillion connections. Although there's a certain amount of plasticity, biological intelligence is essentially fixed. Non-biological intelligence is growing exponentially; the crossover point will be in the 2020s. When we get to the 2030s and 2040s, it will be the non-biological portion of our civilization that will be predominant. But it will still be an expression of human civilization.

Every time we have technological gains we make gains in life expectancy. Sanitation was a big one, antibiotics was another. We're now in the beginning phases of this biotechnology revolution. We're exploring, understanding and gaining the tools to reprogram the information processes underlying biology; and that will result in another big gain in life expectancy. So, if you watch your health today, the old-fashioned way, you can actually live to see the remarkable 21st century.

BEFORE YOU READ: If, either now or in the future, you and your spouse or partner were unable to have a child and were offered the choice of either using an egg donor or adopting a child, which method do you think you would choose and why?

YOUR GAMETE, MYSELF*

Peggy Orenstein

Peggy Orenstein is a contributing writer for *The New York Times Magazine* and author of the memoir *Waiting for Daisy: A Tale of Two Continents, Three Religions, Five Infertility Doctors, an Oscar, an Atomic Bomb, a Romantic Night and One Woman's Quest to Become a Mother.*

Two years ago, when Catherine was in sixth grade, she was given a school assignment that would have been unremarkable for most kids: make a timeline for history class in which half the events occurred before she was born and half after. For a while, she worked quietly at the dining-room table of her family's rambling Northern California home. Then she looked up.

"Mom?" she asked. "What was the year that you and Dad met our donor?"

Sitting with me in May, Catherine's mother, Marie, a 59-year-old therapist, smiled wryly, remembering the incident. The crinkling of Marie's eyes gave her a passing resemblance to the actress Anne Bancroft—but not to her own daughter. Marie, who asked me to use only her middle name and a family name for her daughter to protect their privacy, is dark where Catherine is blond, olive-skinned where Catherine is fair, brown-eyed where the

For Discussion: What comment on the process of selecting an egg donor does this collage of women's faces with labels make?

For Writing: Using the categories offered by this collage, describe what combination of qualities would make a "perfect" child. Would you feel comfortable "engineering" a child by genetic means?

Context: The caption reads: *Your Gamete, Yourself* by Balint Zesko. This image is an illustration to the essay with which it appears, and so comments directly on its themes.

*Reproduced by permission of the author.

girl's are hazel. There is no similarity to their jaw lines, their cheekbones, the shapes of their faces. Of course, lots of kids don't look like their mothers; few people would consider that odd, though they might—often incessantly—comment on it in conversation.

"So, what's going to happen with this project?" Marie recalled responding to Catherine at the time, being careful to keep her voice neutral. "Is it going to be put up in the hallway? In the classroom?"

5   Catherine shrugged. "I don't know," she said. And later, "Mom, this is my timeline."

"I got the message," Marie told me. "But in essence, I was outed on the wall of the middle school. It was there in black and white for everyone to see. They'd all know we used an egg donor. We'd been committed to openness from the beginning, but my first reaction was, 'No!'"

If Marie and Catherine are unusual, it is only because of Catherine's age. In 1992, the year she was conceived, there were just 1,802 attempts by women to become pregnant using someone else's eggs, according to the Centers for Disease Control. Three years later, there were more than 4,738 such cycles; by 2004, the most recent year for which data has been published, there were 15,175 cycles, resulting in 5,449 babies. By comparison, some 22,911 children were adopted from abroad that year, and although there are no official figures, one survey estimated that at least the same number are conceived annually via donor insemination. Donor eggs are now used in 12 percent of all in vitro fertilization (I.V.F.) attempts, making it among the fastest-growing infertility treatments. Despite the portentous hype around women like Frieda Birnbaum, a 60-year-old New Jersey resident who in May used donor eggs to become the oldest American to give birth to twins, the bulk of intended mothers are in their 40s. The birthrate among women ages 40–44 has risen 62 percent since 1990, while the rate among those in their late 40s has more than doubled. Among those

who used I.V.F. in 2004, about a third of the 43-year-olds used someone else's eggs; by 47 years old, 91 percent did. [. . .]

One day this spring, Becky, who is 38, met me at the airy loft in a sketchy neighborhood of Oakland, Calif., where she works in the music industry. She is a tiny woman—just over five feet tall—with dark blond ringlets pulled back in a ponytail and three earrings ascending one ear. A wedding photo on her desk, taken last summer, showed her tucked beneath the arm of her husband, Russell, a public-school teacher who is more than a foot taller than she and who asked that I use only his middle name. [. . .]

Becky, who asked me to use a nickname, sat down and began scrolling through pictures on the Web site of Ova the Rainbow, one of the (regrettably named) agency sites she browsed last fall during her search for an egg donor. "When I first started doing this it was really emotional for me," she said. "I kept thinking about that kids' book, 'Are You My Mother?' I'm looking through these pictures of young women and feeling like: 'Oh, my God! Is this the mother of my future child? Is this the mother of my future child?'"

10   I stood behind her, watching the young women go by. Each was accompanied by an assortment of photos: girls in caps and gowns graduating from high school, sunburned and smiling on family vacations, as preschoolers in princess frocks, sporting supermodel pouts in shopping-mall glamour portraits. Sperm banks rarely provide such visuals, which is just one disparity in the packaging and treatment of male and female donors, according to a study published last month in *The American Sociological Review*. Egg donors are often thanked with presents and notes by recipients for their generous "gift." [. . .]

It was weird to look at these pictures with Becky. I inevitably objectified the young women in them, evaluating their component parts; it made me feel strangely like a guy. Becky clicked on a photo of a 22-year-old brunette with a toothy grin. Each profile listed the donor's age (many agencies consider donors to be over the hill by 30), hair color (there seemed to be a preponderance of blondes), eye color, weight, ethnicity, marital status, education level, high school or college G.P.A.'s, college major, evidence of "proved" fertility (having children of their own or previous successful cycles). Some agencies include blood type for recipients who don't plan to tell their child about his conception. Others include bust size and favorite movies, foods and TV shows. [. . .]

"Why don't you just adopt?" That is the first question most people ask if you say you're considering egg donation. It's the question I asked myself, as had every potential donor recipient I spoke with. Why create a child where none existed? Why spend the money on something that's not a sure bet? Why ask another woman, even (or maybe especially) a friend, to inject herself with drugs—drugs whose side effects, although unlikely, could require hospitalization and even, in extremely rare instances, be fatal. (Recipients of donor eggs are required to buy supplementary health insurance for the donors in case something untoward occurs.)

The answers among the women I met were both deeply personal and surprisingly consistent. Like Becky, these women longed for the experience of pregnancy, childbirth and breast-feeding. Often they (or, more often, their husbands) resisted adoption, reasoning that egg donation would be psychologically easier on the child, who would be born—rather than relinquished—into its family. They wanted the opportunity to handpick a donor's genes rather than gamble on a birth mother's and father's. And they wanted to be able to see at least their husbands, if not themselves, reflected in their children's faces. [. . .]

Yet there is often no way to know whether the information the donor gives, including her medical history and educational background, is accurate. A 2006 study conducted by researchers at New York

University found that donors routinely low-balled their weight, and the heavier they were, the more they fudged. Agencies, too, which are unregulated and unlicensed, can easily manipulate the truth. Many advertise I.Q. and psychological testing as part of their services, though there is no independent verification of either the results or the protocols used. Even if there were, jacking up fees for smarts is a dubious prospect. "Fees for donors are based on time and trouble, so I don't see how someone who goes to Brown has more time or trouble doing this than someone who didn't go to college at all," Feingold, the psychologist, told me. "Parents are vulnerable. People would be willing to do a lot to take charge so that they didn't need to feel so sad, bad, fearful, and out of control. They'll pay more money, do testing. But it's impossible to do intelligence testing on an egg."

15   To discourage both fraud and undue inducement, the ethics committee of the American Society for Reproductive Medicine (A.S.R.M.) issued a position paper in 2006 on donor compensation: $5,000, they determined, was a reasonable, but not coercive fee. Anything beyond that needed "justification," and sums over $10,000 went "beyond what is appropriate." What's more, the committee denounced paying more for "personal attributes," saying that the practice commodifies human gametes. [. . .]

The agency Becky eventually used charged her a flat $6,500 donor fee (there would've been a comparatively reasonable $500 premium if she had requested a Jewish or Asian donor) along with a $3,800 agency fee. Additionally, there were the costs of the donor's medical screening and health insurance; legal fees; reimbursement for the donor's and possibly a companion's travel expenses if the donor was from out of the area (Becky's wasn't); and reimbursement for lost wages and child care. There were also the costs associated with any I.V.F. cycle: not only the fertility drugs, but also physician, clinic, and lab fees. And fees for freezing any unused embryos, in case the transfer failed or the couple wanted to have another child. Becky estimated that she and Russell would eventually be out about $35,000. [. . .]

According to several studies, most donor recipients haven't told their children about their origins, though some researchers argue that this trend is reversing. . . . In truth, it isn't clear that secrecy is necessarily damaging. In the most extensive longitudinal study to date, Susan Golombok, the director of the Center for Family Research at Cambridge University in England, has compared families who have sperm-donor children with those who have egg-donor children, as well as with those who used conventional I.V.F. and those who conceived naturally. In 2006, when her team last checked in with the donor-conceived children, they were 12, and most had not been told the nature of their conception. The kids in all of the groups were equally well adjusted. What's more, parents of donor-conceived kids (and those who used conventional I.V.F.) were more involved with their kids' lives than those who had conceived naturally. [. . .]

Once a child knows she was donor-conceived, what then? How far do her rights extend? Should she be able to meet her donor, and who gets to decide? It was clear to Marie, the donor recipient who is also an adoptee, that knowing one's genetic lineage should not just be an option, it should be an entitlement. . . . [Marie and Catherine] have been in phone and e-mail contact with the donor, who at the time of the donation was a college student interning for an acquaintance of Marie's, ever since. Catherine has known about the woman since preschool. "The comments she'd make about it at 5 were different than at 10," Marie said. "At 5, we'd be driving to Safeway, and this little voice in the back of the car would say, 'Now, what's an egg donor again?' At 10 there were a lot of questions about who she looked like and 'Why don't I look like you?'"

Then, when Catherine was 12, came the moment that all of the donor recipients I spoke to told me they dreaded. "She turned to me in this relaxed, 'Hey, Mom, isn't this interesting' kind of voice and said, 'You know, technically speaking, you're not actually my mother.'"

20   This, Marie said, is where it helped to be a trained therapist—and perhaps an adoptee as well, someone who has understood from experience both the salience and limits of genetic relationships, that DNA doesn't make the mom, but children need to figure out what, if anything, it signifies. "It was her way of acknowledging that this means something to her that's completely independent of her relationship to me. And that's inevitable: no amount of being wanted, planned for or loved eliminates that piece of the experience."

Last winter, the donor, who is now 36, single and childless, began pressing for a closer relationship with Catherine. She invited the girl and her parents to her house for dinner, the first time they had gotten together in several years. Halfway through the meal, and against Marie's explicit instructions, she pulled out a collection of family photos: her mother, brothers, sisters, nieces, and nephews. Catherine recoiled. "The donor has this great need to make Catherine into family because she doesn't have children of her own," Marie said. "My husband and I had to tell her: 'That's Catherine's decision. It's not yours or even ours.' So now the two continue to e-mail but rarely get together." [. . .]

A few days after my conversation with Marie, I talked to Becky. She had just found out she was pregnant with twins. . . . She paused a moment, thinking about her future. "I'm just happy," she said. Finally, Becky would be a mother, her husband a father, the two of them building a family with all the conflict, joy and unpredictability that entails—regardless of whose genes are involved.

BEFORE YOU READ: How do you understand the term "second life"? In your opinion, is it valid to define an online persona as a supplement to or replacement for "real life"?

MAKING A LIVING IN SECOND LIFE*

Kathleen Craig

Kathleen Craig is a frequent contributor to *Wired* magazine.

Jennifer Grinnell, Michigan furniture delivery dispatcher turned fashion designer in cyber space, never imagined that she could make a living in a video game. Grinnell's shop, Mischief, is in *Second Life*, a virtual world whose users are responsible for creating all content. Grinnell's digital clothing and "skins" allow users to change the appearance of their avatars—their online representations—beyond their wildest Barbie dress-up dreams.

Within a month, Grinnell was making more in *Second Life* than in her real-world job as a dispatcher. And after three months she realized she could quit her day job altogether.

Now *Second Life* is her primary source of income, and Grinnell, whose avatar answers to the name Janie Marlowe, claims she earns more than four times her previous salary.

Grinnell isn't alone. Artists and designers, landowners and currency speculators, are turning the virtual environment of *Second Life* into a real-world profit center.

5   "It's not just a game anymore," said online artisan Kimberly Rufer-Bach. "There are businesses, nonprofits and universities" taking advantage of the online world.

With users now numbering over 130,000, game-maker Linden Lab estimates that nearly $5 million, or about $38 per person, was exchanged between players in January 2006 alone. Working in *Second Life* is "the same as working in London and sending money home to pay the rent for your spouse," said company CEO Philip Rosedale.

Just ask Rufer-Bach, known in *Second Life* as Kim Anubus, who works full time making virtual objects for real-life organizations. In a recent contract with the UC Davis Medical Center, Rufer-Bach created virtual clinics in *Second Life* to train emergency workers who might be called upon to rapidly set up medical facilities in a national crisis. The work is funded by the Centers for Disease Control. "In the event of a biological attack? The CDC have to set up emergency 12-hour push sites, to distribute antibiotics," said Rufer-Bach.

To create the most realistic simulation possible, Rufer-Bach crafted about 80 distinct objects, "from chairs (to) a forklift, plumbing, wiring," she said. The end result is a training environment that's not only lifelike, but relatively inexpensive. "There are substantial advantages to doing this training in the virtual world," said UC Davis professor Peter Yellowlees. For one thing, it's "incredibly cheaper."

Of course, most of the business opportunities in *Second Life* don't involve anything as weighty as medical training. The game has a significant market in specialized avatars: People pay as much as 2,200 in-game "Linden dollars," or just over $8, for stock avatars—with custom work commanding prices that can go much higher. Rufer-Bach ordered a special avatar for her mother, "a knee-high lavender warthog, with a tiara and wings and a big fat spleef with smoke effects."

10   The game world's mixture of fancy and serious business can lead to some incongruous scenes. "We joke that you just don't show up at a business meeting as a mermaid," said Rufer-Bach. "One guy is a furry, with an animal head. Another's a ball of glowing fuzz. There's a giant two-story robot transformer."

Once they've perfected their look, *Second Life* immigrants who want to build virtual homes often purchase or rent land from entrepreneurs like Tony De Louise, from Long Island, New York, who gave up the meatspace rat race to become an online landlord. "I've worked two to three jobs most of my life," said De Louise. Now, "instead of coming home at 10:30 at night, I'm home and can help my wife put our new baby to bed."

De Louise and business partner Alice McKeon own d'Alliez Island Rentals, and now lease land on a chain of in-world islands they own. They pay Linden Labs $1,250 for each island, plus a $195 monthly maintenance fee. Renters in turn pay from $15 to $75 for average-size land parcels.

"We have three purely residential (islands), one purely commercial," said De Louise, whose in-world name is Tony Beckett. "Two are for furries," who prefer animal-like avatars.

The landowners act as benign dictators of their property, making sure the islands are calm and protected, and helping renters get started building their own homes or businesses.

15   Even with seventeen islands in their cyber archipelago, De Louise and McKeon don't expect to catch up with *Second Life*'s most famous landowner, Anshe Chung, who reportedly makes more than $150,000 a year in the virtual world.

"We've taken it very slow," said McKeon, known in *Second Life* as Alliez Mysterio. "We reinvested the money we've made and that's how we have the seventeen islands." McKeon said *Second Life* is now her sole source of income.

De Louise said *Second Life* can be difficult to explain to friends, who invariably ask, "People pay you money to rent land that doesn't exist?" "I say, you've got to see it," said De Louise. "Watch the videos off the Web site and after you take your chin off the floor, come on in."

With more and more people cashing in on *Second Life*, the most pressing question may be, how many can benefit before the boom times end?

Wharton professor Dan Hunter, an expert on law and virtual worlds, said *Second Life*'s relatively small size makes its economic future hard to predict. But virtual worlds are becoming spaces where "globalization of services can occur," he said. "In *SL*, services are valued. 'Hey, I can provide something that someone else wants! And I can make money from it!' The expansion of the economy is almost certainly going to be dependent on expanding the service opportunities."

20   This, said Hunter, "can be generalized to a range of services—a tremendously important trend in employment in the 21st century. I confidently predict that my kids (currently 6 and 4 years old) will end up working within one or more of these worlds."

For now, any uncertainty within *Second Life* only seems to energize its entrepreneurs. "It's growing, changing," De Louise said. "And in chaos, there are opportunities. That's what *Second Life* is, it's opportunity."

McKeon agrees. "And you have to be willing to go after that opportunity."

Questions to Help You Think and Write About Modern Technology

1. Morozov worries about the ways digital technology makes us "dumber." Steinberg, conversely, argues that digital tools can serve as a powerful vehicle for fostering new kinds of intelligence. Take one example of digital culture—a blog, a YouTube video, a Facebook profile, etc.—and use it as evidence in an argument in support of either Morozov or Steinberg's perspective.

2. Dick Locher's cartoon and the essay by Carr explore the ways in which our lives are governed by the machines that make social communication simple and easy. For one full day, make a hourly chart and keep a record of how much time you spend doing different kinds of activities: reading, writing, eating, exercising, thinking, catching up on the news, communicating, doing homework, praying, and so on. For which of these activities do you need technology? Is technology making your life easier and more efficient or is it just eating up your time?

3. While Carr and Morozov raise questions about the dangers and limitations of online technology, consider instead the ways in which sites like YouTube or Facebook can give you a glimpse of people, places, ideas, and activities to which you otherwise would not have access. Find one YouTube video on a topic of your choice, then look at four or five videos on related topics that the YouTube search function offers you. Argue the claim that the positives of YouTube outweigh the negatives, using the videos you have watched as your supports. What new information, skills, or social/cultural knowledge have you gained from this activity?

4. Using Matt Kirschenbaum's observation that the line between reading and writing is becoming blurred by computers, consider an online or computer-facilitated method of communication with which you are familiar. List the ways in which the activity could be described as one that involves "reading," then list the ways in which the activity could be described as "writing." What do you think is the relationship between reading and writing in a computer environment?

5. Kurzweil explores the implications of genetic engineering for both individuals and human society. Take one aspect of life that, according to these authors, could be improved by genetic science and consider whether intervening in the "genetic lottery" is a good or bad thing. In what ways can science help to overcome this problem? Are there other ways to accomplish the goal of making people lead longer and better lives? Which way is preferable?

6. **Arguing Like a Citizen:** Orenstein explores some of the key questions raised by the growing prevalence of *in vitro* fertilization. Conduct some firsthand research of your own into the ways *in vitro* fertilization is being debated in the larger culture. What are the key arguments made in favor of this practice? What are the key criticisms leveled against it? Which side of this debate do you find more persuasive? Why?

SECTION 3

Education and Learning

The Issues

A. What Are the Key Problems Confronting Higher Education?

This section considers the challenges currently confronting the world of higher education. Tressie McMillan Cottom looks at the demographic changes transforming the typical college student body, and on this basis argues for a radical rethinking of what college should be. Scott Jaschik, meanwhile, focuses on a more particular aspect of college life, advocating for significant changes in the ways college students are graded. Turning our attention to the economics of higher education, the editorial writers at the *Daily Californian* offer recommendations for making college more affordable, while Kevin Carey directs a critical gaze at the ways higher education has become increasingly commercialized.

B. What Role Should Technology Play in Education?

The readings in this section all examine the ways technology is reshaping the ways we think about and define education. In taking up this question, several of the pieces here focus on online technology in particular. Sarah Perez looks at the unintended consequences Facebook can have on college students' prospects for graduation. David Silver explores the growing prevalence of such online communication tools as Twitter within the classroom. Kerry Soper investigates the ways that teacher evaluation Web sites are changing the relationship between students and professors. And Mira Jacob supplements this focus by taking a look at the ways a different form of technology—educational videos aimed at toddlers—plays a similar role in changing the ways we think about kids and learning.

Exploring Online Argument

The following Web sites present interesting perspectives on education and learning.

No Child Left Behind	National Network of Digital Schools
Race to the Top	Open Source Education: Open Source Initiative
US Charter Schools	*Chronicle of Higher Education*
About Home Schooling	National Education Association (NEA)
Progressive Education Network	STEM Education Curriculum

The Rhetorical Situation

The exigence for the issues related to education has increased markedly over the last few years. With the passage of such legislation as the No Child Left Behind Act and the federal school funding initiative Race to the Top, questions about how best to educate young people, how to make our schools more effective, and how to make American students globally competitive have gained greater and greater public attention. Motivational warrants linked to the needs for quality education and equal opportunity are implicit in many of the arguments about education and school.

Two areas in which contemporary attitudes toward education reform have become complicated are in the question of affordability and the role of technology. As college tuitions have grown exponentially over the last several years, the question of higher education affordability has grown increasingly urgent for a growing number of students. Similarly, the emergence of new educational technologies has raised questions about the true nature and purpose of education. Can online tools like email, texting, and Facebook be utilized to enhance student learning? If so, how? Are there drawbacks or pitfalls to converting part of school into a virtual experience?

A. What Are the Key Problems Confronting Higher Education?

> **BEFORE YOU READ:** How would you define the "typical" college student? Do you think this definition is changing? If so, how?

REDEFINING THE "TYPICAL" COLLEGE STUDENT*
Tressie McMillan Cottom

The author is a staff writer for the online journal *Slate* and a PhD candidate in sociology at Emory University. This piece appeared in *Slate* in 2013.

Our nation's system of over 6,700 colleges and universities is said to be outdated, overpriced, and losing the public's trust. President Obama appears to agree. His college-affordability plan may have been pushed below the fold by Syria and Miley Cyrus when he introduced it a few weeks back, but his proposal continues to make waves. The plan would dramatically alter the form and extent of federal involvement in an arena where states and semi-autonomous institutions have historically reigned supreme. It's an audacious proposal designed for complicated times. But it does not address the real higher education crisis as it is experienced by the majority of college students.

Here's how the Obama administration sees it. College demand is up and the White House wants to see it rise further. Obama previously pledged a 20 percent increase in Americans age 25 to 34 with a college degree by 2020. These reform proposals reflect the administration's belief that degrees spur economic innovation and train workers for the skilled jobs of the future. The problem is that the price of college has been steadily increasing along with demand. Obama's challenge in a nutshell: More people want college, we want more people to want college, but the high cost of college interferes with that goal.

On its own terms, Obama's proposal makes sense ideologically, if not practically.

Among the proposals are fairly benign goals, such as devising a rating system for college quality and experimenting with online learning. The rating system—which would look at the potential earnings of graduates relative to the cost of tuition, for example, or compare outcomes among students from similar demographic backgrounds—is controversial; institutions may fear rankings that pit schools against each other with the authority of the government. Even more controversial are eventual plans to link these ratings to eligibility to participate in federal aid programs. In 2010, 57 percent of all undergraduate students used federal student aid to help pay for college. A college that can't offer federal aid to students may not long be in business.

Ratings haven't worked out all that well at the K–12 level, and there are some good critiques out there of how difficult it will be to pull off the ratings model for colleges and universities. People who study higher education can cry you a river over how difficult it is to objectively measure something as subjective as quality. It is hard to imagine that the federal government will devise standard measures that researchers have struggled to agree upon for years. But the biggest potential problem is that there is little evidence that students make college decisions based on this kind of information. Some students want to attend the most prestigious college they can, while others want to follow friends or go as far away from home as possible.

5   More importantly, typical college students today are not straight-from-high-school young adults. They are older. They've worked or are working. They have families. They care for parents or children. Their lives don't necessarily accommodate a full-time, four-year enrollment. Their educational choices are often about convenience, geography, and access. They're not necessarily looking for the information that the Obama administration wants to give them.

Public policy and debates about the higher education crisis focus on an ideal college student that does not reflect reality. Recent high school graduates taking part in the residential college experience represent just 15 percent of all college students. This trend has been clear to researchers for some time. Even traditional-aged students are more likely to be in nontraditional college arrangements than they are a dorm room, as 50 percent of them are enrolled part-time. Older adult students are increasing their share of higher education enrollment: 38 percent of college students in 2011 were 24 or older. Depending on your definition of a "nontraditional" student, they may account for as much as two-thirds of all college students.

Higher education is serving more students who may take longer to graduate, who may need to cobble together credits from several institutions, and who, as a result, use financial aid differently. These are all trends projected to intensify. Many colleges have responded to these demographic changes by trying to attract a dwindling pool of traditional students. This institutional status contest is related to the increasing cost of college, as institutions spend money to attract wealthier students. This competition diverts attention, resources, and policy away from the needs of the new typical college student.

That same new typical college student faces a range of economic and social pressures that make pursing higher education an imperative. Higher-quality jobs require more credentials while jobs in the middle of the ladder are declining. Labor training is being transferred to the public account, by requiring workers to pay for their own skills training through financial aid programs. Workers caught in this squeeze are receiving an ideological message from the White House that they are morally, personally responsible for attaining credentials that the private sector values. At the same time, the conditions of being a nontraditional student limit the available choices for how to attain these credentials, and almost the only means of paying for them is through federal student aid. Often, the options that are left are the most expensive: The pricier for-profit sector has positioned itself as the flexible, accessible, occupational solution for nontraditional students. Ratings and measures don't address that reality. What these students need are practical choices. Most of those practical choices sound a lot like jobs—good jobs that pay a living wage. Federal higher education policy could stand a dose of economic policy that focuses more on today's job conditions. Higher education policy often neglects significant debates—about minimum wage increases, welfare-to-work policies, and declines in public sector hiring, for example—that inform how students make their educational choices.

We are also overlooking a major ideological shift in what federal student aid is meant to subsidize. It was originally intended to provide equal opportunities to attain a college education. Now, federal aid often takes form as public subsidies of the private sector to provide lifelong career training for workers. We deserve a more robust debate on whether that's what the public wants or deserves. In the meantime, what we'll get is a rating system for students to choose between paying more than they would like and *way* more than they would like to purchase a credential that is, effectively, a lottery ticket for a job.

BEFORE YOU READ: What are your own experiences with grades? In your view, are grades a valid measure of student performance? What are the kinds of things grades can tell us about student learning? What are the kinds of things grades cannot tell us?

GETTING OUT OF GRADING*

Scott Jaschik

A former editor at *The Chronicle of Higher Education*, Jaschik leads the editorial operations of *Inside Higher Education*. He has published articles on colleges in such publications as *The New York Times*, *The Boston Globe*, *The Washington Post*, and *Salon*.

Few parts of their jobs seem to annoy professors more than grading. The topic consumes gripe sessions, blog posts and creates plenty of professorial angst (not to mention student angst).

Cathy Davidson has decided that the best way to change grading is to take herself out of it. Davidson, a Duke University English professor, announced on her blog last week that she was going to give students the power to earn A's or some other grade based on a simple formula in which she wouldn't play much of a role.

"I loved returning to teaching last year after several years in administration . . . except for the grading," she wrote on her blog. "I can't think of a more meaningless, superficial, cynical way to evaluate learning than by assigning a grade. It turns learning (which should be a deep pleasure, setting up for a lifetime of curiosity) into a crass competition: how do I snag the highest grade for the least amount of work? how do I give the prof what she wants so I can get the A that I need for med school? That's the opposite of learning and curiosity, the opposite of everything I believe as a teacher, and is, quite frankly, a waste of my

time and the students' time. There has to be a better way . . ."

Her approach? "So, this year, when I teach 'This Is Your Brain on the Internet,' I'm trying out a new point system. Do all the work, you get an A. Don't need an A? Don't have time to do all the work? No problem. You can aim for and earn a B. There will be a chart. You do the assignment satisfactorily, you get the points. Add up the points, there's your grade. Clearcut. No guesswork. No second-guessing 'what the prof wants.' No gaming the system. Clearcut. Student is responsible."

5   That still leaves the question of determining whether students have done the work. Here again, Davidson plans to rely on students. "Since I already have structured my seminar (it worked brilliantly last year) so that two students lead us in every class, they can now also read all the class blogs (as they used to) and pass judgment on whether they are satisfactory. Thumbs up, thumbs down," she writes.

"If not, any student who wishes can revise. If you revise, you get the credit. End of story. Or, if you are too busy and want to skip it, no problem. It just means you'll have

---

*Used by permission of *Inside Higher Education*.

fewer ticks on the chart and will probably get the lower grade. No whining. It's clearcut and everyone knows the system from day one. (btw, every study of peer review among students shows that students perform at a higher level, and with more care, when they know they are being evaluated by their peers than when they know only the teacher and the TA will be grading)."

Several of those posting comments on Davidson's blog expressed support for her approach or outlined similar strategies they had tried or wanted to try.

One post, "Never underestimate grade orientation," noted a caution. "I can see this working with a small course. I tried something similar several years ago at Buffalo. My mistake was to make it a 'curved' class (though only a positive curve). Two 'gangs' (one a group of fraternity brothers, the other just people who met and formed up) reached an agreement that they would vote up each others' work no matter what, and non-members' work down, no matter what, in order to increase their own grade in the class favorably, and hurt others' grades. I wrote it up a little here. When I intervened, I got complaints: I had set up the rules, several said, if I didn't like the outcome, how was it their fault."

Another posting describes a more successful attempt of a similar approach: "I've done something like this with my big undergrad class, 'Intersections: Race, Gender & Sexuality in US History,' for years now. They do all the work, at a 'good faith' level of quality (earning a check from their TA), show up on time to all classes and participate in discussion sections—they get an A. Grades scale down from there. The greatest thing about it is that many students without previous educational privilege *love* it and often do extremely well when not being judged in the usual way—reading a book a week, writing response papers every week, and ultimately participating at grad student level. Entitled students who try to skate by on a good prose style do not like it at all."

10   In an e-mail interview, Davidson said her announcement represents more than her personal distaste for grading as we know it. Rather, her views relate to ideas she explores in her forthcoming book (from Viking Press next year), *The Rewired Brain: The Deep Structure of Thinking for the Information Age.*

> "Many of us are frustrated with grading as presently, historically constructed and are finding a mismatch between the kinds of learning happening on the Internet (from a five-year-old customizing her Pokemon onward) and the rigid forms of assessment that have become the hallmark of formal education, K–12 and beyond, in the late 20th and now the 21st century. In an era when customizing, process, collaboration, and learning from mistakes are hallmark, when we are all having to revise how we think about the human desire to work together towards a goal—whether a Wikipedia entry or a Netflix software competition—we are saddled with a Machine Age model of assessment which is as rigid, reductive, uncreative, and uncollaborative as we can imagine. We know from early childhood studies that if you tell an American toddler 'here comes the teacher,' he sits up straight, looks up, shuts up, and stops smiling. That is not the kind of teacher I want to be. But by the time young people enter college, they have cordoned off 'education' into 'grading.'"

Her approach to grading, Davidson said, "encourages students to rethink everything they've learned about grading within higher education and encourages them to think about how you evaluate quality and performance—not for a grade but for the respect of one's peers and one's own self-respect. This is one of the important skills of the 21st century."

She stressed that she's not abandoning the role of grading, but having students take ownership of the task in a way that shows that "evaluation, in a serious way, is part of collaborative, interactive creativity. Right now, we have an educational system that encourages 'teaching to the test.' That's appalling as a learning philosophy and a total waste of precious learning time and opportunities in the digital age."

Whatever the results of her grading approach, Davidson is in a secure position—as a highly regarded, tenured professor at a leading university—to try something new. She acknowledged that there would be additional issues for a junior professor or non-tenure-track instructor taking this idea, but said that they shouldn't rule it out. And she noted problems with continuing with the status quo.

"One never knows what one can get away with pre-tenure and that is why I tell all of my [graduate] students to make their department chairs partners in anything they do, from the most traditional to the most experimental—and to keep a paper trail. That is, write to set up a meeting to explain one's pedagogical philosophy in a case like this, send it to your chair, ask to meet with the chair, discuss it, and then write a follow-up note thanking the chair for the meeting, recapping it, and giving her or him credit for any changes you've made in the syllabus (for example) and then send a copy of the revised syllabus. That is a helpful process for everyone involved as well as a wonderful addition to one's tenure portfolio," she said.

15   "Who wouldn't want a teacher who thinks seriously and deeply about what teaching means? I don't believe anything is risky if it is well thought out and well communicated. I happen to believe that just about everything is risky (including playing by the rules) without careful intention and careful communication."

BEFORE YOU READ: Has college become too expensive? Is higher education becoming an option for only the privileged few? If so, what should be done?

MAKING COLLEGE AFFORDABLE*
Editorial Board, The Daily Californian

The Daily Californian is the campus newspaper for the University of California–Berkeley.

It is common knowledge that American higher education is in need of repair. Recognizing the immediacy of the issue, President Barack Obama laid out a plan last week that aims to create a system of affordability ratings for colleges nationwide. The announcement is a positive development, in spite of some serious flaws based on the limited facts available.

The heart of the initiative is to tether the billions of dollars in federal student aid to colleges' ratings, incentivizing administrative reforms that make higher education affordable to more students. Additionally, payments on federal student loans would be capped at 10 percent of the borrower's discretionary income. Capping loan payments is unequivocal progress, as is government

---

*The Daily Californian. Reprinted by permission.

demands for colleges to be honest about the full cost of a degree.

But as positive as all this may be, it remains a Band-Aid on American higher education's broken leg. The fundamentals of the problem have not changed.

As a result of this year's sequester cuts, UC Berkeley lost millions in research funding that otherwise would have gone to invaluable scientific work. Twenty-six years ago, state funding accounted for 54 percent of the campus's budget; today, it makes up less than 15 percent. UC tuition has soared over the last decade, more than doubling to an in-state rate that's more than $13,000 per year. The solution is somewhat more straightforward: Increase federal and state funding for higher education, and expand access to community colleges for those who need them most.

5   Clearly, it is a constructive goal to give prospective college students more information on potential places of study. But wouldn't a simpler and far more effective approach be to advocate for a public education system in which students don't have to take on unmanageable loads of debt in order to get a degree?

While Obama's plan does take on the issue of college affordability, it still ties student aid to an individual college's success. As critics of the plan have noted, incentivizing "good" affordability practices has the unfortunate side effect of placing schools with struggling, debt-ridden students into a trap where they do not get access to necessary resources to strengthen their institutions.

The president's plan has undeniable strengths. But a sketchy ratings system whose central focus lacks a plan to get more dollars into starved public budgets does not a forward-thinking strategy make.

BEFORE YOU READ: Has higher education become too commercialized? Do colleges and universities now treat incoming students as if they were little more than consumers? And if so, is this a bad thing?

COLLEGE CONSUMERISM RUN AMOK*

Kevin Carey

Kevin Carey writes frequently for *The Chronicle of Higher Education.*

Fie upon thee, climbing walls to damnation! We shall not succumb to thy decadent corruptions!

The two dirtiest words in higher education these days are "climbing" and "wall." Seriously, if you spend enough time attending conferences, reading op-eds, etc., you come to realize that climbing walls have somehow come to symbolize all that ails postsecondary education in America today. People are constantly denouncing their proliferation, or loudly noting that their institution refuses to install one, or otherwise employing them as a symbol of consumerism run amok. Students today demand all manner of creature comforts, the thinking goes, forcing colleges to kowtow to their every whim, which is why college is so expensive and academic standards

---

*Used by permission of the author.

are in decline and the academy in general is a pale shadow of its former, greater self, back when students were students and professors were professors and higher learning happened how and where it was meant to happen, that is, in unheated, dimly-lit buildings constructed entirely of large granite blocks quarried no later than the 16th century.

This puzzles me.

First, because of all the things to be upset about, climbing walls don't seem that bad. Are they really that expensive? At least students are getting some exercise. How about dorms that cost nearly $400,000 per unit? *That's* extravagance.

Second, because colleges act as if they have no influence over the consumer preferences of students. Which is ridiculous. For example, some time in the near future I'm going to drive to the Best Buy on Route 1 in Alexandria, Virginia, and buy a flat-screen television. The store offers something like a hundred different models to choose from. In making my selection, I'll be asking a number of questions. How big is it, measured diagonally, in inches? How many HDMI inputs? Ethernet connection? Plasma, LCD, or LED? Are there 1080 lines of resolution? 120 Hz or the more powerful 240 Hz? And so on.

How do I know to ask these questions? And why is every similar customer, regardless of where they live and where they're shopping, asking the same questions? *Because that's how flat-screen televisions are advertised.* I also consulted independent reports like this article in *The New York Times*, which advises that LED's are really just backlit LCD's and I only need 240Hz if I'm going to spend a lot time watching fast-motion programming like pro football. (I won't be; I'm more of an HBO and Showtime guy.) So there's some marketing b.s. to wade through. But it's safe to say that there are no crucial elements of flat-screen televisions that *aren't* readily available for me to understand.

By contrast, let's say I was trying to choose the right college for my (non-existent) 17-year-old daughter. And let's say I'm the perfect higher-education consumer from the academy's perspective—I don't care *at all* about climbing walls or fitness centers or luxury dorms or any of that stuff. I care about all the truly important things I'm supposed to care about: the quality of the teaching, scholarship, and academic environment; how the school will help my daughter become an enlightened, ethical, fair-minded public citizen.

How would I choose? Where would I get that information, in a way that would allow me to decide among hundreds of alternatives? Answer: nowhere, because it doesn't exist.

Colleges may complain about having to market themselves based on dorm-based pilates studios and whatnot, but it's not like they have some other *secret brochure* in a filing cabinet somewhere, filled with all the real information about the true meaning of higher education, materials that they would gladly distribute far and wide if only students weren't so coddled by their helicopter parents and addled by the rap music and the video games.

In fact most colleges don't systematically gather this kind of information, or if they do—via the National Survey of Student Engagement or something similar—they don't release it to the public. Yes, yes, colleges are a lot more complicated than televisions. But nobody can say with a straight face that colleges are doing *nearly* as much as they could to provide consumers with information about teaching and learning that's useful for making consumer choices—that is, presented in a way that allows for institutional comparisons.

Even the data that colleges do gather, like graduation rates, are usually buried on the IR department Web page somewhere. Why? Because graduation rates are frequently terrible.

And that's the real climbing wall scandal: They're *cheap*, compared to the cost of improving the quality of instruction that many undergraduates receive. If colleges want consumers to make choices differently, then colleges have to take the lead in creating, promoting, and standing behind different terms of consumer choice.

B. What Role Should Technology Play in Education?

> **BEFORE YOU READ:** As Silver notes, college students now regularly use Facebook and Twitter during class. Is this true in your own experience? Do you think this practice should be allowed?

TWITTER MEETS THE BREAKFAST CLUB*
David Silver

David Silver is an associate professor of media studies and environmental studies at the University of San Francisco. This article appeared in *The Chronicle of Higher Education* in 2011.

"Be careful," I used to warn my students back in the mid-1990s as I taught them how to make what we then called "home pages." "When you put something on the World Wide Web, you're making it public. And that means future employers may find it."

For the next 15 years, I repeated my warning as I taught students how to build Web sites, craft blogs, use Flickr, and create content on a small but growing site called Facebook.

About three years ago, all of that changed. "Be careful," I said to my students as I taught them how to use Twitter. "Future employers may find your work."

"But Professor Silver," said one of the students as he looked up from his laptop, "I want future employers to find my work."

5   This semester I am teaching "Green Media," a media-studies production course devoted to making media about making food. In the course, students learn about the history of television cooking shows, how to make their own food media, and how to share their work via social media like Twitter, Flickr, and blogs. To give us some context, we read Kathleen Collins's *Watching What We Eat: The Evolution of Television Cooking Shows* (Continuum, 2009); for some contemporary views, we read Novella Carpenter's *Farm City:*

The Education of an Urban Farmer (Penguin Press, 2009).

On the second day of class, I required the 10 students in the course to join Twitter (if they had not already) and to create public Twitter accounts. I further required them to tweet under their real names. And finally, I asked them to follow all their classmates and me on Twitter, and to get into the habit of checking Twitter at least once a day.

While many discussions about Twitter and teaching revolve around the brevity of tweets (140 characters or less), my use of Twitter has more to do with the public nature of its platform.

I have my students begin a Twitter account for a number of reasons.

First, because their Twitter accounts are public, their professor, their classmates, and the larger Twitter community have access to their work. As I learned years ago when my students posted their work on their home pages, the larger the potential readership is, the better they make their work. With Twitter, the stage is bigger and the stakes are higher—and invariably, students' work improves.

10   Second, because they tweet under their real names, they become, I believe, more responsible for their work. Too often, online

anonymity contributes to rude and reckless discourse—witness comments on YouTube and on blogs. By tweeting under their own names, students post with a bit more deliberation and, perhaps, caution—not out of fear of future employers finding their work but rather with hope and expectation that they will.

Third, and most practically, for both my students and me, Twitter simplifies course management by replacing at least three classroom technologies. Twitter replaces the class listserv (or course blog, Blackboard, or discussion group) for our outside-the-classroom discussions and resource sharing. Twitter replaces e-mail announcements for new readings, location changes, and relevant happenings around the city. And Twitter replaces the cardboard box I used to bring to class to collect papers and other assignments. Now my students post tweets with links to their work.

In early February, I (or @davidmsilver on Twitter) tweeted the following: "breakfast project for #greenmedia http://bit.ly/ewCOix."

Roughly translated, the 54 characters announced a project to students in "Green Media" (signified by the #greenmedia hashtag, a method of categorizing, and thus searching for, tweets) and provided them (and anyone else following me on Twitter) a shortened link to the whole assignment posted on my blog (http://silverinsf.blogspot.com).

The assignment was fairly straightforward. First, students had to cook, bake, or prepare something suitable for breakfast or lunch. Second, they had to document the cooking process with digital photos, upload them to Flickr (an online photo-management and sharing application), and curate them into a set that tells a meaningful story about their dish. Third, somewhere within their Flickr set, they had to provide a recipe (title, ingredients, instructions) for their dish. Fourth, once finished with their breakfast project and before class on February 15, they had to tweet a link to their recipes and include a link to their Flickr sets and the #greenmedia

hashtag. Finally, they had to bring their dishes to class and share them with the rest of us.

15   As the deadline approached, breakfast-project-related student tweets began rolling in.

Stephanie Bruno, @princessbruno, tweeted, "Chocolate Chip Banana Muffins for #greenmedia are all done! Don't you wish this was your homework? http://bit.ly/ghVsqx."

Chris Williams, @ChrisUSF, tweeted, "Mmmmmm Blueberry Lemon Bread for breakfast. http://tinyurl.com/4wj7qez #greenmedia now we feast."

Nicholas Ryan, @nryan89, tweeted, "Rice pudding breakfast project . . . cant wait to see everyones #greenmedia . . . http://tinyurl.com/4z3zbld."

What I find especially interesting is that in many of the students' tweets, there is both an announcement of an individually created dish and an anticipation of a collectively created meal ("#greenmedia now we feast"; "cant wait to see everyones #greenmedia"). Students are tweeting as both individual creators and collaborative sharers, a powerful combination for both learning and working environments. Increasingly, being able to operate within a team is a crucial skill for effective citizenship in the 21st century.

20   One student, Sophia Miles (@sophiamiles7), mentions other students' work within her own tweet: "My stomach is growling with excitement for class today #greenmedia! Scones, muffins, banana bread, OH MY! http://tinyurl.com/4qf5kf3."

In all my years of using a cardboard box, I can't recall a student's giving a shout-out to another while turning in a paper.

Each time I saw a breakfast project-related tweet I would "favorite" it—an option which, similar to bookmarking Web sites, easily stores favorite tweets. Because my students used the #greenmedia hashtag, finding and favoriting these tweets was easy. When I arrived in class on February 15, I fired up the classroom laptop, logged in to Twitter, and clicked "favorites." With one click, I had links to all of my students' projects in the order that they completed them, giving us a convenient and ready-to-go order for Demo Day, the day students present their projects to the class.

But before we demonstrated our media, we devoured our dishes.

Through Twitter, Katherine D. Harris, @triproftri, an assistant professor of English literature at San Jose State University, learned about the breakfast project and integrated it into a first-year composition class, "Food and You." As part of an in-class workshop, she had her students create Flickr accounts, visit my students' Flickr sets, and leave comments on their work. Out of the many comments from San Jose students, my favorite was from Dtagaloa90, who commented on Jaime Giacomi's (@jcgiacomi) cinnamon rolls: "The results of this recipe look great. My mouth is watering right now! I appreciate the pictures that are pretty self-explanatory in terms of making the dish. I don't know how to cook anything, but I may try this one soon."

25   Of course, Twitter didn't invent cross-institutional collaboration, but it sure makes it easier. By tweeting my syllabi and then my assignments, I invite and engage with other professors who follow me on Twitter in hope of encouraging more collaborations like the one with San Jose students. Perhaps with Twitter and social media we will begin to witness new forms of the "networked classroom," which not only connects enrolled students to one another but also allows students from different courses to network together, creating larger, more diverse, and more collaborative learning environments.

Although exciting for professors, such open, public pedagogies are even more exciting, I believe, for our students. Making her recipe for cinnamon rolls public is great for Jaime, whose work now involves a very real readership that goes beyond her professor and home institution. And it is great for Dtagaloa90, who, with Jaime's help, may learn how to cook her first dish.

"Be careful," I used to warn my students. "On the Internet, you never know who will find your work."

"Make it great," I now tell them, "because people will find your work."

BEFORE YOU READ: Should we be held responsible for every image of ourselves that appears online? And more specifically, do these kinds of images have any bearing on our qualifications or achievements as students?

SOCIAL NETWORK PROFILE COSTS WOMAN COLLEGE DEGREE*

Sarah Perez

Sarah Perez writes frequently about education and technology.

Forget losing your job, apparently your MySpace or Facebook profile and photos can now cause you to lose your degree. In what may be one of the most frightening rulings regarding social networks and privacy to date, a federal judge has ruled

---

against a former student of Millersville University of Pennsylvania who was denied her college degree because of an unseemly online photo and its accompanying caption found on her social network profile.

The Case of "Drunken Pirate," Stacy Snyder

The woman, Stacy Snyder, sued Millersville in 2007. Snyder was student-teaching at a high school, but had received poor evaluations regarding her professionalism in the classroom. Before her semester-long teaching assignment was up, she was barred from campus. However, it was not the negative reviews that caused her to be barred nor were they responsible for the loss of her degree. *It was a MySpace photo.*

In the photo, Snyder was posed standing with a cocktail. The caption read "drunken pirate." It was accompanied by a note which made reference to her supervising teacher. That led to the school's decision to end her assignment, which in turn meant she now no longer qualified for her bachelor's degree in education.

Instead, the university reclassified some academic credits and gave Snyder a degree in English. She appealed the decision and lost. She then decided to sue. The judge, Paul S. Diamond of the U.S. District Court in Philadelphia, dismissed her free-speech claims, saying that employees' free speech is only protected if it relates to matters of public concern. Snyder's criticism of her supervisor did not.

5 University president, Francine McNairy, agreed with the decision. "This was not about First Amendment rights, it was about performance, and she clearly did not do what was necessary in order to earn a degree in education," she said.

Was the Photo Really to Blame?

Given Snyder's history in this case, the photo of her drinking and the accompanying note may not be really to blame for her lack

of degree. In a way, they were just the proverbial straw that broke the camel's back. If Snyder had been a good employee (student teacher) up until the point the photo had been discovered, she probably would have been disciplined, but not let go, and thus would not have lost her degree.

However, given her prior negative reviews, the photo simply gave the school an excuse for what they wanted to do all along—fire Stacy Snyder. It was tangible evidence of her unprofessionalism in a way that subjective performance reviews are not. She may have been able to argue with the university that her supervisor had a personal problem with her, or something of the like, had her negative reviews come up in a decision regarding her degree. A photo is not as easy to explain away.

Lesson Learned: Use Privacy Controls on Your Social Network Profile

Snyder's real mistake in this situation was not knowing or choosing to turn on any sort of privacy controls on her social network profile page. Given that the photo was found on her MySpace profile, it could have easily been kept out of sight from her supervisors and administrators at the university. It never needed to come into play.

MySpace profiles can easily be set to "private," which would have prevented anyone except those who were accepted as Snyder's friends to have access to the items she posted. Facebook also offers extensive privacy controls that should be configured, especially if your profile is being used for more business networking type purposes.

Don't Be So Quick to Criticize

10 Although it may be easy to criticize Snyder based on the information we've learned so far—negative performance reviews, distasteful photos—the truth is that many younger teachers disagree with their older supervisors, which could have led to the bad reviews.

In fact, if you take the time to review the judge's decision (PDF), you'll see that Snyder's "unprofessionalism" that was cited in those reviews came from accusations that she exhibited "over-familiarity with her students," and "had difficulty maintaining a formal teaching manner." *Really? A college student teaching a high school class? Shocking.* In addition, it seems that students knew of her MySpace page and checked it regularly, another unseemly violation of a teacher's ethical code, in the eyes of her supervisor.

Ironically, one of Snyder's MySpace postings in question began,

> I have nothing to hide. I am over 21, and I don't say anything that

will hurt me (in the long run). Plus, I don't think that they would stoop that low as to mess with my future.

MySpace Lost Snyder Her Degree

Snyder may have needed more coaching in how to be a professional—the very thing that student-teaching is designed for—but it hardly negates her years of completed course work towards her education degree. So in the end, it really was her MySpace mistake that lost her the degree after all. And if that isn't a tale that has you rushing out to manage your profile page's privacy settings right now, then it's hard to imagine what will.

BEFORE YOU READ: What do you think of the recent phenomenon of marketing educational tools for children? Do these products have the potential to truly enhance the learning capabilities of youngsters? What aspirations or anxieties among parents do these products cater to?

THE GREAT BABY EINSTEIN SCAM*

Mira Jacob

Mira Jacob is an editor at the online magazine *Shine.*

Of course it was too good to be true. The *New York Times* reported Thursday that Disney is offering a refund to buyers of its ubiquitous "Baby Einstein" videos, which did not, as promised, turn babies into wunderkinds. Apparently, all those puppets, bright colors, and songs were what we had feared all along—a mind-numbing way to occupy infants.

This news has rocked the parenting world, which had embraced the videos as a miraculous child-rearing staple. Videos that make your kid smarter while you prepare dinner? Genius!

Or not. According to the article, the American Academy of Pediatrics recommends that children under two years old stay away from watching screens. In the letter threatening Disney with a class-action lawsuit for "deceptive advertising," public health lawyers hired by Campaign for a Commercial-Free Childhood cited a study

---

which found a link between early television exposure and later problems with attention span.

5   For many parents, this was the most unsettling of "duh" moments, and a confirmation that nothing, when it comes to child-rearing, is ever as easy as we'd like to make it. So why were we so quick to seize on Baby Einstein videos as technological tutors?

Call it the perfect storm of parenting. Who doesn't want to believe that there is a magical, wondrous, no-parental-guidance-required product that will turn their kids into Mensa members? The combination of our lack of time, our paranoia over our kids

performance, and our faith in technology primed this generation of parents to accept the clever advertising around "Baby Einstein" as truth, just as parents before us have seized on corporal punishment, or the teachings of Dr. Spock.

Still, the idea that a caper this big could be pulled off (according to the *Times*, in "a 2003 study, a third of all American babies from 6 months to 2 years old had at least one 'Baby Einstein' video") is mind-boggling. Disney's refund is about as close as we're going to get to an actual admission that we were sold snake oil, and it casts a pall over the other "educational" toys out there.

BEFORE YOU READ: What role do you think online evaluations of professors should play in college? What are the advantages and disadvantages of this technology?

RATEMYPROFESSORSAPPEARANCE.COM*
Kerry Soper

Kerry Soper is an Associate Professor in the Department of Humanities, Classics, and Comparative Literature at Brigham Young University.

Let's be honest: Most of us are never going to see one of those red-hot chili peppers next to our names on RateMyProfessors.com. Who knows why? Certainly it couldn't be that extra 15 pounds, rapidly graying and/or receding hair, weird teeth, or consignment-quality wardrobe. We may get raves about our senses of humor, our knowledge of an arcane field, or our ability to be "fair" in our grading, but most of us will never have the satisfaction of being considered *caliente*.

It is unfair that only the few youthful, freakishly good-looking faculty members among us get all of those chili-pepper accolades. So I propose that the following consolation icons be included on the site's menu:

The Pizza Slice. This is for faculty members who make an effort, however misguided, to appear youthful and hip after passing the 40-year mark. Students are saying, "Yes, it is embarrassing to observe a middle-aged man (or woman) in expensive jeans, funky shoes,

---

and trendy shirt, but it seems to make you happy—so go for it. Better that you be delusional and cheerful than depressed, grouchy, and fully aware of how old and pathetic you actually look."

The Espresso Cup. The student here is saying, "I can see that you have a coherent style going on there: an array of black and gray clothing that has a vague, critical-theory hipness to it. And good job on finding the right kind of severe glasses and retro haircut to fit the look. Personally, I find this aesthetic dull and pretentious, but it is fun to see you strike self-conscious poses at the whiteboard, like some kind of morose poet in a Sears catalog for existentialists."

5 *The Lump of Tofu.* With this icon, the student is suggesting: "I gather from all of your references to vegan dietary ethics and your frequently expressed contempt for the eating habits of our fast-food nation that you're taking good care of yourself nutritionally. That internal health may not be reflected in your sallow complexion, bird's nest of unkempt hair, and lethargic demeanor, but I'll take your word on this one, nevertheless."

The Half-Eaten Protein Bar. This is a student's way of saying: "You may not be an especially attractive human being, but it does appear that you spend a lot of time at the gym attempting to get into shape. Good job, in other words, for trying. Yes, you may have weird hair, lame clothes, and dorky glasses, but I'm sure that somewhere under the extra 15 pounds you've accumulated over the years, there must be some nicely sculpted delts and pecs."

The Pressed Flower. The student here is suggesting that "it looks as if you may have been hip and attractive at one point in your life. And guessing from your big hair, lavender pantsuit with the puffy shoulder pads, and bright pumps, that year was probably 1986. Thank you for preserving this historical look for future generations."

The Bow Tie. This is for professors determined to maintain an ivory-tower dress code established in a previous century. The student is saying, "Yes, that stuffy little bow tie looks ridiculous on your portly frame; your frumpy oxford shirts are stained and frayed; and I have never seen a jacket that is so depressingly brown and textured. Nevertheless, your stereotypically fussy sense of style does help me feel like I'm getting my money's worth as a college student."

The Cassava Root. The student is acknowledging that "you do, indeed, seem to be a well-traveled, open-minded, and culturally sensitive person, with all of that colorful clothing you wear from various ethnic traditions. Your pale skin color and Midwestern accent place you somewhere north of Des Moines, but from the look of that dress, you may also be an honorary member of a West African tribe. Way to go."

10 *The Pocket Protector.* A student here is congratulating a professor on being unabashedly (or unconsciously) nerdy in his or her appearance: "It's clear that you just don't care, and that's awesome. We get a kick out of your functional polyester slacks; limp, faded shirts; and grimy, heavy-framed glasses. Don't change! We feel comforted knowing that none of your valuable research and class-prep time is eaten up with frivolous concerns over wearing same-colored socks, changing your pants every day, or taking any extra time to match up the buttons with the proper buttonholes in that threadbare shirt."

The Piña Colada with a Little Umbrella. The student is simply pointing out that: "Wow, that is a really casual look you've got going there: cruddy sandals, baggy Bermuda shorts, and some sort of open-collared, vacationy-looking shirt. I also notice that shaving and hair-washing are often optional parts of your morning routine. It's hard to believe that a professor could look more lackadaisical about his appearance than a hung-over freshman, but you've pulled it off. Good job at finding a career where you can get away with that."

The Crystal. This icon allows students to say: "Thank you for entertaining us with your loopy New Age persona and aesthetics. That gauzy skirt, peasant blouse, and wild hair may be a poor fashion choice for a sedentary woman in her 50s, but we are grateful that your enthusiasm for Wiccan healing practices, goddess mythologies, and heavy turquoise jewelry appears to distract you from focusing too closely on our half-hearted attempts at writing."

The Harmonica. This is for the securely upper-middle-class prof who enjoys wearing faux working-class garb: scuffed leather boots, aged denim, faded T-shirts, and Teamster-style plaid button-ups. Students can say: "We don't get your fetish for all things Springsteen, and your folky, left-leaning political references are about 40 to 50 years out of date, but we appreciate the laid-back, democratic ambiance you bring to the class. Indeed, it makes it difficult for you to say no to our requests for grade adjustments when you find out that we, too, are from humble, working-class roots."

The Power Tie. This is for the prof who seems to belong (or perhaps has once belonged) in corporate America rather than academe. The student is saying, "You must be a misguided Republican adjunct—a refugee from the downsized business world—or some kind of weird, moonlighting administrator. How else to explain the worn-out black dress shoes, Brooks Brothers shirts with the frayed collars, silk ties that were fashionable maybe 10 years ago, and that heavily gelled hair? Nice job on keeping me distracted from your dry lectures with this fashion conundrum."

15   In sum, there should be a little something for everyone in my list of alternative icons. I urge the creators of RateMyProfessors .com to adopt these suggestions. The egos of thousands of well-intentioned but fashion- and body-challenged professors are in your hands. I await your response, as I sit here sweating from a recent jog, self-consciously squirming in my expensive jeans, funky glasses, and Peruvian shirt, none of which seem to be doing a very good job at hiding my 15 extra pounds.

Questions to Help You Think and Write About Education and Learning

1. Tressie McMillan Cottom makes the argument that college life needs to be reenvisioned. How do you respond? In your own view, what aspects of contemporary schooling most need to be rethought? How?

2. Scott Jaschik offers an argument in favor of abolishing grades. How do you respond? In your opinion, what role should grades play in evaluating student performance? Student learning?

3. Perez and Soper both offer critiques of the effect that online technology is having on modern educational life. How do their critiques compare? Which do you find more convincing? Why?

4. Carey and Jacob both focus on the intersection between education and commercialism. How do you understand this relationship? Do you think there is a trend toward greater commercialization of education? If so, how do you evaluate the effects of this trend?

5. Using Jaschik's essay as your starting point, write a description of what you would consider to be the ideal grading system. How much or how little would

grades be used to evaluate student work? On what basis would grades be given? Would you supplement grades with other ways to evaluate student performance? Would you eliminate grades altogether? Why or why not?

6. **Arguing Like a Citizen:** Spend a week sitting in on a class on your campus. How would you characterize the educational model being employed? What kind of role does the instructor play? What types of work are students asked to perform? What changes to this educational model would you advocate? Why?

SECTION 4
Race, Culture, and Identity

The Issues

A. How Important Is Race to American Identity?

The first set of essays considers race as cultural construct and genetic makeup. In the visual exercise that follows, two famous Shakespearean lovers are reversed. Emma Daly writes about college students' reactions when DNA tests show that the racial makeup of some of them differs from what they had always thought. One of these students reflects on why that knowledge seems so important. The next three essays provide different perspectives on the role of race in American culture from the 1960s to the present. In a 2013 speech commemorating the fiftieth anniversary of Martin Luther King's famous "March on Washington," President Barack Obama reflects on the achievements and challenges of the civil rights movement. K. A. Dilday recommends abandoning the term *African American* for the more inclusive term *black*, which acknowledges affinities Americans have with the global community of black persons. And finally, Mychal Denzel Smith asks some hard questions about what it means to be viewed as "young and black" in America.

B. To What Extent Does Individual Identity Depend on Ethnic Affiliation?

The essays in this section consider the ways in which cultural identity can shape individuals, how individuals can reject ethnic identity, and the potential benefits and costs of both processes. Dorinne Kondo writes about the confusion in identity that can result when trying to retain one's own cultural identity in a foreign context where there is pressure to conform to social norms.

The final two essays suggest the complexity of ethnic identity for contemporary Americans. Katie Halper argues that she feels most Jewish when connected to the social ideals of her family rather than to the religious rituals of Judaism. Carlos Lozada reflects on the combination of ancestry, geography, culture, and experience that goes into creating a coherent "Hispanic" identity.

Exploring Online Argument

The following Web sites present interesting perspectives on race, culture, and identity.

Interracial Voice	PBS: Genealogy Roadshow
Genetic Genealogy, DNA Ancestry Project	*Crossroads*, AmericanStudiesWeb
Martin Luther King Jr. Research and Education Institute (Stanford University)	National Council of La Raza
Jewish Encyclopedia	National Japanese American Historical Society
Foundation for Jewish Culture	Center for Immigration Studies
Anne Frank House	U.S. Census Bureau
The Muslim News	American Anthropological Association: Race, Are We So Different?
Muslim-Answers	

The Rhetorical Situation

Dorinne K. Kondo, one of the authors in this section, makes the assertion that "race, language, and culture are intertwined." To understand this statement, you might want to think about how your race, culture, and language intertwine to contribute to your own sense of personal identity and how they cause other people to regard you in particular ways. How would you characterize yourself in terms of these categories? What group of people do you identify with primarily? How would you characterize the knowledge, beliefs, and behavior of this group, and how does the group itself influence your values and behavior? What aspects of your identity *cannot* be accounted for by such categories as race and ethnicity?

Throughout the history of the United States, race has been an important factor in defining American national identity. As President Barack Obama reminds us in his speech on the fiftieth anniversary of the civil rights march on Washington, the most fundamental expressions of American idealism, such as the Declaration of Independence, promote the concept of "equality." Nevertheless, the institution of slavery, although in the past, existed and still makes the realization of this ideal difficult. At the same time, science is changing our understanding of race by making it possible for individuals to learn their racial DNA makeup, a process that has produced interesting and even surprising results. African American literary scholar Henry Louis Gates Jr., for instance, recently discovered through DNA testing that his maternal ancestors were European. The essays in this section also question the importance of customs and religion in determining personal identity. The line between religion, values, and customs can be difficult to define. To what degree, for instance, are identities such as "Jewish" or "Muslim" a matter of religion or family, and to what extent are they a matter of shared values and commitments?

A. How Important Is Race to American Identity?

BEFORE YOU READ: What do you know about your own family background? To when and where can you trace your ancestors? Have you ever found out some new, surprising information about your heritage?

DNA TEST GIVES STUDENTS ETHNIC SHOCKS*

Emma Daly

Daly is a former Balkan correspondent for the British newspaper *The Independent* and a foreign correspondent for *The New York Times*.

When Don R. Harrison Jr. was growing up in Philadelphia, neighborhood children would tease him and call him "white boy" because his skin was lighter than theirs. But Mr. Harrison, a "proud black man," was still unprepared for the results of a DNA test, taken as part of a class at Pennsylvania State University, to determine his genetic ancestry.

"I figured it would be interesting. I'm light-skinned and I wanted to know my whole makeup," said Mr. Harrison, a 20-year-old sociology major. But he was shocked by results showing him to be 52 percent African and 48 percent European: "which I had no clue about, considering both my parents are black," said Mr. Harrison. "So I'm half white."

Samuel M. Richards, who teaches Sociology 119, Race and Ethnic Relations, to 500 students each semester, said the DNA tests, which were conducted last year for the first time, were very popular with the class.

"Everyone wants to take the test, even students who think they are 100 percent one race or another, and almost every one of them wants to discover something, that they're 1 percent Asian or something. It's a badge in this multicultural world," he said.

5   About half of the 100 students tested this semester were white, he said, "And every one of them said, 'Oh man, I hope I'm part black,' because it would upset their parents."

"That's this generation," he said. "People want to identify with this pop multiracial culture. They don't want to live next to it, but they want to be part of it. It's cool."

The tests also help to deepen conversations about race, he said.

"When I teach I try to demonstrate to students how complex race and ethnicity are," Dr. Richards said. "My secondary goal is to improve race relations, and when people discover that what they thought about themselves is not true—'I thought I was black, but I'm also Asian and white'—it leads them to have a different kind of conversation about race. It leads them to be less bigoted, to ask the deeper questions, to be more open to differences."

Mark D. Shriver, associate professor of anthropology and genetics at Penn State, took cheek swabs from about 100 student volunteers in Dr. Richards's class for the DNA tests.

10 Many students were surprised by the results of the test, which was created by Professor Shriver and his commercial partners at DNAPrint Genomics Inc. to measure genetic mixing in populations, because of the potential importance of racial or ethnic background to drug trials, and also because of the researchers' curiosity about their own ancestry. The company analyzed the test results free; the results will go into a database for Dr. Shriver's research.

The test compares DNA with that of four parent populations, western European, west African, east Asian and indigenous American, and the company claims it is more than 90 percent accurate.

Many unexpected results can be explained by family history. Mr. Harrison, for instance, recalled a great-grandfather who "would cross for white, he was so fair."

"The white women apparently found him attractive, and black women would flock to him because light was in back then." Mr. Harrison added, "He worked on the railroad, and he looked white in a black-and-white photo."

Natasha Best, a 21-year-old public relations major, has always thought of herself as half black and half white, because her mother is Irish-Lithuanian and her father West Indian. But the test proved her to be 58 percent European and 42 percent African.

15 "I was surprised at how much European I was, because though my father's family knows there is a great-great-grandfather who was Scottish, no one remembered him," said Ms. Best, who grew up in Yonkers. "I knew it was true, because I have dark relatives with blue eyes, but to bring it up a whole 8 percent, that was shocking to me."

But Professor Shriver explained that although a great-great-grandparent would contribute on average 6.25 percent of a person's genes, any one ancestor might be represented at a higher or lower level in today's generation.

Modern migration patterns are also leaving a mark. Ms. Best and Mr. Harrison are members of the fastest-growing ethnic grouping in the United States, one that was acknowledged in the 2000 census for the first time: mixed race.

Yet the two students identify themselves in very different ways.

"I am 48 percent white—genetically I am, at least, but not culturally. And the fact that I'm black is more important because it's something I know. It's who I'm comfortable with," Mr. Harrison said.

20 "Some people think it's funny that I consider myself Irish and celebrate St. Patrick's Day," said Ms. Best, "because no matter how you cut it, when you look at me you don't think, there goes a white girl."

She has noted discrimination on both sides. "Black people have told me I shouldn't date white people," said Ms. Best, whose boyfriend is white. Some of her white friends say their parents, too, disapprove of interracial dating. "Other people have told me I'm not really black, or I think I'm better than other black people because I'm lighter."

Mr. Harrison, who says that as a child he molded himself to be more black, does not want this new information to change his identity.

"Just because I found out I'm white, I'm not going to act white," he said. "I'm very proud of my black side."

But whatever his genes say, or those of Ms. Best, they will most likely be seen as black—at least by white Americans—for the rest of their lives.

25 "I think the test is really interesting; I had to know," said Ms. Best. "But it makes me question, why are we doing this? Why do people, especially in this country, want to know? Why are we, as a people, so caught up in race? Maybe we haven't progressed as much as we thought we had."

Reading Images: Racial Role Reversal in William Shakespeare's *Othello*

Image 1:
A Black Othello

Paul Robeson as Othello and Peggy Ashcroft as Desdemona in the 1930 London production of Shakespeare's *Othello*

For Discussion: Whether or not you have read or seen *Othello*, what is the impact on your awareness of color when the races of two fictional characters (e.g., friends or lovers) are reversed? How does the photo in Image 2 when juxtaposed with the Robeson-Ashcroft photograph, make you conscious of what qualities are stereotypically associated with whiteness and blackness?

Image 2:
A White Othello

Tim McInnemy as Iago and Lorraine Burroughs as Emilia in Wilson Milam's production of *Othello* at the Globe Theatre in 2007.

For Writing: Think of a short story, film, or television show you know that involves both black and white characters, or characters of different ethnicities or color. Describe how the story would be changed if the race, ethnicity, or color of the characters were reversed.

Context: Famous actor, singer, and political activist Paul Robeson was one of the first African American actors to play Othello in Shakespeare's play of that name. The character is a black African Moor who is married to Desdemona, a white Venetian, and race plays a large role in their love tragedy: Othello is persuaded that Desdemona is unfaithful and ends up strangling her. In the 2007 production, the racial identities of the key characters are reversed.

BEFORE YOU READ: Martin Luther King Jr. is an American icon. What is your sense of his importance to American history?

COMMEMORATING THE 50TH ANNIVERSARY OF MARTIN LUTHER KING'S MARCH ON WASHINGTON*

Barack Obama

Barack Obama is the 44th President of the United States.

Martin Luther King Jr. delivering the "I Have a Dream" speech. This speech was delivered August 28, 1963, on the steps of the Lincoln Memorial on the National Mall in Washington, D.C.

We hold these truths to be self-evident, that all men are created equal, that they are endowed by their creator with certain unalienable rights, that among these are life, liberty and the pursuit of happiness.

In 1963, almost 200 years after those words were set to paper, a full century after a great war was fought and emancipation proclaimed, that promise, those truths remained unmet. And so they came by the thousands, from every corner of our country—men and women, young and old, blacks who longed for freedom and whites who could no longer accept freedom for themselves while witnessing the subjugation of others. Across the land, congregations sent them off with food and with prayer. In the middle of the night, entire blocks of Harlem came out to wish them well.

With the few dollars they scrimped from their labor, some bought tickets and boarded buses, even if they couldn't always sit where they wanted to sit. Those with

*Barack Obama, Remarks by the President at the "Let Freedom Ring" Ceremony Commemorating the 50th Anniversary of the March on Washington, Aug 28, 2013.

less money hitchhiked, or walked. They were seamstresses, and steelworkers, and students, and teachers, maids and pullman porters. They shared simple meals and bunked together on floors.

And then, on a hot summer day, they assembled here, in our nation's capital, under the shadow of the great emancipator, to offer testimony of injustice, to petition their government for redress and to awaken America's long-slumbering conscience.

5   We rightly and best remember Dr. King's soaring oratory that day, how he gave mighty voice to the quiet hopes of millions, how he offered a salvation path for oppressed and oppressors alike. His words belong to the ages, possessing a power and prophecy unmatched in our time.

But we would do well to recall that day itself also belonged to those ordinary people whose names never appeared in the history books, never got on TV.

Many had gone to segregated schools and sat at segregated lunch counters, had lived in towns where they couldn't vote, in cities where their votes didn't matter. There were couples in love who couldn't marry, soldiers who fought for freedom abroad that they found denied to them at home. They had seen loved ones beaten and children fire-hosed. And they had every reason to lash out in anger or resign themselves to a bitter fate.

And yet they chose a different path. In the face of hatred, they prayed for their tormentors. In the face of violence, they stood up and sat in with the moral force of nonviolence. Willingly, they went to jail to protest unjust laws, their cells swelling with the sound of freedom songs. A lifetime of indignities had taught them that no man can take away the dignity and grace that God grants us. They had learned through hard experience what Frederick Douglas once taught: that freedom is not given; it must be won through struggle and discipline, persistence and faith.

That was the spirit they brought here that day.

10   . . . And because they kept marching, America changed. Because they marched, the civil rights law was passed. Because they marched, the voting rights law was signed. Because they marched, doors of opportunity and education swung open so their daughters and sons could finally imagine a life for themselves beyond washing somebody else's laundry or shining somebody else's shoes. Because they marched, city councils changed and state legislatures changed and Congress changed and, yes, eventually the White House changed.

Because they marched, America became more free and more fair, not just for African-Americans but for women and Latinos, Asians and Native Americans, for Catholics, Jews and Muslims, for gays, for Americans with disabilities.

America changed for you and for me.

. . . And so as we mark this anniversary, we must remind ourselves that the measure of progress for those who marched 50 years ago was not merely how many blacks had joined the ranks of millionaires; it was whether this country would admit all people who were willing to work hard, regardless of race, into the ranks of a middle-class life. The test was not and never has been whether the doors of opportunity are cracked a bit wider for a few. It was whether our economic system provides a fair shot for the many, for the black custodian and the white steelworker, the immigrant dishwasher and the Native American veteran. To win that battle, to answer that call—this remains our great unfinished business.

We shouldn't fool ourselves. The task will not be easy. Since 1963 the economy's changed.

15   The twin forces of technology and global competition have subtracted those jobs that once provided a foothold into the middle class, reduced the bargaining power of American workers.

And our politics has suffered. Entrenched interests—those who benefit from an unjust status quo resisted any government efforts to give working families a fair deal, marshaling an army of lobbyists and opinion makers to argue that minimum wage increases or stronger labor laws or taxes on the wealthy who could afford it just to fund crumbling schools—that all these things violated sound economic principles.

We'd be told that growing inequality was the price for a growing economy, a measure of the free market—that greed was good and compassion ineffective, and those without jobs or health care had only themselves to blame.

And then there were those elected officials who found it useful to practice the old politics of division, doing their best to convince middle-class Americans of a great untruth, that government was somehow itself to blame for their growing economic insecurity—that distant bureaucrats were taking their hard-earned dollars to benefit the welfare cheat or the illegal immigrant.

And then, if we're honest with ourselves, we'll admit that during the course of 50 years, there were times when some of us, claiming to push for change, lost our way. The anguish of assassinations set off self-defeating riots.

20   Legitimate grievances against police brutality tipped into excuse-making for criminal behavior. Racial politics could cut both ways as the transformative message of unity and brotherhood was drowned out by the language of recrimination. And what had once been a call for equality of opportunity, the chance for all Americans to work hard and get ahead was too often framed as a mere desire for government support, as if we had no agency in our own liberation, as if poverty was an excuse for not raising your child and the bigotry of others was reason to give up on yourself. All of that history is how progress stalled. That's how hope was

diverted. It's how our country remained divided.

But the good news is, just as was true in 1963, we now have a choice. We can continue down our current path in which the gears of this great democracy grind to a halt and our children accept a life of lower expectations, where politics is a zero-sum game, where a few do very well while struggling families of every race fight over a shrinking economic pie. That's one path. Or we can have the courage to change.

The March on Washington teaches us that we are not trapped by the mistakes of history, that we are masters of our fate.

But it also teaches us that the promise of this nation will only be kept when we work together. We'll have to reignite the embers of empathy and fellow feeling, the coalition of conscience that found expression in this place 50 years ago.

And I believe that spirit is there, that true force inside each of us. I see it when a white mother recognizes her own daughter in the face of a poor black child. I see it when the black youth thinks of his own grandfather in the dignified steps of an elderly white man. It's there when the native born recognizing that striving spirit of a new immigrant, when the interracial couple connects the pain of a gay couple who were discriminated against and understands it as their own. That's where courage comes from, when we turn not from each other or on each other but towards one another, and we find that we do not walk alone. That's where courage comes from.

25   And with that courage, we can stand together for good jobs and just wages. With that courage, we can stand together for the right to health care in the richest nation on earth for every person. With that courage, we can stand together for the right of every child, from the corners of Anacostia to the hills of Appalachia, to get an education that stirs the mind and captures the spirit and prepares them for the world that awaits

them. With that courage, we can feed the hungry and house the homeless and transform bleak wastelands of poverty into fields of commerce and promise.

America, I know the road will be long, but I know we can get there. Yes, we will stumble, but I know we'll get back up. That's how a movement happens. That's how history bends. That's how, when somebody is faint of heart, somebody else brings them along and says, come on, we're marching.

There's a reason why so many who marched that day and in the days to come were young, for the young are unconstrained by habits of fear, unconstrained by the conventions of what is. They dared to dream different and to imagine something better. And I am convinced that same imagination, the same hunger of purpose serves in this generation.

We might not face the same dangers as 1963, but the fierce urgency of now remains. We may never duplicate the swelling crowds and dazzling processions of that day so long ago, no one can match King's brilliance, but the same flames that lit the heart of all who are willing to take a first step for justice, I know that flame remains.

That tireless teacher who gets to class early and stays late and dips into her own pocket to buy supplies because she believes that every child is her charge—she's marching. That successful businessman who doesn't have to, but pays his workers a fair wage and then offers a shot to a man, maybe an ex-con, who's down on his luck—he's marching.

30   The mother who pours her love into her daughter so that she grows up with the confidence to walk through the same doors as anybody's son—she's marching. The father who realizes the most important job he'll ever have is raising his boy right, even if he didn't have a father, especially if he didn't have a father at home—he's marching. The battle-scarred veterans who devote themselves not only to helping their fellow warriors stand again and walk again and run again, but to keep serving their country when they come home—they are marching. Everyone who realizes what those glorious patriots knew on that day, that change does not come from Washington but to Washington, that change has always been built on our willingness, we, the people, to take on the mantle of citizenship—you are marching.

And that's the lesson of our past, that's the promise of tomorrow, that in the face of impossible odds, people who love their country can change it. And when millions of Americans of every race and every region, every faith and every station can join together in a spirit of brotherhood, then those mountains will be made low, and those rough places will be made plain, and those crooked places, they straighten out towards grace, and we will vindicate the faith of those who sacrificed so much and live up to the true meaning of our creed as one nation under God, indivisible, with liberty and justice for all.

BEFORE YOU READ: Americans are very familiar with the term *African American*, but try making up a term using a different national or geographic adjective that is less familiar (e.g., French American, Caribbean American). How would such a title alter or not alter your perception of the relation of Americans to other parts of the world?

GO BACK TO BLACK*

K. A. Dilday

K. A. Dilday is a columnist for the online magazine *Open Democracy*, according to *The New York Times* where this column was published.

I'm black again. I was black in Mississippi in the 1970s but sometime in the 1980s I became African-American, with a brief pause at Afro-American. Someone, I think it was Jesse Jackson, in the days when he had that kind of clout, managed to convince America that I preferred being African-American. I don't.

Now I live in Britain, where I'm black again. Blacks in Britain come from all over, although many are from the former colonies. According to the last census, about half of the British people who identify as black say they are black Caribbean, about 40 percent consider themselves black African, and the rest just feel plain old black. Black Brits are further divided by ancestral country of origin, yet they are united under the term black British—often—expanded to include British Asians from the Indian subcontinent.

The term *African-American* was contrived to give black Americans a sense of having a historical link to Africa, since one of slavery's many unhappy legacies is that most black Americans don't know particulars about their origins. Black Americans whose ancestors arrived after slavery and who can pinpoint their country of origin are excluded from the definition—which is why, early in his [presidential] campaign, people said Barack Obama wasn't really African-American.[1] Yet, since he has one parent from the African continent and one from the American continent, he is explicitly African-American.

Distinguishing between American black people based on their ancestors' arrival date ignores the continuum of experience that transcends borders and individual genealogies and unites black people all over the world. Yes, scientists have shown that black means nothing as a biological description, but it remains an important signal in social interaction. Everywhere I travel, from North Africa to Europe to Asia, dark-skinned people approach me and, usually gently but sometimes aggressively, establish a bond.

5   When, early on in the race for the Democratic nomination [in 2008], people wondered if black Americans would vote for Mr. Obama, I never doubted. During the last two years I've learned to decipher his name in almost any pronunciation, because on finding out that I'm an American, all other black people I meet, whether they are

Arabic-speaking Moroccans in Casablanca, French-speaking African mobile-phone-store clerks in the outer boroughs of Paris, or thickly accented Jamaican black Brits, ask me eagerly about him. Black people all over the world feel a sense of pride in his accomplishment.

It's hard to understand why black Americans ever tried to use the term *African-American* to exclude people. The black American community's social and political power derives from its inclusiveness. Everyone who identifies as black has traditionally been welcomed, no matter their skin color or date of arrival. In Britain, in contrast, dark-skinned people who trace their relatives to particular former colonies can be cliquish. Beyond the fact that blacks make up a smaller share of the population here, this regional identity may be a reason that the British black community isn't as powerful a social and political force.

I've never minded not knowing who my ancestors are beyond a few generations. My partner is an Englishman whose family tree is the sort that professional genealogists post on the Internet because it can be traced back to the first king of England in the 11th century. To me, it's more comforting to know that, through me, our children will be black, with all of the privileges and pains.

On Mr. Obama's behalf, American blacks have set aside their exclusive label. Polls show that about 80 percent of blacks who have voted in the [2008] Democratic primaries have chosen him. And all of the black people in the mountains of Morocco, the poor suburbs of Paris, the little villages in Kenya and the streets of London are cheering Mr. Obama's victories because they see him as one of their own.

Black Americans should honor that. It's time to retire the term *African-American* and go back to black.

Editor's Note

1. Barack Obama was a Democratic candidate for President of the United States in 2008, when this essay was written and published as an Op-Ed contribution.

B. To What Extent Does Individual Identity Depend on Ethnic Affiliation?

> **BEFORE YOU READ:** What are some of the stereotypes our culture promotes about "young black men"? Where do these stereotypes come from? And what can be done to change them?

TO BE YOUNG AND BLACK IN AMERICA: ALWAYS CONSIDERED A THREAT*

Mychal Denzel Smith

Mychal Denzel Smith writes about race and popular culture for *The Nation* magazine. This piece appeared in 2013.

Over the course of my twenty-six years, I've developed three responses to most news headlines: "Couldn't have been a black person," "Please, Lord, don't let it be a black person," and "Oh, that was definitely a black person."

Miami-Dade police officers pinned a 14-year-old to the ground and put him in a chokehold after the teen gave them, in their words, a "dehumanizing stare" and clenched his fists. Can you guess which response I had?

Tremaine McMillian was walking the beach on Memorial Day when police officers riding an ATV approached him and another teen to tell them their roughhousing was unacceptable behavior. The officers asked McMillian where his parents were, and as he walked away from them (McMillian says he was walking toward his mother, in an effort to answer the officer's inquiry as to where his parents were) they jumped off the ATV and restrained McMillian. They choked the teen until he could not breathe and he urinated himself. The six-week-old puppy McMillian was holding and feeding when the officers approached him was also injured.

Tremaine is being charged with felony resisting arrest with violence and disorderly conduct.

5   I saw the story making the rounds of my social media networks and knew without clicking any links that the 14-year-old in question was black. And not because the headlines identified him as such, or because I saw that his name was Tremaine, or because I was there and witnessed the whole thing, but because racism is predictable. It's the most consistent thing in my life.

Also predictable is the trying to pretend this isn't racism. Attempting to justify the use of force in this situation, Detective Alvaro Zabaleta said: "Of course we have to neutralize the threat in front of us. And when you have somebody that is being resistant, somebody that is pulling away from you, somebody that's clenching their fist, somebody that's flaring their arms, that's the immediate threat." You see, this had nothing to do with racism, it's just the police doing their job.

But it's a matter of who constitutes a threat. Who but a black teenager has the ability to

---

*Reprinted with permission from the May 31, 2013 issue of *The Nation*. For subscription information call 1-800-333-8536. Portions of each week's Nation magazine can be accessed at http://www.thenation.com.

dehumanize a police officer with a stare? Who but a(n unarmed) black teenager can make (armed) police feel threatened by clenching his fists? Who but a black teenager can simultaneously clench his fists and feed a puppy? Who but a black teenager isn't afforded the opportunity to comply with a request before it's determined that they're not complying? Who but a black teenager is choked to the point they urinate themselves while being handcuffed? When does any of this happen to people who aren't black teenagers?

It happens when a person poses a threat, not when they're walking on the beach. This is what it is to be young and black in America: you are always considered a threat. And that's why, as livid as this makes me, it's so incredibly unsurprising. Racism, in all its predictability, lost its ability to shock me a long time ago.

BEFORE YOU READ: Have you ever visited a place where you felt you were an outsider? How did you respond to this feeling? Did you feel awkward? Did you work hard to fit in with people or the customs of the place? How successful were you?

ON BEING A CONCEPTUAL ANOMALY*

Dorinne K. Kondo

Dorinne K. Kondo, a Japanese American professor of anthropology, is the author of *Crafting Selves: Power, Gender, and Discourses of Identity in a Japanese Workplace.* In this excerpt from her book, she relates her experiences in visiting Japan, where she looked Japanese but acted like an American.

As a Japanese American,[1] I created a conceptual dilemma for the Japanese I encountered. For them, I was a living oxymoron, someone who was both Japanese and not Japanese. Their puzzlement was all the greater since most Japanese people I knew seemed to adhere to an eminently biological definition of Japaneseness. Race, language, and culture are intertwined, so much so that any challenge to this firmly entrenched conceptual schema—a white person who speaks flawlessly idiomatic and unaccented Japanese, or a person of Japanese ancestry who cannot—meets with what generously could be described as unpleasant reactions. White people are treated as repulsive and unnatural—*hen na gaijin*, strange foreigners—the better their Japanese becomes, while Japanese Americans and others of Japanese ancestry born overseas are faced with exasperation and disbelief. How can someone who is racially Japanese lack "cultural competence"?[2] During my first few months in Tokyo, many tried to resolve this paradox by asking which of my parents was "really" American.

Indeed, it is a minor miracle that those first months did not lead to an acute case of agoraphobia, for I knew that once I set foot outside the door, someone somewhere (a taxi driver? a salesperson? a bank clerk?) would greet one of my linguistic mistakes

---

*Kondo, *Crafting Selves: Power, Gender and Discourses of Identity in a Japanese Workplace*. University of Chicago Press. Reprinted with permission.

with an astonished "Eh?" I became all too familiar with the series of expressions that would flicker over those faces: bewilderment, incredulity, embarrassment, even anger, at having to deal with this odd person who looked Japanese and therefore human, but who must be retarded, deranged, or—equally undesirable in Japanese eyes—Chinese or Korean. Defensively, I would mull over the mistake of the day. I mean, how was I to know that in order to "fillet a fish" you had to cut it "in three pieces"? Or that opening a bank account required so much specialized terminology? Courses in literary Japanese at Harvard hadn't done much to prepare me for the realities of everyday life in Tokyo. Gritting my teeth in determination as I groaned inwardly, I would force myself out of the house each morning.

For me, and apparently for the people around me, this was a stressful time, when expectations were flouted, when we had to strain to make sense of one another. There seemed to be few advantages in my retaining an American persona, for the distress caused by these reactions was difficult to bear. In the face of dissonance and distress, I found that the desire for comprehensible order in the form of "fitting in," even if it meant suppression of and violence against a self I had known in another context, was preferable to meaninglessness. Anthropological imperatives to immerse oneself in another culture intensified this desire, so that acquiring the accoutrements of Japanese selfhood meant simultaneously constructing a more thoroughly professional anthropological persona. This required language learning in the broadest sense, mastery of culturally appropriate modes of moving, acting, and speaking. For my informants, it was clear that coping with this anomalous creature was difficult, for here was someone who looked like a real human being, but who simply failed to perform according to expectation. They, too, had every reason to make me over in their image, to guide me, gently but insistently,

into properly Japanese behavior, so that the discrepancy between my appearance and my cultural competence would not be so painfully evident. I posed a challenge to their senses of identity. How could someone who *looked* Japanese not *be* Japanese? In my cultural ineptitude, I represented for the people who met me the chaos of meaninglessness. Their response in the face of this dissonance was to *make* me as Japanese as possible. Thus, my first nine months of fieldwork were characterized by an attempt to reduce the distance between expectation and inadequate reality, as my informants and I conspired to rewrite my identity as Japanese.

My guarantor, an older woman who, among her many activities, was a teacher of flower arranging, introduced me to many families who owned businesses in the ward of Tokyo where I had chosen to do my research. One of her former students and fellow flower-arranging teachers, Mrs. Sakamoto, agreed to take me in as a guest over the summer, since the apartment where I was scheduled to move—owned by one of my classmates in tea ceremony—was still under construction. My proclivities for "acting Japanese" were by this time firmly established. During my stay with the Sakamotos, I did my best to conform to what I thought their expectations of a guest/daughter might be. This in turn seemed to please them and reinforced my tendency to behave in terms of what I perceived to be my Japanese persona.

5   My initial encounter with the head of the household epitomizes this mirroring and reinforcement of behavior. Mr. Sakamoto had been on a business trip on the day I moved in, and he returned the following evening, just as his wife, daughter, and I sat down to the evening meal. As soon as he stepped in the door, I immediately switched from an informal posture, seated on the *zabuton* (seat cushion), to a formal greeting posture, *seiza*-style (kneeling on the floor) and bowed low, hands on the floor.

Mr. Sakamoto responded in kind (being older, male, and head of the household, he did not have to bow as deeply as I did), and we exchanged the requisite polite formulae, I requesting his benevolence, and he welcoming me to their family. Later, he told me how happy and impressed he had been with this act of proper etiquette on my part. "Today's young people in Japan," he said, "no longer show such respect. Your grandfather must have been a fine man to raise such a fine granddaughter." Of course, his statements can hardly be accepted at face value. They may well indicate his relief that I seemed to know something of proper Japanese behavior, and hence would not be a complete nuisance to them; it was also his way of making me feel at home. What is important to note is the way this statement was used to elicit proper Japanese behavior in future encounters. And his strategy worked. I was left with a warm, positive feeling toward the Sakamoto family, armed with an incentive to behave in a Japanese way, for clearly these were the expectations and the desires of the people who had taken me in and who were so generously sharing their lives with me.

Other members of the household voiced similar sentiments. Takemi-san, the Sakamotos' married daughter who lived in a distant prefecture, had been visiting her parents when I first moved in. A few minutes after our initial encounter, she observed, "You seem like a typical Japanese woman" (*Nihon no Josei to iu kanji*). Later in the summer, Mrs. Sakamoto confided to me that she could never allow a "pure American" (*junsui na Amerikajin*) to live with them, for only someone of Japanese descent was genetically capable of adjusting to life on *tatami* mats, using unsewered toilets, sleeping on the floor—in short, of living Japanese style. Again, the message was unambiguous. My "family" could feel comfortable with me insofar as I was—and acted—Japanese. [. . .]

My physical characteristics led my friends and coworkers to emphasize my identity as Japanese, sometimes even against my own intentions and desires. Over time, my increasingly "Japanese" behavior served temporarily to resolve their crises of meaning and to confirm their assumptions about their own identities. That I, too, came to participate enthusiastically in this recasting of the self is a testimonial to their success in acting upon me. [. . .]

The more I adjusted to my Japanese daughter's role, the keener the conflicts became. Most of those conflicts had to do with expectations surrounding gender, and, more specifically, my position as a young woman. Certainly, in exchange for the care the Sakamotos showed me, I was happy to help out in whatever way I could. I tried to do some housecleaning and laundry, and I took over the shopping and cooking for Mr. Sakamoto when Mrs. Sakamoto was at one of the children's association meetings, her flower-arranging classes, or meetings of ward committees on juvenile delinquency. The cooking did not offend me in and of itself; in fact, I was glad for the opportunity to learn how to make simple Japanese cuisine, and Mr. Sakamoto put up with my sometimes appalling culinary mistakes and limited menus with great aplomb. I remember one particularly awful night when I couldn't find the makings for soup broth, and Mr. Sakamoto was fed "*miso* soup" that was little more than *miso* dissolved in hot water. He managed to down the tasteless broth with good grace—and the trace of a smile on his lips. (Of course, it is also true that although he was himself capable of simple cooking, he would not set foot in the kitchen if there were a woman in the house.) Months after I moved out, whenever he saw me he would say with a sparkle in his eye and a hint of nostalgic wistfulness in his voice, "I miss Dorin-san's salad and sautéed beef," one of the "Western" menus I used to serve up with numbing regularity. No, the cooking was not the problem.

The problem was, in fact, the etiquette surrounding the serving of food that produced the most profound conflicts for me as an American woman. The head of the household is usually served first and receives the finest delicacies; men—even the sweetest, nicest ones—ask for a second helping of rice by merely holding out their rice bowls to the woman nearest the rice cooker, and maybe, just maybe, uttering a grunt of thanks in return for her pains. I could never get used to this practice, try as I might. Still, I tried to carry out my duties uncomplainingly, in what I hope was reasonably good humor. But I was none too happy about these things "inside." Other restrictions began to chafe, especially restrictions on my movement. I had to be in at a certain hour, despite my "adult" age. Yet I understood the family's responsibility for me as their guest and quasi-daughter, so I tried to abide by their regulations, hiding my irritation as best I could.

10   This fundamental ambivalence was heightened by isolation and dependency. Though my status was in some respects high in an education-conscious Japan, I was still young, female, and a student. I was in a socially recognized relationship of dependency vis-à-vis the people I knew. I was not to be feared and obeyed, but protected and helped. In terms of my research, this was an extremely advantageous position to be in, for people did not feel the need to reflect my views back to me, as they might with a more powerful person. I did not try to define situations; rather, I could allow other people to define those situations in their culturally appropriate ways, remaining open to their concerns and their ways of acting in the world. But, in another sense, this dependency and isolation increased my susceptibility to identifying with my Japanese role. By this time I saw little of American friends in Tokyo, for it was difficult to be with people who had so little inkling of how ordinary Japanese people lived. My informants and I consequently had every reason to

conspire to re-create my identity as Japanese. Precisely because of my dependency and my made-to-order role, I was allowed—or rather, *forced*—to abandon the position of observer. Errors, linguistic or cultural, were dealt with impatiently or with a startled look that seemed to say, "Oh yes, you are American after all." On the other hand, appropriately Japanese behaviors were rewarded with warm, positive reactions or with comments such as "You're more Japanese than the Japanese." Even more frequently, correct behavior was simply accepted as a matter of course. *Naturally* I would understand, *naturally* I would behave correctly, for they presumed me to be, *au fond*, Japanese. [. . .]

Identity can imply unity or fusion, but for me what occurred was a fragmentation of the self. This fragmentation was encouraged by my own participation in Japanese life and by the actions of my friends and acquaintances. At its most extreme point, I became "the Other" in my own mind, where the identity I had known in another context simply collapsed. The success of our conspiracy to recreate me as Japanese reached its climax one August afternoon.

It was typical summer weather for Tokyo, "like a steam bath" as the saying goes, so hot the leaves were drooping limply from the trees surrounding the Sakamotos' house. Mrs. Sakamoto and her married daughter, Takemi, were at the doctor's with Takemi's son, so Mr. Sakamoto and I were busy tending young Kaori-chan, Takemi-san's young daughter. Mr. Sakamoto quickly tired of his grandfatherly role, leaving me to entertain Kaori-chan. Promptly at four P.M., the hour when most Japanese housewives do their shopping for the evening meal, I lifted the baby into her stroller and pushed her along ahead of me as I inspected the fish, selected the freshest-looking vegetables, and mentally planned the meal for the evening. As I glanced into the shiny metal surface of the butcher's display case, I noticed someone who looked terribly familiar: a typical young housewife, clad in slip-on sandals and the loose, cotton shift called "home wear" (*homu wea*), a woman walking with a characteristically Japanese bend to the knees and a sliding of the feet. Suddenly I clutched the handle of the stroller to steady myself as a wave of dizziness washed over me, for I realized I had caught a glimpse of nothing less than my own reflection. Fear that perhaps I would never emerge from this world into which I was immersed inserted itself into my mind and stubbornly refused to leave, until I resolved to move into a new apartment, to distance myself from my Japanese home and my Japanese existence.

For ultimately this collapse of identity was a distancing moment. It led me to emphasize the *differences* between cultures and among various aspects of identity: researcher, student, daughter, wife, Japanese, American, Japanese American. In order to reconstitute myself as an American researcher, I felt I had to extricate myself from the conspiracy to rewrite my identity as Japanese. Accordingly, despite the Sakamotos' invitations to stay with them for the coming year, I politely stated my intentions to fulfill the original terms of the agreement: to stay just until construction on my new apartment was complete. In order to resist the Sakamotos' attempts to re-create me as Japanese, I removed myself physically from their exclusively Japanese environment.

Editor's Notes

1. See Edward Said, *Orientalism* (New York: Pantheon, 1978). The issue of what to call ourselves is an issue of considerable import to various ethnic and racial groups in the United States, as the term *African American* shows. For Asian Americans, the term *Oriental* was called into question in the sixties, for the reasons Said enumerates: the association of the term with stereotypes such as Oriental despotism, inscrutability, splendor, exoticism, mystery, and so on. It also defines "the East" in terms of "the West," in a relationship of unequal power—how rarely one hears of "the Occident," for example. Asian Americans, Japanese Americans included, sometimes hyphenate the term, but some of us would argue that leaving out the hyphen makes the term "Asian" or "Japanese" an adjective, rather than implying a half-and-half status: i.e., that one's loyalties/identities might be half Japanese and half American. Rather, in the terms *Asian American* and *Japanese American*, the accent is on the "American," an important political claim in light of the mainstream tendency to see Asian Americans as somehow more foreign than other kinds of Americans.

2. Merry White, *The Japanese Overseas: Can They Go Home Again?* (New York: Free Press, 1988) offers an account of the families of Japanese corporate executives who are transferred abroad and who often suffer painful difficulties upon reentering Japan.

BEFORE YOU READ: Do you define yourself primarily as a religious or a secular person? Is this even a useful distinction?

DIGGING FOR ROOTS AT SECULAR CAMP*

Katie Halper

Katie Halper is a comic, writer, and filmmaker based in New York.

My name is Katie Halper, and I am a secular Jew. I've been secular for a little over 26 years now.

I recently went on a young adult retreat, whose aim was to explore the definition of Judaism. When several people assumed I was Reform I explained I was secular. When they responded, "Oh cool. What synagogue do you go to?" or "Nice. Where do you celebrate Shabbat?"[1] I started to think that not everyone was as familiar with secular Judaism as I had thought.[2]

One of the speakers, a female rabbi who wore a yarmulke, spoke about the Jewish tradition of social justice and the importance of the Exodus story. She asked us, rhetorically, "How can we, whose ancestors came out of slavery in Egypt, not care about current-day oppression and injustice, whether that be genocide in Darfur, or pharmaceutical companies denying access to life-saving AIDS medication and killing millions?"

After, one young man was visibly uncomfortable with the rabbi's message. Social justice was not an inherent part of Jewish identity, he said. He was a recovering secular Jew, he confessed, whose parents had desecrated their home with a Christmas tree every winter, and whose grandparents had been . . . Communists. Ultimately, this born-again Jew concluded, it was impossible to be Jewish without believing in God.

A woman agreed: "It's Shabbat," not justice, that defined Judaism. Hearing them, I realized that not only was secular Judaism an unknown for many, it was a rejected unknown. And I, a secular Jew who values activism but does not celebrate Shabbat, was not a real Jew.

5   This wasn't the first time I felt like the odd Jew out. I have never felt comfortable with exclusively Jewish communities. Until I was seven, I went to a Jewish day school. (I still don't know why my secular parents sent me there. They claim that it was for its warmth and minimal snobbishness, but I suspect it was because it was a walkable distance from our apartment.) The roll call gives you a good sense of the type of school it was: Malka, Brahm, Yehuda, Yael H., Yael R., Yael S. (Yes, there were three Yaels in my class of 12), Hannah, Rachel, Sarah, Samuel, Jacob, and . . . Katie. I couldn't quite put my finger on it, but even then, as early as kindergarten, I was aware that in some way or another, I wasn't part of this community.

I really put my un-kosher foot in my mouth when we had to go around the room and state our Hebrew names. This was a no-brainer for my classmates, (especially easy for the Yael trio), who translated effortlessly: "My name is Hannah and my Hebrew name is Chana, my name is Rebecca and

*Katherine Halper, "Digging for Roots at Secular Camp," *JBooks*, April 10 © 2006. Used by permission of the author.

my Hebrew name is Rivka." I, on the other hand, had no idea if I had a Hebrew name, much less what it was. I racked my brain and found nothing. Finally it was my turn. All Yahweh-fearing eyes were on me as I thought to myself, "Come on, Katie: Think, think! Rebecca is to Rivka as Katie is to . . ." And then, like lightning, it struck me. I suddenly remembered a name my uncle sometimes called me, which sounded foreign and, I deduced, had to be Hebrew: "My name is Katie," I bellowed triumphantly, "and my Hebrew name is Katchkalah!" I exhaled a breath of relief and smiled in victory. But the room grew silent, the students looked confused, and the teachers exchanged worried glances. Little did I know that katchkalah was not Hebrew at all but actually the Polish-derived Yiddish word for duckling. [. . .]

The retreat on the meaning of Judaism was the first time I was asked to examine my Jewish identity and my place in the Jewish community. Was I indeed less Jewish than the religious Jews on the retreat, than religious Jews in general? Was I even Jewish? [. . .] While I've found certain Jewish communities and practices alienating, I do feel Jewish. Yet the Jews I identify with are Jews who identify with Jews as well as non-Jews. And this, itself, draws from both a rich tradition of Jewish social justice and, at the same time, a universal sense of solidarity that defies religious, ethnic, and national boundaries. Just as religious Jews connect with the rituals they inherit from their families, I feel a connection to the secular traditions in which I was raised.

My grandmother was raised in The Coops, a workers' housing cooperative in the Bronx, inspired—in spirit and architecture—by a communal housing complex in Vienna, aptly named the Karl Marx apartments. My father's uncle died in Spain during the Spanish Civil War fighting against Franco with the Abraham Lincoln Brigade.[3] My maternal grandfather lied about his age in an attempt to join the Brigade, but a *brigadista*

examining papers saw he was only 16 and sent him home. Stuck in the United States, my grandfather went to jail for climbing the flagpole outside the Austrian embassy and tearing down a swastika. And then, a few years later, as fascism marched along, my grandfather got his chance to fight fascists in Italy and North Africa during World War II.

My parents are almost a parody of Upper West Side [New York] secular Jews. Their apartment is filled with saints, shivas, Buddhas, and the occasional dream catcher. The only Jewish holiday we celebrate— Passover—is based in a historical story of oppression, resistance, and liberation. Until recently, I didn't even know Passover was a Jewish holiday. I thought it was a Black holiday, like Kwanzaa, but much, much older because while my family honors the Jews' Exodus out of Egypt, most of our Seder is spent discussing slavery in the United States, the Civil Rights Movement, and now, the occupation of Iraq. The story of the suffering of Jews in Egypt is a mere starting point for exploring more recent realms of oppression, wherever—and to whomever—they occur.

10   Ultimately, where I felt most connected to my Jewish identity was at summer camp. I went to a camp founded by progressive Jewish immigrants in the 1920s, welcoming Jews and non-Jews alike. Following in the footsteps of my mother and her mother before her, I made that great summertime migration north from NYC to Camp Kinderland. While other camps name their bunks after letters, numbers, or (often fictitious) Native American tribes, Kinderland names its bunks after social-justice activists, Jews like Shalom Aleichem, Emma Goldman, and Anne Frank, and non-Jews such as Joe Hill, Harriet Tubman, and Roberto Clemente. For the World Peace Olympics, Kinderland's version of the "color wars," teams are named after social movements (AIDS Education, Suffragism, Civil Rights) or activists (A. Philip Randolph, Sojourner Truth, César Chávez).[4] My first summer I was on the Martin Luther King team, and I'll never

forget that MLK vs. Ghandi soccer match of '92, when Martin Luther King cleaned the floor with Ghandi. [. . .]

After years as a camper, I became a counselor. To this day, I try to visit every summer, and my friends from camp remain my best friends. And it was and is here, surrounded by Jews and non-Jews committed to social justice (for everyone), drawing from traditions as rich, as authentic, and as Jewish as the religious traditions that offer so much meaning to others, that I felt and feel most Jewish.

Editor's Notes

1. *Shabbat* means "Sabbath," which is celebrated by Jews from sundown on Friday through sundown Saturday.

2. The concept "secular Jew" is open to various interpretations. It refers generally to a person who is ethnically Jewish and identifies with that ethnic identity, but is not religious and perhaps may not believe in God. In this essay, the term suggests an identification with ethical and social ideals learned from the Jewish community, but also implies inclusiveness, a sense of identification as well with non-Jews who share those same ideals (e.g., "social justice").

3. The Abraham Lincoln Brigade was made of American volunteers in the Spanish Civil War against Francisco Franco and fascism.

4. Sholem Aleichem was a famous Yiddish author; *Fiddler on the Roof* is based loosely on one of his stories. Emma Goldman was an anarchist and political activist. *The Diary of Anne Frank* relates the story of a German Jewish girl whose family took refuge in the Netherlands, was betrayed to the Nazis during the German occupation, and deported to the concentration camps; she died in Bergen-Belsen concentration camp. Joe Hill was a radical American labor activist whose execution for murder was controversial and made him a folk hero. Abolitionist Harriet Tubman, herself a former slave, rescued African American slaves through the Underground Railroad during the Civil War. Roberto Clemente was born in Puerto Rico and died tragically in a plane carrying relief supplies to earthquake victims in Nicaragua, the last day of 1972. He is a member of the Baseball Hall of Fame. A. Philip Randolph was a twentieth-century African American Civil Rights leader. Sojourner Truth, an emancipated slave, was an abolitionist and women's rights activist. César Chávez was a Mexican American migrant farmer and labor activist. This diverse list of persons all embody and worked toward the ideal of social justice.

BEFORE YOU READ: Lozada's essay talks about the significance of ethnic labels and identifiers. How useful are these descriptors? Do we need them to understand our own identity?

WHAT MAKES ME "HISPANIC"*

Carlos Lozada

Carlos Lozada is the Outlook editor for *The Washington Post*. This article appeared in the Fort Wayne (Indiana) *Journal Gazette* in 2013.

"Shut up, you stupid Mexican!"
The words spewed from the mouth of a pale, freckle-faced boy, taunting me on our school playground. More than three decades later, I remember only my reply. "Stupid Peruvian," I pointed out, wagging my finger.

My family had emigrated from Lima to Northern California a few years earlier, so

---

my nationality was a point of fact (whereas my stupidity remains a matter of opinion). The response so confused my classmate that my first encounter with prejudice ended as quickly as it started. Recess resumed.

Today, my grade-school preoccupation with nationality feels quaint. Peruvian or Mexican—does it even matter? We're all Hispanics now.

5   And don't call us stupid. Ever since the 2012 election, when the Hispanic vote helped propel President Barack Obama (71 percent) over Mitt Romney (27 percent), Hispanics have become coveted, exciting, DREAMy. When politicians ride Hispanic ancestry to presidential short lists and convention keynote slots, when a stale-mated Congress has a shot at immigration reform because Democrats need to keep us and Republicans need to woo us, and when Univision beats NBC in prime-time ratings, you know that America's 51 million Hispanics are officially marketable, clickable, unignorable.

The attention is nice, I admit. But there's an odd twist: It's not evident what being Hispanic truly means, and most Hispanics, it turns out, don't even identify with the term.

Is being Hispanic a matter of geography, as simple as where you or your ancestors came from? Is it the language you speak or how well you speak it? Is it some common culture? Or is it just a vaguely brown complexion and a last name ending in "a," "o" or "z"? Politicians build Hispanic-voter outreach operations, businesses launch marketing campaigns to attract Hispanic "super-consumers," yet depending on whom you ask—politicians, academics, journalists, activists, researchers or pollsters—contradictory definitions and interpretations emerge.

If all ethnic identities are created, imagined or negotiated to some degree, American Hispanics provide an especially stark example. As part of an effort in the 1970s to better measure who was using what kind of social services, the federal government established the word "Hispanic" to denote anyone with ancestry traced to Spain or Latin America.

"The term is a U.S. invention," explains Mark Hugo Lopez, associate director of the Pew Hispanic Center. "If you go to El Salvador or the Dominican Republic, you won't necessarily hear people say they are 'Latino' or 'Hispanic.'"

10   According to a 2012 Pew survey, only about a quarter of Hispanic adults say they identify themselves most often as Hispanic. About half say they prefer to cite their family's country of origin, while one-fifth say they use "American."

The Office of Management and Budget defines a Hispanic as "a person of Cuban, Mexican, Puerto Rican, South or Central American, or other Spanish culture or origin regardless of race"—about as specific as calling someone European.

"There is no coherence to the term," says Marta Tienda, a sociologist and director of Latino studies at Princeton University. For instance, even though it's officially supposed to connote ethnicity and nationality rather than race—after all, Hispanics can be black, white or any other race—the term "has become a racialized category in the United States," Tienda says. "Latinos have become a race by default, just by usage of the category."

Janet Murguia, president of the National Council of La Raza, listed its basic elements: "Culturally, we're bound by language, a common affection for Spanish—even though we learn English. Strong faith, strong family, strong sense of community. These are values we hold in common."

Sergio Bendixen, a Miami-based strategy consultant on Hispanic politics and media, agrees that a culture exists but defines it entirely differently. It's "not really language or the Catholic Church, or that we come from this country or that," he said. It is "a culture that gives tremendous weight to human relationships and the celebration of life; you are free to show your emotion, more than suppress your emotion. That is what really unites all Hispanics."

15   If most Hispanics are united in something, though, it's a belief that they don't share a common culture. The Pew Hispanic Center finds that nearly seven in 10 Hispanics say they comprise "many different cultures" rather than a single one. "But when journalists, researchers or the federal government talk about" Hispanics, Lopez acknowledges, "they talk about a single group."

Even the Spanish language is losing some of its power as a cultural marker. About 80 percent of U.S. Hispanics say they read or speak Spanish "very well" or "pretty well," according to Pew, but only 38 percent claim it as their primary language.

If language or race or a common culture aren't enough to define or unite us, perhaps politics can help.

A stark vision of a Hispanic political identity emerged from former New Mexico Gov. Bill Richardson, who suggested to ABC News that Sen. Ted Cruz, a Cuban American and conservative Republican from Texas, should not be "defined as a Hispanic" because he doesn't support immigration reform.

(Soon afterward, Richardson told Fox News it was a misunderstanding.)

20   Yes, the notion of a political litmus test for Hispanic identity seems bizarre. But Richardson made clear how, in the political world, that identity has evolved from a broad ethnic and cultural category to include an implied liberal sensibility.

A 2012 Pew survey found that immigration reform was not the key issue for registered Hispanic voters. When asked what subjects they considered "extremely important," Hispanics rated education, the economy, health care and even the budget deficit before immigration.

Not that different from the rest of America.

There is one moment when assuming the Hispanic label feels right, even urgent: when the political debates over immigration turn ugly, when talk of self-deportation and racial-profiling laws and anchor babies permeates campaigns, distinctions and nuances seem to dissipate.

"When one of us is under attack, we identify, we come together," Murguia says. "When one of us is singled out because of their accent, their skin color, our people come together out of a sense of justice. People say, 'That can be me.'"

25   This is why the anti-Hispanic sentiment that has emerged in some quarters of American politics is self-defeating. It fosters unity among otherwise disparate peoples. It strengthens, even creates, the very identity it seeks to dislodge.

Questions to Help You Think and Write About Race, Culture, and Identity

1. Demographers predict that whites will become a minority race by 2050. In the context of the arguments these readings make about race in contemporary America, consider this prediction. What effect on how we think about racial and ethnic difference might it have for white Americans to become a statistical minority?

2. Daly writes about students in a sociology class at Penn State University who participate in DNA tests to determine their genetic ancestry. How would you feel about participating in such a study? How would you adjust to learning that your racial makeup is different from what you had thought it was? Should this information matter to individuals? Why or why not?

3. Imagine that Barack Obama and K. A. Dilday have been invited on a television talk show to consider how Americans can better promote racial equality for all citizens. What position might each of these speakers take? What might be their claims? Would they agree or disagree in their opinions?

4. "Reading Images" in this section of The Reader shows how "photo-negative" images—the reversal of black and white—can alter your perception of familiar figures, groups, and settings. Select a photograph, famous painting, advertisement, or some other image and "recolor" it to change the race/color/identity of the figures. Then write an analysis of your visual argument that examines how the color reversal either makes "whiteness visible" or calls into question some cultural assumptions embodied in the image or in the figures depicted.

5. Halper and Lozada both explore the practice of identifying with a particular religious, ethnic, or cultural group. Identify one group with which you identify. Create a chart: in the left column, list the typical, or even stereotypical, characteristics associated with this group; in the right column, consider whether you see these characteristics in yourself. What are the limits of group identification?

6. Halper's essay is based on an oxymoron, or the simultaneous existence of two incompatible things: secularism and Judaism. Write an essay about an important paradox in your own identity. Begin the essay with this statement completed: "My name is _____, and I am a _____ _____. I've been _____ for a little over _____ years now." For instance, "My name is Josh, and I am a compulsive procrastinator. I've been a compulsive procrastinator for a little over eighteen years now." Or, "My name is Josh, and I am a cheerful pessimist."

7. Try Googling your own name. How many different kinds of people can you find with either your first and last name (or just your last name, if the first attempt does not yield enough examples)? What can you infer or imagine about the group of people who share your name as a cultural "type"? Create your own "label" for this new group or community. Is it possible to find common threads? Describe these threads or, if you find no threads at all, discuss the significance of that lack of commonality.

8. **Arguing Like a Citizen:** Imagine that you are going to live in another country where the race, language, religion, and culture are different from your own. What aspects of your culture would you want to keep? What would you be willing to give up? How do you think your sense of personal identity would be affected by such a relocation? What would you do to try to adjust to your new environment?

SECTION 5

The Environment and Sustainability

The Issues

A. **How Can We Create a More Sustainable Culture of Eating?**

The four authors in this section explore the relationship between sustainability and food from a range of different perspectives. Lisa Hamilton challenges conventional assumptions about the environmental effects of eating meat. James McWilliams examines the growing prevalence of genetically modified food, describing some of the surprising environmental benefits this new technology brings. Uncovering yet another environmental dimension to our eating practices, Josh Viertel makes the case for the importance of the Slow Food Movement. Rounding out these selections, Martha Rosenberg wonders aloud about whether our interest in sustainable food needs to acknowledge the question of "animal rights."

B. **How Can We Resolve the Economy versus Environment Debate?**

The essays in this section consider environmental issues within a global context. Ramit Plushnick-Masti's essay tells the story of one community's effort to stand up to the coal mining interests in her home state. "Reading Images: Coal Mining and the Environment" depicts the impact of coal production in two distant locales. Stuart Price, meanwhile, examines the ways that environmental concerns and economic realities can often conflict, while Brian Wingfield reports on the ways in which the needs of environment and economy are coming together in the green-job sector. And finally, Bill Carter completes our investigation into the economics of environmentalism by uncovering some of the "hidden costs" of going green.

Exploring Online Argument

The following Web sites present interesting perspectives on the environment and sustainability.

U.S. Environmental Protection Agency, Climate Change	Sustainable Table
United Nations Environment Programme (UNEP), Themes, Climate Change	World Health Organization (WHO): Food, Genetically Modified
Pew Center on Global Climate Change	Slow Food USA
Center for Virtual Appalachia	Organic.org
Chinamining.org	Amazon Conservation Team
Mongabay.com, preface page to Rain Forests	USDA: Food Security in the US
World Bank	The Vegetarian Resource Group
World Wildlife Fund	People for the Ethical Treatment of Animals (PETA)

The Rhetorical Situation

Modern debates over the environment stretch back at least to the 1960s. In 1962, nature writer and marine biologist Rachel Carson published *Silent Spring*, which attacked the chemicals industry by imagining a time when pesticides would, through a chain of ecological events, kill off all the songbirds. The activism of pioneers such as Carson led to the establishment of the Environmental Protection Agency in 1970, but many changes in the political climate and the economy have sustained ongoing conflict and negotiation among environmental groups, the government, and the business sector.

One such example of this conflict involves the ongoing debate over the state of the coal industry. For many in the southeastern United States, coal mining remains a vital source of employment. In the eyes of others, however, the environmental costs of coal mining far outweigh the economic benefits this industry brings. The practice of mountaintop removal, for instance, is an efficient and profitable method of mining coal, but it literally flattens mountains, destroys forests, and fills streams with soil. Among the problems that have been blamed on mountaintop removal are water and noise pollution, flash floods, cancer, unemployment, and the loss of community and traditional ways of life. This same conflict is now being played out in places beyond the U.S. In China, for example, massive and rapid industrial growth has been fueled in part by largely unregulated coal mining practices that have led to sulfur dioxide pollution in places as far-flung as South Korea and Hawaii.

In all of the geographical areas pictured and discussed in this section, destruction of the environment is linked in complicated ways to poverty. In those areas of the southern and southeastern United States where domestic coal mining is most prevalent, unemployment can be quite high, rising as high as ten to fifteen percent of the population. Troublingly, although mining jobs pay better than average, it is not clear whether this production practice creates new jobs or further unemployment. Migrants have flocked to the rapidly growing cities in industrialized China, but many harm their health at the same time. In South America and Africa, some of the most delicate ecosystems in the world have been severely damaged as a result of corporate-sponsored efforts to extract valuable resources.

There is hope, however. For Americans there is a rising interest in so-called "green-collar" jobs. This shift can particularly benefit low-income Americans by creating jobs that must be performed here: a job putting up solar panels in homes or constructing wind farms cannot be outsourced to developing countries. "Green careers" for scientists and engineers will also need to be developed to create the environment-saving materials used in these jobs.

International organizations are beginning to acknowledge how small the globe seems to have become. The most recent United Nations Climate Change Conference, held in Warsaw, Poland in 2013, concluded with new agreements among the world's most developed nations to continue addressing such important environmental issues as greenhouse gas emissions and deforestation. In a world that is increasingly interdependent, what happens in one place can have unexpected consequences for other places and peoples. While all countries bear responsibility for the ongoing harm being inflicted on the environment worldwide, there still exist genuine opportunities to create change.

A. How Can We Create a More Sustainable Culture of Eating?

> **BEFORE YOU READ:** In debates over food and eating, proponents of vegetarianism often argue that this mode of eating carries not only individual health benefits but also benefits for the environment. Can you think of ways in which our culture and media either reinforce or challenge this claim?

UNCONVENTIONAL FARMERS: LET THEM EAT MEAT*

Lisa Hamilton

Lisa Hamilton is the author of *Deeply Rooted: Unconventional Farmers in the Age of Agribusiness*.

Last fall, the head of the U.N.'s International Panel on Climate Change, Dr. Rakendra Pachauri, offered a simple directive for combating global warming: eat less meat. Critics might point out that he is a vegetarian, but the numbers back up his idea. A 2006 UN report found that 18 percent of the world's greenhouse gas emissions come from raising livestock for food. Overall, Pachauri's advice is good, though I would add a corollary: At the same time that we begin eating less meat, we should be eating more of it.

*Used by permission of Lisa Hamilton.

More of a different kind, that is. Animals reared on organic pasture have a different climate equation from those raised in confinement on imported feed. That's because much of livestock's emissions come as a result of dismantling the natural farm system and replacing it with an artificial environment. For instance, in confinement systems manure has nowhere to go. Managed in man-made lagoons, its anaerobic decomposition produces millions of tons of methane and nitrous oxide every year. On pasture, that same manure is simply assimilated back into the soil with a carbon cost close to zero.

Some would argue that pasture-raised animals are just the lesser of two evils. Given that livestock make for emissions no matter where they're raised—cows, for instance, emit methane as a by-product of their digestion—wouldn't it be better to have no livestock at all? Not according to farmer Jason Mann, who grows produce and raises chickens, hogs, and cattle on pasture outside Athens, Georgia. In the age of CAFO's [Concentrated Animal Feeding Operations], we have come to regard livestock as a problem to be solved. But for a sustainable farm system like his, animals are essential.

Mann thinks of it like a bank account: Every time he harvests an ear of corn or a head of lettuce, he withdraws from the soil's fertility; if he doesn't redeposit that fertility, the account will hit zero. He could truck in compost from 250 miles away, or apply synthetic fertilizers to make the vegetables grow. But by his carbon calculation the best option is to return that fertility by using livestock, particularly cows. They do more than keep his soil rich. When managed properly, cattle can boost soil's ability to sequester carbon. Their manure adds organic matter to the soil, their grazing symbiotically encourages plant growth, and their heavy hooves help break down dead plant residue. Some proponents argue that highly managed, intensive grazing can shift cattle's carbon count so dramatically that the animals actually help reduce greenhouse gases.

5   In addition to completing the farm's ecology, Mann's livestock also complete the farm's economy with critical revenue for the real bank account—which keeps the farm afloat in a way that lettuce cannot. But that happens only when the animals become meat. That's the thing about livestock: If they stand around eating all day but never produce more than manure, they are a net loss. With the exception of laying hens, in order for animals to be worthwhile in a whole farm system, they must be eaten. That means for Mann's farm to be sustainable, his neighbors must buy and eat the meat.

The same applies on a larger scale: In order for pasture-based livestock to become a significant part of the meat industry, we need to eat more of its meat, not less. As it is, grass-fed beef accounts for less than one percent of American beef consumption, and numbers for chicken and pork hardly register. Even where the industry is growing, it is stunted by inadequate infrastructure. The greatest challenge is a lack of small-scale slaughterhouses (something Bonnie Powell addressed artfully in an article for *Mother Jones*), but the industry also suffers from a dearth of research, outreach for new producers, and investment in breeding for pasture-based systems. And those things will change only as the market grows. So if you want to use your food choices to impact climate change, by all means follow Dr. Pachauri's suggestion for a meatless Monday. But on Tuesday, have a grass-fed burger—and feel good about it.

> **BEFORE YOU READ:** How do you respond to the term "Frankenfood"? What image of genetically modified food does it evoke for you?

THE GREEN MONSTER*

James McWilliams

James McWilliams is an associate professor of history at Texas State University, and the author of *Just Food: Where Locavores Get It Wrong and How We Can Truly Eat Responsibly*. This article appeared in the online journal *Slate* in 2009.

I'm sitting at my desk examining a $10.95 jar of South River Miso. The stuff is delicious, marked by a light, lemony tang. The packaging, by contrast, is a heavy-handed assurance of purity. The company is eager to tell me that the product I've purchased is certified organic, aged for three weeks in wood (sustainably harvested?), unpasteurized, made with "deep well water," hand-crafted, and—the designation that most piques my interest—*GMO free*.

GMO refers to "genetically modified organisms." A genetically modified crop results from the laboratory insertion of a gene from one organism into the DNA sequence of another in order to confer an advantageous trait such as insect resistance, drought tolerance, or herbicide resistance. Today almost 90 percent of soy crops and 80 percent of corn crops in the United States sprout from genetically engineered seeds. Forty-five million acres of land worldwide contain genetically engineered crops. From the perspective of commercial agriculture, the technology has been seamlessly assimilated into traditional farming routines.

From the perspective of my miso jar, however, it's evident that not all consumers share the enthusiasm. It's as likely as not that you know GMOs by their stock term of derision: *Frankenfoods*. The moniker reflects a broad spectrum of concerns: Some anti-biotech activists argue that these organisms will contaminate their wild cousins with GM pollen and drive native plants extinct. Others suggest that they will foster the growth of "superweeds"—plants that develop a resistance to the herbicides many GMOs are engineered to tolerate. And yet others fear that genetic alterations will trigger allergic reactions in unsuspecting consumers. Whether or not these concerns collectively warrant a ban on GMOs—as many (most?) environmentalists would like to see—is a hotly debated topic. The upshot to these potential pitfalls, however, is beyond dispute: A lot of people find this technology to be creepy.

Whatever the specific cause of discontent over GM crops, popular resistance came to a head in 2000, when the National Organic Program solicited public input on the issue of whether they should be included. In response, sustainable-food activists deluged officials with a rainforest's worth of letters—275,000, to be exact—beating the measure into oblivion. Today, in the same spirit, environmentalists instinctively deem GMOs the antithesis of environmental responsibility.

5   Many scientists, and even a few organic farmers, now believe the 2000 rejection was a fatal rush to judgment. Most recently,

---

Pamela Ronald, a plant pathologist and chair of the Plant Genomics Program at the University of California–Davis, has declared herself one such critic. In *Tomorrow's Table: Organic Farming, Genetics, and the Future of Food*, she argues that we should, in fact, be actively merging genetic engineering and organic farming to achieve a sustainable future for food production. Her research—which she conducts alongside her husband, an organic farmer—explores genetically engineered crops that, instead of serving the rapacity of agribusiness, foster the fundamentals of sustainability. Their endeavor, counterintuitive as it seems, points to an emerging green biotech frontier—a hidden realm of opportunity to feed the world's impending 9 billion a diet produced in an environmentally responsible way.

To appreciate how "responsible genetic modification" isn't an oxymoron, consider grass-fed beef. Cows that eat grass are commonly touted as the sustainable alternative to feedlot beef, a resource-intensive form of production that stuffs cows with a steady diet of grain fortified with antibiotics, growth hormones, steroids, and appetite enhancers that eventually pass through the animals into the soil and water. One overlooked drawback to grass-fed beef, however, is the fact that grass-fed cows emit four times more methane—a greenhouse gas that's more than 20 times as powerful as carbon dioxide—as regular, feedlot cows. That's because grass contains lignin, a substance that triggers a cow's digestive system to secrete a methane-producing enzyme. An Australian biotech company called Gramina has recently produced a genetically modified grass with lower amounts of lignin. Lower amounts of lignin mean less methane, less methane means curbed global warming emissions, and curbed emissions means environmentalists can eat their beef without hanging up their green stripes.

Another area where sustainable agriculture and genetic modification could productively overlap involves nitrogen fertilizer. A plant's failure to absorb all the nutrients from the fertilizer leads to the harmful accumulation of nitrogen in the soil. From there it leaches into rivers and oceans to precipitate dead zones so choked with algae that other marine life collapses. In light of this problem, Syngenta and other biotech companies are in the process of genetically engineering crops such as potatoes, rice, and wheat to improve their nitrogen uptake efficiency in an effort to diminish the negative consequences of nitrogen fertilization. Early results suggest that rice farmers in Southeast Asia and potato farmers in Africa might one day have the option of planting crops that mitigate the harmful effects of this long-vilified source of agricultural pollution.

Animals, of course, are just as modifiable as plants. Livestock farmers have been genetically tinkering with their beasts for centuries through the hit-or-miss process of selective breeding. They've done so to enhance their animals' health, increase their weight, and refine their fat content. Breeding animals to reduce environmental impact, however, hasn't been a viable option with the clunky techniques of conventional breeding. But such is not the case with genetic engineering.

Case in point: Canadian scientists have recently pioneered the "enviropig," a genetically modified porker altered to diminish the notoriously high phosphorous level of pig manure by 60 percent. Like nitrogen, phosphorous runoff is a serious pollutant with widespread downstream consequences. But with the relatively basic insertion of a gene (from E. coli bacteria) that produces a digestive enzyme called phytase, scientists have provided farmers with yet another tool for lessening their heavy impact on the environment.

10   When commercial farmers hear about GM grass, increased nitrogen uptake, and cleaner pigs, they're excited. And when they hear about other products in the

works—genetically modified sugar beets that require less water and have higher yields than cane sugar; a dust made from genetically modified ferns to remove heavy metals from the soil; genetically modified and *edible* cotton seeds that require minimal pesticide use—they're also excited. And they're excited not only because these products have the potential to streamline production, but also because GM technology allows them to play a meaningful role in reducing their carbon footprint.

However, with the exception of the modified sugar beets, the GMOs mentioned in this article are not currently on the market. The cutting-room floors of research laboratories all over the world, in fact, are littered with successful examples of genetically engineered products that have enormous potential to further the goals of sustainable

agriculture. Demand for these products remains high among farmers—it almost always does—but food producers fear the bad publicity that might come from anti-GMO invective.

Given the potential of these products to reduce the environmental impact of farming, it's ironic that traditional advocates for sustainable agriculture have led a successful campaign to blacklist GMOs irrespective of their applications. At the very least, they might treat them as legitimate ethical and scientific matters deserving of a fair public hearing. Such a hearing, I would venture, would not only please farmers who were truly concerned about sustainability, but it would provide the rest of us—those of us who do not grow food for the world but only think about it—a more accurate source of scientific information than the back of a miso jar.

> **BEFORE YOU READ:** What do you know about the "slow food movement"? In what ways does the name of this movement suggest a concern for the environment?

THE SOUL OF SLOW FOOD*
Josh Viertel

Josh Viertel is the president of the Slow Food Movement USA. This article was published in *The Atlantic* magazine in 2012.

When my fiancée, Juliana, and I were farming, we grew the most beautiful produce I have ever seen. I do not mean to brag. It is sort of like being a parent, or a pet owner. Anyone who has grown food with love probably feels that way about the product of his or her labor. We grew 300 varieties of fruits, vegetables, herbs, and flowers, many heirloom varieties, and ingredients for cooking food from so many traditions.

We sold them at a farmers' market in a well-heeled neighborhood, and we charged a lot of money. We did not think twice about charging $16 per pound for salad greens. We knew what work went into it, we knew how good it was, and we knew it was worth it. We sold out. And we made $12,000 a year between the two of us. We thought we were doing pretty well.

*Josh Viertel, "The Soul of Slow Food: Fighting for Both Farmers and Eaters," *The Atlantic*, January 23, 2012. Reprinted by permission of the author.

When low-income people came to our stand with food stamps, we gave them two or three for the price of one. But something was broken. At $12,000, we had low incomes ourselves, and the only people we could feed had high incomes. I wanted to change the world, and I saw farming as a piece of that work. Fairness for the farmer seemed to mean injustice for the eater. Fairness for the eater seemed to mean injustice for the farmer. How could we simply choose to fight for one, with the knowledge that it undercut the other?

A few years later, I found myself standing in a room filled with about 300 extraordinary people—people working to take on the same paradox that had troubled me as a young farmer. Slow Food USA was putting on an enormous event in San Francisco in the fall of 2008 called Slow Food Nation. It brought the most inspiring artisan pickle makers, charcuterie curers, and bread bakers together with the most committed food activists and farmers. Alice Waters, Carlo Petrini, Wendell Berry, Eric Schlosser, Michael Pollan, Raj Patel, Van Jones, Vandana Shiva, Lucas Benitez, and many, many other heroes of mine were all in the same place, at the same time, to talk about food, farming, and the movement to transform both. Monsanto and Ronald McDonald would have done well to blow up the building.

But the room I am thinking of did not have any of these well-known leaders in it. It was filled with Slow Food's unsung heroes—the people doing extraordinary work, day in, and day out, in their communities. This was a meeting for Slow Food USA's chapter leaders to come together and talk about where to take the organization in the years that would follow.

5   People like Paula Shatkin, who was working to organize farmers to save the Gravenstein apple, which used to be a mainstay in northern California but had nearly disappeared because of rising property value

for big wineries and real estate. People like Andy Nowak, and Gigia Kolouch and Krista Roberts, parents who would go on to organize over 500 parents and teachers to bring gardens and real food to the cafeterias of more than 60 percent of Denver's public schools. People like Amanda Peden, from Portland, who would go on to bridge a gap between the committed farmers market shoppers in Portland and the farm workers that often picked the food that showed up on the table there.

We came together to commit to a common direction for the years that would follow. I had just been named Slow Food USA's president, and had come there to meet and hear from the people I would be serving. I was impressed by what I heard. Some things did not surprise me. Leaders reaffirmed that the pleasure and power of the shared meal must continue to be central to the work Slow Food does. They talked about the importance of food traditions, biodiversity, and supporting food producers.

All were clear that this is deeply a part of who we are. But at the same time, there was a collective commitment to forwarding work that is explicitly about bettering the world—work that includes a commitment to justice, and that is serious about change. I heard statements like, "I don't want to just be a part of a supper club. I want to change the way food and farming works in my community."

That potential—the possibility of building a movement committed not only to the simple pleasure of the shared meal and paying the farmer fairly but to becoming a force for social change—is what first inspired me about Slow Food. It inspired all of us.

At this initial meeting, many leaders said that a move in this direction was simply becoming more true to Slow Food's roots. After all, we were born at an anti-corporate protest: People gathered to shut down the opening of a McDonald's on the Spanish Steps in Rome, chanting, "We don't want

Fast Food, we want Slow Food." But they did so while serving penne pasta to the passersby. From the beginning, it was protest and pleasure, all in one.

10   Since Slow Food Nation, we have been doing the work and making the change. Most of this work has manifested itself at the local level, as chapters across the country have initiated projects and campaigns to make food in our communities more good, more clean, more fair. Much has happened at the national and state level as well, as we have mobilized initiatives to change school lunch policy, shut down Ag-Gag laws, reform food and farm policy, and to save the honey bee.

Just three years later, there are 1,200 leaders committed to that vision, leading that work. When we first met together, at Slow Food Nation, Slow Food USA had 14,000 members, and reached about 25,000 people on its mailing list. Today, we have 25,000 members and reach over 250,000 people on our mailing list. Together, we are working to build an alternative to the industrial food system. We are proving something better is possible.

This shift has prompted some important and difficult conversations. Lately it has bubbled over into controversy. Some people worry we are turning our backs on our roots. Some people say we are being more faithful to them. There are real, difficult questions at hand. What does it mean to promote paying the real cost of food while also promoting social justice and access? Is asking people to pay more for food elitist? Is exploring affordability an affront to farmers? Can you both fight for the farmer and fight for the eater, or do farmers and eaters have competing agendas? Can we fight for serious change without abandoning our commitment to the simple pleasure of a shared meal? What changes will we seek to make and who will we fight for? Access vs. food

traditions and biodiversity. Farmers vs. eaters. Rural vs. urban. Youth vs. elders.

So far, the basic question has been about our identity: Should we be a movement that meets the interests of those who are naturally drawn to us and who can afford to take part, or should we be a movement that meets the needs of those who are most dependent on our being successful—and who are most vulnerable if we fail?

Underlying is a much deeper question, not just about our identity, but about our soul as an organization and as a movement: Do we have the foresight, the bravery, and the heart to be a movement that does both?

15   I believe we do, and I believe we must. Foresight, because if we choose one or the other, we lose. Bravery, because choosing both will sometimes make us uncomfortable as we face things that are difficult. And heart, because we need to be large-hearted enough to see that if we are only for one, and not for the other, we are not even for the one. That to love and support the farmer necessitates loving and supporting the person who should be able to be her customer.

One day, I want to grow and sell vegetables again. It may be the most satisfying work I have ever done. But we have a lot of work to do first. Because being a farmer should not mean earning a living that prices you out of eating the sort of food you grow. And people in your same income bracket should not be priced out of being your customer.

The only way we can get there is through building a movement that derives strength by being for both. For youth and elders; for food access and for food traditions; for farmers, workers, and eaters. One relies on and strengthens the other. We will come to see that preserving a food tradition, renewing a rare breed, and even just sharing a meal together can all be profound political acts— and that, in the end, good protest can start with a pot of good pasta.

> **BEFORE YOU READ:** What is your opinion of the animal rights movement? In your view, should concerns over animal rights influence our policies regarding food production? Why or why not?

IS ANIMAL TREATMENT ON FARMS OUR BUSINESS?*

Martha Rosenberg

Martha Rosenberg is a health reporter for *The Huffington Post*. This article appeared in 2013.

Did people just discover where meat comes from? Sometimes it seems like it.

Animal rights activists, with the help of miniaturized cameras and the Web, have forced farm animal treatment onto the national front page with a parade of cruel, upsetting and gruesome exposés. To capture the farm verité all they often have to do is get hired at a factory farm or slaughterhouse.

How hard is it to get hired in a slaughterhouse or on factory farm? Can you fog a mirror? Can you start this afternoon? There is not a long line to fill jobs whose descriptions are, "Remove dead animals from 98 degree ammonia-infused pens wearing face mask, $8 an hour possible, depending on experience," or "Determine sex of newborn chicks and grind up unwanted males for dog food: $6 dollars an hour; chance for advancement."

Many farmers and ag professionals are miffed that the days of "it's-none-of-your-business" farming are over. Once upon a time, consumers cared only about price and wholesomeness of food and didn't worry about—or investigate—its origins and "disassembly."

5   Today consumers want to know how an animal lived, died, and even what it ate in between—and think it is their business.

Some of the newly engaged consumers are motivated by health, wanting to avoid hormones in milk, antibiotics in beef, arsenic in chicken and who knows what in seafood. But most are motivated by what meat producers would call sentimentalizing animals—not wanting them to suffer and die.

When food producers are caught red-handed abusing their animals on video, their defenses are often over the top. "That's not our farm," they claim, "and even if it is, those are not abusive practices and even if they are abusive practices, the employees were put up to it by the activists, and even if they weren't put up to it, there were only a few bad apples and we've fired them and even if there were a few bad apples, why did the activists tolerate the abuse and not report it to us and even if they did report the abuse to us, these people have a vegetarian agenda and want everyone to give up meat!"

Some abuse that undercover employees document can be explained by ignorance, cost margins at volume operations that make it cheaper to kill animals than treat their illnesses, and the frustration of degrading, low-paying jobs that seem to be made more difficult by the animals themselves. ("You'll learn to hate them," the mechanic training an undercover animal rights activist

*Martha Rosenberg, "Is Animal Treatment on Farms Our Business?" *Huffington Post*, Aug 16, 2013. Reprinted by permission of the author.

says of the cows.) But other operations seem to harbor employees who enjoy and seek to hurt animals.

Revelations of cruelty on U.S. farms often have immediate, "viral" results. Customers of the operation sometimes suspend their business, consumers may boycott products, and politicians have even introduced legislation to stop exposed cruel practices. Yet prosecuting attorneys almost never bring charges because the victims are just animals and farm animals to boot. Prosecuting attorneys even say they will launch "their own" investigations as if the farm operations would not have been subsequently cleaned up after exposing videos.

Now, Agribiz is attempting to make the depiction of factory farm conditions a crime with "ag gag" bills that clearly violate the First Amendment. Rather than criminalizing undercover animal rights activists who document abuse, meat producers, government regulators, and food consumers need to contemplate the ethics of a system of production that has become so cheap there is no room for the welfare of the animals in the equation. As the activists say, "Are you really that hungry?"

B. How Can We Resolve the Economy versus Environment Debate?

> **BEFORE YOU READ:** Ramit Plushnick-Masti's essay documents some of the threats modern industry poses to a particular community. What natural resources are crucial to your own community and way of life?

DESCENDANTS OF SLAVES IN EAST TEXAS HOLD OUT AGAINST LUMINANT'S COAL MINING PLANS*

Ramit Plushnick-Masti

Ramit Plushnick-Masti writes about environmental issues for *The Huffington Post*. This piece appeared in 2013.

Ida Finley smiles wistfully, recalling how she used to cook for an entire East Texas community—nearly all descendants of slaves. The children would grab cornbread, greens and cookies from her kitchen while their parents grew vegetables in a tiny creekside village hidden among pine forests.

"It's been so long," she muses, gazing at old photos that dot the walls of her nursing home room some 30 miles from Dirgin.

Now, just weeks from her 102nd birthday, Finley faces the prospect of losing the land worked by her husband and his parents, slaves who toiled for a master.

For three years, Luminant Mining Co. has tried to purchase this 9.1-acre plot, which is currently owned by a bevy of relatives spread across the country. The company owns more than 75 percent of the parcel but can't mine it because of a complex

---

*"Descendants of Slaves in East Texas Hold Out Against Luminant's Coal Mining Plans," Ramit Plushnick-Masti, © Sept 1, 2013, in Associated Press. Reprinted by permission of YGS Group.

Jacquelin Finley, right, shows her grandmother Ida Filey, 101, a family photo she recovered during a visit to the house she grew up in with her grandmother in Dirgin, Texas. The Finleys are descendants of slaves holding out against a company's attempt to mine East Texas land for coal. (AP Photo/LM Otero)

inheritance arrangement and the refusal of some family members to let go or accept Luminant's offer.

5   Luminant says it has negotiated fairly with the owners, offering them more than the land's appraised value, plus full compensation to Ida Finley and her granddaughter for homes they have on the land, which the company says they do not legally own. For the first time in its history, Luminant has sued some of the heirs, asking a court to equitably divide the land or force a settlement.

And some of the Finleys are gearing up for a fight.

"I don't want to sell my family's land. If I were to sell it, they would have to offer me a huge amount of money," said Kay Moore, a Fairfield, Calif., woman who says Luminant offered her $3,000 for her piece of property, which the company says is 1/20 of the remainder.

"It belongs to me, and I'm not willing to part with that," she added, recalling horseback riding trips and meals at Aunt Ida's.

The company has acknowledged the family's emotional ties to the land and said in a statement that it "strived for consistency from owner to owner to maintain our credibility. Most people found our offers to be more than fair."

10   In many ways, the family's story is about a way of life that disappeared long ago and a town 150 miles east of Dallas that has vanished into modernity.

Brushing the wispy white hairs from Ida Finley's forehead is her granddaughter, Jacquelin Finley—a force behind the battle against Luminant and for preserving something from those long-gone days. Still living on the property in a decaying trailer with patched siding, Jacquelin remembers Dirgin before Luminant's predecessor built the nearby reservoir. This is where Ida Finley, known to her family simply as Big Momma, raised her children and grandchildren and buried her husband.

In the early 1800s, Dirgin, like much of East Texas, consisted of large cotton plantations worked by slaves. In 1865, when the Civil War ended, Union soldiers entered Texas for the first time. The slaves were freed, and some masters sold or gave them land.

Ida Finley says "Old Man Martin," the master, gave her husband's parents more than 100 acres. Luminant says its records show the family bought the land from two Confederate Army veterans. Either way, sometime in the late 1880s, the Finleys came to own land in Dirgin. Living alongside them were other former slave families: the Menefees, Humphreys, Petersons, Barrs and Reeses among them.

When those Finleys—Dick and Puss—died, they left no will, and the parcel was evenly divided among their five children, including Ida's husband, Adolphus.

15   Ida and Adolphus lived in a small white house with a front porch and a backyard dotted with fruit trees and a basketball hoop. After the crops were harvested, the children played baseball in the cleared fields. On Sundays, they went to church—either in a wagon or by foot.

"It was the best of times," said Jacquelin Finley, who went to live with her grand-parents in the early 1960s, when she was a baby.

In the 1970s, life changed.

Just as Jacquelin Finley was bused from Mayflower Elementary to a newly desegre-gated school in nearby Tatum, Luminant's predecessor moved into the area. It had its eye on a multimillion dollar prize hid-den deep beneath the green grass and pine trees: a low grade of coal known as lignite. To profit from it, the company had to uproot trees and build a power plant.

The company bought land. Ida Finley remembers the pressure applied on her hus-band, who finally sold 9.5 acres for $1,000— the equivalent today of just over $4,300.

20   Feeling duped, he spent his final years sitting on his front porch gazing bitterly at the nearby reservoir that had flooded his land. Barely two years later, he died.

"That bothered him all those years until he died," Jacquelin Finley said. "That's my anger. Do I have a right to be angry? Yes. I want to see them go down."

Life went on, though. The power plant was built. People moved away. The church congre-gations shrunk. Some of the Finleys remained, including Ida and Jacquelin. The crops were gone, but Ida's little white house bustled.

Then, about three years ago, Luminant came knocking. The company needed to expand the mine to meet Texas' growing energy demands.

The company said that because Ida's husband died without a will, their children owned the land, and they had sold it to Luminant.

25   Under Texas law, when a landowner dies without a will, a surviving spouse receives the right to live on part of the land, but ownership passes to blood relatives, usually children.

Ida Finley, Luminant said, owned only the house, its porch now hanging forlornly near overgrown weeds, the steps broken and rotting. The quaint siding is broken and cracked. Looters scattered pictures, stuffed animals, Christmas ornaments, letters, shoes and clothing across the dusty floor, making off with more valuable items, like a refrig-erator. Luminant says it offered Ida money for the home, but she declined.

Jacquelin Finley said Sunday that initially the company only offered her a new trailer but in recent days, through her mother, also offered an acre of land. Luminant denies that account, saying she only owns the trailer she lives in and that the company offered her a new trailer and an acre else-where toward the beginning of the negotia-tions. Either way, Jacquelin has declined to accept it, and doesn't want to move. And for now Luminant can't force her.

Looking recently at the dirt patch and pile of rubble that remains of the Method-ist church she attended as a child, Jacquelin said Luminant would have to give her at least $1 million to leave—enough, she esti-mates, to fix her grandmother's house and care for her there.

"It's like I'm going against the world, and they're the world because they own every-thing," she said.

Reading Images: Coal Mining and the Environment

Context: The caption reads: Coal mining along the Three Gorges of the Yangtze River, Wushan County, Quanqing, China.

Image 1:
Coal Mining in China

For Discussion: Photo journalist Keren Su does not comment directly on the scenes he captures on camera. In this photo, how does the artistic composition of the image itself make a claim about daily life in industrialized China?

For Writing: Artistic photographs such as those by Su can be interpreted in terms of visual argument. Analyze the ways in which this photo employs *logos*, *ethos*, and/or *pathos* to create its argument.

Context: The caption reads: Mountaintop Removal in Appalachia. Vivian Stockman, a project coordinator with the Ohio Valley Environmental Coalition, photographs the effects of mountaintop removal in Appalachia as part of her organization's ongoing fight against what it calls "King Coal." More of her photographs on this subject can be seen at http://www.ohvec.org/galleries/mountaintop_removal/index.html. Like Chang W. Lee, Stockman documents with images of precise clarity and aesthetic merit.

Image 2:
Mountaintop Removal in the United States

For Discussion: This photo, shot from an airplane flying over the mountain landscape, makes a claim of fact. Like Image 1 of China, this image also makes an appeal to *ethos* and *pathos*, giving the landscape a dignity and identity of its own, separate from human industry. How do appeals to *ethos* and *pathos* complicate the claim of fact in this image?

For Writing: Analyze this image as an "argument from sign," visible evidence that supports the claims that coal mining in Appalachia is changing the landscape.

BEFORE YOU READ: This essay not only describes how economic interests are trumping environmental concerns in Africa, but suggests that the wealth made from logging never reaches the community. What is the most important natural resource in your own community and who benefits from it?

CARVING UP THE CONGO*

Stuart Price

Stuart Price is deputy editor of *New African* magazine.

In the murky days of colonial occupation, it was ivory pillaged by Europeans from deep within the jungles of DRCongo [Democratic Republic of the Congo] that formed the core of the exploitation. Over 100 years later, the plunder continues, but this time in the form of timber and other strategic natural resources.

According to an investigation by the environmental pressure group, Greenpeace, international logging companies are conning forest communities with as little as a crate of beer, sugar, and salt in order to gain access to rare and lucrative tropical hardwoods worth hundreds of thousands of dollars.

The Greenpeace report, *Carving Up the Congo*, claims that companies operating in the country are causing social chaos and wreaking environmental havoc while the rainforest is being sold off under the illusion that logging alleviates poverty. According to the report, some companies donate "gifts" to local communities worth as little as $100. In one instance, Greenpeace

Context: Compare the image with Image 3 on page 547.

For Discussion: How does this image contribute to the essay's examination of the conflict between environment and economics in the Congo? What claim does the image make? Does the essay provide evidence in support of the image's claim?

For Writing: Consider this image as a comment on the essay's title, "Carving Up the Congo." How does it contribute to the essay's argument, by supporting its claims or by supplying warrants?

*Carving Up the Congo, IC Publications Ltd., *New African Magazine,* October 2007. Reprinted with permission.

found that: "Sodefor's—an NST Group[1] company—gift package often comprises two sacks of salt, 18 bars of soap, four packets of coffee, 24 bottles of beer, and two bags of sugar, in exchange for rainforest access."

As a result, the communities effectively sign away their right to protection against the Company's activities within their area. "It is crunch time for the DRCongo's rainforests," says Stephan van Praet, Greenpeace International Africa Forest Campaign coordinator. "The international logging industry operating in the country is out of control. Unless World Bank helps DRCongo to stop the sale of these rainforests, they will soon be under the chainsaws." Greenpeace claims that the World Bank's support for development through extractive industries, including logging, is set to compromise the future of DRCongo's rainforests, its people, and the global climate.[2]

5   Two thirds of Congo's population— 40 million people—relies on the forest for food, traditional medicines, and energy. Ironically, the years of political turmoil and war in the Congo protected the forest from major logging companies. During the conflict of 1996–2003, timber production virtually ground to a halt, while corrupt and criminal elites, backed by foreign multinationals, joined a free-for-all to gain control of Congo's natural resources.

During this period, an estimated 43.5 million hectares of forest, an area twice the size of the United Kingdom, fell under the control of the logging industry.[3] At the same time, the World Bank suspended all funding and lending to the Congo, resuming its assistance in 2001. And by mid-2006, having by then approved more than $4 billion in grants, credits, and loans, the Bank was in a "unique position to influence the country's development," says Greenpeace.

Now, however, the relative peace ushered in under the government of President Joseph Kabila means the country has stabilized enough for multinationals to begin extraction and wholesale clearance of one of the oldest and most important areas of natural rainforest in the world. According to a World Bank–led forestry sector analysis earlier this year, industrial timber has a particularly poor track record in Africa. Over the past 60 years, there is little evidence that industrial timber has lifted rural populations out of poverty or contributed in other meaningful and sustainable ways to local and national development. Similarly, a United Nations Security Group of Experts stated that urgent intervention against all forms of illegal natural resource exploitation is required. Figures estimate timber smuggling is so rife that export levels are as much as seven times higher than official figures.

Following the suspension of new logging titles and the renewal or extension of existing ones in May 2002, 163 noncompliant contracts—in areas deemed as dormant and not being logged and which covered 25.5 million hectares of rainforests—were cancelled. Yet since then, few new areas have been granted or afforded any special status protecting them in the future. At the same time, since April of last year, the then transitional government signed 156 new contracts with companies covering over 15 million hectares of rainforest.

Greenpeace alleges that many of these contracts have been "approved under the guise of remapping, exchange, adjustments, and relocations of old titles, as well as out-and-out new allocations." It further charges that in the context of corruption and poor governance in DRCongo, "the World Bank's attempts to reform the forestry sector are currently failing to control the expansion of logging." Behind the granting of logging concessions is the idea that companies pay relevant taxes, which will be used to develop forest communities through the construction of schools, health centers, and improved public services. Even the World Bank admits that in the last three years, none of the forest area taxes paid by companies have reached forest communities.

10   The 156 contracts signed over the last five years cover areas inhabited by forest-dependent communities, two-thirds of which are also populated by pygmy hunter-gatherer communities. As stipulated in the 2002 Forestry Code, companies negotiate directly with communities and agree on the services they will provide in exchange for logging in their area. "These contracts are a shameful relic of colonial times. Millions of hectares of the Congo rainforest have been traded away by local communities to the logging industry for gifts like salt, machetes, and crates of beer while logging companies and their taxes do next to nothing for local development," concluded Greenpeace's van Praet. [. . .]

Like the logging industry, Congo's mining sector offers some of the highest concentrations of strategic minerals in the world. One-tenth of the world's copper reserves and a profusion of diamonds, gold, tin, cobalt, and coltan (today's miracle mineral used widely in electronic gadgets) are all found in abundance. With recent stability in the country, multinational mining companies and many smaller ventures have been scrambling to invest billions of dollars in the extractive sector.

According to the *Bretton Woods Project (BWP)*, a watchdog and critical think-tank on the World Bank and IMF [International Monetary Fund], "a confidential World Bank memo dated September 2005 and leaked to the *Financial Times* [of London] in November 2006 finds that three of the Congo's biggest mining contracts over which the World Bank had oversight were approved with 'a complete lack of transparency.'"[4]

Patrick Alley, director of Global Witness, says the government needs to ensure the highest standards of transparency and independence if the process is to be credible and restore public trust. "This review is a unique opportunity to halt the systematic looting of Congo's resources and to set a precedent for responsible investment practices, in accordance with national and international laws and standards," says Alley.

Editor's Notes

1. NST Group is an international holding company headquartered in Liechtenstein; Sodefor is a Portuguese-owned timber company. A holding company holds or owns controlling amounts of stock in other companies.

2. The World Bank is a group of five institutions formed in 1944 to reduce poverty. Although not technically a bank it provides "low-interest loans, interest-free credit and grants to developing countries for education, health, infrastructure, communications, and many other purposes" (http://www.worldbank.org).

3. A hectare is a unit of measurement commonly used for measuring land; one hectare equals 10,000 square meters or 2.47 acres.

4. The IMF (International Monetary Fund, also formed in 1944) was established to oversee currency valuation and sustainable macroeconomic growth in impoverished countries.

Reading Images: The Rain Forest

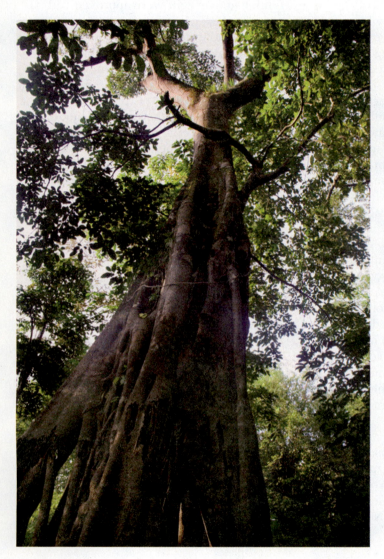

Image 1:
Tree in Lowland Rain Forest in Borneo

For Discussion: The saying "A picture is worth a thousand words" may be a cliché, but this image offers a particular argument about the importance of forests and larger wilderness of which they are a part. From the evidence here, what can you infer about the goals behind this photograph? What *ethos* of the photographer is being communicated, and what claims are being made about what is represented?

Context: Image 1 of the rain forest in Borneo, Indonesia, is reprinted from the Web site of photographer Cagan Sekercioglu, a Turkish photographer who is interested in the conservation of biodiversity. Image 2, which depicts rain forest destruction in southern Brazil, was taken by the photographer Martin Wendler.

Image 2:
Rain Forest Destruction as Viewed from Above, Southern Brazil

The image can be seen at http://www.alamy.com.

For Discussion: How does this image serve to establish the ethos of the photographer? How does this compare to the ethos established in Image 1?

For Writing: This photograph is intended to record damage to the environment, but the image also makes its own argument of fact. What argument is being made, and what evidence supports it?

Image 3:
Deforestation in the Amazon

Image of machinery harvesting logs in the rain forest.

For Discussion: Many writers and artists in the environmental movement appeal to the experience of viewers who live far away from the areas depicted. How does this photograph visually tap into your general feelings about nature?

Context: Most Americans have never visited a rain forest and therefore depend on photos and videos for their visual information. What type of information does this visual present? How does this photo compare to the illustration for the essay "Carving Up the Congo" (pages 543–545)?

BEFORE YOU READ: What careers did you imagine yourself pursuing when you were young? And what careers do you imagine yourself pursuing now? How has the reasoning behind your choices changed?

FOR JOB MARKET, GREEN MEANS GROWTH*

Brian Wingfield

Brian Wingfield writes for *The New York Times.*

In 1999, as the dot-com boom reached new heights, environmental journalist Joel Makower launched an online publication covering business and environmental interests: two areas he believed would become more connected.

Smart bet. The tech bubble burst, but Makower's publication, *GreenBiz.com*, boomed. Providing news and analysis, it's the flagship publication for Greener World Media, a for-profit company he created last year with associate Pete May. "As the greening of business expands, it is filtering into every aspect of business," from procurement to marketing to human resources, says Makower.

According to Kevin Doyle, president of Green Economy, a Boston-based firm that promotes an environmentally healthy workforce, the green industry in the United States in 2005 was about $265 billion employing 1.6 million people in an estimated 118,000 jobs. This information was adapted from the *Environmental Business Journal*, he says, and does not include the organic industry.

Green businesses have also been growing at a rate of about 5 percent annually during the last three years, Doyle says. Two particularly hot areas are global carbon credit trading, which doubled to $28 billion from 2005 to 2006, and construction and services associated with "green buildings" that meet industry standards set by the U.S. Green Building Council. Today, the green building industry is worth $12 billion; 10 years ago, it was unquantifiable.

5   The greening of industry is creating a constellation of new careers, and they're not your everyday forestry professions. Many of them are environmental twists on old professions, like law, or in Makower's case, journalism. Others are engineering careers tied to research in renewable technologies like wind energy and ethanol production. For instance:

- **Emissions brokers:** In a market economy, credits to emit greenhouse gases can be traded on an exchange, and brokers facilitate the deal. If the U.S. ever moves to a mandatory trading system, expect this field to boom.

- **Bio-mimicry engineers:** This new branch of science uses Mother Nature as a model for solving engineering problems. For example, Atlanta's Sto Corp. created a self-cleaning paint that repels dirt whenever it gets wet, just like the lotus leaf does.

- **Sustainability coordinators:** Corporations from AstraZeneca to Wal-Mart are now employing managers to oversee the economic and environmental components of company efforts.

- **Green architects:** With an increasing focus on energy-efficient buildings, a growing number of architects and developers are getting certified to become specialists in green design.

Corporations assume that at some point in the future, governments will put a price on waste, says Doyle. So it's better to invest now in clean technologies than to lose money if new regulations come into play. "People want to get ahead of the game," he says.

Conversely, companies see new revenue streams in green technologies and social responsibility. Goldman Sachs, for example, has invested heavily in the wind industry. Earlier this year, Tyson Foods and Conoco-Phillips jointly announced plans to make diesel fuel from chicken fat. And Silicon Valley venture capital firms, like Kleiner Perkins Caulfield & Byers, are shoveling money into the development of clean technologies.

Universities—particularly business schools—also see opportunity. Schools such as Stanford, the University of Michigan, the University of North Carolina and the University of Michigan offer joint M.B.A./environmental science masters degrees. Derrick Bolton, director of admissions at Stanford's Graduate School of Business, says many students are taking positions with corporations that have a commitment to the environment.

"They're what I call the 'and' generation," he says. "They don't want to make money

or support the environment. They want to do both."

10 Students in Michigan's dual degree program are encouraged to intern with both a nongovernmental organization and a business while in graduate school. "Students coming in are very aware of the sustainability program," says Rosina Bierbaum, dean of the School of Natural Resources and Environment at Michigan. "It's really just a matter of time before we're going to start valuing carbon and valuing pollution."

Makower's advice to students pursuing a green job is to learn all they can about business. The most exciting things are happening in product design, research and development, manufacturing, and buildings and grounds. "If you go into the environmental part of a company, you become ghettoized," he says.

But what if you're no longer in school? Where do you find a green job?

The Web site of Business for Social Responsibility (bsr.org), a group that helps companies navigate sustainability issues, is a good place to start. GreenBiz.com also contains a job board. Others are ecojobs.com, which includes a broad array of positions from conservation to engineering to international opportunities. Greenjobs.com focuses on the renewable fuel industry.

Makower, who survived the dot-com implosion, says the green boom is no bubble. There's a proven market, government backing and corporate buy-in. His take: Expect green business to grow even more over the next decade, and a new generation of green careers to blossom with it.

BEFORE YOU READ: What are some of the ways advertisers use "green" images or ideas to sell their products? How accurate a portrait of the "green" movement do you think such ads provide?

THE HIDDEN COSTS OF GOING GREEN*

Bill Carter

Bill Carter is the author of *Boom, Bust, Boom: A Story About Copper, the Metal That Runs the World.* This article appeared in *The Huffington Post* in 2012.

Go green. Buy a Prius to save money on gas and reduce your carbon footprint. Support wind farms and solar energy farms cropping up in places like the deserts of Arizona and the waters off Massachusetts, and soon we will make a real dent in our carbon-based fuel consumption. So the thinking goes. The green revolution makes perfect sense, but like most things in life, there is a tradeoff. A shift to green technology will increase our reliance on copper mines, the wastes of which "constitute the largest quantity of metal mining and processing wastes generated in the United States," according to the EPA. Copper can be found in nearly every electrical device in the world and is abundant in green technology. At first, only isolated communities near mines will feel this uptick in the demand for copper, but a clash of global priorities looms on the horizon. It will come down to a basic question of what we value more: food and water or minerals.

Gold gets all the attention, but copper is the metal that literally runs the world, because it is a perfect conductor of electricity and does not decay. Here are some numbers: The average car has 50 pounds of copper. An electric car contains three times that amount. The average house has over 400 pounds of copper, mostly hidden in the walls or tucked away in the basement. Every 747 jet has 120 miles of copper wiring, weighing in at 9,000 pounds. Six and a half million miles of copper have been installed in U.S. plumbing since 1963. There are over 1 billion personal computers in the world today, each with an average of 1.5 pounds of copper. There are 16 grams in every one of our world's 6 billion cellphones. Copper can also be found in all tablets, iPads and any electrical handheld device.

As for renewable energy, one modern-day windmill has some 8,000 pounds of copper. A solar farm uses a significant amount of copper to capture energy, and then enormous amounts to ground the installation and move the energy to market.

Currently the world uses about 16 million tons of copper per year. The largest producer of copper is Chile, and the largest consumer is China. With growing economies in Asia, Africa and South America, and with a global population expected to hit 9 billion by 2050, the world consumption of copper will only rise. Add to that the shift to green technology, and by 2020, world annual consumption is expected to reach 27 million tons. To accommodate this increase, industry experts predict that new, large-scale mines will have

---

*Written by Bill Carter. Reproduced with permission.

to be up and running by 2020, but due to a lack of new or "greenfield" mines on the horizon, this will largely be done by opening many small mines and reopening older mines, often referred to as "brownfields."

5   The majority of copper mines in the world today are open pit mines, measuring up to 1 mile long, 1 mile wide and 2,000 feet deep. In these boreholes into the Earth, trucks weighing up to 600 tons move the earth from one spot to another, in hopes of extracting a trace amount of copper. It takes approximately 100 tons of earth to produce half a ton of copper. In Morenci, Ariz., the largest copper mine in the U.S., five open pits produce almost 400,000 tons of copper per year. Meanwhile, the mine continuously spits out waste rock, which creates man-made mountains that now cover 10 square miles and ooze a runoff of sulfuric acid that contains heavy metals such as arsenic, barium, cadmium, chromium, iron, lead, nickel, selenium and uranium.

The majority of gas and oil pollution drifts up to the sky, causing the greenhouse effect. In contrast, pollution created by copper mining has a more direct consequence for people living near mines. Air becomes filled with dust and silica, which residents breathe at their peril. Water tables drop, and aquifers become polluted.

Over the next century, protecting our most basic natural resources, specifically food and water, from our increasing demand for copper will become a heated national discussion. In some places this is already happening. The proposed Pebble Mine in Alaska would tap a deposit of up to 80 billion pounds of copper, making it one of the largest copper mines on Earth. But this proposed mine would be 14 miles from Lake Iliamna, the world's largest natural incubator of sockeye salmon. As many as

40 million sockeye salmon enter Bristol Bay every summer, producing an estimated 12,000 jobs, worth around $600 million a year. The fishery feeds tens of thousands of Alaskan natives and millions of people around the globe. In the next few months the EPA will release a final report regarding their scientific analysis of the proposed mine. If the early EPA draft is any indicator, it will clearly state that even without a mining disaster, Pebble Mine will destroy up to 87 miles of salmon streams and 4,300 acres of salmon wetlands. In layman's terms, the mine would mean the utter destruction of the fishery. No amount of copper is worth that risk.

This is a pivotal moment in our collective decision to take charge of how we manage our resources. Yes, we need green technology to curb the impending danger of greenhouse gases. For that, more copper mines must be built. At current growth projections, it may be impossible to stop large-scale copper mining, especially if we want to go green and reduce our carbon output. Nevertheless, we need to mine as responsibly as possible, taking into consideration the environmental and social consequences to the site. We need to be able say "no" to projects like Pebble Mine, where a global food resource far outweighs the potential of a copper mine.

I am a copper product user. I have a cellphone, a computer and a car. I fly every year and cook with copper pots. I believe the only way forward is to go green. We need to bet the farm on it. Nonetheless, we also need to realize that we will drive the open-pit copper mining industry with a new demand for copper components. Going green is best for the planet, but do not be mistaken: Doing so will mean digging enormous holes in the Earth, all of them bleeding toxic metals into watersheds in the name of clean technology.

Reading Images: "Near-Zero Energy Home" Advertisement*

Home, sweet hybrid home.

If cars are being built to be more energy efficient, why shouldn't homes? At BASF, we've put our energies into building an affordable house in Paterson, New Jersey, to demonstrate how truly energy efficient a home can be. Our Near-Zero Energy Home utilizes BASF's high-performance products in insulating foam sealants, panels and concrete forms, and is 80% more energy efficient than the average American home. Who says a hybrid should only come on wheels? Learn more at basf.com/stories

Helping Make Products Better®

■·**BASF**
The Chemical Company

For Discussion: What green careers would have to be created to either remodel or build new homes that would meet the specifications of a hybrid home? What other types of green careers that could not be outsourced to other countries can you imagine being established in the United States?

For Writing: Compare the image of this hybrid home with the image of the beach house on page 38. Write a short essay in which you develop two or three ideas about human life and environmental change that occur to you as a result of viewing the two images.

Questions to Help You Think and Write About Issues of the Environment

1. Imagine Lisa Hamilton and James McWilliams in a debate over what eating practices are best for the environment. On what points raised in their respective essays would they agree and disagree? How does each of these writers define the relationship between food and environmentalism? Finally, which position do you think is better, or which position would you be able to support and why?

2. As you read the essays by Viertel and Rosenberg, consider not so much the content of their articles, but the argumentation strategies employed by each writer. What strategies do they have in common? Where do they differ? What claims do they make, and what evidence and warrants support those claims? Based on your analysis, which argument is most persuasive?

*Newsweek, February 11, 2008, p. 20.

3. The economies of both China and Texas depend on the mining and production of coal. From what you have viewed in "Reading Images" on page 542 and read in the essay by Ramit Plushnick-Masti, what similarities do these disparate cultures share?

4. Using the method employed by Hamilton to discuss environmental issues related to eating meat, analyze the nature and extent of our obligations as eaters to the larger environment. Are we obligated to consider the environmental effects of our personal eating choices? If so, to what extent?

5. In describing the environmental situation in the Congo, including the disappearance of the rain forest and its causes, Stuart Price suggests that the struggle between the needs of the economy and the environment is a global one. In what ways are the social and economic causes of the environmental situation in the rainforests similar to those governing the controversies in the United States? In what ways are these situations different from the others?

6. Brian Wingfield and the advertisement for the BASF Near-Zero Energy Home describe some "green" careers. If you were advising a college president on how better to prepare students for a world in which green industries will become increasingly important, what recommendations for social and curriculum change in American education would you make?

7. **Arguing Like a Citizen:** Find an example of an ad that uses environmental messages to sell a particular type of food. What rhetorical strategies does this ad use to promote this product as eco-friendly? Then purchase this product yourself. Does your own experience of consuming this food live up to its environmental billing? How or how not?

SECTION 6

Immigration

The Issues

A. **How Should We Respond to the Global Problem of Illegal Immigration?**

While the United States has always been a nation of immigrants and the problem of illegal immigration is by no means new, in recent years it has become a highly charged social and political issue. The first three essays address the economic dimensions of migration in a global context. Marc Cooper investigates the problems and dangers illegal immigrants from Mexico face when crossing the United States–Mexico border. United States Senators Harry Reid and Rand Paul offer contrasting visions of what immigration is, and what federal immigration policy should be. Angela Maria Kelley looks at some of the demographic changes reshaping the way we think and talk about immigration. Rounding out this section, Ellen Wu offers her thoughts on the cultural stereotype often touted as the idealized flip side of the immigration debate: the so-called model minority.

B. **Do Good Fences Make Good Neighbors When Defining National Borders?**

In 2007, in response to concerns about the economic and social impact of illegal immigration, Congress authorized the U.S. president to build a 700-mile wall on the border between the southern United States and Mexico. Jonah Goldberg, who analyzes the symbolic significance of such a wall, refers to Robert Frost's poem "Mending Wall" to suggest that while many people think "good walls make good neighbors," there is something inherently divisive about the wall as a symbol of national boundaries. Miguel Bustillo describes the way in which long-standing Hispanic homeowners along the Rio Grande in Texas respond to the allocation of their familial lands to build the wall. David Aaronovitch, finally, argues that public anxieties around immigration make immigrants the scapegoat for larger fears about societal change.

Exploring Online Argument

The following Web sites present interesting perspectives on immigration issues.

Center for Immigration Studies	U.S. Census Bureau home page
Migrants' Rights Network (U.K.)	*Immigration* . . . (Library of Congress, slide show 1 and 2)
Global Commission on International Migration (GCIM)	Immigration ProCon.org
Compass (U.K.)	National Geographic: The Changing Face of America
Global Forum on Migration and Development	Pew Hispanic Center
Immigration Policy Center (IPC)	

The Rhetorical Situation

The idea that America is a land founded and sustained by immigrants goes back a long way. As early as the late eighteenth century, J. Hector St. John de Crevecoeur identified Americans as a mix of different European nationalities, which "melt" into one another to create a new identity. While the English, Spaniards, and French who colonized parts of the North American continent are at its core, the Africans who were brought here as slaves as well as the Native American peoples already on the continent have also had a major influence on the construction of American national character. The history of nineteenth and early twentieth century immigration to North America has generally been constructed as the story of European immigration: Irish, Scottish, German, Polish, Italian, and Jewish peoples and others who arrived in New York at Ellis Island in the shadow of the Statue of Liberty and (or so the story goes) enthusiastically assimilated into their new home. Such a view ignores the experiences of many nonwhite immigrants, such as the Chinese people who worked on railroads in the western United States during the Gold Rush of the mid-nineteenth century, not to mention the Hispanic peoples who were already long-standing residents of Texas and California. (California, having been colonized by Spain, was not only a Hispanic culture but also a part of Mexico, between 1821 and 1846.)

The highly charged debates about immigration in the United States during the last half-century frequently center around issues of language and economic opportunity. Nativists (those who think that there is an essentially American culture that must be defended and preserved) complain that newer immigrants have kept to themselves and have often failed to learn English, a critique that has led over the years to recurring calls for "English Only" legislation at both the state and federal level. Most recently, though, the debate over immigration has played out along economic lines, with opponents of immigration reform warning about the threat posed by illegal immigrants to "American jobs," and those supporting such efforts responding by pointing out the economic benefits immigrant workers bring. Much of this debate has focused on the traffic in illegal immigrants along the southwestern border from California to Texas. The notion that poor illegals take jobs from Americans by working for very low wages, by increasing the crime rate, and by overburdening schools and the health system are all arguments advanced by Americans who want to curb illegal immigration. Other political activists, scholars, and policy experts suggest that these generalizations are untrue. Solutions to the problem of illegal immigration that are being advanced by both liberal and conservative politicians and lawmakers range from deportation, imprisonment, and stiff fines to exclusion from schools and drivers' licenses to full amnesty for all immigrants currently residing in the United States. One of the most highly charged controversies in this debate is the fortification of the United States–Mexico border with a 700-foot fence. The proposed "Great Wall of America"[†] is part of a general legislative trend to deal with illegal immigration. Over the last ten years, a number of proposals to construct such a wall have been considered by legislators, and over this same time an equal number of protests have been lodged against such plans. The effectiveness of these fences continues to be debated even as portions of it are being built.

A. How Should We Respond to the Global Problem of Illegal Immigration?

BEFORE YOU READ: Marc Cooper's essay has a biblical title that refers to the Israelites' escape from slavery in Egypt. Based on this allusion, what attitude do you expect the author to have toward the illegal immigrants he writes about?

EXODUS*

Marc Cooper

Marc Cooper is a contributing editor of *The Nation* and a senior fellow at the Institute for Justice and Journalism at the University of Southern California's Annenberg School for Communication. This essay originally appeared in *The Atlantic* magazine.

On January 6, which is celebrated as Three Kings Day in Mexico, the flow of border crossers heading north restarts its annual cycle. So when I arrive on the following Wednesday in the dusty, gritty Sonoran Desert town of Altar, two hours south of the border via a liver-jostling dirt road, the local merchants couldn't be more delighted. I have been to Altar before. And on this trip, I can readily agree with the local street entrepreneurs and hustlers that this year's crossing season, barely in its third day, looks to be as bountiful and profitable as ever—in spite of an also cyclical uproar,

---

[†]So named by *Time* magazine on its cover, June 30, 2008.

*Reprinted with permission of the author.

north of the border, over illegal immigration. Once an anonymous bus stop on Mexico's Route 2, Altar—a diesel-marinated ten-block grid of around 10,000 people—has become the primary staging area for Mexican migrants before they make their desperate bounce across the border. And the town's entire commercial life rests on this singular enterprise.

All around the central plaza that skirts the butternut-colored colonial-era church, small groups—mostly men, mostly young, mostly dressed in dark clothing and running shoes, though there are also some women with babies in their arms—await contact with the *coyote* or *pollero* who has promised to push them through a treacherous but in many ways invisible membrane from which they will emerge, almost magically, on the other side as our carpenters, gardeners, waiters, pickers, pluckers, and nannies. The going rate, door-to-door, from the fields of Veracruz or Oaxaca to the orange orchards of Florida or to a Brentwood kitchen: about $1,500. No need, even, to pay it all in advance: installments, with interest, will be drawn from future income.

On the streets adjoining the plaza, tiny, airless shops selling phone cards and converting currency are doing brisk business, as are the occasional youth gangs, who find few other places in Mexico where so many people are walking around with so much folding money in their pockets. Other Mexican migrants fleeing the impoverished south operate a warren of kiosks and stands, offering up for sale everything needed to ease the perilous crossing ahead: plastic gallon jugs of water; plastic baggies of combs, toothbrushes, aspirin tablets, and lip balm; dark jeans; black windbreakers; hooded sweatshirts; athletic shoes; baseball caps; bandanas; backpacks; and the black woolen ski masks favored by the salaried guides who lead the walkers across the desert. Also for sale are black plastic trash bags—$3 each—to

be wrapped around the body; they're said to foil the heat-seeking sensors that the U.S. Border Patrol and the Department of Homeland Security have stitched into the other side of *la linea*. One Oaxacan vendor shows off a black cap with an embroidered green cannabis leaf. "They buy this one a lot," he says. "I tell them I don't think it's the best one to wear."

A few yards away, the Red Cross has just opened its first-aid trailer for this year's season, and its advice is also readily spurned. "I tell them that they run a great risk," says uniformed paramedic Amado Arellano. He even shows them a colorful but macabre wall map—provided by the Tucson-based Humane Borders group—that marks every spot where a migrant has died in the desert. Hundreds of fatal red dots cluster just above the border. "We try to tell them not to go," he says. "But no one listens. The necessity is too great." . . . Approximately 40,000 migrants per month make this trip through and out of Altar.

5   Accompanied by Jorge Solchaga, a thirty-eight-year-old diplomat who works with the Mexican consulate in Phoenix, I walk through a nameless tortilla shop on a side street off the plaza, out its back door, and into a brick-and-cement courtyard teeming with people getting ready to cross. This is one of Altar's countless unregulated and ill-named "guest houses"—tenement flops that offer nothing except a body-sized patch of floor for $5 or $6 a night. On one side of the cramped courtyard, workmen plaster together an add-on to the tenement; its owners clearly realize that they are part of a growth industry. A rickety iron staircase leads us to some second-floor lodgings, a bare twenty-by-twenty-foot room in which about fifty people have put down their sleeping mats and backpacks.

The night before my trip to Altar, I had dinner with the Tucson-based journalist Charles Bowden, author of more than fifteen books, most of them set along the border. In perhaps his most acclaimed work, *Down by the River*, certainly a must-read for anyone researching the border, Bowden describes the poverty that swamps even the more prosperous Mexican border cities and that relentlessly churns the human flow northward. "Over there," he writes of Ciudad Juárez, just across from El Paso, Texas, "most of the streets are unpaved, two thirds of the houses lack any sewage connection. At least 200,000 people in the city live as squatters. . . . At least 35,000 more poor people descend on Juárez each year. Or sixty thousand, no one is sure. They take jobs at $3 to $5 a day that cannot sustain them."

In the courtyard once more, Solchaga spots a dark-skinned girl with a nursing-age infant in her lap. She stares at the ground as Solchaga gently warns her that she is about to put her life and that of her child at risk. When he presses her on the dangers, she barely nods. Almost inaudibly she says that she's twenty, but she looks five years younger and somewhat terrified. However, the die is cast. She's given up everything back home and will be heading out into a new world within a few minutes. "Make sure your husband carries three extra gallons of water for you, you hear?" Solchaga says, nodding to the man sitting behind her. As we exit the flop, Solchaga tells me that the blank look in that girl's eyes will surely haunt him. One of his jobs at the consulate is to process the deaths of Mexicans in the United States. Three years ago in Altar, he tells me, he warned another nursing mother not to make the crossing, and less than a week later, when a call came in to his Arizona office requesting him to help identify a "fatality" that had been found in the desert, he recognized the same young woman. "This is my job, and I am used to it," he says. Last year he processed the

deaths of 219 Mexicans in the Phoenix area; some were migrants who had wandered in the desert for eight or nine days before their souls and bodies burned out. "It's the young women I never forget," he says, shrugging his shoulders.

When they realize that it's only the width of a river—or a twelve-foot wall, or three strands of cattle wire, or a three-day walk, for that matter—that separates them from a First World economy and some reasonable chance at a future, they push north. "The Mexican border is the only place," Bowden writes, "where the cyberspace world of a major economy rubs up against a world of raw sewage and mud huts. The world of mud is failing to sustain its people." [. . .]

With an estimated 11-to-1 manufacturing wage differential between the two countries (some experts put the agricultural wage gap at twice that), why is anyone shocked by what's happening? "You're looking at the biggest story of our lives," Bowden told me over dinner. "This is the largest cross-border human migration in history." Though rarely, if ever, posed in those terms, the staggering numbers tend to bolster Bowden's sweeping vision. Something like fifteen to twenty million migrants have crossed into the United States over the last two decades. An equal number are expected to do so in the next twenty years. "People aren't coming here as much as they are leaving a cratered economy," Bowden said. "The only way you'll stop Mexicans coming to the U.S. is if you lower American wages to the same level as Vietnam. Someone worth maybe $100 a month in Mexico who comes to the U.S. becomes a human ATM machine. McCain-Kennedy, Kyl-Cornyn?" he said, referring to the hodgepodge of current immigration-reform proposals. "It's all bullshit. What we're seeing is something right out of the Bible. This is an exodus." [. . .]

BEFORE YOU READ: What jobs do you think of as low-level jobs? Which ones are high level? Would it surprise you to discover that many illegal immigrants hold jobs that require significant skills and pay better than minimum wage?

Context: This photograph depicts men who are seeking work as day laborers with construction companies. In Dallas, men gathered in hopes of being hired. Construction is attracting many illegal immigrants, but so is manufacturing.

Source: L. M. Otero/Associated Press.

BEFORE YOU READ: Immigration reform remains one of the most controversial political issues of our time. What are your views on how the arguments over this issue have been conducted? Do you think politicians make claims about this issue that are fair, accurate, or valid? Why or why not?

ISSUE: IMMIGRATION*

Harry Reid

Harry Reid (D, Nevada) has served in the U.S. Senate since 1987. He has been majority leader since 2007.

Our nation is a nation of immigrants, where the values of family, hard work, and love of country are what defines us. Our grandparents and great-grandparents came here to pursue the American dream, and we should honor that proud heritage as we try to create an immigration process that works. I have been a strong supporter of reforming our broken immigration system in a way that is tough on lawbreakers, fair to taxpayers, and practical to implement. I have also fought to secure the resources necessary

---

*Copyright 2013 Senator Harry Reid. Rand Paul.

for our country's border and national security, made reuniting and keeping families together a top priority, urged and supported the Obama Administration's decision to provide legal status to DREAMers, and long fought for the protection of refugees.

Our nation was built on the basic principle that all men and women were created equal and that all people have basic rights, no matter what they look like or where they come from. Our nation is a nation of immigrants, where the values of family, hard work and love of country are what defines us. As Americans, we all do our part to contribute; we are all the better for having hardworking new immigrants as contributing members of our communities—shopping as customers in our stores, paying taxes, and giving to local churches and charities.

America deserves a commonsense immigration process, one that includes a roadmap for new Americans who aspire to be citizens. Everyone agrees that the current patchwork of policies and programs is badly broken, mismanaged, and tears families apart. Those who want to become citizens face a maze of regulations and bureaucratic hurdles that often offer no "line" in which they can wait to become fully participating Americans. For aspiring citizens, the essential rights of citizenship should be attainable by passing a test about our country's history and system of government, paying an appropriate fee, and pledging allegiance to our country.

People move their families here to provide a better life for their children, and they want to be fully contributing members of their communities in this country. It is hard to move—to pack up everything and go to a new place takes courage—but people do it in order to provide for their families. Our grandparents and great-grandparents did it. They came here to pursue the American dream, and we should honor that proud heritage as we try to create an immigration process that works.

Rand Paul

Rand Paul (R, Kentucky) has been in the U.S. Senate since 2011.

I do not support amnesty, I support legal immigration and recognize that the country has been enriched by those who seek the freedom to make a life for themselves. However, millions of illegal immigrants are crossing our border without our knowledge and causing a clear threat to our national security. I want to work in the Senate to secure our border immediately. In addition, I support the creation of a border fence and increased border patrol capabilities.

Immigrants should meet the current requirements, which should be enforced and updated. I realize that subsidizing something creates more of it, and do not think the taxpayer should be forced to pay for welfare, medical care and other expenses for illegal immigrants. Once the subsidies for illegal immigration are removed, the problem will likely become far less common.

I support local solutions to illegal immigration as protected by the 10th amendment. I support making English the official language of all documents and contracts.

Millions crossing our border without our knowledge constitutes a clear threat to our nation's security. Instead of closing military bases at home and renting space in Europe, I am open to the construction of bases to protect our border.

> **BEFORE YOU READ:** From your own experience, what is the best way to ensure that newcomers to any community (e.g., a nation, city, neighborhood, religious group) are treated properly?

THE CHANGING FACE OF IMMIGRATION IN AMERICA*

Angela Maria Kelley

Angela Maria Kelley is Vice President for Immigration Policy and Advocacy at the organization, American Progress.

Recent statements by President Barack Obama, Senate Majority Leader Harry Reid and House Speaker Nancy Pelosi indicate a strong likelihood that congressional debate on immigration will begin later this year. Concern about immigrants' integration into U.S. culture is a longstanding tension from past debates that will undoubtedly resurface. Fears that immigrants in modern day America are different and lack commitment to assimilate are pervasive and permeate much of the discussion both inside and outside the Beltway.

Yet, often missing from the debate is an understanding of who today's immigrants are and how they adapt to American culture and see their future in this new homeland.

New public opinion research by New America Media (NAM), a consortium of more than 2,500 ethnic media outlets nationwide, provides valuable insights into today's newcomers and their transformation to new Americans.

The U.S. census data show that more than half of immigrants to the United States are women. And research by the Pew Hispanic Center finds that most immigrants live in families with children. NAM interviewed over 1,000 immigrant women from Latin American, Asian, Arab and African countries, asking in-depth questions about their daily lives, their roles in their families, and how their roles have changed since immigrating to the United States. They interviewed both women who arrived relatively recently (less than 10 years) and those who have lived here longer than 20 years. When asked why they chose to come to America in the first place, the women's answers were perhaps not surprising. The majority responded that they came to the United States to join family members already here—90 percent of respondents live with their husbands and children—or to make a better life for their children.

5   What some might find surprising is the power of American culture and its influence on the newcomer women. For example, 73 percent of immigrant women consider themselves more assertive in America than they had been in their home countries, and 33 percent of women immigrants consider themselves the head of their household, up from 18 percent in their home countries. Fifty-seven percent of these women also report that many of their responsibilities in the United States are handled by men in

their home countries: 82 percent indicated that they share family financial decisions with their husbands or handle them by themselves, and 91 percent indicated a similarly proactive role in family planning. These findings suggest that American culture, which permits women relative independence and influence in their life direction and that of their families—certainly in comparison to many countries where today's immigrants come from—reaches and transforms America's female newcomers.

The research also provides insights into immigrant women's economic roles. A majority of immigrant women from China, Korea, the Philippines, India, Africa and Arab countries describe their last job in their home country as "professional." The research found however that a substantial percentage of them do not initially find comparable employment in the United States and instead end up in low skill positions in hotels and restaurants, or as domestic and textile workers. Why would these women leave positions as nurses to become nannies? The answer lies in their motivation for coming to America in the first place—they sacrifice their own status for their families' future. The good news is that they climb quickly back up the economic ladder. Almost all reported success in increasing their income levels—some dramatically more than others, reflecting differences in education levels. This suggests that immigrant women are successfully managing themselves in America's demanding workplaces.

Women will have an enormous impact on their integration process because they drive their families' transformation from newcomer to new American. This is perhaps best understood in their powerful motivation to engage in America's civic life. Over 90 percent of women arriving from Latin America, Vietnam and Arab countries want their families to become citizens. They cite "securing family stability" as the number one reason for pursuing citizenship, followed by wanting to participate in the electoral process.

These findings suggest that as policy-makers consider a new course on immigration and immigrant integration, their strongest allies may be the fiercely focused women motivated by their love of family to make America their home.

BEFORE YOU READ: How do you understand the term "model minority"? What images or associations does it evoke? In your view, are these images or associations fair? Accurate?

ASIAN AMERICANS AND THE "MODEL MINORITY" MYTH*

Ellen D. Wu

Ellen D. Wu is a history professor at Indiana University and the author of *The Color of Success: Asian Americans and the Origins of the Model Minority.*

Previews of Amy Chua's forthcoming book, "The Triple Package" (co-written with husband Jed Rubenfeld), detonated a social media uproar among Asian Americans. Many were infuriated by the New York Post's report that Chua, the self-styled Tiger Mom, was identifying eight superior "cultural" groups in the United States: Jewish, Indian, Chinese, Iranian, Lebanese, Nigerian, Cuban and Mormon. For Asian Americans, the problem is about another Chua production that seems to perpetuate the "model minority" myth and, in particular, the notion that Asians are culturally—even genetically—endowed with the characteristics that enable them to succeed in American society.

Before the mid-20th century, the Tiger Mom did not exist in the national imagination. Instead, Americans believed that Chinese culture was disgusting and vile, viewing U.S. Chinatowns as depraved colonies of prostitutes, gamblers and opium addicts bereft of decency. Lawmakers and citizens deployed these arguments to justify and maintain the segregation, marginalization and exclusion of Chinese from mainline society between the 1870s and World War II. Those efforts were more than effective: to have a "Chinaman's chance" at that time meant that one had zero prospects.

There is danger in offering culture as a formula for success, because our ideas of culture are hardly fixed. The history of Americans' views about Chinese immigrant behaviors shows that "culture" often serves as a blank screen onto which individuals project various political agendas, depending on the exigencies of the moment.

During World War II, white liberals agonized that racism was damaging the United States' ability to fight a war for democracy against the Axis powers. Many felt that the Chinese exclusion laws, which had barred migrants from China from entering the country or becoming naturalized citizens since the 1870s, risked America's trans-Pacific alliance with China against Japan. A coast-to-coast campaign emerged to overturn the laws. The Citizens Committee to Repeal Chinese Exclusion recognized that it would have to neutralize deep-seated fear of "yellow peril" coolie hordes. So it strategically recast Chinese in its promotional materials as "law-abiding, peace-loving, courteous people living quietly among us." Congress repealed the Chinese Exclusion Act in 1943.

5   In the 1950s, journalists, social scientists and policymakers recycled this fledgling idea, circulating it further and wider as they groped for a solution to what they perceived as a national juvenile delinquency crisis. The New York Times Magazine emphasized that Chinese youths displayed "unquestioned

*Ellen D. Wu, "Asian Americans and the 'Model Minority' Myth," January 23, 2014, *Los Angeles Times*. Reprinted by permission of the author.

obedience" toward their elders, while Look magazine celebrated their "high moral sense." U.S. Rep. Arthur Klein of New York praised his Manhattan Chinatown constituents for their "respect for parents and teachers," "stable and loving home life" and thirst for education.

These narratives gained traction because they upheld two dominant lines of Cold War-era thinking. The first was the valorization of the nuclear family. Popular portrayals of Chinese American households that attributed their orderliness to Confucian tradition resonated with contemporary conservative mores. The second was anti-communism. Observers who lauded stateside Chinese and their "venerable" Confucianism effectively drew contrasts between U.S. Chinatowns and Mao Tse-tung's China to suggest that superiority of the American way of life.

By the 1960s, the concept of strong, disciplined families became the basis of the new racial stereotype of Chinese Americans as "model minorities": domestic exemplars, upwardly mobile and politically docile. In the midst of the black freedom movement of the 1960s, numerous politicians and academics and the mainstream media contrasted Chinese with African Americans. They found it expedient to invoke Chinese "culture" to counter the demands of civil rights and black power activists for substantive change. In 1966, then-Assistant Secretary of Labor Daniel Patrick Moynihan defended his controversial claim that the too-strong emphasis on matriarchy in black "culture" was to blame for the "deterioration" of African American communities by pointing to the "enlightened family life" of the relatively well-to-do Chinese. The magazine U.S. News & World Report unequivocally made the same charged comparison: "At a time when it is being proposed that hundreds of billions be spent to uplift Negros and other minorities, the nation's 300,000 Chinese Americans are moving ahead on their own—with no help from anyone else."

Then, as now, Asian Americans were troubled by what they saw as untrue juxtapositions. For one, the stereotype glossed over the myriad difficulties their communities faced: poverty, drugs, suicide, mental illness. Ling-chi Wang warned in UC Berkeley's Asian American Political Alliance newsletter (1968) that Chinatown's problems "will forever be neglected by the government" unless the community liberated itself from "the tyranny of this Chinese myth."

Moreover, critics disliked the ways in which ideas about Asian Americans reinforced the denigration of African Americans. Writing for Los Angeles-based Gidra magazine in 1969, Amy Uyematsu resented being implicated in "white racism" by being "held up" before other minority groups as a "model to emulate."

10   Today, the "model minority" concept both fascinates and upsets precisely because it offers an unambiguous yet inaccurate blueprint for solving the nation's most pressing issues. The obstacles Americans face in the global economy, our declining prospects for socioeconomic mobility and the uncertainty of parenting in difficult times—all are real challenges. But "culture" cannot explain "success" any more than it can serve as a panacea for the dilemmas of the new millennium.

We've heard enough of specious generalizations about "model minorities." We need to see Asian Americans—and other racial, ethnic and religious groups—for what they are: dynamic, diverse and much more than one-dimensional stereotypes.

B. Do Good Fences Make Good Neighbors When Defining National Borders?

> **BEFORE YOU READ:** One character in Robert Frost's poem "Mending Wall" says that "good fences make good neighbors." The other says, "Something there is that does not love a wall." From your own experience, do walls make for good or bad human relations? Can you give a specific example?

TO WALL OR NOT TO WALL*

Jonah Goldberg

Jonah Goldberg, editor at large for the *National Review Online*, is an American conservative commentator.

I'm torn between two symbolic arguments about the future of this country. Symbolism matters in politics, a lot. That's why political leaders show their respects to certain creeds and faiths by showing up at churches, synagogues, mosques, ashrams, AIDS clinics, NASCAR races, bratwurst eating contests, and the like. We build monuments and memorials for symbolic reasons. The fight over the confederate flag is a symbolic fight.

In short, I get it. Symbolism is important. But it ain't everything. If desecrating the America flag is the only way to stop a guy from setting off a bomb, then *hasta la vista*, Old Glory. And since we're speaking Spanish, I guess I should get to my point. On the one hand, I hate the symbolism of building a wall along our southern border. It would be both literally and figuratively ugly. It would change the narrative of this country in a significant way and send a terrible signal to the world of a fortress America. I don't think that's the only rational interpretation of such a wall, but few can dispute that's how it would be received by the rest of the planet (and our own media).

On the other hand, I think the symbolic significance of what's going on now is destructive and has the potential to poison our politics for a long time to come. Even grade-school textbooks make it clear that a country is defined by its borders. People instinctively understand that a nation that can't control its borders is a nation that lacks the confidence and will to stand up for its principles. It creates a culture of lawlessness, breeds contempt for lawmakers, and activates some of the baser instincts of the public. [. . .] Working on the fairly reasonable—but not definite—assumption that a wall would actually work, one benefit would be that these emotional reactions would subside. But if every politician and movement in America that calls for taking illegal immigration seriously is reflexively denounced as "anti-immigration," never mind racist, then you won't get rid of those sentiments, you'll feed them. In other words, if you don't have a reasonable "anti" immigration movement, you will get an unreasonable one. That's what's happening in parts of Europe.

Opponents rightly say you don't need a wall if you simply enforce the laws we have now. O.K. But there's very little reason to believe that moment is just around the

---

*Jonah Goldberg, "To Wall or Not to Wall," *National Review Online*, Aug 25, 2005. Used by permission.

corner. They sound like the guys watching Noah load the ark, saying, "All that work will be unnecessary once the rain stops." And, whenever politicians suggest actually doing that, many of the same critics object to that symbolism as well. Indeed, enforcing the laws by placing thousands of armed men—troops, in effect—along the U.S. border isn't a great look, either. And, historically, troops on the border is a bigger provocation than concrete. [. . .]

5   It feels unserious to say this is ultimately all about symbolism, but that's where I come down. I think the economic arguments on both sides are usually unpersuasive. Paying busboys $10 an hour, one probable upshot of a complete halt to illegal immigration, isn't major progress in my book. And it's hard to take liberals seriously when they complain about the costs of a wall—estimates vary from $15 to $30 billion—when they regularly champion other grandiose public works projects. Clearly the cost isn't their real objection.

So here I am torn between two bad symbols. Everyone likes to quote Robert Frost's line that "good fences make good neighbors." But they leave out the opening line from the same poem, "Something there is that doesn't love a wall." That sums up my continental divide.

BEFORE YOU READ: This essay presents a challenge to those who believe walling off newcomers to America is the solution. Instead, it offers readers a different way to think about the issue of immigration, framing it less as a question of "who gets to stay" and "who has to go," than as an opportunity to understand the way our society is undergoing dramatic social change. Do you find this argument convincing? Why or why not?

IT'S NOT IMMIGRATION WE FEAR, IT'S CHANGE*

David Aaronovitch

David Aaronovitch is a columnist for the London *Times*.

Overnight my inbox fills up with unsought mail. "Hair straighteners," I was told yesterday, "are the new man-bag essential," and that a "hitherto unknown Jacobean play" by Lord Edward Herbert (to me, a hitherto unknown playwright) has been found in a trunk in an attic in Powis Castle.

Both, however, were more welcome than the e-mails from two organizations that leapfrogged over each other between Thursday night and Sunday. At 28 minutes past midnight on Friday morning Nick Griffin e-mailed me and countless others to offer masochistic highlights of his *Question Time* catastrophe.

Twelve minutes earlier Frank Field, MP, in his incarnation as the Balanced Migration group, wrote responding, not to Griffin, but to Jack Straw's appearance on the same programme. His question was as pithy as it was tendentious: "If the Government," asked

---

*David Aaronovitch, "It's Not Immigration We Fear, It's Change," *Sunday Times*, October 27, 2009. Reprinted by permission.

Mr Field, "is against capping the British population at 65 million, where will they set a cap?"

Mr. Straw and the panel had been asked if Labour's immigration policies were responsible for the rise of the BNP [British National Party]. As I understood the answers, the Conservative and Liberal Democrats said "yes" and Mr. Straw seemed, tentatively, to think not. The question was good but the responses were dreadful, and there was something more. All of them saw immigration as a problem—there was no one to say that it had benefited us economically and enriched us culturally. Surely, I thought, it was this unchallenged and cowardly perception of the negative nature of migration, rather than migration itself, that was a part cause of the growth in votes for the BNP.

5   More of that later as we continue to root around in my mailbox, for Mr. Field's late-night population-cap demand was preceded by another Balanced Migration press release. (I got a third on Friday.) This followed the release of the Office for National Statistics' 2008 biennial population projection. The ONS projected a population increase of 10.4 million to 71.6 million by 2033. Of this 10.4 million the contribution of immigration, directly or in the form of new births, would be 7 million.

The Balanced Migration group (or Frank Field as it should more accurately be called) wanted to tell me that "the official forecasts mean that, if the UK's population is to be held below 65 million, we will have to reduce net immigration from a projected 180,000 a year to zero."

I should say here that the ONS begins every such report with the explicit warning that its projections are not forecasts, as Mr. Field claims, but projections forward of recent trends. When I spoke to him yesterday Mr. Field essentially dismissed this as nit-picking. I think he's wrong.

Anyway, the press release said that "we are on course for an unsustainable and unacceptable rise in population. Over the next Parliament, at a time of public spending cuts, the Government will have to find the money to pay for one million new immigrants—a city the size of Birmingham." Always Birmingham. Never ten Cambridges.

What Mr. Field didn't point out—because his intention is propagandist, not informative—was that the 2008 projection was a reduction (albeit small) from the 2006 one. Nor did he mention that the last actual figures, for 2008, showed net inward migration of only 118,000, far below the ONS projection. And even these numbers are likely to be substantially undercut by figures out next month for April 2008 to March 2009. Broadly the ONS assumptions have been based on an unparalleled period of growth. They don't speculate on what might happen if things change.

10   It's likely that net immigration will fall and the next set of projections will be revised, although they certainly won't get down to Frank's magic 65 million (at which point, I guess, the rivers run out of water, to be replaced by blood). One thing readers should know is that—contrary to tabloid imagination—those emigrating are not all white British citizens escaping the horrors of foreignisation, but are mostly former immigrants going home. But even if no one went in and no one went out, we would still get to around 65 million because of the birthrate and an ageing population.

So the forecasts (rather than the projections) are probably wrong. But even if you accept that, and further accept that there isn't very much that's hugely different between a country of 62 million and one of 70 million, Mr. Field's third objection to immigration has to be dealt with.

It's about cost. All those migrant children with English as a second language (more than half in 1,338 schools, says Mr. Field) cost a lot when budgets have to be squeezed—although he worried about it when budgets were blooming—and the babies need midwifery, houses and so on and on.

One day, I suppose, we will stop having these dialogues of the deaf where the Fields tell you all about how much migrants cost, and the responding Aaronovitches remind you that the economic benefits of relatively free migration are much, much greater. Remind you, too, that the idea that there are only so many jobs in the economy, and that they go either to immigrants or "indigenous" people, is utterly false. In late 2003, just before we opened our doors to the Polish plumbers, for example, there were about 700,000 unfilled vacancies in the UK.

But even if I could convince Mr. Field of this, he has his last, trumping, objection, that, as he put it in an article last week (co-written with Nicholas Soames, MP), there remains the nebulous problem of "social cohesion," that "England is being fundamentally changed." Why? Because, he told me, before 1945, in the Victorian and Edwardian eras—a time of "secularized

Christianity"—we all roughly agreed on what citizenship was, but migration and globalization have changed all that.

15   It occurs to me, in all this, that net inward migration has again become the lightning conductor of people's disgruntlement with change, with the ever more mobile and demanding world of the 21st century. It is utterly false to say that we haven't talked about immigration. Many of our newspapers do very little but talk about it. They don't "debate" it because their operating assumption, like Mr. Field's, is that it is bad; it overwhelms us; floods us; swamps us; it swarms in Sangatte, until it is closed, then infests "the Jungle."

No other point of view is put, just as Mr. Straw failed to put it on Thursday, as he dangled between denial and defense. So when people make the wrong connection between their fears of the modern world and the incomers, no one has slipped an e-mail into their mental inboxes to suggest that they might be wrong.

Reading Images: What Is American?

Image 1:
Grant Wood, *American Gothic*

Context: Grant Wood's well-known painting of the American heartland and its citizens depicts the reigning idea of what it meant to be "American" in 1930 and pokes gentle fun at its subject. The term *American gothic* refers primarily to the architectural style of the house in the background, but it is often applied to the farmer and the woman as well.

For Discussion: What draws you into this painting? What symbols are included? What is the effect?

For Writing: What values would you say these two figures embody? What larger commentary about America in the 1930s do you think Wood is attempting to make?

Source: American Gothic, 1930 (oil on board), Wood, Grant (1892–1942) / The Art Institute of Chicago, IL, USA / © DACS / The Bridgeman Art Library International, Art © Figge Art Museum, successors to the Estate of Nan Wood Graham / Licensed by VAGA, New York, NY.

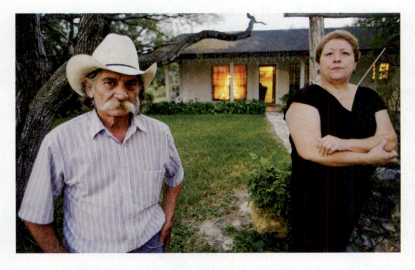

Image 2:
Family Home

For Discussion: What are some of the basic elements this photograph has in common with the painting *American Gothic* above? What draws you into this photo? What symbols are included? What is the effect? How are the photo and the painting relevant to the article that follows?

For Writing: Compare and contrast this photograph with the Wood painting. In what ways are the figures and the values they embody similar and different? What claim do you think the photographer is making about who is an American in the twenty-first century?

Context: The caption reads: Family Heirloom: Eddie and Gloria Garza's two-acre lot "has a sentimental value that is worth more than any amount of money," Gloria says. The composition of this photograph, with a serious man and woman posed against a house, recalls in a subtle way Grant Wood's iconic image of American life and values.

BEFORE YOU READ: The article below discusses how building a portion of the "Great Wall of America" in Texas is creating a conflict between landowners' rights and the government's stated intention to protect the general public. In the abstract, which do you think is more important, the individual's property rights or the public's safety? Do you think that the wall described here will actually provide real protection for Americans?

A TOWN AGAINST THE WALL*

Miguel Bustillo

Miguel Bustillo is a staff writer for the *Los Angeles Times*.

Granjeno, Texas—Gloria Garza doesn't have a whole lot. But what she has, she clings to with pride. She lives in a simple stucco house with a rustic wooden veranda and a well fashioned from odd stones her husband found around the state. Kittens stretch lazily in the sun beside her porch. Armadillos dart across her backyard. Her two-acre lot is her heirloom, her link to a legacy that dates to 1767, when Spain's King Carlos III gave her pioneer ancestors a *porcion* of property that started at the Rio Grande and stretched inland for miles.

So she is not going to be quiet while some bureaucrat in Washington tries to take it— to build a border fence. She doesn't want to become an unintended victim in a war against illegal immigration that she sees as misguided and wrong. "It would be heartbreaking," said Garza, 51, who teaches tots in a Head Start program. "For us, this place has a sentimental value that is worth more than any amount of money."

Granjeno is a frontier town of about 400 people, where everyone seemingly lives a door down from their uncle and descends from the same rancheros. It outlasted the rule of Spain, Mexico and the independent Republic of Texas. But it might not survive the U.S. government's plan to build 370 miles of steel fencing along the border with Mexico.

Blueprints show that about a third of Granjeno's house lots lie in the fence's path, even though the town sits more than a mile from the Rio Grande, the dividing line between the U.S. and Mexico. The fence would run alongside an earthen levee that passes just south of Granjeno because federal officials fear that if it were built by the river it would be worn away by flooding. "I always thought, I'll serve my country, they'll pay me a little money and I'd build my house here and retire," said Mayor Alberto Magallan, 73, a 20-year Air Force veteran. "Now, a government man comes and tells me he's going to take my land? It's not right."

5   Granjeno weathered the racially charged land fights that shook the Rio Grande Valley after the Civil War, when Anglo newcomers acquired property through schemes that included using the Texas Rangers to intimidate the *Tejanos*, earlier Texans of Mexican or Spanish descent. Granjeno persevered again a decade ago, when it fought off Hidalgo County power brokers who decided that the path to prosperity after the North

American Free Trade Agreement was a big bridge to Mexico that would run right over the town and consume much of it. But this fight may be the last for Granjeno, which is named for a thorny shrub with bright orange berries that is said to bloom more beautifully here than anywhere else.

Federal officials stress that the fence's location in Granjeno, just like the rest of the 70 miles of border walls being planned for the lower Rio Grande Valley, is subject to change. "No final decisions have been made in the construction of fencing in that area," said Michael Friel, a spokesman for U.S. Customs and Border Protection in Washington. "The input from the community will be a vital part of the process." Yet Border Patrol leaders have made it clear that they believe places like Granjeno—where drug smugglers and illegal immigrants can cross the river and slip into someone's house within minutes—are where physical barriers are needed most.

Wary locals note that government officials have already been knocking on doors, asking residents to sign release forms granting access to their properties so that surveyors can begin plotting where the fence will go. Many oldtimers refused to sign, worried that if the properties are condemned, Granjeno will be too small to carry on. In response to similar resistance all along the border in Texas, Homeland Security Secretary Michael Chertoff said . . . that he would take landowners to court to seize property if needed, and also pledged that he would not pay more than market price for land.

Some in Granjeno argue that as descendants of the Spanish land grant families, they have property rights that the federal government cannot take away. A few attorneys think they may be right and recently offered to represent Granjeno's citizens *pro bono*. But in a post–Sept. 11 environment, legal experts said, there's virtually no chance of stopping a fence that's touted as a way to make the nation safer. "The way things look, nothing is going to be left," said Garza's uncle, Daniel Garza, 73. "Then two miles west, the fence is going to stop. Do they really think people won't go around?"

Similar complaints are heard from El Paso to Brownsville, in river towns only a football field away from sister cities in Mexico, where the prevailing culture has long been bilingual and binational, and where everyone knows someone on the other side.

10   Many border residents still can't believe that a fence they ridiculed as a politician's pipe dream is about to become reality. They're stunned that the wild river that served as the playground of their youth will soon look like a military zone. But in Granjeno, the mood is especially melancholy. People feel like they are being fenced off from their heritage. Granjeno was once a rambling expanse of small ranchos that spanned thousands of acres of brushy country. The homesteads were owned by descendants of the land-grant families, the Munguias and the Bocanegras, and *Tejano* families such as the Garzas and Anzalduas that got parcels through business deals and marriages. Most existed well before the Treaty of Guadalupe Hidalgo, which recognized the Rio Grande as the border between Texas and Mexico in 1848.

"We didn't come to the United States," said Rey Anzaldua, 62. "The United States came to us."

Citrus farms, housing developments and flood-control projects chipped away at Granjeno over the last century, leaving little but some working-class families with historic last names. Now the town is just a city hall, a church, a cluster of small houses and one business—a bar with cinder-block walls named Cabrera's Place—all crammed into a third of a square mile. Crumbling plaster-coated buildings teeter next to sturdy brick homes. Ponies wander in fenced yards beside broken-down trucks.

Granjeno is so poor that until it recently installed solar-powered lamps, its streets went dark at night. The per-capita income is

$9,022. Half of the population lives below the poverty line. It only got around to incorporating as a city in the last decade, when the border bridge threatened its existence. The town has little political clout in today's lower Rio Grande Valley, one of the nation's fastest-growing regions. "We have no voice in government," said Granjeno's unofficial historian, Yolanda Martinez, 61, who is Rey Anzaldua's sister. "Money talks, and we have none."

Though Granjeno is short on wealth, it is rich in tradition. Families that left years ago dutifully return to bury their dead in pastoral El Granjeno Cemetery. It was founded in 1872 by the heir to a sheep ranch named Don Juan Garza to inter his brother Antonio, who was killed in a gunfight across the river in Reynosa. Fresh flowers adorn family plots memorializing men who served in the Civil War, World War II and Vietnam. Among the marble and brick gravestones is a marker for Sgt. Luis Ramirez, who reportedly meant to sign up for the Confederacy like most Texans but mistakenly enlisted with the Union side instead.

15   Sotero Anzaldua, 39, who trims the trees and keeps the gravestones clean, thinks a border fence may do some good. "The government has a right to do what it wants," he said in Spanish. He blamed river-crossers for a burglary at his brother's house. But most here don't believe illegal immigration is becoming worse, or was ever bad. Gloria Garza fondly recalled that her mother used to leave aromatic plates of tacos on her porch at night—a token of *Tejano* hospitality for the migrants trudging north.

If anything, the clannish Granjeno folk—who shift easily between Spanish and English, often midsentence—seem more leery of newcomers such as the Border Patrol and the Minutemen than they are of illegal immigrants and drug-runners. Anyone not native to Granjeno is always going to be viewed with suspicion by some, no matter how long they've been around. "He's still on probation!" joked former Mayor Vicente Garza, 55, pointing to his 79-year-old neighbor. Felix de la Cruz, who fell in love with a Granjeno girl when Harry Truman was president, has lived in town since 1951.

Napoleon Garza wanted to show off a side of old Granjeno that was fast fading into memory. So the 31-year-old son of Vicente Garza, and nephew of Gloria Garza, hopped into his dilapidated car and headed beyond the earthen levee toward the Rio Grande. The government had condemned many acres in Granjeno to build the levee during the 1970s. But there were still a few isolated homesteads to the south, including one with a perimeter of cactuses serving as a crude fence, and another that was inhabited by a man of scant words whom locals called "The Mexican Redneck." The redneck wasn't home, so Garza drove over a dead cottonmouth snake and kept going until he reached a *resaca*, or abandoned riverbed, where the Rio Grande ran decades ago before shifting course.

Then he headed for the river. "This is what I'm going to miss," he said as he stood by the banks, staring at the slowly moving water. For all his life he has hunted *javelinas*, pig-like critters, at this spot, he explained. Next he drove a few minutes west to the site of another massive public works project that was taking shape. Construction crews were lining up orderly rows of monolithic concrete pillars—the foundation for the international bridge Granjeno had successfully fought against a decade ago. It was being built just outside the town. Called the Anzalduas Bridge, it's expected to ease long wait times at the border when it opens in 2009. With the bridge and the border fence, Granjeno would be walled off by manufactured structures on two sides.

Garza walked down to the slope where the 10-foot-tall Carrizo cane weeds had been cleared in preparation for the final pillars, and began chatting up a Mexican man who sat minding a fishing pole on the opposite bank, which was less than 50 yards away.

"He's a lookout," Garza concluded, and drove back to town. Minutes earlier, Garza had pointed out that he was running over one of the electronic sensors the Border Patrol plants in the ground to detect movements. Soon, he predicted, he'd have company.

20   As he pulled into Granjeno, a white Border Patrol truck raced up. The agent quickly realized he was dealing with locals, not drug-runners, and sped away. But that did not stop a car full of neighborhood kids from pulling beside Garza and shouting *Dame la maleta!* ("Give me the suitcase!") to make fun of the border cop who mistook Garza for a smuggler. Garza ignored them. "Pretty soon, it will all be behind the wall," he said sadly. "I won't even be able to pick blackberries down there no more."

Questions to Help You Think and Write About Immigration

1. Marc Cooper's "Exodus" and David Aaronovitch's "It's Not Immigration We Fear" both examine the situation of illegal immigrants from an ethical perspective. Based on what you have read about illegal immigration as a global phenomenon, create a hypothetical scenario for such an immigrant (migrating from any country to any country) and analyze how that person's situation should be handled as a "human rights issue." What effect would the particulars of this fictional person's life have on your response to his or her situation?

2. Make a list of stereotypes about immigrants that come to mind. Using the essays that you have read in part A of this section on immigration, argue the claim that these stereotypes are not supported by the available evidence.

3. Senators Reid and Paul have radically different views on the issue of illegal immigration. Which view do you find more persuasive? What sort of immigration policy would you advocate as the ideal?

4. Part B of Section 6 is concerned with the ethics and practicality of walling off one nation from another. What are the benefits and the drawbacks of defining the nation by such physical barriers? Can you still be an American if you live on the wrong side of the wall or if you lived in a foreign country? What defines national identity?

5. One thematic thread running throughout the essays by Goldberg and Bustillo are the symbolic and practical importance of home, private property, and the family. Why are home, land, and family such powerful symbols of citizenship, belonging, and personal rights?

6. Assume, for the sake of argument, that you have moved to a new country or community and that you want very much to "fit in" to your new surroundings. What are the most important things a migrant must do to assimilate successfully to a different culture? For instance, consider characteristics like religion, language, clothing, customs, or other factors that might be crucial to this effort of fitting in culturally. When in your life have you been an outsider, and what did you do (or not do) to fit in or become an "insider"?

7. **Arguing Like a Citizen:** Compare any two images from the section on immigration as images engaged in a dialogue about what it means to be an American. What do these visual arguments suggest are the defining qualities of the "American" identity? Next, find an example in our current culture (i.e., op-ed, political speech, public service announcement) that offers its own perspective on this discussion. What specific viewpoint does it advance? Which of these views comes closest to your own?

SECTION 7

War and Peace

The Issues

A. Is War Inevitable? How Does War Become Integral to Society?

In this section, three authors, one of whom is a major American philosopher, one a major figure in anthropology, and one a well-known journalist, provide competing perspectives on the inevitability of war. William James, a self-avowed pacifist, believes that people, and young men in particular, have a need for warfare and, given this view, offers a way to transfer their aggression to other, more productive outlets. James's essay is followed by images of war memorials that illustrate some of the virtues of the martial character alluded to in the James excerpt. Margaret Mead does not agree that the need to fight is a natural condition. Basing her work on research that shows some cultures do not understand the concept of war, Mead argues that war is neither a biological given nor a necessary condition, but is instead an invention. Placing this issue in a more contemporary context, David Goodman casts a critical eye on the strategies currently deployed by military recruiters.

B. How Do People Justify War?

The essays here focus on some ways in which individuals either justify war or try to come to terms with war. Noah Charles Pierce presents us with poems that detail some of the challenges and realities of life within combat. Frank DeFord examines the ways the language of warfare has infiltrated popular sports. And finally, Haim Watzman contemplates the moral ambiguities in warfare of finding yourself the "first one to shoot."

Exploring Online Argument

The following Web sites present interesting perspectives on war and peace.

Images of War: Combat Photography 1918–1971	Witness to War: Preserving the Stories of War Veterans
The Virtual Wall (Vietnam Veterans Memorial)	Carnegie Endowment for International Peace
Institute for War and Peace Reporting	Iraq and Afghanistan Veterans of America
America's Army: The Official Army Game	Nuclear Threat Initiative
U.S. Department of Homeland Security	Nuclear Proliferation International History Project
Veterans for Peace	Fans Against Violence
Voice/Vision: Holocaust Survivor Oral History Archive	Electronic Intifada
War in Context	

The Rhetorical Situation

Few issues are more controversial than whether or not a country should go to war. In the United States, nationalism and patriotism remained strong during World Wars I and II, and almost all of the smaller wars in which this country has been engaged; but the war in Vietnam, like the America Civil War one hundred years earlier, tore the United States in half, changing the face of politics and conceptions of and responses to warfare.

More recently, the wars in Iraq and Afghanistan have led to many deaths on all sides. At the same time, the proliferation of nuclear materials and the movement of both Iran and North Korea to develop nuclear weapons indicate that we may be reliving some of the tensions of the Cold War era, when the United States and Soviet Union were then superpowers poised in military and ideological opposition to one another. Complicating matters still further is the fact that as regimes such as the Soviet Union crumbled, their militaries lost track of these powerful weapons, and many are believed to have fallen into terrorist hands.

Wars, the problem of war itself, and its potential solutions lie in the constitution of human nature. Whether we think that war is innate or invented, war becomes almost an expected feature of life in afflicted nations, and the hostility and violence that characterize war as an event can be communicated and nurtured, both deliberately and accidentally, in activities as innocent as children's games. At the same time, education and conversation between individuals seem as important as national negotiations in reestablishing peace. Finally, lessons learned from wars of the past century ranging from wars for independence to the Holocaust, to the present century, with ongoing fighting in places ranging from Afghanistan to Africa, can help us deal more intelligently with war as a human problem. The lessons conveyed by history are various and even paradoxical: in some cases the past tells us that only force can bring a true and lasting peace and in other cases that the will to survive is itself an act of successful resistance.

The current state of national affairs and recent history will greatly affect the way you and others think about the nature of war. Answers to the questions posed by this section of The Reader may seem difficult to solve, but history shows that people persist in their efforts to solve the problem of war and violence and to restore a global peace.

A. Is War Inevitable? How Does War Become Integral to Society?

BEFORE YOU READ: Do you think war is something we have in our "blood"? Or, do you think that war is a way of resolving conflict people learn from culture and history? Do you know the source of your thinking about this issue?

THE MORAL EQUIVALENT OF WAR*

William James

Philosopher William James (1842–1910), brother of novelist Henry James, advanced pragmatic philosophy through his famous writings, *The Will to Believe and Other Essays in Popular Philosophy* (1897) and *The Varieties of Religious Experience* (1902). In the following essay, James claims that it is necessary to get the desire to fight out of men rather than going to war and proposes a solution. What is that solution? How pragmatic for civil life do you think his solution would be?

The war against war is going to be no holiday excursion or camping party. The military feelings are too deeply grounded to abdicate their place among our ideals until better substitutes are offered than the glory and shame that come to nations as well as to individuals from the ups and downs of politics and the vicissitudes of trade. There is something highly paradoxical in the modern man's relation to war. Ask all our millions, north and south, whether they would vote now (were such a thing possible) to have our war for the Union expunged from history, and the record of a peaceful transition to the present time substituted for that of its marches and battles, and probably hardly a handful of eccentrics would say yes. Those ancestors, those efforts, those memories and legends, are the most ideal part of what we now own together, a sacred spiritual possession worth more than all the blood poured out. Yet ask those same people whether they would be willing in cold blood to start another civil war now to gain another similar possession, and not one man or woman would vote for the proposition. In modern eyes, precious though wars may be, they must not be waged solely for the sake of the ideal harvest. Only when forced upon one, only when an enemy's injustice leaves

---

*First published by the Association for International Conciliation in 1910 and in *McClure's*, 1910. From *The Best American Essays of the Century*, Joyce Carol Oates, ed., and Robert Atwan, coed. (New York: Houghton Mifflin, 2000), 45–49, 52–55.

us no alternative, is a war now thought permissible.

It was not thus in ancient times. The earlier men were hunting men, and to hunt a neighboring tribe, kill the males, loot the village and possess the females, was the most profitable, as well as the most exciting, way of living. Thus were the more martial tribes selected, and in chiefs and peoples a pure pugnacity and love of glory came to mingle with the more fundamental appetite for plunder.

Modern war is so expensive that we feel trade to be a better avenue to plunder; but modern man inherits all the innate pugnacity and all the love of glory of his ancestors. Showing war's irrationality and horror is of no effect upon him. The horrors make the fascination. War is the *strong* life; it is life *in extremis*: war-taxes are the only ones men never hesitate to pay, as the budgets of all nations show us.

History is a bath of blood. The *Iliad* is one long recital of how Diomedes and Ajax, Sarpedon and Hector *killed*. No detail of the wounds they made is spared us, and the Greek mind fed upon the story. Greek history is a panorama of jingoism and imperialism—war for war's sake, all the citizens being warriors. It is horrible reading, because of the irrationality of it all—save for the purpose of making "history"—and the history is that of the utter ruin of a civilization in intellectual respects perhaps the highest the earth has ever seen. [. . .]

5   Such was the gory nurse that trained societies to cohesiveness. We inherit the warlike type; and for most of the capacities of heroism that the human race is full of we have to thank this cruel history. Dead men tell no tales, and if there were any tribes of other type than this they have left no survivors. Our ancestors have bred pugnacity into our bone and marrow, and thousands of years of peace won't breed it out of us. The popular imagination fairly fattens on the thought of wars. Let public opinion once

reach a certain fighting pitch, and no ruler can withstand it. In the Boer war both governments began with bluff, but couldn't stay there, the military tension was too much for them. In 1898 our people had read the word WAR in letters three inches high for three months in every newspaper. The pliant politician McKinley was swept away by their eagerness, and our squalid war with Spain became a necessity.

At the present day, civilized opinion is a curious mental mixture. The military instincts and ideals are as strong as ever, but are confronted by reflective criticisms which sorely curb their ancient freedom. Innumerable writers are showing up the bestial side of military service. Pure loot and mastery seem no longer morally avowable motives, and pretexts must be found for attributing them solely to the enemy. England and we, our army and navy authorities repeat without ceasing, arm solely for "peace," Germany and Japan it is who are bent on loot and glory. "Peace" in military mouths today is a synonym for "war expected." The word has become a pure provocative, and no government wishing peace sincerely should allow it ever to be printed in a newspaper. Every up-to-date Dictionary should say that "peace" and "war" mean the same thing, now *in posse*, now *in actu*. It may even reasonably be said that the intensely sharp competitive *preparation* for war by the nations *is the real war*, permanent, unceasing; and that the battles are only a sort of public verification of the mastery gained during the "peace" interval. [. . .]

In my remarks, pacifist tho' I am, I will refuse to speak of the bestial side of the war-regime (already done justice to by many writers), and consider only the higher aspects of militaristic sentiment. Patriotism no one thinks discreditable; nor does any one deny that war is the romance of history. But inordinate ambitions are the soul of every patriotism, and the possibility of violent death the soul of all romance.

The militarily patriotic and romantic minded everywhere, and especially the professional military class, refuse to admit for a moment that war may be a transitory phenomenon in social evolution. The notion of a sheep's paradise like that revolts, they say, our higher imagination. Where then would be the steeps of life? If war had ever stopped, we should have to reinvent it, on this view, to redeem life from flat degeneration. [. . .]

Having said thus much in preparation, I will now confess my own utopia. I devoutly believe in the reign of peace and in the gradual advent of some sort of a socialistic equilibrium. The fatalistic view of the war function is to me nonsense, for I know that war-making is due to definite motives and subject to prudential checks and reasonable criticisms, just like any other form of enterprise. And when whole nations are the armies, and the science of destruction vies in intellectual refinement with the sciences of production, I see that war becomes absurd and impossible from its own monstrosity. [. . .]

All these beliefs of mine put me squarely into the anti-militarist party. But I do not believe that peace either ought to be or will be permanent on this globe unless the states pacifically organized preserve some of the old elements of army-discipline. A permanently successful peace-economy cannot be a simple pleasure-economy. In the more or less socialistic future towards which mankind seems drifting we must still subject ourselves collectively to those severities which answer to our real position upon this only partly hospitable globe. We must make new energies and hardihoods continue the manliness to which the military mind so faithfully clings. Martial virtues must be the enduring cement; intrepidity, contempt of softness, surrender of private interest, obedience to command, must still remain the rock upon which states are built—unless, indeed, we wish for dangerous reactions against commonwealths fit only for contempt, and liable to invite attack whenever a centre of crystallization for military minded enterprise gets formed anywhere in their neighborhood.

10   The war-party is assuredly right in affirming and reaffirming that the martial virtues, although originally gained by the race through war, are absolute and permanent human goods. Patriotic pride and ambition in their military form are, after all, only specifications of a more general competitive passion. They are its first form, but that is no reason for supposing them to be its last form. Men now are proud of belonging to a conquering nation, and without a murmur they lay down their persons and their wealth, if by so doing they may fend off subjection. But who can be sure that *other aspects of one's country* may not, with time and education and suggestion enough, come to be regarded with similarly effective feelings of pride and shame? Why should men not some day feel that it is worth a blood-tax to belong to a collectivity superior in *any* ideal respect? Why should they not blush with indignant shame if the community that owns them is vile in any way whatsoever? Individuals, daily more numerous, now feel this civic passion. It is only a question of blowing on the spark till the whole population gets incandescent, and on the ruins of the old morals of military honour, a stable system of morals of civic honour builds itself up. What the whole community comes to believe in grasps the individual as in a vise. The war-function has graspt us so far; but constructive interests may some day seem no less imperative, and impose on the individual a hardly lighter burden.

Let me illustrate my idea more concretely. There is nothing to make one indignant in the mere fact that life is hard, that men should toil and suffer pain. The planetary conditions once for all are such, and we can stand it. But that so many men, by mere accidents of birth and opportunity, should have a life of *nothing else* but toil and pain and hardness and inferiority imposed upon them, should have *no* vacation, while others natively no more deserving never get any taste of this campaigning life at all, *this* is capable of arousing indignation in reflective minds. It may end by seeming shameful to all of us that some of us have nothing but campaigning, and others nothing but unmanly ease. If now—and this is my idea—there were, instead of military conscription a conscription of the whole youthful population to form for a certain number of years a part of the army enlisted against *Nature*, the injustice would tend to be evened out, and numerous other goods to the commonwealth would follow. The military ideals of hardihood and discipline would be wrought into the growing fibre of the people; no one would remain blind as the luxurious classes now are blind, to man's real relations to the globe he lives on, and to the permanently sour and hard foundations of his higher life. To coal and iron mines, to freight trains, to fishing fleets in December, to dish-washing, clothes washing, and window-washing, to road building and tunnel-making, to foundries and stoke-holes, and to the frames of skyscrapers, would our gilded youths be drafted off, according to their choice, to get the childishness knocked out of them, and to come back into society with healthier sympathies and soberer ideas. They would have paid their blood-tax, done their own part in the immemorial human warfare against nature, they would tread the earth more proudly, the women would value them more highly, they would be better

fathers and teachers of the following generation.

Such a conscription, with the state of public opinion that would have required it, and the many moral fruits it would bear, would preserve in the midst of a pacific civilization the manly virtues which the military party is so afraid of seeing disappear in peace. We should get toughness without callousness, authority with as little criminal cruelty as possible, and painful work done cheerily because the duty is temporary, and threatens not, as now, to degrade the whole remainder of one's life. I spoke of the "moral equivalent" of war. So far, war has been the only force that can discipline a whole community, and until an equivalent discipline is organized, I believe that war must have its way. But I have no serious doubt that the ordinary prides and shames of social man, once developed to a certain intensity, are capable of organizing such a moral equivalent as I have sketched, or some other just as effective for preserving manliness of type. It is but a question of time, of skillful propagandism, and of opinion-making men seizing historic opportunities.

The martial type of character can be bred without war. Strenuous honor and disinterestedness abound elsewhere. Priests and medical men are in a fashion educated to it, and we should all feel some degree of it imperative if we were conscious of our work as an obligatory service to the state. We should be *owned*, as soldiers are by the army, and our pride would rise accordingly. We could be poor, then, without humiliation, as army officers now are. The only thing needed henceforward is to inflame the civic temper as past history has inflamed the military temper.

Reading Images: War Memorials and Martial Character

Image 1:
Iwo Jima Monument (Marine Corp War Memorial), Washington, D.C.

For Discussion: Each of these monuments has a different *ethos* or concept of the dead men and women that it honors. What values do these American monuments associate with the soldiers they commemorate?

For Writing: Consider these three war memorials as visual arguments about the nature of war and the nation's appropriate response to it. What claim does each monument make and how does its construction provide evidence in support of that claim? In what ways do the memorials offer a consistent idea of how to honor the war dead? In what ways do their arguments differ from one another?

Image 2:
Tomb of the Unknown Soldier, Arlington National Cemetery

Image 3:
Vietnam Veterans Memorial

Context: William James concludes the previous essay by stating, "the martial type of character can be bred without war." James wants to distinguish the civic virtues that military service cultivates from the violent act of war itself. The War Memorial is an important cultural symbol of the martial character and its virtues. Here we see three well-known American examples. The Marine Corps Monument (also known as the Iwo Jima Monument) near the Potomac River in Washington, D.C., was designed by Felix DeWeldon based on Joe Rosenthal's famous photograph of the flag being raised at Iwo Jima. Many nations have one or more tombs of the "Unknown Soldier." The Tomb of the Unknown Soldier in Arlington National Cemetery contains the remains of soldiers from World Wars I and II, the Korean Conflict, and the Vietnam War. The Monument's inscription reads: "Here Rests in Honored Glory an American Soldier, Known But to God." The Vietnam War Memorial on the Mall in Washington, D.C., has a very different character. Designed by sculptor and landscape artist Maya Lin, the Wall is made up of two black granite walls etched with the names of the dead. One wall points toward the Lincoln Memorial, the other toward the Washington Monument. Visitors search for names of friends and family and often leave tokens such as photos, flowers, or flags.

BEFORE YOU READ: Can you imagine a world without war? What important social changes would characterize such a utopian world? Use your imagination!

WARFARE: AN INVENTION—NOT A BIOLOGICAL NECESSITY*

Margaret Mead

A leading cultural anthropologist, Margaret Mead (1901–1978) became a household name in the United States because of her best-selling work, *Coming of Age in Samoa*, about her field research on sexuality among adolescents in Samoa. She went on to write forty-four books. In the following article, Mead argues against the traditional notion that warfare is a biological, not a cultural, drive. While you read, consider whether you think war and/or warring behavior is something we inherit from genetics or from society.

Is war a biological necessity, a sociological inevitability, or just a bad invention? Those who argue for the first view endow man with such pugnacious instincts that some outlet in aggressive behavior is necessary if man is to reach full human stature. It was this point of view which lay back of William James's famous essay, "The Moral Equivalent of War," in which he tried to retain the warlike virtues and channel them in new directions. A similar point of view has lain back of the Soviet Union's attempt to make competition between groups rather than between individuals. A basic, competitive, aggressive, warring human nature is assumed, and those who wish to outlaw war or outlaw competitiveness merely try to find new and less socially destructive ways in which these biologically given aspects of man's nature can find expression. Then there are those who take the second view: warfare is the inevitable concomitant of the development of the state, the struggle for land and natural resources of class societies springing, not from the nature of man, but from the nature of history. War is nevertheless inevitable unless we change our social system and outlaw classes, the struggle for power, and possessions; and in the event of

our success warfare would disappear, as a symptom vanishes when the disease is cured.

One may hold a compromise position between these two extremes; one may claim that all aggression springs from the frustration of man's biologically determined drives and that, since all forms of culture are frustrating, it is certain each new generation will be aggressive and the aggression will find its natural and inevitable expression in race war, class war, nationalistic war, and so on.

All three positions are very popular today among those who think seriously about the problems of war and its possible prevention, but I wish to urge another point of view, less defeatist perhaps than the first and third, and more accurate than the second: that is, that warfare, by which I mean organized conflict between two groups as *groups*, in which each group puts an army (even if the army is only fifteen Pygmies) into the field to fight and kill, if possible, some of the members of the army of the other group—that warfare of this sort is an invention like any other of the inventions in terms of which we order our lives, such as writing, marriage, cooking our food instead of eating it raw, trial by jury, or burial of the dead, and so on. Some of this list any one will

---

Asia 40.8 (August 1940): 402–405.

grant are inventions: trial by jury is confined to very limited portions of the globe; we know that there are tribes that do not bury their dead but instead expose or cremate them; and we know that only part of the human race has had a knowledge of writing as its cultural inheritance. But, whenever a way of doing things is found universally, such as the use of fire or the practice of some form of marriage, we tend to think at once that it is not an invention at all but an attribute of humanity itself. And yet even such universals as marriage and the use of fire are inventions like the rest, very basic ones, inventions which were perhaps necessary if human history was to take the turn it has taken, but nevertheless inventions. At some point in his social development man was undoubtedly without the institution of marriage or the knowledge of the use of fire.

The case for warfare is much clearer because there are peoples even today who have no warfare. Of these the Eskimo are perhaps the most conspicuous example, but the Lepchas of Sikkim are an equally good one. Neither of these peoples understands war, not even the defensive warfare. The idea of warfare is lacking, and this lack is as essential to carrying on war as an alphabet or a syllabary is to writing. But whereas the Lepchas are a gentle, unquarrelsome people, and the advocates of other points of view might argue that they are not full human beings or that they had never been frustrated and so had no aggression to expend in warfare, the Eskimo case gives no such possibility of interpretation. The Eskimo are not a mild and meek people; many of them are turbulent and troublesome. Fights, theft of wives, murder, cannibalism occur among them—all outbursts of passionate men goaded by desire or intolerable circumstance. Here are men faced with hunger, men faced with loss of their wives, men faced with the threat of extermination by other men, and here are orphan children, growing up miserably with no one to care

for them, mocked and neglected by those about them. The personality necessary for war, the circumstances necessary to goad men to desperation are present, but there is no war. When a traveling Eskimo entered a settlement he might have to fight the strongest man in the settlement to establish his position among them, but this was a test of strength and bravery, not war. The idea of warfare, of one *group* organizing against another *group* to maim and wound and kill them, was absent. And without that idea passions might rage but there was no war.

5   But, it may be argued, isn't this because the Eskimo have such a low and undeveloped form of social organization? They own no land, they move from place to place, camping, it is true, season after season on the same site, but this is not something to fight for as the modern nations of the world fight for land and raw materials. They have no permanent possessions that can be looted, no towns that can be burned. They have no social classes to produce stress and strains within the society which might force it to go to war outside. Doesn't the absence of war among the Eskimo, while disproving the biological necessity of war, just go to confirm the point that it is the state of development of the society which accounts for war, and nothing else?

We find the answer among the Pygmy peoples of the Andaman Islands in the Bay of Bengal. The Andamans also represent an exceedingly low level of society: they are a hunting and food-gathering people; they live in tiny hordes without any class stratification; their houses are simpler than the snow houses of the Eskimo. But they knew about warfare. The army might contain only fifteen determined Pygmies marching in a straight line, but it was the real thing none the less. Tiny army met tiny army in open battle, blows were exchanged, casualties suffered, and the state of warfare could only be concluded by a peacemaking ceremony.

Similarly, among the Australian aborigines, who built no permanent dwellings but wandered from water hole to water hole over their almost desert country, warfare—and rules of "international law"—were highly developed. The student of social evolution will seek in vain for his obvious causes of war, struggle for lands, struggle for power of one group over another, expansion of population, need to divert the minds of a populace restive under tyranny, or even the ambition of a successful leader to enhance his own prestige. All are absent, but warfare as a practice remained, and men engaged in it and killed one another in the course of a war because killing is what is done in wars.

From instances like these it becomes apparent that an inquiry into the causes of war misses the fundamental point as completely as does an insistence upon the biological necessity of war. If a people have an idea of going to war and the idea that war is the way in which certain situations, defined within their society, are to be handled, they will sometimes go to war. If they are a mild and unaggressive people, like the Pueblo Indians, they may limit themselves to defensive warfare; but they will be forced to think in terms of war because there are peoples near them who have warfare as a pattern, and offensive, raiding, pillaging warfare at that. When the pattern of warfare is known, people like the Pueblo Indians will defend themselves, taking advantage of their natural defenses, the *mesa* village site, and people like the Lepchas, having no natural defenses and no idea of warfare, will merely submit to the invader. But the essential point remains the same. There is a way of behaving which is known to a given people and labeled as an appropriate form of behavior. A bold and warlike people like the Sioux or the Maori may label warfare as desirable as well as possible; a mild people like the Pueblo Indians may label warfare as undesirable; but to the minds of both peoples the possibility of warfare is present. Their thoughts, their hopes, their plans are oriented about

this idea, that warfare may be selected as the way to meet some situation.

So simple peoples and civilized peoples, mild peoples and violent, assertive peoples, will all go to war if they have the invention, just as those peoples who have the custom of dueling will have duels and peoples who have the pattern of vendetta will indulge in vendetta. And, conversely, peoples who do not know of dueling will not fight duels, even though their wives are seduced and their daughters ravished; they may on occasion commit murder but they will not fight duels. Cultures which lack the idea of the vendetta will not meet every quarrel in this way. A people can use only the forms it has. So the Balinese have their special way of dealing with a quarrel between two individuals; if the two feel that the causes of quarrel are heavy, they may go and register their quarrel in the temple before the gods, and, making offerings, they may swear never to have anything to do with each other again. Under the Dutch government they registered such mutual "notspeaking" with the Dutch government officials. But in other societies, although individuals might feel as full of animosity and as unwilling to have any further contact as do the Balinese, they cannot register their quarrel with the gods and go on quietly about their business because registering quarrels with the gods is not an invention of which they know.

10   Yet, if it be granted that warfare is after all an invention, it may nevertheless be an invention that lends itself to certain types of personality, to the exigent needs of auto-crats, to the expansionist desires of crowded peoples, to the desire for plunder and rape and loot which is engendered by a dull and frustrating life. What, then, can we say of this congruence between warfare and its uses? If it is a form which fits so well, is not this congruence the essential point? But even here the primitive material causes us to wonder, because there are tribes who go to war merely for glory, having no quarrel with

the enemy, suffering from no tyrant within their boundaries, anxious neither for land nor loot nor women, but merely anxious to win prestige which within that tribe has been declared obtainable only by war and without which no young man can hope to win his sweetheart's smile of approval. But if, as was the case with the Bush Negroes of Dutch Guiana, it is artistic ability which is necessary to win a girl's approval, the same young man would have to be carving rather than going out on a war party.

In many parts of the world, war is a game in which the individual can win counters—counters which bring him prestige in the eyes of his own sex or of the opposite sex; he plays for these counters as he might, in our society, strive for a tennis championship. Warfare is a frame for such prestige-seeking merely because it calls for the display of certain skills and certain virtues; all of these skills—riding straight, shooting straight, dodging the missiles of the enemy, and sending one's own straight to the mark—can be equally well exercised in some other framework and, equally, the virtues—endurance, bravery, loyalty, steadfastness—can be displayed in other contexts. The tie-up between proving oneself a man and proving this by a success in organized killing is due to a definition which many societies have made of manliness. And often, even in those societies which counted success in warfare a proof of human worth, strange turns were given to the idea, as when the Plains Indians gave their highest awards to the man who touched a live enemy rather than to the man who brought in a scalp—from a dead enemy—because killing a man was less risky. Warfare is just an invention known to the majority of human societies by which they permit their young men either to accumulate prestige or avenge their honor or acquire loot or wives or slaves or sago lands or cattle or appease the blood lust of their gods or the restless souls of the recently dead. It is just an invention, older and more

widespread than the jury system, but none the less an invention.

But, once we have said this, have we said anything at all? Despite a few instances, dear to the hearts of controversialists, of the loss of the useful arts, once an invention is made which proves congruent with human needs or social forms, it tends to persist. Grant that war is an invention, that it is not a biological necessity nor the outcome of certain special types of social forms, still, once the invention is made, what are we to do about it? The Indian who had been subsisting on the buffalo for generations because with his primitive weapons he could slaughter only a limited number of buffalo did not return to his primitive weapons when he saw that the white man's more efficient weapons were exterminating the buffalo.

A desire for the white man's cloth may mortgage the South Sea Islander to the white man's plantation, but he does not return to making bark cloth, which would have left him free. Once an invention is known and accepted, men do not easily relinquish it. The skilled workers may smash the first steam looms which they feel are to be their undoing, but they accept them in the end, and no movement which has insisted upon the mere abandonment of usable inventions has ever had much success. Warfare is here, as part of our thought; the deeds of warriors are immortalized in the words of our poets; the toys of our children are modeled upon the weapons of the soldier; the frame of reference within which our statesmen and our diplomats work always contains war. If we know that is it not inevitable, that it is due to historical accident that warfare is one of the ways in which we think of behaving, are we given any hope by that? What hope is there of persuading nations to abandon war, nations so thoroughly imbued with the idea that resort to war is, if not actually desirable and noble, at least inevitable whenever certain defined circumstances arise?

In answer to this question I think we might turn to the history of other social inventions, inventions which must once have seemed as firmly entrenched as warfare. Take the methods of trial which preceded the jury system: ordeal and trial by combat. Unfair, capricious, alien as they are to our feeling today, they were once the only methods open to individuals accused of some offense. The invention of trial by jury gradually replaced these methods until only witches, and finally not even witches, had to resort to the ordeal. And for a long time the jury system seemed the one best and finest method of settling legal disputes, but today new inventions, trial before judges only or before commissions, are replacing the jury system. In each case the old method was replaced by a new social invention; the ordeal did not go out because people thought it unjust or wrong, it went out because a method more congruent with the institutions and feelings of the period was invented. And, if we despair over the way in which war seems such an ingrained habit of most of the human race, we can take comfort from the fact that a poor invention will usually give place to a better invention.

15   For this, two conditions at least are necessary. The people must recognize the defects of the old invention, and some one must make a new one. Propaganda against warfare, documentation of its terrible cost in human suffering and social waste, these prepare the ground by teaching people to feel that warfare is a defective social institution. There is further needed a belief that social invention is possible and the invention of new methods which will render warfare as out-of-date as the tractor is making the plow, or the motor car the horse and buggy. A form of behavior becomes out-of-date only when something else takes its place, and in order to invent forms of behavior which will make war obsolete, it is a first requirement to believe that an invention is possible.

Reading Images: Child Soldiers in Combat

Context: The caption to this photograph reads: "Free Syrian army's young fighters pose on April 2, 2013 as they hold positions near the front line during clashes with regime forces in the old city of Aleppo. Photo by Guillaume Briquet."

For Discussion: Think about the composition of this photograph. What does the alignment of these two young boys, dressed in combat garb and set against the background of a war-torn city, suggest about the larger conflict of which they are a part?

For Writing: It's possible to interpret this image in a couple of different ways. One way is to read it as a neutral depiction of combatants in the ongoing Syrian civil war. Another is to read it as a highly subjective (and highly critical) commentary on the way this war has unjustly forced innocent young people into this conflict. Building on your formal understanding of Briquet's photograph, discuss the ambiguities that leave its claim uncertain. After articulating several possible claims that the photo might make, choose the one you think is most accurate and explain.

> **BEFORE YOU READ:** What is your general opinion about military recruiting? Should there be restrictions placed on this activity?

A FEW GOOD KIDS?*

David Goodman

David Goodman is a contributing writer for *Mother Jones*.

John Travers was striding purposefully into the Westfield mall in Wheaton, Maryland, for some back-to-school shopping before starting his junior year at Bowling Green State University. When I asked him whether he'd ever talked to a military recruiter, Travers, a 19-year-old African American with a buzz cut, a crisp white T-shirt, and a diamond stud in his left ear, smiled wryly. "To get to lunch in my high school, you had to pass recruiters," he said. "It was overwhelming." Then he added, "I thought the recruiters had too much information about me. They called me, but I never gave them my phone number."

Nor did he give the recruiters his email address, Social Security number, or details about his ethnicity, shopping habits, or college plans. Yet they probably knew all that, too. In the past few years, the military has mounted a virtual invasion into the lives of young Americans. Using data mining, stealth Web sites, career tests, and sophisticated marketing software, the Pentagon is harvesting and analyzing information on everything from high school students' GPAs and SAT scores to which video games they play. Before an Army recruiter even picks up the phone to call a prospect like Travers, the soldier may know more about the kid's habits than do his own parents.

The military has long struggled to find more effective ways to reach potential enlistees; for every new GI it signed up last year, the Army spent $24,500 on recruitment. (In contrast, four-year colleges spend an average of $2,000 per incoming student.) Recruiters hit pay dirt in 2002, when then-Rep. (now Sen.) David Vitter (R-La.) slipped a provision into the No Child Left Behind Act that requires high schools to give recruiters the names and contact details of all juniors and seniors. Schools that fail to comply risk losing their NCLB funding. This little-known regulation effectively transformed President George W. Bush's signature education bill into the most aggressive military recruitment tool since the draft. Students may sign an opt-out form—but not all school districts let them know about it.

Yet NCLB is just the tip of the data iceberg. In 2005, privacy advocates discovered that the Pentagon had spent the past two years quietly amassing records from Selective Service, state DMVs, and data brokers to create a database of tens of millions of young adults and teens, some as young as 15. The massive data-mining project is overseen by the Joint Advertising Market Research & Studies program, whose Web site has described the database, which now holds

34 million names, as "arguably the largest repository of 16–25-year-old youth data in the country." The JAMRS database is in turn run by Equifax, the credit reporting giant.

5   Marc Rotenberg, head of the Electronic Privacy Information Center, says the Pentagon's initial failure to disclose the collection of the information likely violated the Privacy Act. In 2007, the Pentagon settled a lawsuit (filed by the New York Civil Liberties Union) by agreeing to stop collecting the names and Social Security numbers of anyone younger than 17 and promising not to share its database records with other government agencies. Students may opt out of having their JAMRS database information sent to recruiters, but only 8,700 have invoked this obscure safeguard.

The Pentagon also spends about $600,000 a year on commercial data brokers, notably the Student Marketing Group and the American Student List, which boasts that it has records for 8 million high school students. Both companies have been accused of using deceptive practices to gather information: In 2002, New York's attorney general sued SMG for telling high schools it was surveying students for scholarship and financial aid opportunities yet selling the info to telemarketers; the Federal Trade Commission charged ASL with similar tactics. Both companies eventually settled.

The Pentagon is also gathering data from unsuspecting Web surfers. This year, the Army spent $1.2 million on the Web site *March2Success.com*, which provides free standardized test-taking tips devised by prep firms such as Peterson's, Kaplan, and Princeton Review. The only indications that the Army runs the site, which registers an average of 17,000 new users each month, are a tiny tagline and a small logo that links to the main recruitment Web site, GoArmy .com. Yet visitors' contact information can be sent to recruiters unless they opt out, and students also have the option of having a recruiter monitor their practice test scores.

Terry Backstrom, who runs March2Success .com for the US Army Recruiting Command at Fort Knox, insists that it is about "good will," not recruiting. "We are providing a great service to schools that normally would cost them."

Recruiters are also data mining the classroom. More than 12,000 high schools administer the Armed Services Vocational Aptitude Battery, a three-hour multiple-choice test originally created in 1968 to match conscripts with military assignments. Rebranded in the mid-1990s as the "ASVAB Career Exploration Program," the test has a cheerful home page that makes no reference to its military applications, instead declaring that it "is designed to help students learn more about themselves and the world of work." A student who takes the test is asked to divulge his or her Social Security number, GPA, ethnicity, and career interests—all of which is then logged into the JAMRS database. In 2008, more than 641,000 high school students took the ASVAB; 90 percent had their scores sent to recruiters. Tony Castillo of the Army's Houston Recruiting Battalion says that ASVAB is "much more than a test to join the military. It is really a gift to public education."

Concerns about the ASVAB's links to recruiting have led to a nearly 20 percent decline in the number of test takers between 2003 and 2008. But the test is mandatory at approximately 1,000 high schools. Last February, three North Carolina students were sent to detention for refusing to take it. One, a junior named Dakota Ling, told the local paper, "I just really don't want the military to have all the info it can on me." Last year, the California Legislature barred schools from sending ASVAB results to military recruiters, though Gov. Arnold Schwarzenegger vetoed the bill. The Los Angeles and Washington, DC, school districts have tried to protect students' information by releasing their scores only on request.

10   To put all its data to use, the military has enlisted the help of Nielsen Claritas, a research and marketing firm whose clients include BMW, AOL, and Starbucks. Last year, it rolled out a "custom segmentation" program that allows a recruiter armed with the address, age, race, and gender of a potential "lead" to call up a wealth of information about young people in the immediate area, including recreation and consumption patterns. The program even suggests pitches that might work while cold-calling teenagers. "It's just a foot in the door for a recruiter to start a relevant conversation with a young person," says Donna Dorminey of the US Army Center for Accessions Research.

Still, no amount of data slicing can fix the challenge of recruiting during wartime. Last year, a JAMRS survey identified recruiters' single biggest obstacle: Only 5 percent of parents would recommend military service to their kids, a situation blamed on "a constant barrage of negative media coverage on the War in Iraq." Not surprisingly, more and more kids are opting out of having their information shared with recruiters under No Child Left Behind; in New York City, the number of students opting out has doubled in the past five years, to 45,000 in 2008. At some schools, 90 percent of students have opted out. In 2007, JAMRS awarded a $50 million contract to Mullen Advertising to continue its marketing campaign to target "influencers" such as parents, coaches, and guidance counselors. The result: print ads that declare, "Your son wants to join the military. The question isn't whether he's prepared enough, but whether you are."

Not far from the mall in Maryland, I asked 21-year-old Marcelo Salazar, who'd been a cadet in his high school's Junior Reserve Officer Training Corps, why he'd decided not to enlist after graduating from John F. Kennedy High School in Silver Spring, Maryland, in 2005. Now a community college student, he replied that his mother was firmly against it.

Then, as if on cue, his cell phone chirped: It was a recruiter who called him constantly. He ignored it. "War is cool," he said, flipping on his aviator sunglasses. "But if you're dying, it's not."

B. How Do People Justify War?

> **BEFORE YOU READ:** What makes war justified? And how do these justifications differ depending on how directly warfare touches on our own lives?

IRAQ WAR POEMS*
Noah Charles Pierce

Noah Charles Pierce is an Iraq war veteran.

FRIENDS
I feel bad for the kids
Can't blame them for begging
Can't give them anything, they beg more
This one was different

---

*Noah Charles Pierce, "The Iraq War Poems of Noah Charles Pierce." Used by permission of Cheryl Softich.

5   He was 7
I let him sit next to me on the Bradley
I give him water,
He goes gets me food.
It's great compared to MRE's
10 No english
No arabic
Yet we still understand each other
Then it's time to leave
He wraps his arms around me crying
15 I say it will be ok
I still wonder if he is.

STILL AT WAR
Got home almost a year and a half ago
We were so happy
20 That beer never tasted so good
Iraq was the farthest thing from my mind
That was the best week of my life
It crept up slowly
first just while sleeping
25 more real and scary than when it happened
After, it's on the mind awake
Never 10 minutes goes by without being reminded
Been home a year and a half physically
Mentally I will never be home

30 **DUST**
The wind is picking up a little dust
no big deal
It must be getting worse
Vehicles are upside down all over
35 It's daylight now and we have to stay put
The sky is a weird orange
Just mid-day but it's dark
better tie a rope before you go pee
Seems like someone keeps dumping a bucket of
40 Sand on my lap
I wonder if this is an omen not to wage war
Or is this our glimpse of the hell we are destined to.

BEFORE YOU READ: How does pop culture influence our views about warfare? Can you think of an example that illustrates this?

SWEETNESS AND LIGHT*

Frank DeFord

Frank DeFord is a writer for *Sports Illustrated* and a commentator for National Public Radio.

There's an old cliché that football is a benign substitute for war. Ground attack, flanks, bombs, blitz and so forth.

But it is a truth, not a cliché, that our football has gained in popularity in the United States as we have had less success with our wars. It makes me wonder if, ironically, football doesn't provide us more with nostalgia for the way war used to be—with clear battle maps, focused campaigns, simple battle lines.

And, of course, football games have neat conclusions—they're simply won or lost. But our wars are precisely not settled that way anymore; their goals are vague and imprecise and they just drag on and on, without resolution.

So, ultimately, given our wistful attention span, war bores us; and since so few of us citizens are asked to actively be engaged in our war, most of us are merely citizen-spectators to it, rather than involved compatriots; and, in this television world today, we lose interest in war. Football is better to watch.

5   Of course, all that aside, the increased popularity of football may also be explained by the fact that it has become so much more violent than our other team sports, as indeed we prefer more violence in most all phases of our entertainment today. Mixed martial arts is more violent than traditional boxing, auto racing is more violent than horse racing, and professional wrestling makes comedy out of brutality. Our movies and television, too, are more violent, and our children grow up devoted to incredibly bloodthirsty video games. Even our music, that which soothes the savage beast, is more savage today.

It's been glib to say that violence in America is as traditional as apple pie. I don't think so. The new violence is show biz. Rather than traditional, it's trendy—a fashionably entertaining part of everyday life, not any byproduct of our aggressive heritage. And for all the beautiful excitement in football—the kickoff returns, the long touchdown passes—the one constant is the hitting. We very much enjoy watching football players hit one another. That makes the highlight reel.

The NFL has belatedly begun to acknowledge that the potential for damage to athletes' minds and bodies is probably much more the case than we have been prepared to admit. It is almost as if we didn't want to recognize that in a sport where hits to the head are so common, concussions are bound to happen. But then, since we no longer pay that much attention to our wars, it's easy to overlook casualties there, as well. Football and war today seem to have that in common, too.

*Used by permission of Frank DeFord.

BEFORE YOU READ: Can you describe a hypothetical situation in which it's possible you would feel you have to "shoot first"? Can you think of any examples of when someone shot first but was then held responsible for the act?

WHEN YOU HAVE TO SHOOT FIRST*

Haim Watzman

Haim Watzman is the author of *Company C: An American's Life as a Citizen-Soldier in Israel.*

Jerusalem in the summer of 1984, as we manned a hilltop observation post during my first stint of reserve duty in the Israel Defense Forces, I heard an awful story from a friend whom I'll call Eldad. Like the story of the police officer who killed an innocent man at the Stockwell subway station in London last week, this one had elements that got my liberal hackles up.

Western democracies are supposed to defend the individual against the power of the state. For this reason, democratic governments place strict limits on the use of force by their agents—executives, judges, members of the military, and law-enforcement officers. When someone dies at the hands of one of these agents, citizens are justified in asking: Did the killer abide by the law? Were his motives pure? Was death really the only choice? All too often, the answer to these questions is no.

Eldad's story took place in Lebanon, where he and I had both served for the bulk of our regular army service, before we graduated to the reserves. He was stationed at a roadblock in southern Beirut. A car pulled up to the roadblock and three men jumped out and started spraying bullets at him and his comrades. Within a split second

the Israelis were returning fire and, before they had time to even think through what was going on, two of the assailants were shot dead. The third was also on the ground, badly wounded but conscious.

"I went up to him and raised my rifle and switched it to automatic," Eldad told me. "He put up his hands as if to fend me off, or maybe beg for mercy. But I just pulled the trigger and filled his body up with bullets." "But you killed a wounded and disabled man," I objected. "That's against orders. It's also immoral."

5   "He could still use his hands, and he might have had a grenade," Eldad said testily. "He was going to die anyway. And he deserved it." Eldad's last two arguments were specious. He had no way of knowing how badly the man was wounded, nor was he authorized to mete out judgment. "You would've done the same thing." He glared at me.

I didn't know whether I would have done the same thing. I half thought I wouldn't have. But what I realized at that moment was that, if I hadn't, I would have been wrong. The man had control of his hands and could have had a concealed and deadly weapon.

A terrible thing happened in London last Friday. On his way to work, Jean Charles de Menezes, a 27-year-old Brazilian electrician, was chased down by suspicious police officers. When he tripped and fell, the officers asked no questions and gave him no warning. One of them fired eight bullets point-blank into his head and shoulder and that was that. At first sight, it was an act much more severe than Eldad's because Eldad had been under attack and shot a man he had good reason to think was armed. Mr. Menezes had hurt no one.

On the other hand, it was an easier call. The police saw a man wearing a long coat out of place on a hot summer day jumping over a turnstile and running for a crowded subway train. He did not stop when he had been ordered to do so.

Just two weeks before the killing, four suicide bombers had blown themselves up on subway trains and buses in London. Just days before, there were all the signs of another coordinated attack—and the police had reason to believe that bombers were still at large. The long coat on a summer day was just the sort of telltale clue that the police had been told to look out for. A number of suicide bombers in recent years have used such coats to conceal the belt of explosives strapped around their waists. What's more, the police acted under express orders to shoot in the head someone they thought was about to commit a suicide bombing.

10   Suicide charges are usually built to be set off with the flick of the bomber's finger. The terrorist can be disabled, flat on the ground, and surrounded by heavily armed men and still blow up everything around him. So the officer who killed Mr. Menezes did a horrible thing. But he also did the right thing. One of the tragedies of this age of suicide bombers—indeed of any war—is that the right thing to do is sometimes a horrible thing. Remember: there's an essential distinction between us and the suicide bombers. The suicide bombers perpetrate gratuitous horrors. We do terrible things only when it is necessary to prevent something even worse from happening.

Questions to Help You Think and Write About War and Peace

1. James calls for rethinking military service for young men. He claims that young men required to serve civic rather than military duty will get the desire to fight out of their systems. As a result, young men will become more contemplative and less aggressive after their training. Do you agree or disagree with James's claim? Identify the reasons for your answer. What are the benefits of adopting James's plan? What are the drawbacks? In your opinion, is there a "moral equivalent of war"?

2. After reading Mead's essay, explain how she justifies her position that war is an invention. How do you respond to her justification? Consider as well DeFord's essays about the use of war language in sports. How does this argument support or undermine Mead's concept that war is cultural rather than biological?

3. Compare James's "A Moral Equivalent of War" with Mead's essay. If these two authors were having a conversation on the "nature" of war, what do you

imagine that they would say to one another? In pairs, have one person play the role of Mead and the other of James. Using the essays for support, attempt to persuade the other person of the nature of war. Whose arguments are more convincing? Why?

4. Consider together the selections by Watzman and Pierce. What does each author think that we can learn from the experience of combat? In what ways do they agree or disagree with one another about the ways to use these lessons to deal with the possibility of future war?

5. **Arguing Like a Citizen:** Conduct some firsthand research into one of the three American war memorials represented in this section (page 580). What is the history behind how this memorial was first created? What event was it intended to commemorate? What attitude toward military combat and military sacrifice was the memorial first designed to convey? How does this attitude compare with the ways people respond to this memorial today?

Credits

Text Credits

Jeffrey R. Young, "High-Tech Cheating Abounds and Professors Bear Some Blame" from *The Chronicle of Higher Education*, March 28, 2010. © 2010, Reproduced by permission.

Felix Carrol, "No Escape from 'Helicopter Parents'" from *Albany Times Union*. Used by permission of the selection Felix Carrol.

Abby Ellin, "The Laptop Ate My Attention Span" from *The New York Times*, April 16, 2000. Reproduced by permission of the author.

Prisna Virasin, "The Barbie Controversy." Courtesy of the author.

Rebecca U. Cho, "Groups Hope to Make Bottled Water a Moral Issue" from *The Christian Century*, January 9, 2007, © 2010. Reproduced by permission. Copyright © 2010 Religion News Service. Used by permission.

Ava Guiterrez, "Let's Ban the Cell Phone Ban." Reprinted with permission.

Will Harrell, "A Defense of Grade Deflation" from *The Daily Princetonian*, March 2, 2010, © 2010. Reproduced by permission of the author.

"The Civil Rights Era," *The African American Odyssey*, The Library of Congress.

"As Spy Drones Come to the US, We Must Protect Our Privacy" from *Scientific American*, March 25, 2013. Reproduced by permission.

Council of Writing Program Administrators, http://www.wpacouncil.org

John Dufresne, "That Crucial First Draft," *Writer*, October 1992.

Stephen King, "Everything You Need to Know about Writing Successfully—in Ten Minutes," *The Writer's Handbook*, ed. Sylvia K. Burack (Boston: Writer, 1991).

Blake Decker, "And as for Target Shooting, Well go Purchase a BB Gun or a Set of Darts."

Gina Kolata, "Psst! Ask for Donor 1913" from *The New York Times*, February 18, 2007, © 2007. Reproduced by permission.

Randy Cohen, "When Texting Is Wrong" from *New York Times Magazine*, July 13, 2009, © by 2009. Reproduced by permission of the author.

Prisna Virasin, "The Controversy behind Barbie." Courtesy of the author.

"Flag Protection: A Brief History of Recent Supreme Court Decisions," Congressional Research Service, Library of Congress.

Frank DeFord, "Bust the Amateur Myth" from *The Chronicle of Higher Education*, December 11, 2011. Reprinted by permission of the author.

Mohamed T. Diaby Jr., "Toulmin Analysis of the 'Price of Oranges' Cartoon." Courtesy of the author.

Richard D. Rieke and Malcolm O. Sillars, "American Value Systems" from *Argumentation and the Decision Making Process*, 2nd ed. © 1984, pp. 118–124. Reprinted and electronically reproduced by permission of Pearson Education, Inc., Upper Saddle River, New Jersey.

Stephen J. Handel, "2-Year Students Have Long Had 4-Year Dreams" from *The Chronicle of Higher Education*, September 23, 2013. Reproduced by permission.

Mark Levinson, "Mismeasuring Poverty" from *The American Prospect*, June 25, 2012. Reprinted with permission.

Barry Schwartz, "When It's All Too Much," from *Parade Magazine*, Jan 4, 2005. Reprinted by permission of the author.

"Journalism, Publicity and the Lost Art of Argument," *Gannet Center Journal*. Reproduced with permission of Newseum.

Careen Shannon, "Stop Calling People 'Aliens'" from *Salon.com*, © 2013. This article first appeared in *Salon.com*, at http://www.Salon.com. An online version remains in the *Salon* archives. Reprinted with permission.

"Poverty in America: Consequences for Individuals and the Economy," U.S. Government Accountability Office.

Hannah Sternberg "Conservative Feminism Is Not an Oxymoron" from *The Foundry*, March 11, 2011. Reprinted with permission.

"The Gettysburg Address" from *AbrahamLincolnOnline.org*, 1995–2008, Speeches, April 2008.

Kelly Dickerson, "Minor Problems?" Courtesy of the author.

Karen Hernandez, "Never Again." Courtesy of the author.

Cal Thomas and Bob Beckel, Excerpt from *Common Ground: How to Stop the Partisan War That Is Destroying America*, New York: Harper-Collins, 2007.

Carl R. Rogers, Excerpt from *A Way of Being*, Boston: Houghton Mifflin, 1980.

Mike Rose, "Heal the Academic–Vocational Schism" from *The Chronicle of Higher Education*, September 10, 2012. Reproduced by permission.

Angela Boatwright, "Human Cloning: Is It a Viable Option?" Courtesy of the author.

Dr. Martin Luther King, Jr., "A Call for Unity." © 1963 by Dr. Martin Luther King, Jr., copyright renewed 1991 by Coretta Scott King. Reprinted by arrangement with The Heirs to the Estate of Martin Luther King, Jr., c/o Writers House as agent for the proprietor, New York, NY.

the Environment?" from *Slate*, Jan 1 © 2009 The Slate Group. All rights reserved. Used by permission and protected by the Copyright Laws of the United States. The printing, copying, redistribution, or retransmission of this Content without express written permission is prohibited.

Josh Viertel, "The Soul of Slow Food: Fighting for Both Farmers and Eaters," *The Atlantic*, January 23, 2012. Reprinted by permission of the author.

Martha Rosenberg, "Is Animal Treatment on Farms Our Business?" *Huffington Post*, Aug 16, 2013. Reprinted by permission of the author.

Ramit Plushnick-Masti, "Descendants of Slaves in East Texas Hold Out Against Luminant's Coal Mining Plans." © Sept 1, 2013, in Associated Press. Reprinted by permission of YGS Group.

Stuart Price, "Carving up the Congo." IC Publications Ltd, *New African* Magazine, October 2007. Reprinted with permission.

Brian Wingfield, "For Job Market, Green Means Growth" from *Forbes*, July 3 © 2010 Forbes. All rights reserved. Used by permission and protected by the Copyright Laws of the United States. The printing, copying, redistribution, or retransmission of this Content without express written permission is prohibited.

Bill Carter, "The Hidden Cost of Going Green." Reproduced with permission.

Marc Cooper, "Exodus." Reprinted with permission of the author.

Harry Reid, Statement on Immigration. Copyright 2013 Senator Harry Reid.

Rand Paul, Statement on Immigration.

Angela Maria Kelley, "The Changing Face of Immigration in America" from *newamericamedia.org*, July 14, 2009. Copyright © 2009 by Angela Maria Kelley. Used by permission.

Ellen D. Wu, "Asian Americans and the 'Model Minority' Myth," January 23, 2014, *Los Angeles Times*. Reprinted by permission of the author.

Jonah Goldberg, "To Wall or Not to Wall," *National Review Online*, Aug 25, 2005. Used by permission.

David Aaronovitch, "It's Not Immigrations We Fear, It's Change," *Sunday Times*, October 27, 2009. Reprinted by permission.

Miguel Bustillo, "A Town Against the Wall" from *Los Angeles Times*, December 17, 2007. Copyright © 2007 by Los Angeles Times. Reprinted by permission.

William James, "The Moral Equivalent of War" from *The Best American Essays of the Century*, Joyce Carol Oates, ed., and Robert Atwan, coed. (New York: Houghton Mifflin, 2000), 45–49, 52–55. First Published by the Association for International Conciliation in 1910 and in *McClure's*, 1910.

Margaret Mead, "Warfare: An Invention—Not a Biological Necessity." © August 1940, in *Asia*, Edition 40.8, pp. 402–405. American Anthropological Association.

David Goodman, "A Few Good Kids?" *Mother Jones*, Sept/Oct © 2009, Foundation for National Progress. Reprinted with permission.

Noah Charles Pierce, "The Iraq War Poems of Noah Charles Pierce." Used by permission of Cheryl Softich.

Frank DeFord, "Sweetness and Light." Used by permission of Frank DeFord.

Haim Watzman, "When You Have to Shoot First" from *The New York Times*, July 28, 2005. Copyright © 2005 by The New York Times. All rights reserved. Used by permission and protected by the Copyright Laws of the United States. The printing, copying, redistribution, or retransmission of this Content without expressed, written permission is prohibited.

Photo Credits

Chapter Openers, Image 1: Digitallife/Alamy; **Chapter Openers, Image 2:** David McNew/Staff/Getty Images News/Getty Images; **Chapter Openers, Image 3:** Jan Martin Will/ShutterStock; **Chapter Openers, Image 4:** Patrick Schneider/Newscom; **Chapter Openers, Image 5:** Ben Sklar/Stringer/Getty Images; **Figure 1.1:** Dennis K. Johnson/Lonely Planet Images/Getty Images; **Figure 1.2:** Jan Martin Will/ShutterStock; **Page 20:** Screenshot courtesy of the National Institutes of Health; **Figure 1.4:** Lizette Potgieter/ShutterStock; **Page 38, Image 1:** © Gary Braasch/Artcphotos/ShutterStock; **Figure 2.1:** © The New Yorker Collection. 2004. Lee Lorenz from cartoonbank.com. All Rights Reserved; **Figure 2.2:** JIJI PRESS/Stringer/AFP/Getty Images; **Page 52:** Screenshot used by permission of Greenpeace; **Page 64, Image 1:** Library of Congress; **Page 66, Image 2:** David Silverman/Staff/Getty Images; **Figure 3.2:** Scott Olson/Staff/Getty Images News/Getty Images; **Page 97, Image 1:** Flashon Studio/ShutterStock; **Page 97, Image 2:** Mike Abrahams/Alamy; **Page 97, Image 3:** Stefano Baldini/Alamy; **Page 97, Image 4:** Megapress/Alamy; **Page 109, left:** Rosenthal Joe/LOC; **Page 109, center:** Daily News Pix; **Page 109, right:** Stephanie Frey/ShutterStock; **Figure 4.3:** Cagle Cartoons Inc.; **Page 133:** Screenshot courtesy of the NHTSA and Ad Council; **Page 136:** Navy Visual News Service; **Page 137:** Universal Uclick for UFS; **Page 170:** Screenshot from WhiteHouse.gov; **Page 176, Image 1:** Ben Sklar/Stringer/Getty Images; **Page 176, Image 2:** Larry W. Smith/EPA/Newscom; **Page 177, Image 3:** Dominic Buettner/The New York Times/Redux Pictures; **Page 177, Image 4:** Go Paperless PSA. Reprinted with permission of Ziegler.com; **Page 178, Image 5:** Ann Cutting/Getty Images; **Figure 6.1:** Steve McCurry/Magnum Photos Inc.; **Page 205:** Screenshot courtesy of the Center for Disease Control and Prevention; **Page 208:** Mothers Against Drunk Driving PSA. Used by permission. Copyright © 2013 Mothers Against Drunk Driving. All rights reserved; **Page 218, Image 2:** Denis Tangney Jr./Getty Images; **Page 218, Image 3:** Driendl Group/Getty Images; **Page 231:** Jonathan Austin Daniels, Getty Images, Inc.; **Page 236, Image 1:** Reproduced with kind permission of Unilever PLC and group companies; **Page 237, Image 2:** National Review; **Page 241, Image 1:** National Archives at College Park; **Page 241, Image 2:** Andre Jenny/Alamy; **Figure 8.1:** Eddie Adams/AP Images; **Figure 8.2:** Bettmann/Corbis; **Figure 8.3:** Rizwan Tabassum/Stringer/AFP/Getty Images; **Figure 8.4:** Bob Adelman/Corbis; **Figure 8.5:** Library of Congress; **Figure 8.6:** Douglas Kent Hall; **Figure 8.7, left:** Fabiano/Newscom; **Figure 8.7, right:** Chris Maddaloni/Contributor/Roll Call/Getty Images; **Figure 8.8:** Valery Hache/Staff/AFP/Getty Images; **Page 256:** Screenshot courtesy of Let's Move! **Figure 8.9:** Digitallife/Alamy; **Figure 8.10:** Andrew Stawicki/Getty Images; **Figure 8.11:** Larry Wright/Cagle Cartoons Inc.; **Figure 8.12:** Centers for Disease Control and Prevention; **Figure 8.13:** NASA Goddard Institute for Space Studies; **Figure 8.14:** "Circle Graph Showing How Federal Spending Is Divided into Sectors" by Christopher Chantrill from U.S. Federal Budget. Reproduced by permission; **Figure 8.16a:** Patrick Schneider/Newscom; **Figure 8.16b:** AFP/Getty Images; **Figure 8.17:** Siberia/Fotolia; **Page 269, Image 1:** Ryan Rodrick Beiler/Alamy; **Page 270, Image 2, top:** David McNew/Staff/Getty Images News/Getty Images; **Page 270, Image 2, bottom:** Drew Angerer/Stringer/Getty Images News/Getty Images; **Page 271, Image 3:** Spencer Platt/Staff/Getty Images; **Page 271, Image 4:** Christian Petersen/Getty Images Sport/Getty Images; **Page 272, Image 5:** Sam Abell/Getty Images; **Page 273, Image 1:** Super Stock, Inc.; **Page 273, Image 2:** Bulent Kilic/AFP/Getty Images; **Page 274,**

Subject Index

Author-Title Index